Time Out

Family
Breaks
in Britain

timeout.com

Published by Time Out Guides Ltd, a wholly owned subsidiary of Time Out Group Ltd.
Time Out and the Time Out logo are trademarks of Time Out Group Ltd.

© Time Out Group Ltd 2007

10 9 8 7 6 5 4 3 2 1

This edition first published in Great Britain in 2007 by Ebury Publishing
Ebury Publishing is a division of The Random House Group Ltd,
20 Vauxhall Bridge Road, London SW1V 2SA

Random House Australia Pty Limited 20 Alfred Street, Milsons Point, Sydney,
New South Wales 2061, Australia
Random House New Zealand Limited 18 Poland Road, Glenfield, Auckland 10, New Zealand
Random House South Africa (Pty) Limited Isle of Houghton, Corner Boundary
Road & Carse O'Gowrie, Houghton 2198, South Africa

Random House UK Limited Reg. No. 954009

Distributed in USA by Publishers Group West
1700 Fourth Street, Berkeley, California 94710

Distributed in Canada by Publishers Group Canada
250A Carlton Street, Toronto, Ontario M5A 2L1

For further distribution details, see www.timeout.com

ISBN 10: 1-846700-39-6
ISBN 13: 978-1-846700-39-2

A CIP catalogue record for this book is available from the British Library

Printed and bound by Firmengruppe APPL, aprinta druck, Wemding, Germany

Papers used by Ebury Publishing are natural, recyclable products made from wood grown in sustainable forests.

Time Out Guides Limited
Universal House
251 Tottenham Court Road
London W1T 7AB
Tel + 44 (0)20 7813 3000
Fax + 44 (0)20 7813 6001
Email guides@timeout.com
www.timeout.com

Editorial
Editor Ronnie Haydon
Deputy Editor Elizabeth Winding
Researchers Cathy Limb, Fiona Shield
Proofreader Cathy Limb
Indexer Anna Norman

Managing Director Peter Fiennes
Financial Director Gareth Garner
Editorial Director Sarah Guy
Deputy Series Editor Cath Phillips
Editorial Manager Holly Pick
Accountant Kemi Olufuwa

Design
Art Director Scott Moore
Art Editor Pinelope Kourmouzoglou
Senior Designer Josephine Spencer
Graphic Designer Henry Elphick
Junior Graphic Designer Kei Ishimaru
Digital Imaging Simon Foster
Ad Make-up Jenni Prichard

Picture Desk
Picture Editor Jael Marschner
Deputy Picture Editor Tracey Kerrigan
Picture Researcher Helen McFarland

Advertising
Sales Director / Sponsorship Mark Phillips
Sales Manager Alison Wallen
Advertising Sales Ben Holt
Advertising Assistant Kate Staddon
Copy Controller Baris Tosun

Marketing
Group Marketing Director John Luck
Marketing Manager Yvonne Poon

Production
Group Production Director Mark Lamond
Production Manager Brendan McKeown
Production Coordinator Caroline Bradford

Time Out Group
Chairman Tony Elliott
Financial Director Richard Waterlow
TO Magazine Ltd MD David Pepper
Group General Manager/Director Nichola Coulthard
Managing Director, Time Out International
Cathy Runciman
TO Communications Ltd MD David Pepper
Group Art Director John Oakey
Group IT Director Simon Chappell

Contributors
London Ronnie Haydon; **The North Kent Coast** Melanie Dakin; **West Sussex** Nicola Belfrage; **The New Forest** Deborah Nash; **Isle of Wight** Dorothy Boswell; **The Isle of Purbeck** Ronnie Haydon, Teresa Trafford; **Somerset & Wiltshire** Melanie Dakin; **South Devon's Riviera** Kate Fuscoe; **The Cornish Riviera to the Lizard** Emily Vivas; **Cornwall's Atlantic Coast** Ronnie Haydon, Teresa Trafford; **North Devon** Derryck Strachan; **Staffordshire** Fiona Cumberpatch; **North Norfolk Coast** Phil Harriss; **The Gower Peninsula** Sally Williams of the Western Mail; **The Dyfi Valley to southern Snowdonia** Ronnie Haydon; **Blackpool** Derek Hammond; **The Lake District** Paul Edwards; **Whitby** Jill Turton; **Northumberland** Nan Spowart; **Edinburgh** Kaye McAlpine.

Additional reviews Peter Fiennes, Sarah Guy, Cath Phillips. Thanks to Peter Cave; Angela and Matty Edwards; Jane and Rick Jones; Carey, Jack and Perry Miller.

Maps john@jsgraphics.co.uk

Photography pages 3, 9, 11, 13, 14, 20, 21, 78, 79, 83, 84, 87, 88, 91, 92, 93, 94, 95, 96, 101, 102, 106, 109, 112, 114, 118, 122, 315 Tove Breitstein; pages 5, 20, 150, 151, 152, 155, 161 Michelle Grant; pages 20, 23, 136, 137, 141, 142, 145, 182, 183, 187, 188, 192 Walter Weber; pages 21, 27, 46, 47, 54, 55, 56, 62, 63, 65, 69, 73, 76, 125, 126, 130 Heloise Bergman; page 26 Olivia Rutherford; page 34 Lukas Birk; page 41 Britta Jaschinski; page 42 Tricia de Courcy Ling; page 74 Sussex By The Sea; page 108, 121 Mark Simons; pages 165, 173 Janie Airey; pages 169, 179 Cathy Limb; pages 170, 284, 288, 295, 310 www.britainonview.com; pages 204, 205, 206, 208, 214, 217 Sam Robbins; pages 218, 219, 220, 224, 227, 228, 230 Alex Ramsay; page 233 CADW Crown Copyright; page 234 Kevin Richardson; pages 246, 247, 249, 252, 253, 254, 255 Simon Buckley; pages 258, 259, 260, 265, 271, 286, 287, 291, 292, 293 Sandy Young; page 266 Brian Sherwen; pages 272, 273, 274, 277, 283, 285 Mike Pinches; pages 299, 311 Alan R. Thomson RZSS; page 307 Charles Jencks, Landform, Scottish National Gallery of Modern Art.

The following images were provided by the featured establishments: pages 15, 16, 17, 30, 51, 53, 59, 60, 67, 72, 80, 86, 99, 115, 116, 124, 133, 148, 149, 156, 162, 164, 176, 194, 195, 196, 201, 213, 232, 237, 240, 244, 246 (left), 256, 280, 298, 302, 312, 314.

Contents

Going wild in the amazing theme park

TUSSAUD'S
Alton Towers

Two extraordinary themed hotels!

come and stay at
Alton Towers,
it's bursting
with...

fun!

Chilling out in the Spa

Fantastic entertainment

Getting soaked in the Waterpark

for more information and to book, go to:

www.altontowers.com
or call us on: 0870 990 6665

About the guide

This guide is divided into 20 areas – all ideal destinations for a family break. (If you're looking for a particular hotel or restaurant, see the index *pp316-329*). From city getaways to seaside escapes and gloriously peaceful countryside retreats, each has its own unique appeal. Different as they are, however, each break is centred around hotels, B&Bs, cafés and restaurants that extend a warm welcome to families.

THE DETAILS

Booking accommodation in advance is always recommended: most of the places we feature in this guide require at least several weeks' (and often months') notice. We've tried to indicate where facilities such as baby-listening services and cots are available, but it's always best to discuss this with the establishment in question. Unless otherwise stated, breakfast is included in hotel room prices. Some places offer seasonal deals for families, so it's always worth enquiring when you book.

The maps featured in this book are intended (with the exception of the town plans) for general orientation, and you will need a road atlas or other detailed map to find your way around.

THE LISTINGS

• Throughout this guide we have listed phone numbers as dialled from within the UK, but outside the particular village, town or city.
• The times given for dining are those observed by the kitchen – the times within which one can order a meal. These can change according to the season and the whim of the owners. Booking is recommended at all times.
• Main course prices are given as a range, from the cheapest to the most expensive – these prices can change over the life of a guide.
• Where credit cards are accepted, the following abbreviations have been used: AmEx (American Express); DC (Diners Club); MC (MasterCard); V (Visa).

THE REVIEWS

The reviews in this guide are based solely on the experiences of *Time Out* reviewers. While every effort has been made to ensure the accuracy of the information contained in this guide, the publishers cannot accept any responsibility for errors it may contain. Opening times, owners, chefs, menus and other details can change at any time.

LET US KNOW WHAT YOU THINK

We hope you enjoy this book and welcome any comments or suggestions you might have. Email us at guides@timeout.com.

SPONSORS & ADVERTISERS

We would like to thank our sponsor, Buxton Natural Spring Water, for its involvement in this guide. However, we would like to stress that sponsors have no influence over editorial content. The same applies to advertisers. No attraction, hotel, restaurant or pub has been included because its owner advertised in the guide: an advertiser may receive a bad review or no review at all.

Give us
a break

Be friendly to families says Ronnie Haydon.

Far be it from us to suggest that producing children puts paid to exotic foreign travel, but there's no denying that an appetite for holidays abroad wanes as a family waxes. Staying closer to home seems an infinitely more attractive proposition when every aspect of the holiday – travel ('are we there yet?'), meals (regular, simple), sleeping arrangements (cot required), nightlife (or lack of it) – tends to be governed by the youngest member of your party. And sorry, but however coolly prospective parents opine that having a baby or two will not affect their freewheeling lifestyle one jot, well, it does – but by the time the babies have come they find they don't really mind after all.

Expectations change with parenthood. Holiday time reawakens memories of simple childhood pleasures. It's brilliant to watch your kids getting the same kick out of sandcastle building (which may as well be in Margate as Miami) as you used to. The enormous sense of wellbeing born of the creation a carefully-moated, shell-bedecked fortress, with time off for a cornet and a paddle, is priceless. Such is the great British bucket-and-spade holiday, punctuated by little forays to heritage sites, theme parks, beauty spots and children's farms – that's the sort of family break celebrated in this guide. It's not just beaches, either; a couple of capital cities and a brace of inland rural retreats are also included in this countrywide mission to find the perfect homespun holiday for you and your children.

Take time out...

...to enjoy all that Great Britain has to offer with Europcar.

Whatever your requirements; a small economy car, a large family MPV or something a little special, Europcar have the right vehicle for you!

So, don't just sit there - Great Britain awaits, call us on **0870 607 5000** or visit **www.europcar.co.uk**

Europcar

'Youth hostels have the edge because they are invariably in enviable settings, with gardens for the children and the option to self-cater...'

Some of the destinations we've chosen for the breaks lend themselves to exploration by public transport. Certainly you'd be bonkers to try to do London in the family motor, and Edinburgh and tram-rattly Blackpool are compact enough for walkers; the Isle of Wight, on the other hand, is ideal cycling terrain. Most of the countryside breaks do not, however, reward the carless family. However green your reasons for holidaying in glorious mid Wales, for example, you'll have to compromise your environmentally sound credentials if you want to get around its variously far-flung attractions. Buses are infrequent at best, non-existent at worst in many of Britain's most beautiful rural locations. Railway branch lines and main lines appear to have a pathological antipathy toward each other's timetables, with the result that, having caught a main line train, you're often waiting about an hour for a connection. So the car-free might find themselves restricted in some areas. Take heart from the fact, though, that in every chapter we've included family-friendly hotels that are so brilliant that you and your offspring won't feel like wandering far, so a return train or coach and taxi journey might be all you need.

A family that plays together...

Several of the family hotels listed in this guide run children's clubs, crèches and even nurseries, so that parents can be footloose and fancy free for a few hours. No doubt children have a great time in such places, but they're not exactly the stuff of family memories. Call us old-fashioned, but it's the days spent rock-pooling on a Cornish beach with the kids, rather than the time you popped them in the Kiddy Club while you had a spot of 'me time' in the health spa that will be recorded fondly in the family photo album. So although we've noted the existence of crèches and clubs in hotels listed, such facilities were by no means the only criteria we used while testing hotels for child-friendliness. Kiddie clubs may be a good indicator that children are catered for in an establishment, but they don't tell the whole story. Many parents are horrified by the idea of children's holiday fun being distinct from that of their parents, to be doled out by shouty playleaders in jolly T-shirts, while parents top up their tans and nurse hangovers. It's not the facilities and NVQ-trained staff that they want for their children, it's a friendly welcome – for all

ages. That, of course, should be what all hotels, regardless of star-rating, location, style or price bracket, provide.

Sadly, even in 2007, that is not the case. We discovered a significant number of hotels and guesthouses with a distinctly grudging attitude towards family groups with children, either actively discouraging the custom of young folk under a certain age, or letting them in on the proviso that they're 'well behaved'. This attitude baffles us. After all, most children are pretty wholesome in their habits – they don't smoke, get drunk, complain about unheated towel rails or notice grubby grouting. In fact, most children are generally uncritical and easy to have around, so why the fastidious attitude?

Fortunately, for every frosty reception we encountered on our trips there were delightfully warm ones to take comfort in. Obviously the big names in the lucrative world of the family hotel – Woolley Grange (see p131); the Knoll House (see p116) and Bedruthan Steps (see p172) – can provide a child-centred break with all the home comforts and little luxuries tired parents crave. Such places do a fantastic job and have an ever growing fanbase, but their splendour costs, and many families find the price of a few days in such rural retreats prohibitive. Thank heavens, then, for little B&Bs, especially those run by folk who not only find children rather jolly additions to their guestbook, but who have children, or grandchildren, of their own, so have at their disposal toys, cots, high chairs, Calpol and, most importantly of all,

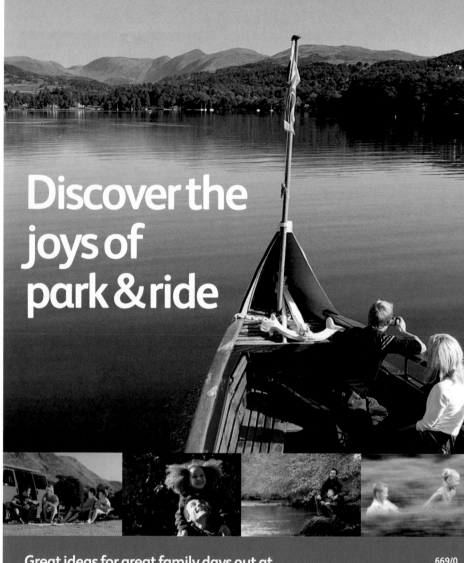

Discover the joys of park & ride

'It's time to wake up to the fact that just because you're on a break with the kids, it doesn't mean you've had your sense of taste surgically removed.'

located, if faceless, chain hotel – such as a Premier Travel Inn – than some of the oppressive, unfriendly guesthouses we discovered in our travels, which is why you'll find some branches of budget chains in our city breaks.

The high-end family hotel and the snug B&B might just not cut it for the family keen to retain a sense of independence, even adventure, on their holiday. The rates in such places might be prohibitive for larger families too. Step up, then, the mighty Youth Hostels Association. Most people are aware that this venerable charitable institution has moved with the times. It may not have progressed as far as fluffy bath robes and heated pools as yet, but the Association's diverse portfolio of properties are becoming serious competition for budget B&Bs and chain hotels. And do banish all thoughts of spartan bunkhouses with serried ranks of walking boots and rainsoaked Gore-Tex in the lobby. Many hostels now have family rooms (many en suite), restaurants, games rooms and comfortable lounges. The five-star ones are a joy to behold. Youth hostels have the edge because they are invariably in enviable settings, with gardens for the children and the option to self-cater using their large and well-equipped kitchens. Many have cots – and no, you don't have to provide your own bedding any more. Bring towels though. We've listed a large number of youth hostels in this guide, but for more on the association, how to join and what each of its properties offers, log on to www.yha.org.uk.

While we're on the subject of budget family holidays, the cool camping frenzy of summer 2006 did not pass us by, so we've included some top campsites in our chosen family breaks. We agree that camping can be very cool, chilled if you will, especially in the teeth of a force nine gale. In the rain. Those of us still trying to dry out our Cath Kidston tents from the previous summer should perhaps investigate the next step up from pitch-your-own camping. Really cool camping is all about tipis, preferably furnished, with a large stove in the middle. Tipi encampments are structurally reliable, totally waterproof, spacious and cuddly – and on pages 174 and 240. Camping for wimps is also the business of Feather Down Farm Days, whom we list on page 126.

a friendly welcome for all. Some of the B&B proprietors we discovered were conscientious about providing a rural idyll for stressed townies, feeding them organic veg and own-baked bread and inviting their junior guests to help collect eggs, bottlefeed lambs and bring in the cows for milking. Others offered lifts from the station, babysitting, foldaway beds, local maps and all sorts of little extra kindnesses to create a home from home.

Youthful good looks

For every B&B that provides a cosy home away from home, however, there is the cold-comfort seafront guesthouse, run along Victorian lines. At these establishments (often booked up in the summer hols) we encountered more 'well behaved children only' attitudes, a horror of any under-five that wasn't strapped down and silent, and some truly cheese-paring attitudes (fun-sized Cornflakes and marmalade in sachets for breakfast, anyone?). Such parsimony would not matter if the B&B wasn't charging a fortune and billing itself as 'homely'. We honestly believe you're better off in a splendidly

Dinner vs din dins

If the family that plays together stays together, the family that eats together may risk indigestion. Much as we believe that the ideal family meal sees all ages around a table reviewing their day over a massive bowl of spag bol (easily arranged if you're

Give us a break

self catering, camping or in a youth hostel), there are some times when adult/infant segregation seems a good idea. We're talking here about the pros and cons of the Children's Dining Room (CDR). These are a great selling point of the top family hotels listed in this guide, and they're much appreciated by most parents of babies and toddlers who believe in bedtime.

Some hotel managers are defensive about their CDRs, however. They've been accused of forcing parents to choose between their dinner and their tot. One manager even told us about the parents who surreptitiously placed their baby, in its childseat, under the dining table, even though they'd been assured that the hotel's baby listening service would alert worried parents to their crying infant immediately. It's perfectly reasonable for hotels to assume that children aged under seven might prefer to have their tea at 5 or 6pm then be bathed and put to bed, before their parents descend to the dining room, safe in the knowledge there's someone listening out for any signs of wakefulness.

Most small children's appetites decrease with tiredness; they're hardly likely to want to chomp their way through a three course meal with wine, coffee and petits fours without kicking up a bit of a kerfuffle. Most hotel restaurants have to consider the rest of their customers, who may want to enjoy a meal à deux, or with their older children, without interruptions from an over-tired high chair dweller in a bait because his parents are trying to make him eat pan-fried sea bass. The CDR in the very best family-friendly hotels serve up organic, own-made dinners for the little ones, and have staff that organise a bit of post prandial play, before bath and sleep. What could be more civilized? We say bring on the CDR for weary tots on their holidays, and let the older members of the family linger over their linguine.

Junior show time

While talking to many parents in the course of researching *Family Breaks in Britain*, we detected a vaguely troubled attitude towards holidaying with children. Many parents agree that fresh air, good food, sandcastles on the beach and picnics in beauty spots, interspersed with the odd castle or museum visit did the ideal family holiday make. Even so, the same parents went on to display a morbid fear of their child's capacity to be 'entertained' by such simple pleasures.

All too often, modern parents' first question when choosing an area for the family break is 'what is there for the children?', as if theme parks and ball ponds were a necessary evil to be endured for the sake of the kiddies. It's time to wake up to the fact that just because you're on a break with the kids, it doesn't mean you've had your sense of taste surgically removed. If you hate chicken nuggets, bouncy castles and petting zoos, eschew them. That's why our breaks promote a different sort of family fun day out. True, each section has its own Places to See, Things to Do section, with the zoos, castles, steam railways and adventure playgrounds we enjoyed listed and reviewed – we'll never forget the bizarre Gnome World (*see p193*) – but such entertainments are optional extras; rainy day plan Bs. It's good to know where they are in the area you're visiting, but it's quite possible, given good weather and a following wind on a coastal break, that you'll never need anything more than sun, sea, sand, a bucket and spade and a good ice-cream vendor.

Slowly but surely, the British hospitality industry is rethinking the whole family-friendliness thing. It's a concept that operates on many levels – from the CenterParcs and Butlins idea, where the family unit holidays as part of a wider tribe, to the green eco-camping family seeking splendid isolation in unspoilt countryside, to the luxurious, family-welcoming country house hotel with health spas and Michelin stars. Most of all, though, it's about warm welcomes for all ages. In these 20 Family Breaks, we've tried to cover most options, but most of all we've tried to convey how this sometimes eccentric, often startlingly beautiful little island can provide the best holiday memories.

All together
now

Sue Webster and family join the tribe.

Family holidays can be exhausting. Maybe we just need to face up to that fact. Sometimes you end up wondering why you spent so much money on a break which only transferred your domestic workload to a more exotic setting. From wading through the websites to waking up in a lumpy bed, every trip away from home tends to be blighted by the awful C-word: compromise. To paraphrase the song, kids just wanna have fun, while adults want to have, well... some fun, some good food, some nice wine, lovely views, excellent service, peace and quiet, interesting sights, comfortable accommodation — oh, and no huge bills at the end.

One way for parents to divest themselves of the daunting responsibility of the vacation agenda is to opt for a holiday park. The two biggest names in the field – Butlins and CenterParcs – promise rest and recuperation for adults, while doling out measured helpings of the freedom that children crave in a safe – detractors would say controlled – environment. Such places, however, are the Marmite of the family holiday industry (parents either love them or hate them). In our experience, young children adore them. Why? Because in the world of the family leisure park, fun for kids comes as standard.

Butlins (advertising slogan 'kids love it') is still the most recognisable name in family fun breaks. Born in 1936 when Billy Butlin opened his first resort in Skegness and introduced the Redcoats to the fun-loving populace, the resorts are still renowned for their teams of brightly-blazered entertainments staff, recruited for their singing, dancing and acting skills. Today, the original holiday camps are being manfully spruced up to meet the discerning gaze of modern parents. Possibly because, in their old incarnation, they can't possibly compete with CenterParcs, the forest-framed holiday destinations whose prices are approximately double those of Butlins – no doubt as part of a concerted effort to appeal to well-heeled folk who prefer wholesome, outdoor activities. After all, it's not just the aesthetics of holiday parks that act as powerful attractants or repellents to potential clients, though they count for a lot. It's the tribal mechanism of wanting to feel you belong.

Boutique it like Butlins

Do people feel they belong at Butlins? They're certainly thrown together in Splash Waterworld. This is the star attraction at Butlins, and everyone goes there. It's curiously gloomy inside, like an airport lounge with no natural light and jungles of plastic plants, but the atmosphere is warm and steamy. It attracts large crowds in high season – so many that there are sometimes no changing cubicles available and you're obliged to don your swimsuit wherever there's a space.

Once at the poolside, you gamely follow your children down a small slide that begins with water thundering on to your head from a not-very-decorative arch. After this moment, you realise there are much bigger and better things to do at the pool – try out the 'Master Blaster', for example, a sort of man-size tube in which you are squirted forwards and downwards in a yellow rubber dinghy. It's 'quite fun, but a bit boring' according to the kids, which probably means they didn't enjoy queuing along a corridor in wet swimsuits for forty minutes to reach their turn.

It's not just the swimming options that have become more sophisticated in the 70-odd years since Billy Butlin started the

craze. The accommodation is now more appealing than in Butlins's 20th-century heyday. In case you thought it was all chalets and glamorous granny competitions, a new 'boutique' hotel has been built at Butlins Bognor Regis, which is really quite smart (*see p73*). Outside it resembles a white ocean liner; inside there are laminate floors, horseshoe-shaped chairs, careful neutrals and strategic strips of determinedly contemporary colours: lime, tangerine, fuchsia. The most expensive rooms have sea views; from the others, you can gaze out through floor-to-ceiling windows over a vast car park, occasionally enlivened by guests taking their 'fun bike' (a four-seater pedalling machine with canopy) for an illicit spin beyond the designated area.

This is not so much loutish behaviour as a necessity, since some things about these holiday resorts – their size, for example – do not compare favourably with the rather wider open spaces of CenterParcs. In your 30-minute fun bike hire period you can easily pedal round the entire Butlins site several times. You go past the 'Deluxe Lodges', where guests get a parking space right outside, past the 'Gold' and 'Silver' apartments (distinguished by the size and number of TVs, kitchen appliances and so on) trundle along the little rows of houses named Oyster Bay and Anchor Boulevard,

'The sense of freedom engendered by being able to ride up and down the road on your own as a young child is priceless — if, at the same time, a sad indictment of modern urban life.'

take in the (unheated) outdoor pool with its quaint, painted concrete fountains, swing by the go-kart track and mini funfair and end up back at the 'traditional pub' next to the sports pitches.

If you like sport, you may notice how weirdly truncated everything is. This is where twenty or so Dads and lads will be kicking a ball around on a dusty surface no bigger than a regular tennis court, while racquet fans are invited to play a game of 'short tennis' on a child-size court. A little strip of sand that might be the walkway to your dustbin turns out to be the boules pitch. You have to pinch yourself quickly, before you start daydreaming of sporting activities for adults, because Butlins is clearly not the place for them.

Nonetheless, the pleasure elicited from watching your children having a good time has to count for a good deal. And in Butlins, everywhere you look there are sprogs enjoying themselves, while their parents and grandparents look on fondly. You have to admire the self-sacrifice, which is greater than mere time. It costs money to provide such enjoyment, as in £1 for five minutes' bouncing on the trampolines; £4 for the go-karts, £8 for the fun bikes and so on. If you have taken the swanky route of staying in the boutique hotel, then hiring a fun bike may cause you to reflect on your good fortune, because as you stand in line you get to stare at the sobering list of hire charges for items apparently not included in 'standard' accommodation, such as 'fridge, £5 per day; toaster, £2; hairdryer, £2' and so on.

There's largesse to be appreciated in other quarters, however. Food, for example, is plentiful – perfect if you've brought a large family group along for the fun. There's plenty of all-you-can-eat going on, which, while it's not exactly the way forward in these obesity obsessed days, is fine for a few days' pigging out on your holiday. In Skegness Butlins, they've factored in a bit of Me Time for the parents too. The Day Spa for men and women (it's out-of-bounds for the under-18s) has proved an enormous draw. Treatments, which range in price from £10 for hand treatments to £60 for a Hawaiian Hot Mineral Stone massage, are good value and professionally executed.

To be fair, lots of things are included in the price of a break at Butlins. The evening entertainment is hugely popular, with people queuing from early evening onwards for ringside seats at pop concerts or WWF wrestling matches. The whole family can go for free, though you may have to fork out a few quid for, say, a giant foam hand with pointing finger. (These are used to keep time in the general chant of 'Lo-ser! Lo-ser!' orchestrated by a bouncy young Redcoat, who skips round the ring, ducking to avoid the falling bodies of wrestlers.) If the kids get bored with the entertainment, they can hang about in the foyer playing on the slot machines or buying lurid sweets from a candy store that stays open conveniently late. Or they can just sleep in their buggies, on chairs and even on the floor of the auditorium, wonderfully oblivious to the noise and movement.

Parc & ride

You don't get any sort of free evening entertainment at CenterParcs, where the 'Sub-Tropical Swimming Paradise' has real rocks, real plants and real daylight. It's busy, but it is still possible to shoot down 'The Rapids'– a twisting miniature river, which causes you to tumble downstream in a hilariously uncontrolled meeting of strangers' limbs – thirty times or more in an afternoon. Other activities, from horse riding to abseiling and sailing to salsa, are controlled by cost. CenterParcs is hardly an exclusive experience. Some eight or nine hundred forest lodges (these rustic holiday homesteads are artfully planted about with trees to give a partial illusion of privacy) may be occupied at any one site on a summer weekend, plus any guests staying at the hotel. If at first the resort appears baffling in its geography –

All together now

and judging by the number of people asking for directions on a Friday night, many spend their first evening going round in circles – that is because it is built in circles. A series of lakes form focal points for the lodges, with each car-free road looping round to lead to the 'Village Square' or 'Piazza', with its multiple eateries got up as outlets for different national cuisines ('Chez Pierre', 'Luciano's'). Most guests take advantage of the strict no-traffic policy to cycle around on hired bikes (around £20 per cycle per day), but quickly discover that,

as in Holland, a nation of pedallers means no one can pedal very fast.

Kids love it, though. Just as they love Butlins – to be honest, ours didn't seem to notice the difference between the two holidays; it's us parents who vote with our wallets. The sense of freedom engendered by being able to ride up and down the road on your own as a young child is priceless – if, at the same time, a sad indictment of modern urban life. In a resort like CenterParcs, that freedom is made possible by strict security. Every car is checked on entry for its corresponding lodge number; early exit (in case you prefer to forego your last day in favour of avoiding the soul-destroying queues to leave) has to be sanctioned by a guard who helps you negotiate the barrier system.

According to most resort clients, the helpfulness of the staff at any venue is crucial. Fans of Eurocamp, a sort of Gallic CenterParcs based around trailer homes, with similar activities ('same plastic garden furniture, but the baguettes are real and there's more chance of sunshine...') say that they appreciate the route maps and children's activity packs sent for their car journey, and the nothing-is-too-much-trouble attitude of the staff. They would not, however, return to certain Eurocamp sites where the young playleaders seemed more interested in their own sex lives than their little charges' enjoyment. The success of your holiday park experience is partly in the hands of the people paid to look after you. Thus, the perky Butlins Redcoat making a fuss of the children, or the CenterParcs refuse collector who chirrups 'Good Morning', has a positive effect. Not so the cleaner we witnessed at Butlins, who kept pausing to sweep cigarette ends into his dustpan but missed them, in a perfect parody of an employee merely going through the motions. This, of course, was just one employee having a bad day, but the image stayed with us.

Is it worth paying more money to be surrounded by people who enjoy their jobs when you are staying in an enclosed resort? The answer has to be 'yes', if only because, for the time you are there, a holiday camp feels like your whole world. You are tied to it by a sense of cost in exactly the same way that an employee is tied to it by his need for income. You have paid handsomely for the facilities on offer, and feel you should make the most of them. So, having swum, skated, climbed, ridden and sailed, you may well be too exhausted to go off-site in search of alternative environments, which sounds rather like the parents' lot in general. So what were we saying about transporting your workload to a more exotic location? Ah well. That's families for you.

THE PROS AND CONS OF FAMILY HOLIDAY RESORTS

Altogether a good thing?

The kids will be happy.

Everything is on site — no need to research an interesting tourist destination.

Food offerings are always geared towards families.

A lively atmosphere means you're never bored.

You can try lots of activities unavailable at home.

Altogether less than appealing?

The adults may not be happy.

Hard to escape a feeling of claustrophobia.

Gourmets will be gagging for a decent meal.

Don't go if you value peace and quiet.

The extras cost far more than you might think.

Butlins

Bognor Regis West Sussex PO21 1JJ
Minehead Somerset TA24 5SH
Skegness Lincolnshire PE25 1NJ
Telephone/website for all (0870 145 0040/www.butlinsonline.co.uk)

CenterParcs

Elveden Forest Brandon, Suffolk IP27 0YZ
Longleat Forest Warminster, Wiltshire BA12 7PU
Sherwood Forest Rufford, Newark, Nottinghamshire NG22 9DN
Whinfell Forest Penrith, Cumbria CA10 2DW
Telephone/website for all (0870 067 3030/www.centerparcs.co.uk)

All together now

Shore thing

From rock pools to surf schools – ten top beaches for all reasons.

BEST FOR ACTIVITIES

Minnis Bay, Birchington, Kent

There's swimming, sea-canoeing, sailing, a fab play area and promenade, beach huts, and a café – children are truly spoilt for choice. *See p51.*

BEST FOR BEACHCOMBING

Compton Bay, Isle of Wight

Fossils are the treasures here – you might strike lucky and find a dinosaur bone. *See p103.*

BEST BLUE-FLAG COLLECTION

Sandbanks, Poole, Dorset

Has won the European Blue Flag (the eco-label for clean beaches) more times than any other British resort – 17 years and counting. *See p118.*

BEST FOR ALL THE FUN OF THE FAIR

Blackpool, Lancashire
The candy floss! The coasters! The donkeys! The bright lights! The sea-and-sand beach and the famed Pleasure Beach shriek at each other across Ocean Boulevard. *See p246.*

BEST FOR PUKKA TUCK

Watergate Bay, Cornwall
Jamie Oliver's Fifteen Cornwall, as well as the more affordable Beach Hut café, means refuelling with great grub is easy-peasy. *See p177.*

BEST FOR ROCK-POOLING

East Portlemouth, near Salcombe, Devon
It's got rockpools galore, but there's also plenty of golden sand for castles. *See p141.*

BEST FOR SAFE PADDLING

West Wittering, West Sussex
Sandy blue lagoons are revealed in 'God's Pocket' at low tide. *See p70.*

BEST FOR SANDCASTLES

Woolacombe Bay, North Devon
This sandy paradise runs a hotly-contested annual Sandcastle Competition, taken very seriously until the post-judgement castle-crushing jamboree. In 2007 the big event is to be held on 1 July. *See p182.*

BEST FOR SURF SQUIRTS

Caswell Bay, Gower Peninsula
Learn how to stay upright while swallowing lots of Blue Flag seawater. *See p224.*

BEST FOR WILDLIFE

Holkham Bay, Norfolk
The Holkham foreshore is birders' heaven. Sanderlings, oystercatchers, ringed plovers and wheatears are just four of the species that feed here. Just make sure you keep your binoculars trained away from the naturists who share this beach with the naturalists. *See p208.*

The Breaks

he Breaks

0   100 miles

0   150 km

© Copyright Time Out Group 2007

LANTIC

OCEAN

NORTH

SEA

SCOTLAND

Edinburgh
(p298)

Northumberland
(p286)

NORTHERN
IRELAND

The Lake District
(p258)

Whitby
(p272)

Irish Sea

Blackpool
(p246)

REPUBLIC OF
IRELAND

Staffordshire
(p194)

North Norfolk
(p204)

WALES

ENGLAND

The Dyfi Valley
to Southern
Snowdonia
(p232)

The Gower
Peninsula
(p218)

London
(p26)

Somerset &
Wiltshire
(p124)

The North
Kent Coast
(p46)

North Devon
(p182)

The New
Forest
(p78)

West
Sussex
(p62)

The Isle
of Purbeck
(p108)

Cornwall's
Atlantic Coast
(p164)

South Devon's
Riviera
(p136)

Isle of Wight
(p94)

English Channel

Cornish Riviera
to the Lizard
(p150)

FRANCE

London

Capital fun for families.

The best city break destination in the world is as stimulating for children as it is for their parents. Families would need to stay a year to see all the bits we could recommend. This chapter can only scrape the surface of this major financial, political and cultural centre, one of the oldest – and youngest – cities in the world. London dates back two thousand years, but nearly a quarter of its population haven't yet celebrated their eighteenth birthday. With that in mind, it's as well that the powers that be, not least the current Mayor of London, Ken Livingstone, are making child-friendliness a priority in this city.

Since the turn of this century, London has become much more fun to explore with your children. The biggest plus point for families was the dropping of admission charges for national museums and galleries (do give a donation though). More recently, Mayor Ken's controversial congestion charge has meant the West End and parts of West London are far less clogged with traffic. All public transport is free for children aged up to eleven; young people aged up to 18 travel free on the buses. This has helped to raise London's profile as a good place to holiday with the kids. Of course, there's an urgent reason for a massive, city-wide refurb. We've only got five or so years until the 2012 Olympics, and parks and sports facilities, not to mention transport links, have to be greatly improved by then. Will this venerable old city scrub up well for the occasion? The race is on.

Covent Garden
Piazza

"we enjoyed the spacious rooms"

**2 Kemplay Road
London
NW3 1SY**

www.hampsteadguesthouse.com

020 7435 8679

HAMPSTEAD VILLAGE GUESTHOUSE

We never planned to start a hotel in our family home but, when life changed, it was a natural development for the house, which had always welcomed a steady stream of visitors, to become a Guesthouse.

Whilst preserving the Victorian character of the house, all rooms have good writing tables, free wi-fi access and guests can use a laptop and mobile phone at no extra charge. Most important for families is the fridge and kettle in each room and, for general use, there are baby monitors, cots, high chairs, changing mat and a selection of toys which most children make a beeline for.

We have a beautiful garden which is a haven in summer. Hampstead Heath, which is very nearby, is an ideal place for children, with a playground just at the bottom of the road and paddling pool within walking distance. Kentish Town City Farm, also a wonderful place for children, is nearby.

"the family atmosphere made us feel welcome"   *"...this is heaven"*

Peaceful setting, close to
Hampstead Heath, yet in the heart
of lively Hampstead Village

~

Close to underground and bus.
Centre of London in 15 minutes.

~

Large rooms full of character, plus
modern amenities: TV, fridge, kettle
and direct-dial telephone.

~

Breakfast in the garden,
weather permitting

~

Accommodation from £50

~

No smoking

"you made our stay very happy"

The Congestion Charging zone (*see p36* Central London map to check the zone's boundary, marked out as a red line labelled 'C') means that car drivers must pay £8 to drive into Central London (do this by text, online at www.cclondon.com, or by phone, 0845 900 1234, 7am-6.30pm Mon-Fri). Parking is difficult and expensive – up to £1 for every 15 minutes. Traffic wardens are ubiquitous and merciless. With this in mind, it's advisable to use public transport or taxis. Better still, invest in a *London A-Z* and walk – you'll see much more of the city.

London's size can seem overwhelming. The tube is the most straightforward way to get around, but if you're not in a hurry, the bus is more picturesque. Good routes for stringing the sights together are the 7, 8, 11 and 12 (all double decker buses) and the RV1, the single-decker river route. Most Routemaster buses have been taken off Transport for London's commuter roster, but two of them – numbers 9 and 15 – run as Heritage Routes, operating between Trafalgar Square and Tower Hill (15) and the Royal Albert Hall and Aldwych (9). Normal fares apply; for more details check www.routemaster.org.uk.

If your sightseeing programme includes more expensive attractions such as the Tower of London (*see p45*) and London Zoo (*see p44*), a London Pass (0870 242 9988, www.londonpass.com), which gives pre-paid access to more than 50 attractions, is worth investing in.

Only a fraction of London's treasures are listed here; for a veritable directory of places to visit, as well as restaurants, shops, and arts and sports venues, arm yourself with a copy of *Time Out London for Children* (£9.99 at all good bookshops).

WHERE TO STAY

The current hotel boom in London is expected to continue till the 2012 Olympics – by which time at least 20,000 rooms will have been added. In the long term, this should provide more much-needed options for the beleaguered family looking for an affordable berth in central London. In the short term, however, London remains one of the most expensive cities in the world where decent hotels are concerned.

The Youth Hostels Association can help here, so we've included the best London branches below. A giant hostel is proposed for Bolsover Street in W1; check www.yha.org.uk for details. Sadly, the most handsome hostel – in a wing of Holland House, a stately Kensington mansion (0870 770 5866) – doesn't have family rooms (dorms for eight to 20 people aren't great for youngsters). Also, the YHA's 'shop tilll you drop' hostel, bang in the middle of Soho, is a wee bit noisy for our tastes.

While scouting for cut-price rooms, don't dismiss the chains. The formula might be corporate, but when you can bag a double room with two extra child beds and a cot on the South Bank for around £90 (Premier Travel Inn, Metro London County Hall, www.travelinn.co.uk) or a family room with access to a swimming pool, free meals for kids and free tickets to London Zoo thrown in for £99 (a recent half term special from Holiday Inn, www.holiday-inn.com), or a normally £89 family room in the heart of touristy Covent Garden (Travelodge, www.travelodge.co.uk) for a bargain price of just £26, who gives a monkey's about feeling a bit institutionalised?

For families looking for a bit of urban swank, budget doesn't necessarily come into it, and some flashy hotels are happy to unbend a little when it comes to children. Our favourite bit of posh – brilliantly placed for shopping, parklife and museums – is the Draycott (*see p31*). The grande dame of the London hotel scene, The Dorchester (53 Park Lane, W1, 7629 8888, www.thedorchester.com), has also muscled in on the child-friendly act. It may have the grandest lobby in town, but its Easter family rate of £265 for a superior double room, plus a free second room for two under-16s, is generous for this place. It also throws in cookies and lemonade, a children's goody bag and a 'Dorchester Kids' pack.

If you prefer self-catering, consider a Citadines apartment (www.citadines.com). Studios, which sleep up to six people, have a kitchenette and baby facilities. The Citadines complex at Trafalgar Square cannot be beaten for location, and the apartments are clean and well equipped, if snug – fine for a sightseeing base.

Amsterdam Hotel

7 Trebovir Road, Earl's Court, SW5 9LS (0800 279 9132/www.amsterdam-hotel.com). Earl's Court tube. **Rates** £90-£148. **Credit** AmEx, DC, MC, V.

We particularly like the rooms with little balconies that overlook the street at this popular, affordable hotel. Its location near the tube has earned it many fans on the tourist trail, as has the bright, clean cut of its gib. An elegant, palm-filled lobby paves the way to 28 neatly decorated en suite rooms with

TOURIST INFORMATION

Visit London
1 Lower Regent Street, Piccadilly Circus, SW1Y 4XT (0870 156 6366/ www.visitlondon.com).
www.kidslovelondon.com
www.london.gov.uk
www.londontown.com
www.whatson4kids.com

City of London Youth Hostel

A few minutes' walk away from the British Museum, Arran House, occupying a couple of Georgian townhouses, is especially welcoming to family groups. The warren of corridors and rooms allow plenty of scope for guests with children. There are huge family rooms with bathrooms, with space to add a couple of bunks or cots, interconnecting pairs of rooms, or double rooms with a twin bed and bathroom across the corridor, which parents with older children may find preferable. Simply furnished and very clean, the rooms all have televisions. Some also have DVD players (for those that don't, the DVD player in the sitting room is connected to the tellies upstairs). The friendly manager keeps a stash of films for children, and is happy to get out the bubble machine for impromptu fun and games in the garden. It's a very beautiful garden, with seats for summer breakfasts, and a pleasant, sheltered spot where children can play safely while their parents plan the day's activities. The communal rooms, such as the downstairs breakfast room and the comfortable lounge with its lived-in leather sofas, bookshelves and television, are also pleasant places to linger. When the kitchen is free, after 3pm, guests can use the facilities to cook up family suppers to eat around the big kitchen table or in the breakfast room (provided they clear up after themselves). It's unusual to find such easy-going homeliness in a central London guesthouse. There isn't a baby-listening service, but hotel staff can babysit if you fancy an evening out on the town.

televisions; innocuous pastel shades give an impression of space, even in the smaller rooms. For guests with children, the suites, with a small sitting area and kitchenette, are in demand. The baby-listening service is free, and babysitting can be arranged with an agency for £8 per hour. Downstairs there's an internet room and a sheltered garden open from April to October. Staff can provide high chairs, cots and pushchairs.

Arran House Hotel

77-79 Gower Street, WC1E 6HJ (7636 2186/www.london-hotel.co.uk). Goodge Street or Tottenham Court Road tube. **Rates** *£72-£130.* **Credit** MC, V.

City of London Youth Hostel

36 Carter Lane, EC4V 5AB (0870 770 5764/www.yha.org.uk). St Paul's tube. **Open** *24hrs daily.* **Rates** *£22.50; £20.95 under-18s; £86-£120 family room.* **Credit** MC, V.
Fancy a room only 100m away from St Paul's Cathedral? That's what you get at this three-star hostel, set in the rather gothic-looking building

that used to be the choirboys' school. The 190-bed hostel has several small rooms for singles and couples, but the majority are four- to eight-bed spaces, which are ideal for families. There are double beds for parents – children sharing the room have comfy little bunks, and there are televisions and basins in the room. Showers and toilets are just across the corridor, each of which is given an iconic London street name – we stayed on Carnaby Street. From Carter Street you can walk to top City destinations and take your pick of the restaurant chains around the cathedral. Breakfast, served in the hostel's restaurant, is included in the price of your stay and is quite a continental spread – cereals, yoghurts, pastries, toast, hard-boiled eggs, cheese, cold meats and fruit. Snacks and evening meals are also available, and packed lunches (£4.30, £3.40 children) can be put together for sightseers on a budget.

Draycott Hotel

26 Cadogan Gardens, SW3 2RP (7730 6466/www.draycotthotel.com). Sloane Square tube. **Rates** *£180-£370.* **Credit** *AmEx, DC, MC, V.*

Quintessentially English, unashamedly luxurious and warmly welcoming, the Draycott sits discreetly in one of London's wealthiest residential areas, just off the King's Road. Taking up three solid late Edwardian houses, it looks for all the world like a wealthy gentleman's club, but softening elements such as the trademark urns of red and green apples in the lobby, vast floral arrangements and a large garden with a perfect lawn and mature shrubbery give it a country manor feel. Service couldn't be more accommodating. Guests are plied with little treats – tea and biscuits at 4pm, champagne at 6pm, cocoa at 10pm – all compliments of the Draycott. Although there's no dedicated restaurant (there are too many good ones in the area), there is a chef on duty to prepare light lunches and room-service suppers (anything from beans on toast to smoked salmon and champagne). The 35 rooms, which include several delightful family suites, are huge and gracious, individually furnished and each glorying in a theatrical moniker – the Noel Coward, for example, or the Ellen Terry, with its star quality Victorian dressing room. The JM Barrie is a good suite for children, with prints of Kate Greenaway's drawings adorning the walls of the bunk-bedded children's quarters off the huge main room. All the comforts that give the Draycott its luxury status – free Wi-Fi, CD and DVD players and satellite television, air-conditioning, bathtubs and power showers and massive double beds – are much appreciated by family groups, but the Draycott likes to go that extra mile come the weekend. Ask about the Family Package, which gives two adults and two children a garden-view double room with an adjacent single room, PlayStation availability, babysitting, Big Bus Tour tickets, teddy bears, children's bathrobes and gift packs and a boiled egg and soldier breakfast for £315 per family. That's doing London in some style.

Earl's Court Hostel

38 Bolton Gardens, SW5 OAQ (0870 770 5804/www.yha.org.uk). Gloucester Road or South Kensington tube. **Open** *24hrs daily.* **Rates** *£20.95; £18.95 under-18s; £53.60-£78 family room.* **Credit** *MC, V.*

The YHA's young and trendy outpost was due to re-open as we went to press, all refurbished after a fire in early 2006. The YHA promised the 186 rooms, including four- to-six-bed rooms, will all be bright and clean, with fresh white walls and new furniture. Its proximity to the Kensington museums, shopping centres and Earl's Court and Olympia, and easy access to Heathrow Airport, are a big draw, particularly with foreign students, although families in the know recommend it too. Breakfast isn't included in the price of an overnight stay, but there is a self-catering kitchen on site and any number of cafés, restaurants and supermarkets just nearby.

Garden Court Hotel

30-31 Kensington Gardens Square, W2 4BG (7229 2553/www.gardencourt hotel.co.uk). Bayswater or Queensway tube. **Rates** *£68-£160.* **Credit** *MC, V.*

TOP 5

SIGHTSEEING TRIPS

Big Bus Company
0800 169 1365/7233 9533/ www.bigbustours.com.
Open-top double decker buses with commentary and a river cruise option.

London Duck Tours
7928 3132/www.londonduck tours.co.uk.
Tours in a DUKW amphibious vehicle take you in and out of the river.

London RIB Voyages
7401 8834/www.londonribvoyages.com.
Rigid inflatable boats skim the Thames.

Original London Walks
7624 3978/www.walks.com.
Themed walks through the historic city with a knowledgeable narrator.

Original London Sightseeing Tour
8877 1722/www.theoriginaltour.com.
This open-top, double-decker bus tour specialist also does Kids Club tours.

This tastefully appointed but unfussy family hotel is one of the best moderately-priced places to stay in town. It's close to Portobello Road market and Hyde Park, which gives it a real London buzz, emphasised by the now legendary antique Beefeater statue standing to attention in reception. The downstairs communal area is pleasant to linger in, with its polished wood floors and squashy leather sofas, and the 34 cheery rooms are even better. They have a bright, modern look, desks and chairs and plenty of space. The three family rooms are particularly comfortable places to set up camp for the weekend. Cots can be provided free of charge, but there's no baby-listening service. As the name suggests, the hotel has a small walled garden of impressive lushness; guests have access to the private square too (a rare privilege in London).

Hampstead Village Guesthouse

2 Kemplay Road, NW3 1SY (7435 8679/www. hampsteadguesthouse.com). Hampstead tube/Hampstead Heath rail. **Rates** *£75-£170.* **Credit** AmEx, MC, V.
Annemarie van der Meer's handsome Hampstead homestead has been one of London's favourite guesthouses for 25 years. Aptly enough for the location, it has a bohemian air. There are lots of toys around, as Annemarie's grandchildren are frequent visitors, and every one of the nine guest rooms has quirky, characterful fixtures and fittings. Some are real collectors' pieces; others are just entertaining. For families, there are plenty of options. One of the big double rooms has a massive antique bath in the corner, as well as the snug little shower and toilet unit, which has been worked into the antique setting in many of the larger rooms. In the smaller rooms, ingenious methods make for increased space. A bed folds out of a giant wardrobe; a little cabinet conceals a fold-out basin salvaged from an old-fashioned Pullman train. Each room has a fridge, basin, direct-dial telephone and Wi-Fi, although there's no baby-listening service. Downstairs there's a sitting room, a music room and a fantastically picturesque kitchen, where a jumble of pots, pans and chinaware create a scene of arty domestic bliss on open shelving. Annemarie's room rates don't include breakfast (£7 extra) – many of her guests prefer to walk to cafés round the corner on Hampstead High Street. The paved garden has places to play and outside seating for family meals. The garage has been converted into a self-contained apartment, which is great for a family; the shed, too, has become a cosy studio flat. Annemarie and her husband Jim were in the midst of refurbishing the downstairs area to create more play space when we called: an enclosed roof garden with play facilities is also planned.

Hart House Hotel

51 Gloucester Place, W1U 8JF (7935 2288/ www.harthouse.co.uk). Marble Arch tube. **Rates** *£95-£160.* **Credit** MC, V.

Handy for London Zoo and Regent's Park, as well as Hyde Park, Oxford and Bond Streets and the tasteful shops of Marylebone, Hart House is, like many of the city's guesthouses, a TARDIS-like Georgian townhouse. The reception area is down a long corridor, liberally festooned with tourist brochures. Upstairs the rooms are gratifyingly bright, thanks to some huge windows and fresh, functional decoration (they're refurbished regularly). The triple rooms are perfectly spacious for a family of four, and cots and Z-beds are easily moved in for larger families. All the rooms have televisions and are en suite. Family suites, with connecting rooms, can be also be arranged. Cots and high chairs can be provided and a bucket of toys keeps the children entertained; staff can babysit for a reasonable £5 hourly rate.

London Thameside Youth Hostel

20 Salter Road, SE16 5PR (7232 2114/www. yha.org.uk). Rotherhithe tube. **Rates** *£20.95; £18.95 under-18s; £42-£51.50 family room.* **Credit** MC, V.
The south London outpost of the YHA's capital family, Thameside is a purpose-built hostel, opened by the Queen in 1993. All its rooms, whether they are little two-person arrangements, rooms for families of up to six, or eight- and ten-bedded dorms, have bunks to sleep in, basic en suite bathroom facilities (shower and toilet) and a little kettle. They're pretty functional, but bright and modern. In the basement there's a television lounge with games, books and toys for children. The communal kitchen has plenty of equipment for people to cook their own meals; otherwise the YHA Taste restaurant provides a continental breakfast (free for all those who book an overnight stay), paninis, salads and light lunches, as well as three-course dinners starring comforting fare such as steak and ale pie and fruit salad and cream. The glass roofed reception area, where the restaurant and bar is located, has computer terminals and tourist information, and there's an outside patio area for summer eating. Budgie bike hire, based in the hostel, lends out wheels for £9 per day.

Meininger City Hostel at Baden-Powell House

65-67 Queen's Gate, SW7 5JS (7590 6900/ www.scoutbase.org.uk). Gloucester Road or South Kensington tube. **Open** *24hrs daily.* **Rates** *£90-£120.* **Credit** AmEx, MC, V.
The Chief Scout's Memorial Hostel has severed its links with the Youth Hostels Association and got into bed with a Berlin company called Meininger City Hostels, self-styled pioneer of the 'boutique' hostel. This means that although prices are low, the word 'hostel' doesn't have to detract from mod cons such as family rooms with en suite facilities, air conditioning, televisions and Wi-Fi (access tokens can be purchased). Other little luxuries include a roof terrace, tea and coffee facilities and on-site parking – a priceless commodity round here. That said, the rooms, though bright and clean,

are functional, and there's no getting away from the fact that you are, indeed, in a hostel. With a location and prices like these, however, who cares about fripperies like fluffy bath robes and complimentary fruit baskets?

New Linden

59 Leinster Square, W2 4PS (7221 4321/www. mayflower-group.co.uk). Bayswater tube. **Rates** £59-£200. **Credit** AmEx, MC, V.
A bit of a budget showpiece, this one. After a major refurbishment the rooms are modern and modish, with white walls, wooden floors and streamlined furnishings with some twirly Eastern influences. It's the location, however, that interests families as much as the tasteful interiors. Just a short walk away from Portobello Road market to the west and Kensington Gardens due south, there's no shortage of fun to be had round here. All 52 rooms are en suite, and some of the marble bathrooms have deluge shower heads. Flatscreen TVs and CD players come as standard. Some of the suites have balconies, and one split-level family room retains elaborate period pillars and cornicing. Then there are three quad-size bedrooms, perfect for a family of four or, for those with older children, double rooms with interconnecting doors. You can borrow a cot at no extra charge.

St Pancras YHA Hostel

79-81 Euston Road, NW1 2QS (0870 770 6044/www.yha.org.uk). King's Cross tube/rail. **Open** 24hrs daily. **Rates** £24.60; £20.50 under-18s; £44-£130 family room. **Credit** MC V.

Right opposite St Pancras Station, and minutes away from King's Cross and Euston stations, the YHA's Euston Road hostel is well set up for transport links in and out of the city centre. For families, the location is a gift. It's fifteen minutes' walk away from every teen's favourite, Camden market, and five minutes away from the London Wildlife Trust's flagship nature reserve at Camley Street (7833 2311, www.wildlondon.org.uk). So depending on their age, the kids can either go pond-dipping, trainspotting (platform 9 and three quarters from King's Cross Station) or coolhunting down the market. Then there's the British Library at 96 Euston Road (7412 7332, www.bl.uk) and London Canal Museum (12-13 New Wharf Road, 7713 0836, www.canalmuseum.org.uk) to consider. The King's Cross hostel is a four-star establishment, which means there are rooms with en suite bathrooms and double beds (often hard to find in YHA-land) as well as family rooms that sleep four, five and six. There's also a cycle store, restaurant and self-catering kitchen. Board games and television are available.

Vicarage Hotel

10 Vicarage Gate, W8 4AG (7229 4030/www.londonvicaragehotel.com). High Street Kensington or Notting Hill Gate tube. **Rates** £78-£140. **Credit** AmEx, MC, V.
This attractive hotel occupies six floors of a handsome Kensington terrace and has some rather grand touches, such as vast Victorian landing windows festooned with foliage and statuary, elaborate cornicing, ornate mirrors and heavy, highly polished antique furniture. Climb the stairs – there are plenty to keep you fit – to reach the

Three-wheeling through car-free **Covent Garden Piazza**. *See p40.*

spacious, tastefully appointed family rooms. There's a very gorgeous double with a smaller twin-bed across the way and a bathroom on the same landing, or you can go for the larger, en suite triple. Cots aren't provided, so you'll need to bring your own. All 19 rooms are individually decorated, though not all of them have televisions. The summery television lounge is a pleasant place to congregate, however. The chambermaids offer babysitting if you're after an evening out.

WHERE TO EAT & DRINK

Benihana

37 Sackville Street, W1S 3DQ (7494 2525/ www.benihana.co.uk). Piccadilly Circus tube. **Meals served** noon-3pm, 5.30-10.30pm Mon-Sat; noon-3pm, 5-10pm Sun. **Set lunch** £8.75-£25 4 courses. **Set dinner** £17-£50 6 courses. **Credit** AmEx, DC, MC, V.

One of three London links in an international chain of Japanese restaurants owned by an ex-Olympic wrestler, Benihana has built its success on creating a performance out of meal preparation. Diners sit at the large, half-moon-shaped teppanyaki tables and make their selection of meat and/or fish (teriyaki steak, tuna or chicken, prawns, filet mignon and lobster tails), after which the red-toqued chefs claim centre stage. Knives are released from holsters, and vegetables and fish are sacrificed for the chefs to show off their (admittedly awesome) cutting skills. The grilled items, spiced up with mustard and ginger dips, are all fresh and healthy-tasting, but it's the preparation that everyone comes for. Pepperpots fly through the air, to squeals of delight from the youngsters. **Branches:** 77 King's Road, Chelsea, SW3 4NX (7376 7799); 100 Avenue Road, South Hampstead, NW3 3HF (7586 9508).

Blue Kangaroo

555 King's Road, SW6 2EB (7371 7622/ www.thebluekangaroo.co.uk). Fulham Broadway or Sloane Square tube, then 11, 19, 22 bus. **Meals served** 9.30am-7.30pm daily. **Main courses** £6.95-£13.80. **Credit** AmEx, MC, V.

Children eat well and play well at this oft-praised family diner, and the adults don't do half badly either. Traditionalists might baulk at the nets, slides, ball ponds and tunnels in the basement – they're not exactly conducive to sitting quietly at the table – but it's great for the grown-ups to be able to linger over their meal while their young companions (four-sevens) play. The brasserie menu focusses on modern classics; we always love the roasted pumpkin risotto and the excellent salmon fishcakes, or the very fine fish in beer batter with chips. The children's menu has own-made versions of kiddy standards: chicken or fish goujons, spaghetti, penne and cottage pie made with organic meat. Puds include ice-cream puzzle pieces, banana boats or simple Petits Filous yoghurts. Service is wonderfully affable and unflappable, even at busy times.

Carluccio's Caffè

St Christopher's Place, W1U 1AY (7935 5927/www.carluccios.com). Bond Street tube. **Meals served** 7.30am-11pm Mon-Fri; 10am-11pm Sat; 10am-10pm Sun. **Main courses** £4.85-£10.95. **Credit** AmEx, MC, V.

This our favourite Carluccio's outpost, because it has plenty of outside tables for watching the world go by. The staff are always pleased to see children, and we're always delighted to pig out on the fabulous classic and regional Italian dishes, such as penne alle luganica, gnocchi gorgozola and lasagne. Main courses are generous, but it's snacky options such as breads, olives, bruschetta, breadsticks and pastries that children enjoy lunching off. Finish off your feast with delicious own-made

London

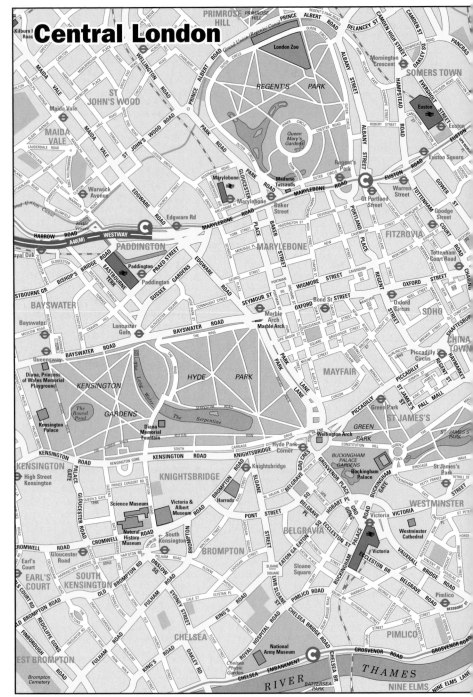

Central London

London

London

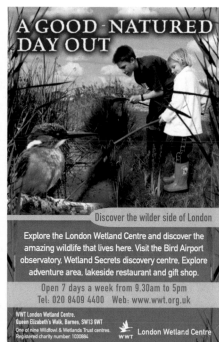

gelati and sorbets, chocolate bread and butter pudding, frothy milk or hot chocolate.
Branches: throughout the city.

Giraffe

Units 1&2, Riverside Level 1, Royal Festival Hall, South Bank, SE1 8XX (7928 2004/ www.giraffe.net). Waterloo tube/rail. **Meals served** 8am-11pm Mon-Fri; 9am-11pm Sat; 9am-10.30pm Sun. **Main courses** £7.95-£10.95. **Set meals** (5-7pm) £6.95 2 courses; (7-11pm) £8.95 2 courses. **Credit** AmEx, MC, V.
There's a Giraffe on every smart London high street, but this is the most central branch. The spacious premises exude warmth, colour and good cheer. This welcome is extended to children, which is why this mini chain is consistently at the top of the Most Child-Friendly Restaurant charts. Generous opening hours mean you can drop in for coffee, brunch or cocktails as well as meals. Children can choose from their own menu (fried or scrambled eggs and beans on toast, salmon fingers and vegetables or grilled or crunchy chicken, with good ice-cream and juice thrown in for £5.50) or opt for a squarer meal from the main menu. The veggie meze starter turns carnivorous with the addition of a lamb skewer, and the spicy chicken wings make a great light lunch. The vegetarian falafel burger, stuffed with grilled pepper, beetroot, houmous, rocket and halloumi is a delight, as are the noodle and salad dishes. The biggest treat is the white chocolate and crushed Toblerone cheesecake. **Branches**: throughout the city.

Hard Rock Café

150 Old Park Lane, W1K 1QR (7629 0382/www.hardrock.com). Hyde Park Corner tube. **Meals served** 11.30am-12.30am Mon-Thur, Sun; 11.30am-1am Fri, Sat. **Main courses** £8.45-£15.95. **Credit** AmEx, MC, V.
Time was when everyone visiting London queued gormlessly to bag a table at this rock 'n' roll-themed restaurant. Everyone's a bit more sensible these days, and the restaurant's bigger anyway, but the Hard Rock still holds a lasting appeal for children, who are treated nicely. It has everything a child could want: face-painting at certain times, a children's menu with all kinds of ketchup-covered pizza, pasta and, of course, burger creations (plus a free colouring book and crayons), as well as themed activities from time to time. Waitresses wear miniskirts and charm the boys. The hamburgers are tasty, the salads huge and quite main-course-orientated and the cheesy nachos truly moreish. When it's busy, each person has to order at least a main course.

Konditor & Cook

10 Stoney Street, SE1 9AD (7407 5100/www. konditorandcook.com). London Bridge tube/rail. **Meals served** 7.30am-6pm Mon-Fri; 8.30am-5pm Sat. **Main courses** £2-£5. **Credit** AmEx, MC, V.

This café is famous for its cakes, and let's face it, once the children have clocked the deservedly legendary brownies, banoffi slices, lemon meringue pies, treacle tarts, Curly Whirly (chocolate and vanilla) double layer cake and the sweet little cup cakes with their coloured icing, that's all they'll want. But you should try the savouries too, such as spinach and ricotta tartlets and salmon frittata. The interior is minimalist, with bare floorboards and bench seating.

Marine Ices

8 Haverstock Hill, NW3 2BL (7482 9003). Chalk Farm tube/31 bus. **Meals served** noon-3pm, 6-11pm Mon-Fri; noon-11pm Sat; noon-10pm Sun. **Main courses** £5.20-£9.60. **Credit** MC, V.
More than 70 years old now, and run by descendants of the original owner, this popular ice-cream parlour and restaurant has a famiglia atmosphere. Children usually have their sights fixed on the traditional gelateria at the back. The more modern restaurant at the front serves pizza, pasta and a few meatier Italian meals. The savoury dishes are hearty, with big bowls of steaming mussels, bresaola and spaghetti alle vongole, and an interesting scampi-based pasta dish. Whether lavished with sauces and toppings in a novelty glass or served as a simple scoop astride a wafer, the ice-cream is something special.

Planet Hollywood

13 Coventry Street, W1D 7DH (7287 1000/www.planethollywoodlondon.com). Piccadilly Circus tube. **Meals served** 11.30am-1am Mon-Sat; 11.30am-12.30am Sun. **Main courses** £10-£21.50. **Credit** AmEx, DC, MC, V.
It's noisy, it's brash, there are screens everywhere, and the menu is all about steaks, shakes, burgers and fries, with double choc-chip brownies for afters. What's there for a tween not to like? Beleaguered parents who would like a chance to enjoy their juicy burger and very good chips in peace tend to be less enamoured. Service is amused and indulgent. The children's menu, including a drink and ice-cream, is £7.95, which isn't bad for this area.

Rainforest Café

20 Shaftesbury Avenue, W1D 7EU (7434 3111/www.therainforestcafe.co.uk). Piccadilly Circus tube. **Meals served** noon-10pm Mon-Thur; noon-8pm Fri; 11am-8pm Sat; 11.30am-10pm Sun. **Main courses** £10.50-£17.50. **Credit** AmEx, MC, V.
Drag them from the ground floor shop, where a talking tree preaches sustainability while you try to sustain equilibrium, to the basement restaurant. Here, animatronic apes, elephants and parrots continue to pump up the excitability levels. Children find the Rainforest Café delightful; indeed they fare better with the menu than the adults do.

BUSY DAYS IN LONDON

This city sprawls, so it's wise to stick to one attraction-filled area per day, or exhaustion beckons. Of our selection of days out below, only Greenwich is out of Zone 1. See map p36 for the areas.

THE SOUTH BANK & BANKSIDE

Promenading along the South Bank of the Thames is a favourite tourist occupation. Capital treasures round here include the British Airways London Eye (Riverside Building, Westminster Bridge Road, SE1 7PB, 0870 500 0600, www.londoneye. com) and the London Aquarium (Riverside Building, Westminster Bridge Road, SE1 2SZ, 7967 8000, www.londonaquarium.co.uk). Further east, the National Theatre (7452 3000, www.nationaltheatre.org.uk) runs a lively June-September open-air performance festival called Watch This Space. Free events might include circus acts, street theatre, music and dance. The Tate Modern looms large on the family agenda. The gallery's weekend and school holiday art activities are free for all ages, as they are at its older sister, Tate Britain, downriver. For more information on both, and the Tate to Tate boat that connects them, log on to www.tate.org.uk. Strike east for Bankside and Tooley Street and the gory frights at the London Dungeon (28-34 Tooley Street, SE1 2SZ, 7403 7221, www.thedungeons.com), which are best for children over ten. All ages get a thrill from exploring warship museum HMS Belfast (Morgan's Lane, Tooley Street, SE1 2JH, 7940 6300, www.iwm.org.uk).

THE CITY

For great views from the Monument (Monument Street, EC3R 8AH, 7626 2717, www.cityoflondon.gov.uk), you'll have to wait for the reopening in late 2007. The best day out in this area is at the Tower of London (see p45), with regular Beefeater-guided tours. The best free day out (with complimentary activity bags for 4-11s), is at the excellent Museum of London (see p44).

BLOOMSBURY & FITZROVIA

The British Museum (see p43) has more than enough to satisfy visitors of all ages. One of London's best playgrounds, Coram's Fields is also in this area; behind it in Brunswick Square is the affecting Foundling Museum (for both see p43). Pollock's Toy Museum (1 Scala Street, W1T 2HL, 7636 3452, www.pollockstoymuseum.com) is full of intriguing playthings and has a brilliant shop.

COVENT GARDEN

This bustling tourist area is best known for its Piazza, where licensed entertainers draw huge crowds and often require volunteers from the audience. Here too is London's Transport Museum (Covent Garden Piazza, WC2E 7BB, 7379 6344, www.ltmuseum.co.uk), in the throes of refurbishment until autumn 2007; check the website for details. The Royal Opera House (Bow Street, WC2E, 7240 1200/box office 7304 4000, www.royaloperahouse.org)

has occasional child-friendly shows and free recitals. The upstairs café is grand for a spot of people watching and relief from the crowds.

TRAFALGAR SQUARE

London's main square has a café, a maritime hero on a tall column, changing public art on the fourth plinth and regular free public entertainments in school holidays. On the north edge of the square, The National Gallery (7747 2885, www.nationalgallery.org.uk) has year-round paper trails and audio tours for children, as well as regular storytelling sessions for under-fives. Just to the west, the National Portrait Gallery (7306 0055, www.npg.org.uk) loans out free activity-filled rucksacks which tie in with the Tudor, Victorian and 20th-century galleries. Across the square, St Martin-in-the-Fields has London's

only brass-rubbing centre and a popular café in the crypt (7766 1100, www.stmartin-in-the-fields.org).

SOUTH KENSINGTON

Hyde Park, the largest of London's Royal Parks, is a delight, but it's the museums that pull in the tourists. Young folk zoom in on the dinosaurs and earthquake simulator at the giant Natural History Museum (see p44) and the hands-on delights of the Science Museum (see p45). Kids' facilities at the Victoria & Albert Museum (see p45) are also a big draw at weekends.

GREENWICH

This World Heritage Site by the river, where Henry VIII's favourite palace once stood, is now dominated by Sir Christopher Wren's Old Royal Naval College (King William Walk, SE10 9NN, 8269 4747, www.greeenwich foundation.org.uk). Get here by train from London Bridge station or on a river trip from central London (Thames Cruises, 7930 3373, www.thamescruises.com) that will take you to Greenwich Pier, by the Cutty Sark (King William Walk, SE10 9HT, 8858 2698, www.cutty sark.org.uk), a 19th-century tea clipper currently being preserved for posterity. More seafaring adventure comes courtesy of the National Maritime Museum (see p45). Glorious Greenwich Park, the south-eastern Royal Park outpost, has fine river views to Docklands, a café, a deer enclosure and a playground – all of which can easily fill a fine day.

London

recycling

Natural History Museum. *See p44.*

London

Dishes such as meatballs, salmon pasta and pork and beef 'jungle spears' use organic ingredients, but others – chicken goujons, bangers and burgers – do not. Puds are a joyous medley of jelly, cream, caramel, chocolate, ice-cream and Smarties.

S&M Café

4-6 Essex Road, N1 8LN (0871 332 5665/ www.sandmcafe.co.uk). Angel tube/19, 38 bus. **Meals served** 7.30am-11.30pm Mon-Thur; 7.30am-midnight Fri; 8.30am-midnight Sat; 8.30am-10.30pm Sun. **Main courses** £2.50-£7.95. **Credit** MC, V.

You choose your sausages from a big list that includes butcher's classics and veggie variants, then select the type of mash and gravy you want. The result is served *Beano*-style, with sausages poking out of a generous mash mountain. Children can choose the same, in smaller quantities, on their menu (£3.50-£3.95), which also offers chicken nuggets or fish fingers and a drink. For afters, tuck into Eton mess, bread and butter pudding or scrumptious hot chocolate sponge pudding. **Branches**: 48 Brushfield Street, Shoreditch, E1 6AG (7247 2252); 268 Portobello Road, Notting Hill, W10 5TY (8968 8898).

Smollensky's on the Strand

105 Strand, WC2R 0AA (7497 2101/www. smollenskys.co.uk). Embankment tube/Charing Cross tube/rail. **Meals served** noon-11pm Mon-Sat; noon-10.30pm Sun. **Main courses** £8.95-£28.95. **Credit** AmEx, DC, MC, V.

To our mind, the main reason for lunching here at the weekend is the children's entertainments (clowns, face-painters and so on). Children love this place, and we're fond of it too; the service is friendly and the food is, on the whole, pretty well presented international fare. Steak is the main attraction, with such options as sirloin with béarnaise sauce and ribeye with peppercorn sauce. On the children's menu (£3.95-£8.50), mini burgers, chicken goujons and penne pasta keep little hands occupied; older children go for rather more serious options of jambalaya or steak with fruit salad to follow. Fun packs are provided.

TGI Friday's

6 Bedford Street, WC2E 9HZ (7379 0585/www.tgifridays.co.uk). Covent Garden or Embankment tube/Charing Cross tube/rail. **Meals served** noon-11.30pm

Mon-Sat; noon-11pm Sun. **Main courses**
£7.45-£17.95. **Credit** AmEx, MC, V.

You can rely on TGI staff to be pleased to see you,
however many buggies and baby carriers you
may be toting. This is especially true at the weekends, when there's sometimes a face-painter in
situ. The children's menu lists tasty burgers, fish
fillets, spaghetti bolognese or penne pomodoro
(from £3.45); sweet teeth are provided for with dirt
and worm pie (ice-cream with chocolate shavings
and jelly worms) or milkshakes and smoothies.

Tas

*22 Bloomsbury Street, WC1B 3QJ (7637
4555/www.tasrestaurant.com). Holborn or
Tottenham Court Road tube.* **Meals served**
noon-11.30pm Mon-Sat; noon-10.30pm Sun.
Main courses £5.65-£14.45.
Credit AmEx, MC, V.

Well placed for sustenance following a hike
around the British Museum, Tas is part of a mini
chain of Anatolian restaurants and is much loved
by families. The food is made for sharing, and
baskets of bread and pots of olives and houmous
arrive as you sit down. Mixed meze menus give
you falafel, feta cheese salad, lamb or chicken
shish, borek (pastries) and more of that delicious
own-made bread, and the children can select a
little sample of each to fill their plates. Staff are
generous with the puddings, such as sticky sweet
baklava or mousse-filled chocolate cake.
Branches: throughout the city.

Tootsies Grill

*120 Holland Park Avenue, W11 4UA (7229
8567/www.tootsiesrestaurants.co.uk). Holland
Park tube.* **Meals served** 9am-11pm Mon-
Thur, Sun; 9am-11.30pm Fri, Sat. **Main
courses** £5.95-£12.50. **Credit** AmEx, MC, V.

At this attractive West London branch of the
family friendly Tootsies chain, the staff are used
to milling children, especially at weekends. The
excellent burgers are served with salad, mayo and
fries, and come in an organic version. Children,
plied with wax crayons and colouring-in sheets
while they wait, have a choice of burgers, hot
dogs or organic pasta meals, with drinks and
a build-your-own sundae option for pudding.
Branches: throughout the city.

Wagamama

*11 Jamestown Road, Camden, NW1 7BW
(7428 0800/www.wagamama.com). Camden
Town tube.* **Meals served** noon-11pm
Mon-Sat; noon-10pm Sun. **Main courses**
£5.95-£9.95. **Credit** AmEx, DC, MC, V.

The original and best noodle chain, Wagamama
has 20 branches in London. This north London
outpost is bright and spacious, a gleaming,
smoke-free environment, where helpful staff
explain the wholesome menu. For children of ten
and under, there's deep fried chicken breast or
mini ramen, vegetarian or prawn noodles or rice

dishes (£2.95-£4.25), with simple puddings of
vanilla pod or coconut ice-cream, or juice ice lol-
lies for afters (£1-£1.50). Green tea is free.
Branches: throughout the city.

PLACES TO SEE, THINGS TO DO

British Museum

*Great Russell Street, WC1B 3DG (7636
1555/www.thebritishmuseum.ac.uk). Holborn,
Russell Square or Tottenham Court Road tube.*
Open *Galleries* 10am-5.30pm Mon-Wed, Sat,
Sun; 10am-8.30pm Thur, Fri. *Great Court* 9am-
6pm Mon-Wed, Sun; 9am-11pm Thur-Sat.
Admission free; donations appreciated.
Credit *Shop* AmEx, DC, MC, V.

Founded in 1753, the vast British Museum's collections are best appreciated in bite-sized chunks.
The Great Court, London's largest covered public
square, makes an impressive starting point for
exploring the Egyptian antiquities – the Rosetta
Stone, statues and mummies – and ancient Greek
treasures, including the Elgin Marbles. Time
should be found for the other collections from Asia
and Europe too. Young Friends of the British
Museum (£20 per year for ages eight to 15) enjoy
various bonuses, including museum sleepovers.

Coram's Fields

*93 Guilford Street, WC1N 1DN (7837
6138/www.coramsfields.org). Russell Square
tube.* **Open** *Apr-Sept* 9am-8pm daily.
Oct-Mar 9am-dusk daily. **Admission** free.

This seven-acre city-centre park dates back to
1747, around the time Thomas Coram established
the Foundling Hospital for abandoned children. It
has lawns, sandpits, a paddling pool, football
pitch, basketball court, climbing towers, play
areas and an assault-course pulley, as well as an
outdoor café, small animal enclosures and indoor
under-fives facilities. Adults are admitted only if
accompanied by an under-16. The park is adjacent
to the Foundling Museum (40 Brunswick Square,
7841 3600, www.foundlingmuseum.org.uk), near
the original site of the hospital.

Diana, Princess of Wales Memorial Playground

*nr Black Lion Gate, Broad Walk, Kensington
Gardens, Bayswater, W8 2UH (7298 2117/
www.royalparks.gov.uk). Bayswater or
Queensway tube.* **Open** *Summer* 10am-7.30pm
daily. *Winter* 10am-dusk daily. **Admission**
free; adults must be accompanied by a child.

Inspired by the story of Peter Pan, this commem-
orative playground is a children's wonderland.
There's a huge wooden pirate ship, mermaids'
fountain, rocky outcrops, wigwams and a treehouse encampment; much of the equipment and
facilities have been designed for use by children
with special needs.

London

Imperial War Museum

Lambeth Road, SE1 6HZ (7416 5000/www.iwm.org.uk). Lambeth North tube/Elephant & Castle tube/rail. **Open** 10am-6pm daily. **Admission** free; donations appreciated. *Exhibitions* prices vary. *Audio guides* £3.50. **Credit** MC, V.
The collection here covers conflicts, especially those involving Britain and the Commonwealth from World War I to the present day. Exhibits range from tanks, aircraft and big guns to photographs and personal memorabilia. Children are particularly fascinated by the smelly old WWI trench and a World War II home front exhibition. The Children's War exhibition is open until 2008. There are trails, quizzes and special events for families throughout the year.

Little Angel Theatre

14 Dagmar Passage, off Cross Street, Islington, N1 2DN (7226 1787/www.little angeltheatre.com). Angel tube/Highbury & Islington tube/rail. **Open** *Box office* 11am-5pm Mon-Fri; 10am-4.30pm Sat, Sun. **Tickets** £6-£9; £6 under-16s. Some pay-what-you-can performances; phone for details. **Credit** MC, V.
Established in 1961, this is still London's only permanent puppet theatre. Performances cover styles and stories from a wide range of cultural traditions, using just about every kind of marionette. Different performances have different recommended lower age limits, so check before you book; details of weekend puppet-making workshops for five- to 11-year-olds can also be found on the website

London Zoo

Regent's Park, NW1 4RY (7722 3333/ www.zsl.org). Baker Street or Camden Town tube then 274/C2 bus. **Open** *Mar-late Oct* 10am-5.30pm daily. *Late Oct-Feb* 10am-4pm daily. Check website for any changes. **Admission** £14.50; £12.70 concessions; £11.50 3-15s; £47 family (2+2 or 1+3); free under-3s. **Credit** AmEx, MC, V.
The country's most famous animal collection, the Zoological Society of London, has pygmy hippos, giraffes (no elephants), big cats, a new gorilla house, loads of birds and reptiles, a children's zoo and BUGS (the biodiversity centre with its fascinating ant empire and cockroach quarters). Get your paws on a map and find out the events timetable; highlights of the zoo day include the Animals in Action talk in the theatre and feeding time for the penguins (they're South African, in a new enclosure near the shop, as the famous listed Lubetkin one didn't suit them). The meerkats, the otters and the Activity Centre, where you can make a badge or brass rubbing for 50p, are much loved by small visitors. Stately Regent's Park, in which the zoo is set, is one of London precious Royal Parks; its open-air theatre runs a family show every summer (details on 0870 060 1811, www.openairtheatre.org).

Madame Tussauds

Marylebone Road, NW1 5LR (0870 400 3000/www.madame-tussauds.co.uk). Baker Street tube/13, 27, 74, 113, 159 bus. **Open** 9.30am-6pm daily (last entry 5.30pm). Times vary during holiday periods. **Admission** *9.30am-5pm Mon-Fri, 9.30am-6pm Sat, Sun* £25; £19 concessions; £21 5-15s. *5-5.30pm daily* £16; £14 concessions; £9 5-15s; £78 family (2+2); free under-5s. **Credit** AmEx, MC, V.
There are even more more grinning celebrities now that Madame Tussauds has done away with the Planetarium that used to be a joint attraction here. That space has been filled by a rather lame show about celebrity, but most people are here for the dummy element of the attraction, with Posh, Becks, Brad, Angelina et al being the main course. The Chamber of Horrors, full of ghastly zombie actors, is pant-wettingly scary – not for for little ones. Children are very fond of the time travel ride, The Spirit of London, which takes you through 400 years of London life in a taxi pod.

Museum of London

150 London Wall, EC2Y 5HN (0870 444 3852/www.museumoflondon.org.uk). Barbican or St Paul's tube/Moorgate tube/rail. **Open** 10am-5.50pm Mon-Sat; noon-5.50pm Sun. **Admission** free. *Special exhibitions* £5; £3 concessions. **Credit** *Shop* AmEx, MC, V.
The large number of exhibits is laid out chronologically, leading you through prehistoric times to the 21st century. Every Sunday and throughout school holidays there is a kids' event, ranging from short film screenings to live music sessions. A major refurbishment, doubling the number of objects on show and building a new family area, sees the entire lower level closed off until 2009.

National Army Museum

Royal Hospital Road, SW3 4HT (7730 0717/www.national-army-museum.ac.uk). Sloane Square tube/11, 137, 239 bus. **Open** 10am-5.30pm daily. **Admission** free. **Credit** *Shop* AmEx, MC, V.
Some eccentric exhibits and displays, together with a great programme of family events, make this museum dedicated to the British Army's 500-year history far more entertaining than its exterior might suggest. Themed weekend events, which usually involve costumed interpreters and craft activities, broaden the museum's appeal. The Children's Zone has a babies' play area, building and music activities for toddlers and a reading and art activity space for older ones.

Natural History Museum

Cromwell Road, South Kensington, SW7 5BD (information 7942 5725/switchboard 7942 5000/www.nhm.ac.uk). South Kensington tube. **Open** 10am-5.50pm daily. **Admission** free; charges apply for special exhibitions. **Credit** AmEx, MC, V.

If you turn left from the main hall in the Life Galleries, you'll find yourself in the Dinosaur Gallery, where most children long to be. Just don't miss Creepy Crawlies, Ecology, Birds and the Mammals galleries in your haste to get there. The Earth Galleries can be reached from Exhibition Road via an escalator that passes through a giant globe – the earthquake simulation is always a winner. The Darwin Centre houses around 22 million specimens. The Centre's final phase of development will store the insect and plant collections and is due for completion in 2008. In winter comes the ice; a 1,000sq m outdoor rink, with a smaller rink for children, in front of the museum.

National Maritime Museum

Romney Road, Greenwich SE10 9NF (8858 4422/recorded info 8312 6565/tours 8312 6608/www.nmm.ac.uk). Cutty Sark DLR/Greenwich DLR/rail. **Open** *July, Aug* 10am-6pm daily. *Sept-June* 10am-5pm daily. *Tours* phone for details. **Admission** free; donations appreciated. **Credit** *Shop* MC, V.
This light, bright museum charting the nation's seafaring history has interactive computer terminals all over, plus games to play in the excellent Life at Sea exhibition on Level 3. Costumed storytellers roam about during school holidays and at weekends, when various activities are arranged.

Science Museum

Exhibition Road, South Kensington, SW7 2DD (7942 4454/booking & information line 0870 870 4868/www.sciencemuseum.org.uk). South Kensington tube. **Open** 10am-6pm daily. **Admission** free; charges apply for special exhibitions. *Science Night Sleepovers* £30. **Credit** AmEx, MC, V.
Children find the Science Museum a thrilling day out, spending hours twiddling about in the museum's six play zones, each created with an age range or developmental stage in mind; under-sixes dig the basement Garden area. The Launch Pad is the museum's largest interactive gallery, the Wellcome Wing, devoted to contemporary science and new technology, also embodies the notion of learning while having fun. There's an impressive five-storey IMAX cinema too. Special Science Night sleepovers are held once a month for eight- to 11-year-olds, in groups of five or more.

Tower of London

Tower Hill, EC3N 4AB (info 0870 756 6060/booking line 0870 756 7070/www. hrp.org.uk). Tower Hill tube/Tower Gateway DLR/Fenchurch Street rail. **Open** *Mar-Oct* 10am-6pm Mon, Sun; 9am-6pm Tue-Sat (last entry 5pm). *Nov-Feb* 10am-5pm Mon, Sun; 9am-5pm Tue-Sat (last entry 4pm). *Tours* Beefeater tours (weather permitting) every 30mins daily. **Admission** £16; £13 concessions; £9.50 5-15s; £45 family (2+3); free under-5s. *Audio guide* £3. *Tours* free. **Credit** AmEx, MC, V.

There are so many parts to the Tower of London (which is, in fact, made up of several towers) that the best way to make sense of it all is to follow a Beefeater. These Yeoman Warders, in their black and red finery, are genial hosts, who tell fascinating stories. The crown jewels are the biggest draw; the Martin Tower's permanent exhibition, Crowns and Diamonds, is a must for lovers of sparkle.

Unicorn Theatre

147 Tooley Street, SE1 2HZ (7645 0560/www. unicorntheatre.com). London Bridge tube/rail. **Open** *Box office* 9.30am-6pm Mon-Fri; 10am-6pm Sat; noon-5pm Sun. **Tickets** £6-£14.50; £3-£9.50 children. **Credit** MC, V.
One of Britain's leading producers of professional theatre for children, the Unicorn's £13-million centre opened in 2005 after a three-year collaboration with local schoolchildren, whose ideas have been incorporated into the design. The 300-seat Weston Theatre is its large-scale performance space, with the Clore providing a more intimate studio for educational projects and new work. Check the website for the 2007 programme.

V&A Museum of Childhood

Cambridge Heath Road, Bethnal Green, E2 9PA (8983 5200/recorded info 8980 2415/ www.museumofchildhood.org.uk). Bethnal Green tube. **Open** 10am-5.45pm daily. **Admission** free. Under-12s must be accompanied by an adult.
Established in 1872 as part of the V&A, this East End museum now holds the UK's biggest collection of toys and childhood paraphernalia, containing some 6,000 games and toys. The play areas and café are popular, and there are several interactive computer stations. Recent refurbishment has given the museum a new entrance hall, more space for community projects and refurbished displays in the mezzanine galleries.

Victoria & Albert Museum

Cromwell Road, South Kensington, SW7 2RL (7942 2000/www.vam.ac.uk). South Kensington tube. **Open** 10am-5.45pm Mon, Tue, Thur-Sun; 10am-10pm Wed, last Fri of mth. *Tours* daily; phone for details. **Admission** free; charges apply for special exhibitions. **Credit** *Shop* AmEx, MC, V.
This imposing museum has vast collections of costumes, jewellery, textiles, metalwork, glass, furniture, photographs, drawings, paintings, sculpture and architecture from cultures across the world. Facilities for children include activity backpacks (available from the main entrance 10.30am-4.30pm Sat). On Sundays (10.30am-5pm) children aged three to 12 flock to the Activity Cart, for various making and doing projects. The V&A is undergoing an extensive ten-year refurbishment, so a number of galleries will temporarily close or relocate; call before your visit to check if particular galleries are open.

London

The North Kent coast

Thanet's entertainment, from Herne Bay to Sandwich.

Sweeping sandy bays, majestic white cliffs, lush rolling fields; it's no wonder a succession of conquerors couldn't resist coming ashore on the Isle of Thanet to lay claim to its charms. Once smitten, the warriors saw fit to guard their prize with a liberal peppering of fortifications, some of which still stand. Today the area attracts visitors from near and far, as it has done ever since the Victorians established a string of resorts along the coast. The genteel piers and bandstands remain – and more modern amusements that continue to tempt well into the night.

One thing that hasn't changed, however, is the area's main draw for children – sand, and plenty of it. Thanet boasts no fewer than ten beaches with Blue Flag status: the prodigiously child-friendly Minnis Bay, West Bay, St Mildred's Bay, Westbrook Bay, brassy Margate's Main Sands, the pride of Broadstairs – Botany Bay, Joss Bay, Viking Bay and Walpole Bay – and Ramsgate Main Sands. For the 'kiss-me-quick' variety of seaside holiday, Thanet's got your number.

The remains of Roman towers can still be seen along this much-tamed northern coast, and robust Norman structures have also stood the test of time. In Tudor times, Henry VIII took his fortifications very seriously indeed. He protected the exposed arm of Thanet with dockyards at Chatham on the north flank and bolstered up the Cinque Ports to the southeast. These coastal bastions continued to serve the country through World War I and World War II, along with wartime tunnels and the round Martello towers so typical of this region.

Kent still bristles with mighty castles to visit while you're surveying the area's charms. The model forts of Deal and Walmer (www.english-heritage.org.uk) are dwarfed by the area's most impressive fortresses, built up from Saxon strongholds: the lovely Leeds Castle in Maidstone (01622 765400, www.leeds-castle.com) and Dover Castle (01304 211067, www.english-heritage.org.uk).

Shingle all the bay

Lying some 12 miles west of Thanet is the modest town of Herne Bay, which can be accessed via train from London Victoria or by car on the new fast-track road, the A299 Thanet Way, which runs from Faversham to Margate.

Once the haunt of smugglers, this quiet resort offers plenty of good walks along the prom, where a well-equipped play area absorbs the children and a shingle beach tests their soles. On the plaza next to the impressive 80-foot clock tower, a 'human sundial' can tell you how much time you have wasted; stand on the correct month and your shadow tells you the time.

If the weather's not up to casting shadows, Herne Bay has a few amusements for rainy days. On William Street you'll find the Herne Bay Museum and Art Gallery (01227 367368, www.canterbury.gov.uk), which has fossils and Roman finds. There are also two theatres with family-friendly programmes: the King's Hall on the East Cliff (01227 374188, www.thekingshall.com) and Herne Bay Little Theatre (01227 366004, www.hblt.co.uk) in Buller's Avenue, by the station.

Just in front of the museum, Central Parade is where the main action takes place. The newly restored bandstand hosts concerts in summer, and there's an ice-cream kiosk and information centre. There's also the arcades of Sandancers Amusements, a seaside shop selling ice-cream, beach goods and body boards, and an outdoor mini golf course.

Herne Bay is blessed with a fine array of family-friendly pubs. There's the Bun Penny

Broadstairs
2 Victoria Parade, Broadstairs, Kent CT10 1QS (0870 264 6111).
Herne Bay
Central Bandstand, Central Parade, Herne Bay, Kent CT6 5JN (01227 361911/ www.canterbury.co.uk).
Margate
12-13 The Parade, Margate, Kent CT9 1EY (0870 264 6111)
Ramsgate
17 Albert Court, York Street, Ramsgate, Kent CT11 9DN (0870 264 6111).
Sandwich
The Guildhall, Sandwich, Kent CT13 9AH (01304 613565).
Thanet Leisureforce
01843 296111/ www.leisureforce.co.uk.
Information on beach activities and chalet and beach hut hire.
Visitor Information Call Centre
0870 264 6111/ www.tourism.thanet.gov.uk.

(46 Central Parade, 01227 374252) which has a beer garden and a seafront restaurant, the Queens Head on William Street (No.44, 01227 361689), which has good, no-nonsense pub grub, and the Druid's Head on the High Street (No.182, 01227 372751), where you'll find a beer garden. The congenial Ship Inn on Central Parade (01227 364638) has outdoor seating with fine views in summer and walls bedecked with smuggling memorabilia; children are welcome for meals, and the food is good.

Macari's Ice-Cream Parlour (54 Central Parade, 01227 374977) is the place to go for coffee and delicious knickerbocker glories. For more substantial but equally traditional seaside fare, visit Ernie's Plaice Fish Bar (77 Central Parade, 01227 366471) which is open on Sundays. If you fancy a picnic, the shady avenue and lawns of Memorial Park, with its model boating lake and duck pond, are a couple of roads back from the seafront.

The rest of the town's attractions lie in the other direction, out at sea (*see p50* **All at sea**). They include the pier head, cut off from the mainland since 1979, the 30-odd wind turbines that form the Kentish Flats Wind Farm and the Maunsell Forts, a series of *Star Wars* Destroyer-style towers built in the 1940s to protect the Thames estuary.

During the summer months, Herne Bay plays host to a two-week carnival, plus music festivals and art markets. Herne Mill

The North Kent coast

ALL AT SEA

One of the best ways to appreciate the Kent coast is by boat. You can take to the water in all sorts of vessels, from jet skis (Jet Ski World, Cliftonville, Margate) to boat tours around Ramsgate harbour with Sea Searcher (0870 264 6111, trips from Easter-Sept). Bayblast in Herne Bay (01227 373372, www.bayblast.co.uk) runs short inflatable boat trips or part day cruises on the open yacht Wildlife from Neptune's Arm, next to Herne Bay pier, every day from April to November. If the children are up for a bit of seal spotting you can take them on a five-hour cruise from Herne Bay, (including one hour at a sandbank for swimming, weather permitting). The seals, who are quite the local celebrities, come up to the boat for adulation. Trips may be under sail both ways if the weather permits, and a short dinghy ride is sometimes necessary. Bring along a picnic lunch and don't forget to pack binoculars and a camera. It costs £160 for 1-9 passengers and between £17-£19 each to hire the boat for five hours.

To take in all Thanet's charms, set sail for a half-day Discovery Tour, also run by Sea Searcher. This takes you around 35 miles out to sea and has an informative commentary throughout. The tour skirts Pier Head, the remains of England's second longest pier and the handsome historical landmark Reculver Towers (www.english-heritage.org.uk), twin 12th-century towers of a ruined church standing amid the remains of an important Roman 'Saxon Shore' fort and a Saxon monastery. This close to the site where bouncing bombs were tested in World War II. The boat then stops off at the Kentish Flats wind farm for a closer look before heading out some 13 miles to visit Fort Knock John (www.undergroundkent.co.uk), one of the Maunsell Army Sea Forts, which were designed to provide anti-aircraft defence in the Thames estuary during the Luftwaffe raids on London in 1940. The Thames estuary presented German bombers with a much easier approach to London for their raids. After everyone has examined these weird, hulking structures (children take note there are no ladders for boarding) the boat returns to the 21st century, and the jolly beach hut-lined seafronts of Tankerton and Hampton.

The waves can be choppy in windy weather, and the boats bouncy, so it's best to bring along some weather-proof clothing – a cagoule and a close-fitting hat, waterproof trousers and shoes with a good grip. There are bench seats so you can position children on the inside to shelter them from the spray and keep them secure. The two-hour trip costs £32 per person or £110 for a family ticket (two adults and two under-tens). Life jacket regulations state that children need a minimum bodyweight of 3st 2lb (20kg) to make the trip.

The eroding chalk cliffs of **Pegwell Bay**. *See p53.*

windmill is also worth a visit (2-5pm Sun and bank hols Easter-Sept, also Thur in Aug, 01227 361326, www.kentwindmills. homestead.com). West of the town, colourful beach huts brighten the walk along the Western Esplanade; to the east lies the Saxon Shore, the ruins of Reculver and the lovely rural sands of Minnis Bay, blessed with great watersports facilities and a children's play area.

A sea change

The brashest resort round Thanet way has to be dear old Margate, a seaside town devoted to having a knees-up. Entertainment is not hard to find here, although the quality might be a tad questionable. Margate boasts five theatres including the second oldest in Britain, the Theatre Royal (01843 293877, www.theatreroyalmargate.co.uk), and the smallest, the Tom Thumb in Cliftonville (01843 221791). The Winter Gardens (01843 296111, www.margate wintergardens.co.uk) also put on shows and entertainments.

For the visual arts, although currently without a purpose-built gallery to call home, there's Turner Contemporary (01843 294208, www.turnercontemporary. org). TC offers a host of exhibitions and workshops for families in the summer at various locations; check the website for details. The £15 million gallery project is due for completion in 2010, with a site on Margate seafront, by the harbour – Turner stayed in a lodging

house that stood on this very spot. It's hoped that the gallery's opening will be the catalyst for major regeneration in the town, so watch this space.

Margate Museum (01843 231213, www.margatemuseum.org.uk), housed in the Old Town Hall, includes displays on the town's policing (housed in four former police cells), maritime past, military history and emergence as a seaside resort. The Walpole Hotel and Museum (*see p59*) offers both a bed for the night and historic insights rolled into one. Dreamland, Margate's most famous (and often troubled) attraction, is a historical relic of another kind, which in the past couple of years has opened for the season, although as we went to press, its future looked uncertain in the extreme. It'll be a sad day for Margate if this doughty old seaside amusement park finally hits the deck. It opened in 1920, and is home to the Grade II-listed Scenic Railway rollercoaster, Britain's oldest (operational) rollercoaster and the first listed amusement park ride in the country. The Save Dreamland campaign would like to see more rides restored and to create themed areas, such as an undersea world, pirate's pier and aquatic exhibits on the site. Visit the website www.savedreamland. co.uk for information.

Margate's most valued tourist draw has to be the beach. The deep sandy strand, which you can practically step onto from the train station, has a tidal pool, bouncy castles, slides, a funfair and donkey rides (www.margatebeach.org.uk) .

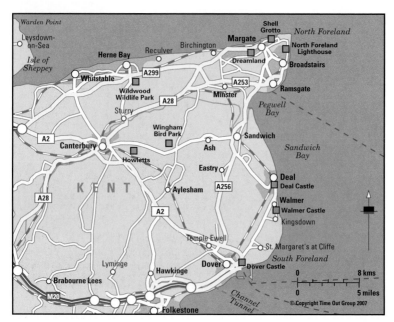

After all that excitement it's time to hit the shops along Queen Street and the High Street, where children can indulge in the delights of the Strokes Adventure Golf course, which is floodlit of an evening, or take a walk with the Rock Doc (01843 577672, www.thanetcoast.org.uk) to discover the prehistory of Thanet's chalk cliffs. The summer holidays are obviously a busy time in Margate, especially if the summer's sunny, and there's no busier day than Margate Carnival Sunday (*see p332*).

Lucky seven

Much has changed around sedate Broadstairs since Charles Dickens spent his summer holidays here. Though it's true that life moves at a quieter pace here than in bustling Margate, this resort is hardly sleepy. It should be noted that the town is not a great place for families to wander around after nightfall; many of its publicans have been granted late licences for live music, which in turn have attracted the stag and hen fraternity. Seek sanctuary in the comfort of your hotel for bedtime stories when the sun goes down.

By day, however, Broadstairs is a child's paradise, with yellow crescent moons of sand, an outdoor bathing pool and lots of beach attractions, including Punch and Judy shows and swing boats. Of the seven bays, Botany Bay is the most northerly, Kingsgate Bay has chalk cliffs and caves and Joss Bay is popular with sunbathers and, when

the wind and tide is right, surfers. Its large car park reflects its popularity. The North Foreland Lighthouse looks out over the sea from here. Stone Bay, the setting for the John Buchan book *The 39 Steps*, is reached via steps down the cliffs or by walking along the promenade from Viking Bay. Now the proud possessor of a Blue Flag, Viking Bay is the main bay in Broadstairs. Horseshoe-shaped, with a small harbour, it has fishing boats, a sailing club, ice-creams and candy floss, a small children's funfair and a café. The beach is easily accessible for all now that a lift has been installed (open daily from Whitsun to the end of Sept). Louisa Bay, just round the southern headland of Viking Bay, is quieter. The most southerly of the seven is Dumpton Gap. You can walk to Ramsgate from here at low tide, or along the cliff top if the tide is in.

Away from the beaches there are any number of welcoming cafés, the best of which is Beaches on Albion Street (01843 600065), a poster-covered haven that plies families with great coffee, cakes and milkshakes and has high chairs, toys and books. Broadstairs has great shopping too. The Continental Corner Delicatessen and Café (11-13 Charlotte Street, 01843 865805) can provide the beach picnic, and Suzanne's (1 Victoria Parade, 01843 862106) has the swimming accessories. Dolls' house enthusiasts can pick through the miniature homes and furnishings in Small World (9 York Street, 01843 862616).

Time and Space on the High Street (No. 82, 01843 866006) with its stock of retro toys and games, is a joy.

For scaled-down pitch and putt fun, Lilliput Minigolf on Victoria Parade has child-sized clubs and a well-designed course. Put the ball through the right final hole to win a free game.

Summer is festival time in Broadstairs. There's Folk Week and the Water Gala in August, and the annual Dickens Festival is celebrated every June (see p331).

Harbour lights

Ramsgate offers lots of scope for eating out and boat trips. The Royal Marina has encouraged a flotilla of smart restaurants, which line the slope down to the harbour and are very attractive at night with their twinkling lights and enticing aromas.

For children, the best fun is either the beach or at Play Bay on Harbour Parade (01843 590591, www.playbay ramsgate.com). Next to the amusement arcade (look carefully for the entrance or you'll miss it), it's an indoor play area with a disco room, climbing wall, soccer net, toddler area, slide and crawl tunnel and ball pool complex – all beloved of small children. The food is cheap and cheerful, probably best avoided. A visit to this rather headache-inducing place (at least for the parents) can be a reward for good behaviour at the rather statelier but interesting Maritime Museum (The

Clock House, Pier Yard, 01843 570622) with its displays of shipwrecks.

Surrounded by nature reserves, the former bustling medieval port of Sandwich reposes on the banks of the River Stour. Here you can roam along the beaches and spot the wildlife in Pegwell Bay Nature Reserve, between Ramsgate and Sandwich, which is managed by the Kent Wildlife Trust (www.kentwildlife.org.uk). This reserve, to the north of Pegwell Bay, with its eroding chalk cliffs, mudflats, sand dunes and saltmarsh, is bird paradise (see p57). Closer to town, Gazen Salts Nature Reserve (01304 611925, www.whitecliffscountry. org.uk), is a series of woodland paths and lake where you can feed the wildfowl. One of the best ways to see the sites is by River Bus (07958 376183, www.sandwichriver bus.co.uk), which runs daily in summer from the Quay by the Old Toll Bridge to Richborough Roman Fort. Weekly seal-watching trips can be booked in advance.

Back in the town, the Elizabethan Guildhall and Museum (01304 617197, www.sandwichtowncouncil.gov.uk), sets out the history of Sandwich with tours of the mayor's parlour and the ancient courtroom. Golfers set their caps at the 18-hole course at Royal St George's (01304 613090, www.royalstgeorges.com). Two miles from town, it's open for visitors on Tuesdays. On a springtime visit in April you can take in the Sandwich food festival; the and Carnival hits town in the first week of September. Contact the Tourist Information office (see p49) for details.

Bell Hotel. See p57.

Brilliant
Broadstairs.
Viking Beach
(right) and the
town (left). For
both, *see p52*.

North Foreland Lighthouse.
See p58.

WHERE TO STAY

Parents with very young children may find the seafront guesthouses tricky because they are invariably built over several floors with steep staircases and don't have lifts. It is strongly advised to check facilities in advance. Away from the front, prices diminish with the view.

Families on a budget choose caravan parks and resorts on the outskirts of the towns. Our two favourites are in lovely settings: Birchington, near Herne Bay, has the Two Chimneys Caravan Park (01843 841068, www.twochimneys.co.uk), with a swimming pool, children's play areas and an entertainment programme. The Wayside Caravan Park (01843 821272, www.waysidecaravanpark.co.uk), near Ramsgate, about a mile from Minster village, offers roomy static caravans in lovely grounds, with a shop, café bar, play area, barbecue and outdoor seating area.

Fancy Canterbury? Many people do, and holiday accommodation is hard to find in this compact, historic little city, but the Cathedral has family accommodation in the shape of the Canterbury Cathedral Lodge (www.canterburycathedrallodge.org), a self-catering pad within the Cathedral grounds.

It's £139 per night for the flat, which has a single room, a twin or double room, a bathroom and a kitchen area. There are also self-catering twin rooms at £89 per night and bed and breakfast twin rooms at £119.

Bay View Guest House

86 Central Parade, Herne Bay, Kent CT6 5JJ (01227 741458/www.bayguesthouse.co.uk). **Rates** £80-£120. **No credit cards**.
A very typical seaside guest house, but The Bay View is well worth a mention because it provided the location for a certain little B&B in the quaint town of Old Haven, where flouncing 'lady' Emily Howard played house in *Little Britain*. In fact several Herne Bay settings featured in the BBC show, including The Bun Penny pub (*see p49*) and Neptune's Arm (not a pub, the 'arm' is part of the sea defences, which creates a small tidal harbour for locals' boats). The rooms in this traditional seaside hotel are spacious, all are well furnished and some have table and chairs overlooking the bay. There's also a pleasant restaurant with a brick fireplace serving good, own-cooked food. All prices include a full English breakfast, and the guesthouse is non-smoking throughout. There are no specific facilities for children, so you'll need to bring your own travel cot.

The Bell Hotel

The Quay, Sandwich, Kent CT13 9EF
(01304 613388/www.bellhotelsandwich.co.uk).
Rates £109-£190. *DB&B* £159-£240.
Credit MC, V.

A member of The Place Hotels group (The Place at Camber Sands and The Ship Hotel in Chichester are its famous siblings), The Bell is being dragged into the modern age with cool linen furnishings, parquet flooring and Egyptian cotton bedding. The rooms also have spa therapy toiletries, radios and remote controlled TVs and Wi-Fi throughout. There are 34 bedrooms, about 15 of which have been updated (they should all be complete by April 2007), including double rooms and suites. Some bedrooms have balconies and river views; all have en suite bathrooms. There is no baby-listening service, but guests can use a recommended local babysitting service; cot hire is an extra £10 per night.

One of the main reasons to stay is for the food. Breakfast brings a choice of freshly baked pastries and mixed breads, fresh fruit salad, local orchard juices, fruit, own-made jams, local honey, yoghurts and cereal, plus a selection of cheeses and own-baked meats or a cooked breakfast, where items are locally sourced where possible. Do stay for dinner (there are room rates to include such a treat). The restaurant has a seasonal approach, with locally caught fresh fish and vegetables. Most dishes can be served as half portions for under-tens – just ask. We loved the autumn salad of organic Cox apples, Kentish cobnuts, cherry tomatoes, yellow peppers and mixed leaves with a sorrel and wholegrain mustard dressing, and the chef's bouillabaisse with local bay fish and shellfish (£6.25). Pan-fried pigeon breast and rack of Romney Marsh lamb are among the other delights. Vegetarian dishes are available and puddings include treacle tart with thick local cream, honey and walnut cheesecake or own-made organic ice-creams and sorbets. The hotel also offers a special Royal St George's golf package. There is a minimum booking of two nights at weekends from June to September; either Friday and Saturday or Saturday and Sunday, with half-price rates for the second night.

Fishermen's Cottages

01843 601996/www.fishermenscottages.co.uk.
Rates £180-£650/wk. **No credit cards.**

Set the children's minds racing with tales of smuggler and shipwrecks by staying the night in Barnaby's Lodge in Broadstairs. Built in 1614, this quirky and charming flint and brick cottage is dotted with beams and ships' timbers and has a secret door. There is a separate lounge, kitchen, courtyard garden, one double bedroom and one bedroom with pine bunk beds. Three other similarly rustic cottages are on offer, with two bedrooms, kitchens and shower rooms. All the accommodation is self-catering. There are no cots so you'll need to bring your own, plus high chairs and toys. All the cottages are a minute's walk away from the beach and amenities.

Margate YHA

3-4 Royal Esplanade, Westbrook Bay, Margate, Kent CT9 5DL (01843 221616/ www.yha.org.uk). **Open** year round.
Rates £14; £10 under-18s. **Credit** MC, V.

Right on the beachfront, this hostel was converted from a hotel, so it's well set up for a bucket-and-spade holiday. The beach outside is gently

TOP 5

WILDLIFE HAVENS

Better known for saucy postcards and candy floss, Thanet's coastline is, a little surprisingly perhaps, recognised as one of the best wildlife sites in Europe. Here are some good areas for rareties.

Broadstairs

Argiope bruennichi, the wasp-eating spider, is one of Britain's largest arachnids. It likes Thanet's eastern edge. *See p52.*

Herne Bay

A boat trip out to sea from here reveals seals on the sandbanks. *See p50.*

North Foreland coast

Montagu's harriers, ospreys and honey-legged buzzards wheel through the skies over the lighthouse. *See p58.*

Pegwell Bay

Plovers, sanderlings and terns glory in the reserve's mudflats. *See p53.*

Wildwood Wildlife Park

Wolves, boar and otters enjoy the parklife. *See p61.*

The North Kent coast

shelving and sandy; Margate's main beach is a stroll down the prom. There are family rooms with four or five beds, and most of the hostel has free Wi-Fi. The two lounges have televisions and DVD players, and there are laundry facilities. Note that it's self-catering only, so be prepared to bring some teabags and cereal. Given the number of cyclists resting up here while doing the coastal route, it's as well there's a cycle store.

North Foreland Lighthouse

01386 701177/www.ruralretreats.co.uk. **Rates** £240/2 nights-£890/7 nights. Prices vary; phone to check. **Credit** MC, V.
Set in lovely rolling countryside just outside Broadstairs, the old lighthouse provides self-catering holiday accommodation in two cottages. The earliest reference to a light on North Foreland was made in a deed dated 1499, when it was a simple beacon; the first lighthouse was built in 1636. Although the original structure burnt down in 1683, a manned lighthouse remained on the site until 1998. The lightkeepers' cottages have now been converted into holiday lets, named Khina and Lodesman. They're surrounded by a large and pleasant garden with decking and a patio, and ample space to sit out. The sands of Joss Bay are a mere three minutes away. Cottages comprise a fitted kitchen, sitting room, dining room, two bedrooms and bathroom with shower attachment. Travel cots and high chairs can be provided. A minimum seven-night stay is required in July and August; at Easter a minimum five-night stay is permitted. Phone for details of other times of year. Book well ahead.

The Priory B&B

203 Canterbury Road, Herne Bay, Kent CT6 5UG (01227 366670/www.thepriory bandb.co.uk). **Rates** £55-£80. **Credit** MC, V.
Just a mile from the beach, this Georgian Grade II listed house, built in the 1750s, is situated in the conservation area of Herne Bay, close to the Thanet Way. It has recently undergone extensive refurbishment to create modern, comfortable en suite accommodation, while still retaining period charm. There's a bright conservatory leading to the garden, plus a large dining room. Cots are available, and there are family rooms as well as doubles and triples.

Royal Albion Hotel

6-12 Albion Street, Broadstairs, Kent CT10 1AN (01843 868071/www.albionbroadstairs. co.uk). **Rates** £83-£207. **Credit** MC, V.
Built in 1760, this lovely old-fashioned seaside hotel has marvellous views of Viking Bay and is just steps away from the sea. Its most illustrious guest was Charles Dickens, who had an enduring affection for Broadstairs. 'Lighthouses, piers, bathing machines and so forth are its only attractions, but it is one of the fresh and free-est little places in the world', he wrote to a friend. All 19 bedrooms have en suite facilities, satellite TV, radios, hairdryers and tea and coffee making facilities. The spacious outdoor patio area is popular with families who like to sit out post breakfast/pre-beach. The bar does light meals, mostly sandwiches and baguettes, and breakfast and dinner are served in a pleasantly refurbished dining room. The restaurant has a pubby sort of menu: ploughman's lunches, jacket potatoes, cod in beer batter, lasagne and the like, with a nuggety sort of children's menu (pizza, sausage and fishfingers are the alternatives). Children can be accommodated in their parents' room with extra beds and inflatable mattresses, and the best rooms for families are undoubtedly those with sea views. The two-bedroom Dickens Suite is the top dollar option. There is a baby-listening service, monitored by reception, and cots can be supplied at no extra cost.

Royal Harbour Hotel

10-11 Nelson Crescent, Ramsgate, Kent CT11 9JF (01843 591514/www.royalharbour hotel.co.uk). **Rates** £88-£195. **Credit** MC, V.
In winter, cosy up to real fires in the dining and sitting rooms of this delightful Georgian townhouse. It's a homely place at any time of year; some of its quirky bedrooms have cabin beds that parents and children often fight over. All ages are catered for: there's a record player with a stack of old vinyls, toys and a tray of sweets for the children and a courtesy bar for the grown-ups. Breakfast is a leisurely affair, with cooked breakfasts, fruit juices, cereals, pastries, fresh fruit and yoghurts served until about 11.30am. Cabin singles with a sea or harbour view are reasonably priced, and a real treat for a teen who wants to be alone. For younger children, babysitting can be provided courtesy of a local agency or one of the hotel's chambermaids. All 17 rooms have en suite showers and a television and video, with a complimentary video library. Rooms have Wi-Fi internet, and the snuggery has a computer with broadband access for guests to use free. There's a garden for the children to play in, and a new 20-seater DVD screening area in the basement for rainy days. Families can club together and book the entire hotel if they wish.

Smiths Court Hotel

21-27 Eastern Esplanade, Cliftonville, Margate, Kent CT9 2HL (01843 222310/ www.smithscourt.co.uk). **Rates** £67-£110; £125 weekend; £375-£616/wk. **Credit** MC, V.
Once part of the Court Hotels group, the recently refurbished Smiths Court, on the seafront, is now owned and operated by Robert and Ann Smith and their family. The bright, individually designed rooms are like a breath of fresh sea air, and there are self-catering suites with fully equipped kitchenettes and dining areas, as well as a daily maid service. Families can also take advantage of the free baby-listening service provided in each apartment, and have access to all

The **Royal Albion** Hotel's terrace view.

the usual lounge facilities plus the recently-refurbished gym. In the freshly completed Orangery dining room, children can choose from chicken nuggets, pizza, mini roast dinners or half portions from the adult menu. The hotel offers a varied entertainment programme; come at Easter and the children can enjoy a spot of egg painting and chocolate hunting.

Walpole Bay Hotel & Living Museum

Fifth Avenue, Cliftonville, Kent CT9 2JJ (01843 221703/www.walpolebayhotel.co.uk). **Rates** £85-£99. **Credit** MC, V.

Part hotel, part museum, the Walpole will transport you back to yesteryear with its collection of curios and historic displays. Built as a genteel hotel by Louisa Budge in 1914 and extended in 1927, the hotel stayed in the family and frozen in time until 1995. Although the elegance remains, the Walpole has come up to date with modern facilities such as en suite bathrooms and satellite televisions. Children enjoy exploring the antique surroundings, particularly the 1920s ballroom, with its original sprung maple dance floor and the 1927 Otis Trellis gated lift. Take a ride in the elevator to the top floor to observe the original workings in action, then admire old photographs of early holidaymakers on the second floor, and the maids' sculleries with their ceramic sinks and wooden drainers and the old kitchens. Families can also join educational walks and talks led by a local geologist. Doubles and family rooms with a baby-listening service are available, and enjoy lovely views out to sea; many of the rooms have balconies. Children will appreciate the cream teas (served from 2-5pm) and hearty Sunday roasts; kids' meals can be rustled up on request. The Walpole is also pet-friendly, and the coastline is walkies-heaven for dogs.

WHERE TO EAT & DRINK

Atlantis Seafood Restaurant & Bar

66 Harbour Parade, Ramsgate, Kent CT11 8LN (01843 581582/www.oakhotel.co.uk). **Meals served** 7-9.30pm Mon; noon-2.30pm, 7-9.30pm Tue-Sat; noon-4pm Sun. **Main courses** £13-£17. *Set lunch* (Tue-Sun) £8.95 1 course; £11.95 2 courses; £14.95 3 courses. **Credit** MC, V.

The Oak Hotel's newly refurbished restaurant specialises in prized fruits of the sea, such as garlic tiger prawns, oyster, grilled scallops wrapped in bacon and mussel soup with deep-fried leeks. For main courses choose from a range of dishes such as grilled skate with lemon and caper sauce, crushed potatoes and watercress, pan-fried monkfish on a Tuscan style stew of white beans and oregano and tomato chargrilled halibut steak with mash in a herb cream sauce. Escape the fish (but not the aquatic theme) with duck breast served pink with a sweet potato mash and a redcurrant, orange and port sauce. Children are welcome until 9pm, and high chairs are available. Kids can choose a half-price half portion, or order from the children's menu in the bar (as long as the adults are eating à la carte).

Broadstairs Pavilion

Harbour Street, Broadstairs, Kent CT10 1EU (01843 600999/www.pavilion-broadstairs. co.uk). **Meals served** *Summer* 9-11.30am, noon-5pm daily. *Winter* 10-11.30am, noon-2.30pm Mon-Fri; 9.30am-4pm Sat, Sun. **Main courses** £4.50-£8.50. **Credit** AmEx, MC, V.

This spacious and very child-friendly pub offers beautiful views over the bay and serves baguettes, pastries, ice-creams and snacks; just right for a midday beach break. Children can have a pasta dish from the main menu for £5, or choose from fish fingers, own-made chicken dippers, vegetable nuggets and sausages from the kids' menu (£3.75). There is outdoor seating and a large garden where they can let off steam after lunch.

Harveys Crab & Oyster House

34 York Street, Ramsgate, Kent CT11 8DS (01843 591110). **Meals served** noon-3pm, 6-8.30pm Mon-Sat; noon-8.30pm Sun. **Main courses** £5.50-£14.95. **Credit** MC, V.
Despite signs that say it is a speciality, steak isn't the best choice on the menu. (We didn't try the oysters, but can report that the crab salad was of substantial proportions and very good.) It's a nice stop-off for a pub lunch and child-friendly service, especially for a Sunday roast. There's a non-smoking dining area, nice toasties for children and a kids' menu with the usual sausage-and-chips choices for around £3.99; colouring books and toys keep younger diners amused. It might be an idea to call ahead if you need a high chair as there's only one up for grabs.

Osteria Posillipo

14 Albion Street, Broadstairs, Kent CT10 1LU (01843 601133/www.posillipo.co.uk). **Meals served** noon-10.30pm daily. **Main courses** £5.95-£13.95. **Credit** MC, V.
You'll find pizza cooked in a traditional stone oven and fish and seafood specials, sourced locally where possible, in this rather full-of-itself Neapolitan restaurant. Next door to the Royal Albion Hotel, Osteria Posillipo offers wonderful sea views from its garden terrace, as well as plenty of additional seating in the dark wood interior. The food is delicious, though the service can be a little on the surly side. That said, the staff were accommodating enough to put two tables together on our extended family visit, and didn't mind the children sharing a pizza. Feast sumptuously on the likes of lobster linguini, fresh mussels, and gnocchi with brandy, butternut squash and king prawns, or more pedestrian spaghetti with meatballs, steaks and chicken dishes. The sister restaurant, Porto Vecchio (23-27 Harbour Street, 01843 862408), is also good.
Branch: 16 The Borough, Canterbury, Kent CT1 2DR (01227 761471).

Le Petit Poisson

Pier Approach, Herne Bay, Kent CT6 5JN (01227 361199). **Meals served** *Summer* noon-2.30pm, 6.30-10pm Tue-Fri; 6.30-10pm Sun. *Winter* noon-2.30pm, 6.30-9pm Tue-Fri; noon-3.30pm, 6.30-9.30pm Sat; noon-3.30pm Sun. **Main courses** £8.85-£12.95. **Credit** MC, V.
Next to the pier pavilion, this was once the Sea View Bar but has smartened up under the present ownership. Plump for classic fish soup, Scottish rock oysters or grilled goat's cheese on prawns, spring onions and crushed new potatoes, all at under a fiver, for starters. For a main course it would be rude not to go for more seafood, with dishes such as salmon fillet on bubble and squeak, whole local crab with lime and coriander mayonnaise and new potatoes, and roasted fillet of haddock on savoy cabbage and smoked bacon. Most mains are under a tenner, which is superb value for a fish restaurant. Younger diners can devour half-portions of fishy grown-up fare if they're feeling adventurous, and impeccably fresh own-made haddock fish fingers, served with chips and salad, if they're not. Seating is available indoors and out, and children love the proximity to the beach and its amusements. They'll be clamouring to go off to explore, unless you can persuade them to sit tight for the tempting puddings – sticky toffee pudding and own-made ice-cream is always a winner. The delightful chef, Darren, recommends the banana and crushed meringue desert, served with cream and butterscotch sauce.

Surin Restaurant

30 Harbour Street, Ramsgate, Kent CT11 8HA (01843 592001/www.surinrestaurant. co.uk). **Meals served** 6-11pm Mon; noon-2.30pm, 6-11pm Tue-Thur; noon-2.30pm, 6pm-midnight Fri, Sat. **Main courses** £5.95-£8. *Set lunch* £5.95 2 courses. **No credit cards.**
This friendly harbourside restaurant is now adding to its charms by offering blond and dark Surin beers, both made in local microbreweries, which compliment the flavours of the Thai cuisine. Children love the sumptuous decor and silk wall

Wildwood Wildlife Park.

hangings and are bound to find something that appeals on the menu, which offers an enormous variety of meat, fish, seafood and vegetarian dishes, along with soups, starters and weekly specials. There are Thai staples such as green and red curry, as well as more exotic couplings such as beef with basil and chili, scallops with garlic and ginger and sea bass with garlic and lime. Families might prefer to graze from sharing plates of spring rolls, dumplings, sesame prawn toast and chicken satay, which offer something to suit pretty much any taste.

PLACES TO SEE, THINGS TO DO

Dickens Museum
2 Victoria Parade, Broadstairs, Kent CT10 1QS (01843 861232/www.dickenshouse.co.uk). **Open** *Apr-Oct* 2-5pm daily. *Nov-Mar* groups only; phone for details. **Admission** £2.50; £1.30 under-16s, concessions; £6 family (2+2). **No credit cards**.

The museum is housed in the former residence of Miss Mary Pearson Strong, the lady who Charles Dickens immortalized as Miss Betsey Trotwood in *David Copperfield*. Dickens frequented Broadstairs during many a summer and visited this modest seafront house, which has been refurbished to match his descriptions. The parlour contains some of his letters, belongings, furniture and memorabilia; elsewhere the house is full of Victorian prints and trinkets in keeping with the era. The house is a hotch-potch of architectural styles: believed to be partly of Tudor origin, it was extensively remodeled with a Georgian frontage and later, the addition of a Victorian balcony. Children enjoy looking at the costumes on the first floor, where Dickens' favourable account of Broadstairs, *Our English Watering Place*, written in 1851, can also be seen. The museum is run by volunteers and opening times are often extended during the summer – it's always worth popping by or phoning to check if they're open.

Howletts Wild Animal Park
Bekesbourne Lane, Bekesbourne, Canterbury, Kent CT4 5EL (01227 721286/www.totally wild.net). **Open** 10am-4.30pm daily (or dusk if earlier). **Admission** £13.95; £10.95 concessions, 4-16s; £42 family (2+2), £49 (2+3); free under-4s. **Credit** AmEx, MC, V.

The aim of the John Aspinall Foundation is to protect and save wild animals and return them to safe areas within their native habitats. The late John Aspinall set up the parks at Howletts and at Port Lympne, near Hythe, more than 40 years ago to conserve endangered species, with a view to breeding them in captivity to be released into the wild. Enclosures replicate specific environments as far as is humanly possible. Almost 50 gorillas are housed here, as well as African elephants, Siberian tigers and many more; a number of the wolves, tapirs and antelopes are endangered species. In the 'Wood in the Park', you can walk

alongside and below a free-roaming family of amazingly agile and lively lemurs. The parks have recently burst into the modern world with web-cam interactivity on the internet and through the BBC children's programme *ROAR!*. Launched in 2006, the show goes behind the scenes of the day-to-day running of the park. The park has all the usual facilities, including a café, restaurant and gift shop.
Branch: Port Lympne, nr Hythe, Kent CT21 4PD (0870 750 4647).

Shell Grotto
Grotto Hill, Margate, Kent CT9 2BU (01843 220008/www.shellgrotto.co.uk). **Open** *Apr-Oct* 10am-5pm daily. *Nov-Apr* 11am-4pm Sat, Sun. **Admission** £2.50, £1.50 under-16s; £7 family (2+2). **No credit cards**.

Children who enjoy collecting shells will find this place a real inspiration. It consists of a series of underground tunnels and chambers, decorated with 4.6 million shells (who counted them?), making up 2000square feet of mosaic. What's most entertaining is the mystery that surrounds this amazing place. It was discoverd by one Mr James Newlove in 1835, while digging a duck pond. No-one knows whether it's some ancient pagan temple, or some weird cultish meeting place, but there was no record of any such thing before its discovery. Newlove opened the place to the public in 1837. The cockle, whelk, mussel and oyster shells are made into patterns of trees of life, gods, goddesses and something that looks ike an altar, which some say points to the fact that the grotto was used as a as a sun temple. Whatever it is, it's fascinating, and visitors love it. A gift shop and the Eighth Wonder Café keep them hanging about to ponder the mystery.

Wildwood Wildlife Park
Herne Common, Herne Bay, Kent CT6 7LQ (01227 712111/www.wildwoodtrust.org). **Open** *Summer* 10am-6pm daily. *Winter* 10am-5pm daily. Last admission 90mins before closing. **Admission** £9; £7 under-18s; £30 family (2+2). **Credit** MC, V.

Kent's woodland discovery park, which lies between Canterbury and Herne Bay, champions the cause of our native furry animals. Visitors can get up close to the shy and furtive little critters that make up Britain's native wildlife, such as otters, dormice, badgers and water voles. Wildwood has also become a safe haven for a host of other creatures like wolves and wild boar, that no longer exist in the wild in this country. Several species such as the konik horse and the beaver have been reintroduced to the UK from Europe. More than 300 animals from over 50 species live here; the children that come to visit them can make the most of a woodland play area, picnic tables and a restaurant; a Saxon settlement is currently under construction. The overall aim of Wildwood is to turn more areas of our countryside back into precisely that – a wild wood.

West Sussex

Arun and about up Downs and downriver.

Tamed and softened by thousands of years of settlement, West Sussex today offers families all they need for a traditional bucket and spade holiday, and much more. From the beaches the flat coastal plain sweeps under chalk Downs – cut through by the rivers Arun and Adur – that grow broader and more wooded the further west you go. Inland, there's the High Weald, with its ancient sunken lanes. This varied terrain has a fabulous network of more than 2,500 miles of footpaths, linking hidden valleys with dense woodland, secluded harbours and remote hilltop ridges.

The county's cities, towns and villages are a mixed bag, ranging from sprawling Crawley and unlovely Gatwick in the north to genteel Worthing on the coast or, inland, the antiques-packed Petworth. The epitome of Sussex charm is the exquisite harbour village of Bosham – the only English place represented on the Bayeux Tapestry, and believed to be the location where King Canute proved to his starstruck court that he could not hold back the waves.

Littlehampton

While many visitors with children would probably opt to stay on the coast, there's a strong case to be made for the historic city of Arundel, lying at the foot of the South Downs on the River Arun. With their backdrop of the country's second biggest castle, Arundel's narrow medieval streets and towering Georgian houses stand alongside traditional Sussex cottages and townhouses, and the magnificent French gothic catholic cathedral stands proud at the top of the hill that is the high street.

One of the town's major annual events is the Feast of Corpus Christi, also known as the Carpet of Flowers. Celebrated in the cathedral 60 days after Easter, it involves a 93-feet display of fresh flowers being laid in the central aisle for two days. In the last week of August, the Arundel Festival (*see p333*) offers classic entertainments such as the All England Marbles Championship, as well as a wide programme of arts events, many geared towards families.

Before leaving the town centre, stroll down 16th-century Tarrant Street and pinch yourself hard when you happen upon Castle Chocolates at No.11 (01903 884419). With its extraordinary range of fudges, sugar mice, old-fashioned boiled sweets in jars, humbugs, toffees, swirly colourful nougat, violet creams, Belgian chocolates and liquorice in all its guises, this place is a sweet tooth's heaven. Even Clive Gardner, who has owned the shop for 19 years, seems too good to be true as he beams out from behind the counter in his colourful bow tie and straw boater.

Out on Mill Road, which leads to the Wetlands Centre and picturesque Black Rabbit pub on the river (01903 882828), river cruises and boat hire are available throughout the year from the Arundel Boatyard (01903 882609). Next door, the Mill Road Leisure Sports Park (01903

TOURIST INFORMATION

Arundel
61 High Street, Arundel, West Sussex BN18 9AJ (01903 882268/ www.arun.gov.uk).
Bognor Regis
Belmont Street, Bognor Regis, West Sussex PO21 1BJ (01243 823140/ www.arun.gov.uk).
Chichester
29A South Street, Chichester, West Sussex PO19 1AH (01243 775888/ www.visitchichester.org).
Cycling in West Sussex
01243 777610/ www.westsussex.gov.uk.
Horsham
9 The Causeway, Horsham, West Sussex RH12 1HE (01403 211661/ www.horsham.gov.uk).
Worthing
Chapel Road, Worthing, West Sussex BN11 1HL (01903 221307/ www.visitworthing.co.uk).
www.sussex-ramblers.org.uk
www.sussexbythesea.com
www.visitsussex.org
www.westsussex.gov.uk

884615, open Easter-Oct) has an 18-hole putting course, tennis courts and pretty tea gardens, with fantastic own-made cakes. Further on, the beautiful Swanbourne Lodge and Lake (01903 884293) is ideal for a duck-feeding jaunt. Rowing boats can be hired out from April to October, and the licensed café is open all year.

During the summer, the Arundel Lido (01903 882404, www.arundellido.com) – with its two heated pools, large grassed areas and views of the castle – must surely be one of the country's most beautiful

West Sussex

Bognor beach.
See p66.

locations for open air swimming. The stunning surrounding countryside and meandering river make Arundel the perfect base for some great walks. In nearby Ford, the Flying Fortress (01903 733550, www.flying-fortress.co.uk) is a good indoor play area for families. In addition to the usual array of slides and soft play areas for young children, it has pool and football tables to keep teenagers entertained, plus comfy sofas and a café for tired parents.

Building a better Bognor

While Bognor's main tourist attraction is, undoubtedly, Butlins (*see p16*), the largest holiday centre in the south of England, the town's other big claim to fame is that it is officially the sunniest place in Britain. In fact, way back in 1787 a wealthy London hatter named Richard Hotham realised how good the climate was in Bognor and built a health resort to attract the aristocracy to the area. His house and gardens still remain in the expansive Hotham Park (01243 830262, www.arun.gov.uk), now also home to an 18-hole putting green and crazy golf course, miniature railway and tennis court with equipment to hire, opposite Butlins. Years later, in 1929, King George V had a lung operation and was advised by his doctors to go to Bognor to recuperate, given the town's health-restoring reputation. Duly recovered, the King was so grateful that he bestowed a royal honour upon the place

and renamed it Bognor Regis. His alleged last words were about the little seaside town too, though they are less than complimentary ('b***** Bognor!').

Nowadays the seafront here offers what many would see as a traditional English holiday, with its own miniature train service, bustling promenade, endless fish and chip shops, a pier, trampolines, water sports, music in the bandstand, crazy golf, putting green and funfair during the summer months. The beach – which boasts a European Blue Flag and Seaside Award – is predominantly pebbly; however, sand can be enjoyed at low tide. During high season, the Kids Care scheme is in evidence: areas of the beach are colour coded, and your children are given the same colour bracelets to wear so that they can find you more easily should they happen to stray.

Bognor offers an imaginative year-round programme of events. From the Clowns Convention in March (*see p330*), something happens here nearly every month, right through to September's International Bognor Birdman Competition (*see p334*).

The alluring Butlins (01243 822445, www.butlins.com), offers day tickets for £15 (£7.50 2-14s). The Bognor Regis Museum (69 High Street, 01243 865636) packs a more educational punch – and admission is free. Another rainy day choice is Captain Oscar's Soft Play (01243 826612, www.inspireleisure.co.uk), which offers indoor fun and games and a crèche.

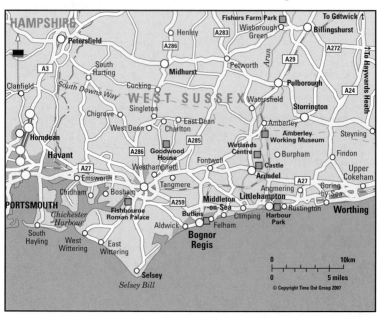

West Sussex

d the troops to
ndel Castle.
 p76.

Compact cathedral city

Chichester's 12th-century cathedral (01243 782595, www.chichestercathedral.org.uk) may not light all children's candles, but two of the city's shops certainly have most kids in raptures. The first is Montezuma's (29 East Street, 01243 537385, www.montezumas.co.uk) – the most amazing conglomeration of all things chocolate. There are some extraordinary creations, viz white chocolate with ginger and chilli. Next, pay a visit to Chichester Toys (53 South Street, 01243 788055), a capacious and traditional toy shop.

This city looks like an archetypal English market town, and an unlikely contender for a child-friendly holiday break, until you realise how much there is to do in the local area. For 17 days during June and July, the Chichester Festivities (*see p332*) provide entertainments for all ages. Nearby, the renowned Goodwood House and Estate (01243 755000, www.goodwood.co.uk) also hosts numerous events throughout the year, including Goodwood Festival of Speed in June. For more information *see p331*. This fine Regency house, set in 12,000 acres of rolling Sussex Downs, has been the home of the Dukes of Richmond for over 300 years. Not only does it contain one of the best collections of English paintings in the country, it also has an organic farm, golf course, hotel and country club (www.marriott.co.uk), plus an award-winning sculpture park set in 24 acres of ancient woodland. As well as providing masses of space for children to enjoy, the park has over 70 large-scale works on display. These include a collection of pieces by Tony Cragg – one of the biggest outdoor sculpture commissions ever given to a British artist (www.sculpture.org.uk).

Chichester is the UK's largest inland harbour – and the somewhat surprising home to a bunch of seals as well as to more predictable wildfowl. Chichester Harbour Water Tours (01243 670504, www.chichesterharbourwatertours.co.uk) run boat trips that show it all off.

Fantastic for cyclists and walkers alike, the Chichester Ship Canal, first opened to navigation in 1822, or the five-mile Centurion Way Railway Path take you from the heart of Chichester to West Dean. The beautiful West Dean House and Gardens (01243 818210, www.westdean.org.uk) are definitely worth visiting. For bike hire try either Shed End Bikes (01243 811766) or Chichester Cycle Hire (07765 565558).

Five minutes from Chichester train station, on Kingsham Road, the South Downs Planetarium (01243 774400, www.southdowns.org.uk/sdpt) has a changing programme of presentations.

Just three miles out of Chichester is the Tangmere Military Aviation Museum (01243 790090, www.tangmere-museum.org.uk), where you can see the speed-record breaking aircraft and try your skills on a flight simulator.

Chichester also has a museum (01243 784683, www.chichester.gov.uk/museum), an impressive leisure centre in Via Ravenna (01243 785651, www.chichester.gov.uk) and the giant Adventure Warehouse (01243 839455, www.adventure-warehouse.co.uk).

West Sussex

Littlehampton's **Seafront Train**

Little wonder

Located at the mouth of the river Arun, Littlehampton's two beaches, harbour and stunning riverside development have a strong appeal for families. Unfortunately, 2007 marks the loss of the European Blue Flag for East Beach, as questions have been raised about the purity of the water flowing down the Arun. While this nevertheless clean beach provides classic south coast shingle and sand, West Beach on the opposite side of the river has unspoilt sand dunes, rare plants and wildlife, and is protected as a Site of Special Scientific Interest (SSSI).

The East Bank riverside development includes the Look & Sea Visitor Centre, a Youth Hostel and a new lifeboat station – with a boathouse tour available on request. The exhibition at the Look and Sea Visitor Centre (63-65 Surrey Street, 01903 718984, www.lookandsea.co.uk) isn't particularly exciting, but its tower affords fabulous views of the harbour, sea and countryside. Tickets for the tower alone are a steal at 99p for adults and 50p for kids.

Exit the Centre and meander down the charming harbour walkway, winner of a Conservation Design Award in 2005. There's a fine collection of boats to admire, along with any number of swans that have learned to love chips and cornets. Among the myriad chippies in Littlehampton, Osca's (58 Pier Road, 01903 715791), on the harbour, stands out. It's open 11am-9.30pm seven days a week and offers a child's portion of cod and chips for £2, and an adult version for £3.35.

Arriving at the seafront, the Harbour Park amusement centre (01903 721200, www.harbourpark.com) hits you right between the eyes. This wallet-drainer is free to enter, but once the slot machines and fairground faves have worked their magic there'll be ruination before bedtime. There's also an indoor synthetic skating rink, a restaurant and a café if you want to offload more cash.

During the summer, the Seafront Promenade Train transports families between Coastguards Tower and Norfolk Gardens, and entertainment on the promenade includes Punch and Judy, live music and magic shows. Annual events include the Arts Festival in May and June; the carnival in July; the Seafront Festival in July and Zap Cats boat racing in August.

Several of the town's parks offer child-friendly activities, ranging from all-weather and grass tennis courts, putting greens, crazy golf, bowls, and a miniature railway to pedal boat hire. Mewsbrook Park has been awarded the Green Flag in recognition of its safe, clean environment and high level of garden maintenance.

Cycling and boating opportunities are arranged by the Littlehampton Dutch Bike Company (47 Pier Road, 01903 730089, www.dutchcycles.co.uk), who hire out bikes, kayaks and pedicabs. The Visitor Centre next to the Look and Sea Centre can provide you with leaflets on the Arun, Dunes and Sea Nature Trail – a fascinating 1.5-mile walk from the Centre that takes in river, saltmarsh, sand dune, shingle and marine habitats – and wildlife identification leaflets. Westward along the coastal path,

West Sussex

WAY DOWN SOUTH

Outstandingly natural and beautiful, the South Downs Way is unlike any other national trail as it is a bridleway, and can therefore be used not only by walkers, but also by riders and cyclists. A linear walk of 100 miles from Eastbourne in the east to Winchester in the west, the trail takes you from one side of West Sussex to the other, sticking largely to the scarp of the South Downs as it goes.

The terrain is not difficult and the hills not too high, but the reward is huge – a bird's eye view of England's gorgeousness rolling gently into the distance. To the south are the sea and the Isle of Wight; to the north, what Rudyard Kipling called 'the wooded, dim/ Blue goodness of the Weald' in his 1902 poem 'Sussex'.

Conveniently placed along the route are numerous Bronze Age barrows, Iron Age hill forts, Elizabethan palaces and classic country houses. This walk is a geography, history, botany, zoology, geology, PE and art lesson rolled into one. The chalk downland is renowned for its rich variety of wildflowers and butterflies, while the skies above contain hovering red kites and other birds of prey.

Even babies and toddlers can join in. The terrain is, for the most part, buggy-friendly, and a decent cross-country model should be able to manage much of the route. We softy southerners have it on a plate.

For further information about tackling the the South Downs Way, phone 01243 558716 or visit www.nationaltrail.co.uk.

Climping Beach offers nothing except itself – pebbles at high tide and a fine expanse of sand at other times. One of only three small sand dune systems in West Sussex, the beach is an SSSI where plants, birds, molluscs, insects, reptiles and mammals living and feeding on the sand flats, shingle and sand dunes are allowed to just be.

'God's pocket'

The Roman army landed on the bit of coast now known as East and West Wittering prior to their occupation of Sussex. When they departed four centuries later, their Saxon successors included a group called the Wihteringas – the people of Wihtere. Their territory is recorded in a charter of AD683 as Wihttringes.

We love winsome West Wittering Beach (www.westwitteringbeach.co.uk). With its European Blue Flag for water cleanliness and a Beach Award from the Tidy Britain Group for its faultless facilities, this beach cannot be beaten for a family day out. The car park (£1-£6, depending on the day of the week and season) covers over 20 acres

of mown grass, with no part of it being further than 100 metres from the beach. One word of caution: the road to the beach can get very busy at times, so early rising is advised if you intend travelling on a hot Saturday or Sunday during the summer without murdering each other. Don't let the volume of road traffic put you off though, as there's space enough for everyone to be accommodated once they arrive.

The locals call West Wittering 'God's Pocket', because it's sheltered by the Isle of Wight and enjoys its own little micro-climate. Even in winter, days here are often warm and sunny when the rest of the country is shivering. The gods of domestic cleanliness also smile on Wittering: the facilities are fab, with three large toilet blocks, showers and fresh water taps. The excellent Beach Café sells everything you would expect, but if the great outdoors has inspired a spot of self catering, barbecues are allowed in the sand dunes – there are even a couple provided.

At low tide, the predominantly sandy beach reveals a series of blue lagoons and pools, which are idyllic paddling spots for youngsters. At the very end of the beach there is a crabbing pool, while the sand dune spit of East Head (another SSSI) is endlessly fascinating. Walkers can explore a series of footpaths, and the 11-mile Salterns Way cycle path (01243 512301, www.conservancy.co.uk), is a peaceful route to Chichester. Bikes and child seats can be hired from 2XS in West Wittering (Rookwood Road, 01243 512552).

East Wittering has puffed itself up as a surfers' paradise. Its Surf School (01243 672292, www.witteringsurfshop.com) takes pupils from age eight. While West Wittering offers little more than the loveliest beach in the world, East Wittering has shops and chippies, as well as the delightful Candies Sweetshop (13 The Parade, 01243 673337) whose 150 neatly ranged jars of sweets contain the nectar of the gods (rhubarb and custard, sherbet pips and chewing nuts). Near the beach, The Shore Inn (Shore Road, 01243 674454) has outdoor seating and an indoor play area with some great games – including giant Jenga. Fresh fish is served up from £5.95, while children's portions start at £3.

WHERE TO STAY

Arundel Youth Hostel

Warningcamp, Arundel, West Sussex BN18 9QY (01903 882204/0870 770 5676/www. yha.org.uk). **Open** year round. **Rates** *Bed only* £19.95; £14.50 under-18s. B&B £80.95-£121 family room. **Credit** MC, V.

Found at the end of a private road, this handsome Georgian mansion has a spacious front lawn and plenty of room for children to run amok. Local entertainments include beaches due south, a riverside path to Arundel and its castle just a mile away, and the more challenging walks along Monarch's Way, which leads to the South Downs Way (*see p70* **Way down South**). There are plenty of family rooms with four, five or six beds, as well as double-bedded en suite rooms that can be booked for parents with children old enough to sleep in twin-bedded rooms on their own. It's very well equipped, with a restaurant as well as a self catering kitchen, barbecue facilities in the extensive grounds, camping spaces outside and, for rainy days, a big lounge, pool table, table tennis and bar football.

Bailiffscourt Hotel

Climping Street, Climping, nr Littlehampton, West Sussex BN17 5RW (01903 723511/ www.hshotels.co.uk). **Rates** *DB&B* £260-£385. **Credit** MC, V.

Fancy the ultimate in pampering *en famille*? Look no further than the glorious Bailiffscourt – a stone's throw from Climping Beach. The building dates from 1927, when Lord and Lady Moyne plumped for a medieval look for their country retreat on a recently-acquired 750 acre plot. The resultant manor house has honey-coloured brickwork, mullioned windows, stone-flagged paths and sturdy oak doors. Decor is appropriately antique, with endless tapestries adorning the walls and heavy oak furniture throughout. Splendid peacocks meander through the estate, and log fires crackle in many of the 39 bedrooms. Modern diversions include a couple of hard tennis courts, a croquet lawn, snooker room, indoor and outdoor pools (with restricted hours for children), several very comfortable sitting rooms and a helipad. The spa and beauty area run the gamut of pampering treatments, while stupendous meals in the restaurant reward every calorie-burning activity. Dinner for parents is included in the rates, but children pay £11 for two courses or £16 for three from the children's menu, or £44.50 for a full à la carte dinner. Dogs are more than welcome here, and can stay in your room at a special canine rate of £12 per night.

Beachcroft Hotel, Spa & Restaurant

Clyde Road, Felpham, Bognor Regis, West Sussex PO22 7AH (01243 827142/ www.beachcroft-hotel.co.uk). **Rates** *DB&B* £107-£113. **Credit** AmEx, MC, V.

East of Bognor, the village of Felpham is a joy waiting to be discovered. Do so while staying at the friendly Beachcroft Hotel – the only beachfront hotel between Brighton and Portsmouth. There are various family rooms, including some with children's quarters in a curtained annex; most have glorious views out to sea. It's a two star hotel, so don't expect luxury facilities, but rooms are spacious and everything is in good condition and spotlessly clean. The indoor swimming pool is a good size, and there's an in-house spa and beauty therapist. In the restaurant, the atmosphere is homely and relaxed. Florian, the manager, is happy to arrange for dishes on the menu to be adjusted to suit junior tastes where possible. If your offspring simply want unchallenging refuelling, a 'Kids Corner' menu lists the usual suspects: sweet battered chicken strips, sausage and mash and pizza with chips and peas (£4.45-£4.95), with an ice-cream boat (£3.25) to follow. Puddings here are well worth the extra 50 lengths required to work them off in the pool.

Beach House

Rookwood Road, West Wittering, West Sussex PO20 8LT (01243 514800/www.beachhse. co.uk). **Rates** £60-£80. **Credit** MC, V.

Susan and Stephen Marks's B&B/guesthouse is very hard to label. While visitors enjoy the intimacy of a family run B&B, there is also a bar, restaurant and sheltered wooden verandah – very colonial – where you can make the most of West Wittering's micro-climate and eat outside. The food is delicious and reasonably-priced; starters such as Sussex smokie and chicken liver and brandy pâté cost under a fiver, and can be followed by the likes of calves liver and parma ham

or a swordfish steak, accompanied by very passable house wine at a mere £10.25 a bottle. Families of six can be comfortably accommodated in a shared room, but travel cots are a must; although children are made to feel extremely welcome, cots are not provided. Dogs are also welcome here – and can bring their own baskets if they like. The resident's lounge is equipped with a fridge and microwave, which is handy for heating up baby food. The Beach House's magical location, within a short walk of the lovely West Wittering beach, means it is one of the most coveted places to stay in the county. Early booking is essential, and there is a two-night minimum stay during school holidays and weekends from April to September.

Chichester Park Hotel

Westhampnett, Chichester, West Sussex PO19 7QL (01243 786351/www.chichester parkhotel.com). **Rates** £70-£85. **Credit** MC, V.

Just on the outskirts of Chichester, this externally somewhat unprepossessing hotel in a not exactly picturesque area was recently acquired from the Ramada Jarvis chain by the energetic Chahboune family. Once you've walked through the doors, any doubts you may have had in the car park will instantly evaporate, thanks to the warm welcome. Most families with children dump their stuff in their rooms and gallop to the good-sized swimming pool. Unusually for a hotel with a pool, there are no time restrictions for children's swimming. In fact, staff do their utmost to engage with the kids, and the hotel's family friendliness extends beyond the external trappings (cots, bottle warming, baby listening service and interconnecting family rooms are all present and correct). Cots are loaned out at no extra cost, and under-16s stay free in their parents' room. Rooms look slightly corporate, but are comfortable, spacious and well equipped. Although the dinner menu isn't particularly extensive, meals are generously proportioned, well presented and reasonably priced at £18.95 for three courses. Children can either eat

from their own menu – a bargain £6.95 for three courses – or sample children's portions from the à la carte. With perfectly quaffable house wines at £12.50 a bottle and staff who clearly enjoy having children around, what more could a parent ask for?

Littlehampton Youth Hostel

63 Surrey Street, Littlehampton, West Sussex BN17 5AW (0870 770 6114/www.yha.org.uk). **Open** *Easter-Oct* advance bookings. *Nov-Mar* phone for details. **Rates** £15.50-£16.50; £11-£12 under-18s. **Credit** MC, V.

Opened in April 2003 as part of the development of Fisherman's Wharf on the east bank of the river Arun, this is a purpose-built four star hostel, the apple of the YHA's eye. There are lots of family rooms, most of which are en suite, and double beds aren't so rare as in other hostels. As a small 32-bed hostel, it's self catering only, but guests aren't going to starve; there's an eclectic collection of restaurants just outside the front door. The town's sandy beach is five minutes' walk away. Facilities include a TV lounge, laundry, clothes drying room and cycle store.

Norfolk Arms Hotel

22 High Street, Arundel, West Sussex BN18 9AB (01903 882101/www.norfolkarms hotel.com). **Rates** £125-£140. **Credit** MC, V.

Built in 1783 as a coaching inn for the tenth Duke of Norfolk, this imposing hotel dominates the centre of Arundel. Its crowning glory is the ballroom, now used for conferences and other events, which has six vast original mirrors and a minstrels' gallery. The hotel is part of the privately owned Forestdale Group, which runs 18 other hotels up and down the country and offers family-friendly rates in all. Under-14s are accommodated at no extra charge if they share your room, and also get free breakfast and dinner during half term holidays, which makes this a good budget option for a midweek school holiday breather. All the usual facilities are provided (cots, high chairs, special menus, even rubber ducks in the bath) and families of four can be easily, if snugly, accommodated in a shared room. The premier grade rooms are the most spacious option; a little chintzy in decor, but comfortable. Children can eat from their own cheaply-priced menu (prawn cocktail £1.45; sausage, egg and chips £2.75; fresh fruit salad £1.25) or choose children's portions from the à la carte menu. The hotel also welcomes animals of all shapes and sizes, including dogs, cats and even the odd parrot.

Royal Norfolk Hotel

The Esplanade, Bognor Regis, West Sussex PO21 2LH (01243 826222/www.royalnorfolk hotel.com). **Rates** £80-£120. **Credit** MC, V.
Everyone is so wonderfully nice and helpful at this Christian-run hotel that you feel blessed you've chosen to stay here. The place is a miracle. Sitting comfortably in three acres of gardens on the seafront, the hotel offers croquet, bowls and its own car park – something of a rarity in Bognor. Built in 1830, it was once known as a genteel hideaway for royalty, and has attracted visitors such as Queen Victoria, King Edward VII, the exiled Emperor Napoleon III of France and the Empress Maud of Russia. Rooms are spacious and light, with big windows and high ceilings, and those with a sea view are blissful. The decor is unfashionable (it's a bit like staying in a very clean maiden aunt's house), with dated dressing tables and bedside lights, but the facilities are good and the en suite bathrooms comfortable and spotlessly clean. The menu in the restaurant is equally unadventurous but sympathetically created for conservative tastes, with a wide variety of specials (option might include classic prawn cocktail, loin of pork, or a vegetable and nut roast for herbivores). Children are made welcome, and the hotel provides cots, bottle warming, a baby listening service and interconnecting family rooms; under-twos stay free.

Shoreline Hotel

Butlins, Bognor Regis, West Sussex PO21 1JJ (enquiries 01243 810099/bookings 810016/ www.butlinsonline.co.uk). **Rates** prices vary; phone or check website. **Credit** MC, V.
Built in summer 2005, the Shoreline is designed for the more discerning Butlins guest *(see p16)*. Satisfied customers approve of the unwonted luxury of the air-conditioned rooms, particularly the pricier 'Nelson's Staterooms', which have games consoles, flatscreen tellies and DVD players, balconies and plenty of room for families. Designed to look like an ocean liner, the Shoreline looms over the seafront. Guests receive an experience pass, so that they can enjoy all the raucous pleasures of the holiday resort – and its endless queues for anything vaguely attractive to children. Butlins devotees who stayed in this swish new hotel in its inaugural summer are full of praise for its ultra modern facilities and sunny ambience (all big windows and laminate flooring), and it's a far cry from the resort's standard apartments.

Stubcroft Farm Bed & Breakfast

Stubcroft Lane, East Wittering, Chichester, West Sussex PO20 8PJ (01243 671469/07810 751665/www.stubcroft.com). **Rates** £54-£70. **No credit cards.**
This secluded Victorian farmhouse, with its welcoming owners, offers an idyllic B&B location. Like the campsite *(see p74)*, the establishment is particularly eco-friendly – organic and fair trade products have a starring role on the farmhouse breakfast table. The house has large period rooms, comfortably furnished with washbasins, central heating, tea and coffee making facilities and a television, if required. For children, cots and a high chair are also available on request. Under-12s pay a half rate, and under-twos stay for free. At the time of writing the B&B was closed for refurbishment with plans to re-open in Easter 2007;

West Sussex

Beach House.
See p71.

new luxury rooms will have king-sized sleigh beds and en suite bathrooms. All around are peaceful private lanes and grounds to explore, making this a delightful countryside base. The farm is run on environmentally friendly grounds, so wildlife watching is rewarding; children can be kept busy spotting deer, rabbits, hedgehogs and over 72 identified species of birds (no tea until they've ticked them all off!). It's great to be able to wander about the farm and see events unfold: in spring and summer there are lambs and calves, and haymaking and harvest make late summer a wonderful time of year to stay.

Stubcroft Farm Camping & Caravanning

Stubcroft Lane, East Wittering, Chichester, West Sussex PO20 8PJ (01243 671469/07810 751665/www.stubcroft.com). **Open** all year. **Rates** £7-£20/pitch (2 adults); £1-£3 additional adult; 50p-£1.50 3-16s; free under-3s. **No credit cards**.

Comprising three paddocks where you put up your tent, Stubcroft is for proper campers. The total lack of shops, nightlife and park wardens is glorious, and means that the skies you sleep under are truly black and star studded. The only sounds you'll hear are birdsong, gentle baa-ing and the contented murmur (and occasional tantrums) of other proper camping families. Oh, and the fevered mutterings of parents praying for dry weather. Stubcroft is run by a friendly farmer, who's mostly busy with the sheep; nonetheless, campers are made to feel very welcome. Children can watch seasonal activities such as lambing,

haymaking and harvesting (not to mention rain-cussing) going on all around them. During high season the place can get quite busy at weekends, but you never feel cramped and can pitch your tent wherever you like. The nearest beach is a 15-minute walk away, there are plenty of shops nearby for supplies, and basic pub grub can be found across the corn field. There are drinking water taps and washing up points, three showers with washbasins, and eight newly-installed electric hook-up units. It's an environmentally friendly site – hence the blocks of waterless eco-loo cubicles, which can save over 1,000 gallons of water on a busy day, alongside two of the more conventional flushing variety. Indeed, the site has been shortlisted for a 'Green Business' award for its conservation planting, waste recycling and eco-loos. Like the farmhouse B&B (*see p73*), the site was closed at the time this guide went to press, but due to open in Easter 2007. Book early to avoid disappointment if you're planning to stay during the high season.

WHERE TO EAT & DRINK

Dolphin Café

5 Waterloo Square, Bognor Regis, West Sussex PO21 1SZ (no phone). **Meals served** 7am-3pm daily. **Main courses** £1.75-£4. **No credit cards**.

This basic café, aptly positioned next to the Fair Trade shop, is unlike many of the other cafés that abound on or near the seafront in Bognor, because it can't claim to offer the otherwise seemingly omnipresent Bognor Grease Aroma. Charmingly decorated in clean blues and whites, the Dolphin's

A perfect pitch in **Wittering**.

large mug of tea will set you back just 50p, while the all day English breakfast costs a mere £3. A decent sized roast can be enjoyed every day, with a traditional pudding to follow. Also on offer are sandwiches, jacket potatoes and fish and chips. If you are here on a Sunday, try the three course Sunday lunch for a risible £6.50.

Lemon Tree

61 Surrey Street, Littlehampton, West Sussex BN17 5BJ (01903 719419/www.thelemontree. uk.com). **Meals served** noon-9pm Mon-Sat; noon-8.30pm Sun. **Main courses** £7.95-£17.75. **Credit** MC, V.

This restaurant, just off the harbour, is quite a few steps up the food chain from the town's endless chippies. Good, fresh starters include warm goats cheese and tomato roulade with pesto dressing, with imaginative vegetarian main courses alongside hearty dishes such as venison steak, red cabbage and potato rosti with redcurrant sauce. There is a wide choice of fresh fish dishes, and children can either eat from their own menu (dishes include mild chicken curry with rice, £4.25) or select small portions from the adults' menu.

Le Zinc Bistro

51 High Street, Arundel, West Sussex BN18 9AJ (01903 884500). **Meals served** 9.30am-9.30pm daily. **Main courses** £7.95-£12.45. **Credit** MC, V.

'Cuisine des tartines' is what le Zinc's all about. Or, if you're trying to tempt the children, 'French pizza'. This good looking café/restaurant is a gem in the heart of Arundel, just opposite the Norfolk Arms Hotel. Serving delicious creations atop *pain Poilâne* (the large, circular sourdough bread usually found in France), the light-lunchy aspect of Le Zinc is particularly attractive to families. Take your pick from toppings such as seasonal grilled Mediterranean vegetables, parmesan shavings and fresh herbs, and scrambled eggs, chives and smoked salmon, or head straight for three scoops of creamy own-made ice-cream. Breakfast is served until 11.30am, then the bistro menu takes over. Adults say the wine list is top notch, while children adore the hot chocolate on a chilly day. There's a patio at the back for sunny lunches.

Oyster Catcher

Yapton Road, Climping, West Sussex BN17 5RU (01903 738620). **Meals served** noon-10pm Mon-Sat; 11.30am-9.30pm Sun. **Main courses** £4.50-£12.50. **Credit** MC, V.

No one in their right mind would visit Climping solely for its gastronomic delights (unless they are staying at the Bailiffscourt Hotel, where the restaurant is brilliant). The Oyster Catcher pub, however, is a decent place for lunch – and our preferred choice over The Black Horse, which is only a stone's throw from the beach. Although clearly part of a chain, the Oyster Catcher has masses of space both inside and out, and the sort of menu

that hits the spot after a busy morning on the beach. It offers a good selection of sandwiches, including the splendid Gloucestershire ham and Wexford cheddar with watercress, tomato, mayo and spicy fruit chutney on ciabatta bread, plus solid gastropub classics such as chargrilled calves' liver in a rich port gravy with peas and cheddar mash. There's no children's menu, but selected dishes from the main menu can be sized down and priced accordingly.

Riverside

Pier Road, Littlehampton, West Sussex BN17 5LP (01903 715966). **Meals served** *Summer* noon-8pm daily. *Winter* noon-8pm Thur-Sun. **Main courses** £4.75-£16. **Credit** MC, V.

Meandering along the delightful harbour in Littlehampton, you'll encounter no end of cheap restaurants and chippies, but the Riverside is the best (though not the cheapest) in this class. With a fine selection of fresh local seafood, it also has a good children's menu with dishes such as meatballs and spaghetti for £4.25 and a mini roast for £4.95. Basics for adults include jacket potatoes and a hearty meal of Cumberland sausages, while the fabulous selection of own-made puddings will soon convince you that the fish and chips didn't really fill you up – there's still space for a spot of local ice-cream or sticky toffee pudding.

St Martin's Tearooms

3 St Martin's Street, Chichester, West Sussex PO19 1NP (01243 786715/www.organic tearooms.co.uk). **Meals served** 10am-6pm Mon-Sat. **Main courses** £5.20-£9.45. **No credit cards.**

Just as older children and adults are more likely to appreciate Chichester's antique charms, so this delightful little labyrinth of nooks and crannies, with its organic and wholefood menu, holds more appeal for those who've lived a little. Children who prefer to run around will be frustrated here, as there are open fires and lots of steps to tumble down. Nonetheless, those who sit down and enjoy their tuck (organic, often vegetarian savouries such as salads, risottos and tarts, plus chunky own-made cakes in chocolate, carrot and flapjack forms) will enjoy the ambience. We certainly do – it's a great place for lunch following a tour around the cathedral or harbour.

PLACES TO SEE, THINGS TO DO

The choice of family entertainments, stately homes, gracious gardens, animal centres and heritage buildings in West Sussex is far too wide for us to include more than our favourites here. To find out about other recommended local attractions such as the Sussex Falconry Centre (01243 512472, www.sussexfalconrycentre.com), Shipley Windmill (www.shipleywindmill.org.uk) and the Earnley Butterfly Centre (01243

West Sussex

Time Out | Family Breaks in Britain **75**

Climping Beach. *See p70.*

512637), contact the Tourist Information Centre (*see p65*) for for a copy of the comprehensive 'Places to Visit' guide.

Amberley Working Museum

Amberley, nr Arundel, West Sussex BN18 9LT (01798 831370/www.amberleymuseum.co.uk). **Open** *Mid Mar-Oct* 10am-5.30pm Wed-Sun (open daily during West Sussex school hols). **Admission** £8.70; £7.70 concessions; £5.50 5-16s; £25 family (2+3); free under-5s. **Credit** MC, V.

Nestling near the South Downs Way, this 36-acre open air museum comprises more than 30 different buildings and hundreds of exhibits from bygone days, when work didn't just mean screens and keyboards. Displays cover transport, print workshops, telecommunications and electricity, and there's a variety of working craftspeople in residence, including a potter, clay-pipe maker and broom-maker. There's a nature and woodland trail, a children's playground and space to run around in. This is a wonderful conglomeration of our artisan and industrial history, splendidly laid out. The museum and grounds are buggy and wheelchair friendly, and you can also travel around the site on a vintage bus and narrow-gauge railway. Even if you don't partake of refreshments in the sympathetically designed Limeburners Restaurant, it's worth popping in to admire its timber frame, artful cedar cladding and hand-made clay tiles. There's so much to see on site that it's best to start your visit by watching the introductory video at the Hayloft Theatre, before drawing up a plan of action for the day.

Arundel Castle

Arundel, West Sussex BN18 9AB (01903 882173/www.arundelcastle.org). **Open** *Apr-Oct* 11am-4pm Mon-Fri, Sun. *Aug* 11am-4pm daily. **Admission** *Castle, chapel & grounds* £12; £9.50 concessions; £7.50 5-16s, £32 family (2+5); free under-5s. *Chapel & grounds* £6.50. **Credit** MC, V.

The picturesque icing on the cake that is the beautiful town of Arundel, the castle was built at the end of the 11th century and has been the family home of the Dukes of Norfolk and their ancestors for more than 850 years. Aside from the occasional reversion to the throne, this is now one of the longest inhabited country houses in England. In 1643, during the Civil War, the castle was besieged by General Waller (for Parliament) and the defences were partly demolished. Happily, many of the original features – such as the crenellated Norman keep, gatehouse and barbican, and the lower part of Bevis Tower – survived. During the late 19th century, the house was almost completely rebuilt. The views of the Sussex countryside from the keep are fabulous, and the grounds include a kitchen garden, rose garden and the Fitzalan Chapel, which is still used as the burial place of the Dukes of Norfolk. Inside, treasures include the fine Regency library and restored bedrooms with their original baths and basins.

Arundel Wetlands Centre

Wildfowl & Wetlands Trust, Mill Road, Arundel, West Sussex BN18 9PB (01903 883355/www.wwt.org.uk). **Open** 9.30am-

4.30pm daily. **Admission** £6.95; £5.25 concessions; £3.75 4-16s; £17 family (2+2); free under-4s. **Credit** MC, V.

Part of a UK network of wetland centres run by the Wildfowl & Wetlands Trust, this one provides succour to Sussex's feathered visitors and residents. Human guests can see, feed and learn about wetland birds on tours or in the Visitor Centre. The 60 acres of ponds, lakes and reed beds accommodate a quacking collection of ducks, geese and swans from all over the world, and the reed bed boardwalk makes it fine for buggies and wheelchairs. The Water's Edge Restaurant, with its child-friendly menus, has floor-to-ceiling windows to ensure you don't miss any wildlife while you eat. The nature reserve at RSPB Pulborough Brooks (01798 875851, www.rspb.org.uk) provides a similarly themed day out.

Fishbourne Roman Palace & Gardens

Salthill Road, Fishbourne, Chichester, West Sussex PO19 3QR (01243 785859/www.sussexpast.co.uk). **Open** *Jan* 10am-4pm Sat, Sun. *Feb, Nov, Dec* 10am-4pm daily. *Mar-Jul, Sept, Oct* 10am-5pm daily. *Aug* 10am-6pm daily. **Admission** £6.80; £5.80 concessions; £3.60 5-16s; £17.40 family (2+2); free under-5s. **Credit** MC, V.

This place is particularly extraordinary because it wasn't discovered until 1960, when a digger driver accidentally cut through the massive wall foundations as he laid a water main. Such serendipity led to the uncovering of the remains of the largest domestic Roman building yet found in Britain. Now you can wander through the palace and admire the fabulous mosaic floors, some almost complete, such as the famous Cupid on a dolphin. Also on view are underfloor heating systems, corridors, courtyards, a bath suite and even a skeleton. Outside, the formal garden has been replanted to its original plan and a display area contains a range of plants that historians reckon were grown at the palace during the first century AD. If you haven't had your fill of Roman remains after Fishbourne, visit Bignor Roman Villa, near Pulborough, for more mosaics and mystery (01798 869259).

Fishers Farm Park

Newpound Lane, Wisborough Green, nr Billingshurst, West Sussex RH14 0EG (01403 700063/www.fishersfarmpark.co.uk). **Open** 10am-5pm daily. **Admission** £7.75-£10.75; £7.25-£10.25 3-16s; £4-£7 2-3s; free under-2s. **Credit** MC, V.

Fishers is consistently voted one of the country's top ten countryside attractions for families, mostly because it's run like clockwork, looks gorgeous and has so much to do beyond cooing at guinea pigs. This is a place where families with children aged up to about 12 could quite happily spend an entire day and still want to come back for more. If you're after the classic cuddly animals, you'll

find all the usual fluffy bunnies, dwarf goats and the like that are happy to be stroked and adored. The cuddlies are just the beginning, however. The sheer variety and quality of the rides, giant sandpits, climbing/clambering features and general activities is quite mind-boggling. Little ones love letting their imaginations run riot in the wooden house deep in the woods (with a bench thoughtfully provided for waiting parents), while older children can try their luck on the climbing wall or massive lighthouse slide complex. Throughout the day there are various other activities on offer, including pony and tractor rides, a ghost tunnel, bumper boats, pedal karts and a mini adventure golf course. If it's hot, go and have a splash in the pool at 'The Beach'; in less clement weather, children can frolic in the indoor play zone. Toilet facilities are spotless and liberally dotted about the park, with the added bonus of offering both hot and drinking water. Refreshments in the licensed café are also excellent; for example, a children's high tea (£3.50) comprises organic and additive-free chicken nuggets, chips made from locally grown potatoes, baked beans and a drink. Just down the road is the delightful Bat and Ball pub (01403 700313) where the food is great and there is a fine selection of good beer and guest ales, plus a beautiful beer garden with separate children's play area. You can even camp in the field next door, enjoy takeaway pub meals under canvas, and spend your whole holiday near Fisher's – which for our young reviewers would be heaven.

Weald & Downland Open Air Museum

Singleton, Chichester, West Sussex PO18 0EU (01243 811348/www.wealddown.co.uk). **Open** *Apr-Oct* 10.30am-6pm daily. *Nov-Mar* varies; phone for details. **Admission** £8.25; £7.25 concessions; £4.40 5-16s; £22.65 family (2+3); free under-5s. **Credit** MC, V.

This extraordinary place celebrates a long lost countryside heritage in just 50 acres of beautiful Sussex countryside. It's a soothing, if slightly sad, place to wander through, dotted with a fascinating collection of about 50 historic buildings dating from the 13th to the 19th centuries. Rescued from destruction, these buildings have been painstakingly dismantled, conserved and rebuilt to their original form. Some also have their own period gardens, showing the herbs, vegetables and flowers grown to meet the needs of our rural forebears. Visitors can see bread, pottage and sweetmeats being prepared in the working Tudor kitchen, marvel at the giant working water mill where stoneground flour is produced daily, admire the skills of early carpenters and watch the heavy horses at work in the fields. Plenty of other farm animals, some rare breeds, await inspection, and there are daily craft activities and special events during the school holidays to further engage the children. December has a particularly busy programme of events, with carol singing, tree dressing and fireside storytelling – plus mulled cider for chilly grown-ups.

The New Forest

Go down to the woods.

For many, a trip to the New Forest means nostalgia. The area resonates with childhood memories of pony treks and picnics, and in a changing world the forest seems comfortingly constant. It's probably the closest that children will get to their storybook images of quaint thatched cottages in wild tulgey woods, where laws are subverted, animals reign and anything might happen...

Such impressions are not so far removed from the truth. For one thing, the New Forest is not new. It is ancient, and made up not only of woodland but also sweeps of sandy brackeny heath, bog and grassland. The area has been protected and carefully managed ever since William the Conqueror arrived from Normandy and set himself up in his castle in Winchester. In 1079 the king brought in laws to preserve the 'Nova Foresta' as a royal hunting ground for deer, forbidding locals from fencing off areas and ordering them to keep their livestock off the land during the summer foaling season and in winter, when food for the deer was scarce. The locals, complaining that beast had become more important than man, were later accorded rights that exist to this day. These include the right to gather firewood and graze their animals in the forest; hence every wild pony and donkey you see wandering nonchalantly down the high street has a local owner. While the forest remains Crown land, it is managed by the Forestry Commission, and became a national park in 2004.

New Forest
Otter, Owl
& Wildlife
Conservation Park.
See p93.

Paultons

The New Forest

Not surprisingly, folklore and fictions abound. From Brockenhurst to Lyndhurst and south to Lymington you will come across the name of 'Brusher' Mills, the legendary local snake catcher, or Mary Dore, the witch of Beaulieu. In the graveyard of St Michael and All Angels in Lyndhurst, beneath a pink rambling rose lies the tomb of the original Alice, who inspired Lewis Carroll. And for a tale set in the woods with lots of local history, there is Captain Marryatt's *The Children of the New Forest*, written in 1847.

The heath and woods cover an area of 145 square miles. They sit in a basin bordered by Dorset to the west, Wiltshire to the north, and are sandwiched between the cities of Bournemouth and Southampton. The Beaulieu and Lymington rivers drain into the Solent, and the area's wildlife-rich coast is one of its key attractions. The coming of the railways in the 19th century saw increased urbanisation and the creation of towns such as New Milton, and a burgeoning tourism industry led to a buzzy boating scene along the waters.

Today, the A31, A35 and A337 wind through the forest like angry snakes, bringing with them their own problems; even out of season. Expect a bottleneck jam on the A337 approach to Lyndhurst, and parking in certain villages during the summer is a game of musical spaces.

But it is worth every bit of the journey. The New Forest has everything except mountains to interest and entertain its visitors: varied wildlife, walking, cycling, horse riding and even a theme park, Paultons, in Romsey (023 8081 4442, www.paultonspark.co.uk). The best advice for parents, however, is to 'let your children run wild like the ponies'.

Trot this way

The village of Brockenhurst sits snugly between the south western railway line and a network of streams. One waterway even crosses the main shopping street, Brookley Road, creating a splash as cars drive through. It reinforces the feeling that nature is encroaching on the human settlement, despite the white picket fences and railings to keep it in check. Wildlife is literally on the doorstep: there are ponies in the streets, cattle in the gateways and grids at practically every entrance to teashops or terraces; it is the ponies, not the foxes, that raid the bins here.

Brockenhurst (an Anglo-Saxon name – 'hurst' means a wooded hill) existed as four manor houses when the Domesday book was drawn up in 1086. The oldest church in the New Forest, St Nicholas Church, is pitched on a steep rise beyond the railway track to the south. Considered mainly Norman, but probably built on the Saxon walling of an earlier church, St Nicholas is worth visiting for its medieval font. More of a draw for the children is the grave of Harry 'Brusher' Mills, known as the snake catcher. His striking white tombstone depicts Harry trapping snakes in the forest beside the charcoal burner's hut in which he lived. The Snakecatcher pub in the village was originally a railway inn, where Harry was served his last bread, pickles and pint before he died in 1905. The graveyard also houses much older stones – we saw one dated 1785.

Also of interest to children is Tatty's (51 Brockley Road, 01590 624442), a toy, sweet and ice-cream shop all rolled into one. Aniseed balls, pineapple chunks and other sugary delights are sold from jars, while ice-cream from Marshfield Farm is the healthier alternative.

Whichever direction you set out in from the village, the spectacle of forest and heath fans out before you beneath expansive, cloud-scudded skies. If you have never ridden a horse before, or spent any length of time on a bike, this is most certainly the place to try. There are three riding stables in the area (*see p92*), which will take absolute beginners on a hack with sessions starting at 30 minutes. Riding is the perfect way to see nature from different heights and angles, but if pony isn't your ideal method of transport, you can hire a bike and explore some of the designated routes. Stop off at a pub along the way or, for an extra special treat, indulge in a cream tea at the Thatched Cottage tearoom on the Brockley Road (01590 623090).

The walks to the west of Brockenhurst are popular with families. The Rhinefield Ornamental Drive takes in the Tall Trees Trail and Bolderwood, where you can view fallow deer from a purpose-built observation platform at feeding time. Here too, you may come across the gigantic Knightwood oak. It's reputedly 500 years old, making it the oldest tree in the forest. The Tall Trees Trail also leads you through soaring redwoods, as well as past rhododendrons and firs. The so-called ornamental trees are the native oak, beech, birch and yew, which preceded the soft wood trees (like firs and pines) planted later in the 18th and 19th centuries to provide timber for fencing, fuel and furniture.

For three days every July, the area gets busy as the New Forest Show (*see p332*) unfolds in New Park.

Capital for tourists

Sitting on a prehistoric man-made mound, the spire of St Michaels and All Angels church pinpoints the beginning of Lyndhurst High Street. The street slopes down, lined

TOURIST INFORMATION

Lymington
New Street, Lymington, Hampshire
SO41 9BH (01590 689000).
New Forest
The main car park, Lyndhurst,
Hampshire SO43 7NY (023 8028
2269/www.thenewforest.co.uk).
Ringwood
The Furlong, Ringwood, Hampshire
BH24 1AZ (01425 470896).

with an assortment of pubs with rooms – the Stag, the Crown, the Fox and Hounds – along with teashops, Mr Whippy ice-cream signs and souvenir shops.

Lyndhurst is the capital of the New Forest, and the only town within its historical confines. To the north of the church stands the mellow brick Queen's House, constructed in the 17th century on the site of an older manor house. The Court of Verderers (from the French word for green, vert) manage the affairs of the forest from here, and still hold regular sessions in the hall attached to the house.

Lyndhurst is a good place to stock up on essentials. Information can be found at the library, tourist office and museum (all under the one roof, located in the car park off the High Street; *see p92*); several leisure stores stock caravan and camping equipment; and toys can be acquired at the charming Down to the Wood on the Romsey Road (023 8028 4428, www.wooden.co.uk). The latter is packed to the rafters with everything wooden, from Noah's ark animals and pullalong crocodiles to puzzles, beaded jewellery and kitchen accoutrements.

When you've exhausted its treasures, there are the sweet shops. There's nothing like spoiling your appetite for dinner with a few sweeties, and the New Forest seems to be sugar overload centre, judging by the amounts of fudge, ice-cream, penny sweets, toffee and humbugs on offer here. Two sweet shops in Lyndhurst really stand out. The Old English Sweet Shop (67 High Street, 023 8028 4949) has skeins of liquorice hanging from the ceiling and is chock-a-block with goodies, from the jars of rum and butter toffees in the window to the colourful array of cola bottles, friendship rings, juicy lips, milk bottles, candy sticks and chocolate satins inside. Chocolatier Isabelle (55 High Street, 023 8028 4999, www.chocolatierisabelle.co.uk) is the polar opposite of its neighbour, but definitely worth a visit – if only to meet the impossibly slender proprietor, Isabelle, who makes Belgian chocolates in the shape of cows, footballs, ponies, fish, hedgehogs, owls, button mushrooms, swans, butterflies, acorns and horse's heads.

The New Forest

If all that shopping has worn you out, you can retreat to local tearooms such as the Lyndhurst Tea House (26-28 High Street, 023 8028 2656) or the slightly posher Under the Greenwood Tree, also on the High Street (No.65, 023 8028 2463, www.underthegreenwoodtree.com), to curl up and wind down.

A few miles north of Lyndhurst, where the A31 to Bournemouth cuts the forest in half, lies Canterton, near Stoney Cross. This is the site of the Rufus Stone, which supposedly marks the spot where William II fell. The unpopular son of William the Conqueror, this William (known as Rufus because of his ruddy complexion) was killed at the age of 40, on 2 August 1100, by a stray arrow shot by Sir Walter Tyrell. Hunting was a dangerous business in those days and grisly accidents were not uncommon; indeed, William lost both a brother and a nephew in similar hunting accidents in the New Forest.

Sir Walter fled to France, while a local charcoal burner by the name of Purkis took the king's body to Winchester Cathedral in his cart. The cast iron Rufus Stone was erected in 1841 – although there is some speculation that William actually met his end in Beaulieu (see p83), and a second Rufus Stone stands on the estate.

Whatever the true location, the Rufus Stone is set in a lovely spot. On the way there you might want to drop in on Furzey Gardens (023 8081 2464, www.furzey-gardens.org), and after your visit to the monument you can enjoy easy forays into the woods and perhaps a picnic. A word of warning: crossing the busy A31 at Stoney Cross is a true test of courage.

You must go down to the sea

Strictly speaking, Lymington is not within the New Forest boundary, but its history is linked closely with the area. Only a five mile drive from Brockenhurst, it has the added advantage of being on the coast. From here you can take a ferry across to the Isle of Wight (see pp94-107) for lunch (Wightlink, 0870 582 7744, www.wightlink.co.uk). If your children are interested in sailing, there are boating lessons from the quay.

Lymington's prosperity, highlighted in the Domesday Book, came from its production of salt. Epsom salts became a speciality of the local salterns (clay huts used for salt production), and the monks of Beaulieu Abbey owned a salt granary in the town to ensure the flavour and preservation of their food. In addition to this medieval industry (which became defunct during the 19th century), Lymington evolved into a major port with a nefarious reputation for smuggling. Today, it is very popular with the yachting fraternity (catered for by the marinas), and continues to be an important boat building centre.

The quaint character of the town is enhanced by pretty pastel-coloured houses, antique lamp-posts and a broad High Street with a busy Saturday market. Leading down

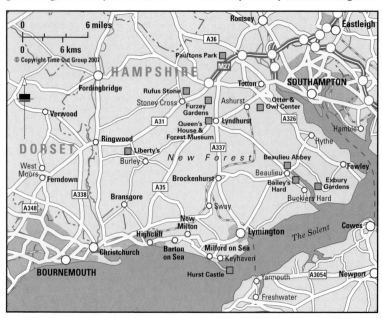

Camping near **Ashurst**. *See p85.*

to the waterfront via the river, the cobbled Quay Hill, lined with bow-fronted shops, makes a pleasant stroll. There are coastal rambles along the marshes, but historians may prefer a walk along the raised spit from Keyhaven to Hurst Castle, where Charles I was imprisoned in 1648 before his trial and execution in London. The shingle walk is over two miles long, however, and not recommended on windy days when the tide is in. The ferry service that runs between Keyhaven Quay and the castle may be a better bet for shorter legs (01590 642500, 10am-5pm daily Apr-Oct). A return ticket costs £4.20 for adults, £2.50 for children.

The Solent is probably one of the best known sailing areas in the world. Regattas and racing events are held during the summer at Lymington, and the Isle of Wight's famous Cowes week is in August (*see p332*). Lymington also offers good-value sailing trips for kids; try Lymington Town Sailing Club (01590 674514, www.ltsc.co.uk) or Lymington Town Sailing School (01590 677478).

Boating enthusiasts also flock to the annual Southampton Boat Show (*see p334*) in September, held in the Marina and Mayflower Park. It's a great big international affair – and hotels and B&Bs in the area soon get booked up for that week.

The estate we're in

The 9,000-acre Beaulieu Estate on the south eastern edge of the New Forest National Park incorporates the picturesque village of the same name, and a fine palace that oversees it from across the Beaulieu river. The palace has been the ancestral home of the Montagu family since 1538, when it was bought from the crown following the dissolution of the monasteries by Henry VIII. It's still home to the current Lord and Lady Montagu, but parts of the house and gardens are open daily to the public. Beaulieu also houses the British National Motor Museum (*see p89*).

The 18th-century hamlet of Buckler's Hard, about four kilometres away, was the birthplace of many of Admiral Nelson's fleet, built using New Forest timber. You have to pay an admission charge – £5.90 for adults, £4.30 for 5-17s – to visit the hamlet, though this includes entry to a museum about the hamlet's history and shipbuilding industry (01590 616203, www.bucklershard.co.uk).

Leisure sailors still ply and tie up along the serene Beaulieu river, which flows down from the village into the Solent. It's a beautiful place to explore. Between Easter and October you can take a 30-minute cruise down the river from the pier

PONY TALE

There are currently about 4,000 ponies roaming the New Forest, so you won't have to travel very far to find them; they're as common as pigeons, and an enduring part of the region's charm.

Ponies are also key to the unique character of the woods and heathland, contributing both to its ecology and traditions. For hundreds of years, these hardy animals have grazed on the rough heathland and woodland, feeding on grass, heather, brambles, holly and the young shoots of gorse bushes (to which they're particularly partial).

While horse-lovers go giddy at the sight of ponies, hitherto seen only in a domestic setting, roaming unharnessed and free, it's important to stress that each animal is owned by a practising commoner, who is exercising his ancient and enduring right of common pasture.

Twice a year they round the ponies up with the help of a team of Agisters, whose role it is to look after the commoners' stock. The Agisters brand the ponies, give them a check-up, worm them and establish the ownership of any new foals. They then acknowledge receipt of each owner's grazing fees by clipping their ponies' tails in particular patterns.

To get a further insight into the custom, you could attend the pony fair on Beaulieu Road (not a wise move if the children are horse-mad though – ponies don't make great

impulse buys). The sales take place in the spring, and then once a month between August and November.

In days gone by, the commoners used their stock for riding and drawing carriages and carts. During the late 19th century and early 20th century the ponies were sold to work in the coal mines, and in World War I they were sent to the Front in France and Belgium. The Victorians tried to improve the breed by introducing Arab stallions, to little effect; today the pedigree of the native stock is carefully regulated by the New Forest Pony and Cattle Breeding Society.

The environment of the New Forest and its ponies is as fragile as eggshell. High density housing threatens from the edges, and increased leisure activity can bring difficulties, from soil erosion to noise pollution. Notices forbid visitors from feeding or touching the ponies, but every year injuries are incurred because someone thought it was a good idea to pat a pony – bad news for the animal who, reacting in a reasonable way when its rump is patted, is deemed aggressive and removed from the forest.

Feeding them also a no-no because ponies, like children, always want more and would be encouraged to stray on to the roads in search of the source of the grub. In 2005, 64 were killed by traffic and 28 injured. There is a 40-mile speed restriction on unfenced forest roads, but if you are unlucky enough to collide with a pony you must report it to the police straight away, or risk prosecution.

at Buckler's Hard (£3 adults, £2 5-17s) which includes a running commentary on the history and wildlife along its banks.

But if you want to engage more actively with the river, canoeing and kayaking courses and trips are on hand. Open boat canoes launch from Bailey's Hard, a little way downstream from Beaulieu village, or you can paddle off on a kayak, hired out to anyone aged 12 and over from Buckler's Hard (01590 624730, www.newforestactivities.co.uk).

WHERE TO STAY

Ashurst Caravan & Camping Site
Lyndhurst Road, Ashurst, Hampshire SO40 7AR (0845 130 8224/www.forest-holidays. com). **Open** 29 Mar-Sept. **Rates** £9.40-£19.70/ unit (2 adults); £3.80-£7.90 additional adult; £1.90-£4 5-15s; free under-5s. **Credit** MC, V.
Ashurst is set mainly on level, open ground, with some cover from the oak trees. It's a five minute walk into Ashurst village and the shops, and not far from Longdown Activity Farm (*see p90*) and the Owl and Otter Wildlife Park (*see p93*). The site has most amenities, including flush toilets, hot and cold water, showers and a launderette.

Balmer Lawn Hotel
Lyndhurst Road, Brockenhurst, Hampshire SO42 7ZB (01590 623116/www.balmerlawn hotel.com). **Rates** £135-£300. **Credit** MC, V.
As the pictures in the sumptuous foyer indicate, the hotel, built in the mid-1800s, was once a hunting lodge. Unusually for its size (55 rooms) it is privately owned, and illustrious former guests include English and Russian royalty and President Eisenhower. It is one of the few establishments to grace Balmer Lawn, a flat grassland in the flood plains of forest streams that has become a grazing ground for ponies, including two Shetlands. In the summer, one of these streams, known locally as 'the beach on the river' becomes a hive of pebble-throwing activity, and is very popular with children. The hotel's interior can't fail to impress – from the smell of lilies to the upright piano (played at weekends), paintings of Hollywood stars on the walls, plush carpets, softly lit chandeliers, stately grandfather clock, swagged curtains and leather chesterfields. Then there are all the attendant luxuries: serene indoor and outdoor heated pools (the latter secluded behind a sculpted hedge); a sauna (children are allowed in with parents); a small Jacuzzi and gym for over-16s; and all-weather tennis courts and squash courts. Most rooms have views over the lawns or forest, and family rooms have solid wooden bunks in an interconnecting room with DVDs, PlayStations, colouring books and a Balmer teddy bear on the bed. There are reduced rates for children (£27.50 3-13s, £37.50 14-17s) and under-threes are accommodated free; cots cost £10 a night. The hushed restaurant with high-backed chairs offers a rather sophisticated children's

Balmer Lawn Hotel. *See p85.*

dinner menu featuring prawn cocktail and honeydew melon fans for starters, but relaxes for the mains (chicken goujons and cheeseburgers). Jazz musicians play here on Sundays during the summer and there's a special three-day Christmas package (including a panto) during the festive season. If all this sounds a touch too formal and upmarket, rest assured that the friendly staff here are the hotel's best asset.

Burley YHA Hostel

Cott Lane, Burley, Ringwood, Hampshire BH24 4BB (0870 770 5734/www.yha.org.uk). **Open** Easter-Oct. **Rates** £13.95; £9.95 under-18s. **Credit** MC, V.
Formerly a family home, Burley is a small hostel, with only 36 beds and a couple of family rooms. Nevertheless, it's set in extensive grounds and is very close to the forest and to Beaulieu Motor Museum (*see p89*). It's down a rough track, so you tend to meet ponies and cattle on your way in. Breakfast is included in the rates, and picnic lunches and hot dinners are also available. Alternatively, there's a self-catering kitchen.

Forest Park Hotel

Rhinefield Road, Brockenhurst, Hampshire SO42 7ZG (01590 622844/www.forestdale. com). **Rates** £125. **Credit** MC, V.
A little out of the village, Forest Park is ideally placed for walks – it's on the Rhinefield Drive route, with the heath and forest opposite – and for riding (there are stables next door). The half-timbered, 38-bedroom hotel was once a vicarage, built in the late 18th century by John Morant, whose family then owned most of the land round Brockenhurst. Apart from a brief spell as a military hospital during World War I, Forest Park has

been a hotel since 1902. The pubby communal areas look slightly faded, but the en suite bedrooms (with plastic ducks in the bath) are clean and spacious. Some have views over the manicured lawn, with its heated swimming pool and patio with potted begonias and rustic log furniture. Under-14s sharing their parents' room can stay free, and cots are available at no extra charge. The hotel's bar pulls in the locals, and all-weather tennis courts, ample parking, space to store bikes and a dog-friendly policy (£7.50 per night) make it popular with families. Romantic photographs of ponies among the bluebells grace the hallway, should you forget where you are.

Hollands Wood Forestry Commission Campsite

off the A337 Lyndhurst Road, Brockenhurst, Hampshire SO42 7QH (0845 130 8224/ www.forest-holidays.com). **Open** Apr-Sept. **Rates** £8.70-£17.80/unit (2 people); £3.60-£7.20 additional adult; £1.80-£3.60 5-15s; free under-5s. *Membership* £12/yr. *Pitch fee* £3/night (non-members). **Credit** MC, V.
You can't get much closer to the wildlife – ponies, squirrels, snakes and woodpeckers – than this campsite, a ten-minute walk away from Brockenhurst village. There are Forestry Commission staff on site to meet you, and an office well stocked with leaflets and brochures on the area. It's pretty basic, with no electrics, but that adds to the tranquility – not many mobile phones go off here. Instead you'll hear children playing, and the camp overlooks grassy plains where wild ponies roam (shut one eye and you could be back in medieval times). The site is cleared in September for the annual turning out of the pigs who forage in the forests for acorns.

Okeover Guest House

12 Forest Gardens, Lyndhurst, Hampshire SO43 7AF (023 8028 2406/www.okeover accommodation.co.uk). **Rates** £50-£60. **No credit cards.**

Off the Romsey Road and within striking distance of both Lyndhurst town centre and the Mill House pub, this Edwardian guesthouse has much to recommend it. Foremost among its advantages is the self-catering unit converted from a former granny flat by owners Anne and Cliff Blake. The flat consists of a lounge with kitchen facilities and a sofa bed, a large bedroom overlooking a spreading oak tree, a bathroom and separate toilet. It's perfect for longer stays with children. The guesthouse also has three double rooms, one of which can accommodate a cot. Having recently becoming a grandmother for the second time, Anne is happy to leave out plenty of toys for when children come to stay.

Rosedale Guesthouse

24 Shaggs Meadow, Lyndhurst, Hampshire SO43 7BN (023 8028 3793). **Rates** £60-£70. **No credit cards.**

Jenny Angel of Rosedale at Shaggs Meadow (I kid you not) is particularly proud of her New Forest breakfast. It uses plenty of local produce, with bread made from flour milled at Alderholt mill and baked in Lymington accompanied by New Forest preserves. Staying here feels rather like coming on a visit to a favourite relative's. The breakfast room and small garden have a comfortable, cluttered look to them, making it a place where you can relax and not stand on ceremony. 'If someone frets about their child dropping food on the carpet, I say, "don't worry about it, just make yourself at home,"' says Jenny. Hallelujah. Rates for children range from £5 to £15, depending on age.

Watersplash Hotel

The Rise, Brockenhurst, Hampshire SO42 7ZP (01590 622344/www.watersplash.co.uk). **Rates** £98-£130. **Credit** MC, V.

This hotel, named after the splash (the local term for the small stream that runs across the bottom of Brockley Road), is both charming and reasonably priced. With its arched windows and alcoves and snug bar with red leather chairs and wildlife clock above the fireplace, the hotel has an air of familiarity and quiet welcome. Children immediately feel at home and play tag on the lawn, then make for the outdoor swimming pool and the small garden with swings and a slide. Dogs are welcome here, with a charge of £4 a day. The en suite bedrooms are sunny and lovely, with fresh flowers and fruit and a wall radio that proved popular at bedtime. Children's high teas can be arranged at an earlier time than dinner, and at breakfast the accommodating staff met our special request for hot chocolate, which wasn't on the menu. The house itself, built around 1895, was bought by the Foster family in 1958 and remained in their hands for two generations. The current owner, Robin Foster, is pleased to report that a large number of the hotel's regular guests are returnees who remember idyllic Watersplash holidays from their own childhood, and come back with offspring in tow.

Watersplash Hotel

WHERE TO EAT & DRINK

Blaireau's

Lyndhurst Road, Brockenhurst, Hampshire SO42 7RH (01590 623032/www.blaireaus. com). **Meals served** noon-2pm, 7-9.30pm daily. **Main courses** £8.75-£16.95. **Credit** MC, V.

Translating to 'Badger's' in English, this French restaurant is a best-behaviour sort of place. Even so, it is open for coffee and pastries in the morning (10.30am-noon) and attracts its fair share of the New Forest's yummy mummies. Booking is advised for the evenings. The interior is a mix of French brasserie and bistro decor, with shiny surfaces, wicker chairs, globe lights and the rather disconcerting presence of a life-size cut-out couple from the 19th century, seated and ready to dine. The kitchen is presided over by French chef Hervé Barbier, whose mission is to serve organic, locally sourced ingredients; Romsey pork, Hampshire lamb and the like often pop up on the menu. Children can partake of ham, chicken, omelette or minute steak with fries and vegetables, or pasta with tomato sauce or ham and cheese sauce (£4.50-£6.95). Despite the 15-minute wait (no microwaves in operation here), the result was delicious. La Dame Blanche – vanilla ice-cream with hot chocolate sauce – is also a hit with the young.

The Buttery at the Brock & Bruin Tearoom

25 Brookley Road, Brockenhurst, Hampshire SO42 7RB (01590 622958). **Meals served** 9.30am-5.30pm Mon-Fri; 9am-6pm Sat, Sun. **Main courses** £4.50-£6.95. **Credit** (over £10) MC, V.

The teddy bear frieze is a telltale clue that this place just might be child-friendly. Indeed it is – a large, relaxed tearoom with takeaway service, rated for its full English breakfasts, own-made cakes, light lunches and clotted cream teas. The enormous and freshly-baked scones are also worthy of note. The children's menu for under-tens (£3.50) consists of chicken teddies, sausages, fish fingers, baked potatoes plus jam sandwiches and, for dessert, 'Toffee Lumpy Bumpy' – a cream-filled, toffee-coated sponge that's certainly not for calorie counters. A sleuth of teddy bears (and a cete of toy badgers) are for sale.

Foresters Arms

10 Brookley Road, Brockenhurst, Hampshire SO42 7RR (01590 623397/www.theforesters arms.org.uk). **Meals served** noon-2.30pm, 6-9pm daily. **Main courses** £6.25-£12.50. **Credit** MC, V.

At the junction between Brockley Road and Lyndhurst Road, the Foresters Arms is easy to stop off at for a bite to eat before heading for the woods. Despite its ordinary pubby exterior, it's more upmarket than the Snakecatcher opposite and has two distinct areas: a bar where the locals hang out with a dartboard, pool table and juke box

Pedal in peace on forest trails

and a family dining area at the back with pew-like wooden seats, fresh flowers on the tables, high chairs and low ceilings. It feels secluded and cosy – a place where you can wear muddy boots and feel at home. You'll find trad pub grub here: beef and Guinness pie for parents and cod fish fingers or chicken with a jacket potato for the littlies (£4.95), plus light bites and sarnies. On Sundays, a separate carvery serves up favourites such as beef and lamb baguettes.

Il Palio 2

Station Approach, Brockenhurst, Hampshire SO42 7TW (01590 622730). **Meals served** noon-2pm, 7-10pm Tue-Sun. **Main courses** £6-£15.50. **Credit** MC, V.

At first glance, this red brick, boxey building overlooking the railway line is about as un-Italian as you can get. But, recommended by locals as 'fantastic for families', it is worth hunting out. Il Palio (named after the horse race in Pisa) is owned by Vito and his wife Susan, who converted this former railway goods shed 20 years ago. The interior retains the layout and fittings of its former life. The upper level still has the crane that unloaded goods from the trains; the narrower, lower strip is where the trains came in. The back of the restaurant – now a conservatory with a wooden pizza oven and marble and granite mix stones on the floor – was once a car park. The menu is comprehensively Italian, with daily specials such as pan-fried lamb cutlets with courgettes, onions, mushroom and pesto as well as the usual pizza and pasta offerings. Decorating the walls are images of Italy and photographs of Il Palio in its former life, as well as a large thank-you letter from the local primary school, whose children had a cookery lesson on how to make pizza here.

La Pergola
Southampton Road, Lyndhurst, Hampshire SO43 7BQ (023 8028 4184/www.la-pergola. co.uk). **Meals served** 10.30am-2.30pm, 6-10.30pm Tue-Sun. **Main courses** £7.95-£15.95. **Credit** AmEx, DC, MC, V.

'We're Italian,' announces Mr Passarelli, the proprietor of La Pergola. 'And Italians love children, take a look at the chef…' (She was in full pregnancy bloom.) A measure of this restaurant's popularity is that it gets so busy in the summer that parents ring to book the high chairs. The menu is traditional Italian cuisine, which can be dovetailed to meet children's tastes and appetites – and if nothing but chips and chicken nuggets will do, the accommodating waiter will whip something out of the freezer (but only if pressed). The restaurant is bright and bold and can be spotted from the main road. Alfresco dining is possible in clement weather, and there's a large secure play pen with climbing frame and swings for your offspring to explore while you down a quick Bardolino.

The Mill
Romsey Road, Lyndhurst, Hampshire SO43 7AR (023 8028 2814/www.millhouseinns. co.uk). **Meals served** noon-9pm Mon-Sat; noon-8pm Sun. **Main courses** £4.45-£11.95. **Credit** MC, V.

The Mill sits on busy, B&B-lined Romsey Road with a patio overlooking a car park, but it's a useful family pub. The sprawling ground floor is cleverly arranged into snuggeries, tucked-away bars and a large sunny room on a separate level, where a children's party was in full swing when we visited. This is the perfect place for a lunchtime bite, particularly if you're waiting for the rain to wear off (or if you want to wear the children out). After a wholesome but standard pub meal (cheese and bacon burger served with chips and salad garnish, for instance) you can leave the children to run riot in the Pirate Pete's indoor play den downstairs, under the supervision of one of the Mill's staff, for the princely sum of £1.50 per hour (open noon-8pm). Here the sprogs can climb up frames and jump down bouncy stairs to their heart's content, and there's also a pen for two to five year olds; meanwhile, you can enjoy a peaceful drink upstairs. The carvery on Sundays provides child portions at half price and a wealth of party cones and goody bags are available at the bar. The children's menu (on Pirate Pete's treasure map) will entertain as they make their way through the trail of fish finger and jacket potato options. Facilities are on hand for changing nappies and reheating baby food. All in all, this is an extremely shipshape operation – and if you'd like to stay, there are nine rooms as well.

Rose & Crown
Lyndhurst Road, Brockenhurst, Hampshire SO42 7RH (01590 622225/www.roomattheinn. info). **Meals served** noon-3pm, 6-9.30pm daily. **Main courses** £8.25-£14.95. **Credit** MC, V.

A pub with rooms catering for the family trade, the Rose & Crown dates back to the 13th century and started life as a coaching inn. There are 14 bedrooms, some in a converted stable, but chief among the pub's attractions is its very large garden, with a yew tree and seven wooden gazebos in different architectural styles. Children flock to these to play while waiting for lunch. The menu delivers good quality, generous quantity food, though the children's menu (quarter roast chicken and chips £5.95, New Forest ice-cream £2.95) is a tad unimaginative – the chips (not French fries) got a big thumbs up, however. If you want a potted history of the area, a blackboard on the wall outside gives the lowdown.

The Mayflower
King's Saltern Road, Lymington, Hampshire SO41 3QD (01590 672160/www.themayflower. uk.com). **Meals served** noon-2.30pm, 6.30-9.30pm Mon-Sat; noon-3pm, 6.30-9.30pm Sun. **Main courses** £6.50-£9.50. **Credit** MC, V.

Close to the marinas and yacht clubs, with views over the Solent and Lymington river, The Mayflower is one of the few places catering for families in Lymington, with the proviso that children are not allowed in the bar after 7pm. The garden has a play area, and the bar and restaurant (recently redecorated) offer comprehensive dining. The accent, unsurprisingly, is on fish; at the bar you can order grilled sardines on toasted ciabatta to start, followed by red snapper or beer-battered fish of the day, rounded off with a Belgian waffle. The children's menu (for under-12s) offers the usual chips and beans with everything.

PLACES TO SEE, THINGS TO DO
Taking to the quiet lanes and minor roads of the New Forest on two wheels offers a wonderfully leisurely way to view the countryside. Cycles can be hired in Lymington, Brockenhurst and Burley, and designated forest cycling tracks can be found throughout the forest.

Beaulieu Palace & National Motor Museum
Beaulieu, Brockenhurst, Hampshire SO42 7ZN (01590 612123/www.beaulieu.co.uk). **Open** *May-Sept* 10am-6pm daily. *Oct-Apr* 10am-5pm daily. **Admission** £15; £14 concessions; £7.75 5-12s; £8.75 13-17s; £41 family (2+3 or 1+4); free under-5s. **Credit** MC, V.

The Motor Museum has a permanent exhibition of over 250 cars and is bang up to date with the latest in vehicle design and technology – great stuff for anyone into concept cars and gangster getaways. When we were there, the Citroën 2006 – claimed to be the safest car in the world, thanks to high-tech wizardry that lessens impact when hitting a pedestrian – was on display. Travel back in time to admire the very first motors, such as the 1897 Bersey Electric cab, which travelled at the genteel pace of 9mph, and look out for the boa constrictor horn in the 1907 Halfords shopfront. If you want to get an idea of Beaulieu's other sights, the ten-minute sky train journey literally takes you through the roof of the motor museum and then down to the abbey and gardens. The roomy Brabazon restaurant is good for refuelling.

Cycleexperience

Brookley Road, Brockenhurst, Hampshire SO42 7RR (01590 624204). **Open** 9.30am-5.30pm daily. **Credit** MC, V.
Take your pick from a variety of bikes at reasonable prices – from £6.50 for half a day's hire, subject to availability, or £11 for a whole day. There are tandems, disabled bikes, trikes, children's bikes and kid cabs for nine-month-olds to five-year-olds, so there's really no excuse for not getting out there. Tag-a-longs are good for four- to nine-year-olds who haven't cycled much before, giving them an idea of balance and the choice of whether or not to pedal. Route maps are provided; most families opt for the eight-mile Ornamental Loop, which takes around two hours (allowing time for a breather at the Oak Inn). The route, which is 99% off-road, explores the Arboretum and also passes a deer sanctuary.

Country Lanes Cycle Centre

The Railway Carriage, Brockenhurst Station, Brockenhurst, Hampshire SO42 7TW (01590 622627/www.countrylanes.co.uk/newforest). **Open** *Easter-Oct* 9.30am-5pm Tue-Sun. *Nov-Easter* 9.30am-4pm Fri-Sun. **Credit** MC, V.
A friendly, professional outfit, staffed by knowledgeable cycling enthusiasts who are confident that they can kit you out with the right bike and helmet (compulsory for 17s and under). Staff are also happy to run through the gears and provide a simple route map to follow. This place is a great resource of knowledge on the local terrain, and the best routes for your capabilities. Prices start at £8 for half day hire of an adult bike, and tagalongs and tandems are there for those who want them.

Exbury Gardens & Steam Railway

Exbury, Southampton, Hampshire SO45 1AZ (023 8089 1203/www.exbury.co.uk). **Open** *17 Mar-4 Nov* 10am-5.30pm daily. *6 Nov-Feb* limited opening; phone for details. **Admission** *Gardens* £6.50-£7.50; £6-£7 concessions; £1.50 3-15s; £15-£17.50 family (2+3); free under-3s *Railway* £3. **Credit** MC, V.
Lionel Nathan de Rothschild, a member of the famous banking dynasty and an enthusiastic gardener, bought the Exbury estate in 1919 and began making his grand horticultural visions a reality. Subsequent generations continued his work, and today the gardens are a magnificent sight. In spring the daffodil meadow is a carpet of blooms, and the famous rhododendron gardens flower in May. With 20 miles of pathways and plenty of different areas, there's lots for children to explore: ponds, a Japanese garden, a rock garden, a water garden – even an ancient Burmese temple bell, said to have been looted from Rangoon. There's also an open-air tearoom. The steam railway runs through the gardens for a mile and a quarter, passing through various green and pleasant sights as it chugs along. Check the website for details of seasonal events, such as April's Easter Bunny Train, October's Ghost Train and the Santa Steam Special in the run up to Christmas. The gardens also stage two free weekends for children: Petal Fall in early June, when they can collect and make a collage from fallen petals from rhododendron and azalea flowers, and the Big Draw in October, which involves creating a collage from fallen leaves and berries.

Liberty's Raptor & Reptile Centre

Crow Lane, Crow, nr Ringwood, Hampshire BH24 3EA (01425 476487/www.libertys centre.co.uk). **Open** *Mar-Oct* 10am-5pm daily (last admission 4pm). *Nov-Feb* 10am-5pm Sat, Sun (last admission 4pm). *Flying courses* Sept-May. **Admission** £5.95; £4.95 concessions; £4.50 3-16s; £18.50 family (2+2); free under-3s. *Flying courses* phone for details. **Credit** AmEx, MC, V.
Given the history of the New Forest as a royal hunting ground, it's apt that this raptor and reptile centre should offer hands-on experience of falconry as well as close-up views of some pretty impressive reptiles, from snakes and lizards to giant tortoises. Named after Liberty, the resident American Bald Eagle, the centre offers full- and half-day flying experiences for children aged 16 and above. Participants are taught how to fly birds of prey – hawks, owls and vultures – and see them return to their gloved hand. The centre also holds demonstrations and talks on the birds at weekends; check the website for details. Liberty's has teamed up with Ringwood Town and Country Experience (www.rtce.co.uk) to offer a combined family ticket for a full day of entertainment for £27.

Longdown Activity Farm

Ashurst, nr Southampton, Hampshire SO40 7EH (023 8029 3326/www.longdownfarm. co.uk). **Open** *17 Feb-28 Oct* 10am-5pm daily. *Nov, Dec* 10am-5pm Sat, Sun. **Admission** £6.50; £5.50 concessions, 3-14s; £23 family (2+2); free under-3s. **Credit** MC, V.
There are plenty of animals for children to feed, pet and cuddle at Longdown, from rabbits (which were introduced to Britain by the Normans; the first colony was recorded in 1176) to alpacas. A visit here is a hands-on experience; children can

Longdown Activity Farm

New Forest Museum

get involved in rounding up and feeding the piglets, handling the chicks (hen and duck eggs are on sale in the shop) and bottlefeeding the goats. If bitten by the bug, eight- to 14-year-olds can be a farmer for a day (£30). They can discover what hard work it is to milk a cow (there are simulated cows to practice on) and, if they're lucky, watch a calving. The farm has an indoor play area with a climbing frame and squeezy tube, plus outdoor go-carts and coin-operated vehicles. There are tractor and trailer rides round the compound, weather permitting.

New Forest Museum

High Street, Lyndhurst, Hampshire SO43 7NY (023 8028 3444/www.newforestmuseum. org.uk). **Open** 10am-5pm daily. **Admission** £3; £2.50 concessions, 8-16s; £9 family (2+4); free under-8s. **Credit** MC, V.
The history and traditions of the New Forest are put under the spotlight at this small museum, opened in 1988. Call in to get your bearings, absorb some local history and pick up maps, postcards, guide books and itineraries from the tourist office next door. At the entrance, there's a film about the ponies and the commoner's rights. The ground floor explores what life in the area was like centuries ago, and looks at the management of the woods and wildlife; there's also a reconstruction of a typical home (with a chair carved with snakes made by Eddie Mills in memory of his uncle, 'Brusher' Mills) and interactive displays on local flora and fauna. Upstairs, you can travel through the area in stitches thanks to a 25ft long embroidery commemorating the 900th anniversary of the New Forest in 1979. Check the website for details of special events, such as conkers and pumpkin-carving sessions in October half term.

New Forest Park Riding Stables

Rhinefield Road, Brockenhurst, Hampshire SO42 7ZG (01590 623429/www.forestpark stable.co.uk). **Rides** £25/1hr. **Credit** MC, V.
Approved by the Association of British Riding Schools (ABRS), these stables next to the Forest Park Hotel (*see p86*), aren't equipped with a mènage, so there are no riding lessons. The staff run hour-long accompanied rides for any standard of rider aged seven and above, however, and two-hour hacks for more experienced visitors. You will be asked the height and weight of each rider and matched to a suitable horse; riding hats are provided. There are various doughty, sensible cobs for nervous riders, and a typical hour-long hack for a beginner will take you through heathland and gorse, among wild pony cousins, into oak and beech woods and across streams – you may even break into a trot. At 12 you are allowed to canter.

New Park Manor Equestrian Centre

Lyndhurst Road, Brockenhurst, Hampshire SO42 7QH (01590 623919/www.newpark manorhotel.co.uk). **Open** 10am-4pm Tue-Sun. **Rides** vary; phone for details. **Credit** MC, V.
A professional outfit attached to an exclusive hotel (in another life, a royal hunting lodge, *see p85*), this centre is British Horse Society (BHS) approved and a member of the Association of British Riding Schools. There's a mènage here, and regular polo matches. All this is reflected in the upmarket prices, but every level is catered for and the centre will take children as young as three for their first outing on horseback. Escorted rides in the New Forest kick off at £15 for 30 minutes, and a group day ride rises to £65 per person. There is tuition too, starting at £20 for a 30-minute

private lesson. Cross-forest pub rides and training courses are also on offer. The stables are set in lush countryside inhabited by wild deer.

New Forest Otter, Owl & Wildlife Conservation Park

Deerleap Lane, Longdown, Marchwood, Southampton, Hampshire SO40 4HU (023 8029 2408/www.ottersandowls.co.uk). **Open** *Summer* 10am-5.30pm daily. *Winter* 10am-dusk daily (Sat, Sun only Jan). **Admission** £6.95; £4.95 2-15s; £20.50 family (2+2); free under-2s. **Credit** MC, V.

Years ago this 25-acre family-owned woodland park was a butterfly farm, but its scope now ranges far beyond that. It covers many of the wild animals associated with this locality, and not just otters and owls either (though there are plenty of both – look out for the British, North American and Asian short-clawed otters, and feathered friends with catchy names like Spook and Spirit the barn owls and Herdi and Orkney the snowy owls). The park has a trail of winding walkways that lead through densely wooded areas and open out onto bracken heaths, giving a real sense of adventure at every turn. There are pens, dens and tall aviaries, with opportunities to watch deer feeding, badgers sleeping and harvest mice building their nests. If you've never understood the difference between a weasel, a stoat and a ferret, you can find out here. A host of other animal inhabitants include wallabies, polecats, pinemartens, a European lynx called Oden and a Scottish wild cat (rather like a large tabby when compared with the moggy back home). The information panels are just right for children – there are not too many of them, and they're humorous and engaging. Bugingham Palace, for instance, is a layered cake

of rotting wood to encourage insect life, and the Talons and Toes sign explains the fearsome feet of owls. The trail passes through indoor accommodation for smaller mammals and insects, with soap dispensers en route for grubby hands. You can finish your visit with a cream tea at the Woodland Bakehouse, or drop in on the souvenir shop stuffed with toys, books and games – a place to avoid at all costs if it's last admissions and you've only just arrived.

St Barbe Museum and Art Gallery

New Street, Lymington, Hampshire SO41 9BH (01590 676969/www.stbarbe-museum.org.uk). **Open** 10am-4pm Mon-Sat. **Admission** £4; £3 concessions; £2 5-15s; £10 family (2+4); free under-4s. **Credit** MC, V.

Housed in a Victorian school, this museum is particularly welcoming to its younger visitors (worksheets are given out and local volunteers are on hand to explain the exhibits). St Barbe explores the unique history of the New Forest coast, looking at the smugglers active in the area during the 19th century and the salt-making industry set up in Lymington in the 11th century, as well as the wildlife that lives in the mudflats and marshes. Children are encouraged to rifle through the exhibits, delve into the secret pockets of a life-size Bob the Barbarous in search of contraband, examine mud patterns and eel spears (used by local fishermen and wildfowlers) and answer a range of quiz questions. Look out for the timeline that links national history to regional events – although children are more likely to make a bee-line for the box of shells to decorate the sandcastle or the wheel house boat reconstruction, while bored parents can pass the time by practising their reef and sheepshank knots.

New Park Manor Equestrian Centre

Isle of Wight

Island of dinosaurs and adventures.

From the moment you step on to the ferry, a visit to the Isle of Wight feels like an adventure. Crossing the Solent, the stretch of water that separates the island from the mainland, might only take 45 minutes or so (much less on the passenger ferry), but it's like travelling in a time machine. Whether you arrive at the bustling ports of Cowes or Yarmouth, the pretty creek at Fishbourne or the long wooden pier at Ryde, the effect is the same – you have left the real world behind and embarked on a *Famous Five* trip, where children are never at a loss for something to do.

If the sun shines, families with young children can happily spend every day on a different beach. There are plenty to choose from – the crumbling coast at Compton Bay has a more rugged appeal than the buckets-and-spade strand at Shanklin; the rock pools of Bonchurch hold a more scientific fascination than the inspirational tiny cove below the Botanic Gardens at Steephill. Sandown is as brash as it gets, although its attractions are rather rundown, even at the height of the season. The beaches are wide and sandy, but if you're not keen on the jingle of fruit machines and the smell of hot dogs you're better off at Yaverland, the more peaceful eastern end of the bay, where the gentle art of fossil hunting can be pursued with enthusiasm.

A minute's walk from the **Seaview Hotel**. *See p100.*

Beaches galore, including **Sandown** (far left) and **Shanklin** (left).

Energetic types won't need any encouragement to take to the water. You can sail, surf, water-ski or kite-surf, go on exciting waterborne safaris around Shalfleet Creek, canoe up the Western Yar or embark on a boat trip out to Hurst Castle or the Needles.

For landlubbers, the island is covered in a network of interconnecting footpaths, bridleways and cycle paths, all well signposted and maintained. In fact, the island has more footpaths per square mile than anywhere else in Britain, and plenty of variety. You can stroll along marshy shorelines, though bluebell woods, across Tennyson Down to the Needles, or stride along the spine of the island, with gorgeous views in every direction. Following the carved stone steps to squeeze though the rocks known as the Devil's Chimney feels like straying into the world of Tolkien. From here, make your way down through the Landslip, a wooded slope formed by the collapse of cliffs two hundred years ago – now a tangled delight of ferns and vines among outcrops of rock that leads down to Monk's Bay.

Whatever key stage your children happen to be at, you can sneak in some painless educational trips. For example, you could visit Yarmouth, Carisbroke and Hurst castles, the Roman villas at Brading and Newport, manor houses at Arreton and Mottistone, or Osborne House, Queen Victoria's holiday home. In the unlikely event that none of the above appeal, there is a steam railway, a tiger sanctuary, ghost walks, rock festivals and the oldest theme park in the country.

Modishly remote

It was Victoria who made the island fashionable in the 19th century. From being a quiet place that was very cut off from the mainland, the island became a must-patronise destination, as visitors flocked from all over Europe to enjoy the healing air at Ventnor. In the 1860s the island played host to Dickens, Marx, the Empress Eugenia, Lewis Carroll and Keats. The Poet Laureate, Tennyson, made his home here at Freshwater, and just down the road Julia Margaret Cameron was busy pioneering the new art of photography.

The decline of the railways and growth in foreign holidays saw a drop in the island's popularity, but after years in the doldrums the Isle of Wight's star is rising again. Articles describing it as England's answer to Martha's Vineyard appear increasingly in the travel supplements, and a boutique hotel recently opened in Ventnor, causing quite a stir around these parts. Inevitably the island will lose some of its time warp charm, but for now it is still like a miniaturised, idealised, version of all England contained in an island just seventy miles around the coast. As in the rest of provincial England, however, public transport is not great and buses are expensive. Unless you are robust walkers or cyclists, you will need a car.

Downtown

Newport, the largest town on the island, boasts an interesting little museum on island life, the Guildhall Museum (High Street, 01983 823366), as well

Isle of Wight

TOURIST INFORMATION

Central Office: Isle of Wight
(01983 813813/www.islandbreaks.
co.uk). For all of the individual tourist
offices listed below, contact this
central number.
Cowes
Fountain Quay, Cowes, Isle of Wight
PO31 7AR.
Newport
The Guildhall, High Street, Newport,
Isle of Wight PO30 1TY.
Ryde
81-83 Union Street, Ryde, Isle of
Wight PO33 2LW.
Sandown
High Street, Sandown, Isle of Wight
PO36 8DA.
Shanklin
67 High Street, Shanklin, Isle of Wight
PO37 6JJ.
Yarmouth
The Quay, Yarmouth, Isle of Wight
PO41 0PQ.

as a farmer's market on Friday mornings,
a multiscreen cinema, Ottakers' bookshop,
the usual chainstores and the Quay Arts
Centre. Don't miss the old-fashioned sweet
shop, Island Treats (142 High Street,
01983 525801, www.islandtreats.co.uk),
with a windowful of glass jars of humbugs
and lemon sherbets (Kate Moss was
spotted spending her pocket money here
recently). Sadly, the traffic-clogged approach
roads and incomprehensible one-way
system make Newport a frustrating place
at the height of the holiday season.

The picturesque village of Godshill
appears in all the brochures, but what the
photos don't show is that the busy road
has no pavements. Tourists find themselves
pressed against the walls of the pretty
thatched cottages to avoid oncoming
traffic. This is not very relaxing when
pushing buggies or shepherding young
children, so the chocolate box village
is best avoided by young families until
the local authority invests in some traffic-
calming measures.

The Isle of Wight Festival in June and
Bestival in September have been
surprisingly family-friendly events in recent
years. In August, the international sailing
set descend on Cowes.

WHERE TO STAY

Many hotels, B&Bs and self-catering places
can arrange ferry tickets at reduced rates,
or even ferry-inclusive deals, so always
ask when booking. Although self-catering
accommodation is only available for weekly
rentals in the high season, shorter breaks

are usually on offer during the rest of the
year. The Farm and Country Holiday group
(www.wightfarmholidays.co.uk) is a
collective of locals offering superior B&B
and self-catering in farmhouses, cottages,
manors, log cabins, barns and dairies.
All the accommodation is inspected by
either the English Tourist Board or the AA,
and many places regularly win awards.
Options such as the 200-year-old converted
barn nestling under St Boniface Down
(www.manorbottom.co.uk) are delightful
for families in search of rural tranquillity,
with great walks on the doorstep.

Bonchurch Manor

*Bonchurch Shute, Bonchurch, Isle of Wight
PO38 1NU (01983 852868/www.bonchurch
manor.com).* **Rates** £90-£110. **Credit** MC, V.
This is a grand early Victorian manor house, built
in the local style from golden island stone, with
gables, glazed verandas and conservatories
galore. The drawing room has huge squashy
sofas, windows opening on to tumbling gardens
(with a swing and outdoor games) and a wonderful view of the sea. Restored by owners Shuba and
Mark, who bought it in 2003 (read their blogs on
the website), this hotel is rapidly gaining a reputation as the place to stay on the island. With no
experience in the hotel trade, the new owners have
brought their own cosmopolitan style, which
leaves guests gushing about the refreshing intel-
ligence of the hosts and the warmth of their welcome. Children are well looked after – bottles are
warmed, cots provided and early suppers prepared – and encouraged to take part in whatever
is going on.

In autumn everyone celebrates Deepavali, the
Hindu Festival of Lights, with fireworks and aus-
picious decorations of petals and coloured pow-
ders. At Christmas, children can help decorate the
tree. There's no baby listening service, but
babysitting can be arranged through a local
agency. Breakfasts are generous and use fresh,
locally produced, organic ingredients wherever
possible, as does its Tiffin Room restaurant (*see
p104*), which serves home-cooked Southern Indian
and Mediterranean food. The delightful beach at
Bonchurch is just a few minutes away, as are the
tiny 11th-century Norman church and the magical wooded hillside known as the Landslip.

Farringford Hotel

*Bedbury Lane, Freshwater Bay, Isle of Wight
PO40 9PE (01983 752500/www.farringford.
co.uk).* **Open** Feb-Dec. **Rates** £100-£174.
Credit MC, V.
Alfred Lord Tennyson fell in love with this imposing pile at first sight, having searched the island
for a retreat from the hurly-burly of literary life.
He stayed 40 years. Set in 33 acres of secluded
grounds (many of which are now devoted to golf),
the hotel in his former abode is a pleasant, old-
fashioned sort of place. Its location in West Wight

means it's a wonderful choice for walkers; a gate behind the house leads directly out onto the down that was later renamed in Tennyson's honour. Although there are some rooms in the hotel that can accommodate them, families are encouraged to stay in the garden suites which have more space for cots and extra beds (these must be reserved in advance). The hotel can provide baby monitors or, at an extra cost, on-site babysitters. As well as a nine-hole golf course, Farringford has an outdoor pool with separate paddling pool (open Easter-Sept), tennis and croquet facilities and a bowling green. Meals can be taken in the hotel restaurant, or, in summer, the more relaxed Shallot's bistro, overlooking the pool.

Little Gatcombe Farm

Newbarn Lane, Gatcombe, Isle of Wight PO30 3EQ (01983 721580/07968 462513/ www.littlegatcombefarm.co.uk). **Rates** £60-£90. **No credit cards**.

Set on a 30-acre working sheep farm, in the heart of an Area of Outstanding Natural Beauty and just down the road from Carisbroke Castle (*see p105*), this very superior B&B offers a relaxing alternative to a hotel. The light and airy en suite rooms have fantastic views of the countryside, and are equipped with tea and coffee making facilities, hairdryers, TVs and Wi-Fi internet. Three-course buffet breakfasts are of the same high quality as the fare on offer at the farm's tearooms (*see p103*). These can can be walked off on the Tennyson Trail footpath, which passes the front door. Riding the farm's horses costs £40 an hour, but you can bring your own horse to stay (full livery is £20 per day). Visit in April and the children can watch the slithery spectacle of lambs being born.

Luccombe Hall Country House Hotel

8 Luccombe Road, Shanklin, Isle of Wight PO37 6RL (01983 869000/www.luccombe hall.co.uk). **Rates** £80-£120. **Credit** MC, V.

It's not hard to see why the the Bishop of Portsmouth chose this site, on the cliffs above the Channel, for his summer retreat. Now a hotel with more facilities than you can shake a crook at, Luccombe Hall bills itself 'the view with a hotel'. The bishop's Victorian home has been extended over the years to accommodate heated indoor and (in summer) outdoor pools, a jacuzzi, sauna, mini gym, snooker, table tennis, squash courts and a solarium. Parents who find it hard to unwind might appreciate some Indian head massage or aromatherapy. There are a variety of relaxed public rooms with board games and videos for children, but it is the gardens, pool and suntrap terraces that make this such a desirable place to stay – along with the outdoor play area, with its swings, trampoline and giant chess set.

An early children's dinner is held from 6-6.30pm, with lasagne, fish fingers, pizza and sausages on the menu. For peckish moments even earlier in the day, a gate behind the swimming pool leads to the hotel's tearooms, perched on the cliff top and aptly named Grand View, where guests take lunch and cream teas. From here you can follow the path down to a quiet sandy beach, or join the cliff walk to the old village of Shanklin with its thatched cottages and esplanade. If you

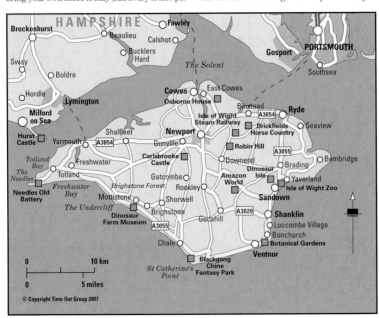

Isle of Wight

prefer somewhere a little quieter, it's a short walk to the Landslip, where you can take the steep steps down to the beach at Luccombe Chine, which is often deserted. Baby monitors are available, though you'll need to hand over a refundable deposit first.

Priory Bay Hotel

Priory Drive, Seaview, Isle of Wight PO34 5BU (01983 613146/www.priorybay.co.uk). **Rates** £90-£210. *Cottages* £402-£1855/wk. **Credit** MC, V.

The Priory Bay is a gorgeous country house, set in acres of grounds (including a golf course and outdoor swimming pool) right on the coast. Outside, a path meanders down through the trees to a sandy beach looking out to the Victorian fort of St Helens. There are two family rooms in the hotel, and five new self-catering 'cottages' in the grounds offering more basic accommodation (the largest of which can sleep up to ten people). Early suppers for children can be pre-booked for 5.30pm, or families can eat together in the downstairs dining room. (If you want to dine in the adults-only restaurant, the hotel can recommend local babysitters, though you'll need to make the arrangements yourself.) The children's menu is a cut above the usual fish fingers and chips affair, offering pea risotto, grilled chicken and new potatoes, and spaghetti bolognese. In July and August the hotel opens a beautifully sited outdoor café in the woods on the shore overlooking Priory Bay, from which you get wonderful glimpses of the sea through the trees. The pool is unheated, and open only during the summer months.

Sandown YHA

The Firs, Fitzroy Street, Sandown, Isle of Wight PO36 8JH (0870 770 6020/www.yha. org.uk). **Open** *Easter-Oct; Nov-Easter* ring for details. **Rates** £13.95; £9.95 under-18s. **Credit** MC, V.

Sandy beaches and shops are just a couple of minutes' walk away from this sensibly placed 47-bed hostel. The hostel is also good for those coming without a car, as it's only half a mile from Sandown train station. It has a few family rooms, and the small garden is a boon for those with young children. As well as the self-catering kitchen, there's a refectory for breakfast and evening meals, and picnic lunches are available. Well located for watersports enthusiasts, the hostel can loan out buckets and spades for those who've forgotten these essential pieces of kit.

Seaview Hotel

High Street, Seaview, Isle of Wight PO34 5EX (01983 612711/www.seaviewhotel.co.uk). **Rates** £120-£155; £240-£445 cottage (4 nights minimum). **Credit** MC, V.

The award-winning Seaview is a small establishment, situated in the centre of a popular sailing village and a minute's walk from the beach. The food in the two restaurants and conservatory is excellent, using local produce to great effect, and there's also a good-sized bar menu. The children's menu has artwork designed by pupils at the local primary school, and lists dishes so sophisticated they will tempt adults like fresh mussels in cream and garlic, Seaview hot crab ramekin, macaroni cheese or fish pie, followed by summer berry Eton mess or warm apple soup, ginger ice-cream and oat biscuits. Who needs nuggets? Prices range from £3.25-£4.95 for starters and £5.50-£6.75 for mains, with desserts at £3.95.

Cots, extra beds and high chairs can be provided (although under-fives aren't allowed in the two more formal restaurants during the evening). Because it doesn't have play areas or grand reception rooms and gardens to explore, the Seaview might be better suited to families with older children who can hit the beach, or babies who stay where you left them.

Totland Bay Youth Hostel

Hurst Hill, Totland Bay, Isle of Wight PO39 0HD (0870 770 6070/www.yha.org.uk). **Open** *Easter-Oct* advance bookings. *Nov-Mar* phone for details. **Rates** £13.95; £9.95 under-18s. **Credit** MC, V.

The island's two main youth hostels are used to catering for families, as well as walkers and cyclists. Earl Mountbatten opened this one in 1975. It's a Victorian pile set in an Area of Outstanding Natural Beauty, much of which is owned by the National Trust. Great for wildlife watchers and beachy folk (you can take the chairlift down to Alum Chine from up here), it has several family-sized rooms, a self-catering kitchen (or meals in the restaurant), a lounge, a cycle store and a TV room. There is another youth hostel at Brighstone, but it only has 12 beds and there are no family rooms (01983 752165).

Wight Mouse Inn

Church Place, Newport Road, Chale, Isle of Wight, PO38 2HA (01983 730431/www. innforanight.co.uk). **Rates** RO £50-£75. **Breakfast** £7.50. **Credit** MC, V.

After a few years in the wilderness, this 17th-century coaching inn is returning to form as a place that really goes out of its way to welcome families. The hotel has been completely refurbished, and now boasts clean and comfortable rooms, many of which have sea views. Cots are provided free, but there's no baby listening service. An adventure playground with swings and a climbing frame awaits at the bottom of the garden, and there's an indoor play area with a ball pond which

is open and staffed at weekends and during school holidays. Situated at the beginning of the Military Road that follows the crumbling south west coastline all the way to Freshwater Bay, the hotel is close to Blackgang Chine Fantasy Park, Dinosaur Farm (for both, *see p105*), the lovely National Trust beach at Compton Bay and the coastal path. You don't have to stay here to enjoy the grub. There's a dedicated children's menu (£3.75), and some of the adult meals are available for smaller appetites. Choose from warm chicken and bacon salad, Tanglefoot ale and steak pie, sausage and mash, or Mediterranean vegetable pot. The pub terrace is a lovely place to sit and watch the sun set behind the Needles and Tennyson Down, after a day on the beach at Compton Bay.

WHERE TO EAT & DRINK

Many tearooms and beach cafés are open only during the tourist season – Easter until autumn half-term at the end of October – so always call before making a special trip. The Seaview Hotel (*see above*) has the best children's menus we've seen.

Some of the smaller tearooms may not be geared towards rampaging younger children, but can definitely be appreciated by older children and teens. One of our favourites is the Horseshoe Café in Ventnor (Shore Road, 01983 856800, www.horseshoebayhouse.co.uk, open daily May-mid-Sept), close to Bonchurch cove and the Landslip. Sitting in the garden when the sun is shining, a pebble's throw from the Channel, you could easily imagine yourself to be on an unspoiled bit of the Cote d'Azur. Crab and lobster come from Wheelers' Bay, right in front of the café, and the cream teas are served with fresh strawberries. Heavenly.

Apple Tree Café

Afton Park, Newport Road, nr Freshwater Bay, Isle of Wight PO40 9XR (01983 755774/ www.appletreecafe.co.uk). **Meals served** 9am-4pm daily. **Main courses** £3.95-£9.45. **Credit** MC, V.

Attached to a fruit tree nursery that produces superb apple juice is this licensed café, serving delicious meals using locally-produced meat, fish, vegetables and (of course) fruit. The menu is ever-changing, but dishes might include carrot and coriander soup, a hot sausage sandwich or a spicy bean hotpot with jacket wedges, with 'hedgerow' crumble or cider and apple pudding to follow. Children can enjoy the same hearty, wholesome fare with the eminently sensible 'half a meal at half the price' deal. From July to August the café opens on Friday and Saturday evenings, serving a more extensive menu; booking is essential. There are meadow walks, an unusual selection of plants, plus a puzzle path and treasure trail for children. Walkers and cyclists have their own entrance off the Freshwater Way.

Baywatch on the Beach

Duver Road, St Helens, Isle of Wight PO33 1YB (01983 873259). **Meals served** *Easter-mid-Nov* 10am-9.30pm daily. **Main courses** £5-£25. **Credit** MC, V.

Right on the beach overlooking Bembridge Harbour, this licensed café uses local fish and seafood, supplementing such treasures with baguettes, steak and fries and pasta. There are plenty of healthier-than-usual-options for little ones on the children's menu (£4.95-£5.95), such as spaghetti bolognaise, mini steaks, chicken strips and salads. In the evenings the food becomes more sophisticated, and booking is essential. There are lots of tables outside, but the Baywatch can get very crowded in the summer. On sunny days outside high season the service can be a bit lackadaisical, but with a gorgeous view and a whole beach to play on the wait shouldn't be too onerous. Skip the pudding menu and buy a New Forest ice-cream from the kiosk next door; blackcurrant or toffee crunch are delicious.

Chequers Inn

Niton Road, Rookley, Isle of Wight PO38 3NZ (01983 840314/www.chequersinn-iow.co.uk). **Meals served** noon-10pm Mon-Sat; noon-9.30pm Sun. **Main courses** £6-£16. **Credit** MC, V.

A free house, highly rated by CAMRA (the Campaign for Real Ale), the Chequers appeals to families as much as serious ale-drinkers. Expect the usual pub grub – steaks, ploughman's lunches and jacket potatoes. The children's menu (£3.25-£6.25) offers cod, steak or scampi, spag bol, bangers and chicken nuggets, all served with a choice of chips or jacket potato and peas, beans or salad. Small appetites would be just as happy with a starter – a bowl of tomato soup or some garlic bread, for example – as with the kiddie menu. Staff are happy to warm up bottles or baby food. As well as lovely countryside views, the inn has a huge log cabin, a games area, a Lego table and a separate play area for under-nines. You can work up an appetite before your meal with a local circular walk that begins and ends at the pub. There are three to choose from, ranging from three to nine miles. Ask for a map at the bar or download one from the pub's website.

Crown Inn

Walkers Lane, Shorwell, Isle of Wight PO30 3JZ (01983 740293). **Meals served** noon-2.30pm, 6-9.30pm daily. **Main courses** £6.95-£13.95. **Credit** (over £8) MC, V.

The Crown is a pretty 17th-century inn, with a trout stream running through its garden and ducks wandering on the grass. Add swings, a slide and a playhouse in the garden into the equation, and it's not hard to see why this place is so popular with families. Specials change daily and might include steak and kidney pie, duck breast

Isle of Wight Zoo. *See p107.*

DEM DRY BONES

The 11-mile stretch of sandstone and clay along the south-western coast of the Isle of Wight is believed to be the richest source of dinosaur bones in Europe. What makes the island even more attractive to fossil hunters is that its crumbling cliffs give up their treasure so easily. The coasts are not just being constantly eroded by the sea – after prolonged rain, the 'blue slipper' clay that runs through the cliffs on the south coast becomes saturated and 'slips', taking the land above it along too. The coast along the Military Road is disappearing at the astonishing rate of a metre every year, and over the decades countless homes, farms and even a grand hotel have slipped into the Channel. But what is a nightmare for homeowners and insurance companies is a joy for fossil hunters, as bones simply fall out of the cliffs on to the beaches below.

The Isle of Wight has been a place of fascinaton for fossil aficionados since Victorian times. The Reverend William Fox (1805-80) was so obsessed with hunting for 'old dragon's bones' on the beach near his parish in Brighstone that his parishioners' souls were sadly neglected, and he eventually lost his position. Fox, a second cousin of Charles Darwin, is the perfect example of the passionate amateur palaeontologist; the fossils he collected are now housed in the Natural History Museum in London, and he has more species

Dinosaur Isle. *See p105.*

of dinosaur named after him than any other Englishman.

Steve Hutt is our modern-day fossil hero. While walking along the beach in 1992, Hutt, curator of the local geology museum, spotted a piece of bone sticking out of the cliff at Barnes High. The bones were taken to the cowsheds of the local farmer on whose land they had been found (see p105 **Dinosaur Farm Museum**), where, on further investigation, they proved to be part of the most complete skeleton of a brachiosaurid ever found in Europe. This dinosaur, part of the family of sauropod, would have lived in the Lower Cretaceous period, using its long neck to reach leaves, which it nibbled with its small, peg-like teeth.

A year after this discovery, in 1993, an single neck bone, three-quarters of a metre long, was discovered along the same stretch of coast. Palaeontologists believe that if a single vertebrae was that large, the sauropod to which it belonged must have been over 20m long and could have weighed as much as 40-50 tonnes; in other words, the bone belonged to one of the largest dinosaur skeletons yet to be discovered in Europe.

Both of these finds can be seen on display at **Dinosaur Isle** (see p105) in Sandown. The best thrill for a young palaeontologist, however, is on the beach at Hanover Point near Compton Bay, where, at low tide, they can hunt for fossils and stand in the giant three-toed footprint of a dinosaur. Wicked!

with plum sauce, or lamb shank with colcannon mash. Local produce is used as much as possible and there is always a vegetarian option. As well as the usual children's menu of nuggets and bangers (£3.50-£5.50), smaller portions of some adult meals are available on request.

Gatcombe Tearooms

Little Gatcombe Farm, Newbarn Lane, Gatcombe, Isle of Wight PO30 3 EQ (01983 721580/07968 462513/www.little gatcombefarm.co.uk). **Tea served** noon-5pm daily. **Set tea** £4.75. **No credit cards**.

Visitors to the island who make a beeline for the beaches miss out on some gorgeous countryside. There aren't many better places to enjoy the scenery than sitting in the gardens of Little Gatcombe Farm, with a generously-proportioned cream tea in front of you. The huge fruit scones come hot from the oven and everything on your plate, from the jam to the cakes, is made by the owner Anita. If you find you eat so much you can't move, you can always stay in the award-winning B&B (see p98).

Olivio's

15 St Thomas Square, Newport, Isle of Wight PO30 1SL (01983 530001). **Meals served** 10am-10pm daily. **Main courses** £9.95-£14.95. **Credit** MC, V.

Situated in the pedestrianised square in the heart of town, this friendly, family-run Italian restaurant is very handy for the farmer's market on Fridays. The restaurant is licensed, so harassed parents can relax with a large glass of wine while their offspring tuck into the children's menu of pasta or pizza with a soft drink (£4.95), followed by ice-cream.

Palm Court Café

Ventnor Botanic Garden, Undercliff Drive, Ventnor, Isle of Wight PO38 1UL (01983 855570). **Meals served** *Nov, Dec* 10am-4pm Tue-Thur, Sat, Sun. *Jan-mid Feb* 10am-4pm Sat, Sun. *Mid Feb-Mar* 10am-4pm daily. *Apr-Jul, Sept, Oct* 10am-5pm daily. *Aug* 10am-6pm daily. **Main courses** £3.45-£5.75. **Credit** MC, V.

Part of the Digby Trout Restaurants company, this licensed café serves sandwiches, own-made cakes and quiches and daily specials such as pasta with mushroom sauce. Children can order smaller helpings of courses from the main menu, or a lunch box containing a sandwich (or a portion of a main course), drink, crisps, fruit and a Penguin bar (£3.95). On sunny days they can explore the winding paths and hunt for lizards basking on the warm stone walls of the gardens, and in the summer holidays they can join Alice and the Dormouse at a Mad Hatter's tea party. Ventnor Botanic Gardens also has a Museum of Smuggling History and secret gardens with extraordinary plants from all over the world. From the gardens you can take the path down to Steephill Cove or go through the gate on the eastern side – just outside is a playground and access to the cliff path.

Quay Arts Café

Quay Arts, Sea Street, Newport Harbour, Isle of Wight PO30 5BD (01983 822490/ www.quayarts.org). **Lunch served** 11.45am-2.30pm Mon-Sat. **Main courses** £3.90-£6.95. **Credit** MC, V.

This arts centre, housed in a converted brewery warehouse, is a real gem. As well as gallery space, a cinema named after local boy Anthony Minghella, comedy, theatre, dance and children's workshops, there's this brilliant café. It's light and airy, with a large terrace overlooking the river Medina. Children can have their own lunch box (£3.75) with fruit juice, yogurt, fruit, own-made cake and a sandwich – peanut butter, Marmite, cheese or tuna mayonnaise. If that doesn't fit the bill, half jacket potatoes with nursery fillings (tuna, cheese) with salad and a piece of fruit on the side are just £2.95. There is always a tempting selection of soups, quiche and salads, as well as own-made cakes and biscuits. Specials on the blackboard change daily and include fish, vegetarian and vegan dishes. On our last visit, smoked haddock and cod fishcakes with a tomato salsa, French onion soup and cheese and lentil bake were on offer. Eggs are free-range, local produce is used whenever possible, and the café prides itself on catering for those with allergies or other special dietary requirements such as low cholesterol, gluten-free and dairy-free. It's also a Wi-Fi zone.

Spy Glass Inn

Esplanade, Ventnor, Isle of Wight PO38 1JX (01983 855338/www.thespyglassinn.com). **Meals served** noon-9.30pm daily. **Main courses** £6.75-£17.95. **Credit** MC, V.

The terrace of the Spy Glass is the perfect place from which to view the pretty town of Ventnor. Perched above the sandy beach, looking out over the Channel, this pub is much appreciated by parents, who sup pints of the local brew, Golden Ale, while older children play on the beach below or lose their pocket money in the not-too-sleazy amusement arcade. As you might expect, seafood and fish feature heavily on the menu, with smoked mackerel salad, jugs of prawns and whole lobsters. The children's menu (£4.50-£5.25) offers own-made cottage pie, ham salad and chips or cheese and vegetable meals, as well as sausages, scampi, chicken or beef burgers and fish fingers. The atmosphere is convivial, and no one turns a hair at muddy boots and dogs on leads. There's live music every night, and booking is advisable on summer evenings during school holidays.

Tiffin Room

Bonchurch Manor, Bonchurch Shute, Bonchurch, Isle of Wight PO38 1NU (01983 852868/www.bonchurchmanor.com).

Dinner served *Apr-Oct* 7-10.30pm Tue-Sat. *Nov-Mar* 7-10.30pm Fri, Sat. **Main courses** £8-£14. **Credit** MC, V.

The accent is on South Indian and Mediterranean dishes at Tiffin, where everything is own-made and the venue – a beautiful Victorian manor house hotel (*see p97*) – imparts a real sense of occasion. When possible, local organic ingredients are combined with freshly ground spices and transformed into delicately flavoured dishes, using owner Shuba Rao's family recipes. The menu changes constantly, but starters might include parsnip and butternut squash soup and masala dosa – crispy lentil pancakes stuffed with spicy potato. Main courses might feature aubergine cooked in a marinade of ground peanuts, coconut, sesame and tamarind; sea bass simmered in a coconut, tamarind and coriander sauce; or lamb tagine with saffron couscous. Desserts include the likes of finely grated carrots simmered in butter, cream and milk laced with cardamom; slow-cooked bananas with sago, coconut milk and saffron; and mango alfonso. Children are welcome, with mini portions available at reduced prices, and; early suppers can be arranged for families. There is a wonderful view from the dining room, and if the weather is good you can eat outside on the lawn. A truly magical experience.

PLACES TO SEE, THINGS TO DO

The island has miles of footpaths to explore, and during May's Walking Festival there are guided walks every day. The coastal path goes right around the island: the section between Shalfleet and Yarmouth is particularly varied, with duckboards over salt marshes, a rickety jetty, tree-fringed beaches, meadows and forest. For more details contact the Coastal Path Visitors' Centre (Dudley Road, Ventnor, 01983 855400, www.coastal wight.gov.uk).

Another great way to see the sights is from the water. You can sign up for a sailing lesson or five-day course at the Medina Valley Centre in Newport (01983 522195, www.medinavalleycentre.org) or the UK Sailing Academy in West Cowes (01983 294941, www.uksa.org). Those who prefer their boats skippered can opt for a boat trip around the Needles or across the Solent to Hurst Castle, leaving from Yarmouth pier; try Puffin Cruises (07850 947618). There are also daily fishing trips from Bembridge harbour.

Amazon World

Watery Lane, nr Arreton, Isle of Wight PO36 0LX (01983 867122/www.amazon world.co.uk). **Open** *Summer* 10am-4pm daily. *Winter* 10am-3pm daily. **Admission** £6.99; £5.99 concessions; £5.50 3-14s; £24 family (2+2); free under-3s. **Credit** MC, V.

This attraction grew out of the owner's desire to educate visitors about the destruction of the Amazon Basin and the endangerment of the creatures that inhabit it. From this worthy aim, Derek Curtis has created a rainforest with rivers, waterfalls, pools and wildlife – avoid getting within chomping distance of the piranhas. This is a great place to spend a wet day, with a huge playground, falconry displays and various animal encounters.

Blackgang Chine Fantasy Park

*Blackgang Chine, Chale, Isle of Wight
PO38 2HN (01983 730052/www.blackgang
chine.com).* **Open** *26 Mar-May, Sept, Oct*
10am-5pm daily. *June* 10am-6pm daily. *July,
Aug* 10am-8pm daily. Closed 28 Oct-25 Mar.
Times may vary during half-term and schools
hols; phone for details. **Admission** £8.95;
£33 saver (4 people); free under-4s. Free return
visit within 7 days. **Credit** MC, V.
Clinging to the side of a crumbling cliff, this theme park has an enduring charm. As one of the oldest theme parks in the country, it is remarkable that it's here at all – particularly considering how many of its attractions have slipped down to the naturist beach below. On a busy day in the holidays, Wild West Town is the place to be. While parents drink strong tea, children of all ages charge around the saloon and blacksmith shop, shooting off cap guns (on sale in the shop) and blasting the living daylights out of total strangers. The newest rides are Water Force, and Cliffhanger – a rollercoaster that climbs high above the sea. But there is plenty of gentler amusement for younger children in the shape of Nurseryland, Sleeping Beauty's Castle and a giant Whale. In Rumpus Mansion, watch out for the beautiful maiden who turns into a hideous hag.

Brading Roman Villa

*Morton Old Road, Brading, Isle of Wight
PO36 0PH (01983 406223/www.brading
romanvilla.org.uk).* **Open** *Mar-Oct* 9.30am-
5pm daily. *Nov-Feb* 10am-4pm daily.
Admission £4.25; £3.75 concessions;
£2.20 5-16s; £12 family (2+3); free under-5s.
Credit MC, V.
The Romans knew a thing or two about location, and would have been attracted to this site by its proximity to Brading harbour and the excellent local food supplies – plentiful oysters and other seafood on the coast, and good hunting (wild boar and deer) in the surrounding woods. This Roman villa, one of the best-preserved in the Britain, was first discovered in 1879 by a local farmer digging holes for a sheep pen. The fine mosaic floor shows peaceful scenes of farming and fishing, but it is the hideous head of Medusa, crowned with its halo of writhing serpents, that sticks in the memory. The award-winning exhibition and visitor centre – an attractive wood-clad building that has been designed to suit the landscape – runs school holiday workshops and activities for children, and there is also a café.

Brickfields Horse Country

*Newnham Road, Binstead, Ryde, Isle of Wight
PO33 3TH (01983 566801/www.brickfields.
net).* **Open** 10am-5pm daily. **Admission**
£6; £5 concessions; £4.50 4-14s; £17 family
(2+2); free under-4s. Free return visit within
four days. **Credit** MC, V.
Paradise for horsey types, Brickfields has been so cleverly planned that you can spend a whole day here whatever the weather. As well as indoor and outdoor riding, catering for all levels of horsemanship, there are tractor rides, a working blacksmith's forge, educational talks, a café, a cider barn and pig racing. Miniworld, with its Shetland ponies, is popular with little ones who enjoy having everything on their scale for a change.

Carisbroke Castle

*Carisbroke, nr Newport, Isle of Wight
PO30 1XY (01983 522107/www.english-
heritage.org.uk).* **Open** *Apr-Sept* 10am-5pm
daily. *Oct-Mar* 10am-4pm daily. **Admission**
(EH) £5.50; £4.10 concessions; £2.80 5-16s;
£13.80 family (2+3); free under-5s. **Credit**
MC, V.
Charles I was held in this hilltop Norman castle before being taken back to Whitehall in London to be executed. The castle's remains are well preserved, and there are towers, courtyards and battlements to explore – the latter offering wonderful views of the island. During the summer, jousting and other events are held here. Don't miss the demonstration of how a donkey trudging around inside a giant hamster wheel can draw water up from the castle's well.

Dinosaur Farm Museum

*Military Road, nr Brighstone (between
Pearl Centre and Atherfield Bay), Isle of Wight
PO30 4PG (01983 740844/07970 626456/
www.isleofwight.com/dinosaurfarm).* **Open**
5 April-4 Nov 10am-5pm daily. **Admission**
£2.95; £2.25 4-16s; £8 family (2+2); free
under-4s. *Fossil hunts* £4; £3 4-16s; £12
family (2+2); free under-4s. **No credit cards.**
The milking parlour where the Barnes High Sauropod skeleton was first taken after its discovery nearby in 1992 is now a charming little dinosaur museum. Here you can chat to volunteers as they clean locally found fossils, or bring your own finds for identification by the museum's expert. New for 2007 is the Treasures of the Earth exhibition, featuring Isle of Wight dinosaurs, fossils and shells, with special events and activities planned for the school summer holidays. The museum also runs fossil hunts on nearby Compton Bay beach (advance booking essential). *See also p102* **Dem dry bones.**

Dinosaur Isle

*Culver Parade, Sandown, Isle of Wight
PO36 8QA (01983 404344/www.dinosaur
isle.com).* **Open** *Nov-Mar* 10am-4pm daily.

Robin Hill Adventure Park

Apr-Sept 10am-6pm daily. *Oct* 10am-5pm daily. Times may vary Jan-early Feb; phone for details. Last admission 1hr before closing. *Fossil hunts* school hols, times vary; phone for details. **Admission** £4.85; £3.60 concessions; £2.85 3-15s; £13.50 family (2+2); free under-3s. *Fossil hunts* £3.50; £3 concessions; £2 3-15s; £10 family (2+2); free under-3s. **Credit** MC, V .

Shaped like a giant pterosaur, it's hard to miss the Dinosaur Isle building on Sandown front. Time travel back to the Cretaceous Period, when the island was a soupy swamp, then enter the dinosaur hall. Here you can peer at the palaeontologists at work in their laboratory and look at exhibits of locally found dinosaurs (*see p102* **Dem dry bones**). There are lots of imaginative interactive exhibits to get children thinking. What colour were dinosaurs? Is that a tooth, a claw or fossilised poo you're feeling? And what on earth is that strange smell? Watch out though; small children might be terrified by the robotic dinosaur with its swivelling eye and bloodstained teeth, and the unexpected roars that rend the air as you move around the hall. You can book to join a fossil hunt on nearby Yaverland beach here.

Ghost Walks

Various locations: Botanic Gardens, Newport, St Catherine's Lighthouse, Arreton Manor, Freshwater Bay (01983 520695/www.ghost-tours.co.uk). **Open** *Walks* 8-9.30pm daily. **Admission** £5; £3 over-fives; £15 family (2+2). **No credit cards**.

These spooky strolls are organised by local enthusiasts who can get quite carried away in their roles. The walks take place after dark in various historic sites around the island, including Arreton Manor and St Catherine's Lighthouse. They're great fun, but not recommended for the very young or those of a nervous disposition. The organisers leave it to the parents to decide as to whether their under-fives can come along, however. Walking in darkness through the Botanic Gardens knowing that at any moment a ghoul is likely to drop down from the overhanging trees is terrifying (even if you know the ghoul probably has a supermarket day job). Booking is advisable; ask about the soon-to-be released Ghost Walk DVD if the walks have you inspired.

GoodLeaf Tree Climbing Adventures

East Wight (01983 563573/07970 033209/ www.goodleaf.co.uk). **Open** *April-Nov* climb times vary; phone for details. **Admission** £40; £25 8-16s. *Individual instruction* £60 any age. **No credit cards**.

Climbing trees, it would appear, doesn't come naturally to our chubby little PlayStation twiddlers. Thankfully, the earthly dryads at GoodLeaf are here to help. They claim that they can enable anyone to make the exhilarating ascent up a 60ft oak tree and, after some relaxing in the leaf canopy,

Isle of Wight

abseil down again. Prices might seem steep (no pun intended), but include all safety equipment and insurance, as well as own-made refreshments back on solid ground at the end of your two-and-a-half-hour climb. Climbs are in groups of three or four, though special arrangements can be made for larger parties. Under-eights generally need individual instruction; call to discuss. The centre's exact location is only revealed once you've booked your climb – the farmer who owns the land is loath to encourage gawpers traipsing across his fields.

Isle of Wight Steam Railway

Railway Station, Main Road, Havenstreet, Isle of Wight PO33 4DS (01983 882204/ talking timetable 01983 884343/www. iwsteamrailway.co.uk). **Open** *mid Mar-Oct* 9.30am-5pm selected days. *26 May-16 Sept* daily. **Fare** £8.50; £4.50 5-15s; £22 family (2+2); free under-5s. **Credit** MC, V.
Restored steam engines and coaches from the island's railway heyday chug back and forth along a five-mile line connecting Wooton to Smallbrook Junction, intersecting with electric trains to Ryde and the passenger ferry. Tickets allow you to ride the trains as much as you like for the whole day. There areplenty of activities for children, including spooky Halloween and festive Santa specials, as well as a play area, steam museum and woodland walks.

Isle of Wight Zoo

Yaverland, Sandown, Isle of Wight PO36 8QB (01983 403883/www.isleofwightzoo.com). **Open** *Apr-Sept* 10am-6pm daily. *Oct-Mar* times vary; phone for details. **Admission** £5.95; £4.95 5-15s; £19.25 family (2+2), £22.85 (2+3); free under-5s. **Credit** MC, V.
This little zoo boasts one of the biggest collections of tigers in Europe. There are even white ones – accidents of nature which would be unable to survive in the wild because of their lack of camouflage. The zoo is currently in the process of creating new enclosures for its tigers, based on the kind of habitat they would inhabit in India. Two phases of the work are already complete; in the area based on Kanha National Park, visitors can sit hidden inside a cave and watch the beautiful creatures though glass. All the big cats here were born in captivity or rescued from negligent owners, and no tigers are bred at the zoo, which aims to educate the public while supporting the conservation of tigers in the wild in India. As well as magnificent African lions, jaguars, cheetahs, panthers and monkeys, the zoo also has a section devoted to the lemurs of Madagascar, with an accompanying video about attempts to reintroduce these creatures to the wild.

Needles Old Battery

West High Down, Totland Bay, Isle of Wight PO39 0JH (01983 754772/www.national trust.org.uk). **Open** *late Jan-Oct* times vary; check website for details. **Admission** (NT) £3.90; £1.95 5-16s, £8.90 family (2+2); free under-5s. **Credit** MC, V.
Looking over the spectacular views of the Needles, the Solent and the Channel, you can understand why this headland is strategically so important to Britain. Built to protect the country from invasion by France, the fort guards the western entrance to the Solent. If you have the energy, this is a great place to end a bracing walk over Tennyson Down from Freshwater Bay (check the battery is open first though). Children can be bribed with a visit to the tacky pleasure park at nearby Alun Bay, where filling glass receptacles with coloured sand has long been a childhood tradition.

Osborne House

East Cowes, Isle of Wight PO32 6JY (01983 200022/www.english-heritage.org.uk). **Open** *Apr-Sept* 10am-5pm daily. *Oct* 10am-4pm daily. *Nov-Mar* 10am-4pm Wed-Sun (pre-booked guided tours only). **Admission** (EH) £9.80; £7.40 concessions; £4.90 5-15s; £24.50 family (2+3); free under-5s. *Grounds only* £5.90; £4.40 concessions; £3 5-15s; £14.80 family (2+3); free under-5s. **Credit** MC, V.
It was to Osborne House, her favourite holiday home, that Queen Victoria retreated after the death of her husband Albert. Built by Thomas Cubitt in the style of an Italian villa, this was the nearest thing the Royals had to a family home. Albert oversaw the construction of the house when he was alive, and the Queen spent much of her time here before her own death in 1901. There's plenty to admire, from the grand state rooms to the odd little domestic details, but for many children the highlight will be the Swiss Cottage. Built as a superior sort of playhouse, the cottage is equipped with forks and spades with which the royal children could work in the vegetable garden, before producing meals for their parents in the little kitchen.

Robin Hill Countryside Adventure Park

Robin Hill, Downend, Arreton, Isle of Wight PO32 2NU (01983 730052/www.robin-hill.com). **Open** *26 Mar-June, Sept, Oct* 10am-5pm daily. *July, Aug* 10am-6pm daily. Closed 28 Oct-25 Mar. **Admission** £7.95; £29 saver (4 people; free under-4s. Free return visit within 7 days. **Credit** MC, V.
This is a country park with a couple of rides attached, but you'll miss the point if you waste much time queuing for the latter. It is the imaginative way that the natural attractions are presented to children that makes Robin Hill a winner. You'll find a labyrinth of underground burrows for crawling in, towers to climb, and, if you're lucky, endangered red squirrels to spot. Then there are all the lakes, bridges and gardens, plus woodland areas and meadows. It's a lovely place to spend a day, and far more refreshing than your average theme park. Dogs on leads admitted.

The Isle of Purbeck

Grockles and cockles.

With more Areas of Outstanding Natural Beauty, not to mention Sites of Special Scientific Interest, than any other county in England, Dorset may be forgiven for seeming a little smug. This county is gorgeous, and it knows it. Its beaches – many of them World Heritage Sites – are garlanded with blue flags and conscientiously coastguarded; several have child-safety zones and family activities throughout the summer. The sea lapping the gentle bays stays warm and welcoming well into autumn. Inland are pretty and prosperous market towns and country parks. The downside of all this charm, however, are the school holiday tourist hordes – described less-than-charmingly as 'grockles' by Dorset folk. It pays to get up early to avoid the crowds round here.

Down to the woods at
Burnbake Campsite.
See p115.

The Isle of Purbeck

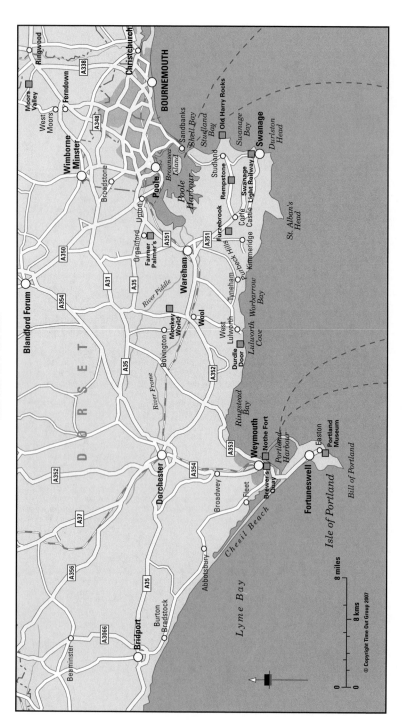

Dorset's southern coastline, from the large natural harbour at Poole west to St Aldhelm's Head, taking in the River Frome's marshy lands to the north, fringes a peninsula known as the Isle of Purbeck. Geologists and paleontologists have an interest in the area because it sits on several parallel strata of Jurassic rocks, including Portland limestone and the Purbeck beds. Purbeck marble is a hard sort of limestone, much in demand during the building of Britain's great cathedrals. The chalky Purbeck hills and Dorset downs are responsible for the area's cliff formations, notably the bizarre rocky landforms around Lulworth Cove and Durdle Door.

This unique geology boils down to a coastline that's postcard perfect and besieged by tourists (Lulworth Cove is particularly hard to spread a towel in during the summer holidays). The area is also exciting for fossil-hunting, walking, beachcombing and paddling that we think it's a family holiday paradise, traffic jams notwithstanding. Enid Blyton thought so too, which is why she placed her most famous adventurers here (see p112 **How absolutely wizard!**)

Big bay, little bay

The big bay in which to start exploring the Isle of Purbeck is Poole Bay, where the bucket-and-spade honeypots of Bournemouth and Poole absorb the greater part of the summer tourist invasion. Poole Harbour, famously Europe's biggest natural harbour and, fascinatingly, too shallow for really hefty ships, has basked in even shallower glory in recent years. Here is some of the most expensive real estate in the country. If you're a millionaire football manager, ex-player or former pop or soap star, this is the place to sit back and count your money.

Arriving in Poole by train (or worse still, coach) it's hard to fathom its desirability. Away from the harbour and beaches, this is an unprepossessing town, whose blockish, utilitarian shopping centre and chip-fat scented bus station are particularly depressing. Poole residents pour scorn on the 'millionaire's playground' tag, then resignedly point their visitors in the direction of the historic old town, the harbour and, more especially, Sandbanks.

This three-mile long sandy spit, just outside the harbour, is the estate agent's nirvana. Its beaches of golden sand and yacht-dotted sea views have prompted quite hysterical comparisons with Palm Beach. The big flashy houses don't score highly in the taste stakes, and although Sandbanks Beach is pleasant, unless where you're staying has direct access to it then parking round here is a nightmare. Families are better off with the greener,

TOURIST INFORMATION

Poole
Enefco House, Poole Quay, Poole, Dorset BH15 1HJ (01202 253253/ www.pooletourism.com).
Portland
Portland Bill, Portland, Dorset DT5 2JT (01305 861233/ www.weymouth.gov.uk).
Purbeck
Holy Trinity Church, South Street, Wareham, Dorset BH20 4LU (01929 552740/www.purbeck.gov.uk).
Swanage
The White House, Shore Road, Swanage, Dorset BH19 1LB (01929 422885/www.swanage.gov.uk).
Weymouth & Portland
King's Statue, The Espalanade, Weymouth Dorset DT4 7AN (01305 785747/www.weymouth.gov.uk).

prettier strands of the Branksome Chines, a little nearer Bournemouth. Chines are little wooded valleys leading to the beach, and the promenade along the beach is a splendid leg-stretcher that takes you to Bournemouth Beach (there's also a landtrain) and the busy pier.

From Sandbanks you have a lovely view of Studland Bay, where there's a delightful beach. Little Shell Bay can be reached via the chain ferry, whose propulsion is achieved by drive wheels pulling along chains on the sea bed. The chains are fixed at the Sandbanks side, where people have been known to queue for hours to board the ferry. During the summer holidays it's a good idea to aim for the 6am crossing.

Studland is also accessible via the depressingly busy A351 from Wareham and Corfe Castle. From Studland's Shell Bay you can follow the South West Coast Path alongside sandy beaches, through the village of Studland, admiring Old Harry Rocks. These famous chalk stacks are named after 17th-century pirate Harry Pay, who used to attack merchant ships as they left Poole Harbour. Old Harry Rocks lie offshore from the Foreland, which leads to Swanage Bay. Here, a clifftop path crosses Durlston Head, where you can admire a 40-ton limestone globe that dates from 1887. On a good day, lucky folk might also spot some dolphins from here.

Note that the northern end of Studland Beach near Shell Bay is reserved for naturists. If you prefer to remain clothed, walk through the dunes to heathland that protects six British reptile species, including adders, sand lizards and slow worms. To enjoy the glories of Studland without the traffic chaos, book a stay at the famous Knoll House (see p117) and live the Enid

The Isle of Purbeck

HOW ABSOLUTELY WIZARD!

Enid Blyton was undoubtedly the JK Rowling of her day. The most successful British author of the twentieth century was born in East Dulwich, London, in 1897, but for many years Enid Mary Blyton's heart belonged to Dorset. She particularly loved the Isle of Purbeck, where she holidayed thrice yearly for 20 years. The area became the inspiration for many of the adventures enjoyed by Blyton's most successful creation, the Famous Five. The smugglers' coves, mysterious islands, ruined castles and rocky bays she saw while exploring the Dorset coastline all found their way into her books.

In the first of the *Famous Five* adventures, Julian, Dick and Anne are packed off to stay with their bad-tempered cousin George, who – rather thrillingly it turns out – stands to inherit an island with a ruined castle. Inhabitants of Corfe Castle proudly claim that George's ruin is modelled on theirs, and Poole people reckon the island has to be Brownsea. In Blyton's day, Brownsea Island was owned by a recluse, Mrs Bonham-Christie, who banned visitors and lived in splendid isolation while nature took over all around her; in her book, Blyton called Brownsea 'Keep Away Island'. The 'mystery moor' the Five go stumbling around in the fog in their thirteenth adventure is considered by locals to be based on Stoborough Heath and Hartland Moor, near Corfe Castle. Eventually, Blyton and her husband bought a farm at Sturminster Newton, which became the inspiration for Finniston Farm, in adventure Blyton dream. The main swimming beach is Knoll Beach, just a short trot away from the hotel, through woodland.

Island of adventure

Enid Blyton was inspired by Brownsea Island – the largest of the islands in Poole Harbour – to write the Famous Five's first ever adventure (*see above* **How absolutely wizard!**). Real life adventures, in the form of scout and guide pack holidays, have been taking place at Brownsea ever since Baden Powell ran his first experimental scout camp here in 1907 (a huge engraved stone marks the spot), so 2007 is a big year, with a flurry of centenary celebrations.

The Brownsea Island Ferry (www.brownsea islandferries.com; *see p115* **Pushing the boat out**) drops you on the south-eastern edge of the island, with Brownsea Castle on your left (this is not open to the public). A National Trust café and shop awaits adventurers disembarking from the ferry (open mid Mar-Oct; landing fee £4.70; £2.40 5-16s; free under-5s). The Visitor Centre runs events for children during the summer holidays, and volunteers equip number 18, where there are yet more castle dungeons for the children to come to grief in.

Today, the spirit of Enid Blyton still stalks the land – kept alive by her most passionate fan, Vivienne Endecott, author of *The Dorset Days of Enid Blyton* and proprietor of Corfe Castle's Ginger Pop Shop (*see p114*), which is, she maintains, 'a shop about childhood, not just a children's shop'. The shop and its proprietor celebrate those heady days of the '50s and '60s when children were able to take off for days at a time without adults to impede their adventures.

Still, with a bit of imagination, children can live the *Famous Five* dream – camping at Burnbake (*see p115*), exploring Corfe Castle and picnicking on Brownsea Island (*see below*) or finding ancient treasures on Chesil Beach (*see p115*). They'll just have to get used to the idea that unlike Aunt Fanny and Uncle Quentin, adults today aren't too chuffed to wave off their ten- and eleven-year-olds as they cycle off for week-long adventures, with just a large dog for protection and not a mobile phone between them.

children with a backpack containing magnifying glasses, notebooks and bird identification guides and tell them to go away and explore the island. It's a lovely thing to do, especially if you've brought a picnic.

In the woodland, look out for red squirrels – Brownsea is one of the few places in the country where they have survived (there was a nasty episode when a grey imposter boarded a Brownsea Island Ferry, but he was apparently dealt with by the immigration authorities). The reds are quite elusive: not so the peacocks, who merrily join forces with the chickens to relieve children of

their sandwiches. The accessible beaches are in the southern section of the island; the northern portion is a nature reserve managed by Dorset Wildlife Trust, so public access is limited. During the summer, al-fresco theatre productions take place in a picturesque clearing (www.brownsea-theatre.co.uk).

Of course, the biggest adventure of all would be to stay here. That's only possible if you're a scout, part of a youth group, a John Lewis employee (the Partnership own the castle), or prepared to put your name on the waiting list to stay in the National Trust's holiday cottage.

Victorian classic

Swanage underwent the transition from fishing village to seaside resort in Victorian times, and has just about managed to keep its composure despite an impressive influx of holidaymakers every summer. Its strategic position at the foot of the Purbeck Hills, looking out on to the World Heritage site of the Jurassic coastline, insures it against overdevelopment. The town looks all the more antique thanks to the remnants of Victorian London that adorn it. Features such as ornate lampposts from Hanover Square and a clock tower from London Bridge were apparently brought back as ballast by the cargo ships that carried the Purbeck marble used in the Victorian restoration of Westminster Abbey.

A host of awards in Britain in Bloom, Tidy Britain and Blue Flag campaigns keep the dear little town spick and span. The beach is crowded, no doubt about it, but its scatterings of shells, millpond bathing, golden sands and Punch and Judy (not to mention strategically placed toilets, beach shops and cafés) are perfect for families. Strolling along the Victorian pier or the beach gardens, with their putting green, tennis courts and café, or paying a rainy-day visit to the museum in the square are simple pleasures to intersperse with a day's paddling and sandcastle building.

Corfe Castle (*see p122*) is just up the railway line, in the heart of the Isle of Purbeck. When visiting with children, it would be a crime not to approach this beauty, and the stone village of the same name, via the Swanage Light Railway (*see p123*). Corfe Castle is a ridiculously picturesque village, and its visitor attractions uphold the correct chocolate-boxy atmosphere. Already entranced by the steam train and castle, small children are further delighted by the giant board games and tiny houses at the Model Village (Corfe Castle Square, 01929 481234, www.corfecastlemodelvillage.co.uk). Opened in 1966, this 17th-century throwback recreates the village and castle in miniature, as it was before Cromwell blasted it to smithereens in 1646. The free Swanage Museum (01929 421427) is open daily from April to October (weekends only the rest of the year).

Don't miss The Ginger Pop shop (The Town House, The Square, Corfe Castle, 01929 477214, www.gingerpop.co.uk, open Apr-Oct) a curious shop run by an Enid Blyton fan who sells lashings of ginger beer, true to form, as well as Enid Blyton's books, tapes and souvenirs, old-fashioned toys and sweets. Visitors are encouraged to sign the Enid Blyton appreciation book.

Upcountry from Corfe Castle, Wareham is a fine old Saxon walled town, sitting prettily between the rivers Frome and Piddle (which always makes children giggle) on their way to the sea. It has a picturesque quay from where you can take a boat trip (see p116), and is famous these days for its foodie nature. The farmers' market is only held once a month, but local produce is sold in delightful old-fashioned shops and there's an auction market every second Tuesday. Be prepared for the road that runs between Wareham and Corfe Castle to be jam-packed in the summer holidays. Some of the traffic is en route to the Blue Pool (Furzebrook, 01929 551408), a lake-and-forest beauty spot whose waters reflect the surrounding seasonal colours to stunning effect. The little café here (open Apr-Oct) does fantastic cream teas with own-made scones. Still more traffic is heading for the now internationally renowned Monkey World near Wool (see p122).

All gone away

In 1943 the seaside village of Tyneham, on the South West Coast Path between Kimmeridge and West Lulworth, was requisitioned by the army. About 250 villagers were evacuated, but told they would be allowed to return to Tyneham when hostilities ceased. That never happened, and the land has continued to be used as a military training area. Helen Taylor, a seamstress, pinned this sad little message to the doors of St Mary's Church before she left: 'Please treat the church and houses with care. We have given up our homes where many of us lived for generations to help win the war to keep men free. We shall return one day and thank you for treating the village kindly.' Taylor was not to know that the buildings and cottages would become derelict. The church and school remain intact, however, and host exhibitions, open from 10am to 4pm when the range walks are open.

From Tyneham village, follow the path down to Worbarrow Bay and descend to the shingle beach. Lulworth Range walks and Tyneham village are accessible most weekends and school holidays throughout the year, but this can be subject to change. Ring the Range Officer (01929 404819) to check access before you set out.

Shingly dells and busy strands

Ringstead Bay, the next beach west from the insanely busy Lulworth Cove, is seldom as packed as its more photogenic neighbour. That's because it's simply 600 metres or so of shingle. Nonetheless, it's a splendid place for a day's fossil hunting and crabbing among the rock pools. The area around Weymouth is, in the best guide book parlance, a place of contrasts. The town is a perfect example of that classic seaside resort made fashionable a couple of hundred years ago, now rather faded in its glamour. The sandy beaches (Weymouth beach is annually named as one of the UK's Elite Beaches for its cleanliness), ornamental gardens, excessive numbers of beachside tat shops, Punch and Judy, fish and chip and ice-cream vendors and gentle surf mean that holidaymakers still come here in their thousands, just as they did when Weymouth was the favoured weekend break spot for King George III.

If you're wandering the shops along the Esplanade, trying to hurry the children past rock, fudge, fridge magnets and yet more crap, look out for the delightful art deco façade of Rossi's Ices at No.92 (01305 785557) to divert them. Mr Figliolini's Italian cornets are a far better thing to squander your pocket money on.

The 17th-century harbour behind the seafront is a delight. Small fishing boats

Kids get their own dining room at **Knoll House Hotel**. See p117.

Moonfleet Manor. *See p117.*

bob timelessly on the water, and the Old Fish Market, built 150 years ago, is still gratifyingly in use. In the Brewers Quay area of the harbour, a network of olde-worlde courtyards and cobbled alleys, there's a gallery, a few chichi shops and children's activities and cafés and pubs with outside seating. Various step-back-in-time attractions, such as the Timewalk and Brewery Days, explore Weymouth's glory days (for events log on to www.brewers-quay.co.uk). Stepping forward in time, Weymouth Bay has been earmarked as home to the London 2012 Olympic Sailing competitions, so book your caravan at Waterside now in time for the rush. Other day-out alternatives to just beaching it include the Museum of Coastal Defence and the Sea Life Park (*see p123* for both).

Don't leave Weymouth without crossing the harbour to Portland, the 'island' made from ancient and much feted limestone, at whose windswept southern tip a lighthouse sits. If the children are over the minimum height of 1.1 metres, they can climb the 153 steps to the top of the lighthouse. The Visitor Centre (01305 861233, www.trinity house.co.uk) is typically illuminating.

The other attraction is the Portland Museum (217 Wakeham, 01305 821804, open Fri-Tue Easter-Oct; daily during school holidays). Housed in two small thatched cottages, this little place was founded in 1930 by Dr Marie Stopes, whose day job as its first curator was eclipsed by her work as a birth control pioneer. Her own cottage is now given over to the shipwreck and smuggling exhibition, as well as a gift shop. The Portland Gallery, in the second cottage, tells of wider Portland history. Local fossils and artefacts adorn the garden, which is a pleasant place to have a picnic.

The fossils picked up for display in the Portland Museum are intriguing pinpoints in an 185 million-year story. The coastline from Portland west for 95 miles as far as Exmouth in Devon is known as the Jurassic Coast. At Orcombe Point in Exmouth, the westernmost part of the stretch, the cliffs are 250 million years old. As you travel east they gradually dip into the sea, and at Portland are a mere 140 million years old.

On the waterline, Chesil Beach, the longest shingle beach in the world, starts at the Isle of Portland's West Bay and stretches 18 miles to West Bay in Bridport. It's stunning, built up of very smooth pebbles that become smaller as you go up the coast from Portland. Inland, the villages get prettier and chintzy cream teas and rose-covered B&B cottages lend themselves to a more sedate sort of family break. Go west to Abbotsbury to feast your eyes on hundreds of swans and acres of fabulous gardens, but be prepared for the now familiar nose-to-tail queuing if you don't get up early enough (*see p121*).

PLACES TO STAY

Burnbake Campsite

Rempstone, Corfe Castle, Wareham, Dorset BH20 5JH (01929 480570/www.burnbake. com). **Open** Apr-Sept. **Rates** £6-£9/pitch (1 adult with tent, car or camper van); £2-£3 additional adult; £1-£2 additional child/tent/vehicle. **No credit cards**.

Set in woodlands with a stream tinkling through, this secluded 12-acre site is about three miles from Studland beach. It's a perfect pitch for families, and was raved about endlessly during last summer's 'cool camping' craze that briefly obsessed the national press. Book early is our advice. There's room for 130 family tents and camper vans; choose a pitch amongst the trees or on the prepared grass. The clean, purpose-built buildings contain washing facilities and toilets, and there are washing-up sinks, a laundry room with washing machine and tumble dryer and a baby room. A safe play area for children has a sandpit and swinging tyres, and there's a sports field next door for games of footie. Pets are welcome. The shop

The Isle of Purbeck

PUSHING THE BOAT OUT

Local Tourist Information Centres (*see p111*) can provide information about exploring Dorset's Jurassic coastline from every angle. By far the most exciting way to see it with young children (for whom geological beach and cliff walks are going to lose their appeal after about 20 minutes) is from the water. A Dorset County Council leaflet entitled *Jurassic Coast By Boat* is available from most tourist information centres, and lists all the boat trips and cruises you can take around Poole Harbour, Swanage, Wareham, Lulworth Cove, Weymouth and Portland. We list a few of the most

useful phone number below; yet more can be discovered in Poole and Weymouth harbours.

Blue Line Cruises

01202 467882/www.bluelinecruises.co.uk.
Poole's Blue Line trips cover Poole Quay to Old Harry Rocks, and run Swanage trips on Tuesdays, Thursdays and Sundays.

Brownsea Island Ferries

01929 462383/www.brownseaislandferries. com.
Poole's festive yellow boats (pictured) have ploughed through the millpond harbour for donkeys' years; their founder carried Scout man Baden-Powell across the water for his unit's first camping trip. The ferries take you to Brownsea Island along the heritage coastline, up and down Wareham's rivers and to and from Sandbanks and Swanage.

has daily deliveries of milk, bread, croissants, cakes, newspapers, Calor gas, charcoal and sundry cooking and camping equipment. Last season a little organic restaurant was set up by some enterprising folk in their on-site yurt.

Cromwell House Hotel

Main Road, Lulworth Cove, Dorset BH20 5RJ (01929 400253/www.lulworthcove.co.uk).
Rates £81-£130. **Credit** AmEx, MC, V.
This century-old hotel has 145 rooms and an enviable, elevated position 200 yards from Lulworth Cove; guests can look on smugly as the grockles sit

in their cars queuing for access to the beach. If the short walk to the sea is too stressful, there's a heated outdoor swimming pool with splendid views. The rooms are simple, homely and affordable enough to allow parents who want their privacy to install their teen in a twin-bedded room of their own. As in most Dorset hotels worth their salt, the chef here goes all out to provide afternoon cream teas. Lobsters, crabs and locally dived scallops gathered by Lulworth's intrepid fishermen are big players on the varied menu, and the food is fresh, nicely presented and served in Dorset helpings. The Cromwell also has a two-bedroomed self-catering flat for £150 per day.

Discoverer

07780 600233/www.underseaworld.co.uk.
This boat has a glass bottom, providing a window on the shallow waters around Weymouth and Portland.

Dolphin III

01929 550006.
The Dolphin is fully equipped to take people with disabilities for free trips around Poole Harbour from May to September.

Dorset Belles

01202 558550/www.dorsetbelles.co.uk.
Cruises around Bournemouth, Poole and Swanage waters, plus evening cruises to Dancing Ledge (near Swanage) to see the puffin colony.

The Fleet Observer

01305 759692/www.thefleetobserver.co.uk.
Explore the Fleet Lagoon and Portland Harbour in a glass-bottomed boat.

Greenslades Ferry Service

01202 669955/www.greensladepleasureboats. co.uk.
A family-run operation, offering one-hour cruises around Portland Harbour and the breakwaters, plus trips to Brownsea Island and around Poole Harbour.

Pequod

07792 334879.
Pequod offer boat trips along the River Frome from Wareham Quay from May to October.

White Motor Boats

01305 785000/www.whitemotorboat.freeuk.com.
White runs a ferry service to Portland from Weymouth Harbour, as well as cruises along the Jurassic Coast to Lulworth Cove.

The Knoll House

Ferry Road, Studland, Dorset BH19 3AH (01929 450450/www.knollhouse.co.uk). **Open** Apr-Oct. **Rates** *DB&B* £176-£206; *full board* £206-£242. **Credit** MC, V.

References to Enid Blyton litter this comfortably eccentric hotel, which is apt, since holidaying here is rather like coming to stay with Aunt Fanny (of *Famous Five* fame). This is the sort of place where children are free to have adventures. There are acres of woodland and heath for them to gallop around, a massive playground, tennis courts, a putting green and a sandy beach just down a grassy slope at the end of the drive. It's also a par-

adise for dogs, so it's not unusual to see a brace of labradors waiting patiently in the flower-filled courtyard while their larger humans supervise the smaller ones playing in the pirate ship playground (no dogs allowed in there). The home-from-home atmosphere, presided over by the Ferguson family, who have run Knoll House as a hotel since 1959, extends to the rooms. Families can book spacious suites (larger ones have three bedrooms and two bathrooms), refreshingly free of gadgetry: there are no TVs unless you hire one, though use of a Roberts radio is free. In lieu of kettles and sachets, early morning tea can be brought to the room. A member of housekeeping staff is on duty until 11pm. Battery-recharging lunches and dinners, without the sprogs, is a Knoll House speciality. Daily changing lunch and dinner menus are strong on locally caught seafood (Poole mussels, local mackerel) and Dorset born and bred meat with seasonal vegetables, all beautifully cooked. Elaborate cold pudding choices are proudly displayed and presided over by a chef, and diners are encouraged to sample more than one. The cheeseboard is laden and unrestricted. This largesse can be shared by children of eight and above, while younger ones eat in the children's dining room. Here they can choose from slightly simpler own-cooked meals (proper handmade burgers, fried fish, salads and a choice of puds). Many children over eight prefer the jolly atmosphere of this more informal dining room, and parents of young children always take breakfast here. The children's dining room and adjoining kitchen are open 24 hours, so parents can use the microwave, baby food, fruit bowl and snacks as if they were at home. Other distractions include games lounges, telly or conversation, a big bar and a large heated outdoor pool with lovely views. Children's discos and entertainers are regularly hosted, and there's a health spa and little beauty treatment room for mummy pampering.

Moonfleet Manor

Fleet, nr Weymouth, Dorset DT3 4ED (01305 786948/www.moonfleetmanorhotel.co.uk). **Rates** £170-£410. **Credit** AmEx, MC, V.

J Meade Falkner's shipwreck and smuggling adventure story, *Moonfleet*, written in the 1880s, was based on the original Fleet House, which became Moonfleet Manor. The hotel's exclusivity is established as you drive miles down a winding country lane, past cottages and farmhouses that might once have been part of the manor. It may have acres devoted to car parking, but that doesn't detract from its movie star looks. The Georgian pile has spacious courtyards and stable blocks at the rear, and smooth lawns with hammocks and steamer chairs looking out over the Fleet lagoon, separated from the sea by Chesil Beach.

Part of the burgeoning von Essen brood of luxury family hotels, Moonfleet plays up its look of antique splendour – although its kiddie appeal is the stuff of many a parenting magazine. From the terrace, parents relax to the merry sounds of their children disporting themselves on the trampoline,

The Isle of Purbeck

Shell Bay Seafood Restaurant. *See p121.*

in the competitive Swanage hotel scene. It also has a reputation for great Dorset dinners – on the menu (£23 for three courses) you'll find local crab for starters, rack of local lamb to follow and cheeses or ice-creams from the county's many dairies among the puds. The garden, perched atop the cliffs, is a wonderful place to enjoy a few sundowners and contemplate dinner, although children are more interested in pounding down the private steps to the beachfront. Staff are accommodating towards children, but make a firm distinction between providing for their needs and going the full-on kiddie entertainment hog. Thus there are children's meal options – if you want to eat separately from your progeny, a high tea is served at 5.30pm (£7); if not, children can choose a reduced priced child's portion in the restaurant from 7pm – but no kiddie clubs or play equipment. It is quite reasonably pointed out that Swanage seafront can provide all the fun any child could need. Under-twos are accommodated free, and there is a baby listening service.

Sandbanks Hotel

15 Banks Road, Poole, Dorset BH13 7PS (01202 707377/www.fjbhotels.co.uk). **Rates** £152-£242; *DB&B* £162-£264. **Credit** MC, V.
Presiding over Poole's millionaire mile, this burly white hotel and its barriered car park look a bit corporate from the outside. Inside, though, it's all smiles for the children. Sandbanks is the family face of the swish FJB chain. Other outposts include the more sophisticated 78-room Haven (01202 707333) on the edge of the peninsula, with its handsome Marconi Lounge (the radio pioneer made his first broadcasts from here), which is good for parents and teens, and the Harbour Heights boutique hotel for the child-free. Residents of Sandbanks can use the Haven's fantastic health club, or retreat here (without the kids) for the critically acclaimed La Roche restaurant.

Sandbanks' prime position next door to the FC Watersports Academy (*see p122*) means that activities such as windsurfing, body boarding and banana boating are easily arranged, but many families come here purely for the beach. The hotel is right on top of the sandiest, safest, Blue Flaggiest beach in Christendom, so if the weather's good, everyone's happy. If it's wetsuit-wearing weather for the older, sportier members of the family, there's still plenty to keep younger children amused. There's a small pirate ship playground outdoors, and in the various playroom and entertainments areas, cheerful playleaders initiate games, competitions and arts activities. The indoor pool is another option.

Interconnecting family suites are bright and spacious, and many have spirit-lifting views over the sea; all have satellite TVs for those times when only Nickelodeon will do. Variously affordable room configurations are available, such as a sofabed or bunks in the parents' room. There's a baby-listening service for parents having dinner in the restaurant. Lunch and high tea for young children is served in the Surf Shack children's dining room;

climbing frame, tennis courts and other outdoor play equipment. Under cover, the indoor swimming pool, skittle alley and Four Bears Den playroom ensure the fun goes on whatever the weather. For walkers, the Dorset coast path is at the end of the garden. Then there's the beach, as well as all the windsurfing, sailing, riding and diving opportunities this part of the coast provides. Keeping the children occupied is half the story (there are children's suppers, babysitters, a crèche and all sorts of fun and games); the other half is the unfrazzling of parents. Professional couples with a brace of young children come here to spend time together and apart. It's not cheap, but the gracious atmosphere, pleasantly adult mediterranean restaurant, spa, bars and handsome, spacious seaview family suites and interconnecting rooms are a tonic for harrassed parents. Children share their parents' room free, but are charged for meals.

Pines Hotel

Burlington Road, Swanage, Dorset BH19 1LT (01929 425211/www.pineshotel.co.uk). **Rates** £117-£141; *DB&B* £144-£176. **Credit** AmEx, MC, V.
The views from this quite high-falluting family hotel at the quieter end of Swanage Bay are heartbreakingly lovely. With its unrivalled position and recent refit – from which it emerged with a series of bright, clean, if conservatively decorated family suites – the Pines has become a serious contender

over-fives pay a surcharge to eat in the Sea View restaurant with the rest of the family. For parents who want to see less of their children than the average family break provides, there's a nursery called Little Rainbows next door, which can be booked in advance for whole days of childcare (01202 709427). Sandbanks has its own spa with beauty treatments by Dermalogica.

Waterside Holiday Park

Bowleaze Cove, Weymouth, Dorset DT3 6PP (01305 833103/www.watersideholidays.co.uk). **Rates** £200-£600 4-berth; £300-£650 6-berth; £400-£900 8-berth. **Credit** MC, V.

Oft praised for the orderliness, friendliness and aura of good, clean fun that pervades it, this huge holiday park in the secluded Bowleaze Cove has been awarded five stars by the Visit Britain inspectors. What's more, unlike many of the more dog-eared caravan parks in the area, it is held in pretty high regard by seasoned seaside caravanners. The caravans are bright, well equipped and pretty spacious, although we'd recommend an 8-berth Dorchester model for a family of five. Family friendly activities abound, with a holiday club in high season. Arts, crafts, music and fun are on offer, as well as evening entertainment. There are indoor and outdoor pools, an internet café, restaurant, soft play area, footie pitch and adventure playground. The site also encompasses Bowleaze Cove funfair, which might be a turn-off (though it's all about gentle rides for children, and payment is by token). Just across the road is a sand and shingle beach that's fine for swimming and playing (the softer sandy beaches of Weymouth with their lifeguards are a mile and a half away). The park has a half-hourly shuttlebus that runs between beaches and local attractions away from Bowleaze, so you can escape quite easily, although many children are happy staying on site. Other nearby facilities include a riding stables next door and some wonderful coastal walks. All the buildings are no-smoking, including the entertainment areas.

YHA Portland

Hardy House, Castletown, Portland, Dorset DT5 1AU (0870 770 6000/www.yha.org.uk). **Open** *Oct-Mar* 8-10am, 5-10pm daily. **Rates** £99 family room. **Credit** MC, V.

A windswept location on Stone Island makes Hardy House a treat for salty seadog families. The early Edwardian building recalls the British Navy's heyday on Portland, when it belonged to the First Admiral. Rooms have fabulous views over Lyme Bay, and this place makes a handy base from which to explore Dorset's southernmost tip, with its castle, museum and lighthouse. Leg-stretching opportunities include the Round Island Coastal Footpath, and guests can choose between Weymouth's sandy beaches or the more dramatic Chesil. The hostel has a kitchen, day room and tourist information centre, and is self-catering only. Portland is graded a three star by the Youth Hostelling Association, as is their Swanage hostel

(0870 770 6058), set in a Victorian house; here, breakfast is included in the price and meals are available. The simpler, one-storey timber building at Lulworth Cove (0870 770 5940) is a two star job. All have family roooms and must be booked way ahead for school holiday stays.

WHERE TO EAT & DRINK

Beavers Restaurant

14 Institute Road, Swanage, Dorset BH19 1BX (01929 427292). **Meals served** 9am-5pm Mon-Fri, Sun; 9am-7.30pm Sat. **Main courses** £3.50-£10.99. **Credit** MC, V.

This is your archetypal cosy café, and a friendly place to indulge in that most appealing west country institution, the cream tea. There are few greater pleasures to beat layering local clotted cream and own-made jam (both served in bowls, not prepacked) onto a wholemeal scone from a Corfe Castle bakery. This exquisite experience can be yours for just £3.99 here. As well as the scones, there are some brilliant cakes and pastries, soups, snacks, sandwiches and hot meals. Staff have a really friendly way with children, and the set children's meal deal is £3.79 (not including a drink).

Café Blue

60 Weymouth Esplanade, Weymouth, Dorset DT4 8DE (01305 787225). **Meals served** 8am-4pm daily. **Main courses** £2.95-£5.50. **No credit cards.**

This is the perfect place to stock up on essentials for your picnic on the beach. There are sandwiches of all descriptions, including own-baked baguettes filled with scrumptious concoctions like avocado and bacon, brie and cranberry and hummus with chargrilled peppers, from about £2 upwards. Then there are cakes and hot snacks such as paninis, toasties and baked spuds. For eaters-in, huge all-day breakfasts or bacon rolls are on offer. It's a splendid, friendly place for seaside-sharpened appetites.

Crab House Café

Fleet Oyster Farm, Ferryman's Way, Portland Road, Wyke Regis, Weymouth, Dorset DT4 9YU (01305 788867). **Meals served** noon-2pm, 6-9pm Wed-Fri; noon-2.30pm, 6-9pm Sat; noon-3.30pm Sun. **Main courses** £12.95-£17.25. **Credit** MC, V.

On a sunny day, this Chesil Beach marvel is inviting to all members of the family. It looks like a wooden shack, but is amusingly decorated with fishing paraphernalia and has a little Derek Jarman-like herb garden on the shingle. Fish lovers are in heaven when they sample Nigel Bloxham's fulsomely praised menu. Bloxham buys from local fisherman, and his purchases – skate, crab, sand soles, mackerel and pollock – find their way onto the daily specials list. The main courses aren't going to wildly excite small children as much as adults (the dishes include skate with chorizo, kipper with ginger topping and sole with guacamole), but kids will enjoy sharing parents' crab meat and Thai fish cakes. The chef will knock up a child's platter of fish and chips for £5.95 and no-one minds if they share your pud.

Fish 'n' Fritz

9 Market Street, Weymouth, Dorset DT4 8DD (01305 766386/www.fishnfritz.co.uk). **Meals served** noon-9pm Mon-Sat. **Main courses** £5.10-£6.50. **Credit** MC, V.

A simply decorated café adjoining a multi-award-winning fish and chip shop, F&F's walls are adorned with the mugshots of appreciative celebrities who have enjoyed post-performance fish suppers after appearing at the Weymouth Pavilion. The fish and chips are freshly cooked and the 'secret recipe' batter is light. As well as a range of options such as salad instead of chips (more chips can be requested at no extra charge), pies and vegetarian dishes, there's a choice of exotic-looking puddings. The whole enterprise is run efficiently and with plenty of smiles all round. Children's fish and chips costs £4.10.

The Greyhound Inn

The Square, Corfe Castle, Dorset BH20 5EZ (01929 480205/www.greyhoundcorfe.com). **Meals served** 11am-3pm, 6-9.30pm daily. **Main courses** £5.25-£16.95. **Credit** MC, V.

With Corfe Castle in the background and Swanage Steam Railway to the fore, you couldn't get a more strategically placed refreshment point for families. It's as well, then, that this historic real ale pub caters for children as well as walkers, golfers, happy campers and beer enthusiasts. The chef uses plenty of fresh local ingredients, and the menu is strong on seafood: scallops, lobster, mussels and sand crab are summer favourites. In the winter, the emphasis is more on the Dorset beef, pork and game delivered daily. Afternoon cream teas are another speciality – no fewer than six types of scone are available on good days – and there are some lovely cakes too. During high season, sandwiches, pasties and the like are sold in the garden Tuck Shoppe, to accompany the real ales and ciders. Meals for children (£5.95) include hot dogs, grilled chicken, fish and chips and filled baguettes with salad.

Hive Beach Café

Beach Road, Burton Bradstock, Dorset DT6 4RH (01308 897070). **Meals served** *Summer* 10am-5pm daily. *Winter* 10am-dusk daily. **Main courses** £6.75-£20. **Credit** MC, V.

Yomp along the South West Coast Path almost as far as Bridport and you'll find the Hive, a wonderful, airy and laid-back beach restaurant. It's a key player in the Bridport and West Bay organic foodie mecca, but isn't remotely poncey. We loved our salmon fishcakes and fresher than fresh sea bass, but you can have a bacon roll for £2.99 if you don't fancy the locally caught seafood. Ice-creams from Somerset dairy Lovingtons are available throughout the summer from a kiosk at the back. If you want an evening meal here, be prepared to book about ten weeks ahead. These foodies know when they're on to a good thing.

Sands Brasserie

Sandbanks Hotel, 15 Banks Road, Poole, Dorset BH13 7PS (01202 707377/www.fjb hotels.co.uk). **Meals served** *Summer* noon-3pm Mon, Sun; noon-3pm, 7-9pm Tue-Sat. *Winter* noon-3pm Sun; noon-2pm, 7-9pm Wed, Thur; 7-9.30pm Fri, Sat. **Main courses** £9.25-£14.50. **Credit** MC, V.

The hotel's brasserie has a smashing beachside location, which makes it particularly popular with lunching families (children can scamper down to the beach when they tire of sophisticated conversation). There's no specific menu for children, but they can enjoy a simple salad and some grilled chicken, starters such as prawn and crab salad or soup, or just opt for the bowl of hand-cut chips (£2.75). Where possible, the chef can prepare a half portion of the lunchtime main courses (cod and chips, pasta dishes or risotto), but items such as whole sea bream (£10.50) have to be ordered in all their glory. Coffee and light bites, such as paninis, scones, cakes and croissants, are served during the day. In high season (particularly a sunny one), evening meals with a Poole Bay sunset as standard have to be booked ahead.

Seagull Café

10 Trinity Road, Old Harbourside, Weymouth, Dorset DT4 8TW (01305 784782). **Meals served** *Summer* 10.30am-10pm daily. *Winter* varies; phone to check. **Main courses** £3.60-£5.99. **No credit cards**.

When a fish and chip shop's 'fresh fish daily' sign looks out over Weymouth's harbourside, where little fishing boats land their catches for local restaurants, you know your fish supper is going to be good. The Seagull is Weymouth's oldest fish and chip purveyor, where enormous portions of cod or haddock and chips can be ordered in the restaurant and taken away to eat outdoors while watching the boats come in. A child's portion of cod and chips costs £3.10.

Shell Bay Seafood Restaurant

Ferry Road, Studland, Dorset BH19 3BA (01929 450363). **Meals served** noon-3pm, 6-9pm daily. **Main courses** £13-£30. *Set meal* £15 2 courses. **Credit** MC, V.

Families who've worked up an appetite on Studland Beach troop along to this near-legendary seafood restaurant, just two hundred yards from the Sandbanks Ferry. Dishes include perfectly executed beer-battered cod and chips or pan-fried salmon, or more attention catching platters of oysters, monkfish with Pernod and dill or line-caught swordfish loin. It can get very busy, but it's worth booking ahead for a coveted table overlooking the water, where the children can watch boats go by as they tuck into cod and chips or smaller portions of dishes from the menu. Evenings are enlivened by twinkling harbour lights and live music. Sadly, the children can't enjoy this unless they're over 12. Fair enough; Shell Bay is a romantic spot for dinner, and high chair diners might spoil the ambience.

PLACES TO SEE, THINGS TO DO

Abbotsbury Swannery

New Barn Road, Abbotsbury, Weymouth, Dorset DT3 4JG (01305 871858/www.abbots bury-tourism.co.uk). **Open** *18-31 Mar, 11 Sept-29 Oct* 10am-5pm daily. *Apr-10 Sept* 10am-6pm daily. **Admission** £7.50; £4.50 5-15s; free under-5s. **Credit** MC, V.

Come here during April nesting time to be dazzled by a white expanse of sociably brooding swans, stretching as far as the eye can see. From early June it's more of a greyness, with cygnets waddling about. There is nowhere else in the world like Abbotsbury, where you're allowed to walk through a colony of thousands of nesting swans. By September they're on the move – either learning to fly, in the case of the cygnets, or taking off for the winter if they're grown up enough. There's a splendid kerfuffle at feeding time – sometimes children are allowed to help give the birds their meal. Once the swans have been fully appreciated (there's a telescope platform to get an aerial view of the colony), children can retire to the play area or bale mountain (May-Sept), or take part in the Ugly Duckling Trail. Abbotsbury's pleasures also extend to a children's farm, where there are goats to feed and ponies to ride (admission £5.50) and some exotic sub-tropical gardens first established in 1765 by the Countess of Ilchester and extending for 20 acres (admission £7.50). A super-saver family ticket (£59) gives unlimited access to all three attractions for 12 months.

Bovington Tank Museum

Bovington, Wool, Dorset BH20 6JG (01929 405096/www.tankmuseum.org). **Open** 10am-5pm daily. **Admission** £10; £9 concessions; £7 5-16s; £28 family (2+ 2); free under-5s. **Credit** MC, V.

If you like your vehicles armoured, you'll love Bovington. Seriously, though, this museum of military hardware has a wider appeal than the name suggests, although it would be safe to assume that army barmy males get the most out of it. The Bovington camp was set up in 1916 by the British War Office as a tank crew training facility. After the war, in 1923, Rudyard Kipling came calling and suggested that a museum should be set up on the site. The collection burgeoned after the Second World War, and in 1947 it was opened to the public. Many of the tanks are in full working order, and can be seen in action throughout the summer months in special displays. The huge site has a play area and picnic area, and various special exhibitions are run throughout the year. An interactive trail for children consists of six separate information stations strategically deployed around the collection, from which you learn about tank mobility, firepower, armour (in the military and animal world), camouflage and life inside a tank in a war situation (smelly, mostly). Heavyweight but strangely entertaining stuff.

Corfe Castle

Wareham, Dorset BH20 5EZ (01929 481294/ www.nationaltrust.org.uk). **Open** *Apr-Sept* 10am-6pm daily. *Mar, Oct* 10am-5pm daily. *Nov-Feb* 10am-4pm daily. **Admission** (NT) £5; £2.50 5-17s; free under-5s. **Credit** MC, V.

Its pleasingly crumbly looks have made Corfe Castle, fortress and village both, the subject of countless fudge box and postcard pictures. Unlike the well-kept village, the castle is feeling its age.

Swanage Railway. *See p123.*

The Isle of Purbeck

Weymouth harbour

Visitors are no longer allowed in the keep because it is dangerously decrepit, and will need £700,000 worth of work over the next few years. You can visit the walls and inner bailey, however, and the visitors centre at the entrance has an exhibition and quiz trails for children.

The castle dates from the 11th century, with more towers added during the reigns of Henry I and Henry III. Besieged by Parliamentarians during the Civil War, the castle was finally captured in 1646, and blown up to ensure it could never again be used as a Royalist stronghold. The defaced structure became a handy source of building materials for locals after its downfall, and pieces of the castle are built into nearby houses.

Bequeathed in the 1980s to the National Trust by the Bankes family, who had owned it for 400 years, Corfe is a grade I listed building. Backpack baby carriers are provided for infants as pushchairs are a no-no up here.

Farmer Palmer's Farm Park

Wareham Road, Organford, Poole, Dorset BH16 6EU (01202 622022/www.farmer palmer.co.uk). **Open** 25 Mar-29 Oct 10am-5.30pm daily. *30 Oct-Dec* 10am-4pm Fri-Sun. **Admission** £4.95; £4.75 3-14s; £18.50 family (2+2); free under-3s. **Credit** MC, V.

A jolly place for young children to pet guinea pigs and rabbits, be shown how to milk cows, groom ponies and go on tractor and trailer rides. Brother and sister Phillip and Sandra Palmer are the farmers; this place was a dairy farm before they diversified into the visitor attraction market; it now draws around 80,000 visitors a year. As well as the popular hands-on animal events there's a playground, a straw mountain, an indoor soft play zone and woodland walks. Farmer Palmer's won the Jim Keetch Farm Attraction of the year award in 2006, so diversification has worked out well, it seems.

FC Watersports Academy

Sandbanks Hotel, Banks Road, Sandbanks, Poole, Dorset BH13 7PS (01202 708283/ www.fcwatersports.co.uk). **Windsurfing lessons** £20-£35/hr; 6-hour RYA courses £99. **Credit** MC, V.

The academy has a classroom where students of the surf arts can learn all about currents, wind directions and techy stuff before donning their wet suits and heading for the beach across the road. Lessons in windsurfing, wakeboarding, kitesurfing, kayaking, diving and powerboat handling take place in the shallow and unthreatening Poole Bay waters. The Animal surf equipment and fashion company, based in Poole, hold their annual Windfest here in September; expect lively demonstrations, displays and races. FC Watersports also hire out mountain bikes.

Monkey World

Longthorns, Wareham, Dorset BH20 6HH (01929 462537/www.monkeyworld.org). **Open** *Jan-June, Sept-Dec* 10am-4pm daily. *Jul, Aug* 10am-5pm daily. **Admission** £9; £6.50 3-15s; £27 family (2+2); free under-3s. **Credit** MC, V.

The cheeky monkeys here are happy ones, and not only because they now have a huge fan base, originating from their weekly television show; these primates have all been rescued. Some have escaped the ignominy of being dressed up and paraded on Spanish beaches (they're killed when they get too bolshy); others liberated from unpleasant pet shops around the world, or were once maltreated pets. The sanctuary was set up in 1987 and works in conjunction with foreign governments from all over the world to stop the illegal smuggling of apes out of Africa and Asia. There are now more than 150 inhabitants at the centre, including 56 chimpanzees – the largest group outside Africa. As well as the chimps there are capuchin monkeys, squirrel monkeys, macaques and gibbons. As Monkey World has grown, so have the number of alternative attractions on the 65-acre woodland site. That's just as well, because the crowds outside the enclosures housing famous telly stars such as Sally and Trudy and cutie-pie orang-utan toddler Gordon mean you often can't get a look in. Coming in poor weather doesn't help: the crowds may be smaller, but the apes stay indoors in their shelters. Still, there are keeper talks every half hour during peak times, the great ape play area, a pets corner, viewing tower, an education centre, café and gift shop, and all kinds of pretty places to go for a pleasant walk and refuelling picnic.

Moors Valley

Moors Valley Country Park, Horton Road, Ashley Heath, nr Ringwood, Dorset BH24 2ET (01425 470721/www.moors-valley.co.uk). **Admission** £1-£7 car parking (free cyclists/pedestrians). *Go Ape!* £15 10-17s (no under-10s). **Credit** MC, V.

About twenty minutes' drive away from Poole, but well worth the journey inland, the terrific Moors Valley Country Park covers 750 acres of river valley. The park provides energetic, wholesome, outdoorsy fun of the very best kind for children of all ages, with adventure play areas, castle and sand areas for young infants, a play trail with wooden play structures and a wonderful wooden walkway through the tops of the trees. For overtens looking for that extra adrenaline rush, there's the Go Ape! high wire adventure course; it has its own admission charges and pre-booking is essential (visit www.goape.co.uk for details). The valley's woodlands and meadows are criss-crossed by miles of footpaths and cycle trails and bike hire is available; a narrow-gauge steam railway runs from the lake around the acreage and is always a big hit. The visitor centre, an 18th century timber barn, houses a restaurant and exhibition area and hosts music evenings throughout the year; phone or check the website for details.

Nothe Fort

Barrack Road, Weymouth, Dorset DT4 8UF (01305 766626/www.fortressweymouth.co.uk). **Open** *1-15 Apr, 22, 29 Apr, May-Sept, 22-29 Oct* 10.30am-5.30pm daily. **Admission** £5; £1 5-16s; £4 concessions; £11 family (2+2); free under-5s. **Credit** MC, V.

With its flags fluttering in the wind and anti-aircraft guns pointing out to sea, this fort salutes the Dorset coast from St Aldhems Head to the town of Weymouth, the isle and harbour of Portland and Chesil Beach. Its commanding views are the biggest attraction, although the historical side of things is pretty interesting and nicely presented. The fort was built between 1860-72 and used until 1956 when it was abandoned, bought by the council and eventually taken over by 'vandals and hippies'. It was rescued by the Weymouth Civic Society, whose volunteers now help to preserve the old place. At ground level is a courtyard, surrounded by 26 large casemates (vaulted rooms) with gun ports for cannons. Below the courtyard lie a maze of passages and tunnels; the ramparts are above. The Caponier, a small fort in its own right, juts out to the south; its role was to protect the main gate. Displays and collections in more than half of the 70 rooms use working models, dioramas and tableaux to illustrate exhibitions on coastal defence and the building of the fort, the garrison soldiers who lived there, local people's World War II experiences and some fascinating stuff about torpedo testing and anti-submarine training in Portland Harbour. Walking down from the ramparts to Weymouth town you pass through the landscaped Nothe Gardens.

Swanage Railway

Swanage Station, Swanage, Dorset BH19 1HB (01929 425800/www.swanagerailway.co.uk). **Open** varies; check website for train running details. **Fares** (return) £7.50; £5.50 5-15s; £21 family (2+2); free under-5s. **Credit** MC, V.

As any enthusiast will tell you, one of the loveliest ways to admire the countryside is from the windows of a steam train, and this top Dorset standard gauge railway certainly has the pick of fantastic views. The trains chuff along six miles of track between Swanage and Norden, through the beautiful Isle of Purbeck, passing through Corfe Castle along the way. It's run, as they all are, by an enthusiastic team of volunteers (the Swanage Railway Trust) whose eventual aim is to get the line going all the way up to Wareham. The Trust lay on various children's events, such as half-term *Thomas the Tank Engine* days, Easter Egg Specials and Santa Specials, which involve mince pie scoffing and presents from Santa along the way.

Weymouth Sea Life Park

Lodmoor Country Park, Weymouth, Dorset DT4 7SX (01305 761070/www.sealife europe.com). **Open** *Summer* 10am-5pm daily. *Winter* 10am-3pm daily. **Admission** £13.50; £8.95 3-14s; £11.50 concessions; £38 family (2+2); free under-3s. **Credit** MC, V.

Weymouth's big-time visitor attraction, as the admission charge attests, performs a useful role as a rainy-day child pleaser and has enough in its seven acres to keep everyone busy all day. Sea life being the main thrust, there's the obligatory pool of fast-swimming rays, a sanctuary for melty-eyed seals, a shark nursery, various tropical tanks and Amazone, where the piranhas lurk. Recent additions include the giant green sea turtles, who glide lazily in their 300,000 litre tanks and get called 'dude' a lot. They look as if they'd rather be in Hawaii, but wouldn't we all? Much is made of Sea Life's rescue work. In Weymouth they have the best equipment for rehabilitating rescued turtles, and also have a refuge for unwanted freshwater terrapins (the *Teenage Mutant Ninja Turtle* craze, circa 1990, has a lot to answer for). The SOS Conservation and Rescue campaign pioneers breeding programmes for endangered and overfished species around the world. SOS is currently raising funds for a Sea Turtle Rescue centre in Zakynthos, Greece, so it's good to think that some profits are going that way. With otter and penguin sanctuaries (both species breed obligingly here) and the seahorse tanks (Weymouth must be the most successful sea horse stable in the country), there's plenty to enjoy for all. With that in mind, don't let the children exert pester power for the extra stuff – there's really no need to shell out for funfair rides, panning for gold and mini golf. If the weather's behaving itself, bring the swimsuits and submerge the kids in the Splash Lagoon's dancing fountains until they stop banging on about bouncy castles.

The Isle of Purbeck

Somerset & Wiltshire

Avon calling.

This is the 'land of the summer people' (as Somerset's Anglo Saxon name translates). The area had a seasonally specific moniker because it was flooded and uninhabitable in the winter, so folk moved elsewhere, but it fits as well today. The influx of holidaying families reaches its peak in the long summer vacation, and warm wet winters produce the greenest hills and valleys a dairy herd ever enjoyed. This is farming country updated for its guests, where barns and byres have been turned into holiday cottages, activity and play centres and environmental education centres to keep everyone busy, whatever the weather. And, in keeping with the images of lushness and fertility of its rolling green hills and valleys, this is the home of the lavishly appointed country house hotel, beacons of tasteful family friendliness nestling within the softly rolling hills.

The counties of Somerset and Wiltshire are imbued with mystery and magic. Every step you take in what used to be the old county of Wessex appears to be on hallowed ground. The story goes that Joseph of Arimathea hid the Holy Grail containing Christ's blood at Glastonbury, the site of the first Christian church in Britain. The legends of King Arthur and his questing knights followed, and many others have come since to on a mission to find the grail.

Ebbor Gorge. *See p135.*

DOWN ON THE FARM

We're used to being scandalised these days by the average modern child's ignorance about all things agricultural. Apparently kids today think milk grows on trees and many aren't sure what part of the chicken the nugget comes from. It's up to concerned parents, of course, to educate them in the ways of our once great farming nation, and there are few better ways of achieving this than staying on a farm in the heart of rural Somerset.

For a break that combines country charm, self-catering freedom and animal encounters, Pig Wig Cottages are the business. These rustic dwellings in the grounds of the idyllic 18th-century Beeches Farmhouse are one mile from Bradford on Avon. All the three-bedroom cottages combine wood burning stoves with electronic mod cons and cosy furnishings. The buildings are surrounded by pasture, where goats, ducks and chickens roam and children can help collect the eggs for breakfast. There's also a games room and play area for family use.

The ultimate farm-based camping experience is run by the chap who brought CenterParcs to the UK, Luite Moraal. He's come up with Feather Down Farm Days, which lets urban families get back to nature in an eco-friendly way in 'tented cottages' on farms. The accommodation is comfortable – under canvas but with wooden floors – and the bonus is that

children can run around on the farm, either helping with the work or just familiarising themselves with the countryside. The Somerset Feather Down is located at Park Farm in Newton St Loe. It's a dairy farm, part of the Duchy Estate, and keeps 140 cows on 330 acres of grass and woodland. The farm is run by the Light family, who like to pass their knowledge and experience on to their guests, and welcome junior apprentices who can help get the cows to and from field and milking parlour. The tents are on a woodland hilltop, with super views. Children can play in the woods and are invited to build shelters if their experiences of running wild in the country have turned them all Ray Mears.

Pig Wig Cottages
Beeches Farmhouse, Holt Road, Bradford on Avon, Wiltshire BA15 1TS (01225 865170/www.beeches-farmhouse.co.uk). **Rates** £300-£400/3 nights; £450-£800/wk. **Credit** MC, V.

Feather Down Farm Days
01420 80804/www.featherdown.co.uk. **Rates** £155-£435/4 nights; £345-£679/wk. **Credit** MC, V.
Details of Park Farm and other Feather Down locations can be found on the website.

For families on a mission for a restorative break, Wiltshire and Somerset's main attractions lie deep in the gorgeous countryside. Many can be reached via Wiltshire's ancient thoroughfare, the Ridgeway. (www.nationaltrail.co.uk). This 87-mile roadway follows a route that has been used since prehistoric times, running north from Overton Hill in Avebury to Ivinghoe Beacon in Hertfordshire. Among the treasures on the southern end of the path are Avebury stone circle (www.english-heritage.org.uk), Silbury Hill, the West Kennet long barrow and the Fyfield Down National Nature Reserve.

The honey and cream coloured limestone of Wiltshire and Somerset continues to be the building material of choice in the area. The pretty towns of Bradford-on-Avon and Castle Combe, not to mention the city of Bath, can all thank judicious use of local materials for their enduring good looks.

Bathtime fun

It may be rather a sedate choice for a family holiday base, but Bath is a pleasant place for a day trip (don't bring the car, though). Visitors can start with a hop-on hop-off 45-minute tour with the Bath Bus Company (www.bathbuscompany.com). It's a relaxing way to get the lowdown on the city's history, with stories of the ghosts of Queen Square – said to include a jilted bride – and the history of the Royal Crescent and Circus. Children should hop off at the imaginatively equipped play area in Royal Victoria Park. There's also a botanical garden, refreshments and toilets nearby. The Bath Children's Festival takes place in the park in May (*see p331*). The Bath Bus Company also run the Skyline Tour, which takes in the lovely National Trust-owned Prior Park Gardens.

Pedallers can find trusty mounts for all at Avon Valley Cyclery, behind the station (01225 442442, www.bikeshop.uk.com), and a ride along the old railway path takes you to the River Avon. Try the pleasure boats alongside Pulteney Bridge (07974 560197, www.bathcityboattrips.com) or the Bath Boating Station on Forester Road (01225 312900, www.bathboating.co.uk) for punt, canoe and row boat hire and also cottage accommodation.

Other attractions include the Building of Bath Museum (The Paragon, 01225 333895), housed in an 18th-century Methodist chapel, and No.1 Royal Crescent, a grand townhouse preserved in all its Georgian splendour (01225 428126, www.bath-preservation-trust.org.uk). Throughout the holidays, art workshops are held at Holburne Museum of Art, Great Pulteney Street (01225 466669, www.bath.ac.uk/holburne). Young

Bath
Abbey Chambers, Abbey Church Yard (www.visitbath.co.uk)
Bradford on Avon
50 St Margaret's Street, Bradford on Avon, BA15 1DE (01225 865797/ www.bradfordonavon.co.uk
Cheddar
The Gorge, Cheddar, Somerset, BS27 3QE (01934 744071)
North Wiltshire
North District Council, Monkton Park, Chippenham, Wiltshire, SN15 1ER (01249 706548/ www.visitwiltshire.co.uk)

fashionistas might also like to pop in to the Museum of Costume (Assembly Rooms, Bennett Street, 01225 477173, www.museumofcostume.co.uk), which offers quiz and colouring sheets and holds regular events during school holidays. A visit to Bath would be incomplete without seeing the Roman Baths and Pump Room (Stall Street, 01225 477785, www.roman baths.co.uk). Children's activity sheets and new audio tours featuring Roman guides are available, and there are free family drop-in activities (10am-1pm, 2-4pm) in summer. The website has a decent children's section with cartoon-illustrated facts about the baths and a game to get kids in the mood for a visit.

Shopping is fab in Bath. Smart stores congregate on Walcot Street. Smaller shops can be found in the old Victorian station in Green Park Road (01225 310418, www.greenparkstation.co.uk), which runs seasonal arts events and activities. A general market is held here from Tuesday to Sunday, with a farmers' market on Saturdays.

There's no shortage of good places to eat, but one of our favourites is Blackstones Kitchen & Restaurant, on Queen Street, which offers reasonably priced meals, using locally sourced ingredients (01225 338803, www.blackstonefood.co.uk).

The broad ford

Chocolate-box pretty Bradford on Avon has been developing a bit of a social conscience of late, and boasts several environmentally sound shops and businesses. One Caring World (33 Silver Street, 01225 866590) offers affordable ethical premises and workshops for local businesses, such as the Bishopston Trading Co (01225 867485, www. bishopstontrading.co.uk). This worker's cooperative provides employment for

Somerset & Wiltshire

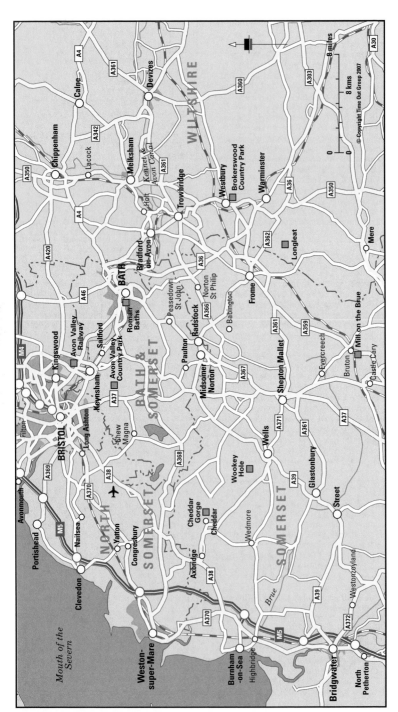

Somerset & Wiltshire

people in India and stocks organic cotton clothes, toys, bedding, pretty soft furnishings, bags and accessories. Housed in a Victorian warehouse just up the street, Ale & Porter (25 Silver Street, 01225 868919, www.aleandporter.org) is a recently refurbished visual arts space that offers exhibitions and children's workshops; the programme of black and white film classics, however, is more geared towards grown-ups.

All-natural fibres and materials – silk, cotton, hemp and ramie – are used in the clothing ranges at The Earth Collection (5 Market Street, 01225 868876, www.theearthcollection.org.uk). Offcuts are recycled into accessories, purses and bags; hand-made jewellery is also on offer. Peapod Childrenswear in the Old Post Office (10 The Shambles, 01225 863733) is good for those who prefer high-fashion children's labels, toys and accessories.

Eating has a environmentally-friendly flavour too. Cottage Cooperative Organic Vegetarian Café (One Caring World, 33 Silver Street, 01225 867444) and Cottage Wholefoods (2 Weaver's Walk, 01225 866590) have health foods, Fair Trade goods and own-baked delicacies.

At Bradford on Avon Museum, above the library on Bridge Street (01225 863280) you can trace the town's history, and admire the immaculate recreation of a 120-year-old apothecary's shop. Also worth investigating are the Saxon Church of St Lawrence; the weavers' cottages where Bradford on Avon's wealth was begun; and the unusual 17th-century stone lock-up on the bridge used to keep drunks in order. The town hosts a market every Thursday morning and a farmers' market on the third Thursday of the month.

The Kennet & Avon Cycle Route is Britain's most popular long-distance waterside cycle route. The first section passes through Bristol and Bath on the traffic-free Avon Valley cycle path and on to the canal path, past Bradford-on-Avon and on to Devizes. A number of self-guided 'Discovery Trail' walk leaflets are available from British Waterways offices (01380 722859, www.waterscape.com).

A short walk from town, Barton Farm Country Park (01225 713489, www.wiltshire.gov.uk) is a lovely place for walks, fishing, birdwatching, rowing and canoeing. Set in attractive meadowland in the Avon valley, the park runs alongside the Kennet and Avon canal. It has an immense 14th-century tithe barn and a series of medieval outbuildings, now home to tearooms and arts and crafts galleries.

This neck of the woods also has a number of shopping villages. To the north you'll find Swindon Designer Outlet (www.swindondesigneroutlet.com); south of Glastonbury in the village of Street (which also has a great lido) is Clarks' Village (www.clarksvillage.co.uk). If you still haven't found retail nirvana, Wilton Shopping Village is near Salisbury (www.wiltonshoppingvillage.co.uk).

WHERE TO STAY

If you're alarmed at the prices of some of the more stately family-friendly hotels, take comfort from the fact that most of the time you need not venture further than the end of the elegantly tree-lined paths within their grounds to find amusement.

Babington House

Babington, nr Frome, Somerset BA11 3RW (01373 812266/www.babingtonhouse.co.uk). **Rates** £395-£425. **Credit** AmEx, DC, MC, V.
Babington House may have started life as a louche country getaway for members of private drinking club Soho House, but has quickly evolved into one of Britain's best hotels and, crucially for our purposes, one of its most child-friendly. It manages what few others attain: it's a soothing retreat for unencumbered adults (well, not too soothing – the bar's open till 3am), but also a happy and welcoming place for families. This notoriously difficult feat is achieved by limiting the number of families (children can only stay in the Stable Block) and the application of a few rules (the little brutes have to keep away from the swimming pool at certain hours and some of the main house's public rooms). Anyway, it works. Spacious family rooms are a short stumble from the pool. Each has bunk beds, an XBox and plasma screens on the ground floor, and a vast bed, balcony and sunken bath upstairs. Nice touches include a disposable camera for every child and milk and a microwave in the rooms. Parents with small children (no under-ones) can drop them off at 'The Little House', a drop-in crèche; older children can play tennis or croquet, swim, watch DVDs or borrow a bike. Dotted around the grounds are wooden huts where parents can be pummelled and smeared with 'Cowshed' beauty products. Meals are served via room service, or in the main house. Breakfast is particularly splendid; you can sit on the covered terrace with sweeping views of the lawns and pond, ducks quacking at your feet, and consume huge portions of fruit, bacon, muffins, kippers, and so on. Staff are relaxed about when (and what) you eat, and how you spend your days. It's a treat.

Burcott Mill

Wookey, nr Wells, Somerset BA5 1NJ (01749 673118/www.burcottmill.com). **Rates** £50-£80. **Credit** MC, V.
This is a great hole-in-the-wall (pardon the pun) if you're planning on visiting Wookey Hole (*see p135*). You can buy some organic flour, help collect the eggs, take a tour or stay the night at

this charming working watermill, which has a large children's play area, a paddock, an orchard and animals such as goats and ducks for children to feed. There's also a tearoom, which is open from Easter to October. Baby-listening and babysitting are available on request, and high chairs and cots are provided. The Mill Lodge has an open-plan kitchen and dining area, twin bedroom, and bathroom. Upstairs is the living room, with exposed beams, natural stone walls, a double sofa bed and a galleried play area. There are various other family accommodation options that sleep up to five people. Child prices for all rooms range from £10 per night (1-10s) to £15 (11-16s).

Centurion Hotel

Charlton Lane, Midsomer Norton, Radstock, Bath, Somerset BA3 4BD (01761 417711/ www.centurionhotel.com). **Rates** £100-£120. **Credit** MC, V.
This is an affordable and child-friendly bolthole for exploring the Mendips and towns of Somerset. Always a good bet for special offers, the 44-room hotel is a favourite for weddings and conferences, but doesn't have an overly corporate air; rooms are spacious and comfortable. There's no babysitting or baby-listening, but cots are supplied free of charge. The Centurion has its own fitness centre, as well as a small and popular swimming pool stocked with inflatable toys, a paddling pool for young children, a sauna and steam room, grounds to run about in and a golf club. Cubros Conservatory restaurant looks out over the golf course and has a menu that ranges from family favourites such as steak and kidney pie to holiday treats like sea bass and moules marinière, along with a good choice of vegetarian dishes. The children's menu offers nutritious starters such as melon and fruit, soup or tagliatelle, with roast of the day, bangers and mash or pizza to follow and fruit crumble or ice-cream to finish. Plain (or just plain fussy) eaters might like the 'party plate' – a choice of sandwiches, crisps and a chocolate bar. Children's meals are inexpensive, with dishes from £1.50.

Cheddar Youth Hostel

Hillfield, Cheddar, Somerset BS27 3HN (0870 770 5760/www.yha.org.uk). **Open** *Easter-Oct* advance booking. *Nov-Mar* limited availability; phone for details. **Rates** £13.95; £9.95 under-18s; £52.50-£65 family room. **Credit** MC, V.
The highest limestone cliffs in England provide an amazing backdrop for this hostel created from a handsome Victorian residence, which sits in the centre of the village below the famous gorge. The dramatic location is perfect for climbers, walkers and explorers of all ages, and the hostel is well set up for young families. A cot is available, and there are plenty of four- and six-bed family rooms. Breakfast, packed lunches and evening meals can be provided, but there's a well-equipped kitchen for self-caterers. Bring the bikes – the hostel has a place you can stow them.

Lucknam Park Hotel

Colerne, Chippenham, Wiltshire SN14 8AZ (01225 742777/www.lucknampark.co.uk). **Rates** £245-£695. **Credit** MC, V.
Set down a long tree-lined drive in the heart of the Wiltshire countryside, Lucknam is about as peaceful as it gets – so much so you might not want to leave the grounds. The hotel is currently undergoing a massive spa refurbishment programme to extend its pool complex, sauna and treatment rooms and make the temperate pool, Jacuzzi and steam room even more luxurious. Yippee! Work is due for completion in December 2007; call before booking to check which facilities will be available. Athletic visitors can make use of the mini five-a-side football pitch, 400m 'Trim Trail' and floodlit tennis courts, or enjoy a sedate game of croquet on the west lawn. Those who fancy pedalling round the park can also borrow bikes. Activities to be booked in advance include clay pigeon shooting and hacking from the equestrian centre; golf, trout fishing and go-karting facilities are also available nearby. Rooms and suites offer spacious accommodation, with cots or extra beds for £25 a night. Note that the room rates given above don't include breakfast, which costs from £12.50-£18.50. There's no baby-listening service, but babysitters can be provided for £11 an hour. In case of rainy days, there are DVDs to borrow and board games in the public rooms. Michelin-starred chef Hywel Jones has left smart Londoners bereft by moving here, and his cooking for the Park Restaurant is the talk of the county. Sunday lunch is reasonably priced for the quality (£30), and might include velouté of broccoli, roast asparagus and soft herb gnocchi or caramelised root vegetables with blue cheese to start, followed by roast sirloin of beef, pot roast chicken with wild

Mill on the Brue. *See p135.*

mushroom cannelloni or pan fried fillet of sea bass with ratte potatoes, Cornish crab and fennel. Desserts are divine and include truffle cream chocolate fondant with basil ice-cream, lemon tart with raspberries and lemon sorbet or a selection of British farmhouse cheeses. The dining room has a smart casual dress code, and under-fives are banned in the evening. It's far more informal at the Pavillion restaurant, where kids can tuck in to cream teas, sandwiches or half portions of main menu dishes – at weekends during the summer there are popular barbecues.

The Sign of the Angel

6 Church Street, Lacock, Chippenham, Wiltshire SN15 2LB (01249 730230/www. lacock.co.uk). **Rates** £105-£155. **Credit** MC, V.
Just south of Chippenham on the A350 is the sleepy, perfectly-preserved National Trust village of Lacock (www.nationaltrust.org.uk). The Sign of the Angel is housed in a 15th-century wool merchant's house, and has been run by the Levis family since 1953. The inn has cosy log fires and oak panelling, a number of beams to duck beneath, a fine staircase and floorboards that echo a wealth of history. Lacock, like many neighbouring villages, was built on cloth, and the house is an example of the prosperity it provided. There's a small courtyard and gardens and six bedrooms, all en suite and with tea and coffee making facilities, telephones and televisions. Some of the rooms have unique beds, including a four-poster and a French antique tented bed, so enquire before booking if you'd like something special. There are no baby monitors or cots, but Z-beds can be supplied and babysitting arranged through an outside agency. Breakfasts are a high point, with eggs from the gardens, locally-cured bacon, own-made bread and Mrs Levis's special recipe marmalade. Lunches are served from Tuesday to Sunday and fireside snacks or picnics by the stream are available seasonally. The evening menu features traditional English dishes such as Lacock beef or Cornish fish served with herbs and vegetables from the kitchen garden. All the puddings are made on the premises. Everything is cooked to order, and children's tastes can be catered for – just say what you're after or want to avoid. Outside is a large, secure garden with a toy tractor for kids to trundle about on. Cottage accommodation is also available.

Street Youth Hostel

The Chalet, Ivythorn Hill, Street, Somerset BA16 OTZ (0870 770 6056/www.yha.org.uk). **Open** *March-Oct* advance bookings. *Nov-Feb* Escape To only. **Rates** £11.95; £8.95 under-18s; £42 family room. **Credit** MC, V.
This chalet-style hostel is one of the smaller, more basic members of the YHA's portfolio. That said, it's a sweet-looking little place, and a quiet retreat near the mystical Glastonbury Tor (always a giggle for hippie-spotting). It also has family rooms, which get booked up way ahead, and a cot you can borrow. If all the rooms are occupied you can camp in the grounds. The hostel is self catering only, so you'll need to stock up on groceries in Street. It's a nice little town, much loved among the less hippie-like fraternity for its shopping village, where you can buy leather school shoes from the huge Clarke's factory outlet and save yourself a packet.

Widbrook Grange Hotel

Trowbridge Road, Bradford on Avon, Wiltshire BA15 1UH (01225 864750/www. widbrookgrange.co.uk). **Rates** £120-£180. **Credit** MC, V.
The blueprint for a Georgian working farm can still be seen at Widbrook Grange, with its imposing main house flanked by stables and barns and its substantial acreage. Now a hotel, Widbrook sits surrounded by 11 acres of gardens and fields in the lush Wiltshire countryside. The grounds have a nature trail for kids to explore, and provide feeding stations for birds, badgers and other wildlife. Best of all, as far as children are concerned, is the heated indoor swimming pool, which has lots of water toys. The playroom is open at weekends, housing games tables, a TV and DVD player and board games. One of the hotel's sitting rooms also has a DVD player and Sky TV for family viewing, along with more board games. Widbrook offers families the option of large, no-smoking family rooms, or doubles with connecting doors to twin rooms. Cots and bottle warmers are provided free of charge, and baby-listening equipment and babysitting can be arranged. Facilities include TVs, video players and children's videos on request. The Kennett and Avon canal is within walking distance; from here, day boats and bikes can be hired for a day out to Bradford on Avon and beyond. Children can have high tea in the restaurant from 6-7pm. The children's menu offers simple stalwarts that even fussy eaters shouldn't sniff at: soup or macaroni cheese to start (£5), perhaps, with cheese-and-tomato pasta, lamb burger or salmon fish cakes with sautéed new potatoes (£10) for afters. Alternatively, the whole family can eat together later on. Main courses such as wild sea bass with parsnip purée or roast pork with apple and prune rosti are probably more appealing to the adult palate – but own-made lemon and thyme tagliatelle with ratatouille and parmesan or tomato and red chilli soup might pass muster. Own-made ice-creams, sorbets and puddings are lovely.

Woolley Grange Hotel

Woolley Green, Bradford on Avon, Wiltshire BA15 1TX (01225 864705/www. woolleygrangehotel.co.uk). **Rates** £110-£370. *DB&B* £180-£440. **Credit** MC, V.
The flagship hotel of the Luxury Family Hotels group may have reached its teenage years, but its charm has not diminished. It's a beautiful place: a 17th-century Jacobean manor house with 14 acres of grounds. Numerous facilities for children

include their very own clubhouse – the Woolley Bears Den, open daily and supervised from 10am-4.45pm. Club nannies are subject to Ofsted checks, and children must be signed in and out by a parent. Suitable for under-eights, the club has games, puzzles, building blocks, role-play areas, dressing up costumes, dolls' houses and a video and music chill-out zone. Calming activities such as arts and crafts and storytime encourage quieter creative play. Children can also make use of the playground, go for walks or cycle in the grounds, or have a go at croquet, outdoor table tennis and football. If the weather threatens, they can retreat indoors for some board games and a go on the PlayStation 2. In summer, guests can enjoy the gardens from the vantage point of the outdoor heated pool, surrounded by loungers; a little way off, a giant trampoline gets the kids bouncing. The Hen House is an unsupervised den for older children, with games tables and squashy sofas. Parents are allowed in if they're really good. Woolley may be kiddie paradise, but it stints not on adult facilities. Room styles range from rustic cosy to contemporary cool, and bathrooms are top of the range. Room-based Swedish massages and other treatments are optional extras. Parents choose whether to dine with their children, book a babysitter or arrange for children to eat earlier with the nannies. The restaurant uses fruit and vegetables from the hotel's organic garden: a typical menu could yield herb soup with crème fraiche or slow-roast pork belly for starters, then Wiltshire lamb with anchovy and caper stuffing, Cornish monkfish or a pear, walnut and blue cheese risotto. Fruit salad with mango sorbet, baked chocolate tart or lemon posset with vanilla cream and shortbread are the finishing touches.

WHERE TO EAT & DRINK

The Bear

6-10 Wellsway, Bath, Somerset BA2 3AQ (01225 425795). **Meals served** noon-9pm daily. **Main courses** £6.45-£8.95. **Credit** MC, V.
You can hardly miss the big polar bear perched on the roof of this cheery pub. Completely refurbished in 2006, the Bear now has a more spacious dining area. The extensive menu features Italian, Indian and Tex Mex dishes, as well as the usual pub staples such as fish and chips, burgers, sausage and mash, pies and roasts. Junior choices such as tomato soup and twisty pasta can be ordered from the children's menu (£3-£4), but small portions from the main menu can also be arranged. Children are welcome until 8pm.

Cocoa House

23 Union Street, Bath, Somerset BA1 1RS (01225 444030). **Open** 9.30-5.30pm Mon-Fri; 9.30am-6pm Sat; 11am-5pm Sun. **Main courses** £3.95-£6.95. **Credit** MC, V.
The children will never forgive you if you don't give this establishment a whirl. Owned by Cadbury's and formerly known as the Cadbury

Café, it's chocolate heaven, with chocolate tart, fondue, cheesecake and ice-cream on the menu. But rest assured, there's more savoury fare on offer. Choose from own-made soup (leek or carrot and coriander, for instance), sandwiches, full English breakfasts and hot snacks. The CocoCubs menu costs £4.50 for two courses and a drink, offering simple comfort food staples such as fish finger sarnies or cheese and beans on toast, with sorbet or ice-cream to round things off nicely.

George Inn

4 West Street, Lacock, Wiltshire SN15 2LH (01249 730263). **Meals served** noon-2pm, 6-9.30pm daily. **Main courses** £8.95-£14.50. **Credit** MC, V.
The George is as historic as the pretty village of Lacock itself; it dates back to the 14th century and has low beams and a lovely old medieval fireplace. Look out for treadwheel built into the wall; traditionally a little dog was tethered to the wheel and made to run in circles, thus turning the meat on a spit. We're not joking – see for yourself. Today the excellent Sunday roasts are cooked in a more conventional manner. The food is pub grub with plenty of child-friendly choices, from simple sausages to more exciting seafood specialities and pasta favourites. There's also a children's menu (£3.50, not including drinks), with scampi, roast chicken breast with boiled potatoes and gravy, and battered chicken fillets with chips, potatoes or waffles, plus vegetables or salad. A scoop of vanilla ice-cream can be had for £1, and a child-sized portion of a pudding from the main menu is £2. Adults are enamoured of the Wadworth's fine ales – perfect with a ploughman's lunch. There's a dedicated family dining area towards the back of the inn and outside tables for clement weather.

Lock Inn Café

48 Frome Road, Bradford on Avon, Wiltshire BA15 1LE (01225 868068/www. thelockinn.co.uk). **Meals served** 8.45am-9.30pm daily. **Main courses** £4.95-£13. **Credit** MC, V.
The Lock Inn hires bikes, including tandems and trailer buggies, and canoes licensed for use on any British Waterways navigations. Its delightful waterside café makes sure you take in sufficient fuel for your boat or bike trip. Big appetites relish the Boatman's breakfast – bacon, egg, smoked sausage, black pudding, beans, mushrooms, chips or fried potatoes, plus toast or fried bread. Children of ten and under can have pasta with meatballs or vegetarian bolognese, a cheeseburger and chips or the usual suspects of egg, sausage, fish fingers or chicken nuggets served with beans and chips, all of which cost under £4. Alternatively, there's a huge variety of sandwiches, salads, jacket potatoes and 'things on toast' to fill up on. The café has a cheerful atmosphere with hanging baskets and picnic tables under shady willows, with further seating on board a boat on the canal.

Longleat. *See p135.*

Sally Lunn's Old English Tea House

4 North Parade Passage, Bath, Somerset BA1 1NX (01225 461634/www.sallylunns.co.uk). **Meals served** 10am-9.30pm Mon-Thur; 10am-10pm Fri, Sat; 11am-9.30pm Sun. **Main courses** £3.98-£9.50. **Credit** MC, V.

It's a bit of a squash packing the family into these diminutive tearooms, but Sally Lunn's does serve exceedingly good buns. The tables are squeezed into the oldest house in Bath, and the somewhat restricted space might necessitate perching in a dark corner on the lower floor. A museum in the basement shows the kind of kitchen Sally would have used when she invented her special recipe here back in 1680. A French refugee, Sally brought her Gallic bread-making skills to Bath and caused quite a stir with her buns, which could accompany both sweet and savoury dishes. We would rather see a whole bun on our plate (servings are half a bun), expecially as the delicacy, served with jam, clotted cream and tea, is a bit pricey at over £5 – but that's Bath for you, unfortunately. Nevertheless, Sally's is a nice place to stop for afternoon tea and a bit of local spice.

Six Bells

33 High Street, Colerne, Wiltshire SN14 8DD (01225 742413/www.sixbells.biz). **Meals served** 7-9pm Tue-Thur; 7-9.30pm Fri, Sat. **Main courses** £8-£14. **Credit** MC, V.

There's no shortage of winsome villages on the Wiltshire/Somerset borders. Colerne, within strik-ing distance from Lucknam Park, is a little more workaday than Castle Combe but just as rewarding for its lovely country walks and heartening lunches. This very family-friendly pub has a big beer garden for children to run about in, and a menu that features pizzas in child and adult sizes, jacket potatoes and salads, as well as more elaborate meat and fish mains at very reasonable prices. Fill up on beef and mushroom pie with new potatoes and vegetables, substantial ploughman's lunches and sizeable plates of fish and chips. A pizza delivery service is also available.

White Hart Inn

Ford, nr Chippenham, Wiltshire SN14 8RP (01249 782213). **Meals served** noon-9.30pm Mon-Sat; noon-9pm Sun. **Main courses** £7.95-£16.95. **Credit** MC, V.

This charming 16th-century former coaching inn sits beside a brook close to the tranquil village of Castle Combe, which was used as the setting for the 1960s film version of *Dr Doolitle*. The pub offers accommodation, and has a courtyard garden with big sun umbrellas for summer dining and a cosy interior with a wood-burning stove for when the weather gets colder. The inn does bar snacks and meals and has a children's menu, with mains of cod and chips, pasta, chicken or steak and chips for around £4.50. The main menu offers sea bass, oven baked monkfish, steak medallions in creamy peppercorn sauce or own-made pie and new potatoes.

PLACES TO SEE, THINGS TO DO

Avon Valley Country Park

Pixash Lane, Keynsham, Bath, Somerset BS31 1TS (0117 986 4929/www.avonvalley countrypark.co.uk). **Open** *Play Barn* Apr-Oct 10am-5pm daily. Nov-Mar 10am-5pm Sat, Sun. *Park* Apr-Nov; phone or check website for details. **Admission** *Play Barn* £3.50; phone for details of park admission. **No credit cards.**

This park has exactly the right ingredients for a fun family day out, including a large wooden play area with slides, tunnels, rope bridges and lookout posts, animals, such as guinea pigs and rabbits to pet, all sorts of rare breeds of cattle and sheep to reminisce over, landscaped picnic and barbecue areas, a café, boating, a miniature railway, tractor rides and quad bikes. The huge, colourful indoor play barn for under-12s has soft play areas, crawl tunnels, a tots play area and the best slides for miles around.

Avon Valley Railway

Bitton Station, Bath Road, Bitton, Bristol, South Gloucestershire BS30 6HD (0117 932 5538/www.avonvalleyrailway.org). **Open** varies; phone for details. **Fares** £5.50; £4.50 concessions; £4 3-16s; £15 family (2+2); free under-3s. *Thomas Days* £8.50; £5 3-16s; free under-3s. **Credit** MC, V.

Somerset & Wiltshire

Steam trains run most Sundays between April and October on the Mangotsfield to Bath Green Park branch of the old Midland Railway. Celebrities turn up on high days and holidays – *Postman Pat* and the much-loved twice-yearly *Thomas the Tank Engine* events are popular with families. Refreshments and snacks are available at the main station in Bitton (between Bristol and Bath), where there's also a picnic area, souvenir shop and children's play area.

Brokerswood Country Park

Brokerswood, Westbury, Wiltshire BA13 4EH (01373 822238/www.brokerswood.co.uk). **Open** *Summer* 10am-6pm daily. *Winter* 10am-4pm daily. *Railway* Easter- Oct Sat, Sun & school hols. **Admission** £3.25; £2.50 3-16s, concessions; free under-3s. *Railway* £1. **Credit** MC, V.

Families can spend a good day out taking in the narrow gauge railway, play trails, heritage centre and two adventure playgrounds – which include an undercover play area for toddlers. Stop off in the café afterwards for own-cooked food or browse in the Bramble gift shop. Outdoorsy families can opt to stay here for the duration of their holiday: there's a camping and caravan park, and lakeside barbecue grills are available for hire. The café offers breakfast, picnics, lunches and is open for evening meals and takeaways; the shop sells camping gear and less essential gifts, sweets and souvenirs. Early booking is advised.

Cheddar Gorge

Cheddar, Somerset BS27 3QF (01934 742343/www.cheddarcaves.co.uk). **Open** *Jul, Aug* 10am-5.30pm daily. *June, Sept-May* 10.30am- 5pm daily. **Admission** *Explorer ticket* £14; £9 5-15s, full-time students; £37 family (2+3); free under-5s. **Credit** MC, V.

The Gorge experience is now a multi-faceted one – hence the admission price. It's expensive but worth it. Start with the open top bus ride (Apr-Sept) from the village to the caves, with guided commentary pointing out all the sights. The first cave is the million-year-old (and counting) Gough's Cave, actually a series of imposing caverns that were carved out by melt waters in the Ice Age and discovered by a retired sea captain in 1890. Next is Cox's cave, discovered by a mill owner in 1837. See the 9,000-year-old skeleton found in the caves and discover what life was like in the Stone Age, gaze into the mirror pools and learn the difference between stalagtites and stalagmites. Children can then venture into the realms of fantasy, doing battle with evil sorcerers and solving the Crystal Quest – a walk-through series of caves with models and voiceovers, inspired by JRR Tolkien's honeymoon visit. The hale and hearty can climb the 274 steps of Jacob's Ladder and take pictures from the lookout tower at the top. Children's audioguides are available and there are plenty of shiny souvenirs to be had in the shop. An on-site café overlooks the gorge.

HorseWorld

Staunton Manor Farm, Staunton Lane, Whitchurch, nr Keynsham, Bath, Somerset BS14 0QJ (01275 540173/www. horseworld.org.uk). **Open** *Easter-Sept* 10am-6pm daily. *Oct-Dec* 10am-4pm Tue-Sun. Last admission 1hr before closing. **Admission** £5.75; £5.25 concessions; £4.75 3-15s; £19.50 family (2+2); free under-3s. **Credit** MC, V.

Guided tours are now running on the last Saturday of the month due to popular demand at this haven for all things equine. The main purpose of the centre is for the rescue, rehabilitation and re-homing of animals. There are plenty of different horses to meet, from the lofty Shires to little Shetland ponies, as well as resident donkeys, goats, sheep, ducks, rabbits and pigs. The complex also houses a play barn, straw dens and an adventure playground.

Lacock Abbey, Fox Talbot Museum and Lacock village

High Street, Lacock, Chippenham, Wiltshire SN15 2LG (01249 730459/www. nationaltrust.org.uk). **Open** *Museum* Nov-late Feb 11am-4pm Sat, Sun. 24 Feb-Oct 11am-5.30pm daily. *Grounds & cloisters* 24 Feb-Oct 11am-5.30pm daily. *Abbey* 24 Mar-Oct 1-5.30pm Mon, Wed-Sun. Last admission 30mins before closing. **Admission** (NT) *Abbey, museum, cloisters & grounds* £8.30; £4.10 5-17s; £21.20 family (2+2) free under-5s. *Garden, cloisters & museum* £5.10; £2.50 5-17s; £12.90 family (2+2); free under-5s. **Credit** MC, V.

Dripping with history, this medieval cloistered abbey and the 13th-century Lacock village are a favoured location for films, including the Harry Potter series, *Pride and Prejudice, Moll Flanders* and *Emma*. The abbey had been converted into a country house by the time William Henry Fox Talbot embarked on his pioneering photographic experiments in the 19th century, and the building now houses a museum dedicated to his work. Children are given a guide and quiz trail to follow during school holidays, but they may prefer to escape all the questions and make straight for the playground adjacent to the site. Aside from his photographic discoveries, Fox Talbot's other consuming passion was for plants, and the abbey's newly restored botanic gardens are a restful spot in which to use your own camera.

Longleat

Warminster, Wiltshire BA12 7NW (01985 844400/www.longleat.co.uk). **Open** *Safari Park* Mid Feb-Oct. Times vary for all attractions; phone or check website for details. **Admission** *All attractions* £20; £16 3-14s; free under-3s. *Safari park only* £11; concessions, £8 3-14s; free under-3s. All other attractions individually priced; see website for details. **Credit** AmEx, MC, V.

There's so much to see at Longleat that the big question is whether you can fit it all into one day.

You can – but only with a bit of careful planning. The grounds and gardens are bristling with attractions; children rate the massive adventure castle complex with its battlements, gate tower and fortress very highly. Be warned – they'll need a towel and change of clothes for the Splashpad area. The Blue Peter maze, hedge maze, steam railway, butterfly garden, pets' corner and an old mine inhabited by Egyptian fruit bats also get a thumbs-up from young children. Infants go a bundle on the *Postman Pat* village, motion simulator and paddle boats. Oh, and did we mention there were animals? Longleat is home to a tiger, two species of camel, deer, Canadian timber wolves, white rhinos, giraffes, zebra, lions and, of course, those mischievous rhesus monkeys. One way to ensure you see the best bits is to join a dedicated guided tour of the park in a 4x4 vehicle. You get to admire the animals at close quarters and learn about them from a park warden, though it doesn't come cheap (£58 per adult and children aged over six, including one guidebook per family group). There are tours of the opulent house almost all year round; the highlights are the great hall, the state dining room and the dress corridor, where robes and gowns are on display. Shops include Lady Bath's souvenir shop and an aspirational cookware and comestibles shop, located down in the Victorian kitchens. There's a café for the obligatory cream tea and the Wessex Pavilion restaurant for hot meals, pancakes and pastries.

Mill on the Brue

Trendle Farm, Bruton, Somerset BA10 0BA (01749 812307/www.millonthebrue.co.uk). **Open** *mid Jan-Nov* 9am-2.30pm daily. **Admission** varies; phone for details. **Credit** MC, V.

If you long to visit stately homes and take country walks in sedate fashion but the children yearn for action, contact the Mill. It's a farm-based activity centre that runs group activities and summer camps for eight- to fifteen-year-olds, and the energetic staff organise the sort of indoor and outdoor challenges and activities that make the average parent want to go and have a nice lie down. A founding member of the British Activity Holiday Association, this family-run, not-for-profit organisation has been been educating and inspiringchildren and adults for nearly 25 years. There's canoeing, vertiginous zip wire adventures, crazy Olympics, archery, camping, high ropes, climbing, crafts, games, barbecues and concerts.

Norwood Rare Breeds Farm

Bath Road, Norton St Philip, Bath, Somerset BA2 7LP (01373 834356/www. norwoodfarm.co.uk). **Open** *Mar-Sept* 10.30am-5pm daily. **Admission** £5; £4.50 concessions; £3.50 3-16s; free under-3s. **Credit** MC, V.

More than 30 different rare breeds live the life of Reilly at Norwood, including pigs, sheep and horses. Local-ish breeds to look out for include

handsome, glossy Red Poll cattle, Exmoor ponies and Wiltshire Horn sheep to name a few. But this place has further strings to its bow: it's also an exemplary organic farm and environmental education centre, which puts into action all the green practices we read about. The hope is that their enthusiasm might rub off on visitors, and it's certainly fascinating to visit the recycling plant and see the wind turbines in motion. Afterwards you can enjoy farm produce in the shop and café.

Somerset Rural Life Museum

Abbey Farm, Chilkwell Street, Glastonbury, Somerset BA6 8DB (01458 831197/www.somerset.gov.uk/museums). **Open** *Apr-Nov* 10am-5pm Tue-Fri; 2-6pm Sat, Sun. *Nov-Mar* 10am-5pm Tue-Sat. **Admission** free.

This is a gentle way to learn about the world of the countryman in days of yore. The exhibition in the farmhouse depicts the social and domestic life of Victorian Somerset via the story of farm worker John Hodges. In the main museum building, a 14th-century barn that once belonged to Glastonbury Abbey, there are displays of farm implements and machinery, as well as exhibits on time-honoured local activities such as willow weaving, peat digging and cider making.

Wookey Hole Caves and Papermill

Wookey Hole, Wells, Somerset BA5 1BB (01749 672243/www.wookey.co.uk). **Open** *Apr-Oct* 10am-5pm daily. *Nov-Mar* 10am-4pm daily. **Admission** £10.90; £8.50 4-14s; concessions; £34 family (2+2); free under-4s. **Credit** MC, V.

Walking with dinosaurs is only part of the attraction to a visit to Wookey, but for most under-tens the stegosaurus, diplodocus and mighty T-Rex are another great reason for heading Wookey-ward. There are 20 life-size models of dinosaurs to encounter. The spooky caves are beautifully illuminated, and guides up the ante with tales of the witch (can you spot her?) and what she might be brewing up in her kitchen. There's an outdoor fairy garden, an indoor pirate play zone for firing foam missiles out of air cannons at unsuspecting landlubbers, a hilarious mirror maze and a collection of operational Victorian penny arcade machines. The hand-made paper mill and museum of early caving equipment complete the trip. Seasonal special events include spook nights during Halloween; Santa's grotto twinkles from late November. A little to the west of the more touristy Wookey lies the beautiful Ebbor Gorge. Only accessible by foot, this area, the amazing limestone gorge, with Neolithic caves, surrounded by enchanting woodland is owned by the National Trust and the nature reserve is managed by English Nature. There are marked trails to follow, and the views to the Somerset Levels and Glastonbury Tor are not to be missed.

South Devon's Riviera

The cream of Devonshire down South Hams way.

Officially, the 'English Riviera' covers the softly undulating stretch of Devon coastline between the River Dart and the Exe Estuary – an area known for its palm trees and mild microclimate rather than its gambling opportunities. Extending downwards to the South Hams, this is glorious seaside, where the warm waters won't turn the children blue. In a period when climate change makes a family holiday in this balmy region a real contender, the past is still with us in South Devon.

Historically it is a fascinating region, with many Domesday Book mentions. The area also creates a yearning for the more recent past – the kind of holidays you used to have, or even the ones you wish you'd had, as portrayed by our gurus Cath Kidston, Boden et al, in a world where everything was simpler, more wholesome and had a 1950s print.

Totnes

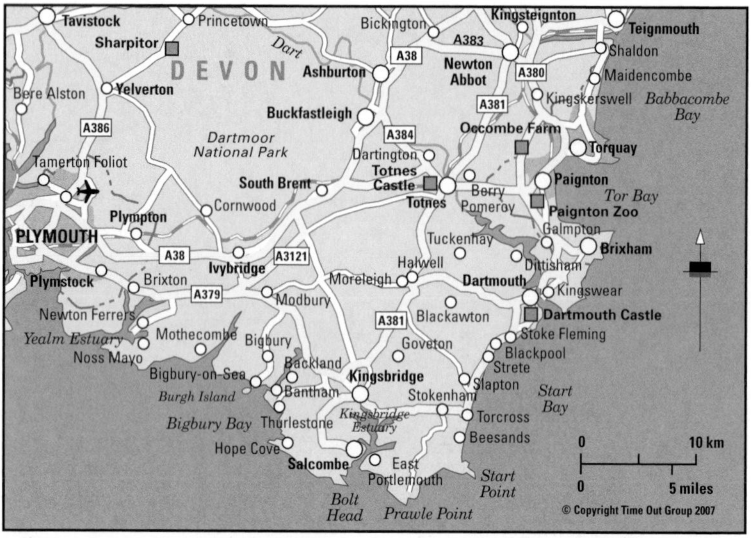
Tavistock
Princetown
Bickington
Kingsteignton
Teignmouth
Sharpitor
Dart
A38
A383
Shaldon
DEVON
Ashburton
Newton Abbot
A380
Maidencombe
Bere Alston
Yelverton
Kingskerswell
Babbacombe Bay
A381
Buckfastleigh
A386
A384
Occombe Farm
Dartmoor National Park
Torquay
Tamerton Foliot
Dartington
Totnes Castle
Totnes
Paignton
South Brent
Berry Pomeroy
Tor Bay
Cornwood
Paignton Zoo
Plympton
PLYMOUTH
Galmpton
Tuckenhay
Brixham
A38
A3121
Ivybridge
Halwell
Dittisham
Plymstock
Brixton
Moreleigh
Dartmouth
A379
Modbury
Kingswear
Newton Ferrers
A381
Blackawton
Dartmouth Castle
Yealm Estuary
Mothecombe
Bigbury
Stoke Fleming
Noss Mayo
Goveton
Blackpool
Backland
Strete
Bigbury-on-Sea
Kingsbridge
Burgh Island
Bantham
Stokenham
Slapton
Start Bay
Bigbury Bay
Thurlestone
Kingsbridge Estuary
Torcross
Beesands
Hope Cove
0
10 km
Salcombe
East Portlemouth
Start Point
0
5 miles
Bolt Head
Prawle Point
© Copyright Time Out Group 2007

One of the big attractions of the area is undoubtedly the food. Delicious seafood comes as standard, and there are a number of major local organic producers such as Luscombe juices and Burts Chips, as well as myriad access to smaller operations through restaurants and cafés. It's hard not to eat well, and the phrase 'locally sourced' appears on many a menu.

Finally, there are many chances to enjoy nature in the area – well documented walks and cycle paths galore, as well as the sea and all the fun associated with it.

Brutus started it

Dartmouth and Totnes are the two key towns of interest, with a rich history and current importance. Smaller developments cluster on the Dart and the Kingsbridge estuary, such as delightful Salcombe.

Described by Pevsner Architectural Guides as 'one of the most rewarding small towns in England' and more recently voted one of the 'top ten funkiest towns in the world', Totnes obviously has enduring charms. Originally a market town, it's a vibrant centre and the self-styled natural health capital of the West Country, so attracts creative types. According to legend, Totnes was named by a young chap called Brutus in around 1200 BC, who landed on this giant-filled island when heading home after the Trojan wars. The Trojans got rid of the giants and named the island 'Britain', after their leader. Check out the Brutus stone, set into the pavement beside No.51 Fore Street. Regardless of this particular legend, the known history of Totnes begins in the tenth century, when it was a walled borough founded by the Saxon kings to defend the area from Viking attacks. The name means the fort ('tot') on the ridge of land ('ness'). After the Norman conquest Totnes belonged to a knight called Judhel, who was responsible for building the castle and priory. Totnes Castle is considered the best-preserved motte and bailey construction in Devon, and affords great views over the town and the river.

Totnes prospered in the Tudor period, largely thanks to the export of Dartmoor tin. A number of merchants' houses from this period remain in Fore Street, though many are hidden behind more recent façades selling all sorts of goodies. The Elizabethan Museum is one such. (70 Fore Street, 01803 863821, www.devonmuseums.net). It's fascinating to take a wander down the central conservation area of Totnes, browsing chakra books and slurping your latte, reflecting on the feet that have trod these stones before yours.

The town's legacy of Elizabethan prosperity is celebrated on Tuesdays throughout the summer, when local traders dress up in period costume and serve as usual. The Totnes Orange Race in August (*see p333*) commemorates a visit by Drake in the 1580s. A pleasant way to admire the lie of the land around Totnes is to take the South Devon railway (0845 345 1420, www.southdevonrailway.org), which follows a scenic route beside the River Dart between Buckfastleigh and Totnes.

Totnes has some restaurants – more 40 at last count. As well as those we review on p144, we recommend Grey's tea shop (The Narrows, 01803 866369) for cream teas. If you want to put together your own picnic try Food for Thought boulangerie (10 The Plains, 01803 862071) or try the Riverford Farm Shop (38 High Street, 01803 86395) for locally sourced produce. Ticklemores (1 Ticklemore Street, 01803 865926) is renowned for cheese. The Good Intent (30 Lower Street, 01803 832157), home of the Dartmouth ice-cream company, also sells tortilla wraps and cream teas.

Check out the old market on Tuesday and Friday for more lunching ideas and have a giggle at the prices on the walls behind, where potatoes cost just one penny a bag.

From Totnes, follow signs for Dartmouth and Kingsbridge (Kingsbridge's Sorley Tunnel Adventure Park in Kingsbridge, 01548 854078, www.sorleytunnel.com, is a great entertainer) and take a turning through Tuckenhay, a sleepy community that was once an important industrial centre, home to a paper mill, lime kilns and busy quays. It was the first place to have gas lighting – even before London. Now a tranquil riverside retreat, it is home to two famous inns. The 18th-century Maltsters Arms (Bow Creek, 01803 732350), once owned by Keith Floyd, has a quayside BBQ. The Watermans Arms (Bow Bridge, 01803 732214), has riverside tables.

Pass through Tuckenhay and continue on to Dittisham ('Ditsum' to the locals). This is a tiny yachting village, with narrow lanes running down to the Dart. Dittisham plums were once famous; there's still a plum tree in practically every garden. The narrow lanes around here are perilous to negotiate by car – parking at the Ham car park allows you to exercise tots at a pleasant open space with a reasonable playground.

Walk to the right to reach the quay, or take the signed footpath behind the swings and follow the green lanes up and down again. The Anchorstone Café (Manor Street, 01803 722365) is a fine place for a bite to eat. Open year-round for breakfast and lunch, in peak season it stays open until 8pm on Fridays and Saturdays. There's a pleasant terrace for sitting out and glugging a glass of rosé, with fishy main dishes such as Caesar salad with local scallops and pancetta, or fish 'n' chips. The café is also home to the Dittisham Sailing School, for sailing lessons and boat hire. A quiet beer or bite to eat can be had at the Ferryboat (Manor Street, 01803 722368), while children amuse themselves crabbing from the jetty in front. Note the bell – to summon the ferryman to take you across to Greenway Quay, a woodland garden where Agatha Christie's house hides. It is due to open to the public in 2008.

Paignton is much changed from its first mention in the Domesday book. As you drift from the multi-storey car park past Aldi, towards myriad tacky souvenir shops, Devon chic seems a million miles away.

The town's redeeming feature, however, is the nicely landscaped Paignton Zoo Environmental Park (Totnes Road, 01803 697500, www.paigntonzoo.org.uk), with its rare black rhinos, white rhinos, elephants, giraffes and beautifully planted gardens, where rare tender plants thrive in the balmy climate. Paignton was much in the news in January 2007 as the BBC trained its cameras on heavily pregnant black rhino Sita awaiting her happy event. The Paignton and Dartmouth steam railway (see p148), runs to Totnes. Nearby Dartmouth has much to offer. Take the river taxi to Dartmouth Castle (see p147) and pootle around the historic town. You might recognise the quayside from Sense and Sensibility, or even from 1970s telly classic The Onedin Line, depending on how historic you are yourself.

Beach to each

One of the most delightful attractions of the area has to be the wide variety of beautiful beaches, each with its own character and many with Blue Flag status.

The nearest beach to Dartmouth (about three miles) is glorious Blackpool Sands (www.blackpoolsands.co.uk). Signposted from Dartmouth on the A379 between Stoke Fleming and Strete, it is also accessible by the coastal path. A far cry from its northerly namesake, this Blue-

TOURIST INFORMATION

Dartmouth
The Engine House, Mayor's Avenue, Dartmouth, South Devon TQ6 9YY (01803 834224/www.discover dartmouth.com).
Devon Farm Accommodation
01271 862588/www.devonfarms.co.uk.
Discover Devon Holiday Line
0870 608 5531/
www.discoverdevon.com
Kingsbridge
The Quay, Kingsbridge, South Devon TQ7 1HS (01548 853195/ www.kingsbridgeinfo.co.uk).
Salcombe
Council Hall, Market Street, Salcombe, South Devon TQ8 8DE (01548 843927/ www.salcombeinformation.co.uk).
Totnes
The Town Mill, Coronation Road, Totnes, South Devon TQ9 5DF (01803 863168/www.totnesinformation.co.uk).
www.southdevon.org.uk

Flagged beach has a sheltered bay and safe swimming – lifeguards are on duty during the summer. A variety of watersports are run by Lushwind Watersports (07849 758987, www.lushwind.co.uk). The Venus Café (see p145) and shop provide for all your worldly needs and for the ultimate accolade, the loos won the 'Best Beach Toilets in England' award.

The pretty village of Slapton lies about five miles south of Dartmouth, off the A379. It is home to the characterful Tower Inn (see p145). Slapton Sands is a splendid beach, with fine shingle; the stones here are just the right size and weight for successful skimming. The nature reserve behind can be walked through, or a pleasant beach walk of about one and a half miles takes you along to Torcross. Buggies might need to be pushed along the path up near the road. Kites and bikes can also be hired at Sea Breeze (see p143). Slapton and Torcross were famously used in practice for the D-Day landings; you can check out a tank that was recovered from the sea in the car park at Torcross, now a memorial to US servicemen.

From Torcross, continuing on to Beesands is a pleasant walk along the coastal path. Steep steps and heights make this unsuitable for wild toddlers or buggies though, unless you have nerves of steel and muscles to match.

More beaches abound. Follow the A381 to Thurlestone, with its two beaches. The one to the south has the view of the 'thyrled' (pierced) stone, said to be the origin of the name of the settlement. The Village Inn (01548 560382) is next door to the Thurlestone Hotel (see p144), and a good child-friendly place for a drink or meal.

From Thurlestone follow the single track road to Bantham, passing through the charming hamlet of Buckland with its biscuit tin-pretty thatched cottages. Bantham was a busy little port until the early 20th century, with sailing barges coming and going; some houses in the village incorporate timbers from wrecks in those bygone days. Nowadays there is a lovely sweep of sand, winner of a rural beach award. A short walk from the beach, the Sloop Inn (01548 560489, www.sloopatbantham.co.uk) is a 16th-century hostelry with historic smuggling connections and five en suite double rooms upstairs, two of which also have single beds and are equipped for families.

Take the B3392 from the A379 and follow signs to Burgh Island and Bigbury on Sea. Bigbury on Sea has a tremendous beach, with Blue Flag status and acres of fine sand for some top bucket and spade work. There is also windsurfing, canoeing, boogie boarding and general surf activity at the South Devon Discovery Surf School

(07813 639622, www.discoverysurf.com), which operates out of the bay. Drop by the Venus Café for an organic lunch – food can be brought down to the beach if work on sandcastles cannot stop – or the Pilchard Inn (Burgh Island, Bigbury on Sea, 01548 810514), for a baguette and a pint of Pilchard's Best. Tables outside look straight onto the beach, so you can watch the kids from above. (The opulent art deco Burgh Island hotel is open only to guests and those who pre-book to lunch or dine.)

Going south

At the mouth of the Kingsbridge estuary, Salcombe is one of the most picturesque harbours going, enjoying a beautiful setting in a warm microclimate. It is the southernmost town in the South Hams – and indeed one of the most southerly in the UK. Salcombe is sometimes likened to Nice, and certainly the approach to the town is similar (in the sunshine at least); you drive down a winding narrow road, with glimpses of the sparkling bay appearing every now and then, until you reach the pastel-shaded villas at the bottom.

Like many other small ports in south Devon, Salcombe had its own area of trading and specialised in importing exotic fruits such as pineapples from the Azores. These days you might still be able to buy a pineapple in Fore Street, though this main drag is packed with restaurants and surfy boutiques (Fat Face and friends).

Children are keen to check out Cranch's Sweet Shop (78 Fore Street, 01548 843493), which has both old fashioned and newfangled sugary horrors. The Tree House toyshop (61B Fore Street, 01548 844133) is a good source of souvenirs and fishing paraphernalia. Casse-Croûte deli in adjoining Clifton Street (10 Clifton Place, 01548 843003) has all the salads, breads and charcuterie to make a superior sort of picnic to take to one of the beaches.

Salcombe is at its bustling peak during the regatta in August, when it becomes completely gridlocked. In winter, things are much quieter – but there are plenty of chances to get out on the water pretty much all season. If you fancy a splash, go to the Island Cruising Club (Island Street, 01548 531176, www.icc-salcombe.co.uk), where you can sail a dinghy on an ad hoc basis. Speeds freaks might prefer the noisy Salcombe Powerboat School (Bartons, Island Street, 01548 842727, www.salcombepowerboats.co.uk), which offers a junior powerboat training programme for the over-eights.

Salcombe's two main beaches are North Sands and South Sands. Both have European Blue Flag status, and are an easy walk from town. When the tide is out,

Soar Mill Cove.
See p143.

North Sands is a sheltered cove, ideal for beach cricket or kite-flying. Rock pools and small inlets form their own mini-swimming pool, making this a good beach for little ones. Just behind the beach, the Winking Prawn (*see p146*) is an excellent spot for lunch or tea. Moult Farm at the other side also serves cream teas in season.

South Sands beach, water sports central, can be reached by ferry from the centre of Salcombe (call Tim Tucker on 01548 561035). Rivermaid ferries also run to what many consider the finer beach of East Portlemouth, from the ferry steps at Salcombe pier (01548 853607/853525). East Portlemouth beach can also be reached by road: take the A379 to Stokenham and follow the signs. The beach is ideal for paddling and rock pool action.

From East Portlemouth you can follow the coastal path to several beaches, including Gara Rock. A westerly path west takes you to Hope Cove, from South Sands. There are two villages here: 'Inner Hope' has a beautiful square of thatched cottages, unspoilt by development; 'Outer Hope' has the cream teas and shops.

WHERE TO STAY

By and large, this is an upmarket corner of England, and the hotels – particularly those that market themselves as family friendly – reflect this in their rates. Many families prefer the freedom of self catering; indeed, Devon is holiday cottage central, as many locals will tell you with a slight rolling of the eyes. The National Trust alone has 126 cottages in Devon and Cornwall, from follies to grand country houses (0870 458 4411, www.nationaltrustcottages.co.uk). Then there's Toad Hall Cottages (01548 853089, www.toadhallcottages.com), which looks after 225 top cottages, mainly around Kingsbridg. Coast & Country (0870 405 0530, www.coastandcountry.co.uk) has over 300 properties in and around Salcombe and Hope Cove.

For information about staying on a Devon farm, see Tourist Information, *p139*.

Café Alf Resco
Lower Street, Dartmouth, Devon TQ6 9JB (01803 835880/www.cafealfresco.co.uk). **Rates** £75-£85. *Self-catering flat* £350/wk (sleeps 6). **No credit cards**.
Year-round accommodation is offered above this extremely popular café in the heart of Dartmouth. The large en suite double (with cot) and twin bunk room would make ideal family accommodation – the bunk room has a toy box, which has done sterling service over the years. There's also a self-catering flat with a double bedroom, plus useful cooking and washing facilities. Fabulous breakfasts or brunches can be taken downstairs in the café, which has an exciting, on-holiday vibe.

MESSING ABOUT IN THE WATER

SEASIDE SAFARI

Children can spend hours dabbling about in rock pools, hoping to nab a crab or flirt with a sea squirt. The best areas to explore are rocky, with a good tidal range. Aquarium nets (from a pet shop) are better than long-sticked fishing nets, which may break. A white bucket is best for viewing. Be aware of local tides so you don't get stranded, and wear non-slip shoes.

Looking for hermit crabs is a good place to start, as they are sea squatters in random shells. You might also spot a starfish; children may know these creatures can grow another limb if one is lost, but in kindness this not an experiment to undertake. Here, too, are limpets, which cling to the rocks and seem immoveable, then suddenly come off. Always put creatures back in the same place in their rock pools once your safari is over.

SAIL AWAY

When the children are old enough to leave the beach and take to the open sea (or a benign bay) they'll need tuition from a qualified instructor. some places, like the ICC (*see below*) offer sailing holidays, short and weekend breaks with tuition or RYA courses for children and adults. Tuition and boat hire is also offered by the other oufits below.

Canoe & Kayak Adventures
12 Riverside, Totnes, South Devon TQ9 5JB (01803 866257/07738 634136).
John Hagger organises tailor-made canoeing and kayaking trips for adults and children. He's based on the River Dart at Totnes.

Island Cruising Club
28 Island Street, Salcombe, South Devon TQ8 8DP (01548 531176/www.icc-salcombe.co.uk).
ICC offers everything from half-day taster sailing lessons to longer Royal Yachting Association-accredited courses. Children aged eight or above can sail without their parents; with parental supervision, the minumum age is five.

Salcombe Dinghy Sailing
John Whitelock offers adult and family sessions, including taster sails for complete beginners. Enquiries and booking via Salcombe Tourist Information Office (*see p139*).

YHA Salcombe
Sharpitor, Salcombe, South Devon TQ8 8LW (0870 770 6016/www.yha.org.uk).
Residential courses during the summer months for children aged 12 and over, as well as a selection of courses for novices and the more experienced, from the age of eight.

South Devon's Riviera

Fingals

*Old Coombe, Dittisham, nr Dartmouth, Devon
TQ6 OJA (01803 722398/www.fingals.co.uk).*
Rates £95-£160. **Credit** MC, V.

Fingals has the feel of an English country house
with an eco-friendly twist. As you approach the
hotel, crossing the croquet lawn and hearing the
gentle thwack of tennis balls on grass court, it's
easy to imagine yourself living some heavenly
Brideshead existence, without the pomp and
snobbishness. Families have a variety of options
including their own suite/room or self-catering in
the purpose-built barn; there's no charge for
under-threes. It's a truly magical place to stay,
where children can have the freedom of the
grounds and the decor is suitably shabby chic to
allow for a few sticky fingers. A highlight is all
the kids sitting down to high tea together at the
big table, while parents idly drift around enjoying
an aperitif. Meals can also be taken a bit later en
famille, or grown ups gather round the same table
for a dinner party feel in the evening. Much of the
food is own-grown, or at least locally sourced and
organic where possible. Dinner is £30 for four
courses (£20 for children) and high tea costs £7.50.
As well as the grounds, indoor attractions include
a mini cinema for early risers and a heated pool.

Royal Castle Hotel

*The Quay, Dartmouth, Devon TQ6 9PS
(01803 833033/www.royalcastle.co.uk).*
Rates £125-£199. **Credit** MC, V.

This characterful hotel, bang in the middle
of Dartmouth, comprises two converted 17th-
century merchants' houses. Built up around an
Elizabethan courtyard, with lots of Tudor
fireplaces, priests' holes and nooks and crannies
to add to the atmosphere, the buildings have been
sensitively restored. Three of the 25 rooms
are family rooms, which can accommodate two
adults and two children. Children are welcome at
the newly revamped restaurant on the first floor,
which majors in fish and can serve up smaller
portions if required. Simpler bar food is also
available in one of the two bars.

The Royal Seven Stars Hotel

*The Plains, Totnes, Devon TQ9 5DD (01803
862125/www.royalsevenstars.co.uk).* **Rates**
£99-£130. **Credit** MC, V.

Daniel Defoe apparently once enjoyed the hospitality of this 17th-century coaching inn. It has been
modernised a bit since he stayed, however, most
recently in 2006, when the hotel changed hands.
There are now 16 attractive, en suite rooms (some
with jacuzzi), with a fresh take on traditional style
using original fabrics. Two rooms are specially
designed to accommodate children. One of these
is a lovely big triple room, with a double bed and
a single; a cot or an extra Z-bed can be added if
required for a small extra charge. A large Premier
double room will also allow an extra bed or cot.
Bistro style food is served all day long at the tables
outside, allowing flexibility for family meals.

Salcombe YHA Hostel

*Sharpitor, Salcombe, Devon TQ8 8LW (0870
770 6016/www.yha.org.uk).* **Open** Easter-Oct.
Nov-Easter 'Escape To' only. **Rates** £14;
£9.95 under-18s; £57 4-bed family room.
Credit MC, V.

This solid Edwardian National Trust property,
set in six acres of gorgeous gardens, has been
converted for use by the Youth Hostels
Association. Only minutes away from the
beaches, it provides information and booking for
sailing courses. Family rooms that sleep four or
six people are available. There's a diner for meals
and a packed lunch service; alternatively, families
can use the self-catering kitchen. Note that this
hostel is spring and summer opening; from
November to Easter, you can only stay here if you
book the entire place out as part of a large group.

Seabreeze

*Torcross, Slapton Sands, Devon TQ7 2TQ
(01548 580697/www.seabreezebreaks.com).*
Rates £60-£90. *Apartment* £200-£500/wk.
Credit MC, V.

At the end of the short promenade at Torcross,
this picture-perfect little beachside café has rooms
to rent as well as bikes and kayaks for hire. The
simply furnished rooms overlooking the sea are
particularly pretty and incredibly peaceful, and
under-12s are accommodated free. Breakfast is
taken downstairs in the homely dining room.
At the beachside café, eats of the panini/latte/
smoothie/ice-cream school are available: the outside tables with umbrellas are a great spot to hang
out and be at one with the world. There is also a
self-catering apartment.

Soar Mill Cove Hotel

*Malborough, nr Salcombe, Devon TQ7 3DS
(01548 561566/www.soarmillcove.co.uk).*
Rates £160-£280. **Credit** MC, V.

This family-oriented hotel has a very special
location, surrounded by National Trust coastline
and with its own access to the cove – hence the
name. All 22 rooms have their own terrace, and
are traditionally furnished. The hotel is small
enough to allow truly personal service, and is not
at all snooty. Younger children (under-15s) can
have a simple high tea between 5-6pm, then settle
down in bed or watch a movie from the DVD and
video library while their parents get stuck in to a
gourmet supper in the dining room. Older children
are welcome to join parents at supper, served from
7.30-9pm. Overall, the food is excellent and
well-sourced, with supplements on the more
expensive items on the menu. The dining room
has a beautiful view of the sun setting over the
cove. The hotel is all on one level, so it could be an
ideal choice for three-generation holidays. Family
friendly facilities include indoor and outdoor
pools, pitch 'n' putt, a grass tennis court and a free
guest laundry. Outside is a play area with a
climbing frame and swings; for rainy days, there's
a games cupboard.

South Devon's Riviera

Thurlestone Hotel

Thurlestone, nr Kingsbridge, Devon TQ7 3NN (01548 560382/www.thurlestone.co.uk). **Rates** £120-£238. **Credit** MC, V.

This large hotel is still family owned after more than 100 years in the business, and checks all the boxes for family friendly fun. As well as the Décleor beauty salon for yummy mummy and golf for daddy, kids have their own games room and playroom, with the bonus of the supervised 'Dolphin Club' for an hour each morning. At this point, parents might take advantage of the squash, badminton or golf facilities, or just slump by the outdoor pool in its gorgeous setting. Traditionally English en-suite rooms have every accoutrement, including fluffy robes for all. There's high tea for the smaller ones, fine dining for those in jackets and a baby-listening service for the tinies; under-twos stay free of charge. Enjoy pre-dinner cocktails on the terrace (kids have their own selection), or try the poolside bistro or the Village Inn for more informal family meals.

WHERE TO EAT & DRINK

Note that a number of cafés are only open in the evening during high season, and if your children like to eat between 5pm and 6pm you may be caught out, as several places stop serving during that tricky hour.

Crabshell Inn

Embankment Road, Kingsbridge, South Devon TQ7 IJZ (01548 852345). **Meals served** noon-2.30pm, 6-9pm daily. **Main courses** £5.75-£22.50. **Credit** MC, V.

Apparently, this traditional pub on the edge of Kingsbridge was originally a bathing hut for the local barracks. Now a free house, it offers an extensive menu, mostly fishy. Seafood platters, sandwiches and a list of daily specials, such as cod and prawn mornay or beef and ale pie, should cater for most tastes. Tables outside have a lovely view onto the estuary and the activity there. Children are welcome in all areas, and there's quite a variety of reasonably priced food, mostly of the pizza-and-scampi variety, on their menu (£2.50-£4), with numerous extras available.

Dusters

51 Fore Street, Salcombe, Devon TQ8 8JE (01548 842634). **Meals served** *Aug* 6.30-9.45pm daily. *Sept, Oct, Dec-July* 7-9pm Mon, Thur-Sun. Closed Nov. **Main courses** £12-£19.50. **Credit** MC, V.

Booking is advisable at this unpretentious bistro – particularly on Sundays, when there are jazz sessions. The owners can provide high chairs and warmly welcome children, but don't believe in separate chips-with-everything menus for them – there's no deep fat fryer on the premises. Instead, they can have pasta, simply grilled fish or meat plus vegetables, or a smaller portion of any dish on the adult menu for half the price. Seasonal, local produce is the focus here, so the dishes scrawled up on the blackboard are constantly changing. Always in evidence, though, are locally-reared beef, pan fried scallops with tomato and herb salsa and crab bisque. Save room for afters, everything on the pudding menu is own-made, including the gloriously creamy ice-cream.

Oyster Shack

Milburn Orchard Farm, Stakes Hill, Bigbury, South Devon TQ7 4BE (01548 810876/ www.oystershack.co.uk). **Meals served** *Summer* 9am-9pm daily. *Winter* 9am-9pm Tue-Sun. **Main courses** £8.95-£15.25. **Credit** MC, V.

Although it's off the beaten track, this place is always full, thanks to its relaxed, Mediterranean vibe and sweet service, as well as super fresh shellfish. It's lovely to lick garlicky fingers while sitting out front under the tarpaulin. Expect dishes like local crab salad with warm bread, onion and cucumber raita and aïoli (half: £8.95, whole: £16.50). A kids' menu is in the pipeline for late 2007, but dishes like whitebait and homemade aïoli, served with warm homemade bread (£4.95), hit the spot in the meantime. A full winelist is now available, though you can still BYO at lunch. A new branch of the Oyster Shack is due to open in Salcombe in spring 2007, with a family restaurant, Jack Spratt's, upstairs as this guide went to press. Telephone the Bigbury branch for details.

Pig Finca Café

The Old Bakery, Kingsbridge, South Devon TQ7 1JD (01548 855777/www.pigfinca.com). **Meals served** 10am-3pm, 6-9pm Tue-Sun. **Main courses** £6.50-£12.95. **Credit** MC, V.

Opposite the quay and set back from the street, two doors down from the Ship, this little place is a hidden gem. There's a lively Spanish vibe, with young staff and cool music, and the food has a Spanish bias with North African and Middle Eastern overtones. Courtyard tables back and front allow you to seek *sol* or *sombra*, whatever your preference. There's a wide ranging day and evening menu, plus specials; although there's no children's menu as such, staff can knock up some pasta or serve up half portions at half the menu price. Meze platters, either mixed or vegetarian – including delights such as own-made houmous and artichoke hearts – are a good choice for grazing. Pizzas are also popular.

Start Bay Inn

Torcross, South Devon TQ7 2TQ (01548 580553/www.startbayinn.co.uk). **Meals served** *Summer* 11.30am-2.15pm, 6-10pm daily. *Winter* 11.30am-2pm, 6-9.30pm daily. **Main courses** £5.80-£14.90. **Credit** MC, V.

This 14th-century pub, at the start of the promenade at Torcross, does excellent fish and chips. In warm weather the tables outside are the place to be, though there's plenty of/ indoor

Willow. See p146.

seating too. Drinks are ordered at the lower bar – the only area where children are excluded – and food in the upper bar. A good value junior menu (£4.30) includes an excellently battered fish with good chips, naturally, and ice-cream to follow. Ploughman's, fresh dover sole and fish platters are other options. The landlord's dad (formerly the landlord here) dives for scallops, and fishermen from the village supply the rest. It's a family business with friendly service and good food. What more could you want?

The Tower Inn
Church Road, Slapton, South Devon TQ7 2PN (01548 580216/www.thetowerinn.com). **Meals served** *Summer* noon-2pm, 7-9pm daily. *Winter* noon-2pm, 7-9pm Tue-Sat. **Main courses** £9.95-£18.50. **Credit** MC, V.
This 14th-century inn in historic Slapton is well regarded among locals, both for its atmosphere and its adventurous ways with local fare. Depending on the weather, a dish such as smoked haddock, mozzarella and spring onion fishcakes or beef wellington can be eaten in the delightful walled garden, or indoors under low-ceilinged interconnecting rooms. The 'Little Bees' children's menu offers pretty standard kiddy food; pizza, burger and chips or pasta for £5.50, not including a drink or pudding. A good range of local beers is available, including Butcombe Bitter and St Austell Tribute.

Venus Café
Branches on the beaches at Blackpool Sands, Bigbury on Sea and East Portlemouth (01803 833338/www.venuscompany.co.uk). **Meals served** *Mar-June* 9am-6pm daily. *Sept, Oct* 10am-5pm Mon-Fri; 9am-5pm Sat, Sun. *Nov-Feb* 10am-4pm daily. **Main courses** £4.50-£7.95. **Credit** MC, V.
Mostly local, organic produce makes this a very desirable spot for the yummy mummy beach set. Organic fresh coffee, baguettes and panini and dishes of the day are among the offerings at the friendly chain of beachside cafés. Only one of the branches, at Blackpool Sands, is open for alfresco dining (6.30-9pm from end of May to the end of September; the reservations number is 01803 839686). All branches do a children's lunch box, which cost from £3.95 and contain, for example, a local ham and cheese sandwich, Burt's no-salt crisps, slices of organic cucumber, organic OJ and an organic yogurt. Sorted. Your conscience can be boosted yet further in the knowledge that you're contributing to local environmental projects supported by Venus, such as the Venus beach wildlife fund. The company has won a number of awards, including one for responsible tourism. Now that's what we call civilised.

Victoria Inn
Fore Street, Salcombe, South Devon TQ8 8BU (01548 842604/www.victoriainnfalcombe.com). **Meals served** noon-2.30pm, 6-9pm daily. **Main courses** £8.25-£15.95. **Credit** MC, V.
Garden tables and a rooftop outdoor area are the Victoria's main draw for families, in a town where space is a key issue. The enclosed and grassy play area, situated three floors up, is suitable for children of five and above under adult supervision. Children have their own menu with own-made mini meatballs, free range chicken breast strips with mash, cod and chips or veggie strudel; all dishes are £5. To follow, there's chocolate bread and butter pudding, a fruit platter or ice-cream for £2.50. Adult food of the open sandwich variety is capably executed, though fish and chips disappointed some of our 'experts'. The no-smoking downstairs bar is good if you're not bothered about staying indoors.

Waterside Bistro
10 Symons Passage, The Plains, Totnes, South Devon TQ9 5YS (01803 864069). **Meals served** noon-3pm, 6-9.30pm daily. **Main courses** £9.95-£14.95. **Credit** MC, V.
Popular all day long, with wooden panelling indoors and alfresco dining at the water's edge if weather permits, this is an excellent place for a family meal. Adults can eat imaginatively prepared fresh seafood such as pan fried tiger prawns with coriander, chilli and garlic; children can choose from their own menu, with generously sized portions of nicely prepared fish and chips or pasta for £5.50. (The children's menu is only available in summer, however.) Drinks of the local

PEDAL LIKE BILLY-O TILL TEATIME

Those of us brought up on the Famous Five and their adventures (*see p111*), or even those more familiar with *The Comic Strip Presents...* version, will have fun scrambling around Devon with bikes or otherwise. Although the panini generation might turn their noses up at the tinned peaches and hard-boiled eggs that 'the Five' get terribly excited about, they can't help but be caught up in jolly cliff adventures, and a visit to one of the farmers markets should furnish you with a scrumptious picnic. What ho!

Geting around South Devon is all part of the fun, with steam trains (*see p148*), boats (*see p142*) and Shanks' pony – yes, walking sections of the coastal path will get you suitably hungry by teatime.

There are also almost 150 miles' worth of National Cycle Network routes in Devon. The Torbay-Totnes trail is well served by public transport, with a parallel bus route and train stations at each end, so you can dip out along the way if need be. The four kilometres from Totnes to Dartington is along a level, shared access path, so it's no sweat for children who've mastered two wheels. You end up at Dartington Cider Press Centre (01803 847500, www.dartingtonciderpress.co.uk). Here, you can refuel with a cream tea or something more substantial at Cranks restaurant.

For a more challenging ride, Totnes to Ashsprington is about five kilometres through farmland. If you are clever and time your visit to coincide with the farmers market at Totnes (last Saturday of the month at the Civic Hall), you can stock up for your picnic. A pie of some description is generally served up to 'the Five' by an apple-cheeked cook, so don't miss the own-made ones at Effings (50 Fore Street, 01803 863435). Kingsbridge, Dartmouth and Ivybridge hold farmers' markets

Luscombe Sicilian lemonade/organic elderflower variety are standard. Charming, informed waiting staff seamlessly do the important stuff like bringing children's meals first and filling the bread basket without delay.

Willow

87 High Street, Totnes, South Devon TQ9 5PB (01803 862605). **Meals served** 10am-5pm Mon, Tue, Thur; 9am-5pm, 7-9.30pm Wed, Fri, Sat. **Main courses** £7.20-£8.50. **No credit cards**.

This vegetarian café is renowned for its use of the finest natural ingredients, with a conscientious menu that indicates where an ingredient or dish is organic, vegan, gluten-free or wheat-free. Expect dishes such as Sharpham homity pie, a delicious combination of tomatoes and potatoes grown on the Sharpham estate. Children may prefer simpler options, such as a filled roll or baked potato, or a substantial 'light' lunch of soup, salad, dip and roll or cheese scone, which at £5.90 represents good value. Airy rooms, toys and a pretty garden out back make this a child friendly place to eat. It's also a no-smoking, mobile-phone free zone, where there's an intelligent attitude towards breastfeeding mothers – who are, after all, giving babies the most wholesome dish of their lives – so are made very comfortable.

Winking Prawn

North Sands, Salcombe, South Devon TQ8 8JW (01548 842326/www.winkingprawn.com). **Meals served** *Easter-Oct* 10.30am-9.30pm daily. *Nov-Easter* Sat, Sun, hours vary. Phone for details. **Main courses** £9.75-£19.95. **Credit** MC, V.

A friendly and relaxed waterside brasserie – and the only eatery at North Sands – this place does a roaring trade. Sit outside in the garden on sunny days and soak in the view and the rays, or head indoors to the wooden tables when evenings get on the first, second and third Saturday of the month respectively. To accompany your pie, lashings of ginger beer can be sourced all over the place from local producer Luscombes.

Bikes can be hired in Totnes at Hot Pursuit (26 The Stables, Totnes Industrial Estate, Ford Road, 01803 865174) or near the start of the Ashsprington cycle path trail at BR Trott (Warland Garage, Warland, Totnes, 01803 862493). Diventure, in Salcombe, also has bikes (Brewery Quay, Island Street, 01548 843663). For more information, visit www.devon.gov.uk/cycling. Details of the Cycle Path Network can be found at www.sustrans.org.uk, and the tourist office will stock leaflets with details of local touring routes.

A selection of 24 circular walks for walkers and cyclists are gathered in Valerie Belsey's *Exploring Green Lanes in the South Hams*, available in local bookshops.

chilly. The lunch menu consists of sandwiches made with white or brown baguettes, salads, simple fishy dishes and excellent skin-on fries. This kind of menu is ideal for families who don't want to compromise – you can work your way through half a dozen chargrilled scallops with lime and ginger dressing, while little ones get their egg mayonnaise. (The chips suit both parties.) The 'Little Winkles' menu features chicken fillet with fries, tomato and basil or cheesy pasta, 6oz rib steak with mushroom sauce and salmon fillet with mash, all at £6.95 (drink and dessert cost extra). The adult's menu is much more extensive in the evening, with flavoursome fish dishes such as sea bass with soy, ginger and lime, more of those scallops, this time dressed for dinner with garlic oil and parmesan shavings . There are meat and limited vegetarian options, plus great puddings of the nursery style. Booking isn't necessary for lunch, but is essential for dinner in the restaurant. From May, there are daily evening barbecues – no need to book, just turn up.

PLACES TO SEE, THINGS TO DO

Berry Pomeroy Castle

Berry Pomeroy (2.5 miles E of Totnes, off the A385), South Devon TQ9 6LJ (01803 866618/www.english-heritage.org.uk). **Open** *Apr-Jun* 10am-5pm daily. *Jul, Aug* 10am-6pm daily. *Sept* 10am-5pm daily. *Oct* 10am-4pm daily. **Admission** (EH) £3.60; £1.80 5-16s; £2.70 concessions; free under-5s. **Credit** MC, V.

On the Paignton side of Totnes is the village of Berry Pomeroy, which has a magnificent ruined castle. It's reputed to be the most haunted place in Britain, and the wooded site certainly feels a bit creepy. The outer walls still stand, encircling the remains of a magnificent residence started by the Duke of Somerset but never completed. Excellent audio tours are available for a small charge, and there is a café offering refreshments.

Dartmouth Castle

1 mile SE of Dartmouth, off B3205, South Devon (01803 833588/www.english-heritage. org.uk). **Open** *Apr-Jun* 10am-5pm daily. *July, Aug* 10am-6pm daily. *Sept* 10am-5pm daily. *Oct* 10am-4pm daily. *Nov-Mar* 10am-4pm Sat, Sun. **Admission** (EH) £3.70; £2.80 concessions; £1.90 5-16s; free under-5s. **Credit** MC, V.

For 600 years, Dartmouth Castle has guarded the Dart estuary. The dramatically situated fortress was erected by Edward 1V after the Wars of the Roses. One of the most exciting aspects of visiting this place is getting there – just down from the ferry landing at Dartmouth, look for the river taxi; 'One of the best loved short ferry rides in Britain,' claims the kiosk. And it may be true – it's a seven-minute journey in a little craft with a maximum of 12 people, steered by a salty seadog skipper. Great stuff. Pleasures at the Castle itself include handling weaponry (!) and watching a projection of guns being fired.

Occombe Farm Project

Preston Down Road, Paignton, South Devon TQ3 1RN (01803 520022/www.occombe. org.uk). **Open** 9am-5pm Mon-Sat; 10am-4pm Sun. **Admission** free.

This 150-acre organic working farm has its own farm shop, butchers and bakery, all selling produce grown and prepared on site. It is a working farm not a petting zoo, so the animals are rotated across the pastures and kids may not get to see their favourite breeds (but at least they'll get plenty of exercise looking for them). Free events take place all year round (for details see the website or call 01803 606035). These include pumpkin carving, 'muddy creative fun', making pottery farm animals, scavenger hunts, puppet making and cupcake-decorating, and should be booked in advance. There is also a resident story teller, a nature trail and a visitor centre.

South Devon's Riviera

Overbeck's

*Sharpitor, Salcombe, South Devon TQ8 8LW
(01548 842893/www.nationaltrust.org.uk).*
Open *Museum* 18 Mar-15 July, 3-30 Sept 11am-
5pm Mon-Fri, Sun. 16 July-2 Sept 11am-5pm
daily. *Oct* 11am-5pm Mon-Thur, Sun. *Garden*
Sept-June 10am-5.30pm Mon-Fri, Sun. July,
Aug 10am-5.30pm daily. *Tearoom* 11.30am-
4.15pm daily. **Admission** (NT) £5.80; £2.90
under-16s; £14.50 family (2+2). **Credit** MC, V.
Formerly the home of Edwardian scientist and
inventor Otto Overbeck, the museum is filled with
his quirky lifelong enthusiasms.With its different
rooms, it is suitable for all ages. Focal points
include Overbeck's curios collection, a maritime
room, and butterfly and taxidermy collections
upstairs. There's also a small room with doll's
houses and old toys, and it is here that the younger
children can look for the 'friendly ghost', Fred.
(This will probably excite under-eights only.)
Various quiz sheets on the museum and garden,
designed for different age groups, are available.
The garden is enthralling for children of all ages,
as there are different 'rooms' with tangles of paths
and unusual plants, such as bananas, cacti, palms,
and tropical greenery. Most of the food served in
the tearoom (light lunches and teas – the only hot
food is soup) can be obtained in children's portions

Paignton & Dartmouth Steam Railway

*Queen's Park station, Torbay Road,
Paignton, TQ4 6AF (01803 555 872/
www.paignton-steamrailway.co.uk).* **Fares**
Paignton-Kingswear £7.40 return; £5.10 5-15s;
£23 family (2+2); free under-5s. *Dartmouth
(including ferry)* £9; £6 5-15s; £28 family; free
under-5s. *Round Robin* £14.50; £9.50 5-15s;
£41 family; free under-5s. **Credit** MC, V.
A great day out for puff addicts, this holiday line
from Paignton to Totnes has steam trains
chugging for seven miles along the coast. The
station staff and announcements are quaintly
old-fashioned. The Round Robin ticket provides a
full day's entertainment, particularly for *Thomas
the Tank Engine* fans, who will be blown away by
the experience. It includes the train journey (from
either direction), the short ferry trip between
pretty Kingswear and Dartmouth, a trip up the
river Dart and finally the bus back to your
starting point. Phew! Sit on the left-hand side of
the train as you leave Paignton for a view of the
coast and look out for Goodrington Sands, with
its pretty string of beach huts. The wild or young
at heart can get off at Goodrington for splashing
at Quaywest water park, or to enjoy the beach.

Riverlink

01803 834488/www.riverlink.co.uk. **Open**
Easter-Oct daily; phone or check website
for timetable. **Fares** *Dartmouth-Totnes*
£7 single, £8.50 return; £4.50 single, £5.50
return 5-15s; £19 single, £23 return family
(2+2); free under-5s. **Credit** MC, V.

With five estuaries in the South Hams, ferries are
an important way of getting around and a
pleasure in themselves. A trip up the River Dart
is an enjoyable way of passing the time,
especially if combined with a trip on the Paignton
and Dartmouth steam train (*see above*). Riverlink
boats cruise up and down the Dart between
Totnes and Dartmouth most days during holiday
season, taking about one and a quarter hours each
way; times vary according to the tides. They
constitute a good outing even in poor weather, as
you can remain under cover. A commentary provides a bit of background, and sights to look out
for include contemporary constructions –
Sharpham vineyard and creamery – and ancient
landmarks, such as Walter Raleigh's house.
Playing 'spot the heron' (cormorant/guillemot) en
route is a great way to amuse small people.

Totnes Castle

*Totnes, South Devon TQ9 5NU (01803
864406/www.english-heritage.org.uk).* **Open**
Apr-Jun, Sept 10am-5pm daily. *Jul, Aug* 10am-
6pm daily. *Oct* 10am-4pm daily. **Admission**
(EH) £2.40; £1.80 concessions; £1.20 5-16s;
free under-5s. **Credit** MC, V.
Perched on top of a hill, with uninterrupted
360-degree views over the town and surrounding
countryside, Totnes Castle is a mighty reminder
of the power of the Normans. Built shortly after
the Norman conquest, it was one of the first stone
forts to be constructed in Devon and an attempt

to strengthen William I's hold over the area. It's an excellent example of a motte-and-bailey design. During the summer months, the Castle hosts all sorts of events, including medieval pageants, archery and performances from court jesters.

Riverford Farm

Riverford Organic Vegetables, Wash Barn, Buckfastleigh, South Devon TQ11 OLD (01803 762074/www.riverford.co.uk). **Tours** *Apr, May* 11am, 4.30pm Sat; 11am Sun. *June, Oct* 11am Mon, Sun; 11am, 4.30pm Thur-Sat. *July-Sept* 11am Mon-Wed, Sun; 11am, 4.30pm Thur-Sat. *Dec* 11am daily. **Admission** *Tour* £4; £3 3-12s; free under-3s. Set lunch £13 (2 courses); £6.50 3-12s; free under-3s. Set dinner £15 (2 courses); £7 3-12s; free under-3s. **Credit** MC, V.

Here's a picturesque way of educating the children about where their grub comes from. Part of the South Devon Organic Producer group, a worthy co-operative of 13 family-run farms in South Devon, Riverford shares its machinery, labour and organic vegetable know-how. Once a traditional mixed farm, it is now home to a dairy, butchery, bakery and farm shop. Riverford land stretches from the edges of Dartmoor down to the coast, where the warm sea air protects the fields from frost; a two-hour guided tour might take in the vegetable fields, a tractor ride and lots of tasting and smelling. Visiting the farm is also a natural precursor to sampling the delights on offer at the Field Kitchen, which started in 2005. The Kitchen is overseen by chef Jane Baxter, who makes imaginative use of the farm produce that's come fresh from the fields. Generous two course meals for adults and children cost from £13 (£6.50 for under 12s) for lunch. In 2006 the national press proclaimed the Kitchen one of the top five organic meal providers in the country. 'Nuff said. Special events at Riverford include cookery demonstrations and seasonal activities such as build-a-scarecrow or pumpkin days in autumn. Advance booking is essential for any visit.

Woodlands Leisure Park

Blackawton, Totnes, South Devon TQ9 7DQ (01803 712598/www.woodlandspark.com). **Open** *mid Mar-6 Nov* 9.30am-5pm daily. *7 Nov-mid Mar* 9.30am-5pm Sat, Sun. Closed 23-27 Dec, 1 Jan. **Admission** *Mar-July, Sept* £8.75. *July-Sept* £9.25. *Oct, Nov* £5.25. Free infants under 92cm; £33.20 group (4 people). **Credit** MC, V.

With the biggest indoor venture centre in the UK, Woodlands comes into its own on rainy days. Under-sevens get their own soft play area and train, while a variety of slides and rapids rides ensure there are plenty of heart-stopping moments for the older ones. Outdoor attractions include a commando course and pedal boats. During school holidays, there are special events and entertainers. Woodlands caravan park residents get free use of the leisure park.

Woodlands Leisure Park

The Cornish Riviera to the Lizard

Bays to amaze from Gribbin to Hot Point.

The south and west of Cornwall rewards those families who are willing to travel that little bit further to see what is round the next corner, or over on the other side of the hill. There are myriad little creeks and coves to explore, a warm microclimate that allows jungly gardens to flourish, and wild moorland heights to scramble up for cracking views over sandy bays. It has been a favourite family holiday destination for generations, not least for the opportunities it offers for messing about in water. Every little town has its regatta week when yachting types come into town, bunting is put up, fireworks organised and flotillas of colourful sails can be surveyed. There is a Cornish beach to meet every need and taste: surf beaches, rock-pooling beaches and gently sloping sandcastle beaches. The area also has fabulous hidden-away strands whose miraculous lack of crowds probably has something to do with the fact that getting to them involves a bit of a clamber, or because there are no loos and ice-cream shops. But if you can leave the pushchair in the car and survive a few hours without a cornet or comfort break, these beaches are the business.

Mevagissey. *See p153.*

Falmouth Harbour: the third deepest natural harbour in the world.

By Tre, Pol and Pen... you may know the Cornish men, goes the saying. It's referring to Cornish surnames such as Trescothick, Poldark and Pengelly. The same goes for place names. 'Tre' means farm, 'Pol' is a pool and 'Pen' a headland. These cause much hilarity, both to tourists and locals, who delight in the mispronunciations of visitors unused to names like Praze-an-beeble, Tregoniggy, Mousehole, Sticker, Vogue and Indian Queens. (You may get to know the last one on the A30 only too well, until the bypass is finished.)

Fowey is another tricky one. You can identify the newcomer to the south Cornish coast by his stated intention to travel to 'Fowee Hall'. In fact, it is pronounced 'Foy', and the place is as intriguing as its name. With its steep winding streets and busy little port, at the mouth of the river of the same name, this natural harbour is always busy with visiting yachts and boats. Fowey's main claim to fame is as the inspirational home of writers Daphne du Maurier and Sir Arthur Quiller Couch, whose friend Kenneth Grahame dreamed up Mr Toad of Toad Hall as he toured the area.

Regatta week here, usually the third full week of August, is said to be one of the best local regattas in the country, with one of the highlights being the spectacular Red Arrows display over the harbour.

You can't visit the town without trying out your sea legs one way or another. Fowey Marine Adventures (www.fma. fowey.com) can take you for an hour's trip up the river estuary and along the coast to spot gannets, cormorants, seals and, if you're lucky, dolphins, whales and basking sharks. Waterproof clothes, life jackets and underwater viewers are all provided. Alternatively, you can chug up the river more sedately in a bright yellow little coal-fired steamer. There are also ferries upriver to Bodinnick, the home of the Du Maurier family, across the river to Polruan or along the coast to Mevagissey – all well worth visiting. Good holiday reading for romantic teenagers would be Du Maurier's *The House on The Strand*, *Frenchman's Creek*, *Rebecca* and *Jamaica Inn*, all of which are set in and around this area.

Landlubbers can visit interesting little shops, galleries, delis and cafés, or stride out along the beaches and coastal walks. Sheltered and sandy Ready Money beach is the closest beach to Fowey, and the big sandy beach at Par Sands, which has plenty of facilities and is popular with families, isn't far. For the more intrepid, the idyllic Lantic Bay is a short drive away. The steep path down to the beach is not suitable for pushchairs and there are no toilets, but this refusal to pander to modern sensibilities makes this one of the best beaches in Cornwall.

Fish and ships

Along the coast a few miles from Fowey sits Charlestown. Built at the end of the 18th century, it was planned and laid out by Charles Rashleigh, after whom it is named. Its little dock was designed to load china clay and copper ore from the nearby pits and mines on to ships for export, and it's still a working port; a small amount of china clay is loaded on to 30 or 40 ships a year. The dock is now home to a collection of old sailing ships, used in film projects all over the world. The elegant houses of the Georgian new town are also a favourite with film and television location scouts.

Mevagissey, also known as 'Fishy Gissy', is an ancient port and fishing village that dates back to the 14th century. In the 19th century pilchards were the main catch here, and the fish were salted and stored in cellars in the town and exported.

The pretty, painted cob houses cling to the hillside overlooking the two harbours, and the old fish cellars have been converted into shops and restaurants. Fishermen these days supplement a meagre fishing income by taking visitors out on fishing trips. There is shark fishing for the adventurous, and more homely mackerel trips suitable for families who want to catch their own supper.

The Mevagissey museum (East Wharf, Inner Harbour, 01726 843568, www.mevagissey.net, open Easter-Sept) is housed in an 18th-century boatbuilder's shed at the end of the north quay, once used for building and repairing smugglers' boats. The museum shows the manacles and huge iron-clad jail door used to imprison smugglers unlucky enough to be caught by the revenue men. The latter would disguise themselves as fishermen and eavesdrop on conversations in pubs about the next consignment of rum or brandy to be brought ashore at quiet coves, in the dead of a moonless night.

Also in Mevagissey is the World of Model Railways (Meadow Street, 01726 842457, www.model-railway.co.uk), which has train tracks laid out for children to play with, and a shop selling all you need to make one yourself.

Nearby Gorran Haven is another lovely, peaceful fishing village with two safe, sandy village beaches, good for swimming and snorkelling.

A right royal harbour

Built on the two hills of a peninsula jutting out into the Carrick Roads at the mouth of the river Fal, the busy port of Falmouth grew up around the two forts that Henry VIII built here, Pendennis Castle and St Mawes Castle. His intention was to protect the entrance to the Carrick Roads, a large waterway created after the Ice Age when an ancient valley flooded with melt waters and caused the sea level to rise dramatically, creating a large natural harbour.

The settlement on the peninsula grew steadily in the 17th century when Sir John Killigrew, the town's creator, realised the potential of what is still the third deepest natural harbour in the world. During the civil war the town took a strong stand on the Royalist side, and the future Charles II set sail into exile from Falmouth. When he later became king, he granted a charter to the town. A church was built and dedicated to his father – King Charles the Martyr church, one of the few churches in England not dedicated to a saint. The assistant priest, Reverend Barrington Bennets, is also landlord of the Seven Stars Pub (The Moor, Falmouth, TR11 3QA, 01326 312111), where he has served behind the bar for over 50 years.

Falmouth became the Royal Mail Packet Station at the end of the 17th century, and the famously beautiful Falmouth Packet sailing ships carried mail all over the world. They're remembered in the name of the local weekly newspaper – the *Falmouth Packet*. Fishing was always an important industry in the town, as was smuggling.

TOURIST INFORMATION

Falmouth
11 Market Strand, Prince of Wales Pier, Falmouth, Cornwall TR11 3DF (01326 312300/www.acornishriver.co.uk). Can also be contacted for information on Helston and the Helford Estuary.
Fowey
5 South Street, Fowey, Cornwall PL23 1AR (01726 833616/ www.fowey.co.uk).
Visit Cornwall
01872 322900/www.visitcornwall. co.uk. Covers the whole of Cornwall.
www.cornwallbeachguide.co.uk
www.cornwall-calling.co.uk
www.go-cornwall.com
www.visit-westcornwall.com

The King's Pipe, a brick chimney by the old Customs House on the quay, marks the place where the contraband was burnt.

The dockyard was built in the mid 19th century; today, the enormous dry docks are still used for shipbuilding and repairs. Bring your binoculars to enjoy the harbour traffic. From Pendennis Point you can see the pilot boat going out to guide big ships to the safety of the harbour or back out to sea. Little tug boats position the bigger vessels for repairs, refuelling, unloading or, with the cruise ships, to allow passengers to embark or disembark. The *Falmouth Packet* publishes all the expected comings and goings in the port for the week, so you will have a good idea of what is going on.

Falmouth, of course, has some lovely beaches. Overlooked by Pendennis Castle (*see p163*), Castle Beach, with its masses of rock pools, is the nearest to the town. Gyllingvase Beach is the most popular, with its gently sloping sands and the excellent Gylly Beach Café (*see p160*). Swanpool beach is a short walk along the cliff path from Gyllingvase. Less busy but just as good, Swanpool has a crazy golf course, a bouncy castle, water sports and a café selling pasties and ice-creams. Just behind the beach is the pool that gives the beach its name, where a resident pair of swans have become quite the celebrities; they nest and raise cygnets here most years.

The town of Falmouth has one long shopping street that runs along the harbour side. The town centre, called the Moor, has a pleasing town square with some grand old buildings, including the Post Office, Old Police Station and Town Hall, a few pubs and a war memorial. An incredibly steep flight of steps, known as Jacob's ladder, leads up from the Moor to the higher terraces of the town.

The presence of Falmouth Art School (recently expanded and renamed University College Falmouth) has meant there has always been a very arty element to the town's population, so there are many little galleries and craft shops along the main street. Falmouth is a top place to buy pasties for lunch too. WC Rowe is a bakery with no less than four shops in town: Old Hill, Arwenack Street, 54 Market Street, and 16 Killigrew Street, all selling truly delicious pasties made on the premises.

The municipal building in the Moor houses the Town Hall, library and the wonderful Falmouth Art Gallery (www. falmouthartgallery.com), which has won various plaudits for its family friendliness, including the *Guardian* Kids in Museums Award in 2006.

Near the Moor is the Prince of Wales Pier, where a huge choice of boat trips, ferry rides and fishing expeditions are on offer. Take the ferry across the river to Flushing,

a settlement built by Dutch seafarers. It was once home to many wealthy Packet captains, whose fine houses can still be seen and probably cost a packet to boot. There is a small playground high above the town, with benches for a breather and a view well worth admiring. The St Mawes and Truro ferries leave from the Prince of Wales Pier, as do various pleasure boats. For details contact Fal River Links (01872 861914, www.falriverlinks.co.uk). At the other end of town stands the smart, newish National Maritime Museum (*see p162*).

If the weather's a bit too chilly for beaching it, many families hire bikes and work off the pasties and clotted cream. There are plenty of bike trails in Cornwall, though the hills can be a challenge. One of the best routes for younger children and older muscles is inland: the Bissoe Tramways route runs from Devoran, on the A39 north of Falmouth, all the way to the north coast, around the edge of Redruth to Portreath Beach. The route follows the tramway that once carried tin and copper to the quays at Devoran or the harbour at Portreath, so it's pleasingly flat.

Mining for tin here dates back to the 1500s. Copper replaced tin in terms of importance in the area in the 1800s, when the Poldice Valley became an important part of the Cornish mining boom. Mining came to an end at the beginning of the 20th century but the old mine workings can still be seen, overgrown with ivy and gorse. From Carnon Downs to the north coast is about seven miles, so you can set off after breakfast and arrive at Portreath Beach in time for a lunchtime pasty.

You can hire bikes of all shapes and sizes at Bissoe Cycle Hire (01872 870341, www.cornwallcyclehire.com). To find the cycleway and Cycle Hire, follow the brown signs off the A39 Falmouth-Truro road near Carnon Downs.

Way down south where camels roam

From Falmouth, the call of the Lizard is too loud for intrepid explorers to ignore. The most southerly point of the British mainland, the Lizard peninsula has everything you'd expect from Cornwall: pretty villages clinging tenaciously on to cliff faces, rocky beaches, rivers and creeks, and high windswept moorland.

The lighthouse on Lizard point was built in 1751 to warn ships of the treacherous coastline. To the west, near Mullion, is Poldhu Cove; in 1901, Marconi sent his first transatlantic radio message from here. The Lizard has far too many gorgeous fishing villages to explore in one holiday, but make a point of seeing Kynance Cove. With a dramatic, rocky beach and an

Charlestown is still a working fishing port. *See p153.*

abundance of screeching seabirds on the cliffs, it epitomises wild, wilful Cornwall.

The nearby Helford river on the sheltered east side of the Lizard has carved out numerous picturesque little creeks – including Frenchman's Creek, where Ms du Maurier from Fowey spent her honeymoon fantasising about dashing French pirates. Helford Passage has some impressive waterside properties and a great pub, the Ferry Boat Inn (Helford Passage, 01326 250625). This quiet corner has been a hideaway haunt of the rich and famous since the turn of last century. The ferry boat (a dinghy with an outboard) runs between Helford Passage and Helford village, and from this hamlet of thatched cottages you can walk to Frenchman's Creek.

Elsewhere on the Lizard Peninsula there are any number of unexpected delights. Helston, the main town, hosts the annual 'Furry Dance' (also called the Floral Dance; see p330). Over at Rosuick Farm (St Martin, Helston, 01326 231302, www.rosuick.co.uk), an organic farm near St Keverne, the owners have imported eight rare Bactrian camels. The friendly camels can take visitors on treks across the Cornish Heathland area of Goonhilly Downs. In addition to camel rides, there's a farm trail, tractor trailer rides, an organic farm shop and a children's play area.

For the sweet-toothed, there is a tiny chocolate factory near Mullion, south-west of Helston, producing hand-made speciality chocolates. You can watch the chocolates being made, then sample the finished article (Trenance Chocolate, Mullion Meadows Craft Centre, Mullion, 01326

241499, www.trenancechocolate.co.uk). The Royal Navy has an airbase near Helston, RNAS Culdrose (01326 574121), from which air-sea rescue operations are launched. Tours of the air base, which is Europe's largest naval air station, take in the hangers, the dog kennels and the bird control unit, which uses falcons to scare off birds and prevent them from crashing into aircraft. Culdrose Air Day is held in July (see p332). The Lizard is also home to south Cornwall's popular theme park, Flambards (see p162).

WHERE TO STAY

Farm holidays are an idyllic way to sample a country life most children only see in picture books. They also educate supermarket-nourished city kids as to the provenance of their full English breakfast. Many farmers who have diversified into the family holiday accommodation business are happy to let younger guests help out with egg-collecting or feeding the lambs. For more on farm B&Bs, log on to www.cornish-farms.co.uk. We've listed a couple of likely farms in this chapter; also note that Rosuick the camel farm (see above) has accommodation to let, as does the organic dairy concern Roskilly's (see p163).

Boswinger Youth Hostel

Boswinger, Gorran, St Austell, Cornwall PL26 6LL (0870 770 5712/www.yha.org.uk). **Open** *Easter-Oct* advance booking. *Nov-Mar* phone for details. **Rates** £13; £9.50 under-18s. **Credit** MC, V.

Fowey Hall Hotel

Boswinger hostel's old farm buildings make a comfortable base for families intent on visiting the Eden Project or the Lost Gardens of Heligan. The hostel is also right near the beaches at Mevagissey and Veryan Bay, and the Cornish Trail coast path. There are three six-bed rooms and four four-bed rooms suitable for families. Breakfast is included in the rates, but for evening meals and lunches you'll have to buy provisions for use in the self-catering kitchen, or eat out in Gorran Haven.

Coverack Youth Hostel

Parc Behan, School Hill, Coverack, Helston, Cornwall TR12 6SA (0870 770 5780/ www.yha.org.uk). **Open** *Easter-Oct* advance booking. *Nov-March* phone for details. **Rates** £13.95; £9.95 under-18s. **Credit** MC, V.

A small, simple youth hostel, set in a Victorian house with spectacular views over the cliffs and coves of the eastern coast of the Lizard, Coverack is much loved by watersports enthusiasts and walkers. It has four family rooms, and plenty of grounds in which to pitch a tent. Breakfast, picnic lunches and evening meals are all available and there's a pool table and a volleyball court if you want entertainment near at hand.

Fowey Hall Hotel

Hanson Drive, Fowey, Cornwall PL23 1ET (01726 833866/www.foweyhallhotel.co.uk). **Rates** *DB&B* £175-£550. **Credit** MC, V.

This luxury family hotel is perfectly situated above Fowey, with views of the river in one direction and the open sea in the other. It is said that this Queen Anne chateau-style Cornish mansion and its river setting were the inspiration for Toad Hall in *The Wind in the Willows*. Rooms are in the main house or in the old stable and coach buildings just behind; you can still see the old granite mounting block in the yard. As you might expect, the rooms are named after Kenneth Grahame's characters – Mole, Ratty, Badger et al. Many have sunny balconies, and you can ring for a complimentary cup of tea to be brought to you before you emerge for breakfast. Under-12s sharing their parents' room are accommodated free, and cots are available. The hotel caters for all ages, from babies to teenagers. There's the Four Bears Den nursery for under-sevens, baby-listening, a games room, a PlayStation room, badminton, croquet and much more. Milly, the friendly dog, is available for walks if you ask for her lead at reception. The indoor heated pool is housed entirely in glass, so you're never without those views. The restaurant is spacious and light with potted palms, floor-to-ceiling windows and a lobster tank to fascinate the children. In good weather, meals can be taken on the terrace, or in summer-evening barbecue form. There are early sittings for nursery tea and kids' supper.

Golant Youth Hostel

Penquite House, Golant, Fowey, Cornwall PL23 1LA (0870 770 5832/www.yha.org.uk). **Open** year round by advance booking. **Rates** £15.50; £10.50 under-18s. **Credit** MC, V.
Children can run free in the three acres of grounds and 14 acres of accessible woodland beyond them, so this is the perfect place for a family holiday. The hostel looks out over the Fowey Estuary and has Bodmin Moor at the back, and is rather off the beaten track, down a long lane from the B3269 Fowey Road. There are plenty of family rooms, including seven six-bedders, so Golant attracts large outdoorsy families who make good use of the space. Breakfast, picnic lunches and evening meals are served (the dining room is licensed), and there's a self-catering kitchen.

Pendraloweth Holiday Village of Gardens

Pendraloweth, Maen Valley, Falmouth, Cornwall TR11 5BJ (01326 312190/ 312689/www.pendra.co.uk). **Rates** £220-£770/wk. **Credit** MC, V.
Hidden away in the pretty Maen river valley, this modern development of traditional Cornish-style two and three bedroom cottages is ideal for families. It recently won the David Bellamy Gold Award for Conservation for its flora and fauna. Kids can ride their bikes around in safety or mess around by the little river, while parents enjoy the wine bar or gym and jacuzzi. The site also has tennis courts, an outdoor play area, a pool table and indoor plunge pool. Safe and sandy Maenporth beach is within walking distance and it's a short drive or bus ride into Falmouth, with its beaches, museum, galleries and shops. Cots, stair gates and high chairs are provided at a small extra cost. Children can choose from the kids' menu in the café-bar, or opt for half-portions of adult dishes.

Pier House Hotel Charlestown

The Pier House, Hotel Harbour Front, Charlestown, Cornwall PL25 3NJ (01726 67955/www.pierhousehotel.com). **Rates** £95-£135. **Credit** MC, V.
This small hotel, right on the harbourside in the enchanting port of Charlestown, can be spotted in numerous Cornwall-based film and television productions, most recently a Walt Disney production of the *Three Musketeers*. The hotel is warm and friendly and has several family rooms that sleep two adults and up to three children. Cots are offered. The restaurant extends to a large patio, where you can watch the world sail by. Fishing

boats are pulled up almost to the windows, so you can be sure that the fish is fresh. For under-12s, the kids' menu offers fusilli pasta with a choice of sauces, alongside the usual fish fingers, jumbo sausage or chicken and chips (£4.45-£4.95). Hearty dishes from the main bistro menu are also offered as child's portions: scampi, fried egg-topped bubble and squeak, bangers and mash or, for more adventurous tastes, spicy seafood jambalaya (all £4.95). Cream teas are another speciality.

The Pollurian

Mullion, Lizard Peninsula, Cornwall TR12 7EN (01326 240421/www.polurrianhotel.com). **Rates** DB&B £106-£206. **Credit** MC, V.
Recently taken over by the owners of the nearby luxury Budock Vean Hotel, this stately old Edwardian building, reminiscent of an old-time cruise liner, is undergoing a much needed face-lift. What it lacks for the moment in stylish decor, it more than makes up for with its stunning location. The hotel is set in 12 acres of rugged coastal moorland, which capture the wild Atlantic atmosphere of this part of Cornwall perfectly. There are notices in the rooms reminding guests to shut the windows during gales, and in the sea view rooms you drift off to sleep to the sound of waves crashing outside. The gardens are full of wild rabbits in the mornings and evenings. For children there is a nursery, and activities in the summer holidays. There are tennis courts, a family putting green, children's climbing frames, a football area, indoor and outdoor pools and the hotel's own sandy beach a quick abseil below. Inside are toddlers' play area and a games room that includes PlayStations, a pool table, table football, table tennis and a separate squash court. Families with fidgety young may wish to forego the main hotel restaurant in favour of the bistro with a large terrace and children's menus.

The Rosevine

Portscatho, Roseland, Truro, Cornwall TR2 5EW (01872 580206/www.rosevine.co.uk). **Rates** £130-£152. **Credit** MC, V.
This luxury hotel with its subtropical gardens looks out over Porthcurnick beach within St Gerran's Bay, and across the bay to the fishing village of Portscatho on the Roseland Peninsula. Family rooms are large and comfortable, and there is a well stocked DVD library. Activities are laid on for youngsters in school holiday time: pirate treasure hunts on the beach in the summer; Easter egg hunts; Santa and magicians at Christmas; and a summer solstice barbecue. The two hotel cats, Tabby and Fizz, love to have their chins tickled. There is a children's play area, a heated indoor pool with a Tiny Tots paddling pool, and a games room. Didier's restaurant looks out across the exotic gardens to the sea, and a pianist will entertain you while you enjoy delicious Cornish produce cooked with flair. Cots and baby monitors are provided at no extra cost, and babysitters can be called in from a local agency.

ONCE UPON A MINE

Nothing is more typical of the wild Cornish landscape than its tumbledown, ivy-clad engine houses, with their granite walls and brick chimneys, which mark the spot where there was once a thriving mine.

There has been mining in Cornwall since prehistoric times. The tin mining industry peaked here in the mid 19th century, after the invention of the steam engine. The new technology allowed water to be pumped out of the mines and ore hauled up. In the industry's heyday there were 2,000 tin mines, many of which were on the coast and worked far out under the sea. Boys as young as ten laboured alongside their fathers underground; mothers and daughters worked on the surface.

When tin was discovered in Australia and South America, however, the industry went into decline, scattering the Cornish miners and their skills all over the world. It left behind only the romantic names of the workings, such as Wheal Mexico, Wheal Prosper and Wheal Jane, and silent engine houses. The last Cornish tin mine, South Crofty near Cambourne, closed in 1998.

It was a Cornishman, Sir Humphry Davy, who invented the eponymous miner's safety lamp. The son of a Penzance woodcarver, Davy created a lamp that replaced the candle-stuck-on-a-hat lighting system that had caused so many explosions and deaths in dark underground tunnels.

Cornish pasties (also known as oggies or tiddy oggies) were the portable lunch of the miners, though they didn't always contain meat; cheese and vegetables were more affordable on a miner's wage. Some mines built huge ovens on the surface to keep the pasties hot, and the miner's wife marked her husband's initials in the pastry of one corner so that it could be identified. The men didn't eat the thick crust of the pasty, but threw it away after eating the rest to avoid being poisoned by the copper, tin or arsenic residue from their fingers.

Perched on a cliff near Land's End, Geevor tin mine survived the competition from Australia in the 19th century. In 1985, though, the international tin price crash meant it fast became an economic liability, and the pumps were finally turned off in 1991. It's now an industrial heritage centre (Pendeen,

WHERE TO EAT

Since Cornwall became a national foodie destination thanks to the input of chefs Rick Stein, Jamie Oliver et al, the quality of the food available has improved vastly, and good meals are much easier to come by than 20 years ago. Most restaurants and cafés worth their salt try to source ingredients locally. Be aware that off-season, opening times may be restricted – so it's a good idea to call ahead.

Budock Vean Hotel

Helford Passage, nr Mawnan Smith, Falmouth, Cornwall TR11 5LG (01326 252100/www. budockvean.co.uk). **Tea served** *Feb-Dec* 3-5pm daily. **Credit** MC, V.

Tea is a hallowed institution at this riverside hotel. You can enjoy the Budock Vean Cream Tea – scones with clotted cream, jam and cakes – or, at £27.50 for two, the Celebration Tea, which also includes sandwiches and champagne. Grown ups go a bundle on the multi-coursed dinners and gourmet breaks in the hotel.

01736 788662, www.geevor.com),
with a museum and underground
tour. The guide takes you to Wheal
Mexico, a small mine typical of the
late 18th/early 19th century, and
recreates the life and work of
Cornish miners. There is a children's
trail, and the whole family can try
panning for gold and test their
strength hand drilling and ore
crushing. The café has spectacular
Atlantic views.

Other mines to visit include Poldark
Mine at Wendron, near Helston
(01326 573173, www.poldark-mine.
co.uk) There are one-hour tours of
the shafts and workings, and ghost
tours on summer evenings.

The National Trust now own
Levant Mine & Beam Engine in
Trewellard (01736 786156,
www.nationaltrust.org.uk), which
clings to the cliff edge not far from
Geevor, and has a working steam-
powered beam engine for pumping
and winding. Copper and tin were
mined a mile out under the sea
here until 1930.

The Cornish china clay industry
still thrives in and around St Austell.
The discovery of this fine clay
and the invention of a method for
extracting it in the 18th century
meant that the English ceramics
industry, which previously produced
only earthenware and stoneware,
could now provide the gentry with
finer porcelain to rival imports
from China.

The production of one ton of china
clay creates five tons of waste,
which can be seen for miles around
St Austell in the form of the white
mountains or 'Cornish Alps'. The
biomes of the Eden Project were
built in worked-out china clay pits.
Nearby is the Wheal Martyn China
Clay Country Park (Carthew, 01726
850362, www.chinaclaycountry.
co.uk). The exhibition here describes
the lives of the people who worked
in the industry, and interactive
displays have visitors driving a
virtual truck to the bottom of a pit
or take part in a tug of war. A history
trail takes in the old workings,
driven by water wheels. Elsewhere
in the 26-acre park there is a
children's play area and commando-
style course for the over-tens, a
nature trail and a viewing platform
over a modern, working china clay
pit hundreds of feet below. There
are picnic areas and a café that sells
food from local producers, organic
ice-cream, local beers and ciders.

The Cove Restaurant & Bar
Maenporth Beach, Falmouth, Cornwall
TR11 5HN (01326 251136/www.thecove
maenporth.co.uk). **Meals served** noon-3pm;
6-9.30pm. *Tapas* noon-9.30pm daily. *Nov-Apr*
closed afternoon. **Main courses** £6.95-£17.95.
Credit MC, V.
This friendly, stylish Falmouth restaurant has a
likely-looking tea, coffee and tapas menu if you
only need a snack, but full lunches and dinners
are worth working up an appetite for. The menu
has a strong emphasis on local ingredients,
especially fish (Helford river mussels and Cornish
mackerel fillets, for instance). The children's menu
aims to tempt the little ones away from their
comfort zone, but not too far – typical options
might include prawns and pesto or penne with
tomatoes, roasted peppers and cheddar as well as
fish or chicken with chips. There are some well
thought out options for vegetarians too, such as
butternut squash and cashew linguine or leek,
spinach and tomato tartlet. The large terrace has
gorgeous views over Meanporth beach, and inside
there is tasteful minimalist decor and an open fire.

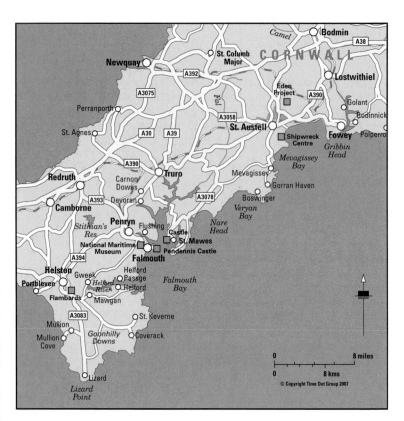

Gylly Beach Café

*Cliff Road, Falmouth, Cornwall TR11
4PA (01326 312884/www.gyllybeach.com).*
Meals served *Summer* 9am-10pm Mon-Fri;
9am-midnight Sat, Sun. *Winter* 10am-4pm
Mon-Fri; 9am-5pm Sat, Sun. **Main courses**
£4-£12.50. **Credit** AmEx, MC, V.

This popular beachside café (try nabbing an outdoor table for a sunny summer lunch) has
welcoming staff, high chairs and a tempting
menu. For snacky-but-filling lunchtime options
try a seafood salad, nachos to share or a sturdy-
looking pizza. Most dishes can be served as half
portions for children, priced at £3.95; herb-topped
seafood pie, own-made burgers in foccacia bread
and crab and coriander fishcakes are among the
options. For more lingering meals, nine wines are
available by the glass, with specials of either substantial brasserie fare (such as grilled sirloin with
seriously thick chips) or vaguely Mediterranean-
influenced dishes (John Dory with Moroccan
spiced potatoes and lime, avocado oil and grilled
vegetables). Plenty of local Cornish produce finds
its way into the menu, and the tapas list makes
the most of local seafood. In the evening musicians
and DJs play, so this beachside haven is best for
young families during the day.

Muffins

*32 Fore Street, Lostwithiel, Cornwall PL22
0BN (01208 872278/www.muffins32.
fsnet.co.uk).* **Meals served** *Feb-Dec* 10am-
5pm Tue-Sat. *Aug* 10am-5pm Mon-Sat.
Main courses £5-£8 **Credit** MC, V.

In summer, the verdant walled cottage garden at
Muffins, in the ancient settlement of Lostwithiel,
is just the place for afternoon tea. If the weather
is inclement, sit in the light and spacious tea shop,
with its pretty tablecloths and pine furniture.
Friendly staff serve a variety of tasty meals, such
as pasty and salad, prawn baguettes, and fish and
chips, based where possible on fresh local produce. The Cornish cream teas, with their delicious
Trewithen clotted cream and strawberry jam, are
just the job for appetites sharpened by fresh air.
This place was a Tea Guild Award of Excellence
winner in 2004, so you can be sure of a decent cup
to wash it down. Muffins serve cream teas with
Cornish Splits, a type of soft white bread roll,
as well as scones. Note that the Cornish
traditionally put the cream on top of the jam,
whereas in other parts of the country the jam is
often put on top of the cream. Own-made muffins
are, of course, another speciality here; most
children plump for the chocolate variety.

The Cornish Riviera to the Lizard

Sam's

*20 Fore Street, Fowey, Cornwall PL23 1AQ
(01726 832273/www.samsfowey.co.uk).*
Meals served *Summer* noon-10pm Mon-Sat;
6-9.30pm Sun. *Winter* noon-2.30pm, 6-9.30pm
Mon-Sat; 6-9.30pm Sun. **Main courses**
£7.50-£14.95. **Credit** MC, V.
The funky decor and lively atmosphere in this
popular bistro make it an ideal place for families.
There is loads of fresh fish on the menu, along
with fabulous burgers and children's portions of
grown-up meals. The food is simple but well cooked.
Pan fried scallops in garlic butter with salad and
bread is a popular choice; the Scooby Burger, piled
high and held together with a skewer, is just the
thing for fish-shy kids. No bookings are taken, but
you can try Sam's Other Place up the road. There,
you can reserve an upstairs table with a harbour
view or people-watch in the café downstairs,
which serves cappuccinos and locally made ice-
cream in a zillion different flavours.
Branch: Sam's Other Place, 41 Fore Street,
Fowey, Cornwall PL23 1AQ (01726 833636).

The Three Mackerel

*Swanpool, Falmouth, Cornwall TR11 5BG
(01326 311886/www.thethreemackerel.com).*
Meals served noon-11pm Mon-Sat; noon-
10.30pm Sun. **Main courses** *lunch* £7.25-
£8.95, *dinner* £11.75-£16.25. **Credit** AmEx,
MC, V.
What a view! Sitting on the potted-palm lined terrace, you could be on the deck of a ship looking
out across Falmouth Bay. The Three Mackerel is

perched above Swanpool beach, and is deservedly
popular; booking is essential for dinner in high
season. The menu is an alluring mix of modern
British and fusion cuisines, combining local fish
and meat with Mediterranean influences to great
effect. Tapas is served throughout the day, and
there is a regular Sunday barbecue in summer.
The children's menu (£4.50) features fettuccine
with tomato and basil sauce, grilled mackerel
fillets with chips and vegetables, sausage and
mash, and fish and chips. Lunch is laid-back and
informal, and kids can run back down the steps
to the beach while mum and dad order that
second bottle of something chilled.

The Lizard Pasty Shop

*Beacon Terrace, The Lizard, Helston,
Cornwall TR12 7PB (01326 290889/
www.connexions.co.uk/lizardpasty).* **Open**
9am-3pm Mon-Sat. **Main courses** 65p-£3.50.
Credit AmEx, MC, V.
Cheap, easy and delicious, pasties are great holiday fast food. Annie's pasty shop at the Lizard is
rightly famous for its delicious own-made prod-
uct. Anne Muller's mother described her offspring's pasties thus: 'I can easily recognise one
of my daughter's pasties. Every mouthful is a
piece of Cornwall – a dream folded in heaven.' If
you can't get all the way down to the Lizard, don't
worry. Countless places bake pasties fresh
throughout the day, filling the towns with their
irresistible smells, and there are different sizes and
fillings to suit all appetites and tastes. For more
pasty options, *see p154.*

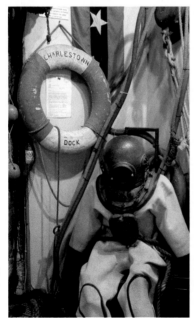

**Charlestown
Shipwreck &
Heritage
Centre.**
See p162.

The Cornish Riviera to the Lizard

PLACES TO SEE, THINGS TO DO

Charlestown Shipwreck & Heritage Centre

Charlestown, St Austell, Cornwall PL25 3NJ (01726 69897/www.shipwreckcharlestown.com). **Open** 10am-5pm daily. **Admission** £4.95; £2.95 10-16s; free under-10s. **Credit** MC, V.

The Shipwreck & Heritage Centre is housed in old china clay loading premises on the waterfront, and you can walk through the tunnels that the clay wagons trundled along before their contents were tipped into the holds of the waiting ships below. The Centre has a fascinating collection of objects rescued from shipwrecks, along with displays of objects relating to local life and industries. Kids can play with remote-controlled boats in a miniature version of the port and dock.

The Eden Project

Eden Project, Bodelva, Cornwall PL24 2SG (01726 811911/www.edenproject.com). **Open** *Summer* 9am-9pm daily. *Winter* 9.15am-4.30pm daily. **Admission** £13.80; £5 5-18s; £34 family (2+3); free under-5s. **Credit** MC, V.

Believe the hype: this place is amazing. Children of all ages will love the Eden Project, and it's worth the queues and crowds. Inside the giant domes there are home-grown play structures, shortcuts and hideaways, stepping stones and rope swings, sandpits and tunnels. There is an 'Around the World in Healthy Ways' trail for kids to follow and find out about the plants that feed the world. The restaurants have child-friendly menus and, of course, source ingredients locally. You can also travel to the Eden Project in an environmentally friendly way. Green buses run from many local resort towns, offering a discounted combination journey and entrance ticket. Or even better, cycle there. Park the car free at Bugle and hire bikes from Bugle Cycle Hire (www.buglecycle hire.co.uk). Staff give you a map of a route that avoids busy roads and hills, and you can arrive at the biomes feeling healthy and virtuous – and claim a £3 discount for your trouble. The Eden Project is on three different cycle trails; see the website for details.

Flambards

The Flambards Experience, Clodgey Lane, Helston, Cornwall TR13 0QA (01326 573404/ www.flambards.co.uk). **Open** *Feb-Mar* 11-4pm daily. *Apr-July* 10.30am-5pm daily. *July-Sept* 10am-5.30pm daily. *Oct-Dec* 10.30am-4.30pm daily. **Admission** *Summer* £12.50; £31.50 family (2+1); £9.55 5-10s; free under-5s. *Winter* £5.95; £3.95 5-10s; free under-5s. **Credit** MC, V.

This theme park was an aviation museum when it opened 30 years ago. Now it's a far more broad-based family fun day out. There are thrill rides (Thunderbolt, Hornet Coaster and Canyon River Log Flume are among the white-ish knuckle ones), an animal section and petting zoo, a Victorian vil-

Eden Project

lage with cobbled streets, an exhibition all about Britain in the Blitz, a live entertainment section called the Kingsford Venue and, hanging on in there, the exhibition of aircraft relics and models. Talking of relics, Gus Honeybun, the now defunct Television South West's popular mascot from the 1960s to the 1980s has a section of the park all to himself. This is an eccentric collection of exhibits and events, but it works well for children of most ages and has a cheery atmosphere.

National Maritime Museum Cornwall

Discovery Quay, Falmouth, Cornwall TR11 3QY (01326 313388/www.nmmc.co.uk). **Open** 10am-5pm daily. **Admission** (unlimited access for one year) £7; £4.80 5-15s; £18.50 family (2+3); free under-5s. **Credit** MC, V.

This magnificent wooden structure houses an amazing range of small sailing craft and maritime objects. The largest space, the Flotilla Gallery, houses temporary exhibitions and collections. New for 2007 is the Survival Zone: among the relics on display are Sir Ernest Shackleton's snow goggles and mug. Also housed here until early 2008 is Mad Dogs and Englishmen – a celebration of eccentricity in boats and on the water. In pride of place is Hugo Vihlen's 5ft 4in boat: the smallest craft ever to cross the Atlantic. In the Tidal Zone you can go underwater and look out into the harbour through two large windows; stand there for long enough and you'll see the tide rise and fall. This gallery also features exhibitions on the effects of the moon and sun on tides. The top floor has a tower called the Look Out, which provides fantastic views over the harbour, docks and estuary, and north to Flushing. There are also interactive computer displays for further information on historic buildings, landmarks, ships and coastal features. Binoculars and telescopes are provided, and a series of maps help you to get your bearings among the rooms and galleries. The museum hosts an extensive programme of events, activities, workshops and exhibitions for all ages, all year round. During school holidays, there is plenty for kids to do here: they can race model boats, learn how to catch a crab or tie knots, and listen to stories of Cornwall's seafaring past.

The National Seal Sanctuary

Gweek, nr Helston, Cornwall TR12 6UG (01326 221361/www.sealsanctuary.co.uk). **Open** from 10am; closing time varies, phone to check. **Admission** £10.95; £7.95 3-14s; free under-3s. **Credit** AmEx, MC, V.
Voted Cornwall's top tourist attraction by local Pirate FM, this sanctuary for rescued seals opened in Gweek in 1975. Rescued seals are brought here to convalesce, before being released back into the wild. There are nursery pools, convalescence pools and resident pools, as well as a hospital. Over the years, the latter has been extended to include isolation pools, as well as treatment and preparation areas. There is a nature trail with other animals to see, and a children's play area.

Pendennis Castle

Pendennis Headland, Cornwall TR11 4LP (01326 316594/www.english-heritage.org.uk). **Open** *Apr-June* 10am-5pm Mon-Fri, Sun; 10am-4pm Sat. *July, Aug* 10am-6pm Mon-Fri, Sun; 10am-4pm Sat. *Sept* 10am-5pm Mon-Fri, Sun; 10am-4pm Sat. *Oct-Mar* 10am-4pm daily. **Admisson** (EH) £4.80, £2.40 5-16s; free under-5s. **Credit** MC, V.
Sitting fatly on the rocky peninsula overlooking one of Falmouth's best beaches, Pendennis cannot be ignored. It was constructed between 1540 and 1545 to form the Cornish end of the chain of coastal castles built by Henry VIII to counter a threat from France and Spain. In the centuries that followed, the fortress was was frequently adapted

to face new enemies, right through until 1945. In 1646, prior to the Civil War, the fort played host to the future Charles II before he sailed to the Isles of Scilly, when it withstood five months of siege, before becoming the penultimate Royalist garrison on the British mainland to surrender. Pendennis helped defend Cornwall from marauders in Victorian times, and saw significant action during World War II. The Guardhouse has been returned to its World War I appearance; underground, there's a network of magazines and tunnels, including the World War II Half Moon Battery, as well as the original 16th-century keep with its recreated Tudor gun. Events in July and August include the ceremonial firing of the Noonday Gun; Christmas holiday shopping and Cornish yuletide events, with quizzes and trails for children, are also held here.

Roskilly's of Cornwall

Tregellast Barton, St Keverne, Helston, Cornwall TR12 6NX (01326 280479/ www.roskillys.co.uk). **Open** *Summer* 10am-8.30pm daily. *Winter* 11am-5pm daily. **Admission** free. **Credit** MC, V.
This is a wonderful organic dairy farm where you can feed the ducks, watch the cows being milked, wander round the farm ponds and walk up to Joes Stones for a view over the sea to St Mawes and beyond. Entrance is free, but you won't be able to hold onto your money when you see the farm shop and the restaurant. There are 24 flavours of Roskilly's organic ice-cream on sale at the Croust House tea rooms and restaurant. There is also the Bull Pen Gallery, selling furniture and glass made on the farm alongside the work of local artists. Reasonably priced wooden toys are also sold. Farm produce on offer includes ice-cream, clotted cream, clotted cream fudge, apple juice in autumn, jams, chutneys and pasties. Check the website for details of Roskilly's farm holidays.

Sea Fans Scuba School

Maenporth Beach, Falmouth, Cornwall TR11 5HN (01326 250100/www.seafanscuba.co.uk). **Open** 9am-5pm daily. **Prices** from £39 per taster session. **Credit** MC, V.
There are plenty of scuba diving centres in this part of Cornwall, and experienced divers can dive on some of the many wrecks that litter the sea bed. Sea Fans is a friendly and affordable centre with taster dives for children over 12 and sometimes as young as ten, depending on their size and swimming ability. You watch a video first in the school Portakabin on the beach, but then you're off into the sea with a wetsuit and tank for anything up to an hour, swimming with the fish, peering into caves and tumbling off underwater cliffs.There's also a four-day course for the PADI Junior Open Water Diver qualification (£299) and two further junior qualifications for those who really get hooked. For younger ones or those not too keen on the idea of all the equipment, Gaynor and her team will organise snorkelling safaris.

Cornwall's Atlantic coast

Around the rugged rocks from
Towan Head to Tintagel Head.

The pleasingly remote south-western corner of the country is
England's family holiday hub. Once defined by its farming, fishing
and mining industries, much of Cornwall now earns its crust, directly
or indirectly, from leisure and tourism. Splendid sandy and rockpooly
beaches, craggy cliffs, unspoilt villages and a temperate climate all
pull in the surfers and walkers. Property developers throng here too,
keen to cash in on the stunning views and SUV-loads of families who
wend their way down the Atlantic highway to fabulous hotels and B&Bs,
rental cottages, campsites and, less happily for the Cornish, second
homes. Then, of course, there is the Rick Stein phenomenon. In the
celebrated seafood master's wake, a colossal wave of gastronomic
tourists has flooded in to the fishing village of Padstow.

The waves that children are more interested in, however, are the
massive breakers that pound the beaches and have made North
Cornwall the surfing capital of the UK – earning this famously
impoverished county £42m a year.

Another hoody, another smashed
sandcastle...**Bedruthan Steps**.

An Oasis of Tranquility and Calm..

Set amidst five acres of beautiful gardens and woodlands this Georgian house has been elegantly maintained and is truly a home away from home.

Just 1 mile from Falmouth and its Blue Flag beach.

- Leisure club with indoor and outdoor heated pools

- Health & Beauty Salon

- Excellent restaurant serving locally sourced foods

- Dining for children in The Manor Bar or The Manor Restaurant

- Family rooms available

Freephone 0800 980 4611

reservations@penmere.co.uk
www.penmere.co.uk

Penmere Manor, Mongleath Road, Falmouth, Cornwall TR11 4PN

Great surf accounts for some of the biggest summer events in the South West, including the English National Surfing Championships and the Rip Curl Boardmasters.

Newquay, the centre of all this surf action, was known as Towan Blystra (sandy hill), until adventurous Elizabethans built the Newe Keye for their sailing vessels. With all the fuss surrounding the town's improbable reinvention as a 'gastrobreak destination' (since the arrival of Jamie Oliver's Fifteen Cornwall, *see p177*), and its established reputation as surf central, the basis of its original claim to fame, the humble pilchard, may get forgotten. Yet until the early 20th century, it was shoals of small herring, not holidaying townies, that provided Newquay's income. Above the western side of the bay perches the Huer's Hut, which provided shelter for the pilchard watcher. His job was to cry 'Heva!' through a long horn when he saw the silvery fish, then direct the sailors as they manoeuvred their boats around the entire shoal. Millions of the plump fish were netted from the boats, and the whole town would turn out to offload the hauls.

Newquay's insignia is still two pilchards (it should really be crossed surfboards these days), even though the town lost its pilchards when they took it into their fishy heads to change their migration pattern. Combined with the coming of the railways, which put paid to maritime trade, the fishes' change of course practically ruined this part of North Cornwall before tourism buoyed it up again.

Gastro-tourism, however, means the demand for locally sourced fish is increasing, so North Cornwall's fishing industry may yet rise again. These days it's local crabs and lobsters that find themselves in the busy kitchens of restaurants like Fifteen Cornwall.

Newquay has been criticised for selling out to the tourist industry, and for its rather downmarket town centre (late at night it's beset by stag and hen parties, and the gastronomic offerings in some quarters appear to be limited to doner kebabs). Nonetheless, it is the wonderful beaches that people come for, and the nightlife scene is neither here nor there for most young families. Furthermore, irrefutable evidence of Newquay's gentrification has arrived in the shape of Prince Charles, who is developing his second ideal village project here. The multi-million pound development, actually planned to consist of a series of villages and hamlets, has been dubbed 'Surfbury'. The project is based on the original Duchy of Cornwall venture in Poundbury, Dorset. Work on Surfbury is due to start in 2007. Early reports say it will have about 1,200 homes and, no doubt, an almost tangible air of smugness.

TOURIST INFORMATION

Boscastle Visitors Centre
Cobweb car park, Boscastle, Cornwall PL35 OHE (01840 250010/ www.visitboscastleandtintagel.com).
Cornwall Online
www.north-cornwall.com
Cornwall Tourist Board Holiday Information Call Centre
01872 322900/ www.visitcornwall.co.uk
Newquay tourist Information
Municipal Buildings, Marcus Hill, Newquay, Cornwall TR7 1BD (01637 854020/ www.newquay.co.uk).
Padstow Tourist Information
The Red Brick Building, North Quay, Padstow, Cornwall PL28 8AF (01841 533449/ www.padstowlive.com).
Tintagel Tourist Information
01840 779084/ www.visitboscastleandtintagel.com
Wadebridge Tourist Information
The Rotunda, Eddystone Road, Wadebridge Cornwall PL27 7AL (0870 122 3337/ www.northcornwall-live.com).

Baywatch

Towan Beach, next to the harbour, is the busiest stretch of sand in high season. It's lined by watersports-hire outfits and beachside tat markets. Tourists also go overboard for the Blue Reef Aquarium (*see p180*). Beyond the harbour, the road continues past the Huer's Hut to the Towan Head clifftop, where the views are terrific.

On the west side of the headland is Little Fistral Beach, followed by Fistral Beach proper, a west-facing strand that bears the full brunt of the Atlantic and where a 'surf's up' vibe prevails. At the far end of the beach, East Pentire Head overlooks the Gannel Estuary as it noses the sea. South of Fistral Bay, Holywell Bay is another popular dune-surrounded beach with parking, toilets and cafés.

Travelling north from Fistral, before you hit the family-friendly Watergate Bay, you pass the sandy Great Western, Tolcane and Lusty Glaze beaches (the latter being by far the best name for a beach we've ever heard). Tolcarne has been in and out of the news since 2003, when there was a proposal to build an artificial surf reef here. That plan appears to have been blown out of the water by Newquay's bigger cheeses, much to the disappointment of the many wetsuited entrepreneurs who ply their trade round the beaches.

Porth Beach, with Porth Island at its eastern end, was the site of an Iron Age

Cornwall's Atlantic coast

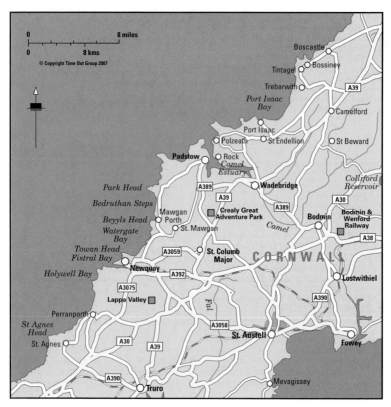

settlement and is linked to the mainland by a footbridge. It's quiet compared to the mighty Watergate Bay up the hill, but it does have ice-cream shops, loos and cafés. Stop by the Lookover Cottage Tearoom on Porth Beach Road (01637 876725), where the scones for the cream teas are made in a tiny little kitchen, and Cornish pixie knick-knacks seduce the small child who's brought her ice-cream money along.

They might be giants

Inland, the woods of the beautiful Vale of Lanherne take you to the village of St Mawgan in Pydar, where the Carmelite convent, ancient church and rickety slate-roofed cottages make you feel you've stepped back two centuries. The seaboard extension of this tranquil spot is Mawgan Porth, which like most bays round here, is well equipped with hotels, cafés and surf shops. Nonetheless, it has a rather thrilling, secretive air about it. The coastal footpath crosses the beach, and following the enchanting coastline brings you to Carnewas Island, where a beautiful clifftop walk runs along the

site of the historic Carnewas Iron Mine. There's a National Trust-run car park, café and gift shop. The cliff walk takes you around to Park Head, passing the beach at Bedruthan Steps. Legend has it that the volcanic rock stacks were stepping stones used by the giant Bedruthan to cross the bay between Park Head and Berryls Point in the south. They were actually created by cliff erosion over the years, but most children prefer the giant story.

Another Cornish giant said to have made his mark on this coastline is Bolster, who was so big he could stand with one foot on St Agnes Head (west of Newquay) and the other on Carn Brea, six miles inland. Bolster was in love with fair St Agnes, and wouldn't leave her alone. She told him that if he wanted to prove his love, he should fill a hole in the cliff with his blood. Bolster didn't think it would takelong to fill the hole, but he didn't realize it was bottomless, and his blood poured into the sea until he lost consciousness and died. A trail of red marks the place where the unfortunate giant's blood flowed. With such stories are Cornish cliff walks spiced, and the best of them all is King Arthur's (*see p170*).

Ferry between Rock and a posh place

The scenic beach theme continues as you follow the coast road north, round spectacular Trevose Head and Constantine Bay, named after the chapel dedicated to that saint, which dates from the 14th century and now lies in ruins on the golf course. The big breakers that come tanking in here make it another surfers' favourite, but the rip tides are dangerous for swimmers. Treyarnon Bay is another good spot for surfing. Bathers might prefer the open-air swimming pool here, although the presence of a caravan park means it's very crowded in summer.

Continuing up the coast, a series of incredible beaches endear themselves to holidaymakers. There's Porthcothan, with its dramatic cliffs, caves and blowholes; Booby's Bay, with the skeletal remains of a World War I German ship preserved in the sand; and Mother Ivey's Bay, which takes its name from a farmer's widow who claimed the rights to all the shipwreck pickings along this part of the coast.

Today's rich pickings come from any sort of property around the tourist honeypots of Padstow and Rock. These two delightful Cornish settlements outsmug each other across the Camel Estuary, with stolid market town Wadebridge looking on to see fair play from the inland tip and acting as a stepping stone to the more glamorous resorts at the estuary mouth.

Once a medieval wool town, Wadebridge has grown into a sizeable community, and is a midpoint of the famous Camel Trail. This cycling and walking path follows a disused railway line between Padstow (six miles from Wadebridge) and Bodmin (eight miles on). You can hire bikes from Bridge Bike Hire in Wadebridge (The Camel Trail, 01208 813050, www.bridgebikehire.co.uk), which has a range of machines including tricycles, child and adult trailer bikes, tandems and bikes for special needs.

Just along the coast is Rock. It's actually very sandy, but takes its name from the quarry that used to provide the rocky ballast for sailing ships emptied of cargo across the river. The village has become increasingly popular with wealthy folk from the city since it became associated with royalty (William and Harry came here for watersports, and now numerous public school pupils follow suit). Rock is reputed to be the home of more millionaires than anywhere else in Cornwall, and has to endure the label 'Kensington-on-Sea' – which irritates the locals no end. It is lovely, however, especially out of season, when the beach that stretches along the

May Day at **Padstow's** 'Obby 'Oss festival

WHERE'S ARTHUR?

There couldn't be a more atmospheric place on which to pin a legend than the craggy coastline of Tintagel Head, where Atlantic breakers crash and gales lash a ruined fortress. The legend that Tintagel claims for its own is that of King Arthur. Many believe that Arthur was a flesh and blood hero warrior, but historians are sceptical about a chap who was supposed to have ruled for 100 years in a pious yet warlike fashion, defeating giants and strange beasts. Not to mention singlehandedly slaying 960 warriors, being cuckolded by Lancelot and enjoying the assistance of a wizard. In any case, Welsh legend also claims Arthur as its own (*see p235*).

Nevertheless, Tintagel Castle is claimed to be the birthplace of King Arthur, and the area derives a good deal of mileage from this fantasy. According to one story, Merlin the magician disguised Arthur's father so that he could enter the fortress at Tintagel and seduce a duke's young wife, Arthur's mother. Another version has Arthur washed ashore and found by Merlin in a cave below the castle (Merlin's Cave, which can be accessed via a footpath from Tintagel Castle).

Evidence to link Arthur to the area is centred on an ancient piece of slate. Excavated on the island in 1998, the 1,500-year-old fragment bears the inscription 'Artognou, father of a descendant of Coll, has had [this] made'. Could Artognou be Arthur? That speculation was enough to give it the moniker 'the Arthur Stone', and pride of place in the Museum of Cornwall in Truro.

Tintagel Castle is just the first stop on a tour in search of King Arthur, and a number of other sites in North Cornwall add spice to the legend. Bossiney Mound, a mile west of Tintagel Castle, is all that remains of a Norman motte and bailey castle. For Arthur followers, this is the burial place of the king's golden round table. Moreover, says Cornish tradition, on midsummer night, 'the table rises up and a flash of light from it for a moment illuminates the sky, after which the golden table sinks again. At the end of the world it will come

to the surface again and be carried to Heaven, and the Saints will sit and eat at it and Christ will serve them.' Your next quest on the Arthur trail is to squelch across the boggy wastes of desolate Bodmin Moor in search of Dozmary Pool. Like many ghostly lakes, Dozmary is rumoured to be bottomless (although it has proved to be pretty shallow during summer droughts). This is where the Lady of the Lake emerged, holding aloft the sword Excalibur to give it to the young King. Here, too, Sir Bedivere reluctantly threw Excalibur back into the pool as Arthur lay dying. Dozmary itself is a still, mysterious outflow from the larger Colliford Lake, just south of Bolventor. Here, bleak Jamaica Inn, the smugglers' refuge made legendary by Daphne du Maurier, lures hapless tourists with its famous fudge.

The final port of call for fans of the warrior king is Slaughter Bridge, near the historic town of Camelford and halfway between Tintagel and Bolventor. A 6th-century inscribed stone marks the spot as a likely contender for the battlefield where King Arthur was killed by Mordred. Some say it also marks his tomb, but since it's rumoured that Arthur's remains are also buried in Glastonbury and various sites in Wales, the king's final resting place is as much a matter for enjoyable speculation as anything else to do with him. For much more on 1,500 years of legend, visit the Arthurian Centre (Slaughter Bridge, Camelford, 01840 212450, www.arthur-online.com; open Apr-Oct).

side of the Camel all the way around to Daymer Bay at low tide is empty of all but dog walkers, hardy windsurfers and lots of pre-schoolers, unrestricted by term dates and enchanted by the rockpools. You can get to Rock's beaches via a coastal walk across the 18-hole golf course at St Enodoc, named after the diminutive church with a crooked steeple nestling in the valley. St Enodoc's is probably best known through its association with John Betjeman, who is buried in the graveyard alongside the bones of sailors and fishermen who lost their lives on the infamous Doom Bar at the entrance to the Camel Estuary.

The posh place is Padstow, just across the estuary. There is a regular foot ferry across the water during daylight hours (£3.50 per person), and a water taxi for those staying out late. For a zippy trip around the estuary, take a speedboat (£4 per person). Padstow is a working port and a number one resort, which makes its harbour in high season a happy melée of holidaying families (children enjoy crabbing off the sea wall), moneyed types off their yachts and red-faced fishermen and pleasure-boat skippers. The Tourist Information Centre by the quay (see p167) is a good starting point for exploration.

The town's patron saint, Petroc, is supposed to have come bobbing up the estuary in the sixth century. Today Padstow's patron saint is considered to be Rick Stein, whose seafood restaurant spawned a clutch of others (see p178), as well as cookery schools and holiday accommodation. The National Lobster Hatchery (South Quay, 01841 533877, www.nationallobsterhatchery.co.uk) is a must-see. The hatchery, a charity, nurtures giant crabs and lobsters for release into the Cornish seas. It's the only place where you can see baby lobsters up close, and learn about the crustaceans that end up in the Stein kitchens.

Come to Padstow in May and you're in for a treat – the world famous 900-year-old 'Obby 'Oss Festival, a bizarre parade led by two monstrous, prancing effigies, takes place on May Day (see p330).

The Camel Estuary is fab for watersports. Rock's sheltered waters are home to a smart sailing club, although there are no breakers for surfing. Polzeath, overlooking Padstow Bay, is a good place for novice surfers, as the waves are gentle and the sand is very fine. The picturesque Port Isaac, further north, doesn't attract the hordes of beach-bound holidaymakers that Rock and Polzeath do, but does suffer from a wearying infestation of second-homers. In this little fishing village, with its white slate-hung cottages clinging to a steep incline above a 700-year-old harbour, it seems every other home belongs to someone described distinctly un-Cornish. Explore the little alleyways between the cottages (look for the one called Squeeze-ee-belly Alley) and banish all thoughts of estate agents.

Headlands of mystery

Tintagel revels in its holiday visitors every summer. In the village, the National Trust (01840 770024, www.nationaltrust.org.uk) looks after the Old Post Office, set in a 600-year-old traditional Cornish longhouse surrounded by cottage gardens. You have to pay to enter (£2.70, £1.35 5-16s, free under-5s) to see the medieval kitchen, early oak furniture and 17th-century needlework samplers, but the kids enjoy exploring the restored Victorian post room.

Most visitors to Tintagel come to honour a king who probably never existed, and Tintagel's beautifully-located ruined castle (*see p181*), accessible via a spit of rock and a bridge, is often called King Arthur's Castle. But aside from the boisterous commercialism that the Arthurian legend has inspired, this is an extraordinary settlement. Come on a stormy day out of season, and you'll see a village that blends in with its bleak setting. Surrounded by moorland and crashing seas, its dark slate cottages look both menacing and mystical.

Tintagel Island was once occupied by a medieval monastic settlement, linked to the mainland by a natural causeway which was gradually worn away by the elements. The huts and religious buildings were abandoned until the 12th century, when Earl Reginald of Cornwall started to build a castle. It was further developed by Richard, the younger brother of Henry III, but was neglected and finally abandoned, resulting in the blackened fragments that survive today. Earlier ruins than those of the monastery have also been unearthed on the island, along with thousands of pieces of pottery dating from the Dark Ages.

It's wild round here. South of Tintagel, the waves at Trebarwith test the skills of young surfers, with the hump of Gull Rock looming offshore. The beach, a long stretch of sand backed by cliffs and caves, is only accessible at high tide. Ferocious storms and heavy seas suit the spiritual types who like to hang out round here, ghost watching and spirit raising.

The little resort of Boscastle, three miles north of Tintagel, attracts more than its fair share of daytrippers, poets, artists and hippies. A tiny harbour on the rocks where the River Jordan reaches the sea, Boscastle has endured worse onslaughts than a tide of holidaying humanity; in 2004 it was practically washed away by flash floods. No one was seriously hurt, but some ancient cottages were damaged

irreparably. The Museum of Witchcraft (*see p181*) had no spells strong enough to withstand the water that washed through it, but it survived to be refurbished in 2005.

Off the road between Tintagel and Boscastle (the B3263) you'll see signs for Rocky Valley. A parking place leads you to this beauty and towards St Nectan's Kieve (www.stnectan.currantbun.com), where a 60-foot waterfall plunges into a deep rock basin. The kieve has been a place of reverence and healing since pre-Christian times, and is reputed to be the site of St Nectan's holy cell. It's also said to be Cornwall's most haunted place, subject to eerie chanting and the apparation of a hooded figure. A great place to visit for October half term, then.

WHERE TO STAY

We've listed the Boscastle Youth Hostel because the building is newly refurbished and in a cracking location. Other youth hostels in the area include one near Padstow, in Treyarnon (01841 520322), which isn't suitable for under-threes, and another at Perranporth (01872 573812). A little to the west of Newquay, the latter is quite basic, with family bunk rooms only.

Bedruthan Steps

Mawgan Porth, Trenance, Cornwall TR8 4BU (01637 860555/www.bedruthanstepshotel. co.uk). **Rates** DB&B £136-£248. **Credit** MC, V. From the airy heights of this mod-con filled hotel's playground, you can look out over the famous giant's stepping stones. Inside, the bustling reception area and austere corridors, where you can hear the Cornish wind howling, are rather reminiscent of a university hall of residence. But that's all forgiven when you step into your family room, with huge windows opening out on to the seascape. Family rooms can either be open plan for young families, or come with two or three bedrooms, and have large, generously-appointed en suite bathrooms. The scramble down to the beach (you won't manage with a pushchair) is the only entertainment many families need, but there's no shortage of activities on offer. The hotel has a big indoor pool, three heated outdoor pools with exotically scattered palm trees, tennis courts, a snooker room and a gymnasium. Then there's Laser Zap and Laser Clay shooting, Surf School and Junior Baywatch for the children, along with the more sedentary Cyber Café and arts and crafts sessions. Animal encounters provided by Mark's Ark (a ubiquitous Cornish travelling show starring spiders, snakes, iguanas and more) are a favourite evening entertainment. Five OFSTED-inspected children's clubs cater for guests aged from nought to 12 (for an extra fee). Likewise, children and babies can take tea separately from the aged Ps, although over-sevens can dine with the rest of the family. On the menu is Padstow seafood, locally reared beef,

**Bedruthan
Steps**.
See p172.

chicken and lamb, and Cornish clotted cream and local cheeses. Special dinners (at a supplementary charge) can be booked ahead at the Indigo Bay à la carte restaurant. Once the baby listening service is performing its magic, there's a Balinese-influenced, wood-panelled cocktail bar to get legless in.

Boscastle Harbour Youth Hostel

Palace Stables, Boscastle, Cornwall PL35 0HD (0870 770 5710/www.yha.org.uk). **Open** Mar-Oct. **Rates** £15.50-£18.50; £10.95-£12.45 under-18s. **Credit** MC, V.

Located in the prettiest harbour in the world, this comfy little hostel is housed in a former stables, once occupied by horses that pulled the boats ashore. The full force of the 2004 floods devastated the hostel's interior, but it has been completely refurbished and looks reborn. Modernisations include a number of great two-, three- and four-bed family rooms, sparkling new bathrooms and a self-catering kitchen. Meals aren't provided, but if you don't fancy using the catering facilities there are any number of cafés and tea shops in the village, where slap-up feeds are on the menu.

Bossiney House Hotel

Bossiney Road, Tintagel, Cornwall PL34 0AX (01840 770240/www.bossineyhouse.co.uk). **Rates** £68-£80. *DB&B* £86-£96. **Credit** MC, V.

Half a mile from Tintagel village centre, Bossiney House and all its modern luxuries come as rather a treat after all the history and mystery pedalled in Arthursville. From its lofty position in private grounds, the hotel commands heart-racing views above Bossiney and Benoath Coves. In the grounds, a nine-hole putting green and a Scandinavian log chalet with an indoor heated swimming pool, a sauna and solarium provide rest and relaxation for South West Coast pathwalkers. At the Cedar Tree restaurant, fresh fish from the day's catch at Port Isaac play a starring role on the menu, with locally farmed beef and lamb and vegetables from the surrounding fields. Sausages made in the village are on the breakfast menu, along with own-made muesli and organic eggs. An early supper can be provided for junior residents who can't keep their eyes open until dinnertime. They can tuck into reduced-priced portions of pasta with own-made pesto or tomato sauce, sausages with mash or chips, and grilled organic chicken breast. As well as 17 doubles, the Bossiney has an airy family suite for four, and a family room suited to parents with pre-schoolers, which sleeps three. Extra single beds and cots are provided where necessary, under-fours are accommodated free. Rooms have TVs and Wi-Fi.

Cornish Tipi Holidays

Tregeore, Pendoggett, St Kew, Bodmin, Cornwall PL30 3LW (01208 880781/ www.cornish-tipi-holidays.co.uk). **Available** Apr-Oct. **Rates** £225-£375/1-3 nights; £325-£720/wk. **Credit** MC, V.

If the cool camping bug has bitten but you just-can't be doing with all the paraphernalia, take the family for a week-long pow-wow in a tipi. Only 15 minutes' drive from Boscastle and Tintagel, where it's pretty difficult to find an unstuffy hotel that accommodates small people, these tipis are an exciting, comfortable self-catering option. Accommodation consists of medium (sleeping two to three) and larger (sleeping six) tipis, constructed along traditional Native American lines. Tipis are colourful or unbleached, their supporting poles are made from local wood and give the structures height – some are 18ft tall, and spacious to boot. Tipis are furnished with rugs and candle lanterns, as well as full cooking gear and camping gas. You can be sociable and rent a tipi standing in a semi-circle in the village field, or keep to yourself in a private clearing. It's a wonderfully peaceful spot, and the lake surrounded by nearby woodland is a fresh, if bracing, swimming spot, where you can also catch a trout for supper. To really immerse yourself in the outdoor life, borrow lifejackets and take a canoe out on the water.

Headland Hotel

Fistral Beach, Newquay, Cornwall TR7 1EW (01637 872211/www.headlandhotel.co.uk). **Rates** £83-£358. **Credit** MC, V.

Looming over Little Fistral Cove from its own promontory, the Headland's slightly aloof air may be remembered from the unsettling film adaptation of Roald Dahl's *The Witches*. Despite its size, Victorian grandeur and purported ghosts, however, there's nothing sinister about Carolyn and John Armstrong's hotel. In fact it's a cheerful place; the staff are smiley and children are made welcome. The refurbished family suites have inspirational views and a second bedroom for the children. If you're holidaying with teens who aren't bothered about views but crave privacy, a budget single room (from £78) might be the answer to their prayers. Five-and-overs are welcome to eat in the restaurant with their parents, but the hotel also provides an early tea at 5.30pm for those who like to get the kids to bed and use the baby listening service during the evening. In the school holidays, staff are available to supervise the children during dinner. Headland has ten acres of grounds, as well as two heated pools, a sauna, a small gym, snooker, croquet and a nine-hole golf approach course and putting green. Teenagers have their own club room with table tennis, a pool table and table football; their younger siblings have a playroom and, in high season, various organised events. These include cut-price entry to the Lusty Glaze Junior Baywatch course for 7-14s and Baywatch Babes for 2-6s. Alongside the hotel is a 'village' of 40 holiday cottages, overlooking Newquay Bay and Little Fistral beach, which can be rented for a minimum of three nights. Shortlisted in 2006 in the RIBA Town and Country Design Awards, the cottages are built in traditional stone and slate, and are nicely appointed. Guests in the cottages can use the hotel's facilities, while enjoying a private space and more economical self-catering holiday.

Higher Lank Farm

*St Breward, Bodmin, Cornwall PL30 4NB
(01208 850716/www.higherlankfarm.co.uk).*
Rates £79-£114. No credit cards.
Lucy Finnemore, her husband 'Farmer Andrew'
and their four children run 'toddler dream holidays'
from their farm near Bodmin Moor. As the idea
is to cater specifically for the needs of families
with babies and young children, the holidays are
reserved for families who have at least one child
under six. The en suite rooms and self-catering
Nursery Rhyme Barns come with all the baby
equipment you could ever need: cots and high
chairs, toys, feeder cups and even nappies; Higher
Lank's green policy means that washable nappies
are lent free of charge, and there's a laundering
service. The farm has its own woodland and river
walks, as well as farm-themed play areas. But the
best fun of all for the young guests is joining in
with feeding the poultry and collecting their eggs,
giving bottles to spring lambs, grooming and
riding the pony and putting the livestock to bed
at the end of a busy day on the farm. Lucy provides
a nursery tea for tinies (£4.50) and suppers for
grown-ups (£15.95), and substantial breakfasts
are included in the price of the room. Babysitting
is also available – Higher Lank Farm may be all
about providing dream holidays for the urban
toddler, but parental fantasies of peaceful evenings
in Cornish country pubs are also indulged.

The Hotel & Extreme Academy, Watergate Bay

*On the beach, Watergate Bay, Cornwall TR8
4AA (01637 860543/www.watergatebay.co.uk).*
**Rates £70-£220. DB&B £90-£270. Credit
MC, V.**
One of the original players in the child-friendly
hotel game, Watergate Bay Hotel appears to have
morphed into a massive surf complex, reminiscent
of a ski resort. The hotel, self-catering cottages
and beachside apartments, surfing school, surf
equipment hire, Beach Hut Bistro and Jamie
Oliver's Fifteen outpost all seem to be under the
Watergate Bay brand. The idea is for families to
find everything they need concentrated in the one
bay: adrenaline sports, relaxation and grub. The
hotel spent much of 2006 and the first few months
of 2007 being refurbished, so its grand old
Victorian exterior now conceals a series of chic
family rooms and suites decorated in beach house
style, with solid oak floors and shutters, as well
as technological treats such as Wi-Fi internet and
flatscreen TVs. Rooms with sea views are the
most coveted (and expensive). The Coach House
has decidedly smaller, less la-di-da family suites
with no views as a budget option. As well as
adrenaline sports, there are all sorts of children's
activities and entertainments during the school
holidays (animal encounters, clowns, discos, arts
and crafts and the like), heated pools, tennis and
squash courts and indoor games rooms. Young
children can have an early supper and bedtime,
while parents dine à la carte in a restaurant overlooking the bay and use of the baby listening

service. Children under a year old are accommodated free. Watergate Bay welcomes dogs, and
this is one of the few pooch-friendly beaches in
Cornwall. The hotel bar has a decked terrace
where you can get drinks and bar snacks all day.
If you don't want to eat in the hotel restaurant,
Fifteen Cornwall (*see p177*) is two minutes away.

Sands Resort Hotel

*Watergate Road, Porth, Newquay, Cornwall
TR7 3LX (01637 872864/www.sandsresort.
co.uk).* **Open** 29 Dec-3 Jan; mid-Feb-Oct.
Rates £96-£190. *DB&B* £128-£212. **Credit
MC, V.**
With the beachy pleasures of Porth Bay to the
fore, rolling green farmland aft and vast tracts of
play area in the middle, Sands is well postioned
and equipped to keep pint-sized holidaymakers
busy. This might give it the air of a holiday village
rather than a top banana hotel, but our children
weren't complaining as they worked their way
through the treats and diversions laid on for them.
Sands is a big, bright block of a hotel, with a playground, mini golf, large outdoor pool, maze and
tennis courts all set out proudly round the back.
Inside are games rooms, playrooms, a steamy,
jungle-themed indoor pool, various lounge areas,
an entertainments hall called the Atlantic Suite
and a large, canteen-like restaurant. Service is
friendly, and activities laid on for children are
prodigious; the Atlantic Suite sees shows and
activities for the children every evening from
5.45pm during high season, and once a week hosts
visits from small, handleable residents of
Newquay Zoo. During school holidays guests can
arrange for their kids to be whisked away and
organised into clubs: Nippers (for under-ones),
Pirates (two to threes), the Adventure Club for four
to sevens and the organised activites of the O-Zone
Club for children of eight up to 11. While their
progeny are thus diverted, grown-ups can let their
hair down (or have it whisked away) at the Ocean
Breeze Spa. Young children can opt for an early
tea-time; older ones can eat later with their parents. The food is a bit of a curate's egg, but the
fish is good and children adore the canteen breakfast. Family suites are large, and most have sea
views. Children are further enraptured by the
widescreen televisions, DVD players and Sony
PlayStations that come as standard in the facili-
ties-plus rooms. Generous price reductions are
available for stays of over six nights and for those
holidaying out of season.

St Enodoc

*Rock, Wadebridge, Cornwall PL27 6LA
(01208 863394/www.enodoc-hotel.co.uk).*
Rates £115-£360. Credit AmEx, MC, V.
For a family friendly hotel, St Enodoc's is a breath
of fresh air, and a bastion of taste and decorum.
Not for St Ned's a team of jolly play leaders and
toddler clubs. Instead, it accommodates children
with excellent grace, but restraint. The hotel is
impeccably chic without being frosty. From the

Watergate Bay Hotel.
See p175.

airy reception and adjoining lounge with slate floors and original art, you climb up stairs and landings carpeted in candy stripes to equally bright rooms. (There are 16 in total, a quarter of which are family sized.) The grounds are pleasantly landscaped and the sheltered outdoor pool, heated from May to September (and sometimes during October half term; phone to check), with wooden steamer chairs dotted around it, is a delight. The largest family suites have plenty of room for big litters and separate children's rooms have bunk beds and sofa beds, plus cots or Z-beds if needed. There are small kitchens, massive wardrobes and seasidey driftwood mirrors and wooden chests. Baths are big, showers torrent forth, handbasins are double-sized and fluffy bathrobes and decent toiletries are provided. The split-level restaurant has wooden floors, efficient staff and a smart menu of Cornish seafood (pan-fried skate or seabass, for example) and locally produced meat, vegetables and cheese. Outside, the terrace looks over the gardens and pool to the Camel Estuary. Children of any age are allowed in the restaurant and are welcome to choose an item from the menu, cooked plainly (grilled organic chicken breast or sea bass with gorgeous chips, for example, for £10.95 instead of the £19.95 average adult main price). Under-sevens of partake of the children's menu (served 12.30-2.30pm and 5.30-6pm), which has delicacies such as French toast with bacon, own-made fish cakes or pasta and broccoli, with strawberry meringue or treacle tart to follow. Although there's no des-

ignated outdoor play area, a cricket set and football are available for games in the grounds, and the rather dark playroom bulges with toys and games. A little gate in the garden sets you on the footpath for the golf course, the beach and dunes and St Enodoc church, saving you the ghastly road down to the beach – it's crammed with 4X4s and has little or no pavement.

Tintagel Youth Hostel
Dunderhole Point, Tintagel, Cornwall PL34 0DW (01840 770334/www.yha.org.uk). **Open** Easter-Sept. Oct-Easter 'Escape To' only. **Rates** £11.95; £8.95 under-18s. **Credit** MC, V.
This place is remote, and families who've stayed here say it feels as if it's on the edge of the world. The views out to sea are incredible, so you can understand why competition for the two four-bed and two six-bed rooms is so fierce during school holidays. Tintagel Hostel has a little shop where you can buy the wherewithal for a cook-up in the kitchen (no meals are served). It's staffed mainly by volunteers, who are friendly and helpful.

Trevornick Holiday Park
Holywell Bay, Newquay, Cornwall TR8 5PW (01637 830531/www.trevornick.co.uk). **Open** Easter-Sept. **Rates** Pitches £4.50-£14.75. *Nightly rates* £4.90-£8.85; £1.25-£6.25 4-14s; £1.20-£1.60 cars. **Credit** MC, V.

A big, jolly touring park, winner of South West Tourism's Holiday Park of the Year Award in 2006, Trevornick is ideal for a budget holiday for happy campers. It has all sorts of facilities to keep children amused – an outdoor pool, Kanga's Holiday Club activities (May-Sept), a large adventure playground and various cafés. Holywell Bay beach, looked after by the National Trust, is a walk through the park and across the golf course. Bang next door is Holywell Bay Fun Park, a small-scale family fun park with go karts, bumper boats, crazy golf and rides of a gentle nature. Teens and adults might enjoy a small round of golf or an afternoon's fishing in the lakes (rods and nets can be hired). In the evening it's all go with the Farm Club, where spangly mini discos, magic shows and fancy dress competitions are laid on for the little ones. A cabaret, comedians and bands take over once the children have conked out. If you like camping but have mislaid your tent, there are pre-erected Eurotents for hire (these are replaced every two years, so are in pretty good nick), which have microwave ovens and televisions.

WHERE TO EAT & DRINK

Beach Hut

On the beach, Watergate Bay, Cornwall TR8 4AA (01637 860877/www.watergatebay.co.uk). **Meals served** *Summer* 10am-9.30pm daily. *Winter* 10am-6pm daily. **Main courses** £11.50-£15.95. **Credit** MC, V.
Downstairs from the rather more pricey Fifteen, the Beach Hut, which used to be a bucket and spade shop, retains a lighthearted vibe. It's open all day and for much of the night, and fresh fish, burgers, salads and mugs of hot chocolate for après-surf comfort troughing are the order of the day. The children's menu, served until 7pm, lists the own-made mini Extreme hamburger with chips for £5.65, a veggie version of same for £4.95, beans on toast or fish goujons. Children under 12 can also have half-priced portions from the main menu (nachos, chilli, chips, moules, seafood specials). The Cornish cheese plate with baguette or the pasty with salad are great lunch fillers; chocolate fudge cake with hot chocolate sauce is our favourite. There is a takeaway window for those who want to picnic on the beach.

Fifteen Cornwall

On the beach, Watergate Bay, Cornwall TR8 4AA (01637 861000/www.fifteencornwall. co.uk). **Meals served** 8.30-9.30am, noon-2.30pm, 7-9.45pm daily. **Main courses** £12-£19. *Set lunch* £24.50 3 courses. *Set dinner* £50 6 course tasting menu. **Credit** MC, V.
Despite mutterings from some quarters about foodie incomers descending on the area, Fifteen Cornwall has proved a worthy success on the beachfront at Watergate Bay. You'll find it on the first floor of the handsome barn that houses the Extreme Academy (*see p176*). The light, airy restaurant has been booked up well in advance since it opened in May 2006, and for good reason – the food is excellent. Part of the Fifteen Foundation charity, and spearheaded by the indomitable Jamie Oliver, it employs 21 local people as student chefs (chosen from more than 300 applicants, trained at Cornwall College). Even more impressive is the fact that 80% of the ingredients these chefs work with are sourced locally. Being devised by Mr Oliver, many dishes often have an Italianate slant, but are unfussy and well executed. The menu changes regularly: when we visited, starters included bruschetta of sardine and flavoursome Cornwall-grown tomatoes, Cornish crab or native lobster with salad from the garden round the corner. Among the mains were Megrim sole (a quintessentially Cornish fish) cooked with cockles and broad beans (£17) and Primrose Herd porchetta with spiced roasted butternut squash. Every day there's a simple but impressive children's lunch for which no reservations are required, which often stars small portions of the meals on the adult menu. There are fruit smoothies (£2), a rich spaghetti bolognese (£6.50), baked Cornish cod with potato gratin (£8.50) and grilled Angus rib-eye with baked potatoes and green beans with gorgonzola butter (£10). Children's puddings are £3.50 – and it's hard to resist apple and blackberry crumble with clotted cream, a delightfully rich dark chocolate tart or a bowl of Cornish ice-cream.

Fistral Blu

Fistral Beach, Headland Road, Newquay, Cornwall TR7 1HY (01637 879444/ www.fistral-blu.co.uk). **Meals served** *Summer* 8.30am-10pm Mon, Tue, Sun; 10am-3pm, 6.30-10pm Wed-Sat. **Main courses** £7.95-£19.50. *Set dinner* *Oct, Nov* £15 2 courses. **Credit** MC, V.
Fistral Beach is an exceedingly popular place, and it can be tricky snagging an early evening sunset and seascape-view table at this restaurant and bar, upstairs from the stylish new Fistral Blu International Surf Centre. The café downstairs is accomodating at all times, however. It serves breakfast, lunch, afternoon teas and snacks to stoke the shivering, snot-streaming children who have fallen off their boards once too often. There are nachos, chips, chicken wraps, and bacon sandwiches; upstairs in the restaurant, the menu changes monthly and offers slightly fancier fare. The own-made burgers are good; you'll also find tapas plates for sharing, deep-fried prawns, Thai spiced local mussels, smoked haddock, lemon and basil fish cakes and catch of the day, served in a light crispy beer batter with mixed leaves and fries. A traditional Sunday roast with all the trimmings costs £8.95. Adult mains cost from £7.95; children can chooose pasta with own-made sauce or chicken and chips for £4.95. Fistral Blu often offer good-value Early Bird specials, giving two adults two courses for £15 while their children chow down gratis. Check the website for details of other seasonal offers, such as cream teas (£4.95) and afternoon tapas.

Golden Lion

Fore Street, Port Isaac, Cornwall PL29 3RB (01208 880336). **Meals served** 6.30-9.30pm Mon-Sat; noon-4pm, 6.30-9.30pm Sun. **Main courses** £3.95-£12.50. **Credit** MC, V.

This delightful old pub, one of only two in the comely village of Port Isaac, overlooks the harbour and played a starring role in the ITV series *Doc Martin*. It seems incredibly aged and rickety, with a sloping floor and pictures of ancient mariners and RNLI heroes on the walls. The fish and chips are excellent – you get an enormous piece of freshly battered cod fried to perfection, with the kind of chips you dream about on brisk coastal walks. Many of the dishes on the pub food menu (Port Isaac seafood is a speciality here, naturally) can be halved for children: a child-sized plate of cod and chips costs around £5. Children eat downstairs in the bar area.

Lusty Glaze Restaurant

Lusty Glaze Beach, Lusty Glaze Road, Newquay, Cornwall TR7 3AE (01637 879709/www.lustyrestaurant.com). **Meals served** *Summer* 10am-9pm daily. *Winter* 10am-2pm Mon, Tue; 10am-2pm, 6-9pm Wed-Sat; noon-4pm Sun. **Main courses** £6.95-£16.95. **Credit** MC, V.

A friendly café attached to a surf and adventure centre on its own beach, Lusty Glaze is renowned for its ultra-fresh fish; its own-made Lusty burger (£6.95) ain't half bad either. Customers can snack on Cornish tapas and bacon baps and a beer, or warm up with hot chocolate and marshmallows if the weather's less than balmy. Daily specials include fish and chips, prawns and salsa, swordfish strips and pan-fried mackerel, although the fish dishes available are dependent on the catch that day. Lusty puds include such delights as pecan and praline tart with honeycomb ice-cream and white chocolate and blueberry cheesecake with a compote of winter berries.

Mill House Inn

Trebarwith, Tintagel, Cornwall PL34 OHD (01840 70200/www.themillhouseinn. co.uk). **Meals served** 12.30-2pm, 6.30-8pm daily. **Main courses** £12.75-£16.50. **Credit** MC, V.

This 18th-century corn mill is set in pretty woodland, halfway up the valley from the surfing beach at Trebarwith Strand. It's an informal, family-friendly place with slate floors and a wood-burning stove for chilly days. Dishes are made from locally sourced meat, fish and produce, such as Cornish field mushrooms stuffed with cheese and sun-dried tomatoes, local haddock with prawn risotto, or pan-fried Cornish hake with a Port Isaac crab sauce. Children can choose small portions from the main menu or select from their own menu. All dishes cost £4.95, and include local haddock, fried or poached with new potatoes, pasta, chicken goujons with chips and good old-fashioned scampi and chips.

The Tea Shop

6 Polmorla Road, Wadebridge, Cornwall PL27 7ND (01208 813331). **Tea served** 10am-4pm Mon-Sat. **Credit** MC, V.

Don't just visit Nicky Ryland's lovely establishment for tea (although it did win a Tea Council award of excellence in 2006); the fresh local produce makes for great elevenses and lunches too. Everything served here is own-made. As well as a selection of 40 different types of tea, there are about 30 cakes on the menu, including boiled fruit cake, chocolate fudge cake and apple and almond cake. Ice-creams are also big sellers, and lunch choices include child-pleasing staples such as jacket potatoes, own-made pizza, ploughman's lunches with local cheese, sandwiches and salads. Cream teas are just the job mid-afternoon, and cost £3.20. A high chair is available.

Terrace Tearoom (Prideaux Place)

Prideaux Place, Padstow, Cornwall PL28 8RP (01841 532411/www.prideauxplace.co.uk). **Open** from Easter for 1wk; 13 May-4 Oct. *Tearoom* 12.30-5pm Mon-Thur, Sun. *House* 1.30-4pm Mon-Thur, Sun. **Credit** MC, V.

It's the teas we like best at this Elizabethan stately home, and you don't have to pay the entry fee to enjoy a proper Cornish spread in the Terrace Tearoom. Outdoor seating overlooks the ancient deer park, with distant views of Bodmin Moor. It's one of the few places you can sample a tea with Cornish splits (soft white rolls) rather than Devonshire scones. They're served with Rodda's clotted cream, another Cornish delicacy, and cost from £4. Tom Petherick, who was instrumental in the restoration of the Lost Gardens of Heligan, has been helping to restore the beautiful woodland grounds of Prideaux, but to have a look at the formal gardens around the house you'll have to pay £2 (£1 5-14s; free under-5s).

Rick Stein's Café

10 Middle Street, Padstow, Cornwall PL28 8AP (01841 532700/www.rickstein.com). **Meals served** 8-10am, noon-2.30pm, 7-9.30pm daily. Closed Mon, Sun out of season. **Main courses** £9.50-£16.95. *Set dinner* £19.95 3 courses. **Credit** MC, V.

This comfortable café has a nautical theme and, despite being part of a celebrity chef's empire, reasonable prices. The food is terrific. Favourites such as burgers and chicken supplement the (naturally) fishy theme, and there are exotic specials such as Vietnamese pho, a light, zingy noodle broth, garnished with gherkins and tomato relish, plus charcuterie, Scottish rib-eye steak with chips and a vegetarian option. Desserts include Quenby Hall stilton with walnuts and honey and lemon posset with raspberries. The children's menu, which changes regularly, might list goujons of plaice with salad and chips, spaghetti with fresh tomato sauce and grilled chicken breast with salad and chips or new potatoes for £5.95, followed by Roskilly's ice-cream or sunken chocolate cake.

The Rock Inn

Ferry Point, Rock, Cornwall PL27 6LD (01208 863498). **Meals served** noon-10pm daily. **Main courses** £7.25-£12.95. **Credit** MC, V.
Just up the road from the beach, this bar and café has huge windows and balcony tables, looking out over the estuary to the wind farms on the horizon. It's a pleasant place to have a beer and a prawn, crab or cheese-and-pickle doorstep sandwich after a busy morning's rockpooling down on the strand. Chips are a steal at £1.75, and reasonably-priced hot daily specials might include seafood pie or fruity chicken curry.

St Petroc's Bistro

4 New Street, Padstow, Cornwall PL28 8EA (01841 532700/www.rickstein.com). **Meals served** noon-2pm, 7-10pm daily. **Main courses** £10.50-£18.95. **Credit** MC, V.
Mr Stein's more affordable alternative to the famed Seafood Restaurant is child friendly and a treat for adults too. The menu is an interesting blend of posh nosh and perfect bistro staples, such as pan-fried calves liver, steak, grilled lemon sole, coq au vin and moules marinière (which children love as much as adults do). If half portions from the main menu aren't what the little 'uns require, their own menu lists comforting favourites such as fish fingers with mushy peas and thick-cut chips (thin if they prefer), spaghetti with own-made tomato sauce (both £7.50) or steak with seasonal vegetables and chips (£8.50). They also go a bundle on desserts such as steamed chocolate pudding with hot chocolate sauce and clotted cream, or banana and custard pavlova.

Stein's Fish & Chips

South Quay, Padstow, Cornwall PL28 8LB (01841 532700/www.rickstein.com). **Meals served** noon-2.30pm, 5-9pm Mon-Sat; noon-6pm Sun. **Main courses** £6-£11.45. **Credit** MC, V.
OK, this is positively the last Stein-run joint we mention (although his pâtisserie on Lanadwell Street, 01841 533901, does exceedingly good cakes, chocolates and pastries…), but this is a very superior sort of chippie. The sheer range of fish available is mind-boggling, with the menu changing according to the day's catch. When we visited, mackerel, oyster, sea bass, gurnard and scallops were listed alongside the more predictable cod and haddock. Cod and chips for an adult is £7; the beef dripping on the fish is a dark, crunchy treat. Children's portions, cod chunks or goujons with chips are £4. If funds are tight, chip butties are a mere £1.85.

Trevathan Farm

St Endellion, Port Isaac, Cornwall PL29 3TT (01208 880164/www.trevathanfarm.com). **Meals served** *Summer* 9.30am-6pm daily. *Winter* 9.30am-4.30pm daily. **Main courses** £4-£9. **Credit** MC, V.
A working farm with nine holiday cottages to let, Trevathan also has a shop with locally produced food and wine, a pick-your-own soft fruit business, and this jolly tearoom and restaurant. Perched on the hillside outside St Endellion village, the tearoom and conservatory have splendid views over the valley to St Austell. On Sundays it's worth booking in for the traditional roast of Trevathan-

Mmmmm… fish and chips.

reared lamb or beef with homegrown vegetables, but during the week you're safe enough just turning up for the daily specials menu of salads and filled paninis. These may well star the legendary Cornish Yarg cheese (also sold in the shop), with its covering prepared from stinging nettles. Breakfasts, own-made cakes and cream teas (scones not splits) are also on the agenda. The biggest draw for children is the play area with zip slide, mini diggers and tractors to play on, and a pets corner with rabbits, Angora goats, guinea pigs, poultry and, in spring, lambs.

PLACES TO SEE, THINGS TO DO

When the weather's good, you need look no further for entertainment than a Cornish beach. Many happy hours can be spent, paddling, boogie boarding, digging, and looking for wildlife in rockpools. If surfing is your reason for being here, you don't even need good weather – surfers are happiest when it's a bit blustery. Almost every bay here has its own surf school and wetsuit and board hire shack.

Children who want to learn to ride the waves can have lessons at the Extreme Academy in Watergate Bay (01637 860840, www.extremeacademy.co.uk), a surf school and action gear shop, where traction kiting, kite buggying, kite landboarding, kitesurfing, waveskiing and mountain boarding are also taught. Surfing lessons cost from £25 for a half day for both adults and children. The surf-wear company O'Neill (01637 876083, www.oneillsurfacademy.co.uk) also opened a surf school back in spring 2006 on the beach in Watergate Bay (children's group lessons from £14/90mins). The National Surfing Centre at Fistral Beach (01637 876474, www.nationalsurfingcentre.com) is one of the best places for beginners to build their confidence (group sessions from £25/2.5hrs for both adults and children).

For non-beach days, the attractions below have their moments.

Blue Reef Aquarium

Towan Beach, Newquay, Cornwall TR7 1DU (01637 878134/www.bluereefaquarium.co.uk). **Open** *Jul, Aug* 9.30am-6pm daily. *Sept-June* 10am-5pm daily. **Admission** £6.99; £4.99 3-16s; £5.99 concessions; £19.99 family (2+2), £23.99 (2+3); free under-3s. **Credit** MC, V.
These days every seaside resort worth its salt has an aquarium for rainy days, and Newquay is no exception. We'd take issue with the attraction's billing itself the 'ultimate undersea safari', but it holds many sources of fascination and is child-friendly. Our favourite bits are the world of the jellyfish, with the Jelly Babies Nursery, the enchanting displays of captive-bred species, such as clownfish and seahorses, and Turtle Creek, for

which Blue Reef has won international acclaim, largely thanks to its rescue work with stranded sea turtles. Local marine life is also bigged up, with mock-ups of rocky Cornish habitats created for lobsters, spider crabs, gurnards, pipefish and conger eels. Children are treated to a programme of free events during school holidays.

Bodmin & Wenford Railway

General Station, Bodmin, Cornwall PL31 1AQ (01208 73666/www.bodminandwenford railway.co.uk). **Open** timetable varies; phone or check website for details. **Fares** *return tickets* £7.50; £4 3-15s; £21.50 family (2+2); free under-3s. **Credit** MC, V.
Cornwall's only full-size steam railway connects with the main line at Bodmin Parkway, and can be accessed via the Camel Trail cycle and walking path at Boscarne Junction. The Easter Steam Weekend is a lovely opportunity to take the 13-mile round trip through the freshly unfurling countryside from Bodmin down the steep track to Boscarne. The railway runs a full timetable throughout school holidays, and there are various Thomas and Santa specials for children – for details, check the website. The railway runs a few diesel locomotives too, generally on Sundays.

Cornwall's Crealy Great Adventure Park

Trelow Farm, Tredinnick, Wadebridge, Cornwall PL27 7RA (0870 116 3333/www.crealy.co.uk). **Open** *Apr-Oct* 10am-5pm daily (10am-6pm daily half term & summer hols). **Admission** £8.65-£8.95; free children under 3ft 1in. **Credit** MC, V.
Theme park-lovers will do well at Crealy, because once you've invested in a family ticket you can come back as often as you like for the next ten days. Children like it very much, and adults are rather beguiled by the animal attractions, which include noble Shire horses, sucky-mouthed Koi carp that feed from your hand, bunnies, calves, piglets, lambs, guinea pigs, ferrets and bumptious goats. The rides are especially good for tinies, and there's a big sandpit, helter skelter and adventure playground, as well as mini diggers to ride and an indoor playzone. A little safari train takes you though the 100 acres of the woodland and meadows in which Crealy sprawls. Check out the glorious sunflower maze in the summer months. Previous visitors advise taking your own picnic rather than shelling out for the cafés offerings.

Dairyland Farm World

Summer Court, Newquay, Cornwall TR8 5AA (01872 10246/www.dairylandfarmworld.com). **Open** *Easter-Oct* 10am-5pm daily. **Admission** £7.75; £6.75 3-15s; £5.75 concessions; £27 (2+3); free under-3s. **Credit** MC, V.
Dairyland was born back in 1975, when the Davy family, owners of Tresilian Barton Farm, decided to upgrade their milk production using a form of

milking parlour, called the Rotary, pioneered in America. A source of fascination for the public, the milking parlour attracted increasing numbers of visitors and Dairyland was born; it was the first farm-themed tourist attraction to open in the UK. Today it's a delightful, reasonably priced animal attraction for families. There's an indoor fun centre called the Bull Pen, where children shriek down astra slides and into ball pools, as well as a soft-play area, playgrounds and climbing nets. For all this, the attraction is still a working dairy farm, and the milking demonstration educates supermarket-nourished children. The cows are milked in a new space age parlour, with flashing lights, music and information about milking. Pat-a-pet, pony riding, animal feeding and pet parades also keep the children amused – not to mention the farm museum, nature trail and rather sweet gift shop. Work on an ambitious £3 million expansion began in 2007; when it's complete (scheduled for Easter 2008), the farm will have a pub, restaurant, hotel and 25 self-catering cottages. The work is taking place on land that adjoins the current site, and shouldn't affect visits in the interim.

Lappa Valley Railways

St Newlyn East, Newquay, Cornwall TR8 5HZ (01872 510317/www.lappavalley.co.uk). **Open** *Easter-Oct* departure times vary; phone or check website for details. **Fares** *return tickets* £8.80; £7.20 concessions, 3-15s; £28 family (2+2); free under-3s. **Credit** MC, V.

The stars of this family attraction, which covers a huge expanse of wooded valley between Newquay and Newlyn, are the miniature steam trains that chug round it. Varying in size from the 15in-gauge Zebedee to the tiny 7in-gauge petrol-powered Mardyke Miniature APT, they chuff around merrily, taking families from the café and pedal car track to the boating lake and crazy golf, then round to the play castle and brick path maze. A little further on are gypsy caravans, picnic areas, adventure playgrounds and woodland walks. The railway used to carry wagons of ore from the East Wheal Rose mine and engine house, which stands in the centre of the valley and now houses a Cornish mining exhibition and film.

Museum of Witchcraft

The Harbour, Boscastle, Cornwall PL35 0HD (01840 250111/www.museumofwitchcraft.com). **Open** *Easter-Oct* 10.30am-5.30pm Mon-Sat; 11.30am-5.30pm Sun. **Admission** £3; £2 concessions, under-16s. **No credit cards**.

This spooktastic collection of witchy history has been giving children the heebie geebies for 50 years, and is the main reason for a visit to Boscastle. It's not a place to bring young or easily perturbed children, but over-tens and teens love its collection of spells, tableaux, pickled foetuses, charms, curses, paintings, woodcuts, satanism and shapeshifting paraphernalia, witches' equipment such as cauldrons and herbs and nasty devices used to persecute witches. The museum was refurbished after extensive damage caused by the summer floods of 2004.

Newquay Zoo

Trenance Gardens, Newquay, Cornwall TR7 2LZ (01637 873342/www.newquayzoo.org.uk). **Open** *Apr-Sept* 9.30am-6pm daily. *Oct-Mar* 10am-5pm daily. **Admission** £6.45-£8.95; £4-£6 3-15s; £17-£25 family (2+2); free under-3s. **Credit** MC, V.

Opened in 1969 as a pets' corner in the ornamental gardens, Newquay Zoo was a small, undistinguished affair until about a decade ago, when new ownership and redevelopment upped the ante in the visitor attraction stakes. It's now a much loved small zoo, with a strong conservation and captive breeding programme for lemurs, red pandas and Siberian lynx, among many others. There's plenty to do and see for all ages. The African plains area, a mixed species exhibit for zebra, porcupines and a group of meerkats, is a big favourite with everyone. Black lemurs, capybaras and golden lion tamarins live on island enclosures on the lakes. Primates include sooty mangabeys (rarely seen in British zoos), diana monkeys and a group of black and white colobus. The tropical house contains a slice of jungle that can be viewed both from ground and first-floor level; every so often, a man-made rainstorm deluges it to keep it steamy. Children love the walk-through aviary, the breeding group of Humboldt's penguins, and the farmyard and petting corner.

Tintagel Castle

Tintagel Head, Tintagel, Cornwall PL34 0HE (01840 770328/www.english-heritage.org.uk/tintagel). **Open** *Apr-Sept* 10am-6pm daily. *Oct* 10am-5pm daily. *Nov-Mar* 10am-4pm daily. **Admission** (EH) £4.30; £3.20 concessions; £2.20 5-16s; free under-5s. **Credit** MC, V.

Like many of Cornwall's loveliest places, the blackened remains of this ancient castle reward visitors who come out of season. A blustery day in December is a great time to experience its full power. The fact that it's a bit of a challenge to reach (there are 100 steps, a lot of uneven ground and a vertiginous bridge over the rocky valley to Tintagel Head) makes it even more enchanting. Pushchairs aren't a good idea, however – take a baby backpack or sling. What's left of the 13th-century castle – steep stone steps, stout walls and a lofty space where there once was a Great Hall – contribute to the overall drama. Tintagel was thought to have been a trading settlement in the 5th century (pottery has been unearthed by archeologists to back this up). Less empirically, the site is rumoured to be where King Arthur was conceived, a legend resurrected by Victorian poet Alfred Lord Tennyson in his *Idylls of the King*. Nevertheless, the potential for fantastic stories and great games of noble knights and holy grails are endless. Children will love it.

North Devon

England's Gold Coast.

From lovely Clovelly in the West round to Lynton in the North East, the North Devon coastline is a winner. The beach at Woolacombe is widely acknowledged as a world top ten, and the cove-pocked cliffs overlooking the Bristol Channel are outstanding natural beauties. It's the top quality seaside that attracts families, and numerous attractions have sprung up around the coast to keep children occupied when the weather turns inclement.

In Exmoor, North Devon has an inland rival to the rugged beauty of the coastline – the countryside here is extraordinarily varied, from salt marshes to soft, rolling hills and ancient woodland.

A big hit with the Victorians, the bracing seaside towns of Ilfracombe, Woolacombe and Lynmouth suffered a setback in popularity when competition from cheap package holidays and budget air fares turned English tourism on its head. But like all homespun destinations, they've ridden the wave and reinvented themselves to welcome a new influx of young families fighting shy of airport security palaver and carbon emissions. All year round they come, for swimming when it's warm, coastline walking when it's not, surfing when the breakers suit and eating and drinking heartily when the sun sets. Then there's the ever-swelling shoal of weekend breakers travelling down from Bristol, Cardiff, Birmingham and London, escaping city pressures to breathe Devon's sweet air and revel in her clotted cream.

The best guides to enjoying London life

(but don't just take our word for it)

'More than 700 places where you can eat out for less than £20 a head… a mass of useful information in a geuinely pocket–sized guide'

Mail on Sunday

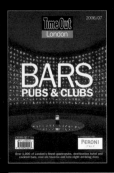

'Armed with a tube map and this guide there is no excuse to find yourself in a duff bar again'

Evening Standard

'I'm always asked how I up to date with shopping and services in a city as as London. This guide is the answer'

Red Magazine

'Get the inside track on the capital's neighbourhoods'

Independent on Sunday

'A treasure trove of treats that lists the best the capital has to offer'

The People

Rated 'Best Restaurant Guide'

Sunday Times

Available at all good bookshops and imeout.com/shop from £6.99

100% Independent

Just off the A39 (the main road from Bideford to Bude in Cornwall), Clovelly is a curiosity that begs exploration. Thanks to the uniquely protected nature of this almost impossibly picturesque fishing village, Clovelly has an atmosphere verging on the surreal. For one thing cars are banned; for another you have to pay to get in – how's that for reducing congestion?

From Elizabethan days until the 1830s the village was reliant on herring and mackerel fishing. It was then rescued from decline by the Victorian tourism boom and Charles Kingsley, author of The Water Babies and Westward Ho!, who was brought up in Clovelly and did much to popularise the village in his novels.

Car parking is free in the plateau above the village, and visitors descend the vertiginous (and, for those with buggies, prams, wheelchairs or walking sticks, somewhat perilous) cobbled path to the narrow, cottage-lined street below, known as the up-a-long, down-a-long. Fear not – there is a Landrover service to take visitors from top to bottom and vice versa.

Make a beeline for the 14th-century harbour (stopping, of course, to admire the stunning view over the bay from Mount Pleasant), where the pebble shore should provide an immediate distraction for restless children, and the Red Lion (The Quay, 01237 431237) an inviting proposition for adults. Small boats bob cheerfully in the bay, their owners gently hustling the tourists for (actually very reasonable) boat trips around the bay and even further afield to Lundy Island.

The steep climb on the way back necessarily affords more leisurely opportunity to check out some of the intriguing alleys that beckon you off the main street, as well as the Fisherman's Cottage (a reconstruction of family life in the 1930s) and the Kingsley Museum, where visitors can watch an animatronic display of the eponymous author at work.

Child-pleasing attractions are only a swift car journey away from Clovelly. The nearest of these, The Milky Way (see p193), is part fairground and part farm-park. With a full-size dodgems, indoor adventure playground and 'Clone Zone' thrill ride, it's a winner for all age groups. As most of the attractions are located indoors, it's a no-brainer when the weather is unleashing hell.

Barnstaple is perhaps most famous for its large concentration of military personnel and, while not renowned for its shopping, is pretty well stocked with cafés, restaurants, bars and the usual high street names, as well as a few nice little boutiques. It's an enjoyable town for strolling – the Pannier Market being probably the most impressive edifice in the centre. Now one of the UK's top food markets, it dates back to Saxon times. The current structure was built after the Great Cholera Epidemic of 1849, which forced food sellers to clean up and move indoors. Friday and Saturday are good days for local produce, although the market is open Monday to Saturday for crafts and antiques – check local papers for details.

A whole lotta otter

One way to discover more about Henry Williamson's Tarka the Otter story – and otters in general – is to visit the Museum of North Devon (see p193). Here, the Tarka gallery offers a pictorial story of biodiversity and ecology in the region that features our fictional web-footed friend, as well as collections of pottery, furniture and archaeological finds.

Away from busy Barnstaple, the North Devon Biosphere Reserve is the first such reserve in the UK, and one of only 400 in the world. Awarded by UNESCO to an area around the Taw and Torridge Estuary that includes Barnstaple and Bideford, the Reserve status aims to help conservation and develop sustainable activities in the area. The Reserve includes parts of the Tarka Trail (see p190) and the South West Coastal Path, as well as the Sites of Special Scientific Interest at the Taw and Torridge Estuary and at Braunton Burrows.

The latter is one of the most outstanding features in the region and a must-see for anyone visiting North Devon. Recognised as the premier dune system in the UK, the Burrows is a naturalist's paradise, boasting

TOURIST INFORMATION

Barnstaple
Museum of North Devon, The Square, Barnstaple, North Devon EX32 8LN (01271 375000/ www.staynorthdevon.co.uk).

Bideford
Victoria Park, The Quay, Bideford, North Devon EX39 2QQ (01237 477676/www.torridge.gov.uk).

Exmoor National Park Centre
Dulverton, North Devon TA22 9EX (01398 323841).

Ilfracombe
The Promenade, Ilfracombe, North Devon EX34 9BX (01271 863001/ www.visitilfracombe.co.uk).

Lynton & Lynmouth
Town Hall, Lee Road, Lynton, North Devon EX35 6BT (01598 752225/ 0845 660 3232/www.lyntourism.co.uk).

South Molton
1 East Street, South Molton, North Devon EX36 3BU (01769 574122/ www.visitsouthmolton.co.uk).

nearly 500 different kinds of flowers and 33 species of butterfly. It's also famous as one of the locations where American troops practised the Normandy landings; the beach itself is one of the finest in the UK.

On the other side of the estuary is Northam Burrows Country Park, another SSSI lying within an Area of Outstanding Natural Beauty, with 625 acres of dunes, grassland, rushes and saltmarsh, as well as England's oldest links golf course. Guided walks throughout the Biosphere area are run by West Country Walks (01271 883131, www.westcountrywalks.co.uk).

Mane attraction

North Devon's coastline is the main draw, of course, but a large part of the area is covered in the moorland regions of Exmoor, famous for its shy, mealy-nosed ponies.

Designated a national park in 1954, it covers 267 square miles, one third of which are in Devon. Eight thousand years ago, most of Exmoor was covered with oak woodland. Since then the landscape has changed, largely due to human intervention, – no wonder it attracted Coleridge, who lived in a small village in the Quantocks and now lends his name to an official walk.

The Exmoor pony breed is one that's changed little since the Stone Age. These days the chances of seeing one are slim though; only around 150 animals still roam free on the moor. The Exmoor Pony Centre

(Ashwick, Dulverton, 01398 323093, www.exmoorponies.co.uk) lets visitors (of less than 12 stone) ride one of these sweet-natured creatures, or simply find out a bit more about them. The Centre runs regular taster sessions and treks for riders.

The moor affords plenty of opportunities for walking, cycling and horse riding, but it may be difficult to occupy younger children beyond the duration of an enticing picnic. When the tether's end is reached, try Exmoor Zoo – a well-maintained zoo specialising in smaller animals (*see p193*).

A hop, skip and a jump to the north, the South West Coastal Path offers some incredible views over the Bristol Channel. In theory, you can yomp all round the Cornish peninsula to Dorset, a journey of six hundred miles or so. We preferred stopping for an ice-cream, clotted cream fudge and a trip on a water-powered cliff railway.

All along the spectacular North Atlantic coast there are quiet coves and bays – it's an area whose history is rife with piratical tales. Situated in the north east corner of the county, Lynmouth and Lynton were havens for smugglers, who brought in rum, brandy and wine from France and tobacco, salt and soap from Ireland. Shelley, Wordsworth and Coleridge all visited the area – it's said that Coleridge was inspired to write *The Rime of the Ancient Mariner* after seeing Lynmouth harbour.

The 450-foot-high cliff made travel between the two towns a tad tricky until the late 19th century, when the growth of

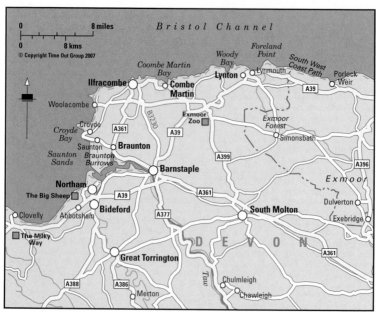

Tunnel vision: the unusual approach to the beach at **Ilfracombe**

tourism inspired Sir George Newnes, a philanthropic newspaper publisher, to fund the construction of the cliff railway. Powered by two large water tanks, which let out just enough water to make the highest car heavy enough to move both cars along the track, it still seems an awesome engineering feat.

On the board

The Victorians may have discovered the leisure possibilities of the North Devon coast, but in recent years the fabulous beaches here have drawn a very different kind of visitor – one more likely to have sun-bleached hair, drive a VW camper van and talk about shooting tubes.

A torrent of surfers head down to the region throughout the year to ride the North Atlantic waves, with the beaches at Saunton Sands, Woolacombe and Croyde proving a big draw for board riders of all shapes, ages and sizes – so much so that the area is now known as the Gold Coast.

Croyde, in particular, seems to have allied itself firmly to surf culture, with cafés, restaurants and bars like Blue Groove, Atlantico and Mai Tai Tiki Lounge and numerous surf shops providing boards, wetsuits and other essentials. There's even

an annual Ocean Festival in June (*see p331*) inspired by the flourishing surfing scene down here.

Beginners might be glad of a surf school – far easier than going it alone. Courses run at both the Surf School in Woolacombe (www.surfersworld.co.uk) and Surf South West (www.surfsouthwest.com), who use both Saunton Sands and Croyde.

WHERE TO STAY

Barnstaple Hotel

Braunton Road, Barnstaple, North Devon EX31 1LE (01271 376221/www.brend-hotels.co.uk). **Rates** £90-£105. **Credit** MC, V.
Part of the Brend Hotels group, the trendy Barnstaple offers a high standard of service and facilities. Conveniently, rather than picturesquely, situated a short distance from Barnstaple town centre, the beach at Saunton is a car journey away. There are more urban entertainments available on the doorstep though, including the North Devon Karting Centre and Let's Go Superbowl ten-pin bowling centre, as well as indoor and outdoor pools in the hotel itself. Interconnected rooms and family rooms are available, with a baby-listening service if needed; babysitting can be arranged with advance notice, using the childminders that

serve Barnstaple's sister hotel at Saunton Sands (*see p189*). The Brasserie has modern favourites such as pan-fried salmon or chicken, tiger prawns, daily fish specials, steaks, roasts and vegetarian choices. The children's menu is impressive, with a choice of nine main courses that include roast of the day, tuna and pasta bake or chicken salad, served with veg, fries, baked beans or salad, all for around the £4 mark.

Broomhill Art Hotel

Muddiford Road, Barnstaple, North Devon EX31 4EX (01271 850262/www.broomhill art.co.uk). **Rates** £70-£80. *DB&B* (Fri, Sat) £105. **Credit** MC, V.
Just outside Barnstaple, Broomhill is an unexpected and rather pleasing find in an area not renowned for its creativity. This small, late Victorian hotel has its very own sculpture garden with a stunning private collection of contemporary works of art. With only six bedrooms (two of which are family rooms), a chic restaurant serving locally sourced, organic and fair trade food (shellfish risotto or local Angus beef stew with chorizo, for example) and a relaxed attitude, this is a real one-off. Children are welcome (the owners have two young children of their own), and the hotel attracts a large number of families. Extra beds are available and there's one cot, which must be reserved in advance. The restaurant offers a dedicated sprog menu, with prices starting at £4.50, and staff are happy to cater for children with half-price half-portions from the main menu.

Lynton Youth Hostel

Lynbridge, Lynton, North Devon EX35 6AZ (0870 770 5942/www.yha.org.uk). **Open** year round for advance booking. **Rates** £11.95; £8.95 under-18s; family rooms from £40. **Credit** MC, V.

Westwell Hall

Deep in the heart of the countryside, this small, friendly hostel is perched on the side of a steep wooded gorge in the perfect picnicking country of Exmoor Forest, not far from the Lynton & Barnstaple railway (01598 763487, www.lyntonrail.net2media.co.uk), a little narrow gauge that runs within the Exmoor National Park above the Heddon Valley near Parracombe. Children will love it here, as there are any number of other jolly holiday attractions in the district, and it's close enough to the sea to make it special. There's a restaurant, shop, laundry and cycle store, but no garden (hardly a problem given the wide open spaces). Family rooms and cots are available.

North Cliff Hotel

North Walk, Lynton, North Devon EX35 6HJ (01598 752357/www.northcliffhotel.co.uk). **Rates** £68-£110. **Credit** MC, V.
Perched 500ft above sea level on the side of a cliff, Northcliff Hotel overlooks Lynmouth Bay and the Watersmeet Valley. Equally well placed for Exmoor and the coast, the hotel offers a taste of a bygone era – particularly the charming 'Teapot' tearooms. The decor is old-fashioned, but you're assured a warm welcome and the views are breathtaking. Children of all ages are accommodated, with a number of dedicated family rooms and discounts for children under 15 sharing a room with two adults. Cots are available, and babysitting is offered. The hotel also tries to be flexible in terms of both menu and mealtimes when it comes to catering for youthful visitors.

Saunton Sands

Braunton, North Devon EX33 1LQ (01271 890212/www.brend-hotels.co.uk). **Rates** £174-£384. DB&B £200-£424. **Credit** MC, V.
Perched high on a cliff overlooking one of Britain's best beaches, Saunton Sands Hotel has one of the most impressive views anywhere on North Devon's Atlantic coast. For location alone it's worth booking right now – a two minute totter down the precipitous slope leading from the hotel swimming pool and you're on the Sands. Miles of windswept dunes abut the vast beach, with the surf attracting both board riders and families (it's a great place for sandcastles). The hotel is as child-friendly as you can get, with an Ofsted registered crèche and plenty of children's activities, as well as a baby-listening service and great family rooms. Indoor and outdoor pools are another major draw. The self-catering apartments are a good alternative to the hotel – equipped to a high standard and decorated in contemporary style, they offer the intimacy of a family environment with the benefits of a modern hotel complex; most come with the same stunning view. As for eating, whether you're self-catering or full board you can dine in the hotel's bar or restaurant, where a children's high tea is available between 5pm and 6pm. In high season it's served buffet-style, with crowd-pleasing delights such as lasagne, freshly crumbed salmon fingers or stir-fried vegetables with noodles.

Westbeach Studios

Beach Road, Woolacombe, North Devon EX34 7BP (01271 870634/www.westbeach accommodation.co.uk). **Rates** £75-£882. **Credit** MC, V.
If you're heading down to the Gold Coast to do a spot of surfing, check into one of Westbeach's funky self-catering studios or flats. There are nine apartments in all above this landmark Woolacombe restaurant (*see p192*), most with sea views. Children are welcome, with a number of cots available and a babysitting service if you book in advance. Think trendy London pad via Californian beach chic and you'll get the right idea.

Westwell Hall

Torrs Park, Ilfracombe, North Devon EX34 8AZ (01271 862792/www.westwellhall.com). **Rates** from £70; phone for details of family rooms. **Credit** AmEx, MC, V.
Surfers may head for Croyde and Woolacombe, walkers for Exmoor and the Tarka trail, but the old-school seaside of Ilfracombe, with its Tunnels Beaches (www.tunnelsbeaches.co.uk) is our delight. Standing amidst the Torrs, a National Trust-owned coastal path, and with easy access to the town, Westwell Hall is a reminder of the splendour of high Victoriana, decorated in period style but without the stuffy formality. It's the kind of place Mum and Dad would happily come back to without the kids. However… children of all ages are welcome, and hotel staff strive to make it as easy as they can for parents during their stay. There are only two family rooms, but most of the others are large enough for extra beds or cots. The conservatory area has games and puzzles, and provides a more informal space for kids to hang out; as for food, staff are happy to discuss what families' requirements are and cook to order.

WHERE TO EAT & DRINK

The Glasshouse & Claytons

2 Cross Street, Barnstaple, North Devon EX31 1BA (01271 323311). **Meals served** noon-3pm, 7-9pm daily. **Main courses** £9.95-£15.95. **Credit** MC, V.
Trendy brasseries and modish café-bars aren't a common feature in Barnstaple, so coming across The Glasshouse and Claytons right in the town centre is a surprise. Downstairs is all dark wood and assignations over cappuccino, while upstairs the Glasshouse offers the polar opposite – a rooftop conservatory with a fashionably retro, affordable menu. We relish the fish finger sandwiches, but those with more sophisticated palates might prefer Caesar salad or moules marinière.

Grove Inn

Kings Nympton, nr South Molton, North Devon EX37 9ST (01769 580406/www.the groveinn.co.uk). **Meals served** noon-2pm, 7-9.30pm Tue-Sat; noon-2pm Sun. **Main courses** £6-£13. **Credit** MC, V.

ON THE TRAIL OF TARKA

Henry Williamson first came to North Devon by motorbike, escaping suburban London and his experiences in World War I. His forays into the local countryside and, in particular, his experiences of caring for an abandoned otter cub inspired his classic novel *Tarka the Otter*.

Originally published in 1927 and subsequently adapted for film, the novel is based on a number of locations in North Devon. It has now been taken as the inspiration for the promotion of an area that's popularly known as Tarka Country, comprising Exmoor, the North Devon coast and, in particular, the Taw and Torridge River valleys and the Estuary, a designated Site of Special Scientific Interest.

The unspoiled countryside that provides the backdrop for the trials and tribulations of the eponymous mustelid (a family that also includes weasels and skunks) is perhaps best seen via the impressive Tarka Trail, an 180-mile long path, roughly in a figure of eight with Barnstaple at the centre, the fringes of Dartmoor to the south and Exmoor to the north. The trail traces the journeys of Tarka, and passes many of the locations mentioned in the book.

This gives walkers a unique view of the lovely North Devon countryside and, if you're lucky, some of its wildlife. Heading north from Barnstaple to Croyde along the top section of the figure of eight (the smaller of the two loops) covers some truly breathtaking scenery, including a large section of the South West Coastal Path, before dipping down through the heart of Exmoor and round to Barnstaple once again.

The lower part of the eight is more ambitious still – although one option is to visit the Tarka Trail Cycle Centre (01271 324202) at Barnstaple railway station and pedal off on the adjacent cycle path. A large section of the trail from Braunton to Petrockstowe is suitable for both walking and cycling – the stretch from Barnstaple down the river Taw toward Bideford is particularly beautiful and comparatively easy going, with the visitor's centre at Fremington Quay providing a natural stopping place for some refreshments and wildlife-spotting.

From Petrockstowe, the going is a little tougher as the path swoops down as far as Okehampton, touching the edge of Dartmoor before climbing up the Taw Valley. Much of the trail is formed from disused railway lines, but the easiest part of the journey comes as you reach Eggleston. Here, the footpath gives way to the Tarka Line, a welcome, working rail link that runs from Exeter to Barnstaple, following the Yeo and Taw valleys. Sit back and enjoy the view with a cup of train buffet tea and – if you've completed all 180 miles – a satisfied smile.

The Mason's Arms (*see below*) may have won the bouquets, but insiders know that the Grove Inn is definitely a contender for best newcomer. This 17th-century thatched inn has become an unpretentious gastropub (if that's not a contradiction in terms) run by two evacuees from the London rat race. It combines the charms of a working village pub with a thoroughly modern restaurant. Browse the supplier list to see just how seriously local sourcing is taken on the menu of robust British dishes – individual beef Wellington with dauphinoise potatoes, for example, or Lundy plaice served with Braunton new potatoes. Kids can choose mini-portions of dishes from the adult menu, but a full children's menu is also available. Options include fresh fish pie, quarter spit-roast chicken or sausage and mash, all using local (and, they claim, perhaps contentiously, 'as good as organic') ingredients. Puddings like banoffi pie, Devon ice-creams and apple and raisin crumble are yummy.

Lathwells

4 Cooper Street, Bideford, North Devon EX39 2DA (01237 476447/www.lathwells.com). **Meals served** 7-9.30pm Wed-Sat. **Main courses** £9.50-£18. **Credit** MC, V.

Just a short stumble along a cobbled street leading from Bideford Quay to the town centre, Lathwells is a relatively recent addition to Bideford's dining landscape. The food centres on tried-and-tested flavour combinations using local ingredients – prawn risotto with lobster sauce for example, or pork stuffed with apple and sage; there's also a good range of locally-caught fish on the menu. Chef/proprietor John Emms is fully supportive of families all eating together, although because of the opening hours and intimate nature of the dining room it's more suitable for children of five and over. There's no set children's menu, but the kitchen can easily rustle something up, with the guarantee that it's fresh, locally sourced where possible and free from artificial nasties.

Mason's Arms

Knowstone, North Devon EX36 4RY (01398 341231/www.masonsarmsdevon.co.uk). **Meals served** noon-2pm, 7-9pm Tues-Sat; noon-2pm Sun. **Main courses** £12.80-£17.50. **Credit** AmEx, MC, V.

After 18 years (13 as head chef) in the kitchens alongside Michel Roux at the Waterside Restaurant, chef Mark Dodson decided to start his own place in the unlikely environs of Knowstone, between Tiverton and South Molton. It wasn't long before the critics announced its arrival, and the Mason's Arms has been crammed with appreciative North Devon foodies ever since. Eschewing unnecessary elaboration, Dodson has concentrated on creating a menu that celebrates the wealth of local produce in the region in dishes that sparkle with imagination – sea bass with sweet peppers and balsamic dressing, for example, or Devon beef fillet with oxtail and parsnip purée. There is no specific children's menu, but the kitchen offer simpler dishes – roast chicken with potatoes or pasta with tomato sauce, for instance – or smaller portions of some à la carte dishes for older children (from £5.50). Families are welcome, although those with younger children are encouraged to come early in the evening.

The Quay Restaurant

11 The Quay, Ilfracombe, North Devon EX34 9EQ (01271 868090/www.11thequay.co.uk). **Meals served** *Bar* noon-3pm, 6-9.30pm daily. *Dining room* noon-2.30pm, 6-9.30pm Wed-Sat; noon-3pm Sun. **Main courses** *Bar* £6.50-£9. *Dining room* £16-£25. **Credit** AmEx, MC, V.

Acquired by Damien Hirst in 1999, The Quay may not have lived up to the hype generated around its opening, but compared to many of its neighbours it's nothing short of trailblazing. Architecturally it's wonderful – particularly the upstairs à la carte Atlantic dining room, with its 'upturned boat' design and fabulous views (a window seat at sunset is something special). Children are always welcome and staff try to ensure that families are served quickly, although the restaurant prefers parents with younger children to come early at dinnertime. The food is contemporary, local, British fare, with seared skate, roast guinea fowl and Muddiford smoked trout among the mains, some of which can be served in half portions. Downstairs, the White Hart Bar area offers bistro-esque versions of classic dishes – beef daube with horseradish mash, for example, or pappardelle with sunblush tomatoes and black olives. It also has more child-friendly dishes, such as meatballs and spaghetti or sardines on toast (available on request in the Atlantic room). Families enjoy the nibbles platter – a feast of crunchy fried broad beans, roasted corn kernels, Spanish olives, anchovies, pitta bread and houmous.

Sands Café Bar

Saunton Sands Hotel, Braunton, North Devon EX33 1LQ (01271 891288). **Meals served** 10am-9pm daily. **Main courses** £6-£15. **Credit** AmEx, MC, V.

This clifftop café certainly lives up to its name. What's more, at peak season it has the added atmospheric touch of sandy floors, courtesy of a motley crew of surf types, families and walkers coming in off the beach. The balcony with views over the Atlantic is fantastic on a summer's day and the menu delivers, with a choice of accessible crowd-pleasers – steak and chips, sandwiches, pasta and the like. There are plenty of child-friendly options; staff are quite happy to do half-size (but still enormous) pasta dishes.

Squires

Exeter Road, Braunton, EX33 2JL (01271 815533). **Meals served** *Sept-June* 11.45am-9.30pm Mon-Sat. *July-Sept* 11.45am-9.30pm Mon-Sat; 11.45am-7pm Sun. **Main courses** £4.60-£6.80. **Credit** MC, V.

A short drive from the coast, Squires is a chippy par excellence that's widely regarded as one of the best in the county. This is the place that locals proudly take their up-country friends to show off the best of Devon. Decor-wise Squire's is more Pizza Express than old school fryer, while the efficient service and a chic bar area add to the sense of occasion. If you're put off by the idea of modish rock salt and balsamic vinegar-style reconstruction at work, fear not; Squires is as authentic as it comes, and the fish and chips are to die for. For the full seaside vibe, the splendid knickerbocker glories will make Devonshire dumplings of us all.

Westbeach

Beach Road, Woolacombe, North Devon EX34 7BP (01271 870877/www.westbeachbar.co.uk). **Meals served** *Summer* noon-10pm daily. *Winter* noon-10pm Sat, Sun. **Main courses** £9.50-£22. **Credit** MC, V.

The gorgeous beach at Woolacombe is a magnet for families and surfers. The cool, cosmopolitan feel is more Bondi than North Devon – a theme that runs through the seafood-heavy menu at Westbeach. Start with tuna ceviche with tomato and avocado dressing, then a main of grilled fillet of Atlantic sea bass with braised fennel, spiced aubergine and chorizo. Half portions are available for many of the dishes, including steaks, roast chicken and seafood. In the summer, the barbecue menus are a very popular family option, and include the 'soul food Sundays' buffet – sitting out on the decked patio in the summer is heavenly. Westbeach offers apartments too (*see p189*).

PLACES TO SEE, THINGS TO DO

The Big Sheep

Abbotsham, nr Bideford, North Devon EX39 5AP (01237 472366/www.thebigsheep.co.uk). **Open** *Easter-Oct* 10am-6pm daily. **Admission** £7.95; £6.95 concessions, 4-15s; free children under-3ft. **Credit** MC, V.

Just up the road from the Milky Way (*see p193*), another enterprising (beleaguered?) farmer has created The Big Sheep, a former winner of South West Attraction of the Year. In essence it's more farm-based fun for the kiddywinks. While away the afternoon with sheepdog trials, horse whispering, tractor racing, duck trials and a brewery, much appreciated by parents driven to drink by poor half-term weather necessitating trips to endless farm-based attractions. Further into the realms of incongruity we have The Battlefield and its live combat games, the same system used by special forces around the world for combat training, apparently. The under-fives prefer dodging ball pond missiles in Ewetopia, the indoor play area with slides, climbing nets, and the nuggety Bo Peep café. Visit during lambing season and you can see the newborns in the Nursery Barn.

Combe Martin Dinosaur & Wildlife Park

Combe Martin, North Devon EX34 0NG (01271 882486/www.dinosaur-park.com). **Open** *Easter-Oct* 10am-3pm daily. **Admission** £12; £8 concessions; £7 3-15s; £34 family (2+2); free under-3s. **Credit** MC, V.

The **Torrs Walk**, near **Ilfracombe**

There's always going to be something slightly artificial about arbitrarily themed attractions like this, but when they're done well, as Combe Martin is, it makes suspension of disbelief that much easier. It seems perfectly reasonable to have an otter sanctuary; after all, Devon will be forever associated with otters, and they're the most watchable creatures in the world. Why, though, should North Devon have a *Jurassic Park*-style animatronic dinosaur enclosure? Or an underground Pharoah's tomb? Or a grizzly gulch mini railway? No reason, but the kiddies love it, and it's a good way of making a living. Nicely landscaped, well maintained and with a packed timetable of events, this place has enough to keep a family with young children entertained for most of the day. The free special bus service that runs to the park from Barnstaple and Ilfracombe is another bonus. Those who are in any way health-conscious should consider bringing a packed lunch.

Exmoor Zoo

South Stowford, Bratton Fleming, Barnstaple, North Devon EX31 4SG (01598 763352/www. exmoorzoo.co.uk). **Open** *Apr-Sept* 10am-6pm daily. *Oct-Mar* 10am-4pm daily. **Admission** £7.95; £6.95 concessions, £5.95 3-16s; £25 family (2+2); free under-3s. **Credit** MC, V.
This small zoo is just a short journey from Barnstaple. What it lacks in the size department, both in terms of the zoo itself and the animals therein, it makes up for in quality. Staff are interested and well informed and a half-hourly activity schedule brings you face-to-face with the animals, including – if you're brave enough – skunks, insects and snakes, which children (or intrepid adults) can hold. For those of a more cautious nature, there's a small petting area with friendly rabbits. Exotic zoo residents include cheetahs, penguins, maned wolves, otters, arctic foxes, lemurs, gibbons and wallabies. There are daily keeper talks, and special events take place throughout the year; the National Insect Day in June is particularly good for young entomologists. Check the website for details.

Gnome Reserve

West Putford, nr Bradworthy, North Devon EX22 7XE (01409 241435/www.gnome reserve.co.uk). **Open** *21 Mar-Oct* 10am-6pm daily. **Admission** £2.75; £2.50 concessions; £2.25 3-16s; free under-3s. **No credit cards**.
There's something quintessentially British (in the sense though eccentric), about a woodland populated with over a thousand diminutive ceramic folk. Gnome hats and fishing rods are loaned free, so you can wander incognito among the pint-sized pottery populace and view the Gnome Airport, Rocket Launch Pad and Motor Bike Scramble, or sit in the gnomically titled Circle of Imagination. Bizarre, but children get a kick out of it. Adults may prefer strolling through the tranquil wildflower garden or sampling the cream teas and own-made cakes at the Gnome Kitchen.

The Milky Way

Clovelly, Bideford, North Devon, EX39 5RY (01237 431255/www.themilkyway.co.uk). **Open** *Apr-Oct* 10.30am-6pm daily. *Nov-Mar* 11am-5pm Sat, Sun, school hols. **Admission** £8; free under-3s. **Credit** MC, V.
Whatever the weather, the Milky Way has its attractions – in fact, it's almost better to hold it in reserve for a rainy day, as the most exciting parts are all indoors. It's a farm, fun-park and space-themed adventure park, which works pretty well to absorb children up to unimpressed teenager stage. Entertainments range from the Time Warp, Devon's largest adventure play area, with its ball pits, amazing vertical slide and foam-lined assault course, to the old school dodgems. Add to that a pets' corner with chick hatchery, an indoor archery range and Clone Zone, a fantasy ride that has children exploring a crashed spaceship, making contact with the mothership and flying away on a suspended coaster, and you're laughing.

Museum Of Barnstaple & North Devon

The Square, Barnstaple, North Devon EX32 8LN (01271 346747/www.devonmuseums.net). **Open** 9.30am-5pm Mon-Sat. **Admission** free.
Intrigued by Tarka? This museum focuses on the intrepid otter, with a series of tableaux of stuffed animals as well as interactive exhibits following Tarka's route, guessing the animal tracks and feeling around for mystery items along the way. The quiz sheet encourages children to ramble through all of the permanent exhibits, including the Victorian collection, the Kiln Room (a recreation of the interior of a 17th-century merchant's house) and the ever-popular Exploratorium, with its (dead) scorpions, rhino beetles, tarantulas and drawers full of pinned butterflies and moths. Recent special exhibitions have included exploring the undersea floor, optics and er… a collection of poo. *See p190* **On the Trail of Tarka**.

South West Mountain Board Centre

Abbotsham, nr Bideford, North Devon EX39 5AP (07866 398599/www.sw-mbc.co.uk). **Open** *Easter-Oct* 10.30am-dusk daily. *Nov-Easter* 10.30am-dusk Sat, Sun. **Admission** £12 1st hr (inc. compulsory training); £9/hr thereafter; £25/4hrs; £30/full day; £9 1st hr (inc. training); £6/hr thereafter; £20/4hrs; £25/ full day 7-16s. No under-7s. **No credit cards**.
Sensible folk may decide that life's too precious to spend it hurling oneself down a hill on a giant skateboard. Mountain boarders would say sensible folk should stick to Gnome Reserve (*see left*). Adventurous speed freaks love the buzz here. The centre offers one of the largest selection of runs in the country – from gentle learner slopes to the competition border cross, a devilishly tricky run which has been used for national competitions. Board hire and lessons are both available.

Staffordshire

Queasy does it –in England's pretty theme-park county.

Alton Towers, the second most-visited attraction in the country, is probably already high on most parents' radars. But Staffordshire, the county it inhabits, isn't so well known. Perhaps that's not entirely surprising – an industrial past and a network of motorways and ring roads don't make for an enticing image. Yet once you leave the main thoroughfares, prepare to be very pleasantly surprised.

One sixth of the Peak District lies in friendly Staffordshire, including parts of Dovedale. Then there's the Staffordshire Moorlands, which encompass beautiful, rolling countryside east of Stoke-on-Trent. Central to this area is the unmissable Churnet Valley, which runs through smooth undulating upland pasture with steep wooded valleys, where tranquil walks lead to pretty hamlets and farms, old mills and lime kilns. Here families can delight in any number of steam railways, gentle walks, canal trips, cycle trails, secluded campsites and open farms, as well as the über child-friendly Alton Towers.

Alton Towers. *See p202.*

Moat House Hotel.
See p198.

Staffordshire's rural areas are under the spotlight in this chapter, but Stokey's merits first deserve a mention. Once described by the town's famous son, early 20th-century author Arnold Bennett, as 'scenery of coal dust, pot shards, flame and steam,' the city is now in the process of reinventing itself. Made up of six older towns – Burslem, Hanley, Tunstall, Stoke, Fenton and Longton – the regeneration project still has some way to go (it's still difficult to navigate the city by car). But with a high concentration of excellent museums – as well as the stately Trentham Gardens – and as a reminder of England's industrial past, it's definitely worth a look.

Ridiculous to sublime

Chances are that Alton Towers (*see p202*) will be at the top of your to-do list – and with good reason. The adrenalin-fuelled thrills on offer, together with the theme park's sensational setting, make the experience a sure-fire bet for families.

Named after the country mansion that once sat on the same site, the land was the main seat of the Earl of Shrewsbury, until he had to sell up in 1922 after a string of misfortunes. The site, located next to the village of Alton, has housed a theme park since 1980. Although the original house no longer stands, the landscaped gardens – at one time the biggest in Western Europe – have been impressively maintained. Their presence ensures that a sense of the original grandeur remains, despite the plethora of candy floss vendors and (reasonably discreet) fast-food stalls.

Once you've had your fill of the teeming hordes of over-excited toddlers, loved-up teens and stag and hen parties who throng the park, a bracing country walk might be in order. Follow the small road that runs alongside the River Churnet from Alton to Dimmingsdale, and you'll discover a network of easily negotiable trails on Forestry Commission land. Children love to play on the pebbly beaches by the Churnet or scramble up the steep valley side and through the National Trust's Toothill Wood to reach Toothill Rock, from which you can enjoy amazing views of the enchanting Churnet Valley.

Just north of the valley lies the Peak District National Park, best approached along the network of minor roads that offer stunning vistas of the beautiful Staffordshire Moorlands. Situated at the Southern tip is Ashbourne, an appealing rural market town with some very pretty Georgian architecture and great shops. The Market Place is a good place to stop and people-watch, especially on market days (Tuesdays and Saturdays).

Spencers the Bakers (35-39 Market Place, 01335 342284), one of Ashbourne's oldest family firms, has a prime position and outside tables, where you can sample some traditional gingerbread or grab an all-day breakfast.

Recently designated a Fairtrade town by the UK's Fairtrade organisation, one of Ashbourne's most ethical traders is Pacahuti on Dig Street, which stocks clothes and charming accessories from the Andes for both children and adults. It's also the UK's only stockist of fairly-traded and organic cotton school uniforms (visit www.cleanslateclothing.co.uk for more information). Next door, stock up on picnic ingredients from Cheddar Gorge (No. 9, 01335 344528), which sells a fabulous selection of own-made scones, quiches, cakes, sausage rolls and pies. Pack up your spoils and drive north along the A515 out of Ashbourne to the glorious former estate villages of Ilam, Tissington and Osmaston. There are superb walks and picnic spots to be found in and around all of these historical gems.

Manifold pleasures of the shire

Just as lovely as the beauty spots of Derbyshire, but without the tourist hordes, are the lesser-known Manifold and Hamp valleys, which offer a mix of rolling countryside and wild moorland. They're an ideal location for unchallenging cycle rides, and bikes can be hired at various points to follow the surfaced Manifold Track, formerly the Leek & Manifold Light Railway. The old station at Hulme End is now a Visitor Information Centre.

Thor's Cave, in the central section of the valley, is the most spectacular sight. The cave is ten metres in diameter, forming a dark gash in the landscape that's visible for several miles. Archaeologists have found stone tools that suggest that the cave was inhabited as long as 10,000 years ago. Huff and puff your way up the 76 metres to the cave from the track and you'll be rewarded with fabulous views.

There were once over 20 big copper and lead mines in the Manifold Valley. In 1904, almost nine miles of railway was built from Hulme End to Waterhouses. The train transported farmers to the market in Leek and milk to the creamery at Ecton, as well as daytrippers from the potteries. But the venture was not a financial success, and the line closed in 1934. Steam train fans can still get their fixes, however, at the lovely Churnet Valley Railway (see p197) or on the miniature narrow-gauge steam railway (www.rudyardlake.co.uk) that runs around Rudyard Lake, just north of Leek on the Staffordshire-Derbyshire border.

WHERE TO STAY

Alton Towers Hotel

Alton Towers, Alton, Staffordshire ST10 4DB (0870 458 5182/www.altontowers.com). **Rates** £139-£359. **Credit** AmEx, MC, V.
Built to resemble a colonial-style home, there's a calmer ambience here than in the neighbouring Splash Landings (see p200), though you can still gain access to the unmissable Cariba Creek Waterpark (see p202) via a connecting corridor (book ahead for cheaper entrance fees). Outside space comes in the shape of a lake and fountain, overlooked by the hotel's Secret Garden restaurant. If you want to push the boat out, snag one of the eight themed rooms. The Cadburys-sponsored Chocolate suite sleeps up to six and is kitted out like a railway carriage, complete with sound effects. Chocolate is hidden in fake books, and unlimited amounts of the sweet stuff is available from the free vending machines – this place may not be good for your health or your teeth (never mind your wallet), but it's certainly good fun. Younger children will delight in the Peter Rabbit Burrow – interconnecting rooms with magical murals, which house four people. Or go for the Big Pyjamas suite, with a technicolour sky, boat-shaped beds and ships' barrels for tables. Book ahead to secure a reasonable time for dinner at the in-house restaurant, which has an à la carte menu.

Beechenhill Farm

Ilam, Ashbourne, Derbyshire DE6 2BD (01335 310274/www.beechenhill.co.uk). **Rates** £64 (2 nights minimum). *Cottage* £350-£680/wk. **Credit** MC, V.
Sue Prince has become a local heroine (with an OBE) for her work promoting local enterprises. She's a keen proponent of organic methods, and runs this 92-acre organic dairy farm and B&B with her husband Terry. As well as stunning views of the Manifold Valley, the limestone farmhouse boasts tasteful furnishings and friendly sheepdogs and cats. Expect excellent breakfasts with own-made bread, locally-reared bacon and Sue's famous organic porridge, made with Beechenhill milk. Children are genuinely welcome, but accommodation for families with under-fives is only available if you book the family room and the double bedroom (as their close proximity could otherwise mean noisy neighbours for other, non-related guests). Cots can be hired for £5 per night. There's also a self-catering cottage, a converted milking barn, that sleeps six. Kids love the sloping garden with giant chess, rope swings and table tennis. There's a farm trail, walks into nearby Dovedale and a sensationally-positioned Swedish hot tub – where the whole family can wallow under the stars by night, or enjoy panoramic views across the valley during the day.

TOURIST INFORMATION

Ashbourne
13 Market Place, Ashbourne, Derbyshire DE6 1EU (01335 343666/www.visitpeakdistrict.com).

Leek
1 Market Place, Leek, Staffordshire ST13 5HH (01538 483741/ www.staffsmoorlands.gov.uk).

Stoke-on-Trent
Victoria Hall, Bagnall Street, Hanley, Stoke-on-Trent, Staffordshire ST1 3AD (01782 236000/www.visitstoke.co.uk).

Best Western Stoke-on-Trent Moat House Hotel

Etruria Hall, Festival Way, Etruria, Hanley, Stoke-on-Trent, Staffordshire ST1 5BQ (01782 609988/www.moathousehotels.com). **Rates** RO £64-£129. **Credit** MC, V.

When you have young children in tow, large and efficient hotels like this 147-roomer can sometimes provide a less stressful experience than intimate B&Bs. And while no one could claim that Stoke-on-Trent is the loveliest place on earth, this imposing building, which incorporates the former home of pottery king Josiah Wedgewood and stands in the city's Festival Park complex, is a stone's throw from the superb aqua park Waterworld (01782 205747, www.waterworld.co.uk), with its rides, multiplex cinema and bowling alley. There's a choice of restaurants on the premises, including JWs Café Bar, with a toddler-friendly ball pool. A well-run leisure club, with a pool, jacuzzi, steam room and spa offering massage and aromatherapy for frazzled parents is a further draw. Under-16s sharing their parents' room are accommodated free (but pay £5 each for breakfast). Younger children get a goodie bag at check-in but note that there is no baby-sitting service. Alton Towers packages are available; phone for details.

Glencote Caravan Park

Station Road, Cheddleton, Leek, Staffordshire ST13 7EE (01538 360745/www.glencote. co.uk). **Open** Feb-Dec. **Rates** £17.50/pitch (2 adults); £4 additional adult; £2 5-16s; free under 5s. **Credit** MC, V.

This small, well-tended caravan and camping park sits alongside the wonderful Churnet Valley Railway (*see p203*), so if there's a *Thomas the Tank Engine* fan in your party, it should go down a treat. As well as the idyllic setting – a quiet, wooded valley with the river Churnet wending its way past – the site has all the essentials for comfortable camping, including laundry rooms, a communal barbecue area, dish-washing sinks and sparklingly clean toilets and showers. The waterside Boat Inn is a short walk away and serves decent hot meals, while the attractive ancient village of Cheddleton, with a chemist, a grocery shop and off-licence, is a pleasant kilometre stroll away.

Heywood Hall

College Road, Denstone, Staffordshire ST14 5HR (01889 591747/www.heywoodhall.co.uk). **Rates** £150 apartment. **No credit cards**.

Louise and John McCann's large Victorian home is minutes away from Alton Towers, and you can get in the mood for pleasure-seeking with its gloriously OTT themed rooms. Each of the three spacious family suites is different. 'Sally' features a kids' twin-bedded room with jungle mural, fake furry animal skins and zebra cushions (plus PlayStation and TV). An artist has been at work in the adult quarters too – this time the backdrop is Tuscan ruins. Attention to detail is clearly of importance here, with chocolates on the stacks of towels and well-selected DVDs. Breakfast is self-catering: the kitchen has a microwave, hob, dishwasher and fridge crammed with sausages, bacon, mushrooms, tomatoes, eggs, milk, croissants and fruit. After a hard day's theme parking, eat at the pub a few doors down, or have a splash in the hot tub or steam in the sauna and order in pizza. Two minutes down the road is construction manufacturer JCB's world headquarters, with its open-to-the-public landscaped gardens, lake, fountains and spectacular digger and heron sculptures.

Ilam Hall Caravan Site
Ilam, Derbyshire, DE6 2AZ (01335 350310). **Open** Mid Mar-Oct. **Rates** £13-£16. **Credit** MC, V.
You need to be a member of the National Trust or the Caravan Club to stay at this small 20-pitch site. It's worth joining, though, because the setting, in Ilam (pronounced eye-lam) Park, couldn't be lovelier. There are child-friendly walks along the banks of the river Manifold, with a small, railed grotto to discover, or through the gentle parkland and woodland, part of the National Trust's South Peake estate. Note that there are no showers or loos on site (though National Trust public toilets are open nearby), but it's a thoroughly peaceful place to spend a night.

Ilam Hall Youth Hostel
Ilam Hall, Ilam, Ashbourne, Derbyshire DE6 2AZ (0870 770 5876/www.yha.org.uk). **Open** year round. **Rates** £16; £12 under-18s; £49-£56 family room. **Credit** MC, V.
It's not often you get the chance to stay in a stately home for just a few pounds, but Ilam Hall, a Gothic-looking mansion built in the 1820s, was bought for the National Trust by Sir Robert McDougall in 1935 on the understanding that it would be used as an International Youth Hostel. There's a lovely notice in the foyer welcoming families, 'including those with under-fives'. Given the stunning location, it's hardly surprising that the family rooms, some of which have en suite facilities, need to be booked well in advance. The accommodation isn't luxurious, but the stately wood panelling and creaky stairs and landings lend an air of faded grandeur. There's a games room with table tennis and pool, communal kitchen and laundry facilities. And you're well placed for visiting Dovedale and exploring the Manifold Valley by bike; cycle hire is available in the village of Waterhouses.

TOP 5

WHITE KNUCKLE RIDES
In Alton Towers, and beyond.

Nemesis
Alton Towers' superfast coaster exacts its revenge on wimps. *See p202.*

Oblivion
This Alton Towers ride climbs over 60 metres then drops to the ground with a force of 4.5G. Hysteria rules for a few seconds. *See p202.*

Pepsi Max Big One
Blackpool's finest – 74mph and 3.5 G Force. *See p257.*

Rita
Our favourite speed queen plays fast and loose with your innards at Alton Towers. *See p202.*

Wild Mouse
The turns are so quick and sharp your life flashes before you right there on Blackpool Pleasure Beach. *See p257.*

Manor House Farm Bed & Breakfast
Quixhill Lane, Prestwood, Denstone, Uttoxeter, Staffordshire ST14 5DD (01889 590415/ www.towersabovetherest.com). **Rates** £50-£90. *Cottage* £160-£425/wk. **Credit** MC, V.
This Jacobean farmhouse with mullioned windows and sloping floors is a real charmer, and owners Chris and Margaret Ball are friendly and relaxed hosts. There's one family room and two doubles inside the house and a self-catering cottage that sleeps four in the grounds. All rooms have four-poster beds and there are antiques and tasteful knick-knacks all around the place, which give it

an atmosphere probably best suited to families with older children, although cots can be provided free for babies. In the fields, rare breed Irish Moile cattle graze, and you can play croquet or tennis on the large lawns. There's also a Victorian summerhouse in the fabulous garden. Alton Towers is only three miles down the road, though like many parts of underrated Staffordshire, this place feels beautifully remote.

Splash Landings

Alton Towers, Alton, Staffordshire ST10 4DB 0870 4585182/www.altontowers.com/splash). **Rates** £139-£359 (4+4). **Credit** AmEx, MC, V.
To get the most from a theme park-based weekend, it's worth considering staying on the premises. Guests at Alton Tower's on-site hotel are allowed on three selected rides an hour before the gates open for Joe Public. And try dragging the children out of Cariba Creek *(see p202)*, the hotel's huge Caribbean-themed indoor waterpark, visible from almost every angle in the hotel. Book your tickets for this when you make your reservation – the price for guests is £8 per person (under-4s are free) instead of the usual £12 (£37 for a family ticket). Pre-booked and discounted theme park entrance tickets are also available. A Caribbean nautical theme is present throughout the busy hotel, from the crab and seaweed print carpets to the strains of the *Captain Pugwash* theme tune in the lift. The family rooms are surprisingly small but well equipped, with a jolly beachcomber theme. Restful it's not, but children feed off the buzz. Be sure to book your preferred buffet mealtime slot at the hotel's Flambo's Feast restaurant *(see below)* as soon as you check in or you may find yourselves limited to visiting at a late hour.

WHERE TO EAT AND DRINK

Bramhall's

6 Buxton Road, Ashbourne, Derbyshire, DE6 1EX (01335 346158/www.bramhalls. co.uk). **Meals served** noon-2.30pm, 6.30-9.30pm Mon-Sat; noon-2.30pm Sun. **Main courses** £8.95-£12.95. **Credit** MC, V.
An informal brasserie within a converted 250-year-old coaching inn, Bramhall's offers diners a no-nonsense approach to modern fusion cooking. The weekly changing menu is augmented by a daily specials board that usually has fresh fish of the day (normally the first option to run out). On Sundays a traditional lunch menu is served. It's a popular and friendly place, with perky staff who do their best to make you feel welcome. The steaks are always fabulous; our fillet of Derbyshire beef with mashed potato, green beans and crisp fried onions was a memorable meal for all the right reasons. For the sweet-toothed, the almond tarte or dark chocolate torte are good bets for dessert. There's no specific children's menu, but the chefs are happy to provide small portions of whatever's on the main menu, or to prepare sausages, beans, chips and the like. There are two high chairs for junior diners.

Eileen's Pantry

The Trading Post, 2 Froghall Road, Ipstones, Staffordshire ST10 2LA (01538 266228). **Meals served** 8am-4pm daily. **Main courses** £2.35-£3.80. **Credit** MC, V.
Eileen and Geoff, proprieters of the Ipstones village shop and this simple, lino-floored café, must be the county's friendliest hosts. Their premises are a meeting place for villagers and the ideal drop-in for visitors to the Staffordshire Moorlands. People come from miles around for huge portions of the warming soup, made fresh daily. Simple snacks such as cheese on toast, bacon baps and hot Staffordshire oatcakes (large flat pancakes) with savoury fillings are also served. Giant slices of own-made sponge cost a mere 80p. A children's menu is available, but Geoff says they'll adapt anything on the menu for small appetites. There's also great Italian coffee and ice-cream sundaes.

Flambo's Feast

Alton Towers, Alton, Staffordshire ST10 4DB (0870 4585182/www.altontowers.com). **Meals served** *Alton Towers' hotel guests* 3-10pm daily. **Main courses** £18.95; £6.95 4-15s; £1.95 under-4s. **Credit** AmEx, MC, V.
You needn't worry about your toddlers letting rip in Splash Landings' restaurant – the dining room is a riot of noise and activity. Collect a plate and then help yourself to a selection of food from the hot buffet, arranged by a series of 'pods'. There's enough choice to ensure that fussy eaters are accommodated, with an emphasis on comfort foods such as chilli con carne, lamb stew, veggie crumble and roasts, with every kind of potato, rice and wraps. It's not fine dining, but it's certainly decent enough. The chocolate fountain with stacks of fresh strawberries, pineapple and marsh-mallows for dunking is a huge draw. There's wait-ress service for drinks (the non-alcoholic children's cocktails slip down very well), and the army of Hawaiian-shirted staff remain good humoured and unflappable throughout the organised chaos.

Kingsley & Froghall Station Tea Rooms

Churnet Valley Railway, Froghall, Staffordshire ST10 2HA (01538 360522). **Meals served** *phone to check.* **Main courses** £2-£3. **Credit** MC, V.
Eating here feels like being stuck in an extremely pleasant timewarp, which is just what the good people who run this charming moorlands railway hope for. Smiling ladies serve snacks, including Staffordshire oatcakes, Cornish pasties, sausage rolls, toasties, and fruit crumble. Care has been taken to provide period touches, such as vintage luggage in the waiting room and old-fashioned adverts. There are tables outdoors, so you can watch the steam trains shunt slowly past, or cosy up to an open fire inside in the winter months. Mummies can dream of getting a smut in their eye and having it tended by a Trevor Howard-like hero. Children dream of Thomas, Gordon, et al.

CRUISING THE CANALS

You're never far from a canal in Staffordshire. Not surprising, as this county has more miles of waterways within its boundaries than anywhere else in England. Children adore watching the brightly-coloured narrowboats gliding over the water, especially if they're *Rosie and Jim* devotees.

Nowadays, the canal system is just for pleasure. But during the Industrial Revolution, in pre-rail times, waterways formed a crucial network for transporting raw materials and finished goods.

The **Caldon Canal**, which opened in 1779, was built to ship minerals from the Peak District to the potteries. It joins the Trent and Mersey Canal at Etruria, Stoke-on-Trent, before winding its way east to the lush Churnet Valley. **Froghall Wharf** (01538 266486) three miles north of Cheadle at the end of the Cauldon Canal is a great setting-off point for a trip, with rides on offer twice a week between May and September. Boatmen are dressed in period costume, and you can get a cream tea on board too.

Once a hive of industry, in the days when iron ore was mined from the valley and smelted, it's now a wildlife haven. There's a reminder of the area's industrial past at the fascinating Flint Mill (01782 502907) at Cheddleton, a museum of industrial archaeology. Walks along the towpath are buggy-friendly and easy to negotiate, and everyone enjoys watching the boats.

It's worth paying a visit to the **Etruria Industrial Museum** in Stoke-on-Trent, which hosts an annual canal festival on the first weekend in June (*see p331*). The museum sits at the junction of the Trent and Mersey and Caldon Canals and has a canal warehouse and Britain's last remaining steam-powered potters' mill (built in the mid-19th century to provide materials for the pottery industry). It's a potent way to bring England's industrial past alive for history-resistant youth.

Longnor Fish & Chip Shop

Market Place, Longnor, nr Buxton, Derbyshire SK17 0NT (01298 83317). **Meals served** *Summer* 11.30am-1.30pm, 6-10pm Tue, Thur, Fri; 6-9pm Sat. *Winter* 11.30am-1.30pm, 6-9pm Tue, Thur-Sat. **Main courses** £2.80-£3.80. **No credit cards.**

This lovely village in the Staffordshire Moorlands also plays host to a tiny and very special fish and chip shop. Set on the corner of the main square, it has pretty red and white checked tables for eating in – but many visitors like to take their fish supper away and munch it in the market place. Wherever you eat, you'll find the fish fresh, the batter crisp and the chips golden and perfectly soft inside. Mushy peas or curry sauce provide the lubrication.

National Trust Tea Room

Ilam Park, Ilam, Ashbourne, Derbyshire DE6 2AZ (01335 350503). **Meals served** *Mar-Oct* 11am-5pm Mon, Tue, Fri-Sun. *Nov-Feb* 11am-4pm Sat, Sun. Phone for details of prices.

These lovely tearooms have toys for children, and plenty of room to sit inside. In fine weather, go for the tables outdoors overlooking Ilam Hall's pleasantly restored Italian gardens, the village, the flat-topped Thorpe Cloud Hill and Bunster Hill (the two hills mark the gateway to Dovedale). An appetising menu features frittata topped with local cheese and quiche with seasonal veg, plus exceptionally fresh salads. Jacket spuds and chunky sandwiches are also on hand for those in need of some carb loading – but save room for the unmissable cakes and cream teas.

Rambler's Retreat

Red Road, Dimmingsdale, Alton, Staffordshire ST10 4BU (01538 702730). **Meals served** *Winter* 10am-4pm Wed-Sun. *Summer* 10am-5pm Wed-Sun. **Main courses** £3.50-£8.95. **Credit** MC, V.

Rambler's Retreat is the kind of place you always hope you'll stumble across after a family yomp in the countryside. The early 19th-century lodge, which sits alongside the wooded Churnet Valley trail, was rescued from dereliction by its current owners Gary and Margaret Keeling. Breakfast, lunch and afternoon tea are offered, all made with local produce. Staffordshire roast of the day is an excellent deal at £6.95, and there's steak pie and oatcake pizza, among other options. Don't miss the damson pie (made with local fruit) and lemon meringue. Eat in the conservatory or outdoors, surrounded by ancient woodland and a pretty garden complete with tumbling waterfall. Booking is advised for lunch and tea in summer.

The Secret Garden

Alton Towers, Alton, Staffordshire, ST10 4DB (0870 458 5182/www.altontowers.com). **Meals served** *Alton Towers & Splash Landing hotel guests* 5.30-9pm daily. **Main courses** £8.75-£18.25. **Credit** MC, V.

After a hectic day in the theme park, this restaurant offers a calmer atmosphere than its neighbour, Splash Landings' Flambo's (*see p200*), with a more sophisticated children's menu (£6.95 for 3 courses) that includes soup, pasta, chicken fillets, cod, sausage and mash, jacket pots, sundaes, fruit salad. For adults, there's an à la carte menu with a reasonably ambitious selection of dishes; melon, proscuitto and honey roast figs (£4.65) for starters, while mains are of the grilled chicken breast with thyme sauce and oak-smoked fillet of beef with mash variety. For dessert, there's comforting warm marmalade and chocolate bread and butter pud, and banana, toffee and chocolate ice-cream sundae.

PLACES TO SEE, THINGS TO DO

Alton Towers

Alton, Staffordshire, ST10 4DB (0870 444 4455/www.altontowers.com). **Open** *Mid Mar-Oct* 10am-5pm Mon-Fri; 10am-6pm Sat, Sun. (9am start for hotel guests). **Admission** £29; £20 children above 1m-12 yrs; £78 family (2+2). **Credit** AmEx, MC, V.

It's often a surprise to people with an aversion to theme parks that Alton Towers is actually very pleasant. It's not just the 500 acres of lushly wooded grounds, but the way that the park is split into cleverly screened and landscaped areas. There's nothing subtle about the rides though. Take your pick from a plethora of rollercoasters: the shockingly fast Nemesis; Oblivion, which shoots you below ground; Air, in which you experience a 360 degree barrel roll; the symbolic Corkscrew; and Rita – Queen of Speed, voted the best ride by visitors. There's stacks for younger children, too, the latest highlight being Charlie and the Chocolate Factory: The Ride, complete with glass elevator and chocolate river (it's worth enduring the huge queues). Kids love getting splashed in the Congo River Rapids and being slightly scared in the Blade, a giant swing boat. Duel, a futuristic ghost train, is also a hit, as is the cable car that transports you between areas. Avoid peak season if possible for less overwhelming crowds. There are fast food outlets throughout the park, but bring your own picnic if you fancy ingesting something less stomach-churning (and vastly cheaper).

Amerton Farm

Amerton, Stowe-by-Chartley, Stafford, Staffordshire ST18 0LA (01889 270294/www.amertonfarm.co.uk). **Open** *Winter* 9am-5pm daily. *Summer* 9am-5.30pm daily. **Admission** free. **Credit** *Shop* MC, V.

You've heard of farms diversifying, but Amerton is a positive powerhouse of enterprise. As well as a traditional farmyard with cows, pigs, sheep, goats and ponies for children to feed and stroke, there's a covered adventure play area and a farm shop. What's more, there's a craft centre with artists who work on site, a bakery and sweet shop, a tearoom, a garden centre and even a small steam railway (not to mention the complementary therapy centre). Bring a picnic or eat in the tearoom, and don't miss the Amerton Farm ice-cream, sold at the farm shop. If you just can't get enough of the place, consider sleeping on site, in the 18th-century farmhouse that's now a thriving B&B.

Cariba Creek Waterpark

Alton Towers, Alton, Staffordshire, ST10 4DB (01538 707344/www.altontowers.com). **Open** 10am-6pm Sun-Thur, Sun; 10am-8pm Fri, Sat. **Admission** £12; £37.50 family (2+2); free under-4s. *Towel hire* £1. **Credit** MC. V.
You can do pretty much anything in this Caribbean-themed waterpark – except swim. But with so many gadgets and devices on hand, serious exercise is the last thing on your mind here. Children love the watery paradise, with its jets and plumes, towers, ladders, pumps, fountains, water pistols and buckets, handily placed to dump over unsuspecting passers-by. Best of all is the Master Blaster rollercoaster water ride that propels you, in a rubber ring, through a twisting labyrinth of tunnels before depositing you in an outside pool. Older kids will find hours of pleasure here, but it's also an easy environment for babies and toddlers, who get their own play area – the tropically heated Little Leak. There's a private parent and baby room just by the pool, and there are poolside lockers for baby paraphenalia.

Churnet Valley Railway

Cheddleton Station, Cheddleton, nr Leek, Staffordshire, ST13 7EE (0870 766 6312/ www.churnet-valley-railway.co.uk). **Open** *Mar-Oct* 10.30am-3.50pm Sat, Sun. *July* 10.30am-3.50pm Wed. *Aug* 10.30am-3.50pm Mon, Wed. *Jan* 10.30am-3.50pm Sun. **Admission** £9; £5 4-16yrs; under 3s free; £25 family (2+2). **Credit** AmEx, MC, V.
There's no better way to discover Staffordshire's beautiful moorlands than through this 10.5 mile (17km) return trip along the Churnet Valley. Board your train from the flower-filled platform at the charmingly-named Cheddleton Station, and enjoy threading through banks of willowherb, passing woodland and narrowboats on the Caldon Canal along the way. There are tea shops at both Cheddleton and Kingsley and also at Froghall. Get off at Consall, in the heart of the valley, for a walk in the oak and hazel woodland of Consall Nature Park before taking another train home. Children should enjoy chugging through tunnels – the longest of any preserved railway. There's a little shop at Cheddleton (open on all running days) that sells *Thomas the Tank Engine* memorabilia.

Emma Bridgewater Factory Shop, Decorating Studio & Café

The Courtyard, Lichfield Street, Hanley, Stoke-on-Trent, Staffordshire ST1 3EJ (Studio 01782 269682/Shop 01782 201328/www.emmabridgewater.co.uk).

Open 9.30am-5.30pm Mon-Sat; 11am-4pm Sun. **Cost** £10/person average (inc unlimited studio time & pottery to take home). **Credit** MC, V.
Stoke-on-Trent is steeped in ceramic history. Let the children discover what all the fuss is about by letting them make their own creations. This attractive studio is owned by Emma Bridgewater, designer of cheerful *Country Living*-style pottery. It's located near the town centre of Hanley, which is struggling manfully to shed its sooty industrial image. The whole family can have a go at designing their own cups, plates or bowls, with help from the trained studio assistants. A pleasant café, along with a shop selling discontinued lines and slight seconds at reasonable prices, provide all the more reason to pop by.

Potteries Museum & Art Gallery

Bethesda Street, Hanley, Stoke-on-Trent, ST1 3DW (01782 232323/www.stoke.gov.uk/ museums). **Open** *Nov-Feb* 10am-4pm Mon-Sat; 1-4pm Sun. *Mar-Oct* 10am-5pm Mon-Sat; 2-5pm Sun. **Admission** free. **Credit** *Shop* MC, V.
An outstanding museum, with plenty to please both boys and girls of all ages. The Reginald Mitchell Spitfire gallery houses a real Mark XVI aeroplane, while the Changing Fashions area highlights flights of fashion fancy from the 18th century to the present, where you can try on clothes. Animal lovers enjoy the natural history's section, with interactive exhibits for busy fingers. Even the vast collection of Staffordshire pottery, not the most obvious draw for kids, is presented imaginatively, with exhibits including a large collection of ceramic cow-creamers. Small shrines to Stoke boys Robbie Williams and Sir Stanley Matthews complete the picture. The gift shop has a fine selection of pocket-money toys.

Trentham Monkey Forest

Trentham Estate, Stone Road, Trentham, Staffordshire ST4 8AX (01782 659845/ www.monkey-forest.com). **Open** *Feb half term* 10am-4pm daily. *Mar, Nov* 10am-4pm Sat, Sun. *Apr, May, Sept, Oct* 10am-5pm daily. *June-Aug* 10am-6pm daily. Last entry 1hr before closing. **Admission** £5.50; £4 3-14s; concessions; free under-3s. **Credit** MC, V.
Stoke-on-Trent is a city currently enjoying a wave of restoration projects. The transformation of the historic landscaped gardens at nearby Trentham, which were the height of fashion in the 19th century, is one such initiative. Part of the estate has been turned into a sanctuary for 140 Barbary macaque monkeys, who roam free over 60 acres of forest. Observe baby monkeys, born between May and July; by autumn they are weaned from their mothers and start branching out to play with other members of the group. Pick up a family quiz sheet to find out more about the species. Guides are stationed at regular intervals along the paths, and there are hourly talks. There's a self-service café and gift shop on site, plus picnic tables with a covered area for rainy days.

Staffordshire

North Norfolk coast

Norfolk is a foreign country:
they do things differently there.

To mangle the famous opening line of *The Go-Between*, LP Hartley's
rites-of-passage novel set in Norfolk before World War I, helps get
to the gist of this singular county. Though you'll find modern amenities
and technical gadgetry if you look for them, the pleasures of the north
Norfolk coast are, in the main, old-fashioned and idyllic: the vast sky,
the jumble of quiet villages, and above all the glorious coastline.
Travelling here with a family requires an adjustment of pace from
city living, yet it's surprising how even world-weary teenagers can
find something to spark an interest.

However short your stay here, it's worth spending some time
acclimatising to the physical and social surroundings. If you're a
motorist (and it's difficult, though not impossible, to explore north
Norfolk by public transport) don't let it be long after arrival before you
spend some time away from the car. A walk through woodland or along
the desolate coastline is the best introduction – for all ages – to this
amazing part of the world.

Wells Harbour

Where the smart set shop: one of **Burnham Market's** delis

Likewise, if you're keen to discover Norfolk's wealth of villages, try not to let the trip become a procession of cottages and country lanes seen through car windows. Rather, choose to explore a village when it's staging an event: the annual fête, perhaps, or a pantomime, or even a simple jumble sale or 'open gardens' day. Not only will you then see the village at its best and get to mix with the locals, but you'll usually find plenty of entertainment for children – even if that consists of spending a few pence on jumble sale junk, then playing on the village recreation ground.

Norfolk is blessed with a first-rate weekly events guide, covering everything from fungi forays to beetle drives. It comes as an insert in the Friday edition of the *Eastern Daily Press*. The *EDP* is read more widely than any national newspaper in Norfolk, and provides a fund of fascinating nuggets about life in the county. From May to September, you won't have to travel far for a fête or carnival; the village pantomime season starts in early December and lasts until March (be prepared for copious in-jokes, bewildering acting, sweets pelted at the audience by the dame and a raffle during the interval). In between, various autumn bazaars and spring fairs are held in village halls throughout the county.

If you plan to spend time on the coast, it's very important to know your tides. At low tide, the 'beaches' on the Wash (Snettisham, Heacham) are mere mud flats; from Hunstanton to Wells, you'll get vast expanses of sand and will need binoculars to see any waves. Yet at points east of Weybourne (including the resorts of Sheringham and Cromer), low tide is prime time, when, as well as pebbles, you'll get a hundred yards of castle-builder's sand before the sea. At high tide, when the Wash becomes quenched, the beaches from Hunstanton to Wells reduce dramatically in size (the currents are dangerous; sirens at Wells sound to warn bathers against being cut off on the dunes), while crabbing boats flood into the harbour to unload their snapping cargo. At high tide too, the sand at Weybourne, Sheringham and Cromer is completely covered and only pebbles remain on view, though in winter you might enjoy a windswept walk scored to the explosion of waves against the sea defences.

Links to local tide tables can be found online at http://new.edp24.co.uk and www.lynnnews.co.uk. Times of high tides are also published on page two of the *EDP* from Monday to Saturday and, on Fridays and Tuesdays, page two of the *Lynn News*.

A very Victorian resort

Even vehement republicans will find plenty of interest at the Sandringham Estate (*see p216*). North of the estate is the large village of Snettisham (mercifully bypassed by the A149). Here you'll find a few shops, a couple of pubs (including the Rose & Crown, *see p212*) and Snettisham Park (*see p217*).

Hunstanton, or 'sunny Hunny' is an archetypal Victorian seaside resort. Its rather austere buildings, made from dark-brown local carrstone, look down on a triangular green (with a bandstand where summer concerts are held), a wide expanse of sandy beaches and the rump of a pier. Rebuilt after a 2002 fire, the latter no longer stretches out into the sea; it does, however, house an amusement arcade, a 90-seat diner and bar and a first-floor ten-pin bowling centre (01485 534960). In summer, pony rides take place on the sands and amphibious vehicles take tourists to explore the coast and see the seal colonies (Searles, 07831 321799, www.seatours.co.uk).

You won't find much in the way of fine dining or high fashion in Hunstanton, but prices are low and there's a fair range of shops, plus a market on Wednesdays and Sundays. Cassie's Fish and Chip Restaurant (21 The Green, 01485 532448) fits the bill for a family feed. After lunch, further entertainment can be had at the crazy golf course on Cliff Parade, at World of Fun, which claims to be 'England's largest joke shop' (2A St Edmund's Terrace, 01485 532016) and at the permanent funfair on the Southern Promenade. Just next door is Hunstanton Sea Life Sanctuary (see p216). Hunstanton also has a theatre, the Princess (The Green, 01485 532252, www.princesstheatrehunstanton.co.uk), where professional pantomimes are held in winter, and a varied diet of films, amateur dramatics and easy-listening musicians is served the rest of the year.

Second-home heaven

Leaving Hunstanton on the A149 coastal road, you soon come to the village of Old Hunstanton. The sandy beach here is quieter than at the resort, and the village shop, Old Hunstanton Stores (38 Old Hunstanton Road, 01485 533197), has become a foodie attraction, with its local grub-rich deli. Away from the main road (signposted on the right, down Church Road, as you leave the village heading east) is the beautiful 14th-century church of St Mary the Virgin – of more interest to young children is the duck pond opposite.

Continuing east along the A149, you'll pass through the attractive village of Holme-next-the-Sea. The beach here has sand dunes and a boardwalk that allows for easy walking with a buggy or wheelchair. There's also a car park and shop (selling Norfolk-made ice-cream, plus beach-found objects that children can look at and touch), but no toilets close by. The next village, Thornham, is home to two family-friendly pubs, the Lifeboat Inn (Ship Lane, 01485 512236, www.lifeboatinn.co.uk) and the Orange Tree (High Street, 01485 512213, www.theorangetreethornham.co.uk), both of which have accommodation. After a couple of miles you'll come to Titchwell (home to the Titchwell Marsh Nature Reserve, see p217), before reaching Brancaster.

Lovers of wild windswept coastlines away from the crowds adore Brancaster beach, reached via Broad Lane, off the A149. After about half a mile you'll find a car park (£3.50 a day; £1 after 4pm), then it's only a hundred metres to the sands. Apart from a golf course, some public toilets and a little shed selling beach gear and ice-creams, there's little in the way of amenities, but even at the height of summer you won't need to walk far to have acres (and at low tide miles) of beach to yourself. Beware of the strong currents; the plaque at the entrance to the beach is a memorial to a child who was swept away.

East of Brancaster is Brancaster Staithe, which has photogenic creeks (where small sailing boats are moored), salt marshes and the welcoming Jolly Sailors pub (see p215). At the next village, Burnham Deepdale, there's a pleasant, peaceful campsite, for tents and small camper vans (see p212). There's also a new parade of shops on the A149 at Deepdale, including the Deepdale Café (see p215).

A short detour off the A149 from Deepdale will take you to the good-looking little town of Burnham Market. Here you'll find high-quality boutiques, bookstores, some very good food shops, and the Hoste Arms (see p212). You'll also notice that many of the customers patronising these establishments aren't from Norfolk. Burnham Market is at the centre of north Norfolk's gentrification, and many of its properties are now second homes to folk from London and the home counties. These new arrivals have started to have an impact on the villages surrounding the Burnhams and on the nearby town of Wells, with several pubs in the vicinity serving classier (though more expensive) food, but not much further afield – so far.

TOURIST INFORMATION

Cromer
Cromer Bus Station, Prince of Wales Road, Cromer, Norfolk NR27 9HS (0871 200 3071/www.visitnorth norfolk.com).

Sheringham
Station Approach, Sheringham, Norfolk NR26 8RA (0871 200 3071/www.north norfolk.org/tourism). Open May-Sept.

Walsingham
Shirehall Museum, Common Place, Little Walsingham, Norfolk NR22 6BP (01328 820510).

Wells
Staithe Street, Wells-next-the-Sea, Norfolk NR23 1AN (0871 200 3071/ www.northnorfolk.org/tourism). Open May-Sept.

PINCER MOVEMENT

Cancer pagurus or the edible brown crab is abundant along the north Norfolk coast, with Cromer crabs being famed throughout Britain. These are sold freshly boiled at markets and fishmongers along the coast, and can also be bought directly from fishermen's houses (look out for signs along the A149). The adult crabs are orangey-brown in colour, but it is their offspring, which are of a much darker purpley-brown hue, that concern us here. These young crabs are too small to eat (laws forbid the commercial landing of crabs with a shell diameter of less than ten centimetres), but catching them is often one of the highlights of a child's Norfolk holiday.

The best crabbing locations are the quays at Wells and Blakeney – find a space between the tethered boats. Come at high tide if you can, when the sea is near the top of the harbour walls and you won't have far to reach down and net your catch. Don't let young children get too close to the edge; deep water at high tide, a long drop at low tide and strong currents in between are real dangers.

Buying the wherewithal to go crabbing is easy and cheap. First you'll need a line with a weight attached. Don't use a hook as these can get lost and cause injury to sea birds; simply tie the bait to the line or put it inside the little net provided. Then you'll have to buy a decent-sized bucket to hold your spoils. Best are the see-through versions, which allow you to view the little snappers at close quarters; partially fill the buckets with sea water, in anticipation of your first crab. Landing nets are also virtually essential, especially if you're crabbing near low tide (when the blighters tend to drop off the line before you can haul them up to the quay).

Back on the main coast road east of the Burnhams, you'll be travelling through land owned by the Coke family, the Earls of Leicester. Their stately home, Holkham Hall (rebuilt in the Palladian style during the 18th century), is open on selected days during the summer (01328 710227). The gardens stay open longer, and boat trips are run around the lake. Holkham also has a beach; a charming sandy inlet that's a fine venue for kite-flying. If you haven't come equipped, there's a great selection for sale at Windseekers on Staithe Street in Wells (01328 710718). The beach can be reached from the pay and display car park via a walk through pine woods. By the car park, a refreshments stand serves up high-quality snacks, including own-made sausages and ice-cream. The beach can also be reached from the Victoria (*see p213*), though the walk's an extra half mile.

East of Holkham, the lovely little town of Wells-next-the-Sea contains a beach resort, fishing port, picturesque shopping street and tree-lined green (The Buttlands, where the carnival is held in summer) within its small circumference. Gentrification has only recently had an impact here, so though there's fine dining to be had at the Crown Hotel (The Buttlands, 01328 710209,

Finally, there's the question of bait. You can buy it (usually squid) from the beachware shops, but you'll get just as good results for less outlay (around 50p) with bacon off-cuts from a butcher's: Arthur Howell's on Staithe Street in Wells, for instance. Purists can go in search of free bait in the form of winkles or mussels.

You won't need to spend more than a fiver for all the equipment. ML Walsingham & Son in Wells (Staithe Street, 01328 710438) can supply the essentials. Near high tide, you'll find you're catching a new specimen every couple of minutes; hauls of 50 crabs per expedition aren't unusual.

Often, tourists come to gawp and it's hard to resist the temptation to assume an expert air. Bluff your way through by picking the crabs up from behind, with finger and thumb (to avoid pincer nip), and talking knowledgeably about cock and hen crabs and how to sex them (the male's abdomen is more pointed than the female's).

At the end, gently tip over the bucket and allow the crabs to escape. Their sideways scuttling as they head for the sea is hugely entertaining.

www.thecrownhotelwells.co.uk) and continental foodstuffs at the Wells Deli (15 The Quay, 01328 711171, www.wells deli.co.uk), there are also old-fashioned independent shops. A butcher's, a baker's, a fishmonger's and a hardware store stand on Staithe Street, the narrow high street running uphill from the quay; at the top is the Corner House (see p214).

The quay is lined with fishing and pleasure boats, and is an ideal spot for crab fishing (see **Pincer movement** p208). Another highlight is the Albatross (The Quay, 07979 087228), a large sailing vessel built in Holland in 1899. Below decks you'll find a

cosy (if rough round the edges) bar where savoury and sweet Dutch pancakes are served. Across the road, facing the quay, is French's Fish Shop (10 Quayside, 01328 710396), which has been selling fish and chips for over 75 years.

Wells' sandy beach is a mile away from the town (there's a car park near the beach, plus toilets and a café/shop). In summer, a little narrow gauge train carries passengers most of the way from the town to the beach. Old-fashioned beach huts line the seafront; these can be hired through Pinewoods Caravan Park (01328 710439, www.pinewoods.co.uk). At low tide you'll have a long walk to the sea, but there are many shallow pools and streams to explore. Be sure to heed the sirens, though, and keep to the landward side of these channels when the sea races in.

Wells also has a small theatre, the Granary Theatre (Staithe Street, 01328 710193) which occasionally stages productions for children. The town's other main attraction is off the A149 just to the east of the centre: the Wells to Walsingham Light Railway (see p217).

The train's destination, Little Walsingham, is a handsome medieval village five miles or so inland from Wells. It has been an important place of Christian pilgrimage for almost 1,000 years; devout members of the Catholic and Orthodox churches are still are drawn to the (rebuilt) shrine of Our Lady of Walsingham. Although there's little specifically geared to children here (unless you count brass rubbing), an enjoyable couple of hours can be spent wandering the narrow streets, admiring the half-timbered medieval buildings, popping into the tea shops and gift shops (religious souvenirs a speciality), or grabbing a meal at one of the pubs. Alternatively, great picnic food can be purchased at the Walsingham Farm Shop (Guild Street, 01328 821877, www.walsinghamfarmsshop.co.uk), before catching the train back to Wells. The ruins and peaceful gardens of Walsingham Abbey are particularly popular for snowdrop walks in February – ask at Walsingham Tourist Information Office (see p207) for details.

Far from the madding crowds

East of Wells, salt marshes, where samphire grows in summer, block the way to the sea. Soon after you leave the town, you'll notice a sign to Warham, about a mile inland off the coast road. It's worth visiting for the splendid pies and own-made puddings at the Three Horseshoes pub (see p215). Back on the A149, Stiffkey (pronounced 'Stukey' by locals) also has an enticing old hostelry with decent food and a little garden, the Red Lion (44 Wells Road, 01328 830552).

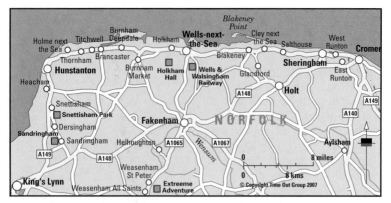

Trips to view the seals at Blakeney Point are run from the next village along the coast, Morston; try Bean's Boats (01263 740038, www.beansboattrips.co.uk) or Temple's Ferry Service (01263 740791). Morston's creeks are splendid for muddy paddling at low tide. However, we'd recommend continuing to the idyllic coastal village of Blakeney, which is peacefully sited off the main road. The sea proper can be seen in the distance, but the creeks leading to the quay fill at high tide. Motor boats carry passengers out to a spit of land where a sizable colony of seals reside. Trips cost about £7 for adults, £4 for children with Bean's Boats (*see above*), Roy Moreton (01328 830394) or Bishop's Boats (01263 740753).

Just to the east of the pay-and-display car park at Blakeney quay there's a large duck pond. Though there's wire mesh around the pond, it's easy to throw bread over the top; a green box at the roadside end of the pond contains a wildfowl species identification book. Across the road are some well-kept public toilets with nappy-changing facilities and, towards Back Lane, the vaulted cellars of the 14th-century Guildhall, which, back in the 19th century, were used as a mortuary for drowned sailors.

Blakeney's two narrow streets down to the quay contain a handful of shops, pubs and restaurants, including a deli and Westons fishmonger's (5a Westgate Street, 01263 741112, www.westonsofblakeney.co.uk). Here you'll find own-made enticements such as potted shrimps, fresh crab and seafood quiches. If you're after local delicacies to take home, continue along the A149 to Cley-next-the-Sea, home of the Cley Smoke House (High Street, 01263 740282, www.cleysmokehouse.com). This modest-sized shop is famous for turning North Sea herring into buckling, kippers, bloaters and red herring. Cley's other foodie haven is Picnic Fayre (The Old Forge, 01263 740587, www.picnic-fayre.co.uk).

Here, exotic cakes share shelf space with locally-made pickles, chutneys, speciality breads, cheeses and pies.

If you travel down Church Lane, by the side of Picnic Fayre, you'll pass Cley's impressive church. Built in the 13th century when the village was a prosperous port, it has a stunning south porch with traceried battlements and a fan-vaulted roof. Follow signs to Glandford from here, and after a mile or so you'll reach the Shell Museum (Church House, Glandford, 01263 740081), built in 1915 to house a collection of shells that was assembled over a period of 60 years by Sir Alfred Jodrell.

Cley's shingle beach can be reached just east of the village, about half a mile down Beach Road (there's a paying car park).

Crab sarnies on the seafront

As you head east out of Cley, you'll notice the Cley Marshes Nature Reserve (*see p215*). The next coastal village is Salthouse, home of Cookie's Crab Shop (*see p214*). Shortly before Weybourne, you'll notice signs to the Muckleburgh Collection (01263 588210, www.muckleburgh.co.uk) where displays of military hardware are held, including tanks and a Harrier jump jet. Weybourne itself has a pebbly beach, but for paddling and castle-making it's best to continue along the coast to Sheringham.

There's plenty to interest children in this attractive little resort town, from the putting green at the top of Church Street to the specially built model boat lake, off the Esplanade – buy little boats for about £15 from Starlings toy shop (31-33 High Street, 01263 822368). Sheringham's Esplanade also has attractive public gardens, fine views out to sea, free car parking (though spaces are at a premium in summer), and public toilets on the way down to the beach.

The beach here is one of Norfolk's most picturesque, featuring plenty of sand at low tide, heaps of pebbles for chucking at the waves at high tide, a line of beach huts and a walkway over a yard where the crabbing boats are kept. The town is a bustling centre of activity (especially on market day every Saturday), where you can buy everything you'll need for the beach. It gets thronged during the annual summer carnival (held in early August).

The best crab sandwiches in Norfolk are served at 'Joyful' West's shellfish bar on the High Street, 30 metres up from the seafront. The Wests, one of Sheringham's oldest fishing families, make the sandwiches to order from freshly boiled crustaceans. Otherwise, there's a decent fish and chip restaurant (Dave's, 7-11 Co-operative Street, 01263 823830, www.davesofsheringham.com) and pub meals served at the Windham Arms (15 Wyndham Street, 01263 822609) and the Two Lifeboats (2 High Street, 01263 822468), which also has accommodation and sea views. Opposite the Windham Arms, a little nugget of history is commemorated by a blue plaque in the diminutive Whitehall Yard; here, at 8.30pm on 19 January 1915, the first bomb dropped on Britain in World War I fell.

A useful standby on a rainy day is Sheringham's Splash swimming pool (Weybourne Road, 01263 825675), which has a 150-foot waterslide, a wave machine and a café. Another alternative is the Little Theatre (2 Station Road, 01263 822347, www.sheringhamlittletheatre.co.uk) which often stages children's events, as well as music, film and theatre productions.

Near the Tourist Information Centre (*see p207*) at the top end of the town are Sheringham's two rail stations, the line to Holt run by the North Norfolk Railway (*see p216*) and the national network station on the Norwich to Cromer line.

The gem of the north

Travelling east of Sheringham, you'll arrive at the villages of West and East Runton. Both have beaches reached via lanes off the A149, featuring sand, sea defence barriers, rock pools at low tide and paying car parks. East Runton is also notable for having a village shop that stays open until 9pm (rare in these parts) and, inland down Green's Lane, a duck pond and large green with a children's play area. Close by, down Mill Lane, is the peaceful Manor Farm Camping and Caravan Site (01263 512858, www.manorfarmcaravansite.co.uk). The village of West Runton, meanwhile, contains a few shops, the Shire Horse Centre (*see p216*), and a train station (on the Norwich to Cromer line).

Cromer, the self-styled 'gem of the north Norfolk coast', is a splendid old-fashioned seaside resort, still boasting guesthouses of blessed cheesiness: flock wallpaper, candlewick bedspreads and tinned tomatoes with your egg and bacon. Children are generally welcome at these establishments, and prices are low. Look along Alfred Road and Cadogan Road (both off the A149) for some likely contenders.

The beach (sandy then pebbly) is Cromer's prime attraction, but you'll soon discover plenty of other child-friendly diversions. In summer, there's a small boating lake, crazy golf course and trampoline area operating just off the A149 (here called the Runton Road), while Cromer pier has a range of amusements: the Pavilion Theatre (staging Seaside Special variety performances, and said to be Britain's last traditional 'end of the pier' show), a modern café and snack bar and a fishing area. Buy the wherewithal from Angling Direct (21 New Street, 01263 513676) in the town centre. Right at the end of the pier stands the Lifeboat Station. Here, plaques dating back to 1923 list all the boats rescued by Cromer's Lifeboat; there's also a shop and a video showing the boat in action. New Street, just in from the seafront, contains an amusements arcade (with some 10p slot machines), J Lee's fisherman's cottage at No.15, where you can buy dressed crab, and a small bookshop (Bookworms, 9 New Street, 01263 515078) with a children's section.

It somehow seems fitting to eat fish and chips when you're visiting Cromer (*see p215*), but alternatives include the courtyard restaurant of the Wellington Hotel on Garden Street (01263 511075), where children have room to play and the daily-changing menu is nothing if not inventive (aubergine stuffed with blackberries, mushrooms and cherry tomatoes, say).

In rainy weather, find out what's on at the Movieplex Cinema (Hans Place, 01263 510151, www.regalfilmcentre.co.uk) or visit the newly refurbished Cromer Museum (East Cottages, Tucker Street, 01263 513543, www.museums.norfolk.gov.uk), which contains a reconstruction of a Victorian fisherman's cottage, displays of old photos, and details of the Cromer Lifeboatmen's exploits. Cromer Market takes place on Fridays, and the town's carnival day is held on the third Wednesday in August (*see p333*).

WHERE TO STAY

Cley Windmill

The Mill, Cley-next-the-Sea, Holt, Norfolk NR25 7RP (01263 740209/www.cleymill.co.uk).
Rates £23-£69. **Credit** MC, V.
In location, the Cley Windmill has few equals. Dating from the early 18th century, it stands just outside the village (and away from the main road), with supreme views of the reed-rustling salt

marshes and the distant sea. The mill has been converted into a guesthouse containing five rooms on the ground, first and second floors. Further accommodation is available in the former boat house, across a small courtyard from the mill, and at two converted outhouses (which can also be let on a self-catering basis). Children's beds can be placed in the outhouses or in the mill's first-floor Barley Bin (originally a storeroom), which has views of the Old Customs House and Cley village. The Barley Bin also has twin beds (or a king-size double), a sofa bed and coffee- and tea-making facilities, plus an en suite wood-panelled bathroom with a claw-footed antique bath. Communal spaces at the mill include a grand, circular sitting room, a beamed dining room (three course dinners are available), an observation room (containing historic photos), a wheel room (where much of the original machinery can be seen), a balcony that encircles the building, and, for the most spectacular views of all, the fan stage, which can be accessed via the windmill's cap.

Deepdale Farm

Burnham Deepdale, Norfolk PE31 8DD (01485 210256/www.deepdalefarm.co.uk/ camping). **Rates** *hostel* £28-£35 family (2+1); £48-£60 family (2+2). *Camping pitch* £3-£6 per person per night. **Credit** MC, V.
This environmentally-friendly farm, right in the heart of an area of outstanding natural beauty on the north Norfolk coast, runs a backpackers' hostel in its stables and granary. It also has a famously quiet, family-friendly campsite that sits discreetly in two well-kept paddocks. A strict noise policy in the late evening means that party animals don't bother with Deepdale, and the caravan ban keeps it cosy (camper vans are permitted). It's simple stuff, with no electrical hookups or generators. The Borthwicks, who run the business, can organise guided farm walks for those who want to find out more about the agricultural side of things.

Hoste Arms

The Green, Burnham Market, Norfolk PE31 8HD (01328 738777/www.hostearms.co.uk). **Rates** £150-£238. **Credit** MC, V.
Paul and Jeanne Whittome brought this yellow-painted 17th-century inn on Burnham Market green in 1989, and paved the way for the village's subsequent gentrification and reputation as a holiday hotspot. Formerly a coaching inn, livestock auction house and assizes, it's now a pub, restaurant and hotel rolled into one appealing package. The conservatory, with its deep leather armchairs, is ideal for afternoon tea or pre-dinner cocktails, while the convivial pub area offers an open fire and real ales. Work by local artists – ornithological paintings by Bruce Pearson and coastline photos by Harry Cory-Wright – are scattered about, and there's also a small art gallery. Meals served in the wood-panelled dining room are a real draw, from the lavish breakfast (porridge with honey is

recommended) to the extensive dinner menu. Local ingredients (Brancaster mussels, Burnham Creek oysters, Holkham Estate venison) and homely dishes (steak and kidney pudding, burger and chips) mix with more international flavours (swordfish sashimi, chicken pad Thai) – plus a 300-bin wine list. Jeanne is responsible for the exuberant (some might say eccentric) decor: the country house style of the bedrooms makes much use of boldly-patterned fabrics and draped beds (including some four-posters), while the Zulu Wing reflects her South African heritage, with dark leather furniture, assegais, masks and native artworks. There are 35 rooms in all – including 14 spacious rooms suitable for families – plus an annex, the Railway Inn. A five-minute walk away, the latter has smaller bedrooms with en suite shower only and no phone. Families keen to self-cater might be interested in the separate holiday cottage, which sleeps eight. Facilities for kids could be better (cots are available, but there's no baby-listening service or nappy-changing facilities) and the Hoste's literature stresses that 'well-behaved' children are welcome. Under-14s pay £25 per night.

Rose & Crown

Old Church Road, Snettisham, Norfolk PE31 7LX (01485 541382/www.roseand crownsnettisham.co.uk). **Rates** £85-£95. **Credit** MC, V.
A curious mixture of old and new, the Rose & Crown combines the functions of village pub, smartish restaurant and well-appointed hotel with admirable dexterity. Three snug bars (low ceilings, pamment floors, Woodforde's ales, loquacious locals) are at the centre of the pub, the oldest part of which dates to the 14th century. Food, from an ample and enticing menu, can be eaten in a variety of locations: at bar tables, in a modern and vividly coloured restaurant room, in the capacious garden room, or outside at picnic tables (the latter two options being best for families). The choice of dishes changes regularly, but might include Brancaster mussels in Sandringham cider, thyme and crème fraîche, or butternut squash and mascarpone risotto, followed by steamed sea bass with warm basil potato salad and roast red pepper paste, or Holkham beefburgers. The children's menu is also a nudge above the norm, with beef lasagne and garlic bread, and mini fish and chips (£4.50). The 16 bedrooms vary in style – from richly coloured oak-beamed spaces to contemporary, pastel-hued rooms in the new extension; two ground-floor rooms have full disabled access. Power showers, Molton Brown toiletries, bottled mineral water and Wi-Fi access, all laid on for free, add a note of luxury. Hairdryers and TVs are provided, as are coffee- and tea-making facilities (Thermos flasks containing fresh milk are a nice touch). Camp beds for children can be set up in the larger rooms. There's ample choice for breakfast, including a vegetarian option or a whole kipper served with poached egg and spinach, as well as a hefty full English. The enclosed garden (a former

Rose & Crown

bowling green) is great for kids, and includes an extensive play fort, complete with wooden walkways. Inside, a new residents' lounge is due to be completed early in 2007.

Titchwell Manor

Titchwell, Norfolk PE31 8BB (01485 210221/ www.titchwellmanor.com). **Rates** £180-£220. **Credit** AmEx, MC, V.

There's a very welcoming vibe at Titchwell Manor, and it's one that extends to families. Staff talk to the children, rather than over their heads, one of the lounges has a large basket of toys, there are lovely leather sofas to collapse in after a walk on the beach (or for a pre-dinner drink) and there's space to romp around in the grounds. There's even a children's comments book. The place is undergoing a gradual refurbishment, meaning that some rooms are currently much nicer than others (though all are spick and span) – when you book ask for one of the new rooms. Those at the front have excellent sea views and a new extension at the back looks over the fields. There are TVs and a selection of children's books in the bedrooms, but no video or DVD players (and it does rain in Norfolk...). There are two dining rooms: the one that families are encouraged to eat in looks similar to the other, more formal room but is more child-friendly. You don't feel like second-class citizens dining there though, and the menu is the same. The children's menu has 'real' food on it – the likes of Norfolk ham with egg and chips, or Lincolnshire sausages with crushed new potatoes and beans. Note that the hotel's baby-listening monitor only works if you have rooms in the main hotel; reception also offer a listening service. A number of rooms are set aside for visitors with pets – one family even brought their hamster!

Victoria Hotel

Park Road, Holkham, NR23 1RG (01328 713230). **Rates** £120-£275. **Meals served** noon-2.30pm, 7-9.30pm Mon-Fri; noon-3pm, 7-9.30pm Sat, Sun. **Credit** MC, V.

At least 50% of the attraction here is the location – walking distance from Holkham beach, and on the edge of the Holkham Estate. The rest comes from the easy-going charm of this small hotel and restaurant. Decor is low-key but stylish, with furniture from Rajasthan mixing with modern TVs and gleaming bathrooms; there's a big fire in the lounge area, together with squashy, lived-in sofas and a bar. It's not aimed specifically at families, but has the air of somewhere pleased to have children on the premises, and the young staff are very sweet with them. As far as the rooms go, no two are the same, and there are various family-friendly options – such as interconnecting rooms, a put-up bed in the same room as parents, or the hotel's attic suites. There are two-bedroom 'lodges' (effectively small houses) elsewhere on the Estate. There's an extra £20 charge for children staying in a lodge (although it's free for babies sleeping in their own cots), and a £15 rate applies to the normal rooms. Breakfast is free for children; early dinners can be arranged for them from 6pm or they can eat in the dining room from 7pm with everyone else. The children's menu costs £6.50: excellent value for very good food (fish and chips followed by chocolate ice-cream in our case, but other choices include pork sausage and mash then fresh fruit or banana milkshake for pudding).

White Horse Hotel

4 High Street, Blakeney, Norfolk NR25 7AL (01263 740574/www.blakeneywhitehorse. co.uk). **Rates** £70-£120. **Credit** MC, V.

Just up from the quay on Blakeney's quaint High Street, the White Horse has an enviable setting. It's an old, pebble-clad pub and hotel that's rightly renowned for its food, though the little yellow restaurant is a mite stuffy and not really suitable for children. Better by far is the light, spacious garden room with its stripped pine furniture, pebbled walls, brick flooring and glass roof. Here the food can be as simple as a lunch of pea and ham soup, with good baked ham piled in the centre of a thick, wholesome broth. Main courses might be roast cod fillet on flageolet bean casserole, or local mussels marinière. Children can have tagliatelle carbonara (£4.50) or 'proper' sausage and mash (£4.25). With luck, plum crumble will grace the pudding menu. Service can be slapdash, but prices (from £9 to £17 for adult's mains) are fair for such accomplished pub food. Drinks include a long list of wines, courtesy of Adnams, and local ales. Happy families tuck in at weekends, with older diners predominating in the week. Accommodation consists of nine en suite rooms, some of which have views of the marshes. The designated family room is a ground-floor space with a king-size bed, bunk beds and a sitting room, furnished in a light, modern style; two of the other rooms can also accomodate a Z-bed or travel cot. All rooms are equipped with TVs, hairdryers, telephones and coffee- and tea-making facilities. Hotel guests also have use of a spacious ground-floor sitting room with comfy armchairs and free internet access. There's a two-night minimum stay at weekends.

WHERE TO EAT & DRINK

Cookie's Crab Shop

The Green, Salthouse, Holt, Norfolk NR25 7AJ (01263 740352/www.salthouse. org.uk). **Meals served** *Summer* 9am-7.30pm daily. *Winter* 9am-5pm Mon-Thur, Sun; 9am-7.30pm Fri, Sat. **Main courses** £4.60-£9.50. **No credit cards**.

'Royal' salads, crammed with mouth-watering seafood, overflow from quaint tearoom plates that look as if they've seen good service during Cookie's 50-year history. You'll find no frills at this jewel of a café. Seating is at cramped tables in a garden shed, or outside in a pagoda or under parasols. Otherwise, you can take your food onto a small piece of green near the road, and picnic while gazing across at the salt marshes. Soft drinks, including Norfolk apple juice, are sold, or you can bring your own alcohol. The menu is limited to a couple of soups (including the smoky and highly savoury kipper and tomato), takeaway sarnies and a wide array of seafood salads. The aforementioned 'Royal' salads include a wealth of ingredients – smoked mackerel, anchovies, prawns, crayfish tails, own-made coleslaw – as well as the star turns (crab, smoked salmon, smoked eel, lobster). Royal crab salad costs less than £6 and even lobster is under a tenner. Non-salad-eating children can order eat-in sandwiches, but few will turn their noses up at the fab sticky toffee pudding. Staff are remarkably patient, given the weekend crowds.

Corner House

Staithe Street, Wells-next-the-Sea, Norfolk NR23 1AF (01328 710701/www.cornerhouse atwells.com). **Meals served** noon-2.30pm Sat, Sun; 6-9.30pm Mon-Sat. **Main courses** £8.50-£22. **Credit** MC, V.

Occupying that laid-back territory between a bar, a pub and a restaurant, the Corner House comes into its own for relaxed Sunday lunches. Two slightly scuffed blue dining rooms decorated with modern art lead off from the cosy bar (where Leffe lager and Greene King ales are on draught).

Cookie's Crab Shop

Cookie's Crab Shop
50th Anniversary Established 1956

Execution of dishes is not always as polished as the alluring menu of seasonal and locally sourced British food (including fresh fish and seafood) might lead you to expect, and service can get stretched, though it's always amenable. Free-range roast chicken came as slices of breast with too-thick mushroom gravy and rather dry roast spuds, but with a spicy stuffing and a wealth of fresh veg; a special of Irish stew (with the unusual addition of black-eye peas) was splendid. For pudding there's the likes of mint chocolate sponge with black cherry coulis. Parents are warned against letting young children go into the back yard, where lurks a deep fish pond.

Deepdale Café

Main Road, Burnham Deepdale, King's Lynn, Norfolk PE31 8DD (01485 211055/www. deepdalecafe.co.uk). **Meals served** *Summer* 7.30-9pm daily. *Winter* 7.30am-3.45pm daily. **Main courses** £5-£15. **Credit** AmEx, DC, MC, V.

Opened in April 2006, the Deepdale Café quickly gained quite a following. That's hardly surprising given the prices charged for what can be outstanding food. The location is unprepossessing (behind a garage forecourt) and the premises are simple but modish, with tiled floor, arty photos on white walls, and a couple of sofas to appease those waiting for a table. It keeps the hours of a transport caff and serves all-day breakfasts, but here you'll get local organic, free-range eggs, locally baked bread and naturally smoked haddock and kippers – or perhaps something as simple as fresh figs served with yoghurt and Norfolk honey, or a warming bowl of porridge (from the 'more yummy things' section of the menu) with a cup of Fairtrade tea. Sandwiches, omelettes and cakes are a cut above the norm, and lunches, from a blackboard list, are yet more ambitious: a tapas plate, say, featuring top-notch ingredients (tapenade, chorizo, houmous, feta, olives, potato wedges and more – all for £7.95), or a smartly dressed salad of crayfish tails and bacon for little more than a fiver. Bring your own wine. Sunday lunch, with locally-sourced roast beef, Yorkshire pudding and 'proper' gravy, is especially popular. Staff are clued-up and amenable, giving good reductions for children's portions.

Jolly Sailors

Main Road, Brancaster Staithe, Norfolk PE31 8BJ (01485 210314/www.jollysailors.co.uk). **Meals served** noon-9pm daily. **Main courses** £8.50-£18.95. **Credit** MC, V.

Highly desirable as a pub (serving its own-brewed beer in a congenial old bar), the Jolly Sailors also has a pretty back garden with a children's play area, and two sizeable rooms where families can eat. True, a little of the bar's bonhomie is lacking in these spaces, but the surroundings (big wooden tables, high-backed settles and terracotta-hued walls) are pleasant enough, and the food more than fills a gap. Meaty sausages, mash and gravy

is the best bet from the children's menu, easily beating the lacklustre pizza. The full menu (on a blackboard) holds more interest, including decent steak and kidney pie, a fair version of roast peppers stuffed with king prawns and pesto, and creamy amaretti cheesecake. The staff are well-meaning, though can be forgetful.

Mary Jane's

27-29 Garden Street, Cromer, Norfolk NR27 9HN (01263 511208). **Meals served** 11.30am-8pm Mon-Sat; noon-8pm Sun. **Main courses** £5.30-£7. **No credit cards**.

With its pink walls and frilly net curtains, Mary Jane's serves up a measure of seemliness with its fish and chips. Family photos and landscape prints decorate the walls, and there's a small bar tucked in a corner (with fizzy keg beer). Queues often form at the adjoining takeaway, and tables in the restaurant are highly prized during the summer rush. Plaice, flaky and fresh, comes clothed in a light eggy batter with decent chips. Order it with a ladle of mushy peas and you'll pay £5.30 for the lot (though sauce sachets are 10p extra). Children's cod and chips is just £3.45, and there's pizza for the awkward squad.

Three Horseshoes

Bridge Street, Warham All Saints, Norfolk NR23 1NL (01328 710547). **Meals served** noon-2pm, 6-8pm daily. **Main courses** £7.50-£10.50. **No credit cards**.

This tiny gem of a pub serves up excellent food, in exceedingly generous portions – the pies are a real highlight, but you should do your best to save room for the supremely old-fashioned desserts too. Bread and butter pudding, spotted dick and golden syrup steamed sponge are among the delights. The pub has a family room and a large garden for the children to explore. There's no set children's menu, but small fry can choose starters or smaller portions from the main menu offerings. They'll love playing on the (working) 1930s one-armed bandit slot machine too.

PLACES TO SEE, THINGS TO DO

Cley Marshes Nature Reserve

Cley-next-the-Sea (01263 740008/www.norfolk wildlifetrust.org.uk). **Open** *Members* dawn-dusk daily. *Non-members* 10am-dusk daily. **Admission** £3.50; free under-16s. **Credit** *Visitor centre* MC, V.

Half a mile east of Cley, this is one of Britain's top bird-watching sites, where hides looking out over reed beds and pools enable you to spot avocets, bitterns, terns, marsh harriers, oystercatchers and more. A new visitor centre that will incorporate a café, shop, and displays on coastal history and stories is currently under construction, and due for completion in April 2007. CoastHopper buses (01553 776980, www.passengertransport. norfolk.gov.uk) stop outside the reserve.

Extreeme Adventure

High House, Weasenham All Saints, King's Lynn, Norfolk PE32 2SP (01328 838720/ 07775 593477/www.extreemeadventure.co.uk). **Open** *Mar-Oct* 9am-4pm daily. **Admission** £20; £18 10-18s. No under-10s. **Credit** MC, V.
If you're over ten years old, are more than 1.4m tall and have a good head for heights, you can experience the adrenaline-provoking pleasures of this extensive high-ropes course. The setting, south of Weasenham All Saints and just off the A1065 (though mostly away from the traffic noise), is impressive. The New Wood contains some of the highest trees in eastern England; signs give details about the main species to be seen. Participants can clamber up rope ladders, navigate their way along 20ft- or 40ft-high walkways, and whizz down a 1000ft zip wire. There are more than 20 different elements to conquer. Less intrepid adults can stay in the covered picnic pavilion, where refreshments are served and a log fire burns in cold weather. Near the pavilion there's a little walkway and tyres for clambering along, suitable for younger children.

Hunstanton Sea Life Sanctuary

Southern Promenade (off Seagate Road), Hunstanton, Norfolk PE36 5BH (01485 533576/www.sealsanctuary.co.uk). **Open** *Summer* 10am-5pm daily. *Winter* 10am-3pm daily. **Admission** £9.50; £7.50 3-14s; free under-3s. **Credit** AmEx, MC, V.
The sanctuary rescues, cares for and rehabilitates sick marine animals found on Britain's shores. While convalescing, the wildlife can be viewed by the public. Star attractions are the rescued seal pups, given names like 'Peter Crouch' and 'Houdini', but there's also an otter enclosure and an aquarium where you can get up close to the likes of bamboo sharks, seahorses and skate. Talks and feeding demonstrations are given. Among the 30 permanent displays is a small colony of Humboldt penguins, bred in captivity, and a new exhibition, 'Claws', featuring unusual clawed creatures from around the world – including lobsters, mantis shrimps and giant Japanese spider crabs with a fearsome one-metre claw span. There's plenty to see indoors, so the sanctuary is a handy option for rainy days.

Norfolk Shire Horse Centre

West Runton Stables, West Runton, Cromer Norfolk NR27 9QH (01263 837339/www. norfolk-shirehorse-centre.co.uk). **Open** *Apr, May, Sept, Oct* 10am-5pm Mon-Thur, Sun. *Jun-Aug* 10am-5pm Mon-Fri, Sun (last admission 3.45pm). **Admission** £6.50; £4.50 3-16s; free under-3s. **Credit** AmEx, MC, V.
Various breeds of shire horses, including the powerful Ardennes strain, are kept in these stables, as well as ponies (rides are available) and vintage horse-drawn machinery, wagons and carts. There are daily demonstrations of harnessing the horses at 11.15am and 3pm, as well as

parades of the animals, showing them at work. Informative staff are happy to answer questions. A small 'children's farm' on the site includes goats, ducks, geese, chickens, pigs and donkeys; feeding times are at 10.45am and 2.30pm.

North Norfolk Railway

Sheringham Station, Sheringham, Norfolk NR26 8RA (01263 820800/talking timetable 01263 820808/www.nnrailway.co.uk). **Open** phone for details. **Tickets** £9.50; £6.50 5-15s; £29 family (2+2); free under-5s. **Credit** MC, V.
The 'Poppy Line' takes passengers on a 5.5-mile trip between Sheringham and Holt, with stops at Weybourne and Kelling Heath. It's a scenic route, going close to the coast before heading inland through heathland to Holt. The vintage carriages are mostly pulled by steam locomotives, but classic diesel trains are also used. Various events are staged by the railway through the year, including 'Day Out With Thomas' events and Santa Specials in December. The buffet and gift shop at Sheringham Station, which is close to the town centre (and near the national network station on the Norwich to Cromer line) is open daily. Holt Station is about a mile outside the centre, though the 'Holt Flyer', a vintage Routemaster bus, will (for an extra charge) take passengers into the town. Holt itself is an enjoyable, if slightly genteel, Georgian town with plenty of interesting shops. Don't miss the department store Bakers & Larners of Holt (8-12 Market Place, 01263 712244, www.bakers and larners.com), which has a marvellous food hall and tearooms. Alternatively, the Owl Tearooms on Church Street has alluring own-made pastries and cakes.

Sandringham Estate

Sandringham, Norfolk PE35 6EN (01553 612908/www.sandringhamestate.co.uk). **Open** *7 Apr-20 July; Aug-Sept House* 11am-4.45pm. *Gardens* 10.30am-5pm. *Museum* 11am-5pm. *Oct House* 11am-4pm. *Gardens* 10.30am-4pm. *Museum* 11am-4pm. *Visitor Centre* all year 10.30am-5.30pm daily. **Admission** *House, museum & gardens* £9; £5 5-15s; £23 family (2+3); free under-5s. *Museum & gardens* £6; £3.50 5-15s; £15.50 family (2+3); free under-5s. **Credit** MC, V.
The Queen's winter residence, a vast Victorian mansion, makes an intriguing day out. Of the ground floor rooms that are open to the public gaze, the dining room, where the royal Christmas dinner is scoffed, is the most memorable. Visitors can also view the gardens and the museum. The highlight of the latter is its collection of vintage royal motor vehicles, which includes a gleaming 1930s Merryweather fire engine (used by the Estate's fire brigade, rather than for transporting royal personages). Admission includes access to Sandringham Country Park, 600 acres of beautiful woodland featuring two nature trails, an abundance of picnic sites and a children's adventure playground, featuring wooden boats, trains and

Snettisham Park

swings. Tractor rides chug around the park and last about 40 minutes (£4 adults, £1 children). The grounds also include a visitors' centre (with a gift shop where some of the ingredients for a posh picnic can be purchased), an ice-cream booth and a restaurant selling snacks, sandwiches and lunches. Regular events such as food festivals and craft fairs are held here, and in autumn the Sandringham fruit farm is open for apple-picking.

Snettisham Park

Park Farm, Snettisham, King's Lynn, Norfolk PE31 7NQ, follow signs off the A149 (01485 542425/www.snettishampark.co.uk). **Open** *Feb-21 Dec* 10am-5pm daily. **Admission** £5.20; £4.20 3-16s; free under-3s. **Credit** MC, V.

Very much geared towards children, Snettisham Park encompasses 150 acres of farm and woodland. A highlight is the large herd of deer, which can be viewed on the 45-minute 'safari' by tractor and covered trailer. Other livestock include sheep (visit in March or April to bottle-feed the orphaned lambs), piglets and kid goats, as well as rabbits to cuddle, guinea pigs and newly hatched chicks. There are two adventure playgrounds: one for under-sevens with 'sit and ride' tractors; and an impressive construction of walkways, ropes and clambering nets for seven to 13s. Pony rides are available (book in advance on 01485 543815), and there's also a leather workshop and a wildlife discovery and archaeology trail. You can bring your own picnic and eat it under the trees in the orchard, or buy lunch and own-made cakes at the Orchard Tearoom. The gift and farm shop sells everything from soft toys to fresh venison.

Titchwell Marsh Nature Reserve

01485 210779/www.rspb.org.uk/reserves/ guide/t/titchwell. **Open** *Apr-Oct* 9.30am-5pm daily. *Nov-Mar* 9.30am-4pm daily. **Admission** free. **Credit** MC, V.

The Royal Society for the Protection of Birds runs this popular nature reserve, located just off the A149. There's a car park (£4, free for RSPB members) with toilets nearby, and a visitors' centre where you can hire high-quality binoculars. The walk to the beach from the car park is about a mile, past reed beds, shallow lagoons and a series of observation hides with pictures and information. A wide variety of wetland birds can be seen through the year: marsh harriers and avocets in summer, wigeons and brent geese in winter. The autumn and spring migration periods are especially good times to visit. There's a shop and café on the site.

Wells & Walsingham Light Railway

Wells-next-the-Sea, Norfolk NR23 1QB (01328 711630/www.wellswalsinghamrailway.co.uk). **Open** *Apr-Oct* times vary; phone or check website for details. **Tickets** £5.50-£7; £4.50-£5.50 4-14s; free under-4s. **No credit cards**. This is the world's longest 10.25in narrow gauge steam railway. At a little over five miles long, the half-hour journey is scarcely arduous. The diminutive train pulls its carriages (some enclosed, others open-topped or part covered) through the Norfolk countryside, with stops at two little villages before its destination on the outskirts of Walsingham. Refreshments are sold at Wells Station.

The Gower Peninsula

Gower powers ahead in the beauty
spot and surfboard stakes.

With its curving white sand beaches, the Gower Peninsula looks as good as any seaside in the world – even if it feels a darn sight chillier. Indeed, it was the first place in Britain to be designated an Area of Outstanding Natural Beauty, more than 50 years ago. Surfers say that when the rollers are on their side, Gower is the top place in the UK for board riding, and it certainly has the best junior surfing academy. For families, it's easy to get to, affordable to stay in and extraordinarily beautiful – not least because it has never attracted tourist crowds on the scale of those endured by trendier surf spots such as Newquay and Croyde in the West Country.

Although Gower is a peninsula, it has an intimate, island feel. It's not unlike the Channel Islands – but handier, because it's just off the M4. Despite its proximity to the industrial heartland of Wales, Gower retains its unspoilt and richly diverse seascape. The 19-mile long, eight-mile wide peninsula is fringed by some of the UK's cleanest and most attractive beaches, and family-friendly walks along its coastal paths lead to dramatic cliffs, waterfalls, leafy woodlands, dunes and marshes.

The Bay
Hot & cold food
Served everyday
OPEN
Cream Teas
Cakes
Lasagne chilli
Spag Bol
Take away food
Tea
Coffee
Cappuccino
Latte
Espresso
Wine
Beer (cold)
Coke Presse orange

Rhossili Bay and village

Rhossili Bay

Today, the National Trust cares for 75 per cent of Gower's coastline and some 5,500 acres of its countryside. It's an idyllic place for a good old-fashioned bucket and spade holiday; Langland Bay, Caswell Bay, Bracelet Bay and Port Eynon, together with Swansea marina, all have Blue Flag status, Europe's highest award for beach quality, water cleanliness and facilities. From June until September, professional lifeguards are on patrol seven days a week, with advice about bathing conditions and tides.

The 300 million-year-old limestone cliffs along the coast are dotted with caves, once home to elephants, cave bears, wolves and hyenas; the oldest dated modern human remains discovered in Britain were found at Paviland Cave. Near the summit of Cefn Gwyn, Arthur's Stone is a burial chamber dating back to 2,500 BC, topped with a massive 25-ton capstone. According to legend, Saint David split the capstone with his sword (or staff) to prove it was an altar to false gods, then commanded a spring to flow from under it.

The Romans made it to Gower and built a fort, Leucarum, near the estuary of the River Loughor on the north coast. They harvested cockles on the nearby sand flats, which stretch for four miles at low tide. Cockle pickers still gather the sea's bounty at Penclawdd, using traditional methods. On the other side of the peninsula, perched on the edge of Pennard Pill, stand the ruins of the 13th-century Pennard Castle. It's well worth a visit –

not least for the dramatic views over the wooded valley and Three Cliffs Bay beneath.

Just along the coast is Port Eynon Bay. Now a popular beach resort and surf spot, it was a centre for smuggling during the 18th and 19th centuries, when a heavy customs duty was imposed on tobacco, spirits and tea.

A Worm's eye view

Rhossili's breathtaking three-mile stretch of sand joins Llangennith beach, one of the UK's best surf destinations. The sea picks up the Atlantic swell, and the gently sloping beach provides long waves that surfers can ride for a hundred metres or more. This is a great place to swim, take a first surfing lesson, or try kite-surfing, beach buggying or hang gliding. Eddie's Restaurant in Llangennith (01792 386606) is a popular lunchtime retreat. For the latest on weather conditions, check www.llangennithsurf.com.

At nearby Rhossili village, you'll find a shop, toilets and a field car park. By the beach, a National Trust Visitor Centre (Coastguard Cottages, 01792 390707, www.nationaltrust.org.uk), has a shop, an exhibition and information about the area. In 1980 an archeological dig in the Warren, a strip of ground next to the beach, revealed that an earlier village and sixth-century church once stood there; both were buried under the sand centuries ago. The area is now protected as an ancient monument, and all that can be seen are a few excavated walls. In the 13th century a new church, St Mary's, was built on the clifftop – a safe distance away from sand and sea. Look out for the marble memorial plaque dedicated to Petty Officer Edgar Evans, who was born here and died in Scott's doomed trek to the Antarctic.

To the north of the village is Rhossili Down. Its summit, the Beacon, is the highest point on the peninsula. The energetic climb allows you to appreciate the spectacular promontory of Worm's Head, and the intricate medieval open field system of the Vile. At low tide, a causeway emerges out to the Worm (from the Viking word 'wurm' for dragon), but visitors need to check tide times to avoid getting stranded. The beach here is one of the most photographed and iconic images in Britain, with a tiny, white-fronted cottage nestled in the surrounding grassy dunes. But the most spectacular view of the Worm's Head and coastline far below is from the Worm's Head Hotel (01792 390512, www.thewormshead. co.uk). The restaurant's picture windows frame enchanting views: admire them over a spread of Penclawdd cockles and lava bread. Time seems to slow down in this peaceful spot, where the landscape is perfectly unspoilt and seemingly endless.

Rhossili was recently voted one of the top ten places to photograph the sunset. It is exceptionally attractive. From the headland to the west of the village (described by Dylan Thomas as 'rubbery, gull-limed grass, the sheep pilled stones... pieces of bones and feathers') you can see the wreck of the Helvetica. The ship ran aground here in 1887, and her bones still stick out, rib-like, from the sandy sea bed.

From the National Trust car park in Southgate, head east towards Pwlldu Head past two of the Gower's larger coastal caves, Bacon Hole and Minchin Hole. Reaching the latter is a real scramble, and only for the stout of heart and shoe. Access to certain caves is restricted at various times of the year to protect the wildlife, so contact the National Trust before planning a visit (01792 390636, www.nationaltrust.org.uk).

Catch the big one

The Gower coastline kicks off at Bracelet Bay, presided over by a 200-year-old lighthouse and a short walk away from Mumbles. Children love throwing pebbles in the waves; older siblings can have a bash at sea kayaking, a popular sport here.

Just along the coast, Langland Bay has a sandy beach with a few scattered rocks, with picturesque beach huts and toilets. It has always had a healthy surfing scene and can get crowded, especially when onshore winds favour the riders. Close by is the legendary Crab Island, a reef break best left to experienced surfers.

The vast beach at Caswell Bay is hugely popular with families, with everything you need close at hand. Although only ten to 15 minutes' drive from Swansea, it retains a tranquil and remote feel; a young Dylan Thomas felt its romance when he courted Pamela Hansford here. The bay boomed in Victorian times, when day trips were organised for underprivileged workhouse children. Today, there's plenty to keep the modern child fed and entertained: souvenir and sweet shops, buckets and spades, mini surfboards, dinghies, ice-cream stalls and a snack bar. Watch out for the area of 'sinking sand' a few hundred yards in front of the GSD (*see p224* **Get on board**) Surf Shed. In this metre-wide spot, freezing spring water bubbles up as gravity sucks surprised children's shins down into the sand – scary! The car park at the entrance of Bishop's Wood nature reserve is big enough on all but the hottest days; take extra care when crossing to the beach, because of the unusual road layout.

West of here, Three Cliffs Bay is another Gower stunner. Here the Penmaen valley leads down to the sea through the salt marshes and sand dunes. Voted Best Beach by the BBC Holiday Hit Squad, it has the honour of being one of irascible *Newsnight* presenter Jeremy Paxman's favourite places. It's a bit of a hike to get to: you can park at Southgate and take the footpath down to the beach, or approach it from Penmaen, down what must be some of the steepest sand dunes in Britain. Rips can be a problem for swimmers, so don't bathe at high tide. At low tide you can walk to the more secluded Pobbles Bay. Pwlldu (Welsh for 'black pool') Bay can be reached via a bracing walk along the Pennard cliffs, or from Brandy Cove.

With a seafront car park, Oxwich Bay is more easily accessible. It has two miles of sand, plus great surf and an uprising of attractive dunes. Dog walking is permitted all year round (unlike other local beaches that ban dogs from May to September). Oxwich is another watersports mecca, attracting the sailing, skiing and surfing –

both kite and wind – set. Fishermen catch squid and mackerel from Oxwich Point.

On the north-west tip of the peninsula is the large and sandy Broughton Bay, accessible at its southern end from the lane that leads from Llangennith via a caravan site. Strong tides along with powerful waves and shifting sandbanks make it too dangerous a place for most watersports, although in calmer conditions experienced wind- and kite-surfers zip along the waves. The strong undertow means swimming isn't recommended.

A touch of the Med

There's something magical about Mumbles, on the western edge of Swansea Bay and five miles from the city. On a summer's evening it takes on an exotic, almost Mediterranean quality, as sailing boats and catamarans return to their moorings. Later on, when the moonlight hits the water and white lights twinkle along the three-mile promenade, it's equally lovely. With Newton Road at its heart, Mumbles has an impressive line-up of restaurants, cafés and bars – eat your heart out, Brighton!

The area is both cosmopolitan and unmistakably British. The Victorian era bequeathed the resort a wealth of attractions, including a pier, traditional boutiques, craft shops and seemingly endless ice-cream parlours. Stretching 225 metres out into the bay, Mumbles Pier (www.mumbles-pier.co.uk) was built

in 1898 and makes a quaint tribute to Victorian architecture. Steamers once docked at the end, unloading tourists who would then make the journey to the Mumbles via the world's first passenger railway. Today the pier is used as a fishing point, or a viewpoint for splendid Mumbles Bay, the lighthouse and Port Talbot. It's home to a lifeboat station, as well as classic seaside diversions: ice-cream cafés, amusements, ten-pin bowling and a small iceskating rink (01792 365230). Little ones who feel uneasy on their skates will love it, but confident teenagers will probably want more room. Special offers mean that a family of four can go skating, bowling and have a pizza all in for £20.

Mumbles, 'the Gateway to Gower', is the original stamping ground of actress Catherine Zeta Jones. Her ladyship still enjoys regular escapes to her parents' home, which overlooks Swansea Bay from Limeslade. Last year when the Douglases were in town, Michael caused a stir by taking their children to Singleton Boating Lake, where paddleboat rides to the small island in the middle cost between £4-£5 for 30 minutes. Across the Mumbles Road is a small crazy golf course (a round costs £1.50, clubs are provided) and play area.

Next to the promenade at nearby Blackpill is a shallow lido, with lifeguards on patrol during high season. The Swansea Bay Rider train (01792 635436) runs along the promenade from the lido to Southend Gardens in Mumbles every day in summer,

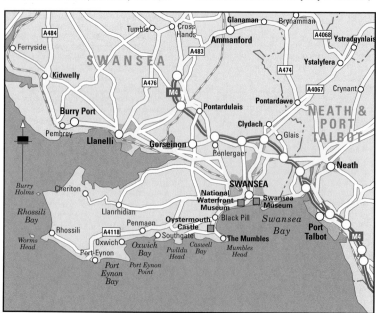

making regular stops along the bay. On bank holiday weekends, the Swansea Society of Model Engineers (01792 775809) operate a beautiful small gauge railway just off the Derwen Fawr Road.

Oystermouth Castle (www.castlewales. com/oyster), one of the best preserved castles in Wales, is nearby. The present structure is a 12th-century Norman stronghold, restructured in 1215 following Welsh attacks. Patronised by Edward I in 1284, the castle commands magnificent views of Swansea Bay and Mumbles and is open to the public during the tourist season (£1, 60p children).

Sea views city

Scandinavian invaders built a fortress at Swansea in the tenth century, naming the area after their leader, Swein. By the 14th century the Welsh had established ship building here, accompanied by a sea fishing tradition that endures to this day.

The attractive seafront promenade goes on for miles, and everyone wants a piece of it. Joggers listening to iPods, cyclists, entwined couples, dog walkers and fast-paced skaters make the most of the scenic walkway, as waves crash against the sea wall and sailing boats move to the arc of the bay and beyond.

Acclaimed as one of the top three waterside developments in Europe, Swansea's Maritime Quarter is bustling. Business types and academics rub shoulders with ambling sightseers, while fishing nets dry out in the sun and yachts sail in and out. The National Waterfront Museum and Swansea Museum (for both, *see p231*) are both found here, along with art galleries, a theatre, bars, restaurants and an observatory.

Swansea's most famous son is Dylan Thomas, born on 27 October 1914. The poet lived at No.5 Cwmdonkin Drive, in the Uplands district of the city, until he was 20. During this time, he wrote two thirds of all his poetry as well as numerous short stories and letters, so it's fair to say that Swansea was an inspiration. The Dylan Thomas Centre (Somerset Place, 01792 463980, www.dylanthomas.com), opened in 1995, is housed in a grand civic building just behind the marina and is open daily from 10am to 4.30pm. It has a permanent exhibition on Thomas and his life, a café, bookshop and restaurant and hosts the annual Dylan Thomas Festival in October. Admission is free, and there are quiz sheets for children to complete.

The ruins of Swansea Castle (www.castle wales.com/swansea) stand on Castle Street, where Wales' second city began – almost a millennium ago. Founded in 1106, the castle was fiercely fought

TOP 5

GOWER BAYS
FOR GROMMETS

(a grommet is surf speak for an adolescent surfer)

Caswell Bay
This is the best beach for learning. *See p224.*

Oxwich Bay
Gentle and sheltered for new surfers. *See p221.*

Llangennith
Where the surf schools are; busy but safe. *See p220.*

Langland Bay
Try it when you've gained experience. *See p221.*

Rhossili Bay
Some scary rips. *See p221.*

over by the English and Welsh, and repeatedly razed and reconstructed through the centuries. By the late 16th century it had fallen into disrepair, and briefly became a debtor's prison in the 19th century. Today, the surviving tower looms over Castle Square, where the city market traded 500 years ago.

Swansea's covered market, opened in 1961, is the largest indoor market in Wales. It's a lively place to take the family on a Gower gourmet journey to learn about local produce, including Welsh cakes served straight off the griddle. Those looking forward to a fish supper can see the catches of the day coming in fresh from the bay, including dogfish, bass, mackerel, plaice, sole and shrimp, destined for Swansea's better restaurants. Children enjoy visiting Swansea Community Farm (2 Pontardulais Road, Fforestfach, 01792 578334, www.swanseacommunityfarm.org.uk). One of only two community farms in Wales, it was devised by ex-Londoners in the 1990s, to show children (and adults) where their food comes from.

Gower Peninsula

GET ON BOARD

When young families make for Caswell Beach, Gower, they're more likely to be armed with surfboards than a bucket and spade. Dressed in wetsuits and ready for action, they're bound for the well regarded Gower Surfing Development (GSD) Junior Surfing Academy.

This seat of learning has produced British and Welsh surfing champions, and is considered by many to be the best surf school in Britain. The only surfing school in Wales to be awarded four stars by the British Surfing Association, GSD offers courses for absolute beginners all the way up to elite level. Its 13 staff work from three beaches, teaching their wetsuit-clad pupils on high-quality flexi surfboards from California.

Children can learn lifeguarding, water skills and surfing, and play paddling race games. GSD also run holiday surf clubs and can arrange birthday surfing parties. It's a fantastic way to keep children fit and confident. All that's required is a swimsuit, bottle of water, towel, packed lunch, sunscreen and a sense of adventure; GSD provides the wetsuits and boards.

Most people book lessons in advance, but it's worth accosting tutors at the Surf Shed to see if there's any chance of joining in on a group lesson. Caswell Bay has Blue Flag status, so you are guaranteed excellent bathing water quality and sustainable environmental management. The beach offers a

huge expanse of sand, and the easterlies provide ideal surfing conditions; waves can be high but manageable, sweeping along in rapid and thrilling succession.

At the Academy, safety always comes first. Children are warned how the tide can be dangerous, told how to get help if in distress, and taught to always keep their 'board to the beach' to avoid it flipping up in the wind. After a warm-up run along the beach and some stretching exercises, the lesson begins with bodyboarding to test water confidence. There is the 'fast dynamic' or pop-up route to standing on the board; a flowing movement intended to take you from lying down to standing on your feet in a trice. Others may prefer the three stage one-knee-first approach of kneeling before standing up.

Young pupils are amused by the jokey surfer instructors and have a real lark. One tip, though: bring plenty of post-lesson sustenance – everyone gets hungry when they learn to surf, even if they've swallowed a good deal of Caswell Bay's briny in the process.

Surf GSD
01792 360370/www.surfgsd.com. **Open** by appointment. **Rates** standard lesson from £30; £25 children; concessionary rates for groups. **Credit** AmEx, MC, V.
The 'family learn 2 surf weekend' and the 'Half and Half' surf day, which involves a learn to surf session in the morning followed by lunch, then use of the equipment for the rest of the day (phone for prices); a day of surf coaching costs £45. Participants must be at least eight years old and able to swim 50 metres in open water. All courses are carried out by BSA accredited coaches.

WHERE TO STAY

Hillend Camping Park
Llangennith, Swansea SA3 1JD (01792 386204). **Open** Apr-Oct. **Rates** £12-£20/tent. **Credit** MC, V.
Hillend's proximity to the sea means that tousle-haired surfing families are keen to set up camp here; at this high vantage point, your tent can overlook the beautiful beach just 200 yards away. There's also the option of sleeping under the stars in a wool-lined yurt; for details, call Adam or Tricia on 01792 371279. These are known as 'ger' in Mongolia, where people cosy down in winter temperatures of minus 40 – so warm Welsh winds make little impression. The structures sleep ten, and are very popular with partying dudes.

North Gower Hotel
Llanrhidian, North Gower, Swansea SA3 1EE (01792 390042/www.northgowerhotel.co.uk). **Rates** £60-£75. **Credit** MC, V.
This 17-room hotel overlooks the Loughor Estuary, and some rooms have views across the whole of the northern peninsula. It's a great location for children – not to mention handy for the M4. Six of the seven en suite family rooms contain a double and a single bed and accomodate two adults and one child; the other is suitable for a family of four. A camp bed can also generally be squeezed in if required. Children are made welcome, and there is a play area with swings and slides in the gardens. The restaurant offers relaxed, inexpensive and informal eating, with Rumbling Tum Kid's Meals (available noon-6pm Mon-Sat) priced from £2.50. The hotel restaurant is also signally proud of its signature dish: chicken breast, with a spinach, tomato, cream and garlic sauce. Its public areas and bedrooms win no prizes for style, but this represents a reasonable deal for families trying to keep costs down.

Oxwich Bay Hotel
Oxwich, Gower Peninsula, Swansea SA3 1LS (01792 390329/www.oxwichbayhotel.co.uk). **Rates** £66-£88. *Cottage* £65-£95. **Credit** MC, V.
If close proximity to sea and sand are important, the Oxwich Bay Hotel is well worth considering. It's set in eight acres of private grounds at the western end of the bay, so close to the sea that the garden is surrounded by a high protective wall (not great for the ground floor rooms, but some of the upstairs rooms offer sweeping views of the long bay). Although all of the rooms are en suite, the hotel doesn't feel terribly modern, and it is the kind of place where you need a little patience because things may not happen as fast as you might require. The restaurant offers sea views and traditional, locally-sourced food, with dishes like Welsh fillet steak, Gower cockles and Welsh lamb chump chops. The children's menu (£4.95) features ham, sausage, or chicken nuggets with chips, baked or new potatoes and beans or peas, or own-made spag bol; high chairs are available. Weather

Gower Peninsula

permitting, guests can eat in the hotel garden at the edge of the beach. Book well in advance in summer, because rooms soon fill up. The hotel also lets out rooms in some nearby cottages (two with four bedroooms; one with five bedrooms and a communal lounge). Larger families may be able to rent out several rooms, or an entire cottage.

Port Eynon

Old Lifeboat House, Port Eynon, Swansea SA3 1NN (0870 770 5998/www.yha.org.uk). **Open** *Apr-Oct* room bookings taken. *Nov-Mar* bookings only (0870 770 8868). **Rates** £13.95; £9.95 under-18s. **Credit** MC, V.
This Swansea hostel was once the lifeboat station, and couldn't be in a lovelier position – it has an award-winning beach right on its doorstep. It's a popular choice for surfers and watersports fans, as well as walkers following the Gower Coastal Path. Don't expect luxury: this is an unpretentious little 28-bed hostel with a self catering kitchen. There are a few family rooms, however, and the location is picture perfect. Book ahead!

St Annes Hotel

Western Lane, Mumbles, Swansea SA3 4EY (01792 369147/www.stannes-hotel.co.uk). **Rates** £80-£135. **Credit** MC, V.
St Annes Hotel is situated in its own grounds in the heart of Mumbles. The hotel's best asset is its elevated position; most of the 35 en suite rooms have views of Swansea Bay. Catering for up to 100 guests, it has a resident DJ and is the kind of place that could appeal to a cross-generation family, including the grandparents. There's no baby sitting or listening service though, and you'll need to bring your own toys and games. The hotel has two sets of spacious family rooms, with a television and tea-making facilities. It has disabled access, and broadband is available. Playgrounds, Mumbles pier and sandy beaches are all nearby, and the ten-screen UCI cinema is six miles away. Breakfast is served in a restaurant with panoramic views of the bay (Mumbles is the home of picture windows) and there is private parking.

Shoreline Hotel

648 Mumbles Road, Southend, Mumbles, Swansea, SA3 4EA (01792 366322/ www.shorelinehotel.co.uk). **Rates** £70-£105. **Credit** MC, V.
This 11-room seafront hotel is scheduled for a thorough refurb in early 2007, after having recently changed hands. The new owners have great plans for the place, intending to make it stand out among the rather poor quality of hotels in Mumbles and create a modern, boutique hotel feel. It offers spectacular panoramic views across Swansea Bay and easy access to the Mumbles promenade, even for buggies. There's a play area just across the road, and the seafront is alive with jet- and water-skiing, sailing, and fishing holiday-makers. Bedrooms are clean, and the communal

lounge area is contemporary and comfortable. You can start the day with a cooked breakfast and round off a trip to the beach with a frothy hot chocolate, a cookie and an evening chat. Parking is on the street in front of the hotel, so arrive early to claim a space. The Shoreline's small scale, intimate feel and friendly owners also make it a good choice for lone parents.

Swansea Marriott

Maritime Quarter, Swansea, SA1 3SS (0870 400 7282/http://marriott.co.uk). **Rates** £94-£139. **Credit** AmEx, DC, MC, V.
City types who want to stay in the heart of Swansea, with all mod-cons and a touch of luxury, will appreciate this link in the Marriott chain. In a prominent position in the city's Maritime Quarter, the hotel has 122 airy, contemporary rooms, some with marina views. Amenities include air conditioning, satellite television with pay movies and high-speed internet access. Guests can swim in the indoor pool (also with great views), work out on fitness equipment and relax in the sauna and spa tub. There are laundry facilities, all-hours room service, a restaurant overlooking the marina, a babysitting service and complimentary parking. The Maritime and Industrial Museum and the Glynn Vivian Art Gallery are both close by, while the start of Gower peninsula is an easy 7.5 mile drive away.

Three Cliffs Bay Caravan & Camping Site

North Hills Farm, Penmaen, Gower, Swansea, SA3 2HB (01792 371218/www.threecliffsbay. com). **Open** Easter-Oct. **Rates** £12-£15/tent; £15/caravan. **Credit** MC, V.
The major attraction of this site is its spectacular clifftop location, which offers panoramic views of the Gower coastline. The golden sanded beach below is easily, if steeply, accessible via a private path. Facilities are modern and well maintained, and an on-site warden keeps campers happy. There's ample opportunity to take bracing cliff walks, so children and dogs can be exercised heartily. The site has a family room with baby-changing facilities, token-operated showers, a laundry room, a kitchen area, recycling facilities and electricity hook-ups at the back of each caravan space. A small shop sells groceries, ice-creams, toys and souvenirs, and replenishes gas and ice supplies.

Western House

Llangennith, Swansea, SA3 1HU (01792 386620/www.llangennith.freeserve.co.uk). **Rates** £50-£60. **No credit cards.**
This family-run business is the epitome of shabby chic, and is popular with surfers, climbers and outdoor types. Proprietors Steve and Pippa, themselves keen surfers, say that guests of a 'more laid-back nature' suit Western House, though the house is also their family home. There are two guest rooms, the largest of which sleeps parents

Oxwich Bay Hotel.
See p225.

and smaller children; the other has a double bed and a washbasin. Both rooms have colour televisions and tea and coffee making facilities. The charge for children is worked out according to how much breakfast they consume, and well behaved dogs are welcome. There is a treehouse, a trampoline and chickens for children to feed. The house is about half a mile from the main beach and just down the road from the village pub, the King's Head (01792 386212).

Winston Hotel

Church Lane, Bishopston, Gower, Swansea, SA3 3JT (01792 234304/www.winstonhotel. com). **Rates** £85-£110. **Credit** MC, V.
The Winston is ideal for families with a yen for the great outdoors and a taste for adventure, organising a range of action-packed activities for guests. Grown-ups can take surfing lessons, learn about bushcraft in the Gower wilderness and go quad biking or sailing, thanks to the hotel's close relationship with a local outdoor sports, events and party planning company. There's a health suite to soothe aching muscles, with a steam room, sauna, jacuzzi, hot-bed and resident beautician. The hotel also has a seven metre by four metre heated swimming pool, plus a concept rower and Nordic rider stepping machine. Children aged six and above can attend storytelling and craft workshop sessions (from £12) and adventurous over-eights can take part in Wilderness Courses (from £40), building sand sculptures and shelters on the beach, learning about sustainable living and cooking outdoors. Pamper and Spa parties can also be arranged groups of up to 15 children, featuring mini facials, mini manicures, a swim and watching a DVD (from £40). The Winston has

three en suite family rooms, set at the rear of the hotel and equipped with a television and tea tray, but no babysitting or listening service. A la carte and bar meals are available at all times of day, with children's meals at £4.95, and there's a hearty Sunday lunch to round off the week.

WHERE TO EAT & DRINK
Bay View Bar

400 Oystermouth Road, Swansea SA1 3UL (01792 652610/www.bayviewbar.co.uk). **Meals served** noon-3pm, 6-10pm Mon-Sat. **Main courses** £5-£9.95. **Credit** AmEx, MC, V. This Thai bar and restaurant, overlooking the scenic Mumbles lighthouse, has three dining areas to choose from: smoke-free and formal, spacious and relaxing or comfortable in the lounge. The children's menu includes dishes made from fresh, authentic ingredients but without too much spice: chicken nuggets-Thai style, fried rice with meat and veg, pork balls, chicken satay sticks or chicken noodles. At £4.95, including a soft drink and dessert, it's something of a bargain.

Castellamare

Bracelet Bay, Mumbles, Swansea SA3 4JT (01792 369408). **Meals served** *Café* 10am-9pm daily. *Restaurant* noon-2.30pm, 6-9.30pm daily. **Main courses** *Café* £4-£10. *Restaurant* £8.95-£17.95. **Credit** MC, V.
A popular, spacious Italian restaurant and café-bar, Castellamare overlooks the pretty Bracelet Bay and is just a short walk from the beach. It's a truly romantic spot, where motorists park up to admire the view of the islands and lighthouse in

Gower Peninsula

Gower Heritage Centre. See p230.

the moonlight. Children's meals include the usual fish fingers, chicken nuggets or sausage and chips, but they can also have a rather more nutritious pasta bolognese or Napoli (£4.) More filling than fancy, Castellamare is ideal for big family groups who want to be served quickly. Adult mains include the so-naff-it's-cool surf and turf (two crevettes and a 5oz sirloin minute steak) and sardines drizzled with lemon and garlic oil. For dessert, try the fontanelle (eight scoops of ice creams and sorbets, whipped cream and chocolate flakes for two to share). Parking is easy – a real bonus in this area – and the views from the large windows and outside seating area are superb, day or night. There is a modern playground nearby.

Frankie & Benny's

Unit 14, Salubrious Place, Wind Street, Swansea, SA1 1EE (01792461774/ www.frankieandbennys.com). **Meals served** 11am-11pm Mon-Sat; noon-10.30pm Sun. **Main courses** £5.95-£14.95. **Credit** MC, V.

Winner of the Menu Masters Family Dining Award 2005 from the Food Association, the menu for children at this lively New York-style 1950s pizzeria is bound to please. As well as a varied range of pizzas and pasta (of all varieties, including vegetarian options), there's fish and chips, saucy BBQ ribs served with corn on the cob, cheese hot dogs with fries, sausage and mash and as a healthier option, chicken Caesar salad. The children's (£3.95) and junior (£6.25) menus include one dessert, fresh fruit of the day or an ice-cream sundae and limitless soft drinks. It feels rather like a cross between TGI Fridays and the Hard Rock Café – always a hit with children – and its unstinting bonhomie and generous portions go down well with families.

Joe's

85 St Helens Road, Swansa SA1 4BQ (01792 653880/www.joes-icecream.co.uk). **Meals served** *Summer* 11am-9pm Mon-Fri; noon-8pm Sat, Sun. W*inter* 11am-8.30pm Mon-Fri; noon-7.30pm Sat, Sun. **Ice-creams** 90p-£7.35. **Credit** (over £10) MC, V.

Joe Cascarini first started making his inimitable Italian ice-cream in Swansea in 1922. Today the recipe regularly scoops top prize in national ice-cream awards, and people all over the country can't get enough of it. This parlour offers the full range of frozen delights, from the luscious chocolate swirl to the demure, award winning vanilla. Sit down and have a whole heap of flavours in sundae form, garnished with fruit, chocolate sauce, wafers and nuts, or grab a cornet to stroll along with. Joe's is a must for the children; there's no ice-cream to match it in South Wales.

Branches: 524 Mumbles Road, Swansea SA3 4DH (01792 368212); The Piazza, Parc Tawe, Swansea, SA1 2AL (01792 460370).

Mermaid Restaurant & Coffee Lounge

686 Mumbles Road, Mumbles, Swansea SA3 4EE (01792 367744). **Meals served** noon-2.30pm, 7-9.30pm Mon-Sat; noon-2.30pm Sun. **Main courses** £9.95-£16.95 **Credit** AmEx, DC, MC, V.

This former pub was a favourite haunt of Dylan Thomas and it plans to stock Dylan's Ale, as well as Welsh gin, Welsh vodka and Welsh rosé. The quality restaurant serves salt marsh lamb from Penclawdd, and locally caught fish. Children's meals are cooked to order, and include spaghetti bolognese, fish or chicken goujons, own-made beef burgers and pasta (£5.95).

Patrick's with Rooms

638 Mumbles Road, Mumbles, Swansea SA3 4EA (01792 360199/www.patrickswithrooms. com). **Meals served** noon-2.20pm, 6.30-9.50pm Mon-Sat; 6.30-9.50pm Sun. **Main courses** £14.90-£20.80. **Credit** MC, V.

Patrick's speciality is good old-fashioned food, prepared to high standards and served with a modern twist. There's a colonial-style lounge bar and a menu of worldwide cuisine; typical starters might include grilled Pantysgawn Welsh goats cheese on celery, walnut and beetroot salad, or own-made breads and oils to share. Local ingredients are key: the Welsh Black mountain beef has a heritage that can be traced, the seabass is served a few hours after being caught, and a trio of Welsh lamb (cutlets, liver and a mini shepherds pie) takes pride of place on the menu. At lunchtime and in the early evening, children can order any dish from the menu, cooked as plainly as they like (so, chicken breast with tomato sauce, pasta with a cheesey one, or a nice piece of recently caught fish). Everything is cooked to order, service is friendly and children's portions are at a reduced price. Puddings such as chocolate fondant tart or honeycomb chocolate nut sundae are a delight, but many adults go for the Welsh cheese platter. Those considering coming back to Mumbles for a grown-up break might like one of the eight bedrooms upstairs. Overlooking the bay, the rooms are of the crisp white linen, waffle dressing gowns and luxury toiletries variety.

The Restaurant @ Pilot House Wharf

Trawler Road, Swansea Marina, Swansea SA1 1HN (01792 466200). **Meals served** 6.30-9.30pm Mon; noon-2.30pm, 6.30-9.30pm Tue-Sat. **Main courses** £10.95-£18.95. **Credit** MC, V.

Set in one of the most eye-catching buildings of Swansea Marina, this former lookout and weather station offers diners something a bit special. Welsh lamb and beef are specialities of the house, and Dover sole, brill and hake are among the 15 catches of the day from Gower. The fruits de mer platter, with oysters, king prawns and dressed crab on a bed of crushed ice, is ideal for families who like to push the boat out. This is also a great place for lobster and crab. Children's portions of fresh fish and pasta cost around £5.

Surfside Café

Caswell Road, Caswell Bay, Swansea SA3 4RH (01792 368368). **Meals served** 9.30am-4.30pm daily. **Main courses** from £4. **No credit cards.**

At the top of steps above Caswell beach, this place is a suntrap from morning until early evening. At low tide the sand stretches far out to the sea; when the tide comes in, the water reaches half way up the steps. Comfortable and chic, the Surfside has a patio outside and sofas and picture windows indoors. Newspapers and surfing magazines are scattered around to positively encourage lounging,

so no one leaves in a hurry. There are ample breakfast ciabattas, bacon buns, and paninis stuffed with such delights as Welsh brie and cranberry. The café bakes its own cakes, ciabatta, croissants, and pastries, importing Proper Cornish pasties and clotted cream from Cornwall. It also serves up a delicious hot chocolate with cream, or a flavoured latte with vanilla, hazelnut or Irish cream syrup, and has to be one of the best places in Gower for kids to enjoy scones with clotted cream and their own personal pot of jam. The extensive choice of Marshfield Farm ice-creams, including triple choc, sticky toffee and marshmallow and blackcurrant, are guaranteed to make them drool. Parents can opt for unusual flavours like ginger.

Verdi's

Knab Rock, Mumbles, Swansea SA3 4EN (01792 369135/www.verdis-cafe.co.uk). **Meals served** *Summer* 10am-9pm daily. *Winter* 10am-6pm Mon-Thur; 10am-9pm Fri-Sun. **Main courses** £3.75-£8.95. **Credit** MC, V.

Verdi's offers a flavour of Italy and the beauty of Wales, with attractive outdoor seating that catches the afternoon and evening sunshine and spectacular views across Swansea Bay. The unpretentious menu lists authentic pizza and pasta, available in children's portions for £4.50, or own-made filled focaccias for around £5. But the real highlight of a visit has to be the award-winning ice-cream sundaes, from £3, and eye-catching knickerbocker glories – all are made to exacting secret recipes. Coffees are another speciality; at Verdi's, the cappuccino is an art form.

PLACES TO SEE, THINGS TO DO

Chocolate Factory

Kingsway, Swansea West Industrial Park, Fforestfach, Swansea SA5 4DL (01792 561617/www.thechocfactory.com). **Tours** daily during school holidays; times vary. Phone or check website for details. **Admission** £6; £4.50 3-16s; free under-3s. **Credit** MC, V.

Michelle and Tony Wadley's Michton brand began with a handcrafted lollipop in 1991, and has now become a Swansea tourist attraction. Tours of their factory last about an hour, kicking off with a talk on the history of chocolate and a demonstration of how various chocolates are made. The really exciting part, however, is when parents and children are togged up in hats and overalls and walk through the factory, tasting along the way – especially around the glorious melting tank. At Christmas time the tours are replaced by a walk through a grotto. This leads children, *Hansel and Gretel*-like, through a fairy-light lit maze of sugar and candy to the man of the season with his bag of goodies. Normal tours resume in January; Easter, naturally, is a very chocolatey time too. Tours are popular, and must be booked ahead. There's also an on-site café and confectionery shop if you still haven't had your fill of the sweet stuff.

Coastal Rib Tours

PO Box 69, Bridgend CF31 2YD (01656 668667/www.coastalribtours.co.uk). **Open** Easter-Sept. Trip times vary; phone or check the website for details. **Trips** £12-£60; £8-£40 under-14s. **No credit cards.**

Sea tours around the Gower Pensinsula come courtesy of a 7.5 metre rigid inflatable boat, similar to those used by the RNLI. The '4x4 of the sea' is crewed by suitably rugged individuals, who promise speeds of up 40 knots on longer trips. The shortest trip, known as the Swansea Bay Experience, lasts an hour and reaches cruising speeds of 20-25 knots. Six people can be taken round the coastline at one time. Trips further afield take explorers to the Somerset and Devon coastlines, and parties chartering the boat for a whole day can reach Lundy Island. Wildlife to spot ranges from seabirds to harbour porpoises and bottle-nosed dolphins. Longer trips on the Gower coastline take in its magnificent bays, beaches, cliffs and sea caves and the Worm's Head; en route, you might see colonies of guillemots, razorbills, choughs, kittiwakes, terns, shearwaters and gannets, plus a few Atlantic grey seals.

Gower Coast Adventures

07866 250440/www.gowercoastadventures. co.uk. **Open** *Easter-Oct* during daylight. Trip times vary; phone or check the website for details. **Trips** £32-£20; £16-£20 under-14s. **Credit** MC, V.

Explore the South Gower Coast from the belly of the Sea Serpent, a 10m purpose-built RHIB (rigid

hulled inflatable boat). The boat is fitted with water jet propulsion, which is kind to marine wildlife and enables passengers to embark from shallow water. Cruising speed is around 20 to 25 knots, and the boat can take a dozen passengers. The crew are a mine of excellent local history and wildlife knowledge, and have fascinating tales to tell as the boat skims along. Children are encouraged to keep their eyes peeled for grey seals and bottle-nosed dolphins.

Gower Heritage Centre

Parkmill, Gower, Swansea SA3 2EH (01792 371206/www.gowerheritagecentre.co.uk). **Open** *Summer* 10am-5.30pm daily. *Winter* 10am-5pm daily. *Gower Heritage tour bus* Apr-Sept. **Admission** *Heritage Centre* £3.95; £2.80 concessions, 5-12s; £12.80 family (2+2); free under-5s. *Heritage Centre & Gower Heritage tour bus* £10; £5 5-16s; £20 family (2+2); free under-5s. **Credit** MC, V.

Based around a working 12th-century watermill, this rural life museum has craft shops and activities, play areas and small animals to feed. Children can also tackle the sand-pit adventure playground, try out traditional Victorian games and learn to throw a pot on the wheel, aided by the resident potter. At weekends and during school holidays there are shows by Poppet Puppets, followed by craft workshops. Guided tours of the corn mill and saw mill include demonstrations of wood-turning and flour-milling, and an obliging blacksmith fires up the forge for metalwork demonstrations. If watching other people

National Waterfront Museum

at work becomes all too much, you can stop for coffee and Welsh cakes in the tearoom. During the summer, hop on the open-top double-decker bus which trundles through leafy lanes via Kittle, Fairwood Common and Cefn Bryn and picks up punters in Swansea and Mumbles.

National Waterfront Museum

Queens Buildings, Cambrian Place, Swansea SA1 1TW (01792 638950/www.waterfront museum.co.uk). **Open** 10am-5pm daily. **Admission** free. **Credit** *Café & shop* MC, V.

Opened in October 2005 and housed in an intriguing glass and slate building, Wales' £33.5m National Waterfront Museum was marketed as 'a museum for people who don't do museums'. Its broad mission is illustrate the effect of industrialisation on the Welsh nation – as well as to help regenerate the city centre. History is brought to life using real stories, artefacts, archive footage, 2-D graphic panels, video diaries and interactive computer displays. Every imaginable aspect of Wales' industrial and social history is covered, with areas devoted to its early copper and steel works and maritime heritage. Here, exhibits include a scale model of the 1865 steam ship Zeta, the inspiration behind a certain Swansea-born leading lady's middle name. A wing of the building is given over to traditional machinery, including a working replica of the first steam locomotive in Wales. Modern industries, including new technologies, science and animation, are covered in the 'Frontiers' area. Politicians Aneurin Bevan and David Lloyd George and modern-day sports stars Dame Tanni Grey-Thompson and Gareth Edwards have pride of place in an interactive hall of fame – visitors can vote for other Welsh luminaries to join them. As you'd expect, there's loads for children to do: storytelling sessions on the museum's Magic Carpet, arts and crafts events, seasonal festivals and Waterfront Nippers play sessions for under-fives. The Princess Way link with the city centre gives access to nearby shops, cafés and restaurants. The museum overlooks the city's marina, and is almost within touching distance of the SA1 development, one of Europe's most exciting waterfront projects.

Oxwich Castle

Swansea SA3 1EG (01792 390359/ www.cadw.wales.gov.uk). **Open** *Apr-Sept* 10am-5pm daily. Last admission 30mins before closing. **Admission** £2.50; £2 concessions; £7 family (2+3); free under-5s. **Credit** MC, V.

Perched on a pretty wooded headland above Oxwich Bay, 11 miles south-west of Swansea, the 'castle' is actually a Tudor manor house. Arranged around an enclosed courtyard, it was constructed in the 16th century by the ambitious Sir Rice Mansel and his son Edward. The castle's faux-military design was for effect – no armies besieged its mock-fortified walls. The Mansels abandoned the castle in 1630, after which it fell into disrepair. It's now maintained by Cadw, the Welsh historic conservation body; on-site facilities include parking, toilets, a shop and an exhibition.

Parc-Le-Breos

Penmaen, Gower, Swansea SA3 2HA (01792 371636/www.parclebreos.co.uk). **Open** 10am-4pm daily. **Rates** half day rides from £22; full day rides £35. **Credit** MC, V.

This family-run trekking centre has been taking its guests for idyllic canters along the sandy beaches of Gower for more than 35 years. Based in a 19th-century hunting lodge, the centre is surrounded by 70 acres of land – once the deer park of William de Breos, Lord of Gower. Accredited by the British Horse Society, the riding centre has ponies for children – riders need to be ten years old or above for half and full day rides. This is also a riding holiday and trekking centre, offering full accommodation and riding weekends; children of four and above staying here are allowed a ride in the paddock, with parental supervision.

Swansea Museum

Victoria Road, Maritime Quarter, Swansea SA1 1SN (01792 653763/www.swansea heritage.net). **Open** 10am-5pm Tue-Sun. **Admission** free. **Credit** MC, V.

Dylan Thomas used to wander, perhaps soberly, through this establishment and reflect that it should be 'put into a museum'. He had a point. Opened in 1841, this is the oldest museum in Wales, celebrating the second city's industry, famous people, maritime links and treasures in a beguilingly old-fashioned way. Nonetheless, the education team work hard to make exhibitions come alive for vistors of all ages – a recent 'Egyptian Day' to mark the Beasts of the Nile exhibition had children belly dancing, drumming, practising hieroglyphics and getting hennaed. That's a far cry from the fusty museum Thomas remembered from his perambulations in what he described as this 'ugly, lovely town'.

Watersports4:all

Euphoria Sailing, 34 Eastlands Park, Bishopston, Swansea SA3 3DQ (01792 234502/www.watersports4all.com). **Open** *Easter-Sept* days and times vary; phone for details. **Rates** vary; phone for details. **Credit** MC, V.

Get wet safely with Euphoria Sailing's courses for all ages. Children can be booked into one-, three- or five-day courses with the Dinghy Sailing Club to give them a basic understanding of the basic principles of sailing, boat maintenance, rigging and storage. They're also shown some rope work, and get to learn about tides and the weather. Over-eights can be left unsupervised, but under-eights must be accompanied by an adult. Euphoria can also organise group days, which can incorporate dinghy sailing, water skiing and ocean kayaking. The centre is licensed under the Adventure Activity Licensing Authority.

The Dyfi Valley to southern Snowdonia

The green way to the red dragon's heart.

With beaches, mountains, castles, farms and steam railways all within a few miles of one another, there's no denying mid Wales's child appeal. Our green way through its many attractions follows the steep sided valleys of the rivers Dyfi and Dysynni, from the gentle seaside resorts at their mouths, north to the foothills of Snowdonia National Park and east to the ancient town of Machynlleth.

The settlements of the Dyfi valley grew up around the twin industries of mining and quarrying and, as far as the village of Aberdyfi was concerned, shipbuilding. During the 19th and early 20th centuries, Aberdyfi's harbour and long jetty were always busy, as ships moored to take on cargoes of slate from the surrounding quarries. During the world wars the area went into decline as the shipping industry faltered. These days, the only vessels tying up round here are yachts and pleasure boats in the marina, and tourism is the main source of revenue.

Castell-y-Bere

Ironically, that which makes the tourists hesitate on their pilgrimages to the wild shores of underpopulated North Wales – the weather – is a lifesaver for the English. Welsh Water supplies much of England with water, as well as green and unspoilt countryside for the school holidays. As the drought hit south-east England in the summer of 2006, the subject of plentiful Welsh water once again hit the headlines, as English MPs hotly denied rumours of plans to flood Welsh valleys to replenish the dwindling Thames. The Welsh have a right to be edgy about the subject; their protests had no effect in the 1960s, when Tryweryn Valley and the village of Capel Celyn were drowned to supply Liverpool.

Beside the seaside

A drowned kingdom is the subject of one of many legends wreathed around the village of Aberdyfi (Aberdovey is the English spelling). A folk song, the Bells of Aberdovey ('Clychau Aberdyfi'), tells of the legend of a submerged kingdom under Cardigan Bay, whose bells can be heard ringing beneath the water. Thomas Love Peacock based a novel, *The Misfortunes of Elphin* (1829), on the legend. The ghostly bells also inspired Susan Cooper's *The Silver on the Tree*, the last book in her mysterious *The Dark is Rising* sequence, parts of which are set in Aberdyfi.

Approaching Aberdyfi village from the green valley road inland, or the more windy A493 coastal road, its attractions are immediately apparent. It presides over huge sandy beaches and is sheltered by steep wooded slopes that take visitors to breathtaking viewpoints over the estuary. With its jolly pastel-painted guesthouses and seaside shops, yacht club, seafront gardens and dune-fringed beach, Aberdyfi is every bit as photogenic as its surroundings.

The village itself has some browsable little shops along Sea View Terrace and around the Wharf. The Lifeboat Shop has secondhand books and RNLI souvenirs, and there are a couple of typically seasidey purveyors of crafts, gifts and essentials. The sweetest thing, however, is obviously The Sweet Shop (2 Sea View Terrace, 01654 767222) with its own-made fudge, chocs and ice-creams.

Far and away the best activities round here are of the sporting variety – sea fishing, estuary fishing, crabbing with lines (Aladdin's Cave gift shop sells them) from the jetty, taking a boat trip with Dyfi Discoveries (*see p245*) or canoeing, rafting, abseiling and climbing at the Outward Bound Centre (0870 513 4227, www.outwardbound.org.uk).

As well as bathing and sandcastle building when the weather is beachy, Aberdyfi is a fine starting point for gorgeous walks, both coastal and into the ancient

Cader Idris, a Welsh giant's armchair. *See p236.*

Welsh hillsides. The signposted Roman Road along the estuary is a reminder that there was once a Roman fort in the village of Pennal, five miles away, but there's no evidence that the rough track is really Roman. Whoever made it, the steep walk out of the Dyfi Valley takes you up to the Panorama Walk, which goes to Llyn Barfog (Bearded Lake, named after a hairy monster that was purported to live in the lake until it was dragged out by King Arthur's horse); there are delightful views over Cardigan Bay all the way.

Arthurian Legend hangs about much of North Wales, most likely because the word for Arthur may come from the Welsh 'Arth Fawr' (the Great Bear), a title which may have been given to any warlord in the Dark Ages possessed of bear-like strength. Early stories of such Arthurs can be found in the Welsh tales known as the *The Mabinogion*. A shorter walk than that to Bearded Lake takes you through Cwm Maethlon or Happy Valley, as Victorian tourists named it.

The town of a prince

About eight miles from Aberdyfi is the handsome market town of Machynlleth (pronounce it 'Mahunclef', but try to add a Germanic guttural note). Its centrepiece, a tall memorial clock tower, was built by the townspeople in 1874. Despite this lofty architectural tribute to mark the coming of age of the Marquess of Londonderry, the town looks too small to be a big noise in Welsh history, but it has ancient claims to being the first capital of Wales. The reason? This was the place that the country's most charismatic Welsh nationalist, Owain Glyndwr, chose to assemble the first Welsh parliament. Visitors can find out all they need to know about this hero at the Owain Glyndwr Centre, housed alongside the

Tourist Information Centre in the medieval Parliament House. This long, low building, a late medieval Welsh townhouse, is a Grade I listed building.

A little south of the centre, Plas Machynlleth is a mansion and grounds that was presented to the townspeople in 1948. It was briefly the home of a vistor attraction called Celtica, which closed down a couple of years back. From the West Lodge, walkers wishing to trace the footsteps of Glyndwr can walk his way via the 'Roman Steps'. Machynlleth is the mid-way point of Owain Glyndwr's Way (OGW). The trail takes you from the town up to Llyn Glanmerin (Lord Herbert's Lake) and Hyddgen, where the beleaguered Glyndwr won his most famous victory.

Glyndwr's Way was granted National Trail status in 2000. The 135-mile (217-kilometre) trail is a long distance walk (it takes nine days, a little hard for the children) beginning at Knighton on the English border and finishing by the Montgomeryshire Canal in Welshpool. For more details on Glyndwr's Way, call its National Trail Officer (01597 827562).

If pottering around town is more your thing, there are antique shops to rummage through, a smart Aga store and a Cath Kidston-esque home shop (it's gentrified round here – Robert Plant is a Mach man) and various little gift shops that children find so appealing. Cariad (2 Penrallt Street, 01654 703555), specialises in Romanian crafts, Christian and Celtic jewellery and knick-knacks (including the ubiquitous Welsh love spoons). All its profits go to the Myosotis Trust, which helps the poor in eastern Romania. Foodies go to William Lloyd (5-7 Maengwyn Street, 01654 702106), the award-winning butcher, for local lamb for the freezer.

The Tabernacle, a former Wesleyan chapel, opened as a centre for the performing arts in 1986 and is home to MOMA (Museum of Modern Art, www.momawales.org.uk), which has six exhibition spaces for modern Welsh Art. Maengwyn Steet has plenty of child friendly, pleasant places to eat to fuel up for your trip to the Centre for Alternative Technology (*see p243*).

To the mountains

Keep marching in a northerly direction from Mach and you'll find yourself at the foot of Snowdonia National Park, one of eleven such protected areas in England and Wales, and the second largest after the Lake District. The park covers 823 square miles (2132 square kilometres) and includes towns, villages, hill farms and several million sheep that look as if they've been Velcro-ed to its slopes.

Dyfi Valley

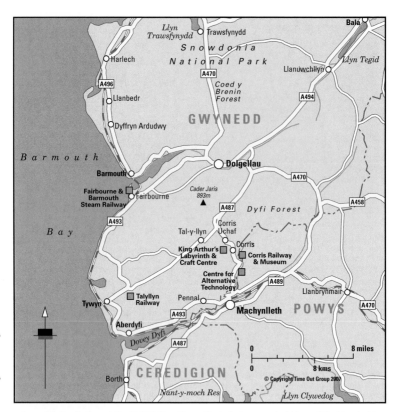

From Machynlleth and the Dyfi Valley, the mountain trail takes you to the brooding bulk of Cader Idris. Snowdon's junior by a couple of hundred metres, Idris is, at 892 metres, not even the second highest mountain in the National Park. It's harder work to climb, however – not least because, unlike Snowdon, it doesn't possess a handy steam train to haul exhausted climbers up to its summit. It's also a lot less troubled by walkers in high season. Walking the eight miles up the mountain and down again isn't too difficult. You need to be fit and well-equipped, however, and children will require a few bribes to maintain their interest.

The name Cader Idris translates as 'the chair of Idris', because one of its cwms looks like an enormous armchair that your typically Welsh giant – called Idris – might once have sat on. The mountain has its fair share of legends, one being that anyone who sleeps on its slopes will wake up either mad or a poet. The name of the mountain is also sometimes translated as Arthur's Seat, presumably with reference to King Arthur, who seems to have made his mark everywhere in North Wales, and is as

likely to have rested his mythical backside on a mountain top as anyone else.

There are several named paths to the summit, which is called Pen-y-gader (Welsh for 'top of the chair'). Long ago, a man used to ride a pack mule to the summit to sell lemonade and sandwiches to panting tourists; the route he took is the safest one, which families with children should attempt, it's now called the Pony Path.

The two highest glacial lakes near Idris, Llyn Cader to the north and Llyn Cau to the south, are walkers's's favourites. Scaremongers say that Llyn Cau has no bottom and a monster in its depths – that'll put the kids off their swim.

Getting to Idris takes you through lonely countryside on the 'Cadr' road about three miles out of Dolgellau. There's a car park at Pont Dyffrydan from where you follow the Pony Path from the Ty Nanant farmhouse. Two miles west of Idris is the eastern end of the Talyllyn Railway (see p245).

You're never far from a great castle in Wales. The mighty Harlech, inspiration for the stirring song 'Men of Harlech' and scene of a long siege during the Wars of the Roses, is a few miles up the A496 from coastal Barmouth (information 01766 780552, www.cadw.wales.gov.uk). The most impressive fortress in Wales, it's a perfectly concentric castle in a truly breathtaking position, and well worth a detour north. Another castle, a lot more ruined, granted, but free to scramble around, is Castell-y-Bere. Y Bere was a fortress built by Llywelyn ap Iorwerth (Llywelyn the Great) who was Prince of Gwynedd in the early 13th century. The castle is now a hulking ruin, standing guard on the valley floor not far from Cader Idris and its less lofty companions near Abergynolwyn (you can take the steam train from the Talyllyn Railway). The castle ruins make a fantastic spot for a picnic; the views are enchanting, and the castle's history fascinating. Edward I seized the Castell-y-Bere in the late 13th century, when it was the last castle to fall during his incursion into Wales.

Castell-y-Bere is looked after by Cadw (www.cadw.wales.gov.uk), an organisation set up by the Welsh Assembly to look after the historical monuments of Wales, including what's left of Edward I's 'iron ring' of fortresses. Cadw means 'to keep' in Welsh; it's not an acronym, as some wags in the Tourist Offices would have it (Come And Do Wales).

WHERE TO STAY

The Centre for Alternative Technology (see *p243*) is a leading light of the Dyfi Valley eco-tourism initiative. Its website has links to environmentally friendly guesthouses, campsites and hostels in the mid-Wales area. CAT also has accommodation of its own; this is usually taken up by students on residential courses, but it's worth ringing to see if they can put you and your family up for a night or two. CAT also recommends the holistic Corris Hostel (*see below*), whose recycling and composting efforts have earned it much praise from the green people of the Dyfi Valley.

Corris Hostel

Canolfan Corris (Old School, Corris), Machynlleth, Powys SY20 9TQ (01654 761686/www.canolfancorris.com). **Rates** Room only £13-£15. **No credit cards**.

If you like a low-cost, low-emission, rather bohemian atmosphere, the greener-than-thou Corris has a bunk for you. Housed in a former school, this 42-bed hostel used to be part of the Youth Hostel Association's empire, until it became independent in 1992. Accommodation can either be in the dormitories, or, if booked ahead, family bunk rooms, which have an en suite shower and toilet.

helters
nlimited
.vite you to tipi.
ee p240.

THE CREAM OF THE OLD STEAMERS

Few families with young children holiday in Wales without planning at least one steam train ride for their little *Thomas the Tank Engine* fan. Talyllyn Railway is the route to choose in this neck of the woods. This steam attraction has special significance for those familiar with the collected works of one train-obsessed cleric. One of the volunteers on the historic line in the 1950s was none other than the Reverend Wilbert Vere Awdry, creator of Thomas, Gordon, James et al. The Skarloey Railway of Awdry's books is thought to be based on Talyllyn, and the museum at the Wharf Station, which explores more than 200 years of the narrow gauge railway's history, also finds space for displays all about the Reverend Awdry and his passion for the railways.

The stories about the steam-puffing characters that made this trainspotter famous were dreamed up by Awdry in 1942 to amuse his son Christopher during a bout of measles. In one, a narrow gauge engine called Duncan gets star billing; Duncan was based on Talyllyn's locomotive, Douglas. Today, the railway casts Duncan as its children's favourite and run special Duncan days throughout the year, on which children and their families can ride the train from Tywyn Wharf Station to Abergynolwyn. Special activities such as storytelling, badgemaking and photo opportunities with Duncan mark the occasion.

With its celebrity train and famous literary connections, Talyllyn Railway is one of the best steam attractions in Wales, but there are 17 others across the country vying for children's attention and affections.

In the little coastal town of Fairbourne, nearby, steam trains run by the small-scale Fairbourne & Barmouth Steam Railway (www.fairbournerailway.com) chuff the short distance to Penrhyn Point; from there, passengers can take a ferry to Barmouth. Not far away in Porthmadog, the Welsh Highland Railway (01766 513402, www.whr.co.uk), along with its sister branch in Caernarfon, is part of the mighty Ffestioniog Railway, (01766 516024, www.festrail.co.uk). Ffestiniog is the oldest independent railway company in the world; its trains run through Snowdonia National Park.

The Snowdon Mountain Railway (www.snowdonrailway.co.uk), provides a painless, if pricey, access to Snowdon's summit. SMR is the only public rack and pinion railway in the British Isles. Of the four coal-fired steam locomotives that run up the steep line, three are originals, dating from 1895 and 1896. The trains run chimney-first up the mountain, pushing a single carriage in front: it's safer that way, given the tricky gradient. Thomas could never have done it.

All the rooms are carpeted and it's comfortable enough for winter stays, as there's central heating and a log fire in the main hall. Lockers are provided, along with quilts, pillows and sheet sleeping bags. There's a small play and picnic area in the grounds, and you can even bring the family dog (provided it's happy to sleep in the main hall only). Breakfast costs £3 and isn't included in the overnight rate; packed lunches and evening meals can also be provided, with prices from £5-£7. Alternatively, knock up your own meals in the self-catering kitchen or try the nearby Slaters Arms. The hostel grounds are sensitively landscaped to encourage wildlife; the children and the dog should have a good time exploring nature immediately outside.

Dovey Inn
Aberdyfi, Gwynedd LL35 OEF (01654 767332/www.doveyinn.com). **Rates** £60-£80. **Credit** MC, V.
This eight-bedroomed hotel is in the heart of Aberdyfi, looking out over the harbour. It's an excellent base for a traditional bucket and spade holiday, with wide sandy beaches and safe bathing a couple of minutes away. The family rooms have adjoining bedrooms for children, and there are plenty of family-only areas away from child-free bars. For sunny days, there are pretty terraces and beer gardens. For rainy ones, The Dovey Inn's reciprocal relationship with the Plas Talgarth Health & Fitness Country Club (a Macdonald holiday resort a couple of miles away) comes in very handy. Dovey Inn residents get a pass card that gives them access to the swimming pools, sauna, jacuzzi, gym and squash courts.

Garthyfog Farm
Arthog, Gwynedd LL39 1AX (01341 250254/ www.garthyfog.co.uk). **Rates** *Camping* £7-£10/ tent; £10/caravan. *Log cabins* £340-£510/wk. **No credit cards**.
This beautiful little camping and caravan site also has two Norwegian log cabins (Caban Idris and Caban Mawddach), with gas-fired central heating, full fitted kitchens and bathrooms, television and stereo. The farm has the Cader Idris mountain range as a backdrop and fabulous views over the Mawddach Estuary. The beaches of Barmouth and Fairbourne and their little steam railway are a couple of miles away. Otherwise, this area is perfect for walking, mountain biking, pony trekking and climbing.

Golgarth Hall Farm
Pennal, Machynlleth, Powys SY20 9LB (01654 791235/www.golgarthhallfarm.co.uk). **Rates** £50-£64. **Credit** MC, V.
Deilwen and Ron Breese run a cattle and sheep farm, but diversified into tourism back in 1990 as their panoramic views of the Dyfi Estuary were lost on the livestock. Happily, English tourists were more appreciative of both the views and Mrs

Breese's cooking, and keep coming back to enjoy the friendly, farmy atmosphere and enormous Welsh breakfasts and dinners. Accommodation could be in the main farmhouse, a handsome, white painted family home with large guestrooms. There's also a coach house with three bedrooms, further cottages and a caravan standing in its own grounds. Up in the hills, away from everything but the river, valley and some sheep, is Cwm Ffernol, another farmhouse with an oil fired Rayburn and loads of space. Children love to walk around the farm and see the animals when they're not being advised by the Breeses about the myriad other attractions in the area – steam trains, castles, watersports and quad bikes. Many guests enjoy getting together in the farmhouse dining room for a jolly meal and informal Welsh lessons.

Penhelig Arms Hotel
Aberdyfi, Gwynedd LL35 0LT (01654 767215/www.penheligarms.com). **Rates** £78-£140. *DB&B* £122-£190. **Credit** MC, V.
This hotel has won so many awards and rave reviews for its food, accommodation, situation and all-round 'perfection' (*Time Out*'s last verdict on it), you must be prepared to book well in advance. We didn't the last time we took the children to Aberdyfi, and couldn't get a room for the night. We know it's lovely though. A range of rooms are available in the main building, plus a private cottage 250 yards away and a posh new addition known as Penhelig House. Bodhelig is the best part of the hotel for families, as it's a self-contained building of four suites, with balconies and a big patio. The view – overlooking mountains, estuary and sea – is enchanting.

Plas Dolguog Hotel
Felingerrig, Machynlleth, Powys SY20 8UJ (01654 702244/www.plasdolguog.co.uk). **Rates** £85-£145. **Credit** MC, V.
The meadowlands around the ancient Plas once belonged to Cuog, a warrior son of one of the Princes of Wales, back in the sixth century. He didn't run a hotel as far as we know, but this building is impressively old, dating back to 1632. It's set overlooking the Dyfi Valley, where the Rivers Dulas and Dyfi converge – a great place for salmon and sea trout fishing (which the dining room makes the most of). Plas Dolguog also has the distinction of being within what is to all intents and purposes a nature reserve. The nine acres of grounds around the hotel are resplendent with wildflowers, ancient trees and rocky outcrops, attracting so many avian and mammalian species, that they have won the David Bellamy award for Conservation. The gardens, known as Grandma's Garden, incorporate an arboretum, sculpture garden and peace garden. Children like to wander around the copses and stone circles in the Children's Enchanted Garden, looking for the fairy statues and dolphin fountains. Inside the old-fashioned hotel there are log fires for chilly evenings, Cu Og's restaurant

for traditional Welsh dishes and eight bedrooms. A stables annexe provides a further six rooms. This is a great place if you don't mind staying at close quarters with the offspring: up to two under-12s can share their parents' room free; each additional child pays £10 (up to four kids in total).

Shelters Unlimited

Rhiw'r Gwreiddyn, Ceinws, Machynlleth, Powys SY20 9EX (01654 761720/www.tipis. co.uk). **Open** campsite year round; phone for times. **Rates** from £20pppn (free under-5s) unfurnished tipi (sleeps 8); £50 pppn (free under-5s) furnished tipi (sleeps 8). **Credit** MC, V.

A family firm that makes and supplies authentic tipis, Bedouin and Berber tents and their furnishings, SU also run a very distinctive campsite in the ancient oak woodland of the sheltered valley. The campsite has shower and toilet facilities and the tipis are designed to have fires lit inside them, should the night feel particularly chilly. Otherwise, there are facilities for outside fires. The tipis are beautiful to look at, designed to be in keeping with the scenery, and strong enough to withstand fierce storms. They're also surprisingly comfortable and spacious. There's lots of space on the site, too, so no one need feel their tipi is overlooked. On balmy nights, people often gather together around campfires, although there is no entertainments schedule. Be prepared to bring your own sleeping bags, ground mats and pillows for the basic unfurnished tipis. Families that fancy a bit of luxury can go for the furnished option and nestle down into sheepskins on coir matting, enjoying the warmth of a stone fireplace and cuddling up in Mexican blankets. If it all sounds a bit Glastonbury, you're right: Shelters Unlimited supply the play tipis for the festival. They also provided three for the famous Diana Princess of Wales Memorial Playground in Kensington Gardens, London.

Talbontdrain Guest House

Talbontdrain, Uwchygarreg, Machynlleth, Powys SY20 8RR (01654 702192/ www.talbontdrain.co.uk). **Rates** £50-£60. **No credit cards**.

The energetic and hospitable Hilary Matthews runs the deliciously remote Talbontdrain, whose name means 'thorn tree at the edge of the bridge'. Every window looks out onto the wild and woolly landscape; fantastic walking country starts right at the front door. Hilary's keen on families, so makes every effort to accommodate them: extra beds and cots can be squeezed into any room, kids go free if they share with the parents, and there are tents for children to use – some regulars sleep in the barn. There isn't a set price for children for this reason – you can't charge much if the kids are out roosting with the chickens, can you? Children can choose to eat early or with their parents and other guests. Again, meal prices are dependent on appetites. The food is good and plentiful; Hilary's an accomplished cook who uses local produce (often from her kitchen garden)

Views to amuse at the **Trefiddian Hotel**.

when in season and eggs from her own hens (children might get a chance to help collect them). At breakfast, own-made jam and local honey are on the table. High chairs and a baby carrier are available for the youngest guests. Hilary will babysit in the evening if you want to go out, and with enough notice can organise childcare during the day if you're planning a long walk. There is a pianola with a large selection of rolls to play, a dressing up box, a huge selection of books and games, a doll's house, and a trampoline in the garden. Goggle eyes take note: there is no television at Talbontdrain. The house is geared up for walkers, with easily followed maps for hikes and plenty of OS maps to borrow. Drying facilities and waterproofs are available for those unprepared for wet Welsh walks. Hilary provides packed lunches, a dog to walk if you're hankering for canine company, a lift for the stranded and restorative cups of tea for muddied returnees.

Trefiddian Hotel

Aberdyfi, Gwynedd, LL35 OSB (01654 767213/www.trefwales.com). **Rates** *DB&B* £124-£228. **Credit** MC, V.

Feasting its many windows over the golf course and the wide sandy beach of Aberdyfi, the 59-room Trefiddian has been run by the same family for almost a century. Its solid reputation is proudly celebrated in the hotel history book, available to read in the main lounge, in which devoted returnees recall several decades of idyllic holidays here. Between hotel and beach, the Aberdyfi golf course is independent of Trefiddian, but hotel residents enjoy concessionary rates during their stay – or can stick with the pitch and putt in the grounds. It's a minute's walk across the road up through the dunes to the beach, a trail well worn by hundreds of flip-flopped feet throughout the summer. If the weather's dodgy, the heated swimming pool, in an outbuilding across from the main entrance, is the preferred alternative. Children have always been welcome at Tref; these days they get an indoor playroom with giant Connect 4, slides and playhouses, plus a games room with a pool table, ping-pong and air hockey. Outside there's a playground area and tennis courts. Very young children are offered an extensive nursery tea menu (pasta, roast chicken, sausage and beans, pizzas and the like) in case they can't hang on for the 7pm dinner. Main meals are served in a spacious dining room with a degree of formality that most children over four can cope with. It's gently suggested that cot-sleepers take their tea earlier. Grandparents with happy memories of 1960s Trefiddian now accompany their children and their kids to enjoy a post-prandial sunset over Cardigan Bay, but many are content to watch it from the dining room and lounges, where massive windows make the most of the seascape. Most people spend from five nights to two weeks in Trefiddian, taking advantage of holiday deals that include dinner, bed and breakfast, all of which we can thoroughly recommend. For more on eating at Trefiddian, *see p242.*

Wynnstay Hotel & Restaurant

Maengwyn Street, Machynlleth, Powys SY20 8AE (01654 702941/www.wynnstay-hotel. com). **Rates** £80-£110. *DB&B* £130-£160. **Credit** MC, V.

This 18th-century coaching inn, once a favourite stopping-off point for the Shrewsbury stage, is often praised for its atmosphere, top chefs, outstanding menu, fabulous wine list and brilliant beers. None of that would really matter much to people travelling *en famille*, except that it is also welcoming and has a clutch of family rooms at reasonable prices; cots are provided and under-fours go free. The relaxed atmosphere harks back to its beginnings as a wayfarers inn, it's now a social centre for locals and Snowdonia walkers with a penchant for the finer things in life. One of the lounges sports a massive Romantic engraving of Cader Idris.

WHERE TO EAT & DRINK

Bear of Amsterdam

9 Seaview Terrace, Aberdyfi, Gwynedd LL35 0EF (01654 767684). **Meals served** *Summer* 10am-8pm Tue-Sun. *Winter* 10am-3pm Tue-Thur, Sun; 10am-7.30pm Fri, Sat. **Main courses** £4-£7.95. **No credit cards**.

Brilliant breakfasts at the Bear include big fry-ups, available all day. This is a small but welcoming café, very handy for the village centre. Its cod and chips won an 'Eat Well in Wales' award, so you know where to come after a hectic morning on the beach. Children are made very welcome.

Dick's Diner

44-46 Maengwyn Street, Machynlleth, Powys SY20 8DT (01654 703346). **Meals served** noon-2pm Mon; noon-2pm, 5-9.30pm Tue-Sat. **Main courses** £2-£5.50. **No credit cards**.

A simple, wipe-clean caff with a mostly deep-fried menu, Dick's is a useful place for economical refuelling after a busy morning's hill walking. A big plate of cod and chips is a bargain £4; the children's portion (under-13s only) a mere £2. You can go vegetarian and have the cheese pasty or bean burger if you've a robust digestive system; or go for the students' favourite, chips with curry sauce. It's not sophisticated, but sometimes a large plate of something and chips is just what you need. With tea a mere 65p a mug, you can afford to go mad and have the plaice.

Dylanwad Da

2 Ffos-y-Felin, Dolgellau, Gwynedd LL40 1BS (01341 422870/www.dylanwad.co.uk). **Meals served** *Summer* 10am-3pm, 7-9pm Tue-Sat. *Winter* (closed Feb, 1st 2wks Mar) 10am-3pm, 7-9pm Thur-Sat. **Main courses** £11.50-£15.50. **Credit** MC, V.

During the day you can have coffees, hot chocolates, snacks and own-baked cakes and pastries in this light, bright dining room, but the cheerful staff have no problem serving up half portions on the dinner menu too. Expect national favourites (leek soup, Welsh lamb and smoked salmon among them), as well as bistro fare such as chicken with coconut and spinach, and mediterranean fish stew. We recommend honeycomb ice-cream for pud, but leave room for the Welsh cheese plate (£5.80) and coffee and chocolates, both of which children are happy to share.

Hennighan's Top Shop

123 Maengwyn Street, Machynlleth, Powys SY20 8EF (01654 702761/www. hennighans.co.uk). **Meals served** *Summer* noon-2pm, 5-10.30pm Mon, Thur-Sat; noon-10.30pm Wed; 5-10.30pm Sun. *Winter* noon-2pm, 5-10.30pm Mon, Thur-Sat; noon-2pm Wed. **Main courses** £2.30-£4.65. **No credit cards.**
A terrific fish and chippie, consistently voted one of the best in Wales by roving gourmets, Hennighan's is mostly takeaway, although there are benches outside for fair-weather chomping.

Penhelig Arms Hotel

Aberdyfi, Gwynedd, LL35 0LT (01654 767215/www.penheligarms.com). **Meals served** noon-2pm, 7-9pm daily. **Main courses** £8.95-£16. **Credit** MC, V.
Ask anyone where you can eat well in Aberdyfi and they'll point you in the direction of Penhelig. So many favourable reviews mean only one thing though – book ahead. The best thing about this roadside inn and brasserie is that it remains refreshingly un-poncey. A commitment to good eating doesn't have to mean formal dining, and children are as welcome to sample the legendary dishes, from exemplary fish and chips to lamb shank braised in red wine, red onions, rosemary and balsamic vinegar, as anyone else. Renowned for its seafood, especially dressed Aberdyfi crab, seared scallops and crevettes and dressed lobster, Pehhelig also has a Fisherman's Bar where seafood is available. The restaurant has won awards for its well-chosen wine list.

Quarry Café

27 Maengwyn Street, Machynlleth, Powys SY20 8EB (01654 702624/www.cat.org.uk). **Open** *Summer* 9am-5.30pm Mon-Sat; 10am-4pm Sun. *Winter* 9am-4.30pm Mon-Wed, Fri, Sat; 9am-2pm Thur. **Main courses** £2.50-£6.15. **No credit cards.**
The good people of the Centre for Altenative technology (*see p243*) run this café from their earthly paradise high in the green hills above Machynlleth. This downtown café is a friendly, vegetarian place with a toy box and nappy changing room for its younger customers. The menu changes daily, but expect two or three hot main dishes such as vegetable lasagne, alongside spicy beanburgers and own-made pizzas with salad (a popular children's option). The cakes, some bought in, some baked here, are mostly

organic, as are the bread and own-made rolls. Fruit crumbles are a popular autumn pudding, particularly if the CAT smallholding has provided plenty of apples and plums. The coffee and tea, beans and biscuits are Fair Trade, the soft drinks organic and there are ice-creams from Green & Black's and even vegan cornettos.

Sea Breeze Tearooms

6 Bodfor Terrace, Aberdyfi, Gwynedd LL35 0EA (01654 767449/www.seabreeze-aberdovey.co.uk). **Open** *Easter-mid Sept* 10.30am-6pm daily. **No credit cards.**
Lisa and Julian Price run a friendly little bed and breakfast here in Aberdyfi, and their six rooms fill up quickly. Everyone is welcome, however, in their tearoom and ice-cream parlour. The Welsh afternoon tea, which replaces the cream scone and jam combo (also available) with Bara Brith (Welsh fruit cake) and Welshcakes, costs just £3.95 with a big pot of tea. Children go a bundle on the milkshakes with own-made cookies, but there's also chocolate fudge cake and cream doughnuts, not to mention ice-cream sundaes and treacle tart, to consider. There's outdoor seating for sunny afternoons, or a sofa and newspapers for chilly ones.

Trefiddian Hotel

Aberdyfi, Gwynedd LL35 0SB (01654 767213/www.trefwales.com). **Meals served** 12.45-1.30pm (bar snacks), 7-8.45pm daily. **Set lunch** (Mon-Fri) £13.75 3 courses; (Sat, Sun) £15.50 3 courses. **Set dinner** £25.50 5 courses. **Credit** MC, V.
If you get a chance to eat in the dining room, with its lovely Aberdyfi views, take it; the food here is of a very high standard. The restaurant is open to non-residents for afternoon tea, lunch and a splendid five-course dinner, but you need to book in advance. A three-course lunch might include beef consommé, prawns or marinated mushrooms, followed by Welsh beef with Yorkshire pudding or gilthead bream with courgette noodles, with citrus tart or *pot au chocolat* to finish. Dinner offers a few more choices, and the chance of a wonderful sunset to accompany your meal of, for example; salmon roulade, steamed sea bass, Welsh lamb served with a piquant tomato jus, plenty of vegetables and a longer pud list. Children are welcome, although under-fives may not get much out of the experience.

Wynnstay Restaurant & Pizzeria

Maengwyn Street, Machynlleth, Powys SY20 8AE (01654 702941/www.wynnstay-hotel. com). **Meals served** noon-2pm, 6.30-9pm daily. **Main courses** £9-£15. **Set dinner** £25 3 courses. **Credit** MC, V.
A most satisfying place to appreciate the best of Welsh produce. Most good restaurants serve locally reared lamb and beef, but Wynnstay's celebrated chef goes the whole hog with fresh seafish landed at Borth and Aberdyfi, freshwater fish from the River Dyfi, Llynlloed pheasant and

Bacheiddon mallard. Locally grown vegetables from Mach's Wednesday market are also thrown into the mix. Expect dishes like Sunday roast lamb, linguine with cockles, salmon fillet with broad beans and risotto with wild mushrooms. With the chefs coming from France and Italy, a Mediterranean slant is evident in much of the grub. Children are welcome to choose a small portion of simpler dishes – a piece of poached salmon with pasta, perhaps, or some beef fillet with fried potatoes. The waiting staff are happy to discuss the options. Alternatively, everyone can trot to the rear of the hotel to have one of the best pizzas in Wales. They're own-made, prepared in traditional wood-fired fashion and include Italian classics such as margherita and fiorentina, as well as some special Wynnstay variations, depending on the ingredients available.

PLACES TO SEE, THINGS TO DO

Animalarium

Ynisfergi, Borth, Ceredigion SY24 5NA (01970 871224/www.animalarium.co.uk). **Open** *Apr-Oct* 10am-6pm daily. *Nov-Mar* 11am-4pm daily. **Admission** £7; £6 concessions; £5 3-15s; £22 family (2+3); free under-3s; . **Credit** MC, V.

With a collection of disparate, often exotic and unusual animals from all over the world, Animalarium prides itself on providing its vistors with 'the best snake encounter in the UK', so has children running in all directions. One of its hands-on snakes is a massive, obviously very patient Burmese python called Grumpy, who is frequently called upon to drape himself over the tentative hands and trembling shoulders of volunteers. Crocodile feeding is another attraction. Older children go around talking in pronounced Aussie accents (you're sadly missed, Steve Irwin) as they view crocs, wallabies, creepy crawlies, snakes and kookaburras. Most of the animals here have come from pet rescue centres, pet shops and other zoos, or were unwanted or abandoned pets, which makes us all feel better about gawping at them. As well as the animal enclosures, there's a petting barn with your requisite moribund guinea pigs and rabbits, pony rides, a big ball pool and playground. Refreshments and ice-creams are available.

Bird Rock Cycle Hire

Cefn Coch Tywyn, Gwynedd LL36 9SD (01654 712193/www.southsnowdoniacyclehire.co.uk). **Open** 9.30am-6pm daily. **Bike hire** £2.50-£7.50/hr; £12-£18/day. **No credit cards.**

Forgotten your bikes? The chaps at Cefn Coch will hire you wheels that can take on the tough Welsh terrain. Children's bikes and tag-along attachments for nervous small riders are also available, so there's no excuse for not taking the National Cycle Route from here to Castell-y-Bere (*see p237*).

Bwlchgwyn Farm

Fairbourne, Gwynedd LL39 1BX (01341 250107/www.bwlchgwynfarm.co.uk). **Treks** £15-£25; phone for details. **No credit cards.**

Pony treks from Bwlchgwyn take you out to beautiful Fairbourne Beach for a canter through the gentle surf (good for the fetlocks), or along the picturesque Mawddach Estuary. Keen riders book into in the well-equipped caravans and cottage available for hire on the farm, but visitors staying elsewhere are welcome to join one of the one- or two-hour rides. Children aged from six can take part; novice riders go on the lead rein. If riding's not your thing, stay at this friendly farm and use it as a base for fishing, walking and shinning up Cader Idris, whose brooding outline can be seen in the distance.

Centre for Alternative Technology

Machynlleth, Powys SY20 9AZ (01654 705989/www.cat.org.uk). **Open** *Apr-Oct* 10am-4.30pm daily. *Nov-Mar* 10am-dusk daily. Closed 2wks mid-Jan; check website for dates. *Cliff railway* open Apr-Oct. **Admission** £6-£8; £5-£7 concessions; £3-£4 5-16s; free under-5s. **Credit** MC, V.

The alternative looks perfectly splendid up here among the trees above the Dulas Valley on the edge of Snowdonia National Park. Getting to the Visitor Centre is the first adventure. You pay your dues, then are shown on to a water-powered railway carriage. It's one of two; the railway works on the principle of water balancing. When water is run into a tank beneath the upper carriage, the weight eventually sends it down a 35° slope, and the cable connecting it to the lower carriage pulls that one up. From the upper station, visitors are treated to fabulous views to Tarren-y-Gesail, the southernmost peak in Snowdonia. From here on in, your ecological education – and the fun – begins in earnest.

An introductory video describes the CAT beginnings in the 1970s. Today, there's a pleasantly landscaped lake, whose hungry carp like picnic leftovers; wind generators; the self-build whole home display; and organic gardens of all varieties, with loads of information about growing your own vegetables. Children love diving down into the molehole and exploring underground chambers with lit displays of over-large soil inhabitants. The busiest area is all about recycling, composting and exploring renewable energy. Children can try to light up bulbs using pedal power, slide merrily into the composting area, indulge in splashy water play and really get stuck in to the eco-interactive experience. You need to leave at least two hours to fully appreciate all the displays, as well as plenty of time for the kids to monkey about in the eco-adventure playground and, during school holidays, take in a workshop or show in the strawbale theatre. We saw a colourful environmental film in the Gaiascope, whose reflective screens deliver a kaleidoscopic cinematic experience. The food in the café is Fair Trade, vegetarian, grown on site where possible

Centre for Alternative Technology. *See p243.*

Dyfi Valley

(CAT would need acres of vegetable patches to provide for all its visitors and staff) and strong on wholesome homebakes and salads. The shop takes a good long time to explore too. As well as an extensive book section, there's organic clothing and toiletries, loads of toys (many pocket money-priced), stationery and tempting investments such as a wind-up DAB radio.

Coed y Brenin

Visitor Centre, Dolgefeiliau, Dolgellau, Gwynedd LL40 2HZ (0845 604 0845/www. mbwales.com). **Open** *Summer* 9am-5pm daily. *Winter* 10am-dusk daily. **Admission** free.
If you're keen mountainbikers, pedal over to the Forest of the King, near Dolgellau, for some of the best rides in Britain. There are five routes of varying difficulty (from a 12km fun route to the strenuous 38km technical single track with its 1110m climb; not one for the tag-along brigade). If you've forgotten to bring your own bikes, you can hire them (Beics Brenin, 01341 440728). The Visitor Centre for pushbikers is quite Teutonic in its pine-clad beauty and efficiency, and provides picnic tables, a café and an information centre. There's a playground for the little ones, but don't be tempted to leave them there while you speed off for some technical rollercoaster riding through mountain views and along the coast.

Corris Craft Centre

Machynlleth, Powys SY20 9RF (01654 761584/www.corriscraftcentre.co.uk). **Open** *Easter-Oct* 10am-5.30pm daily. *Nov-Mar* varies; phone for details. **Admission** free.
The craft centre consists of a series of workshops where craftspeople make, display and sell their wares. Patchwork, quilting, glass giftware, rustic furniture, handmade designer cards, candles, jewellery, leather goods, pottery, wooden toys and turned wood are the skills and products shown off. The Agau Jewellery Studio specialises in Celtic knot patterns in gold and silver; Tawny Owl makes wooden toys such as skipping ropes, building blocks, doll's houses, mobiles and abacuses. Wood turners at Corris use local sycamore, ash and beech to make plates, bowls and kitchen utensils. Children have a play area to retreat to while the grown-ups deliberate over the goods. There's a Tourist Information Centre and a café at the centre, which is the starting point for King Arthur's Labyrinth (*see below*).

Dyfi Discoveries

Unit 2, Canolfan Dyfi, The Wharf, Aberdyfi, Gwynedd LL35 0EE (01654 767676/ www.dyfidiscoveries.co.uk). **Open** *Boat trips* Mar-Oct. **Fares** *1hr* £18; £8 5-12s; £5 under-5s; £48 family (2+2). *2hrs* £30; £16 5-12s; £10 under-5s; £88 family (2+2). **Credit** MC, V.
One- and two- hour trips around the bay and into the open sea take place on a fast, 12-seater rigid inflatable boat. It's extremely exhilarating and

children love the ride (everyone wears seatbelts). The crew give their passenges a tour of Aberdyfi waters and take the boat out to sea in search of wildlife: shearwaters, gannets and cormorants, and, more excitingly (though they can't be guaranteed to put on a show), dolphins. Whatever you see, you learn an awful lot about this beautiful area of Wales on the trip.

King Arthur's Labyrinth

Corris, Machynlleth, Powys SY20 9RF (01654 761584/www.kingarthurslabyrinth. com). **Open** *Apr-Nov* 10am-5pm daily. **Admission** *Labyrinth* £5.50; £3.90 3-15s; free under-3s. *Bard's Quest* £3.90; £2.25 3-15s; free under-3s. *Combined Labyrinth & Bard's Quest* £7.45; £5 3-15s; free under-3s. **Credit** MC, V.
In the abandoned slate mines of Braich Goch, something stirs... It's a monk, in a boat, and he's taking visitors to a magical waterfall, behind which mystical tales of King Arthur are told with much drama and judicious use of tableaux and light and sound effects. However tenuous the link between King Arthur, old Merlin and the spooky mountains of Wales, this is an entertaining trip into the Dark Ages. As you wander through a series of dimly lit chambers you learn about the legend of King Arthur and the role of Merlin. The tour of the Labyrinth includes a walk of half a mile through the quite chilly caverns, so sensible shoes and a sweatshirt even in the summer (and coats in the winter) are advisable. Visitors are taken into the Labyrinth in groups of 20, with boat trips leaving every 15 minutes. Tour over, you emerge at the Corris Craft Centre and another part of the Arthur attraction. The Bard's Quest (with its own admission fee) sends you on a mission through the maze of time to hear favourites from the ancient collection of Welsh stories, the *Mabinogion*.

Talyllyn Railway

Wharf Station, Tywyn, Gwynedd LL36 9EY (01654 710472/www.talyllyn.co.uk). **Open** timetable varies; phone or check website for details. **Fares** £11 Day Rover (unlimited travel); £2 5-15s accompanied by an adult, otherwise £5.50; free under-5s. **Credit** MC, V.
This historic narrow gauge steam railway runs seven miles from Tywyn to Abergynolwyn and Nant Gwernol, passing the uncommonly beautiful Dolgoch Falls and the forests of Nant Gwernol. The 2ft 3in-gauge railway, opened in 1865, is one of a number of lines established in the 19th century to carry slate. When the line's owner died a group of enthusiasts campaigned to keep the the railway open, and the Talyllyn Railway Preservation Society (the first of many such organisations throughout the world) was born. Today, volunteer members of the TRPS make up much of the train crew and station staff. The engine Duncan, of course, has a special place in their hearts. Why? *See p238* **The cream of the old steamers** for details.

Blackpool

That's entertainment.

Ever since Victorian times, when the cotton-mill workers of Lancashire first started to descend on Blackpool on rare days off from the dark satanic production line, the town has stood for fun and frolics. With the coming of the railways it quickly grew into the biggest and best holiday resort in England, and arguably remains exactly that. Here are not just one but three piers, a Golden Mile of beautiful safe sands and a giddying range of theatres, with the UK's ultimate funfair and the landmark Tower forming the perfect backdrop for all the classic seaside holiday pastimes. In Blackpool they've got thrills and spills, glitz and glamour, spectacle and sensation in spades. Most importantly, from our perspective, the town remains a child's dreamland.

Fairhaven Lake.
See p251.

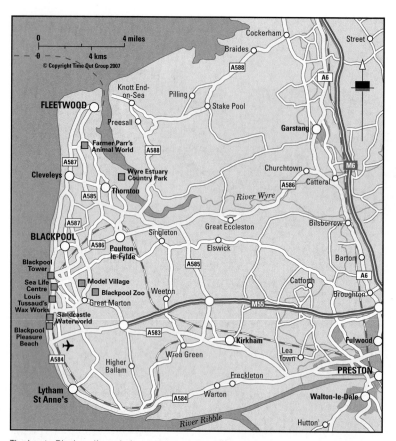

The key to Blackpool's enduring success has been knowing how to move with the times. It was back in the 1970s, when the Brits first started holidaying in the sun en masse, that Blackpool's first rethink was forced. The city reinvented itself partly as a conference centre for politicos, then a stamping ground for stag and hen parties and, more recently, a hotel-splattered centre for all sorts of punter-pulling events. In 2006, these ran to classic car rallies, northern soul and punk weekenders, dance festivals, world pool and town criers championships, forces reunions, fun runs and the George Formby Society convention.

Now the masterplan is to 'transform the resort physically and in spirit, to create an entertainment destination of national and international significance'. Airport and shopping centre investment, together with the reconstruction of the promenades and seafront tramways, is laudable – but it can only be hoped that Blackpool hasn't piled too many chips on the hope of being

granted a supercasino licence (the final verdict hung in the balance as this guide went to press).

Emerging on to the Promenade by the North Pier, the clash of competing markets is evident. Cahoots pole-dancing club rubs shoulders somewhat uncomfortably with Roberts' Oyster Rooms – a Rick Stein-recommended restaurant and a treat for the now-largely absent stag parties – and some of the many ultra-traditional seaside attractions that bring to mind the cover of a *Dandy* or *Beano Summer Special* in the '70s. On the beach there are donkey rides; on the Prom there are ice-creameries, chipperies and luminous rockeries, with hundreds of shops and stalls selling novelties, buckets and spades and Kiss-Me-Quick headgear. The amusement arcades here, Coral Island (01253 293133) and Funland (01253 620820), are enormous.

In autumn, the Blackpool Illuminations (*see p334*) are a dazzling sight – bright, brash and a definite crowd-pleaser. In

2006, Bolton's own Peter Kay threw the switch, ably assisted by the glamorous Dale Winton. Ronan Keating, Paolo Nutini and Liverpool's Zutons topped the Big Switch-On bill, leaving behind a million megawatt legacy to light up the seafront until the closing bash on Guy Fawkes' Night. It's quite a spectacle, as the trams, Prom, Tower, piers and Pleasure Beach all shimmer with electric light, neon, LED technology, lasers and fibre optics.

Three piers on the front

Built in 1863, the North Pier is the oldest of the three piers. Nowadays it's home to the Merrie England bar and beer garden, an amusement arcade and a famous old theatre – in 2006, the latter was closed for the first summer season in living memory and may face an uncertain future. Instead, the summer's entertainment came courtesy of the Merrie England, which offered free nights out with the likes of Jimmy James and the Vagabonds and '70s glam-rockers The Sweet, presumably with a new singer.

Right under the Tower is the first of Blackpool front's three gypsy fortune-tellers called Petulengro, all of whom press credible claims to be the one you once saw on telly. An addictive blast from the past comes courtesy of Slots of Vintage Fun on the Promenade (www.melright.com/bpslots), which has slot machines the way grandma and grandad knew them, using big old pre-decimal pennies.

Timewarp trams clatter all the way along the wide Promenade. A pleasant tram ride

TOURIST INFORMATION

Blackpool
1 Clifton Street, Blackpool, Lancashire FY1 1LY; Central Promenade, Blackpool, Lancashire FY1 4BJ (01253 478222/www.visitblackpool.com).

north takes you along the coast until Cleveleys, goes inland awhile then reaches the sea again at the Fleetwood terminus. This quiet seaside town at the end of the line has one historic pier (redeveloped in 2003) and no fewer than three lighthouses. After dark, from September to November, Blackpool's trams are specially decorated and play a major part in the famous Illuminations, both as a spectacle in their own right and as a favoured method of taking in the surrounding storm of electricity. And to think it all started off in 1879, when they cranked up eight arc lamps and garnered reviews which likened the effect to 'artificial sunshine'.

The Central Pier was built soon after its northerly neighbour, becoming known as the 'people's pier' because of its pavilion dances. The theatre is now better known for its Legends shows, which in 2006 featured Shirley Bassey, Robbie Williams, Lionel Ritchie and Elvis tribute acts, but the focal point remains the 108-foot Big Wheel.

There are more dizzy heights on the South Pier, where you can pay £15 to shoot into the sky on the Skyscreamer, then reverse the sensation on the Skycoaster free-fall tower. For more sedate tastes, there are

Blackpool

Fleetwood Pier

BLACKPOOL TOWER

The entrance to Blackpool Tower leads straight into the cavernous aquarium, where sub-aquatic light and weird music set the mood for retro thrills; this could easily pass for a '60s *Star Trek* set. Every tank has a backdrop with luminous plastic coral, and fish swim dozily among the miniaturised ruins of Atlantis.

The Tower opened in 1893, when parts of 'Dr Cocker's Aquarium & Menagerie', which originally stood on the site, were built into its foundations, then slowly surmounted with 2,586 tons of steel and cast iron in an audacious, 518-foot remodelling of the Eiffel Tower.

Up at the ballroom level, you'll find a beautifully vaulted selection of the building's five million bricks, inset with jade-coloured Burmantoft tiles with images of birds, animals and angels. The ballroom is a Victorian faux-baroque masterpiece, with two ornate gilt balconies and a trompe l'oeil third balcony, which bleeds into a ceiling painted with allegorical and flying figures. 'Bid me discourse and I will enchant thine ear' is emblazoned over the stage, with its backdrop of an idyllic Edwardian Amalfi coastline. The Wurlitzer organist hammers at his keys, grinning over his shoulder into the warm, twinkling ballroom, where hundreds of elderly dancers swoon and spin in unison as the beats blend seamlessly from cha-cha-cha to *Van der Valk*.

There's yet another timewarp on the Dawn of Time ride, a four-minute spin through steamy swamps (a blast of warm compressed air) and the ice ages (cold), taking in animatronic mammoths, mooing dinosaur heads and hydraulic sabretooth tigers. A plummy, old-style BBC talkover is almost enough to convince you it's educational.

On Sea View Terrace level, the Heritage Trail's collection of old photos traces the Tower's evolution and its long-faded stars. Little Emmie danced and sang with the Children's Ballet between 1908 and 1936; Reginald Dixon was organist from 1930 to 1970. Trapezes once hung from the ballroom ceiling, and long before Jungle Jim's ballpark, the space adjoining the smoky family bar and food court was Ye Olde Englishe Village in Edwardian times. Next it was Chinatown Oriental Village until

talking telescopes, traditional stalls (Every Lady and Child Receives a Prize, Win or Lose!) and the Laughing Donkey Family Bar with its nightly cabaret and irresistible wallful of vintage seaside postcards.

On past the vast blank plastic bricks containing a casino and a waterworld (*see p257*), the Pleasure Beach looms in the shape of the Pepsi Max rollercoaster – until recently the highest rollercoaster in Europe, and visible for miles down the coast. It's extremely good news for anyone who likes the idea of teetering on the top of a 213-ft scaffold fence, or hurtling down a banister rail at 74mph. Even from outside the park you can see the generations of rollercoasters stacking up over incidental roads: humpback woodies with little fake stations, dwarfed by steely '60s and loop-the-looping '70s updates, and finally the Pepsi Max, the great Wailing Wall of Blackpool. There are 13 rollercoasters in total; unlucky for any bright individuals who decide to get tanked up on pop and candyfloss and then attempt to ride them all. Not a pretty sight.

being replaced, in 1970, with the Apollo Playground, the Tower Ascent lift rigged up as a rocket blast-off.

On a clear day you can see forever from the top of the Tower – or the Isle of Man, at least. You can also stand on a thick pane of glass set in the floor and picture yourself plummeting down to the Prom, 380 feet below. It's awesome. But at two o'clock it's time to peel yourself away and file downstairs for the big finale: the big-top circus, set in the baroque gilt vault between the Tower's legs. No animals have been involved since 1990, but Mooky the Clown carries on the red-nosed tradition of Charlie Cairoli, and there's a showband and a real sense of glamour and excitement. The international line up includes a German strongwoman, a Mongolian contortionist, an Italian balancing act, a Chinese acrobatic troupe, a Hungarian troupe who walk on giant balls and – kaboom! – the heroic American human cannonball.

And as you emerge into the daylight, thine ear, eye and funny bone enchanted, thou too will agree with the billboards: Blackpool Tower's Too Big To Miss.

Adoloscent boys will be disappointed to hear they're excluded from the adult pleasures of the South Shore's casinos and glitzy Mystique cabaret – a 'magical, mysterious and sexy cabaret of illusion' – leaving them with their noses pressed to the window at Ripley's Believe It Or Not (Units 5-6, South Promenade, 01253 341033, www.ripleysblackpool.com), where fertility statues, touted for titillation alongside 'freaks of nature' such as Siamese Twin calves, are set out for gawpers. Watch out inside, mind: one particularly potent fertility symbol claims some 2,000 pregnancies.

North of the seafront, Blackpool Grand Theatre (33 Church Street, 01253 290111, www.blackpoolgrand.co.uk) is a historic landmark building, dubbed 'the prettiest theatre in the Kingdom'. First opened in 1894, it serves up everything from drama and opera to musicals, variety and panto all year round. More culture, of sorts, comes courtesy of the Winter Gardens, just up the road from the Grand (97 Church Street, 01253 292029). Originally intended as a centre for off-season entertainment for the people of Victorian Blackpool, the Winter Gardens now house one of the largest theatres in Europe and 12 other venues used for exhibitions and events throughout the year. 2006 posters flagged up the likes of New Order, Simply Red, Chubby Brown and Tonight's The Night.

Saintly calm

On past the disco pavements under the world's largest mirrorball is the road to St Annes, and the more genteel pleasures of its Prom, bandstand and uncluttered pier. Tranquillity and golf are the primary pleasures on offer in classy St Annes and its joined-at-the-hip neighbour Lytham, which has a windmill on the coastal green and a particularly bijou shopping drag.

There are four championship golf courses under five miles from Blackpool; St Annes Old Links, Fairhaven, Lytham Green Drive and the British Open venue Royal Lytham & St Annes – all a light year from the pitch 'n' putt and crazy golf at Blackpool's Stanley Park (see p257). This is beauty spot country. Fairhaven Lake on the Ribble Estuary (Ansdell, Lytham St Annes, FY8 1BD, 01253 725610) is a peaceful, unflashy antidote to Blackpool, with boating, tennis, putting and bowling. It only takes a breezy lakeside walk and a well earned cuppa in the café to get the glitz out of your system.

WHERE TO STAY

The question is whether to stay in Blackpool and immerse yourself in the holiday vibe, or go a little out of town and mix and match your pleasures. All the rated hotels on the front at Blackpool – the Norbreck Castle (www.norbreck-castle-hotel.com), the Hilton (www.hilton.co.uk), the Lyndene (www.lyndenehotel.com) and so on – can be relied upon for child-friendliness in such a family-orientated resort, but we've pulled out three with special attractions for kids.

Lytham St Annes is only a ten-minute drive from Blackpool, and offers a far calmer base. Fleetwood, scene of John Lennon's childhood holidays, is the same

Windmill at Lytham. *See p251.*

distance to the north. There are many upmarket hotels; again we've selected the number one for children. Staying outside Blackpool will give access to the Wyre and Fylde countryside – then there's Morecambe, Lancaster and the Lune Valley, and the Forest of Bowland on the eastern side of the M6. Visit to the excellent website www.visitlancashire.com to check out the self-catering cottages and farms, and caravan and camping parks away from it all.

The Big Blue Hotel

Ocean Boulevard, Pleasure Beach, Blackpool, Lancashire FY4 1ND (0845 367 3333/ www.bigbluehotel.uk.com). **Rates** £80-£208. **Credit** AmEx, MC, V.
The vast majority of young teenagers would probably rate the possibility of sleeping over on-site at the Blackpool Pleasure Beach right up there with a birthday pony or a snog with Lily Allen. Like the BBH, the kids might well quote Aristotle at you as a reason to escape here: 'The highest purpose of a civilisation was to create meaningful forms of leisure for its citizens – and for the individuals the ideal to be sought was leisure as an exploration of the good life.' Blackpool Tourism's Hotel of the Year 2005 has a unique take on child-friendliness, involving a separate children's area in every family room and bunk beds for children (up to 12), each with their own television and PS2 connection. There's a DVD player in each room with DVDs, games consoles and a selection of games available for hire from reception. Cots are provided on request, and there's a baby-listening service, via the internal phone system. In the brasserie, the children's menu delivers the standard chicken nuggets, burgers and fish fingers; more enticing is the opportunity to create their own pizza.

The Cliffs Hotel

Queens Promenade, Blackpool, Lancashire FY2 9SG (01253 595559/www.choice-hotels.co.uk). **Rates** £65-£132. **Credit** AmEx, MC, V.
An imposing Edwardian pile on the Queen's Prom, the Cliffs is big on tradition, but also scores highly on facilities and amenities available for kids at weekends and during school hols. There's an indoor heated swimming pool and nightly cabaret entertainment for everyone's enjoyment, along with 'Jungle Club' activities for over-fours. The latter can offer you a well-deserved break as the children dive off to discos, parties and games rooms, all under fully trained supervision – though parents do have to stay on the hotel premises. There's also a soft play area for under-fours where kids must be accompanied. All 160 bedrooms are en suite, and 50 are family rooms; the largest can accomodate families of five, with a double bed, bunk bed and single bed.

Dalmeny Hotel

19-33 South Promenade, St Annes on Sea, Lancashire FY8 1LX (01253 712236/ www.dalmenyhotel.co.uk). **Rates** £89-£177. **Credit** AmEx, DC, MC, V.
Owned and managed by the Webb family since 1946, the last 60 years have seen the Dalmeny empire extend all the way back from the main coast road right through to the South Prom. It's a vast, mainly modern complex, with high standards of accommodation, food and facilities for children. A family room with a balcony overlooking the Prom and coast is airy, comfortable and vast, with a huge wetroom shower; all rooms are equipped with cots and baby-listening facilities. The second B in a B&B deal involves a superb, fresh-cooked self-service selection of all the full English regulars, with cereals and a DIY fruit salad – including gorgeous fresh figs to counterbalance that irresistible black pudding. There are three high-class restaurants on site, along with nightly entertainment, a swimming pool, a gym and a sauna. The expertly-run Pebbles crèche allows three-hour sessions, at no extra charge; an impressive array of weekend and holiday activities for older children includes discos, parties, Funky Fashion crafts, creative modelling, sport in the pool, mini-Olympics in the squash courts and a final Chillout Zone. It's enough to make you wish you were ten again. Babysitting is on offer for £6 an hour (£7 after midnight), though parents have to stay on the hotel premises.

Guy's Thatched Hamlet

St Michaels Road, Bilsborrow, Preston, Lancashire PR3 ORS (01995 640010/ www.guysthatchedhamlet.co.uk). **Rates** *Room only* £52-£71. **Credit** MC, V.
An unusual thatched hamlet, custom-built in the 1980s, this place offers a carefully controlled step back in time at the M6 end of the M55 – handy for Blackpool as well as roaming the countryside in every direction. So what do you gain by visiting or

staying here rather than just down the road in the real-life idyllic market town of Garstang, where there are genuine olde-worlde pubs and entertainments? That's up to you to decide; this is a place you'll either love or hate. The hamlet sits sweetly on the canalside, clustered around a small square of craft shops, with the very popular Owd Nell's Tavern, Guy's Eating Establishment (the children's menu features pizza, spaghetti bolognese, bbq spare ribs and the like for £3-£4.50), and a cricket pitch and bowling greens to boot. There are Morris Dancers and Punch and Judy shows for the kids. Cots are provided free of charge, but there's no baby-listening service, equipment or toys.

Ribby Hall Village

Ribby Road, Wrea Green, nr Blackpool, Lancashire PR4 2PR (01772 671111/ www.ribbyhall.co.uk). **Rates** *Hotel* £110-£205. *Cottages* £245-£1,120/wk. *Pine lodges* £570-£1,380/wk. **Credit** AmEx, MC, V.

Ribby Hall Village is set in 100 acres of landscaped grounds, where hotel guests can take up the offer of numerous sport and leisure activities, from riding, racquet games or boating to relaxation in the sauna, steam room and spa. There's also a nine-hole golf course and separate adult and family swimming pools, along with an outdoor adventure playground, a 25ft climbing wall, an acrojump bungee trampoline and an indoor soft play area with ball pool, tumble tower, crazy mirrors, basketball, mini football and a maze. An FA-qualified trainer supervises a football school, plus there are pony rides, mini golf, an arcade room and pool tables. Hotel accommodation is modern and three-star, overlooking a lake and fountain – or you can stay in one of the self-catering cottages, or the new four- to six- berth Scando pine lodges, with outdoor hot tubs. Book well ahead – the lodges get snapped up fast.

Sparkles Hotel

37 Station Road, South Shore, Blackpool, Lancashire FY4 1EU (01253 343200/ www.sparkles.co.uk). **Rates** £70-£100. **No credit cards.**

Set up as a 'fantasy-themed hotel for families and celebrations', Sparkles is garnering a big reputation as the kind of holiday accommodation that you probably won't have enjoyed before. It's a one-off boutique hotel, with eight years' investment of love, deep thought and hard work poured into it. The eight suites have stunning decor, and your fantasy landlady Su, aka Mrs Sparkle, is the perfect hostess to guests of all ages. The Narnia, Ruined Castle, Barbie, Teddy Bears' Picnic, Cruella de Ville and 101 Dalmatians Suites are all chock-full of atmosphere, not to mention exquisite fittings and details ranging from jacuzzi-style bathtubs and walk-through wardrobes to Disney costumes, books and toys. Children love tucking into a full English in the mock-underwater breakfast room. Then there are the hundreds of dressing-up costumes, toys and books spread around the place, a ballpit and playroom, plus children's activities in the morning and evening led by former teacher and party entertainer Mrs S. In all, fantastic fun – and good value too, with frequent special offers on the website.

Lytham
St Annes
beach.
See p251.

Blackpool

Sparkles Hotel. *See p253.*

WHERE TO EAT & DRINK

It doesn't have to be fish and chips, but you've got to try them just once during your stay in Blackpool. For a really good fish supper, you may have to look a little beyond the vendors lined up on the piers and Promenade.

The Cottage

31 Newhouse Road, Marton, Blackpool, Lancashire FY4 4JH (01253 764081/www. cottagefishandchips.co.uk). **Meals served** *Summer* 11.30am-2pm, 4.30-9.30pm Mon-Sat; 11.30-2pm, 4.30-8.30pm. *Winter* 11.30am-2pm, 4.30-9pm Mon, Tue; 11.30am-2pm, 4.30-10pm Wed-Sat; 11.30am-2pm, 4.30-8pm Sun. **Main courses** £4.95-£9.90. **Credit** MC, V.
Superlative fish suppers are the reason to travel a little out of the way to the village of Marton. Among the prizewinning meals you'll find organic fish caught in well managed fisheries and incredibly good haddock in light batter, served with Lincolnshire potato chips (twice fried for flavour and crispness). Regulars also rave about the gourmet fish cakes with their lemony finish. The Cottage has been rubberstamped over the years by a curious array of celebs. 'I enjoyed my meal greatly,' opined John Major. 'To all at The Cottage, best in the country,' scrawled sometime World Snooker champion Steve Davis. The Cottage's sister restaurant in Lytham, Whelan's, is the only fish and chippery mentioned in Rick Stein's *Seafood Lover's Guide*, and last year was graced with the presence of Gordon Ramsay, who enjoyed his birthday fish supper in the restaurant. **Branch**: **Whelan's** 26 Clifton Street, Lytham, Lancashire FY8 5EW (01253 735188).

Mamma's Ristorante

40 Topping Street, Blackpool, Lancashire FY1 3AQ (01253 622345/www.mammas restaurant.co.uk). **Meals served** noon-2pm; 5.30-11pm Mon-Sat; 5.30-11pm Sun. **Main courses** £5.95-£14.95 **Credit** MC, V.
The original Blackpool Mamma's is in a poky part of town, but it's worth braving the strip club next door to find this cosy, busy old-school Italian with its classic red-white-and-green tablecloths, pictures of Italian landmarks and exceptional rustic cooking with peerless ingredients. Go for the staple treats – own-made spaghetti or lasagne, tournedot Rossini or fish – and you won't be disappointed. The naughty photo art in both sets of loos are by now the stuff of Blackpool legend, a fine tradition carried on at the spacier St Annes branch, run by members of the same bustling family clan.
Branch: **Mamma's Too** 37-39 St Andrews Road South, St Annes on Sea, Lancashire F18 1PZ (01253 712233).

Moghul Premier

12 Orchard Road, St Annes on Sea, Lancashire FY8 1RY (01253 712114/www.moghul tandoori.co.uk). **Meals served** 5pm-midnight Mon-Sat; 1-11pm Sun. **Main courses** £5.95-£12.95. **Credit** AmEx, DC, MC, V.

Every generation of Anglo-Indian food is covered at the Moghul, from tandoori classics via sizzling balti dishes to modern, even less traditional stabs at European fusion. The greatest recommendation is that this is a restaurant that's always busy; the staff, and manager in particular, are always on hand and welcoming, and ingredients are up to scratch and freshly cooked. As far as child-friendliness goes, our children were given a new mild honey-based dish to test, and extra choccies with the bill. They want to know when we're going back.
Branch: The Red Fort 15 Park Street, Lytham, Lancashire FY8 5LU (01253 737799/ www.redfortoflytham.co.uk).

Outside Inn

Hallam Way, Whitehills Industrial Estate, Blackpool, Lancashire FY4 5NZ (01253 798477/ www.outsideinnblackpool.co.uk). **Meals served** noon-10pm Mon-Sat; noon-9.30pm Sun. **Main courses** £7-£15. **Credit** AmEx, MC, V.
Never mind the industrial estate address. The Outside Inn promotes itself as 'a world of its own under one roof', and that's not a bad description of the Funky Forest play area, lit up as if it were night-time with shooting stars, waterfalls and trees enclosing a giant wooden construction of pathways that lead kids over bridges and through tunnels. It's great for over-fours, but toddlers will need assistance. Healthy eating options include jacket spuds, carrot sticks, carrot and swede mash or wacky salads instead of chips to go with the mains – all presented as DIY, empowering fun. Under-tens can get a main meal, ice-cream and drink for £4.25, while under-14s have a separate menu with mains from £4.50 to £6.

Portofino & Zest

Henry Street, Lytham, Lancashire FY8 5LE (01253 795890/www.portofino-zest.com). **Meals served** noon-2.30pm, 6-11pm Mon-Fri; noon-10.30pm Sat, Sun. **Main courses** £7-£20. **Credit** AmEx, MC, V.
Yes, they're child-friendly, with charming waiters and a fishtank to hold the children's attention for a while. But Portofino's really warrants inclusion because the food is exceptional, with fresh pasta, fish and seasonal veg providing solid starting points. For example, *capesante arrosto* (brochette of sea scallops wrapped in pancetta over rocket salad) was wonderful, ditto grilled roast seabass with fresh rosemary and sunblush tomatoes. Downstairs from the fine dining room is Zest, a more informal brasserie where you might be more comfortable with younger children – here, own-made pizzas, Italian breakfasts, coffee and deli options are the order of the day.

The Seafood Restaurant

25 Bond Street, South Shore, Blackpool, Lancashire FY4 1BQ (01253 342251/ www.seafoodblackpool.co.uk). **Meals**

served 5.30pm-late Mon; noon-1.30pm, 5.30pm-late Tue-Sat; noon-late Sun. **Main courses** £9.95-£15.95. **No credit cards**.
An agreeably unpretentious restaurant, run by Colin and Alison Ellis, that's well known for drawing in crowds of journos and politicos during conference season. Signature dish scampi thermidor, along with menu items such as steak diane, banana split and 'glass of milk', contribute to a slight timewarp feel, but sea bass, oysters, lobster and all the fish dishes are very fresh and expertly prepared. The popular menu for under-8s (dishes cost about £3-£4) includes pizza, sausages and fish fingers; a Junior menu for 8-13s charges £5 or so for own-made lasagne or a mini mixed grill.

West Coast Rock Café

5-7 Abingdon Street, Blackpool, Lancashire FY1 1DG (01253 751283/www.westcoast rock.co.uk). **Meals served** noon-1am Mon-Sat; noon-11.30pm Sun. **Main courses** £6.20-£13.50. **Credit** MC, V.
Blackpool's only Tex and/or Mex eaterie, the West Coast Rock Café offers a straightforward menu of ribs, chilli, steaks, burgers, pizza and chicken wings. The quality is good and the service is excellent. Families are made especially welcome, and the older kids among us will appreciate the noisy music and 1980s MTV videos that form the backdrop to the food.

Fleetwood Lighthouse. *See p249.*

Pleasure Beach

PLACES TO SEE, THINGS TO DO

Blackpool Tower

Promenade, Blackpool, Lancashire FY1 1BJ (01253 292029/www.theblackpooltower.co.uk). **Open** 10am-4pm daily unless there is a show on. **Admission** £12-£20. **Credit** MC, V.
The timewarp cha-cha-cha pleasures of the ballroom, the thrills of a genuinely first-rate circus, the horrors of the tower top and much, much more. *See also p250.*

Blackpool Zoo & Dinosaur Safari

East Park Drive, Blackpool, Lancashire FY3 8PP (01253 830830/www.blackpoolzoo.org.uk). **Open** 10am-3pm daily. **Admission** *Zoo* £11; £8.50 concessions; £7 3-15s; £32 family (2+2), £38 (2+3); free under-3s. *Dinosaur Safari* £6.50; £6 concessions; £4.75 3-15s; £20 family (2+2), £24 (2+3); free under-3s. *Combined ticket* £13.50; £12 concessions; £10.50 3-15s; £42 family (2+2), £50 (2+3); free under-3s. **Credit** MC, V.
Trust Blackpool Zoo to go beyond the usual tigers and orang-utans, underwater weirdoes and creepy crawlies. As wonderful as the Zoo is, with its award-winning Gorilla Mountain, miniature railway and 1,500 animal inhabitants, it didn't seem quite complete without the addition of a set of awesome extinct beasts in the Dinosaur Safari. What better way to hammer home the conservation message of the Zoo than inviting kids on a landscaped garden walkway featuring a volcano, 13,000 plants, erupting geysers and 30 life-size monster models from 150 million years ago. Just be careful the kids don't lean too far over the railings and feature in dinosaur feeding time.

Doctor Who Exhibition

Doctor Who Museum, The Golden Mile Centre, Central Promenade, Blackpool, Lancashire FY1 5AA (01253 299982/www.doctorwho
exhibitions.com). **Open** *Summer* 10am-6pm daily. *Winter* 10.30am-5pm daily. **Admission** £7; £5 3-15s; £20 family (2+2), £22.50 (2+3); free under-3s. **Credit** AmEx, MC, V.
Look out – there's a Cyberman, a Draconian and a Tetrap behind you! This is an interactive walk-through experience, featuring hundreds of genuine props, baddie suits and memorabilia from the classic and revamped BBC series, including star turns K9 and Bessie the Roadster. It's not cheap, mind, and the 'small prize' for kids who spot all the little TARDISes in the exhibition is a disappointment.

Farmer Parr's Animal World

Rossall Lane, Fleetwood, Lancashire FY7 8JP (01253 874389/www.farmerparrs.com). **Open** 10am-5pm daily. **Admission** £4.25; £3.50 concessions; £3 3-16s; £12 family (2+2); free under-3s. **Credit** AmEx, MC, V.
In this cute and cuddly farmyard attraction, there are 50 species of animal to gaze upon and possibly even pet in the new playbarn. Here are cows, guinea pigs, rabbits, hawks, sheep, reptiles, wallabies and chinchilla, to name but a few – plus ancient farm equipment, a playground, a picnic area, water gardens, a café and a gift shop. Phew.

Louis Tussaud's Waxworks

89 Promenade, Blackpool, Lancashire FY1 5AA (01253 625953/www.louistussauds waxworks.co.uk). **Open** *Summer* 10am-6pm daily. *Winter* 10am-4pm daily. **Admission** £8.95; £6.95 concessions; £21 family (2+2), £25 (2+3). **Credit** MC, V.
There's been a waxworks in the line-up of wonders on the prom at Blackpool ever since 1870, with the great grandson of the original Mme Tussaud setting up shop in 1900. Even today, at a certain angle in a certain light, there's no denying the frisson you feel standing next to Michael Jackson, Bobby Moore or Marilyn Monroe. Here are historical figures, royalty through the ages,

movie and rock stars and a neat horror section, set out over five floors, with an unforgettable *Coronation Street* recreation for Bet and Alec Gilroy fans. Younger children simply don't get it.

Pleasure Beach

525 Ocean Boulevard, Blackpool, Lancashire FY4 1EZ (0870 444 5566/www.blackpool pleasurebeach.com). **Open** *10 Feb-28 Mar* 11.30am-8pm Sat; 11.30-7pm Sun. *Apr-Jan* times vary; phone or check website for details. **Admission** wristband prices vary; phone or check website for details. **Credit** MC, V.
Blackpool Pleasure Beach is the UK's most popular single tourist attraction, with over six million visitors per year, so you can expect big rides, singular thrills and serious crowds at peak times. The record-breaking Pepsi Max rollercoaster looms over the 42-acre site, while Valhalla is rated the best water ride in the world, throwing in extremes of climate as well as disorientation. You can travel to 20 storeys high on Ice Blast – in a cool two seconds. It's easy to while away the best part of a day here, provided your innards are up to the task of defying gravity on the 145 rides while also making the most of the 35 bars, restaurants and cafés scattered around the park. There's also an ice-skating auditorium and, from July 2007, a new family show entitled 'Forbidden'.

Sandcastle Waterworld

South Beach, Blackpool, Lancashire FY4 1BB (01253 343 6020/www.sandcastle-waterworld. co.uk). **Open** times vary throughout the year; phone or check website for details. **Admission** £10.50; £8.50 6-13s; £6.50 concessions, 2-5s; £25 family (2+1), £32 (2+2), £40 (2+3), £48 (2+4); free under-2s. **Credit** MC, V.
Housed in what looks like a vast plastic brick, Sandcastle Waterworld makes a lot more sense on the inside. Here, the world of Monkey Island, Ushi-Gushi River Creek, Typhoon Lagoons and Shimmering Shallows opens out for kids to explore, in 84 degrees of sub-tropical stickiness. To say that there are wave machines, white-knuckle waterslides and water cannons would be understating the splashtastic value of the place. The Masterblaster is the world's longest indoor rollercoaster waterslide, and every five minutes there's a tropical deluge as 600 gallons of water are tipped out of a giant coconut into the water below.

Sea Life Centre

Promenade, Blackpool, Lancashire FY1 5AA (01253 621258/www.sealifeeurope.com). **Open** *Summer* 10am-8pm daily. *Winter* 10am-4pm Mon-Fri; 10am-5pm Sat, Sun. **Admission** £11.50; £9.95 concessions; £8.50 3-16s; £34 family (2+2), £40 (2+3); free under-3s. **Credit** MC, V.
Even if there is a tendency to fit tanks with magnifying glass, it takes a very cynical parent not to be impressed with the tank-bottom walk-

through tunnel, which affords some uncomfortably intimate views of 7 and 8ft sharks. If you've never experienced one of these subaquatic walkways before, you really do need to – and the same applies to coming face to face with a shoal of unmoving, casually psychotic-looking piranhas, and some of the weirdest jellyfish Mother Nature has to offer, including UV and upside-down models. It's educational, okay?

Stanley Park & Model Village

East Park Drive, Blackpool, Lancashire FY3 9RB (01253 763827/www.blackpoolmodel village.com). **Open** *Mar-Nov* 10am-dusk daily. **Admission** £4.50; £3.25 3-16s; £14 family (2+2); free under-3s. **Credit** AmEx, MC, V.
A mile inland from the coast lies this idyllic 256 acre oasis of lawns and lakes, formal gardens and quiet corners – and yet another checklist of things to do. Bowl on the crown greens, go boating on the lake or try your hand at the pitch 'n' putt and crazy golf. There are also kids' play areas, a café and a gift shop. The model village is really something special, occupying two and a half acres of superb gardens and incorporating loads of great detail and humour. The kids are given an I Spy-style sheet to fill in with notes on escaped prisoners from the jail, the wedding at the church, café punch-ups, garage owners Hugh Crashum and WE Mendum, and so on. Started up in the late '60s, the model village and gardens won the Blackpool Tourism Attraction Of The Year Gold Award in 2006.

Sudden Impact Leisure

Whyndyke Farm, Preston New Road, Blackpool, Lancashire FY4 4XQ (0870 777 5909/www. sudden-impact.co.uk). **Open** according to demand. **Admission** *paintballing* £43/game incl kit & balls; *quad biking* £30/hr; *air rifles/ archery/laser tag* £15/hr. **Credit** AmEx, MC, V.
If you're taking a group of children to Blackpool (you need a minimum of ten participants for each activity), the centre is friendly, safety-conscious and fun. It offers paintballing for children of 12 and above, air rifles, archery, laser tag and, for over-16s, quad biking. Older speed demons might also enjoy Karting 2000 in central Blackpool (New South Promenade, Blackpool, Lancashire FY4 1TB, 01253 408068).

Wyre Estuary Country Park & Wyreside Ecology Centre

River Road, Thornton, Cleveleys, Lancashire FY5 5LR (01253 857890/www.wyrebc.gov.uk). **Open** *Nov-Mar* 11am-3pm daily. *Apr-Oct* 10.30am-4.30pm daily. **Admission** free.
There's a popular riverside visitor centre set right in the middle of the Wyre Estuary Country Park, just north of Blackpool. Explore the countryside and riverside on well-marked nature trails, or do a little bit of homework at the centre and gear up for some serious twitching. It's all free – including the car park.

The Lake District

Pottering around the poets' manor.

Even if they're fans of Wordsworth (daffodils), Arthur Ransome (*Swallows and Amazons*) or Beatrix Potter (dressed-up animals), the main reason that country-loving families come to this part of Cumbria is the same as it always was. It's an Area of Outstanding Natural Beauty (and that's official). Twelve million visitors come every year, and though they may spend time on the streets of Windermere buying postcards, ice-creams and Peter Rabbit dinner plates, they mostly come for the fresh air and the peace and quiet.

There is nothing in England quite like these wooded lakeside valleys under the bulging fells. To prove it, round every bend in the road there is a guesthouse, roadside inn or, at the end of a driveway, a country house hotel. Sixteen lakes of all shapes and sizes adorn a central core of mountains. Each lake forms part of a wonderful interplay between water, mountain and sky. Here are some of the highest peaks in England, such as Sca Fell and Helvellyn. Ten-mile long Windermere is the largest lake in England and Wasdale is the deepest. Thirlmere, now a reservoir, feels remote and brooding; Grasmere looks serene and pastoral, taken straight from a Victorian oil-painting. Ullswater, at the centre of classic walking country, is where Wordsworth found his daffodils. It's also where Sir Paul Macca proposed to Heather (though this last fact may not be a recommendation).

Coniston Water

This area is perfect for luxury-seeking couples, with its fluffy-towelled country house retreats; for foodies (plenty of rosetted wannabes and actual Michelin chefs at work in the hotels); and most obviously for walkers and nature-lovers. Its child-friendliness may be concealed under a well-to-do veneer, but it's there. Attractions for all the family include taking a steamer ride on lake Windermere, a sprinkling of wildlife parks, watersports on the lake, several steam railways (operational mainly in the summer), a climbing centre, the Beatrix Potter sites and some interesting museums and history. And that's before you've persuaded them out on a walk.

There are plenty of junior hikes alongside the ascents of major peaks; even young children can cope with a tour of Grasmere lake. Older children scamper up Helvellyn and Easedale Tarn, a small lake formed by glaciers. Family groups have different priorities to the gnarled ramblers in their uniforms of breathable Gore-Tex, but you'd be mad to come here and not walk at all.

The lure of the lakes

The list of writers and artists associated with the area is long and distinguished: Wordsworth, Coleridge, Southey, Ruskin, Constable and, er, Melvyn Bragg. It was Wordsworth and the other Romantic poets who created a kind of English icon out of the English lakeland, never realising their work would end up on tea towels. Painters such as Constable and Ruskin swelled the legend of an English paradise.

Up until then the region, settled by the Romans and the Vikings (Windermere is a Norse name), was largely dependent on farming and a spot of slate mining, until Victorian times. Once the railway came to Windermere (the only railway station in the core of the Lake District), even daytrippers were suddenly able to share the idyll.

Since Wordsworth, others have fallen in love with the lakes. Beatrix Potter has added to the Lakeland mythology, and spawned a multitude of gift shops selling anything from Mrs Tiggywinkle fudge to Peter Rabbit golf accessories. Potter was a Londoner who stayed, bought property and became a successful farmer and breeder of the hardy local Herdwick sheep. She bequeathed large tracts of land to the National Trust, including her former home at Hill Top (see p264). The job of preserving Lakeland's unique character as a farming area and wildlife habitat has become more important since her death – as an exhibition at the National Park's visitor centre at Brockhole illustrates (see p261).

Arthur Ransome is another children's author of international repute whose work derives from the area. His father loved the countryside, and carried the baby Arthur up to the top of Coniston Old Man (later to become 'Kanchenjunga' in the *Swallows and Amazons* books). There are also links with the Windermere Steamboat Museum at Bowness (Rayrigg Road, 01539 445565, www.steamboat.co.uk), which has the original Amazon and the Esperance, which was one of the prototypes for Captain Flint's houseboat. At the Museum of Lakeland Life (see p270), housed in the Abbot Hall Art Gallery in Kendal (www.abbothall.org.uk), there is a recreation of Ransome's study and assorted memorabilia.

Arthur Wainwright was a writer of a different kind. He devised walks, as a way to escape his dull job at Blackburn town hall. Without Wainwright, a grumpy pipe-smoking personality, and his walking guides of the 1950s and '60s, the Gore-Texed hordes wouldn't be here at all.

A tour of Lakeland

Kendal, eight miles from Windermere, is a slate-grey market-town ringed by hills. It has a ruined Norman castle and several museums, including one that's devoted to Quaker tapestry (Friends Meeting House, Stramongate, 01539 722975, www.quaker-tapestry.co.uk) and another that's all about chocolate, 1657 Chocolate House (54 Branthwaite Brow, 01539 740702, www.chocolatehouse1657.co.uk). In the centre of Kendal, Castle Hill Park involves a very steep walk, but has superb views and assorted ruins to play on. If you're in need of sustenance after the climb, the Brewery Arts Centre (122A Highgate,

Armathwaite Hall Hotel. *See p263.*

01539 725133, www.breweryarts.co.uk) has an excellent café, where children can feast on own-made breaded chicken strips and potato wedges, cod goujons, and mini-portions of pasta and pizza.

Kendal, in common with other large towns on the periphery of the Lake District, such as Keswick and Carlisle, boasts historic houses, museums and other attractions. These towns all yearn to attract some of the Dove Cottage (see right) and Beatrix Potter passing trade. Sizergh Castle (01539 560951, www.nationaltrust.org.uk) and Levens Hall near Kendal (01539 560321, www.levenshall.co.uk) are two wonderful period properties, medieval and Elizabethan respectively, but without child-specific attractions to call their own.

North-west of Kendal, the town of Windermere acts as a kind of gateway to the Lake District proper. A mile from the lake of the same name, it offers hotels with imposing façades, the normal Lakeland shops (selling climbing gear mostly) and plenty of traffic. A bike hire centre, Country Lanes, is conveniently located next to the railway station (01539 444544, www.countrylanes.co.uk); they also organise cycling holidays. The Visitor Centre here (01539 446601, www.lake-district.gov.uk) has a great café at the back, whose terrace has superb views.

Windermere merges into the lakeside town of Bowness a mile away, and this is where the daytrippers tend to end up. You can stroll along a pleasant lakeside promenade between the water and the ample Glebe Park, or catch one of the white steamer boats across to Lakeside (from where a steam railway operates in summer) or up to Waterhead at the top of the lake, near Ambleside. This is England's premium tourist area, and the prices reflect that. What makes it so pleasant is the stunning view across Windermere, but it isn't really Wordsworth country. Peter Rabbit fans should visit the World of Beatrix Potter attraction at the Old Laundry (see p264).

Four miles beyond Windermere-Bowness, further along the arterial A591 into proper Lakeland territory, Ambleside is a sort of HQ of the walking industry and a major refuelling stop, full of restaurants and food shops. The food on offer is a mish-mash of metropolitan and traditional. Among the many outlets are Lucy's, a highly-regarded deli on Church Street (01539 432288) with a café operation next door (see p269).

Ambleside is at the dead centre of the Lake District National Park, which has its Visitor Centre on the lakeside at nearby Brockhole (www.lake-district.gov.uk). Also close by is Waterhead, where you can board the steamer; there's a watersports and activity centre (01539 439441, www.elh.co.uk/watersports) opposite the Low Wood Hotel. Troutbeck Bridge, not far from here, has the area's only public swimming pool (01539 443243, www.tbsp.org.uk). Around here, hotels are best for swimming; those without an indoor pool will often give guests a pass to use the leisure facilites of a grander establishment down the road. There are fine walks here into the Troutbeck valley; Troutbeck Park Farm is among the properties in the area that once belonged to Beatrix Potter. Ambleside also boasts a Roman fort and the tiny, much-photographed Bridge House.

Pastoral perfection

Beyond Ambleside one road leads down the west side of the lake towards the Coniston area, past where Beatrix Potter lived in Hill Top Farm, near Sawrey. The continuation of the A591 in a north-west direction towards Keswick takes you past two lovely little adjoining lakes, Rydal Water and Grasmere, into deepest Wordsworth-land. The setting of the village of Grasmere next to the lake under two vast brooding fells is sublime; 'the most loveliest spot than man hath found' said Wordsworth, forgetting his grammar in his excitement. His home, Dove Cottage, and the adjoining Wordsworth Museum are at Town End (01539 435544, www.wordsworth.org.uk). It's a short walk from here to the village, where Sarah Nelson's famous gingerbread shop (01539 435428, www.grasmeregingerbread.co.uk) occupies the old village schoolhouse where Wordsworth taught as a young man. This is situated in one corner of the lovely St Oswald's churchyard, where the poet is buried. This bit is on everyone's itinerary, so be prepared to wrestle through tourists on auto-pilot in summer.

TOURIST INFORMATION

Ambleside
Central Buildings, Market Cross, Ambleside, Cumbria LA22 9BS (01539 431576/www.amblesideonline.co.uk).

Bowness
Glebe Road, Bowness, Cumbria LA23 3HJ (01539 442895/www.lake-district.gov.uk).

Coniston
Ruskin Avenue, Coniston, Cumbria LA21 8EH (01539 441533/www.conistontic.org).

Kendal
Town Hall, Highgate, Kendal, Cumbria LA9 4DL (01539 725758/www.lakelandgateway.info).

Windermere
Victoria Street, Windemere, Cumbria LA23 1AD (01539 446499/www.lakelandgateway.info).

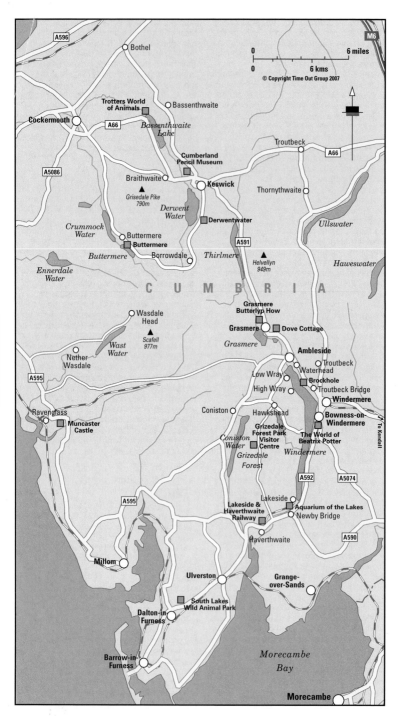

To have one taste of the wonders of Lakeland, take the walk anti-clockwise from Grasmere village around both lakes, across Silver How and Loughrigg (on Loughrigg terrace there are fine views and caves to explore). This is the 'round of Grasmere', favourite walk of the MP Chris Smith, president of the Ramblers' Association.

The A591 continues from Grasmere past massive Helvellyn and remote Thirlmere to Keswick, an attractive market town. Several family-friendly attractions have been imposed on the landscape, and you can take a tour of Honister Slate Mine (Honister Pass, Borrowdale, 01768 777230, www.honister-slate-mine.co.uk), Cumberland Pencil Museum (*see p270*) or Trotters World of Animals (*see p271*). There's walking country around the three-mile-long Derwentwater, known as the Queen of the Northern Lakes.

Beyond Keswick is Cockermouth, Wordsworth's birthplace, but here you are coming out of Lakeland proper. Turn west and you come to the bleak Cumbrian coast near Workington; turn north-east and it's Hadrian's Wall (the end of the line in every sense). The A591 runs like an artery through the lakes' heartland between Windermere and Keswick. Tremendous fun, especially for children, is a jaunt on the open-top 599 bus that plies this route. Windblown on the top deck and jolted at speed over every hump in the road, children end up hysterical with laughter.

There are areas worth a detour on either side of the A591. Down twisting roads and under humped hills nestle country hotels, inns and small guesthouses; walkers and holidaymakers tramp the roads and the fells. The scenic drive along the A592 hugging the shoreline of Ullswater came second in a nationwide competition to find the loveliest route in the UK.

There are dramatic walks around Aira Force waterfall at Ullswater, a celebrated Victorian times beauty spot. In the other direction, south from Ambleside, the area west of Windermere lake is rich in unspoiled woodland, much of it National Trust-owned. Hawkshead is a classic Lakeland village, home to the Beatrix Potter Gallery (*see p264*). Further in this direction lies Coniston Water, with its gondolas and steamers, and Ruskin's house, Brantwood (01539 441396, www.brantwood.org.uk). Strike out from here to the fells around Buttermere and, beyond, the Cumbrian coast for really handsome scenery: the words 'wild and rugged' hardly do it justice.

Cumbria's bleak coastline conceals many attractions, including the town of Barrow (www.barrowbc.gov.uk), Walney Island and Sellafield – yes, an attraction, why else would it have a Visitor Centre (01946 727027, www.sellafield.com)? There's

also Muncaster Castle (*see p270*), the pretty Georgian town of Whitehaven (www.whitehaven.org.uk) and St Bees, the starting-point for Wainwright's coast-to-coast walk (www.coast2coast.co.uk). This area is perhaps a bit beyond the orbit of most Lakeland visitors, but it does lead you to that feature loved by all holidaying families: the beach. The beaches here are unpopulated and spectacular with their distant mountain backdrop, but must be visited only on days when gale-force winds don't make standing up impossible. Pick your road to the coast carefully. The road which heads west from Grasmere towards the coast over Hardknott Pass should only be attempted by an experienced rally driver, or perhaps on the back of a mule.

WHERE TO STAY

It is taking a while for the Lake District's more starchy hotels to unbend themselves sufficiently to give a warm welcome to families. Some say they admit children, but we detect a shudder in their tone. Turns out they'll accept over-eights only. Persevere, however, and you'll find places that will welcome younger guests, without alienating the vast numbers of well-heeled childless folk that bring the money up here.

Once again, the Youth Hostels Association proves a saviour. There are 22 hostels in the Lake District – far too many to list below, but we've included a few of our favourites. For more details, and to find out about the most isolated hostel in England, the Black Sail hostel (a favourite with mountaineer Chris Bonnington, but sadly not suited to the under-threes), log on to www.yha.org.uk.

Armathwaite Hall Hotel

Bassenthwaite Lake, Keswick, Cumbria CA12 4RE (01768 776551/www.armathwaite-hall.com). **Rates** DB&B £125-£175. **Credit** AmEx, MC, V.

This four-star former stately home is in a remote location at the top end of Bassenthwaite Lake, north of Keswick and therefore on the outer fringe of what most would consider the core Lakeland area. It's a classic of the country house hotel type. Driving up the long driveway and entering the great mansion on a stormy night feels deliciously like the first frames of a horror movie. Inside, there is the predictable wall-panelling and stags' heads. The family rooms are large, luxurious and equipped with all mod-cons (flat-screen TV and PlayStation, games obtainable from reception; paradise for Kevin the Teenagers). This is a place for those seeking to be pampered in old-fashioned surroundings. The beds are huge and the bathrobes impeccably fluffy; in winter the fires roar comfortingly. Under-12s can stay free in their parents' room, and get breakfast into the bargain.

POTTERING ABOUT

The recent film about Beatrix Potter's life, starring Renée Zellweger, will only help to fuel an already-thriving Lakeland industry. The Japanese, for some reason, are obsessed with the author and illustrator of the celebrated bunny tales, even using her books as English-language textbooks. The film's release in early 2007 had even more packed tourist coaches heading down the area's twisty lanes in search of Potter's version of English country life.

You can see the attraction. Potter's books present a rosy picture of quaint cottages, gardens and wildlife wearing natty little blue jackets. But Potter was more interesting than her body of work would perhaps suggest. A lonely, middle-class woman, she was born and brought up in London. After visiting Lakeland, she fell in love with the place and stayed for the rest of her life. She became a farmer, sheep-breeder, landowner and keen embracer of local tradition – much like the many fell-enthusiasts today, who look and speak like Lakelanders but actually hail from Salford.

Potter's tales began as illustrated letters to a child she knew, but her career only took off in 1902, when Frederick Warne agreed to publish her work. She fell in love with his son Norman, who died before the wedding; she later married a solicitor from Hawkshead, Mr Heelis – much to her family's disapproval.

Potter died in 1943, leaving vast swathes of land to the National Trust. There is a fascinating little film about her at the **World of Beatrix Potter Attraction** in Bowness. It consists mainly of a walk through reconstructions of scenes from her books, such as Mrs Tiggywinkle's cottage. There's also the inevitable gift shop with Peter Rabbit china.

For a more serious experience, you can visit Potter's lovely little farmhouse at **Hill Top**, near Sawrey. Now preserved as a National Trust-run museum, it can get very busy in summer. At Hawkshead, a 17th-century house that was once her husband's office has become the **Beatrix Potter Gallery**, which displays much of her artwork. It's clear she was a legend round here well before the inevitable Zellweger effect took hold.

Beatrix Potter Gallery
Main Street, Hawkshead, Cumbria LA22 ONS (01539 436355/www.nationaltrust.org.uk). **Open** *Mar-Oct* Times vary; phone or check website for details. **Admission** (NT) £3.80; £1.90 5-17s; £9.50 family (2+3); free under-5s. **Credit** MC, V.

Hill Top
nr Sawrey, Hawkshead, Ambleside, Cumbria LA22 OLF (01539 436269/www.nationaltrust.org.uk). **Open** *Mar-Oct* Times vary; phone or check website for details. **Admission** (NT) £5.40, £2.70 5-17s; £13.50 family (2+3); free under-5s. **Credit** MC, V.

World of Beatrix Potter Attraction
The Old Laundry, Bowness-on-Windermere, Cumbria LA23 3BX (01539 488444/www.hop-skip-jump.com). **Open** 10am-4.30pm daily. **Admission** £6; £3 4-14s; free under-4s. **Credit** MC, V.

Take to the lake at **Windermere**. *See p260.*

The six-course table d'hote menu is served in a room worthy of *Brideshead Revisited* and the food, mostly Frenchified and formally served, is excellent. A more relaxed children's dinnertime takes place in the Leisure Club from 4.30pm until 6.30pm, for those wanting to feed small folk a simpler menu of salads, soups, pizza, chips and the rest. Adults can then organise an early bedtime and make use of the electronic baby listening service while lingering over their haute cuisine. You're not obliged to choose this option, however, as the six courses can be served in half portions in the restaurant. The Leisure Club, with its pool, sauna, and gym, is open to all. Trotters World of Animals (*see p271*) is in the grounds.

Belsfield House

Belsfield Terrace, Kendal Road, Bowness-on-Windermere, Cumbria LA23 3EQ (01539 445823/www.belsfieldhouse.co.uk). **Rates** £50-£107.50. **Credit** MC, V.
This is a straightforward guesthouse with nine en suite rooms, four of which are suited to families, with cots available. Some rooms overlook Lake Windermere. There are toys and colouring books for children, and videos in the lounge. Breakfast in the dining room is a hearty affair; the full fry up can be halved for smaller appetites. This is a perfect base for a weekend of Beatrix Potter, shopping and a cruise on Windermere, but if all that seems too touristy, you have free access to Parklands Leisure club, two minutes' walk away.

Butharlyp How Youth Hostel

Easedale Road, Grasmere, Cumbria LA22 9QG (0870 770 5836/www.yha.org.uk). **Open** Feb-Oct daily. *Nov-Feb* Fri only. **Rates** £16.50; £12 under-18s; £58-£82.50 family room. **Credit** MC, V.
This 84-bed hostel is a Victorian house set in extensive grounds, with family rooms, a safe play area for children and outdoor games equipment. Hostel staff can help guests book a wide range of outdoor activities, including watersports, climbing, orienteering, cycling and fishing. Or you can hire a YHA Budgie Bike. Facilities include a restaurant, shop, kitchen, showers, laundry, TV lounge and internet access.

Great Langdale & Low Wray Campsites

Great Langdale, nr Ambleside, Cumbria LA22 9JU (01539 437668/www.ntlakescampsites.org. uk). **Open** year round. **Rates** £4.50; £2 5-16s; free under-5s; £3 vehicle.
Low Wray, nr Ambleside, Cumbria LA22 0JA (01539 432810/www.ntlakescampsites.org.uk). **Open** Easter-Oct. **Rates** £4.50; £2 5-16s; free under-5s; £3 vehicle.
These are two of the three Lakeland campsites run by the National Trust (the other is Wasdale). They are both nicely located near Ambleside, and family-friendly. Great Langdale has a separate field and play area for families, and is open all year round; Low Wray is open from Easter to October. Low Wray has boat launching access on the lakeside and is ideal for canoeing and dinghy sailing. Both sites have a shop, laundry facilities and showers, and all profits go towards conservation work. If showers and flush toilets seem too luxurious, stay in a bothy. The National Trust's Holme Wood Bothy is a converted fish hatchery offering 'extremely basic accommodation' on the secluded shores of Loweswater, whose facilities are enhanced by a composting toilet and Dowling stove (a welded steel, fuel efficient woodburner).

High Wray Farm B&B

High Wray, Ambleside, Cumbria LA22 0JE (01539 432280/www.highwrayfarm.co.uk). **Rates** £56-£75. *Cottage* £290-£510/wk. **No credit cards**.
What could be better than being surrounded by the sounds and smells of rural life? With chickens in the yard, horses in the fields, and sheep and cows grazing yonder, High Wray is a working farm with a nice little B&B sideline and a self-catering stable cottage that sleeps up to four people. You have to book way ahead for the cottage, though; with views city folk dream about and comfortable living quarters (as well as local milk and meat deliveries), it's a little bit of paradise. Happily, the 17th-century farmhouse, with its oak beams and creaky floors, is also gorgeous. High Wray nestles in the rolling hills above Lake Windermere, with lovely walking country all around. Parents can borrow a baby monitor or book babysitting, and there are some toys around the place.

The Lake District

An owlish inhabitant of **Muncaster Castle**. See p270.

Keswick Youth Hostel

Station Road, Keswick, Cumbria CA12 5LH (0870 770 5894/www.yha.org.uk). **Open** year round. **Rates** £17.50; £13.95 under-18s; £63 family room. **Credit** MC, V.

A favourite family hostel in downtown Keswick, this 86-bedder stands on the the banks of the River Greta, with great walking country all around. Skiddaw, one of the highest mountains in the Lake District, isn't far away either. The YHA's Budgie Bike scheme will lend you wheels from as little as £1.50 a day. There's also plenty to do in the evenings. Just a few minutes' walk away are a cinema, numerous restaurants, pubs and a theatre, so wet weather needn't be too much of a dampener. The hostel is looking spick and span following a revamp partly financed by one Dr Graham Pink, a retired Manchester schoolteacher who donated generously to the work, which has brought the place up to four star status. There are now smaller private rooms, as well as a redesigned ground floor with a new reception, kitchen and dining room, so it's top notch for families.

The Regent by the Lake

Waterhead Bay, Ambleside, Cumbria LA22 OES (01539 432254/www.regentlakes.co.uk). **Rates** £99-£170. **Credit** MC, V.

This 30-room hotel has a family-run, family-friendly vibe and is right on the lake by the Waterhead steamer pier, five minutes' walk from the centre of Ambleside. It has an indoor pool, PlayStation and Gameboy and a variety of room shapes and sizes that are perfect for adults and children to share. The garden rooms have their own patio, and courtyard rooms, near the swimming pool, are dog-friendly too as they lead straight outside onto a courtyard. Garden suites are more spacious, and the one with views over Lake Windermere is much requested. Children can choose from a simple supper menu, available earlier in the evening, if they're too tired to eat with their parents – they can choose from soup, salad, prawn cocktail, fish of the day, spaghetti and meatballs, plain pasta, chocolate pots, ice-cream or sticky toffee pudding (£8 for 1 course, £15.95 for 3 courses). Breakfast is a big event. Available until noon, it fills you up in inimitable Lakeland style with free range eggs, Garside Cumberland Sausage, Plumgarth's bacon and Bury black pudding or Deveroux Manx Kippers, or locally smoked salmon. There'll be no need for lunch after that lot. For wet days, the back lounge is stocked with board games.

Rothay Manor Hotel

Rothay Bridge, Ambleside, Cumbria LA22 0EH (01539 433605/www.rothaymanor.co.uk). **Rates** £135-£210. *Lodge* £210/night. **Credit** MC, V.

This three-star family-run hotel is in a listed Regency building with landscaped gardens. Families are well provided for with family rooms (doubles with two chair beds), suites (with a separate room for the children) and lodges – two- and three-bedroom bungalows in the grounds. Travel cots and a baby-listening service are provided. The restaurant, which does a mean afternoon tea and filling lunches, goes all candlelit and award-winning for dinner (smoked salmon, sea bass, venison and the like) and infants are banished from the feast. Which is, after all, what many parents of pre-schoolers want to happen after a day of running around after them across the fells. Rothay provides a children's high tea for under-sevens (as kids this young aren't permitted in the dining foom for dinner). It's served between 6.15pm and 6.30pm, giving a rather small window of opportunity, and must be booked at breakfast time. Delights such as soup, melon, prawn cocktail, pasta, pizza, omelette, burgers and ice cream are dished up (£4.50 for 1 course, £8 for 3 courses). The on-site Leisure Club has a heated pool and children's paddling pool, and guests also have access to the Leisure Club at the nearby Low Wood Hotel, the premier pool-gym-sauna facility in the neighbourhood.

Skelwith Fold Caravan Park

Ambleside, Cumbria LA22 0HX (01539 432277/www.skelwithfold.co.uk). **Open** Mar-15 Nov. **Rates** £17.50-£20/pitch per night; £110-£125/wk. **Credit** MC, V.

This award-winning holiday park takes pride in what it doesn't offer. There are no bars, discos or outdoor heated pools. Instead, there's a twice-daily chorus of birdsong, plus the odd guest appearance by a badger, squirrel or deer. Set in 130 acres of wooded estate near Ambleside, its manager, Henry Wild, is aiming at sustainable tourism. Guests can recycle their waste, there's shielded illumination so that the night sky can be properly enjoyed, and local skills such as dry-stone-walling and coppicing are used to maintain the site's character. The place also boasts its own tarn, home to dragonflies and kingfishers. The aptly-named Mr Wild's efforts have won his site a David Bellamy Conservation Award. The pitches are for caravans only, so don't roll up here with a tent.

Waterhead Hotel

Lake Road, Ambleside, Cumbria LA22 0ER (01539 432566/www.elh.co.uk). **Rates** £175-£280. **Credit** MC, V.

A classy refurbishment here aims at a sophisticated Soho feel with the odd nod to the Lakeland locale. There is art everywhere and giant pebbles under glass in the bar area; even the towel-rail looks like a work of art. Martin Campbell's photographs of local waterfalls adorn the doors of the 41 rooms. The almost aggressively lit restaurant, The Bay, has striking blue glass tableware and superb views of the lake. Fell-bred beef and lamb and Grizedale venison are on the menu (from £13 and upwards). Children who want to sample this largesse must pay the full price for their dinner; otherwise the children's menu has tagliatelle, sausage and beans, chicken strips and the rest (£3.95-£5.95 for 1 course, £7.95 for 2 courses, £9.95 for 3 courses). Waterhead has nicely appointed family rooms and a baby listening service; under-fives can share their parents' (note the plural, two full paying adults) room for free, with breakfast included. Fives to 15s sharing with the aged Ps are charged £15 each per night. Children can join Sam's Club, an activity club that gives them a goodie bag on arrival. Guests can use the leisure facilities and pool at the Low Wood Hotel down the road, where scheduled children's splash times involve inflatable fun and frolics; there's also a Watersports Centre.

White Moss House Hotel

Rydal Water, nr Grasmere, Cumbria LA22 9SE (015394 35295/www.whitemoss.com). **Rates** £78-£98. **Credit** MC, V.

This little hotel is a gem, perfectly situated at the north end of Rydal Water (close to the south end of Grasmere lake). You couldn't get closer to the Wordsworth idyll; the house, which dates from 1730, was once owned by the poet, and his descendants lived here until 1930. It also lies between Wordsworth's other famous homes at Dove Cottage and Rydal Mount. Sue and Peter Dixon have run this place for 23 years, and the hotel and restaurant have won every award going. There are only five bedrooms in the main house, but there are more in Brockstone cottage, a little way up the hill, which children love. It's a relief to find such a classy place so children-welcoming and family-friendly. There's a large garden to play in, and the hotel may be able to provide babysitting if you ask in advance. Guests can use the local pool and gym free of charge, or try their hand at fishing in the nearby lakes and rivers.

Windermere Youth Hostel

Bridge Lane, Troutbeck, Windermere, Cumbria LA23 1LA (0870 770 6094/www.yha.org.uk). **Open** year round advance booking. **Rates** £13.95; £9.95 under-18s; £40 family room. **Credit** MC, V.

If you want a view of the District's most famous lake, book ahead (sometimes way ahead is necessary) for this 69-bed hostel. It's set in a peaceful location, deep in the countryside two miles outside Windermere. Children of all ages are most welcome, and cots are available. There's a garden, a barbecue area and a self-catering kitchen, or you can partake of dinner in the dining room.

WHERE TO EAT & DRINK

Note that the Waterhead, the Regent by the Lake, Armathwaite Hall, Rothay Manor and White Moss House hotels all have highly regarded restaurants (*see above*). Many of the hotels also serve afternoon tea. A word of caution about food in Lakeland: it's hard to find an unpretentious budget restaurant in these parts. Instead you must rely on the odd café and pubs, plenty of which offer superior pub-grub (at superior prices).

Drunken Duck

Barngates, Ambleside, Cumbria LA22 0NG (01539 436347/www.drunkenduckinn.co.uk). **Meals served** noon-2.15pm, 6-9.15pm daily. **Main courses** £14.95-£24.95. **Credit** AmEx, MC, V.

This much-lauded 400-year-old pub has a lovely unspoilt setting. There is rustic decor, award-winning own-brewed beer and a very popular menu of modern British cooking. Much of the produce is local, such as Cartmel Valley smoked salmon or Cumbrian air-dried ham, and portions are huge. Puddings are traditional and intricate (summer pudding is accompanied by Pimms jelly and strawberry shortcake ice-cream, while crème brûlée is scented with saffron and served with sesame caramel and mango salsa), and promise to live a lifetime on the hips unless you run up and down the hillside after the kids all afternoon. Children are welcome here, but the no-high chair policy would suggest that babies and toddlers might have to stay in the car. For those that can perch on their own chairs, simplified half-price portions of most dishes can be arranged. This is seriously good cooking; not cheap, but it certainly makes you cheerful. Most people seem to agree – there are not many better pubs than the Drunken Duck.

Low Sizergh Farm Shop & Tea Room

Sizergh, Kendal, Cumbria LA8 8AE (01539 560426/www.lowsizerghbarn.co.uk). **Meals served** *Jan-Mar* 9.30am-4.30pm daily. *Apr-Dec* 9.30am-5pm daily. **Main courses** £3.95-£6.50. **Credit** MC, V.

Foodies flock to this organic dairy farm outside Kendal for its award-winning farm food shop, as well as the tearoom. The shop is housed in an 18th-century barn, and was voted Farm Retailer of the Year 2005; among its wares are a fantastic array of cheeses, along with own-made jams and pickles, locally-sourced meat and game and organic vegetables. On the menu in the tearooms are own-baked quiches and pies, proper Cumberland sausage, soups, sandwiches, cakes and cream teas. The great attraction here is that there are viewing windows onto the milking parlour, so if you're there at 3.45 in the afternoon you can watch as the cows come in to be milked and show the kids where the cream for their scone comes from. In the summer, the Windermere ice-cream company sells its wares from a cart in the yard – made with Low Sizergh milk, of course.

Lucy's on a Plate

1 Church Street, Ambleside, Cumbria LA22 0BU (01539 431191/www.lucysofambleside. co.uk). **Meals served** 10am-9pm daily. **Main courses** £6.50-£18. **Credit** MC, V.
This friendly café is next door to the well-regarded Lucy's deli, set up in 1989 by a woman who was dismayed to find the Lake District a 'food desert' when she first settled in Cumbria. The café opened in 1996, with a varied menu that concentrates on hearty rib-stickers, such as proper beefy burgers spilling juices on to fresh ciabatta, focaccia bread filled with goats cheese and roast vegetables, Cumberland sausage for breakfast and macaroni cheese for lunch. Portions tend to be big, so children might want to share to leave room for a slab of own-made chocolate cake, scones, pecan tart or treacle sponge. Drop by the evening for substantial dishes, which have silly names but seriously good ingredients. To start there might be fig in the middle (plump figs stuffed with cheddar) or a dollop of scallops. Mains include lamb rumpy pumpy – pan-roasted Lakeland lamb with sweet potato mash and veg – and well-fed fell-bred filly (pan-fried local beef fillet with gratin potatoes). Children are welcome day or night, and can order starters or half-portions of mains.

Queens Head Hotel

Townhead, Troutbeck, Cumbria LA23 1PW (01539 432174/www.queensheadhotel.com). **Meals served** noon-2.30pm, 5-9pm daily. **Main courses** £12.95-£16.95. **Credit** MC, V.
As well as plying customers with real ales such as Bluebird Bitter or Old Faithful, this stone-flagged and oak-beamed coaching inn also has a fantastic restaurant. Its menu of wholesome mouth-waterers – butternut squash soup, Thornby moor goats' cheese, roast rack of Lakeland lamb, steak, ale and mushroom cobbler or grilled salmon, for instance – are a walker's dream. There are a few smaller, simpler dishes prepared for children, such as pork and leek sausages, vegetarian spaghetti bolognese, or cheddar cheese omelette, all £3.95.

Travellers Rest Inn

Grasmere, Cumbria LA22 9RR (01539 435604/ www.lakedistrictinns.co.uk). **Meals served** noon-9.30pm daily. **Main courses** £5-£14.95. **Credit** MC, V.
This whitewashed roadside inn outside Grasmere is distinguished by friendly and efficient service, a stone-floored and oak-beamed bar serving the very best real ales, and great food served in the large dining room adjoining the bar. Steak and Jennings' Ale pie and Waberthwaite sausage are representative. Puddings tend to be similarly traditional, and are usually first-class. Outside tables (next to the fields at the foot of the fell) and two back rooms for pool and TV make this pub hard to beat. The food on the children's menu is good quality, and the portions are of a decent size; scampi, gammon, Cumberland sausage, fish goujons, spag bol and macaroni cheese are all £3.95, with ice-cream, doughnuts or fudge cake and chocolate ice-cream (£2.25) for those with room left.

Tweedies Bar

Dale Lodge Hotel, Grasmere, Cumbria LA22 9SW (01539 435300/www.dalelodge hotel.co.uk). **Meals served** noon-3pm, 6-9pm daily. **Main courses** £8.50-£18.95. **Credit** MC, V.
We're not so interested in the Lodge Restaurant attached to this hotel. It may have a chef who trained under Raymond Blanc, but that's nothing exceptional round here. The point for us is that Tweedies serves good quality gastropub food and has a beer garden – a pleasant spot to eat en famille when the weather's up to it. Beers served include old familiars such as Coniston Bluebird, and meals might range from Cumberland sausage and creamy mash to spicy Thai fishcakes. We had quite a wait for the food when visiting one Saturday lunchtime, but it was worth it.

Zeffirelli's

Compston Road, Ambleside, Cumbria LA22 9AD (01539 433845/www.zeffirellis.co.uk). **Meals served** 10am-4.30pm daily, 5.30-10pm daily. **Main courses** £4.95-£10.50. **Credit** MC, V.
A popular place, well situated for passing trade in the middle of Ambleside, Zeffirelli's sits next to the cinema and has a jazz bar for good measure. The Italian-Mediterranean menu will satisfy any pizza or pasta cravings, or provide a simple lunch of jacket spuds and salad, soups, ciabatta and other family essentials. Mini-portions can be served up for smaller appetites, priced at around £5 – pasta with own-made pesto, linguine with puttanesca sauce and parmesan or pizza with a face on it always go down well. If you fancy the flicks, there's a joint ticket that covers cinema entry plus a two-course meal for £17.95; ask for details of special deals for children. Come in the afternoon for warm scones, jam and cream before the big picture. In the evening, the lower dining area becomes the setting for proper dinners.

PLACES TO SEE, THINGS TO DO

Aquarium of the Lakes

Lakeside, Newby Bridge, Cumbria LA12 8AS (01539 530153/www.aquariumofthelakes.co.uk). **Open** *Summer* 9am-6pm daily. *Winter* 9am-5pm daily. Last admission 1hr before closing. **Admission** £7.50; £5 3-15s; £22 family (2+2), £26.25 (2+3); free under-3s. **Credit** MC, V.

This freshwater aquarium at Lakeside isn't a huge place, but very informatively takes you through the watery journey from mountainside spring to lake bottom. Along the way the various habitats are well explained, featuring riverbank mammals such as otters, voles, harvest mice and rats along with fish. There are also toads, huge pike, eels and sharks (of the small British variety – don't expect Jaws). The emphasis is Lakeland-orientated with no showy tropical fish, but it's impressive in its own understated way.

Cumberland Pencil Museum

Southey Works, Greta Bridge, Keswick, Cumbria CA12 5NG (01768 773626/www.pencils.co.uk). **Open** 9.30am-4pm daily. **Admission** £3; £1.50-£2 concessions; £1.50 5-16s; £7.50 family (2+3); free under-5s. **Credit** (over £10) MC, V.

Marvel at the World's Longest Pencil! Yes, it's easy to sneer, but one finds oneself drawn (no pun intended) to this sort of place after a thorough soaking on a wet Easter vac, and in fact the children loved it. The museum, on the same site as the pencil making factory (although you can only see a video of the works, rather than the pencil making practice per se), covers the history of the writer's tool, which started life in the graphite mines of Borrowdale. Visitors can admire machinery and a mock-up of a mine, and children get involved in all sorts of arty activities, such as brass rubbing, sketching, the testing of various pencil types and themed art workshops.

Go Ape!

Grizedale Forest Visitor Centre, Grizedale, Hawkshead, Cumbria LA22 OQJ (0870 458 9189/www.goape.co.uk). **Open** *Feb half term, 23 Mar-Oct* daily. Times vary; phone for details. **Admission** £25; £20 10-18s. **Credit** MC, V.

The Lakes outpost of the popular Go Ape! high wire forest adventure empire is exhilarating. Under-18s must be accompanied by adults, the very young can't join in; children have to be over ten years old and more than 4ft 7in tall. Swing high on the eleven courses of rope bridges, tarzan swings and zip slides. Pre-booking is required.

Lake District Visitor Centre

Brockhole, Windermere, Cumbria LA23 1LJ (01539 446601/www.lake-district.gov.uk). **Open** *10-25 Feb, 31 Mar-Oct* 10am-5pm daily. **Admission** free; £2.20/2hrs, £4 4/hrs, £6/day on-site car park. **No credit cards.**

This slice of lakeside between Ambleside and Windermere, a kind of open-door HQ for the National Park, has an exhibition centre, café, shop, adventure playground and also a pleasant walk past wildflower meadows to the lakeside, where there is a steamer pier. There are children's quizzes and trails, and the eco-conscious and child-friendly exhibition centre describes how local wildlife, farming and culture are under threat from hordes of visitors like us. Whoops. The noticeboard here is the best place to find details of guided walks and seasonal children's events.

Lakeside & Haverthwaite Railway

Haverthwaite Station, nr Ulverston, Cumbria LA12 8AL (01539 531594/www.lakeside railway.co.uk). **Open** *31 Mar-28 Oct* 10.40am-4.45pm daily. **Tickets** £3.10-£5.20; £2.10-£2.60 5-15s; £14.20 family (2+3); free under-5s. **Credit** MC, V.

A jaunt on one of these small gauge steam railways is a must on a UK family break. Younger children are entranced by the bells and whistles and *Thomas the Tank Engine* associations, and tired parents can sit back and enjoy the countryside without being chivvied by the kids. This line, from Lakeside through the Leven valley, works well because it departs from one of the drop-off points of the Windermere Lake steamer (*see p271*). There's a more frequent service in the peak summer season, as well as the usual seasonal specials (Santa, ghosts, Thomas and the like).

Muncaster Castle

Ravenglass, Cumbria CA18 1RQ (01229 717614/www.muncaster.co.uk/www.owls.org). **Open** *Feb-Dec Gardens, Owl Centre & Maze* 10.30am-6pm daily. *Castle* noon-5pm Mon-Fri, Sun. **Admission** *Castle, Gardens, Owl Centre & Maze* £9.50; £6.50 5-15s ; £27 family (2+2); free under-5s. *Gardens, Owl Centre & Maze* £7; £5 5-15s; £22 family (2+2); free under-5s. **Credit** MC, V.

This place is a bit off the Lakey track, on Cumbria's 'Heritage Coast', but well worth a detour. There are four elements: a castle, its gardens, the World Owl Centre and the Meadow Vole Maze. To get to it you walk through the Himalayan gardens, which are full of unusual plants and trees. Don't miss the owls: this is a kind of world HQ for owl conservation. Every size, type and nationality is represented here, and it's a fascinating collection. Afterwards you can embark on the maze, an interactive trail that younger kids will really enjoy. It all adds up to a lovely day out.

Museum of Lakeland Life

Abbot Hall, Kendal, Cumbria LA9 5AL (01539 722464/www.lakelandmuseum.org.uk). **Open** *Summer* 10.30am-5pm daily. *Winter* 10.30am-4pm daily. **Admission** £3.75; £2.75 concessions, 2-18s; £11 family (2+2); free under-2s. **Credit** MC, V.

Trotters World of Animals

they wander their grassy enclosures – you can meet the giraffes head on from up here. Visitors can join in a daily programme of events which includes feeding the giraffes and lemurs, along with fascinating rhino talks by the zoo owner, who stands shoulder-to-shoulder with the great beasts. For lunch, there are picnic areas or a restaurant.

Steam Yacht Gondola

Pier Cottage, Coniston, Cumbria LA21 8AJ (01539 441288). **Open** *Apr-Oct* 11am-4pm daily (weather permitting). **Tickets** £6; £3 5-15s; £15 family (2+3); free under-5s. **Credit** MC, V.

This is a daily 45-minute cruise on Lake Coniston, on a steamboat rebuilt from the Victorian original. It stops at Brantwood (01539 441263), the home of John Ruskin, which has gardens, an art gallery and a restaurant. Suffice to say, explaining how Donald Campbell met his end breaking the land-speed record in Bluebird on Coniston might open your children's eyes wider than learning about the eminent artist and critic.

Trotters World of Animals

Bassenthwaithe Lake, Keswick, Cumbria CA12 4RD (01768 776239/www.trottersworld.com). **Open** *Easter-Oct* 10am-5.30pm daily. *Nov-Easter* 10am-4pm daily. **Admission** £5.95; £4.50 3-16s; free under-3s. **Credit** MC, V.

This is a pleasant (if small) zoo under the fells in the grounds of Armathwaite Hall Hotel (*see p263*), at the north end of Bassenthwaite Lake, north of Keswick. There are otters and a reptile house, and the monkeys are rather good – especially the gibbons roaming loose in a grassy meadow. On our last visit there was also an excellent flying demonstration involving a buzzard, an owl and a vulture. It's not a whole day out; more a pleasant two hours, at most.

This small museum in the stable block of an art gallery in Kendal has the distinction of being the first establishment ever to win the Museum of the Year award back in 1973. The permanent collections include displays linked to the Arts and Crafts movement, *Swallows and Amazons* author Arthur Ransome, and Cumbria in Victorian times, with an antique street scene for atmosphere. A number of the temporary displays are accompanied by themed workshops for children, as well as costumed storytelling. The coffee shop has outdoor seating, alongside the croquet lawn.

South Lakes Wild Animal Park

Broughton Road, Dalton-in-Furness, Cumbria LA15 8JR (01229 466086/www.wildanimalpark.co.uk). **Open** *Sept-Mar* 10am-4.30pm daily. *Apr-Oct* 10am-5pm daily. **Admission** £7; £4 concessions, 3-15s; free under-3s. **Credit** MC, V.

Venture outside the core Lakes area to visit this wildlife park at Dalton, on the road to Barrow – its tigers, lions, giraffes, rhinos, bears, lemurs and snakes may be just the spectacle children need after a few days of soggy crag clambering. The park is the home of the Sumatran Tiger Trust, and there are two tigers here as part of a captive breeding programme. Visitors highly recommend the thrilling spectacle of the tiger feeding. The cats are encouraged to work for their food, which is placed on top of 6m-high poles to ensure they use all their muscle groups. The park also has an elevated giraffe, rhino and baboon viewing walkway that affords a birds' eye view of the animals as

Windermere Lake Cruises

Winander House, Glebe Road, Bowness-on-Windermere, Cumbria LA23 3HE (01539 443360/www.windermere-lakecruises.co.uk). **Open** *Apr-Oct* 9am-7pm daily. *Nov-Mar* 10am-4pm daily. **Admission** £5.25-£7.70; £3.15-£4.10 5-15s; £21.50 family (2+3); free under-5s. **Credit** AmEx, MC, V.

These elegant ferry-boats ply the lake several times daily between Ambleside, Bowness and Lakeside. Extra stops in the summer include Fell Foot (where there's a large, restored Victorian park owned by the National Trust) and Brockhole. It's much more peaceful these days, now that a ten-mile-an-hour speed limit has been enforced on Windermere, putting paid to the speedboats – a victory for the conservation lobby that still has the tourism brigade moaning because of lost business. The Lakeside stop (where you'll find the Aquarium of the Lakes) connects in summer with the delightful Lakeside & Haverthwaite Railway (for both *see p270*).

Whitby

Take the 'plein air' of the North East.

The old harbour town of Whitby, the ten-mile stretch of Heritage Coastline either side from Robin Hood's Bay to Staithes, and the North York Moors in the immediate hinterland combine adventure, natural beauty and fun. Small surprise that in 2006 Whitby was voted England's best seaside resort in *Holiday Which?*. Barring a really good hotel, it's got the lot: knockout scenery, from long beaches to windswept moorland; great local produce, from legendary fish and chips to live lobster; steam trains and river trips; dinosaur footprints and Dracula trails; Goth Weekends and a Wizard Workshop; world music festivals and whale-watching. What more could a family want?

It's a town stuffed with history. Here Captain Cook served his apprenticeship before sailing away in a Yorkshire collier to put Australasia on the map, and Captain Scoresby startled his neighbours by bringing a polar bear home from a whaling expedition. Bram Stoker unveiled Dracula among the sea-scoured gravestones of St Mary's churchyard, and Lewis Carroll was inspired to compose The Walrus and the Carpenter, 'who wept like anything to see such quantities of sand and sea'. And no sea-going community was more evocatively recorded than by the great Victorian photographer Frank Meadow Sutcliffe, and the 'plein air' artists of the Staithes Group.

Runswick Bay

The history and character jumps out at every turn, overlooked by the brooding clifftop ruin of Whitby Abbey, for 1,300 years one of England's most significant sites of Christian worship. Below, the working harbour remains the heart of the town, and is still in the serious business of landing fish and building ships while tourists pack its narrow lanes.

For many families Whitby means the call of bucket and spade. At West Cliff, take the zig-zag paths 200 feet down to the long, clean sands stretching two miles away to Sandsend. There are no cafés, no donkeys and no dogs (on designated sections at least), so hire a deck chair, a windbreak, or a brightly painted beach hut until high tide forces you back to the top with an easy ride in the cliff lift.

There's no short cut up the famous 199 steps of East Cliff, or the adjacent Donkey Path, to visit the Abbey and the remarkable St Mary's church, but it must be done. Walk, too, the mighty double-decker piers that arc out into the North Sea like lobster claws, or take a guided walk to find real dinosaur footprints among the low tide rock pools. Explore alleys so narrow that smugglers passed their contraband from house to house without it ever touching the ground, or wait for the harbour swing-bridge across the Esk to open for a sailor who has precedence over you and your car.

A number of pleasant, low-key entertainments congregate happily on Whitby's West Cliff: a sweet art deco paddling pool, water dodgems, crazy golf, trampolines, go-carts and a leisure centre with an indoor pool (01947 604640, www.discoveryorkshirecoast.com).

Rainy days are no problem. Apart from the quintessential Whitby Museum and Pannett Park Art Gallery (01947 602908, www.durain.demon.co.uk), there's Whitby Lifeboat Museum (Pier Road, 01947 602001), Captain Cook's house, a Dracula experience, the Whitby Jet Heritage Centre and the Abbey Visitor Centre, (for all, *see p285*). Other child-friendly options include the delightfully homespun Wizard's Workshop (01947 810470, www.whitbywizard.com), a whimsical science museum created by a modern Viking settler, Dag Kjelldahlin, in which every exhibit is hands-on, sturdy and guaranteed to occupy any age group for a good value hour or two, Doodlepots (5B Skinner Street, 01947 825824) for pottery painting, and the charity-run Whitby Coliseum (Victoria Place, 01947 825000) for arts and craft workshops and a charming little cinema. The year-round live music scene is notably strong in folk and world music, and for half the year the Grand Turk, a full size replica 18th-century man o'war, is berthed in the harbour.

Garish, gothic, glacial

Whitby has always been popular, so there are the inevitable tacky corners. The trashiest stretch of candyfloss and slot machines is sensibly confined to Pier Road, while much more interesting shopping can be found on Skinner Street, Flowergate and Church Street. Whitby's artistic heritage is reflected in quality galleries like the Reading Room (24A Flowergate, 01947 820771, www.thereadingroom.biz) and Pybus Fine Art (127 Church Street, 01947 820028, www.mpybusfinearts.co.uk). There are two honourable independent bookshops, Holman's (19-21 Skinner Street, 01947 602372) and the Whitby Bookshop (88 Church Street, 01947 606202, www.whitbybookshop.co.uk). Try Bothams (35-39 Skinner Street, 01947 602823, www.botham.co.uk) for cakes and Poachers Pocket (3 Skinner Street, 01947 606166) for good value outdoor gear, and take time to explore the elaborate profusion of antique, jewellery and gift shops and small boutiques.

For shopping, Flowergate on the west side is emerging as one of the best streets in Whitby for quirky individual shops. The Reading Room Gallery at No.24A (01947 820771) sells good quality paintings and photographs and the Sutcliffe Gallery (1 Flowergate, 01947 602239, www.sutcliffe-gallery.co.uk) holds the photographic archive of Victorian photographer Frank Meadow Sutcliffe. The Porthole fair trade gift shop is the centre for Whitby's estimable World Music Festival (01947 603475, www.whitbymusicport.com) which runs for three days in October and attracts top names in world music.

The bi-annual Whitby Goth Weekends (*see p335*) make for great people watching, as hundreds of black-clad devotees descend on town. They shop at Pandemonium (29 Flowergate, 01947 821955) and rest their weary bones in Bats and Broomsticks (11 Prospect Hill, 01947 605659), probably Britain's only goth guest house.

If the bank holiday and peak summer crowds become oppressive, it's easy to find open space and skies around the local coast and countryside. The dramatic cliff top that extends both north and south of Whitby can be walked on the Cleveland Way (www.nationaltrail.co.uk). Descend to sea level for the beaches at Sandsend, Runswick Bay and Boggle Hole, the cliff-hanging fishing villages of Staithes and Robin Hood's Bay, and the eerie lost harbour of Port Mulgrave. Better still, hire a bike and cycle from Whitby to Ravenscar and back, enjoying the spectacular views from the safety of a disused railway line.

For active railways, the North York Moors Steam Railway (01751 472508, www. nyr.co.uk) sets off six miles away at

TOURIST INFORMATION

Langbourne Road, Whitby,
North Yorkshire YO21 1YN
(01723 383637/
www.discoveryorkshirecoast.com).
www.moors.uk.net
www.whitbyonline.co.uk
www.whitby-holidays.com

Grosmont and cuts through glacial valleys to Pickering. Various events and galas are held throughout the year, details of which can be found on the website. From Whitby's own little terminus, the Esk Valley Railway's diesels (0845 748 4950, www.eskvalleyrailway.co.uk) follow the course of the sparkling river Esk, crossing it 17 times in as many miles. The trains halt at a string of unspoiled villages, which offer a pub lunch or a launch pad for a brisk walk on the heather-clad moors.

Hit the beach running

Six miles south of Whitby, Robin Hood's Bay is so popular on sunny weekends that the single (pedestrian) lane into it can become quite a procession – but the jumble of pretty cottages that cascade down to the tiny harbour make it worth the jostle. The beach at low tide makes for great rock-pooling, and the further you venture around the curving bay, the emptier it gets. At high tide, mug up on the coastline at the National Trust's Old Coastguard Station or take tea and cakes at Swell (01947 880180), a converted chapel with a sea-view verandah and its own cinema.

One of the best ways to see Robin Hood's Bay is to cycle along the disused railway track that runs from Whitby to Scarborough. Trailways Bike Hire (01947 820207, www.trailways.info) has 120 bikes in every configuration: adult, junior, infant or even tandem, with child seats, buggies and tagalongs. Book your bike of choice for anything from two hours to two days, with junior bikes a bargain £1 an hour in the evenings. Spin along *Famous Five*-style on the safe, car-free track, spoilt for choice when it comes to picnic spots and with ever-changing vistas of one of the most dramatic seascapes in the British Isles.

Exploring the dinosaur coast

Five miles north of Whitby is Sandsend. A timewarp seaside village with 1950s charm, Sandsend has a handful of tearooms, a couple of shops and the Turnstone Gallery (East Row, 01947 893289, www.turnstonegallery.net). The shallow estuary allows for safe

Whitby

bodyboarding and has great views back to Whitby Abbey. The pretty cottages of 'millionaires row' are a pretty sight, as are Mulgrave Woods and their ruined castle (01723 383637, open Wed, Sat, Sun Jan-Apr, June-Dec), part of the Marquis of Normanby's estate. For a weirder walk, follow the Sandsend trail through the lunar wastes of the area's industrial heritage of alum and ironstone mining.

Yorkshire was a tropical lagoon 160 million years ago. Its crumbling cliffs have disgorged dinosaurs, and continue to release all sorts of fossils. A programme of activity days, fossil hunts, walks with geologists and fossil masterclasses run throughout the summer, aimed at children, adults and families (01723 232572, www.dinocoast.org.uk). But there is no better fossil than the one you find yourself (www.discoveringfossils.co.uk). Drive to Port Mulgrave, nine miles north of Whitby, then take the steep footpath down to the silted-up harbour. Scramble northwards round and over the rocks until the remote curve of Brackenbury Wyke opens up, and the first little rocky beach after the big landslip is littered with ammonites and belemnites. Beware of cliff falls and check tide times though, or you could be cut off.

Runswick is prettier still; a steep-sided village of pantiled roofs, sandstone cottages, tumbling window boxes and a gem of a beach. In 1664 a disastrous landslip sent every house but one tumbling into the sea, and the whole village had to be rebuilt. Today, its picture-postcard appeal has made Runswick somewhat sterile, with permanent residents long outnumbered by weekenders. In prime location is the white-washed and immaculately thatched Lady Palmer's Cottage, the subject of a thousand paintings. Sadly it's not for hire: it's part of the Normanby Estate again. Drown your sorrows at the village pub or tearoom.

In contrast to Runswick, Staithes has a more rugged, hard-working saltiness about it. Set in a deep gorge cut in half by Roxby Beck, its mish-mash of cottages still burn coal as if it was the 1950s, while seabirds scream from their ledges on Cowbar Nab. It's easy to believe its history of smuggling, and to understand its enduring appeal to artists. The remnants of a once vibrant fishing industry are evident in the distinctively curved red, white and blue painted cobbles (boats) that still fish with line and pot during the summer. You'll find the freshest seafood, dressed crab or live lobster in the depots behind the car park; try Whitby Sea Fish (01947 841236) or Tim Turnbull the Lobster Man (01947 840917).

There's a small sandy beach and, at low tide, a fine expanse of flat rock. Known locally as rock 'steel' or 'scar', it's ideal for walking and rock pooling. At high tide, buy a line from the Kessen Bowl and go crabbing off the pier, or buy a blow-up dinghy and mess about in the beck or the harbour. See the practice lifeboat launch (Mon evening in summer, Sun morning in winter). For the history of Staithes and its most famous son, the Captain Cook Museum (*see p283*) is a wonderful treasure house. The best of a new generation of artists are celebrated in Staithes Gallery (01947 841840).

Moor countryside

Within a couple of miles inland, the scenery changes. The North York Moors National Park stretches across 554 square miles, it's one of the largest stretches of heather moorland in Britain. It's unmissable in August, when the purple heather is in bloom, but has its own wild beauty at any time. Red grouse, merlin, golden plover and curlew wheel over ancient crosses and standing stones. Pannier Ways, stone paths laid centuries ago, recall the days when pack horses crossed the moors carrying goods to market.

Travelling further, the tourist honeypot village of Hutton le Hole is too prettified for some, but the less cynical (children) enjoy the recreation of an ancient village at the Ryedale Folk Museum (01751 417367, www.ryedalefolkmuseum.co.uk). Duck your head inside the tiny crofter's cottage and admire the manor house, the village shop and the Victorian photographer's studio. There's also a model farm, Highfields, which has fields containing rare cornfield flowers and livestock, including rare-breed, mud-bathing porkers and pecking poultry.

Enjoy the wilderness on a badger watch or a family star watch at night in Dalby Forest (www.forestry.gov.uk,dalbyforest), or, more exotically, while trekking with llamas at Staintondale near Scarborough (01723 871234, www.llamatreks.co.uk). Explore the moors with a guided bike ride with Purple Mountain (01751 460011, www.purplemountain.co.uk), who also run events throughout the year (including Junior Riding Skills days). The ambitious can walk the Cleveland Way (or a section of it), a 110-mile (177-kilometre) national trail, taking in dales, moor and coast.

For a quirky end to your stay, attend a gig at 'England's tiniest major venue'. The Band Room at Farndale (01751 432900/ www.thebandroom.co.uk) is a small hall built for the local silver band, and now a respected music venue in one of the best-looking corners of the National Park. The criteria for playing is that a band must have released at least one critically acclaimed CD; past performers include Cerys Matthews and the Handsome Family.

Whitby

Ship-shape
in **Whitby
Harbour**.
See p282.

WHERE TO STAY

One of the biggest new attractions to open in Whitby in 2007, and of particular interest to families, is the Abbey House Youth Hostel (*see below*). Developed next to the historic Whitby Abbey, thanks to funding from the Heritage Lottery Fund (HLF) and the European Regional Development Fund, it's an exciting new addition to the hitherto rather limited accommodation options for families in the area. Now all that's required is a luxurious family-friendly hotel, of the type that fill up so quickly during the school holidays around the south coast of England. At present, it must be said that Whitby isn't over endowed with high-end hotels for family treats.

Abbey House Youth Hostel

Whitby Abbey, East Cliff, Whitby, North Yorkshire YO22 4JT (0870 770 6088/ www.yha.org.uk). **Open** phone for details. **Rates** £18.50-£20; £13.50-£14.50 under-18s; £48-£78.50 family rooms. **Credit** MC, V.
Set high on the headland next to Whitby Abbey, with panoramic views over the historic town and down to the river Esk and the harbour, Abbey House was due to open as we went to press, following a £2.5m restoration programme. The house is a Grade I listed landmark building with a fascinating history and the surrounding Grade II listed gardens are also being restored, making this particular affordable berth all the lovelier.

Accommodation in the flagship 100-bed youth hostel includes twin and family rooms, some en suite. A restaurant, bar and communal facilities are also available – the bar is a useful alternative to walking down the 199 steps to find a pub.

Boggle Hole Youth Hostel

Boggle Hole, Mill Beck, Fylingthorpe, Whitby, North Yorkshire YO22 4UQ (0870 770 5704/www.yha.org.uk). **Open** year round. **Rates** £13.95; £9.95 under-18s; £48-£78.50 family rooms. **Credit** MC, V.
Six miles from Whitby, the bay in front of this hostel was once a smugglers' haunt. Now it's full of children beachcombing, all year round. You can walk part of the Cleveland Way to Whitby from here, or hire a bike and cycle along the old Whitby to Scarborough railway line. Note that this place is on a steep hill with no vehicle access for the last 600 metres, so it's not the easiest place to get to, but it's well worth the effort for the cliff walks; glorious Robin's Hood Bay is on your doorstep too. The hostel has four- and six-bed family rooms, some of which are in an annexe, a comfortable lounge and a licensed dining room. Picnic lunches can be booked.

La Rosa Campsite

Murk Esk Cottage, Goathland, Whitby, North Yorkshire YO22 5AS (07786 072866/ www.larosa.co.uk). **Open** Apr-Sept; rest of year by arrangement. **Rates** £24; reduced rates 7-16s; free under-6s. **No credit cards.**

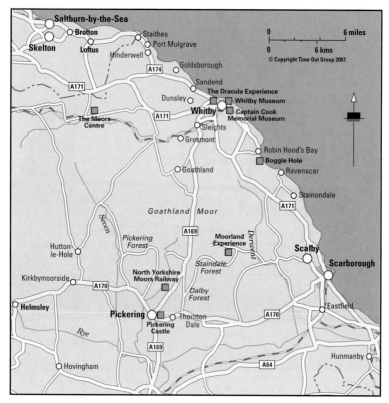

On a 20 acre site, deep in the woods of the North York Moors, La Rosa is a secret little bit of heaven for hardy campers – and a lovely find. It's a low impact, environmentally friendly and delightfully kitsch campsite, made up of a dozen vintage, themed caravans with names like Psycho Candy, Safari Suite, Viva Espana and Elvis Presley. Choose from genuine gorgeously ornate Romany caravans, all etched glass and decorated mirrors, or green 1960s vans done up with vintage wallpapers, nostalgic fabrics and old-fashioned puffy eiderdowns. Power showers are in the cow byre, where there's also a writing desk and arm-chairs; it's heated with paraffin stoves and lit by candles. The compost toilet is housed in an antique wooden shepherd's hut. Guests – often groups of friends – cook and eat in a communal red and white striped circus tent, decked out with funky sofas and Formica tables. Here, too, are a dressing-up box and retro games to keep the children amused. Hang out in a hammock or meditate in a tipi while the kids bounce on the trampoline or raid the sweet shop (found in another period caravan). Be advised that facilities are simple, hippy-ish even, but at night when bats swoop, owls hoot, and the only light come from oil lamps, candles, a glowing wood-fire and the stars, this is truly a magical part of the world.

Number Five

5 Havelock Place, Whitby, North Yorkshire YO21 3ER (01947 606361). **Rates** *£46-£50.* **No credit cards.**
A clean, friendly guest house in the popular B&B quarter on West Cliff. Pleasingly unchintzy, its seven bedrooms are mostly en suite, furnished with old pine and iron bedsteads; under-fives are accommodated free in their parents' room. Breakfast is served in a basement dining room, crammed with ephemera that ranges from old tin advertising signs to an ancient rocking horse.

Raven Hall Hotel

Raven Hall, Ravenscar, Scarborough, North Yorkshire YO13 0ET (01723 870353/ www.ravenhall.co.uk). **Rates** *£65-£84* **Credit** MC, V.
At the southern end of Robin Hood's Bay, perched on a dauntingly high clifftop, this gaunt stone 52-en suite bedroom pile wins no prizes for fine dining or contemporary styling. The setting, however, is amazing. It's surrounded by ten acres of landscaped grounds, and the fabulous views are made much of, particularly in the Panoramic Room restaurant. Big on conferences, corporates

and weddings (there's a medieval banqueting hall), the hotel also lays on a good break for families. Staff can help to arrange all sorts of activities, including pony trekking, trail riding and llama trekking. With an indoor swimming pool, croquet lawn, tennis courts, nine-hole golf course, battlements and an eccentric history (it provided a retreat for King George III in his madness), Raven Hall has all the ingredients for a fun weekend. Cots can be provided if you put in a request at the time of booking, but there's no baby listening service or children's activities. Children's portions are available in the restaurant from 6.30pm onwards, or you can choose from the bar food menu if the kids get peckish before then.

Robin Hood Bay Holiday Cottages
4 Princess Place, Whitby, North Yorkshire YO21 1DZ (01947 821803/07721 630294/www.robinhoodsbaycottages.co.uk). **Rates** £50-£650. **No credit cards**.
This small local agency offers a good selection and high standard of self-catering cottages. Star turns include the Studio, in Robin Hood's Bay, which has views towards Fisherhead from the front and stunning sea and coastal views from the back and side windows. It's perfect for children, with a secluded garden and a decking area that overlooks the sea. The second double bedroom has bunk beds and a single. All of the holiday cottages are well equipped – a fridge freezer, washing machine, telly and DVD player comes as standard. Some of the cottages have games, toys and equipment, including high chairs, travel cots and stairgates, so call to to discuss what you're after.

Shoreline Cottages
Exhibition House, Grape Street, Leeds LS10 1BX (0113 244 8410/www.shoreline-cottages.com). **Rates** £350-£1550. **Credit** MC, V.
Choose from 18 superior, well-equipped self-catering cottages in Whitby and attractive local villages. The decor is cool and contemporary, and most locations have fabulous sea or river views. Cots and high chairs are provided free on request, but you'll need to pack your own baby monitor and toys. One of the most gorgeous and spacious options is Bakehouse Cottage, a Grade II listed building. Tucked away in a quiet yard only a hundred metres from Whitby's bustling quayside, it sleeps eight.

White Horse & Griffin
87 Church Street, Whitby, North Yorkshire YO22 4BH (01947 604857/www.whitehorseandgriffin.co.uk). **Rates** £60-£200. *Cottages* £95-£340. **Credit** MC, V.
This former coaching inn, only a short stroll away from the Abbey ruins, is Whitby's most atmospheric hotel. The main building was built in 1681, and positively creaks with age. Downstairs is dark, moody and candlelit, but the antique

charm stops with the staircase: the ten bedrooms, which including a family room, are smartly furnished and equipped with CD players, TVs and bathrobes. Nearby are three family-sized cottages and the tiny one-bedroom Boathouse, a romantic eyrie with a deck right over the water. Cots can be provided at a cost of £10 a night, and there are a few games in the main lounge. Specials in the cosy candlelit restaurant/bistro major on fresh seafood, brought in to town daily by the local fisherman; moules marinière are a good bet, but there are meat and vegetarian options too.

WHERE TO EAT & DRINK
Bridge Cottage Café
East Row, Sandsend, North Yorkshire YO21 3SU (01947 893111). **Meals served** *Apr-Oct* 9.30am-7pm daily. *Oct-Dec, Feb* (closed Jan) 9.30am-4.30pm Wed-Sun. **Main courses** £7.75-£9.75. **Credit** MC, V.
A pretty little whitewashed cottage with a sweet garden, over the bridge and set back from the road on the edge of Mulgrave Woods. It's a good stop for light meals, soups, snacks and sandwiches with a separate menu for children. They can start the day with sausage, bacon and scrambled eggs on toast or muffins with jam; for lunch, there's soup, ham and cheese salad, toasties, pizza or 'real' fish fingers and chips, with ice-cream or chocolate brownies to round off proceedings (£3.45-£4.95).

Chocolate Falls
153 Church Street, Whitby, North Yorkshire YO22 2BH (01947 604192/07900 957933). **Open** *Summer* 9am-9pm daily. *Winter* 9.30am-5pm daily. **No credit cards**.
The perpetual cascade of melted chocolate often has a crowd of children glued to the window. About turn and cross to the other side if you want to avoid temptation, or indulge in a kebab of strawberries or marshmallow, expensively dipped in melted chocolate. Sadly, you don't get to dip yourself – the staff do it for you. No fun at all!

Endeavour
1 High Street, Staithes, North Yorkshire TS13 5BH (01947 840825/www.endeavour-restaurant.co.uk). **Dinner served** 7-9pm Tue-Sat. **Main courses** £12.25-£16.95. **Credit** MC, V.
With only 14 covers, a Friday or Saturday night table at the Endeavour is one of the hottest dining tickets along the coast. Book in advance to dine here on turbot, halibut, haddock, pollack and local shellfish, landed by Staithes' cobbles or Whitby's inshore fleet. Dishes are unfussy, so the quality of the fish shines through. There are some meat options (including excellent steaks) and a vegetarian dish or two. Children can order one of the starters as a main, or have a smaller portion of one of the main menu offerings. Desserts impress, with crème brulée, port jelly, own-made ice-creams and chocolates with confidence.

Whitby

WATERWORLD

On a cold grey day, the North Sea could not be less inviting. Few yachts sail the waters around Whitby. This wrecking coast has a chequered history of heroic lifeboat rescues and tragedy. But when the sun comes out and the wind drops, the sea turns blue and you're safe to take to the water.

On the quays north of the swing bridge, the old Whitby lifeboat, Mary Ann Hepworth (www.oldlifeboat whitby.co.uk); along with the small replica of Captain Cook's Endeavour (01723 364100, www.endeavour whitby.com) and the bright yellow Esk Belle II (01947 601385, www. whitbycoastalcruises.co.uk) are all ready to carry you out to sea. If the tides are right and the sea is calm, the Esk Belle II offers evening cruises round the bay or to Staithes and back.

Whitby also has a dozen licensed boat owners who run fishing trips. These can last from between two hours to two days, with bait and rods provided. The local wrecks have some hefty ling, cod and conger eel. At Staithes, Sean Baxter runs family-friendly fishing, sunset and birding trips aboard All My Sons (01947 840278, www.sea-angling-staithes.co.uk). Feathered attractons include nearby colonies of kittiwake, gannet, cormorant, razorbill and puffin. Global warming has brought recent local sightings of porbeagle sharks, dolphins and minke whales.

Don't let the sharks stop you making the most of the surf. Body boards and surf gear are available from Zero Gravity (01947 820660) in Flowergate, and to buy or hire at the Surf Shop in Saltburn (01287 625321, www.saltburnsurf.co.uk), where they also run a surf school suited to youngsters, on a gently shelving beach. There is more good surf at Skinningrove, Sandsend and Whitby. Strictly for experts, Staithes has a 'world class rolling barrel' which crashes on to Penny Steel, a reef of highly dangerous rocks.

Less intrepid souls can hire a canoe or rowing boat with Ruswarp (01947 604658, www.ruswarp-pleasure-boats.co.uk). Paddle upstream on a lovely stretch of the Esk, looking out for heron and kingfisher, tie up for tea at the century-old wooden tea hut at Perry's Garden Centre at Sleights, then idle back downstream.

Back in Whitby, The Grand Turk, a replica 18th-century man o' war, is usually berthed in Endeavour Wharf; clamber aboard to see the captain's quarters, climb into hammocks, and watch the cannon firing.

If you want no more to do with water than to dangle a line in it, try baiting a crab line with a morsel of bacon and holding out for a bucketful of shore crabs. Rock angling – fishing from the shore – for cod and whiting is permitted on the lower part of the west pier (check that no safety restrictions are in operation) and on the beach. An area by the swing bridge is reserved especially for children's fishing.

The river Esk is Yorkshire's premier salmon and sea trout river. Fishing in the tidal stretch of the river is banned, but you can fish from the Weir at Ruswarp with a licence (from the post office or 0870 850 6506, www.environment-agency.gov.uk) and a permit. Day permits are available from Mill Beck in Ruswarp (The Carrs, 01947 604658) or from the boat shed. Sleights has a fish pass (which lets them swim upstream): the fish do this in October and November, so this is the time to see one of nature's most fascinating shows.

Fox & Hounds

Goldsborough, North Yorkshire YO21 3RX (01947 893372). **Meals served** noon-2pm, 6.30-8.30pm Wed-Sat; 6.30-8.30pm Sun. **Main courses** £9-£18. **Credit** MC ,V.

It's well worth the five-mile drive north to Goldsborough for the district's first and finest gastropub, now nationally acclaimed. The board outside proclaims that 'Everything is fabulous', and so it is. On the menu are pea and mint risotto, ham hock terrine, turbot, halibut, crab and lobster, and chef Jason Davies exploits the best of local ingredients with deceptively simple skill. This place is genuinely welcoming to children (there's a toy box in the back room and a rocking horse in the hall), and will adapt most items on the menu. Sirloin steak with herb butter and fat chips needed no compromising for some recent small diners, who wrote in the visitor's book that it was the best they'd ever had.

Green's

13 Bridge Street, Whitby, North Yorkshire YO22 4BG (01947 600284/www. greensofwhitby.com). **Meals served** *Summer* 6-10pm Mon-Thur; noon-2pm, 6-10pm Fri, Sat; noon-3pm, 6.30-9.30pm Sun. *Winter* 6.30-10pm Mon-Thur; noon-2pm, 6.30-10pm Fri, Sat; noon-3pm, 8-9.30pm Sun. **Main courses** £13-£22. **Credit** MC, V.

Just over the swing bridge on the Abbey side of town, this enticing, intimate restaurant serves the best seafood in Whitby. Rob Green buys straight from the quay and sources his fish by the boat that landed it. Turbot, brill, halibut, crab and lobster are all in their prime, and there is also good local beef, ham and game. Children are welcomed and Green's will happily simplify and adapt the menu, – not that anyone needs to minimize a sticky toffee pudding with own-made ice-cream.

Magpie Café

14 Pier Road, Whitby, North Yorkshire YO21 3PU (01947 602058/www.magpiecafe.co.uk). **Meals served** *Mar-Nov* 11.30am-9pm daily. *Dec, Feb* 11.30am-9pm Mon-Sat; 11.30am-6.30pm Sun. **Main courses** £6.95-18.95. **Credit** MC, V.

Whitby fish and chips are legendary. So, too, is the Magpie, famous for its no-booking policy and queues so long they have become politically contentious in the town. Some would argue there are better fish and chips in Whitby, but for a granny's parlour of a restaurant, classic views over the harbour from the bay window tables, cheerful waitresses, crisply battered cod and thick-cut chips, it's an essential stop. Haddock, plaice, skate, Whitby woof (catfish), Dover sole, lobster and crab come in resounding portions, served with white sliced bread and butter and a pot of tea. The children's menu offers sausage, egg, chips and beans, plus meatless dishes like vegetarian shepherd's pie or cheesy pasta (all around £4.95), with occasional specials on the blackboard.

Whitby

Children with grown-up tastes can order more polished dishes such as salmon Caesar salad, seafood chowder or lemon sole, with prices peaking at £8.95. Simple fare for toddlers such as soup or boiled eggs is also available – and you can't go wrong with a bowl of jelly and custard for dessert.

Mister Chips

68-69 Church Street, Whitby, North Yorkshire YO22 4AS (01947 604683/www. misterchipswhitby.co.uk). **Meals served** *Summer* 11.30am-9.30pm daily. *Winter* 11.30am-9pm Mon-Thur, Sun; 11.30am-9.30pm Fri, Sat. **Main courses** £5.45-£16.95 **Credit** AmEx, MC, V.
A smart and cheery little fish and chip shop and restaurant at the bottom of Church Street on the Abbey side of Whitby, popular with locals and boasting numerous awards – including the *Whitby Gazette*'s Chip Shop Challenge. Children's meals include cod pieces, sausages, fish fingers and beefburgers with chips, beans and a drink (£4). The restaurant is licensed , so you can wash your cod and chips down with a restorative glass of wine or two.

Moon & Sixpence

Marine Parade, Whitby, North Yorkshire YO21 1PR (01947 604416/821071). **Meals served** noon-10pm daily. **Main courses** £7.90-£16. **Credit** MC, V.
Sipping champagne and slurping oysters feels decadent for Whitby, but makes sense at this delightful bar and brasserie overlooking the harbour. Bar alternatives include steak sandwich, grilled mackerel or own-made burger and chips. In the evening the dining room opens up, and a pianist accompanies the appreciative noises of diners sampling crab gumbo, salt and pepper red snapper, stuffed sea bass and steak from the daily changing menu. Dishes can be adapted for children – or give them a thrill with snails or frogs' legs in garlic butter.

Royal Hotel

Runswick Bay, Saltburn-by-the-Sea, nr Whitby, North Yorkshire TS13 5HT (01947 840215). **Meals served** *Easter-Sept* noon-2pm daily, 6-8.30pm daily. *Oct-Easter* noon-2pm daily; 6 - 8.30 Fri-Sun (times vary in school hols). **Main courses** £6.95-£8.95. **Credit** MC, V.
The Royal occupies a prime site in the centre of Runswick village, with great views round the bay to Kettleness and out to sea. The bar menu is normally pub grub, with options for children including sandwiches, baked potatoes, plaice goujons, fish fingers, cheeseburgers and pasta specials. It's undoubtedly a child-friendly place, with high chairs, books and traditional games in the back bar – including Trivial Pursuit, Twister, Monopoly and draughts. If you're lucky you might catch local chef Lisa Chapman (owner of To Dine For, *see below*) serving one of her evening three

course specials in the upstairs dining room. These take place once every six weeks or so, and are probably better for older children who will appreciate the grub. Booking is essential.

Sanders Yard Restaurant

Sanders Yard, Church Street, Whitby, North Yorkshire YO22 4BH (01947 825010/www.sandersyard.co.uk). **Meals served** 9am-5pm daily. **Main courses** £3.95-£7.50. **Credit** MC, V.
Venture down a cobbled passageway to find picturesque Sanders Yard, tucked away behind the Shepherd's Purse emporium opposite the market cross. The Yard has a simple menu of light meals, soups, sandwiches and snacks, with an impressive variety of delicious cakes. The comfy sitting room is particularly welcome on days when bustling Church Street becomes all too much. Bliss out on the sofa with tea, cake and newspapers, aiming small children at the box of toys.

Sandside Café

Runswick Bay, North Yorkshire TS13 5HT (no phone). **Meals served** *Easter-Sept* 10am-5.30pm daily. **Main courses** £2.95-£3.85. **No credit cards.**
This simple, flat-roofed hut is beautifully situated overlooking Runswick Bay. Although it doesn't serve hot food, it's a pleasant and useful stop-off for sandwiches, tea, cakes and scones, ice-creams and beach toys. Sit inside or take a tray out to the benches and admire the beautiful crescent beach stretching out below.

Sea Drift Café

Seaton Garth, Staithes, North Yorkshire TS13 5DH (01947 841345). **Meals served** *Summer* 10am-5pm daily. *Winter* times vary, phone to check. **Main courses** £2.50-£5.50. **No credit cards.**
A tiny but excellent little café on the harbourside, where you can sit inside or out to enjoy good own-made soup, sandwiches and fab cakes. Cinnamon-scented, apple-filled Coble cake is the star turn, served warm with cream. Coffee cake, chocolate cake, florentines and scones with cream are all good too. Children will soon spot the old fashioned sweets in glass jars behind the counter.

To Dine For

21 Porret Lane, Hinderwell, North Yorkshire TS13 5JT (01947 841321/www.todine for.org.uk). **Open** phone enquiries 24hrs daily. **Prices** on application. **No credit cards.**
Lisa Chapman, for twelve years the chef/patron of the Endeavour at Staithes (*see p279*), provides outside catering and superior take-aways. For a no-hassle holiday, stock up on Lisa's ready-prepared dishes or order quiches or pies for a superior picnic. She can bake a cake or make a dinner party – just let her know what you want.

Dracula Experience. *See p284.*

Trenchers

New Quay Road, Whitby, North Yorkshire YO21 1DH (01947 603212/www.trenchersrestaurant.co.uk). **Meals served** *Summer* 11.30am-8.30pm Mon-Fri, Sun; 11.30am-9pm Sat. *Winter* noon-3pm Mon-Thur; noon-7.30pm Fri; noon-8pm Sat; noon-6pm Sun. **Main courses** £7.95-£14.75. **Credit** MC, V.

For good fish and chips without the Magpie's queues (or atmosphere), this bright, bold room with trademark Tiffany lampshades offers a huge menu, a salad bar and small portions for children.

Wits End Café

Lythe Bank Bottom, Sandsend, Whitby, North Yorkshire YO21 3RJ (01947 893658/www.witsendcafe.co.uk). **Meals served** *Summer* 10am-5pm daily. *Winter* 10am-4pm Mon, Tue, Thur-Sun. **Main courses** £2.95-£10. **Credit** AmEx, DC, MC, V.

Clapboard cosiness close to the slipway and the main pay-and-display car park. Pull in for espresso, cappuccino, Yorkshire ice-cream, snacks on toast and great cakes. Sit outside and close your eyes as the local ducks waddle blithely across the busy main road to reach their beck.

PLACES TO SEE, THINGS TO DO

Captain Cook Memorial Museum

Grape Lane, Whitby, North Yorkshire YO22 4BA (01947 601900/www. cookmuseumwhitby.co.uk). **Open** *Mar* 11am-3pm daily. *Apr-Oct* 9.45am-5pm daily. **Admission** £4; £3 5-16s; £10.50 family (2+2); free under-5s. **Credit** MC, V.

It's hard to avoid the salty Captain Cook, explorer, navigator, cartographer and one-time haberdasher's apprentice of Staithes. His statue surveys the world from atop the West Cliff, and it's easy to imagine him as a young man, striding purposefully through these streets. Amid the numerous Cook trails, the best starting point is his former lodging house in Grape Lane, which has been converted into a small but impressive museum. There's a fascinating collection of exhibits about Cook's Whitby years, when he learnt his seaman's skills. The quaint old house is a most appealing example of an 18th-century shipowner's dwelling, with a sloping back yard leading from its cellar all the way to the edge of the river Esk, from where Whitby-built ships were serviced and repaired. Cook lodged in the spacious attic and studied under a roof formed from old

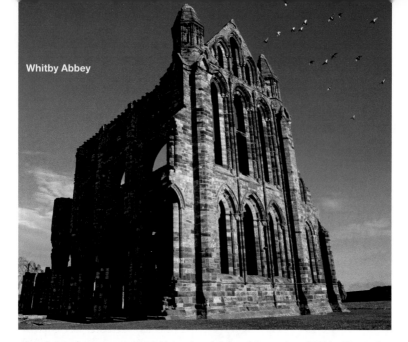

Whitby Abbey

ship's timbers. A programme of activities at the museum includes a family fun day, which this year is part of the Captain Cook Festival and takes place with much face painting and sea-shanty singing on 28 May 2007. In the school-holidays there's storytelling, music and exhibit handling – there's a vicious-looking cat o' nine tails that sends shivers down the spine.

Dracula Experience

9 Marine Parade, Whitby, North Yorkshire YO22 3PR (01947 601923). **Open** *Nov-Mar* 11am-5pm Sat, Sun (also Easter and Christmas hols). *Apr-Jul* 10am-5pm daily. *Jul, Aug* 10am-9pm daily. *Sept, Oct* 10am-5pm Sat, Sun. **Admission** £1.95; £1.50 5-16s, concessions; £6 family (2+2); free under-5s. **No credit cards.**

This is no literary exploration of Bram Stoker's gothic novel, but it is possibly more exciting. Scary models, spooky noises, coffins and live actors frighten the living daylights out of all; sensitive children beware. Whitby and *Dracula* are gently exploited in Whitby Walks' 'In Search of Dracula' with Harry Collett (01947 821734, www.whitbywalks.com). Mr Collett, an expert on Whitby, is entertaining on the subject of Dracula as he takes you round the landmarks. Goth Weekends (*see p335*) also focus on the legend.

Fortune's

Henrietta Street, Whitby, North Yorkshire YO22 4DW (01947 601659). **Open** Jan, Feb, Dec 9am-noon, 1.30-3pm Mon-Sat; 10am-noon, 1.30-2.30pm Sun. *Mar-Nov* 9am-3pm Mon-Sat; 10am-noon, 1.30-2.30pm Sun. **No credit cards.**

Another of the wonders of Whitby. You can buy fresh fish at a number of places in town, but the century-old smokehouse on Henrietta Street is the compulsory stop for a pair of oak-smoked kippers wrapped in newspaper. While you're buying these delicacies, peep into the unimaginably tarred blackness of the smokeroom.

Moors National Park Centre

Lodge Lane, Danby, Whitby, North Yorkshire, YO21 2NB (01439 772737/www. moors.uk.net). **Open** *Summer* 10am-5pm daily. *Winter* 11am-4pm Sat, Sun. **Admission** free. **Credit** (shop) MC, V.

A useful starting point for all sorts of information on the moors, staff at this Visitor Centre regularly run activity days for both adults and children. The shop has a great supply of maps and books and staff can also provide information about cycle routes and bridleways. There is a pleasant tearoom and a new, state of the art children's playground. Don't miss the bird hide in Crow Wood by the car park.

North York Moors Railway

(Customer services 01751 472508/Timetable 01751 473535/www.nymr.co.uk). **Open** phone for details. **Tickets** *Pickering-Grosmont* £11 single, £14 return; £8.50 single, £12 return concessions; £5.50 single, £7 return 5-15s; free under-5s. **Credit** MC, V.

One of the loveliest ways to appreciate the desolate beauty of the moors is from a railway carriage. The North York Moors Railway runs for 18 miles between Grosmont and Pickering, passing through a series of delightful stations and halts. Goathland is famous as the location for TV's

Heartbeat, and is transformed into Hogsmeade Station for the Harry Potter films. Newtondale Halt and Levisham stations are the starting point for some bracing walks. Grosmont, a 1950s railway junction, is where the enthusiasts gather to see restoration work in progress on the old locomotives in the engine shed. This station also has a café. The company run special themed weekends throughout the year: the *Thomas the Tank Engine* goes down very well with the youngest visitors – check the website to find out when Thomas will next puff on down. Otherwise, there are 'Return to the '60s' and 'Wizard Weekends' for the Potter fans.

St Mary's Church

Abbey Plain, East Cliff, Whitby, North Yorkshire YO22 4JR (01947 603421). **Open** *Summer* 10am-4pm daily. *Winter* 10am-3pm daily (weather permitting). **Admission** free.
Next to the Abbey and next to unmissable, this is one of the loveliest churches in England, reckoned Pevsner (who saw just about all of them). Who could argue? Its magnificent interior is like a great wooden ship, a jumble of galleries and high-sided box pews with a three-tiered pulpit and accompanying ear trumpet, all lit by candlelit and warmed by a roaring pot-bellied stove. The windswept cliff top graveyard – where Dracula met Lucy Westenra – is more chilling, with black rows of tombstones gradually being eroded by North Sea salt. See if you can find the epitaph to Francis and Mary Huntrodd, who were born on the same day, married each other and, 88 years later, died on the same day.

Whitby Museum

Whitby Jet Heritage Centre

123B Church Street, Whitby, North Yorkshire YO22 4DE (01947 821530/www.whitbyjet.co.uk). **Open** 10am-5pm daily.
Admission £1; free under-12s. **Credit** MC, V.
Not every jet shop in Whitby sells true Whitby jet. These days it's easier to import it than to find it in the cliffs, but when Queen Victoria wore black it meant big business for the town and the trade survives to this day. For the real thing, start at the little museum and workshop at the bottom of the 199 steps. Here you can see the black stone, carved from the fossils of the monkey puzzle tree, being ground and polished.

Whitby Abbey

Whitby, North Yorkshire YO22 4JT (01947 603568/www.english-heritage.org.uk). **Open** *mid Mar-Sept* 10am-6pm daily. *Oct* 10am-5pm daily. *Nov-mid Mar* 10am-4pm Mon, Thur-Sun.
Admission (EH); £4.20; £3.20 concessions; £2.10 under-16s; £10.50 family (2+3). **Credit** MC, V.
On a visit to Whitby Abbey, the headland on which it stands is the natural place to start. Pay for the car park and the entrance fee, then take your bearings over the town, harbour, and history. The monastery was founded in 657AD by Abbot Hild, and it was at Whitby Abbey that two thorny issues were finally resolved: the arcane formula for calculating the dates of Easter, and the style of pudding-bowl haircuts for monks. Should children (and adults) tire of old stones and early Christian doctrine, they can enjoy the interactive exhibits and 'hard garden' at the handsome Cholmley House, English Heritage's expensively restored visitor's centre.

Whitby Museum & Art Gallery

Pannett Park, Whitby, North Yorkshire YO21 1RE (01947 602908/www.whitbymuseum.org.uk). **Open** 9.30am-4.30pm Tue-Sun (also Mon Feb & Oct half term, bank hols). **Admission** £3; £2.50 concessions; £1 under-16s; £7 family (2+4). **No credit cards**.
Some glass-case museums are dull. Not the Pannett. It presents bizarre and breathtaking proof of Whitby's reach around the world and into history. Here a massive stuffed albatross, there a narwhal tusk and a Chinese pirate's pigtail. Native spears from the South Seas sit next to Eskimo canoes and a model ship in a light bulb. In the next case you might find a weather machine powered by leeches, or the macabre 'hand of glory', a robber's lucky charm – the pickled hand of a hanged man. To top it all is a world-beating collection of fossils: icthyosaurs, plesiosaurs, huge ammonites and the fearsome Jurassic crocodile, all locally found. The gallery has a collection by the Staithes Group, a set led by Harold and Dame Laura Knight, who captured the lives and tragedies of the local fishing families at the turn of the last century.

Whitby

Northumberland

Get back to nature.

It's no surprise that sections of the Harry Potter films were shot
in Northumberland: it really is a magical place both for children and
adults. Not only are there fabulous castles to explore, but also miles
and miles of sandy beaches, clean sea, picturesque villages, great
walks and a host of other outdoor and indoor activities.

As Northumberland is the most northerly region on the east coast
of England, people living in more populous areas tend to regard it
as being a bit remote. In fact, it's served by the east coast rail route,
and Berwick-upon-Tweed, the county's farthest flung outpost, is easily
reached by train from London. There's also a perception that it's much
colder here than in the south. It's cooler, yes, but look on it as a
refreshing escape from the humidity of the cities. What's more, it
rains much less here than in the west.

The pace of life is pleasingly slow. This is an area built round farming
and fishing, and its people are markedly down to earth, unflappable
and welcoming to visitors. After all, they have plenty of space to share
– Northumberland is the least densely populated county of England,
and there are five times as many sheep as there are people.

Bamburgh Castle

Blessed peace at **Holy Island** – apart from the tourists, that is.

Berwick-upon-Tweed makes a great base for touring the Northumberland coast. Family-friendly attractions are plentiful in and around the town, and Alnwick Castle (*see p296*), famed for its Harry Potter connection, is only 40 minutes away by car.

Rich in history, Berwick is an extremely attractive town. Not only does it have a seaside location, but the River Tweed flows through it. The three bridges that span the river, with the red roofs of the town's Georgian buildings stacked around them, combine to make a winning view.

To appreciate Berwick at its best, stroll round the Elizabethan walls. It doesn't take long, and there are steps back down into the town centre at various points. From this vantage point, the bridges can be admired properly. The red sandstone Old Bridge, also known as Berwick Bridge, was built between 1611 and 1634 and has 15 arches. Next came the Royal Border Bridge, an impressive rail viaduct that was designed by Robert Stephenson and opened by Queen Victoria in 1850. The concrete Royal Tweed 'New Bridge' was built in 1928; much of the traffic for which it was designed now takes the Berwick bypass, avoiding the town altogether.

Berwick was a Royal Burgh of Scotland in 1120 and has a stormy history; during the many centuries of Border warfare it changed hands no fewer than 13 times, the last being in 1482. The border is now a couple of miles north of Berwick on the A1, and it's quite easy to hop in the car and go and snap each other standing to attention beside the Welcome to Scotland and Welcome to England signs.

Although it's still a popular holiday town, Berwick is spoiled by its town centre which, like many a modern British town, has a surfeit of charity and downmarket shops on its main street. You have to dig deeper to find any decent independents for souvenirs – try West Street and Bridge Street, which are just off the main drag. It's not such a chore finding somewhere to eat; thankfully, Berwick has lots of good, child-friendly cafés and restaurants.

Place of pilgrimage

No visit to Northumberland would be complete without a trip to Holy Island, otherwise known as Lindisfarne. Only 20 minutes' drive from Berwick, the island is linked to the mainland by a long causeway, accessible only at low tide. The island is famous for being the first seat of Christianity in England, and also for its picturesque 16th-century castle (*see p297*). Built to guard the English-Scottish border, it was later restored by Sir Edward Lutyens as an Edwardian country house, with a lovely garden designed by Gertrude Jekyll.

As well as a visit to the castle, spend some time in the spooky ruins of the ancient priory, before repairing to the excellent, but sadly seasonal, Café Bean Goose (Selby House, Holy Island, 01289 389083), which has a pretty sheltered garden at the back, and a great line in fresh-baked scones and cakes, organic lunches and satisfying teas.

Locally, the island has been known as Holy Island ever since a murderous attack on the monastery by the Vikings in 793AD. After the monks were slaughtered, it was said that the place had been 'baptised in the blood of so many good men' that it was truly a Holy Island. Now tourists are the only invaders, and the tiny population of just over 150 inhabitants is swelled by an influx of over 500,000 visitors from all over the world every year.

The island is a joy to explore: small (only two square miles) but full of interest. Walk from the harbour, with its quirky upturned-boat huts, to the fascinating castle. Past the disused lime kilns is the northern shore and its wide sandy beach, where children love playing hide-and-seek and flying kites. The quaint village has some interesting little shops, where you can buy the monks' honeyed Lindisfarne Meade. Always pay close attention to the safe crossing times on display at the causeway. The tide comes

Northumberland

in extremely rapidly, and every year catches out a number of foolish tourists who have tried their luck and have to be rescued from their sodden cars.

Bring your wand

Looking across from Holy Island, along the Northumberland coast, the imposing outline of Bamburgh Castle (*see p297*) dominates the coastline. Built on a massive basalt outcrop, this fantastic fortification overlooks undulating dunes and miles of sandy beach. The little village below the castle is ridiculously picturesque, its shortbread-box cosiness a stark contrast to the grim fortress that towers above.

Bamburgh was once the ancient capital of Northumberland, and is the cradle of the county's history. A castle was first built here in the 6th century by the Saxon Monarch Ida. It was followed by the kingdom's first church, built in AD635 by St Aidan and King Oswald, a Christian convert. The present fine Norman church, which dates from the 12th century, is throught to have been built on the site of the original.

There's an effigy of the heroic Grace Darling in the church, and her grave is in the churchyard. Born in 1815, Grace was the daughter of the keeper of the Longstone lighthouse on the nearby Farne Islands. When a violent storm swept the *Forfarshire*, a steamship heading for Dundee, onto the rocks, Grace and her father rowed a boat through the heaving seas to the wreck and rescued nine passengers. The 23-year-old's heroism fired the imagination of the British public and she became a heroine. She died just four years later of TB. Opposite the church, the RNLI-run Grace Darling Museum contains the original 21ft rescue boat, a Northumberland fishing cobble. Currently undergoing major building work, it's due to re-open in late 2007 – call the RNLI for updates (0845 122 6999).

In true best-kept village style, Bamburgh also maintains a good cricket pitch, tearooms, pubs with beer gardens, a proper butcher's, various gift shops and a plant nursery.

A few miles to the north, Budle Bay is a twitchers' and golfers' paradise. The birding fraternity make their own pilgrimages to this, the esturarine southern section of English Nature's Lindisfarne National Nature Reserve, whose varied bird life is legendary. The receding tide reveals extensive mud and sand flats, and is a safe haven for wintering wildfowl. At last count the bay sustained about 225 species, including wigeon, shelduck, teal and shovellers. The golf course, on the high ground above the bay, is considered one of the most beautifully sited in England.

A couple of miles south along the coast lies Seahouses, where many visitors dig in for the duration of their holiday. It's easy to see why; the place is well set up for a family break, with great beaches, decent fish and chip restaurants, cosy cafés, pubs, good ice-cream and souvenir shops, not to mention a pretty harbour, from which daily boat trips set out to the Farne Islands to spot grey seals and birdlife.

There has been a harbour here since 1318, if not earlier, and fishing has long been the lifeblood of the town. It is said that the world's first kipper was produced in Seahouses, when someone absentmindedly left their split herrings in a shed where a fire was burning.

Fishing vessels as well as tourist boats work out of the harbour. Some combine the two moneyspinners: sea fishing trips can be enjoyed by all but the very young. The RNLI lifeboat station is a reminder that this isn't easy sailing water – there are treacherous rocks off the mainland. The station is open to the public (01665 721604, www.seahouseslifeboat.org.uk). On display is the modern offshore lifeboat named after local heroine Grace Darling. From the sublime to the ridiculous; just beyond the lifeboat station is the town's very popular and well-designed crazy golf course – truly addictive, we find.

South of Seahouses lies the little village of Beadnell, whose small harbour and 18th-century lime kilns sit sweetly alongside a magnificent sheltered sandy beach. At the end of Beadnell Bay is the charming Low Newton-by-the-Sea. Along with its lovely beach, the village is almost entirely owned by the National Trust (no penthouse flats with stunning views round here, thank you very much). The Trust also owns five miles

Northumberland

of the surrounding Northumberland coast, including the beach at Embleton Bay. Recommended in the Marine Conservation Society (MCS) Good Beach Guide, these beaches are not only clean and sheltered, but have fantastic views of the romantic medieval ruins of Dunstanburgh Castle. Wildlife watchers are rewarded with the sight of hundreds of toads feeding on insects on the beach in summer evenings and there are well-maintained hides for birdwatchers at Newton Pool Bird Reserve.

There is nothing much in the way of shops and cafés, but the Ship Inn here (01665 576262) serves hot meals, good beer and is family-friendly. Ramblers can explore footpaths going north to Beadnell or south to Craster, another picturesque village that's famous for its kippers.

The busy market town of Alnwick is about 15 minutes' drive inland. As well as being home to Alnwick Castle and Garden (see p296), the town also has a number of secondhand book shops, housed in the old train station building. Barter Books (Alnwick Station, 01665 604888, www.barterbooks.co.uk) has a good children's section, and a little toy train chugs round a long track suspended from the ceiling. Browsers are encouraged with armchairs and fresh coffee and biscuits, payable by donation.

Nearer the coast is the delightful town of Warkworth, also dominated by its castle (see p297). It's lovely to walk along the riverbank or row along the River Coquet

in one of the boats on hire just below the castle. Some small galleries and interesting shops add to the town's charm.

Alnmouth lies on the coast, and has a pretty beach and bracing cliff walks. The town is quite well-to-do, so is well served with gift shops and galleries for souvenir shopping. It's hard to believe that in 1748 Methodist John Wesley described this now rather sedate little place, with its clean streets and well-maintained buildings as 'famous for all kinds of wickedness', but in his era – pre-custom house days – Alnmouth was a big smuggling centre, and Wesley wasn't big on life's little comforts.

WHERE TO STAY

Beadnell Towers Hotel

Beadnell, Chathill, Northumberland NE67 5AU (01665 721211/www.beadnelltowers.com). **Rates** £65-£133. **Credit** MC, V.

Tucked away in the centre of the village, the Towers has no views to speak of, but the sea and picturesque harbour are only a few minutes' walk away. The hotel's exterior is fairly unprepossessing, but inside it is cosy and comfortable, with a big open fire in the lounge. Family rooms are bright and roomy, and the rainbow curtains and bedcovers are obviously designed to appeal to children. Indeed, the hotel gets many repeat bookings because children love the rooms so much. You'll need to bring your own cot, however. The food is good – so much so that locals bring their families here for bar meals. The menu is the same in the large, book-ahead dining room and spacious

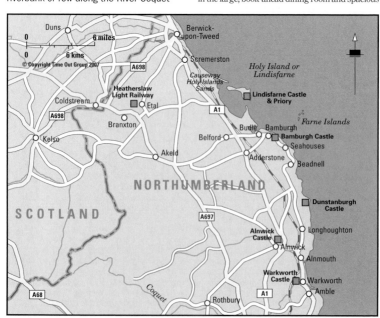

Pot-a-Doodle Do Wigwam Village

BOREWELL

lounge; dishes of note include cod in Northumbrian nettle cheese sauce, Beadnell Bay lobster and roasted Jenny of Northumbrian lamb with honey, mint and thyme. Children can order a half-portion of what's on the menu for a flat £6 rate, or go down the well-worn nugget/pizza/fish goujons route for £5.25 on the children's menu. Breakfasts are worth getting up for, with a choice of cereals, fruit and juice followed by scrambled eggs with smoked salmon, Seahouses kippers or a full English with very good quality sausage, black pudding and bacon. Just what's needed to set you up for a good walk along the bay to Dunstanburgh Castle.

Gainslawhill Farm Cottage

Gainslawhill Farm, Berwick-upon-Tweed, Northumberland TD15 1SZ (01289 386210/ www.gainslawhill.co.uk). **Rates** £300-£450/wk. **No credit cards.**
Children and pets are welcome at this lovely cottage, which has its own walled garden and looks out over the River Tweed to the Cheviot hills. Part of a 300-acre farm (mostly arable, but with 40 cows and 200 sheep), the cottage is comfortable and tastefully decorated, with a well-equipped kitchen diner and three bedrooms; a travel cot is available. Short breaks are available in low season, as well as the usual weekly hire throughout the year. Children enjoy the hour-long Farm Walk, and there are several excellent walks off the farm, following the rivers in each direction.

Pot-a-Doodle Do Wigwam Village

Borewell, Scremerston, Berwick-upon-Tweed, Northumberland TD15 2RJ (01289 307107/ www.potadoodledo.com). **Rates** £13-£17; £7.50-£9 children. **No credit cards.**

Pot-a-Doodle Do Wigwam Village at Scremerston is the only establishment of its kind in the area. The village, which consists of 12 wooden wigwams, goes down a treat with children. In fact, all the family like the set up because it offers all the joys of camping (cheapness, fresh air and a sense of adventure) with none of the discomforts (basic facilities, the cold and a sense of incipient rheumatism). The dozen wigwams, more like little chalets, sleep up to five and are all insulated and double-glazed. They have electric lights and a fridge as well as foam mattresses, so all you need to bring are the sleeping bags. There's a clean shower and toilet block on site, as well as a communal kitchen and eating area. Even more fun is the barbecue hut; a wooden tipi with benches and furs to recreate the thrill of the Wild West. This can be booked for the evening and staff will light the indoor barbecue, so all guests have to do is grill their meal and relax. Breakfasts with a Wild West theme are available at the very nice café/restaurant and there is a play park on site as well as an arts and crafts activity centre (*see p297*). The beach is nearby and the village is handy for Holy Island and Bamburgh. The restaurant is licensed and has a cosy, rustic interior filled with the smells of homebaking – prices start at £1.30 for a scone with jam and cream, but more substantial snacks, baguettes and freshly-made main meals are also available. The whole place is closed in January.

Seafield Caravan Park

Seahouses, Northumberland NE68 7SP (01665 720628/www.seafieldpark.co.uk). **Rates** from £205/3 nights (4-6 people). **Credit** MC, V.
This plush caravan settlement won holiday park of the year in 2005 in the North East of England Tourism Awards. Well deserved, we reckon; the

Beadnell Bay:
a perfect spot
for sandcastles
or windsurfing.

The little harbour
at **Seahouses**
(opposite). For
both, *see p289*.

park is extremely clean, and the grass so well kept that it would be suitable for the Ryder Cup. Both children and adults love the facilities, which include a swing park, a spick and span swimming pool and the Ocean Club health and beauty club, which helps happy campers to maintain a well-honed face and body in the face of those whipping north-easterly winds. Prices for caravan parking include the club facilities (although beauty treatments are extra) and gas and electricity. The newly-built coffee shop will provide a warming soup of the day for £2.95 and a bacon baguette for £1.95. Then there are panini, tortilla wraps and a fine platter of cakes and traybakes for afters. The café is licensed, which is another bonus. In the immaculate caravans, thoughtful welcome packs include coffee, tea, sugar, milk, bread and butter, as well as mod cons such as a DVD player and TV with six satellite stations. Each little homestead possesses its own patio and picnic table and the park has a well-equipped centrally heated launderette. You're right in the centre of the village here, just across the road from the harbour.

Victoria Hotel

Front Street, Bamburgh, Northumberland NE69 7BP (01668 214431/www.victoriahotel. net). **Rates** £100-£150. **Credit** AmEx, MC, V.
Set in possibly the most picturesque village in Northumberland, the Victoria is a perfect base for a break in the area. Bamburgh's fantastic beach and castle are within minutes of the hotel, which has been refurbished to an extremely high standard. In keeping with its stately exterior, the interior is graceful but still offers modern comforts. Family rooms are spacious and beautifully decorated, with en suite bathrooms and flatscreen TVs. One offers luxurious sleigh beds (a double and two singles); the other has an interconnecting double and twin-bed room. The hotel keeps two cots for younger visitors (book one before you turn up!) and has baby-monitors, so parents can relax downstairs. There are two comfortable lounges for residents, one with internet access and the other with a large widescreen TV and boxes of board games. Guests dine beneath a domed glass atrium in the brasserie or adjoining lounge bar; the latter has a simpler menu, but the food served in both is excellent. Main courses use seasonal produce from suppliers and growers in north Northumberland, and signature dishes in the brasserie include a rack of spring lamb from the delightfully-named Glororum Farm. A children's menu of simple fare like plaice and chips and pizza is available; otherwise they can have half portions of the posher food. The lovely lounge bar's wide-ranging menu also has some child-friendly options such as scampi and chicken curry, and is where the not-to-be-missed breakfast is served, with award-winning sausages from the village butcher. The hotel has a garage and is happy to store bikes and kayaks, and has an arrangement with the privately-owned Seafield Ocean club in Seahouses for the use of its new swimming pool, gym and sauna at a minimal daily charge.

West Coates Bed & Breakfast

30 Castle Terrace, Berwick-upon-Tweed, Northumberland TD15 1NZ (01289 309666/ www.westcoates.co.uk). **Rates** £100. **Credit** AmEx, V.
So gorgeous that it has a gold award from the tourist board, West Coates is a luxurious place to get away from it all. The big Georgian house sits in two acres of beautiful gardens – the scene of many a genteel croquet match in the summer. Older children like playing on the swing rigged up in one of the larger trees (it's not suitable for under-fives). The Pool House, containing a large indoor swimming pool and hot tub, is a huge draw, and children are welcome to swim at any time (under parental supervision). Karen Brown, the proprietor, is a serious cook, so children's convenience food is a no-no. In fact the excellent cooking is a major attraction – dinner, should you opt for it, might include seafood canapés, roast monkfish and warm chocolate tart (£35 a head). A wonderful bonus is that Karen gives cookery classes for adults and children (by arrangement). The bedrooms are tastefully furnished and have TVs and CD players, but no cots. It's safe to surmise that it's older children and teens – especially those who appreciate good tuck – who will get the most out of this place. Other thoughtful touches in the rooms include fresh flowers, Crabtree & Evelyn toiletries, Egyptian cotton sheets and a collection of books and magazines. Packed lunches and picnic hampers are available with prior notice.

WHERE TO EAT & DRINK

Many of the organic and rare breed farms making a patchwork of the countryside around Berwick and Alnwick are open to visitors from February to about November. Places like Conundrum Farm and Oxford Farm near Berwick also have excellent shops and cafés, where produce from the fields is on the menu. For more on the agricultural attractions in the area, log on to www.farmshopping.com.

Carlo's

7-9 Market Street, Alnwick, Northumberland NE66 1SS (01665 602787). **Meals served** *Summer* 11.30am-10pm Mon-Sat. *Winter* 11.30am-2.30pm, 4-10pm Mon-Fri; 11.30am-10pm Sat. **Main courses** £2.25-£4.60. **No credit cards**.
This friendly town-centre chippy has been run by Italian Carlo Biagioni and his wife Laura for the past 15 years. It's a clean, modern-looking set up, with a thriving takeaway trade. All the fish comes from suppliers in the region. Cod and chips is the favourite dish, but haddock and plaice are on the menu too, along with sausages, pies and fishcakes; more unusual non-fishy items include haggis and smoked sausage. The chip buttie – a bargain £1.30 – comes highly recommended. The kids' menu has hotdogs, sausages, chicken nuggets, fish bites and fishcakes with chips for £2-£3.35.

BE A HARRY SPOTTER

Take your children to see the real Hogwarts Castle and they'll be spellbound. Alnwick Castle starred as Hogwarts in the first two Harry Potter films, and the castle is making the most of its newfound celebrity status. Its 'Battleaxes to Broomsticks' tours take you round the sites of some famous cinematic scenes, as well as recounting the stories of real-life local heroes.

In the first two Harry Potter films, many of the exterior shots of Hogwarts were of Alnwick, and its grounds appear in the scenes where the students are learning to ride their broomsticks, and again when the actors venture into the Enchanted Forest. The library and staterooms were also used.

Robin Hood, Prince of Thieves and *Blackadder*, also filmed here, get a mention too. Then it's back to real life with the story of Henry Percy (nicknamed Harry Hotspur), the most famous knight to live at the castle. A boy of action, he joined the army at the tender age of seven and became a knight at 11.

Once the tour has drawn to a close, children can become knights (or ladies) through the Knight's Quest roleplay. There's dressing up, swordfighting and jousting, after which they're eligible for a certificate pronouncing its holder to be a Knight or Lady of Alnwick Castle. The Dragon's Quest, introduced in summer 2006, involves youthful volunteers ridding Northumberland of a fearsome beast.

At peak times there's a magician in the grounds, as well as birds of prey which you can stroke and a court jester, whom you probably can't. Have-a-go archery sessions give parents a chance to say 'you'll have someone's eye out with that'.

With so many extra entertainments going on, it's tempting to forego a tour of the castle. Make time: the sumptuously decorated staterooms are splendid, and the battlements house various exhibitions.

All of the children's activities are included in the entry price, making it very good value for the parental pound. But there is one drawback – children are reluctant to leave, even if they're bribed with ice-creams and cakes in the courtyard bistro.

Mason's Arms

3 Dial Place, Warkworth, Northumberland NE65 0UR (01665 711398). **Meals served** noon-3pm, 5.30-9pm Mon-Sat; noon-3pm, 6-8.30pm Sun. **Main courses** £6.25-£14.95. **Credit** MC, V.

A pub that's as popular with the locals as the visitors is always a good bet. People with children like the Mason because there's a decent beer garden and a reliable – if unremarkable – food menu. The own-made steak pie, lasagne and chicken curry are popular favourites; hungry carnivores can plump for the large mixed grill with rump steak, lamb chops, sausage, black pudding, mushrooms and tomatoes. Simpler meals such as baked potatoes or baguettes might be a better choice for the children, rather than their own inexpensive (£3.10) but unimaginative menu.

Oaks Hotel

South Road, Alnwick, Northumberland NE66 2PN (01665 510014/www.theoaks hotel.co.uk). **Meals served** 11.30am-2.15pm, 5.30-9pm daily. **Main courses** £6.95-£17.25. **Credit** AmEx, MC, V.

Alnwick is a busy market town, and there are a number of hotels and cafés to choose from. One of the locals' favourites is the Oaks, which sits on the edge of town and has a patio, large bar and dining room. Starters include fish soup or grilled wood mushrooms and goat's cheese. Vegetarian options are more interesting than the norm, but the children's menu follows the well-trodden path of pizza, fish fingers and sausages (£3.50). Steak and ale pie is a hearty choice for hungry grown-ups, or there's the popular Lamb Jennings, a house speciality. This is a half shoulder of lamb, marinated in mint and garlic then slow cooked and served with a redcurrant and mint jus. The monumental mixed grill and steaks are worth a try, and fish lovers are also well catered for; seafood linguine, lemon sole and good old-fashioned scampi with tartare sauce are among the offerings.

The Red Lion

22 Northumberland Street, Alnmouth, Northumberland NE66 2RJ (01665 830584/ www.redlionalnmouth.co.uk). **Meals served** 9am-9pm Mon-Sat; 9am-3pm Sun. **Main courses** £6.95-£13.50. **Credit** MC, V.

This pub on the main street doesn't look much from the outside, but has a lovely long, sheltered beer garden with raised decking, where you can sit back and enjoy the sea views. Children are welcome and the food is freshly cooked. Fish dishes and roasts go down well, and not just because the prices are so reasonable (roast topside of beef with all the trimmings is £6.95; pan-fried cod and haddock £8.95). Portions are generous and come with a colourful selection of vegetables. The enormous seafood platter is always in demand, and there's also a decent lasagne or stilton and broccoli pasta bake. Panini are served with salad and coleslaw, with fillings such as hot beef, cajun chicken and

tuna and cheese. The children's menu includes pasta with cheese sauce as well as the usual sausages/fishfingers/scampi combination (£3.25). The pub has a cosy interior and offers the influential (on an empty stomach) Farne Island Ale.

PLACES TO SEE, THINGS TO DO

Alnwick Castle

Alnwick, Northumberland NE66 1NQ (01665 510777/www.alnwickcastle.com). **Open** *Apr-Oct* 10am-6pm daily. **Admission** £9; £8 concessions; £4 5-14s; £24 family (2+4); free under-5s. **Credit** MC, V.

Awarded a gold medal for its sterling work in the line of duty (attracting tourists), Alnwick is regularly besieged by excited children waving broomsticks. Why? *See p295* **Be a Harry Spotter.**

Alnwick Garden

Denwicklean, Alnwick, Northumberland NE66 1YU (01665 511350/www.alnwickgarden. com). **Open** *Apr, May, Oct* 10am-6pm daily. *June-Sept* 10am-7pm daily. *Nov-Mar* 10am-4pm daily. Last admission 45mins before closing. **Admission** £8; £7.50 concessions; free under-16s (up to 4 children per adult). **Credit** MC, V.

Fast becoming one of northern England's most popular tourist attractions, this enchanting garden has been created over the last few years on land beside the imposing Alnwick Castle (*see above*). Reminiscent of formal Italian gardens, the centrepiece is the Grand Cascade, the largest water feature of its kind in the country. Children enjoy dodging the spray as well as playing on the toy tractors at the foot of the cascade. Further distractions include the Bamboo Labyrinth maze and a giant treehouse – a wooden structure of turret-topped cottages, wooden bridges and suspended walkways, all accessed by a ramp. This is so far removed from the usual touristy gardens that it's sheer magic for children. There are, of course, gift shops and tearooms galore both in the gardens and at the treehouse.

Aqua-Trax

Seahouses Harbour, Northumberland (07803 006593/www.aqua-trax.co.uk). **Open** Apr-Oct. **Admission** £12/hr; £9/hr under-12s; £38/hr family (2+2). **No credit cards.**

High-octane, adrenaline-fuelled, white knuckle… You name the clichés, Aqua-Trax will provide the thrills, taking you on a zippy speedboat trip from Seahouses to the Farne Islands off the Northumberland coast. The 300 horsepower boat, which seats 12, has speeds of up to 50 miles an hour and reaches the islands much faster than conventional boats. That means there's plenty of time to see the seals (who come right up close to the boat), nesting puffins and other seabirds, as well as (if you're lucky) dolphins, porpoises and whales in the open sea. Skipper Lloyd Currie is a mine of information about the islands and wildlife, and stops near the lighthouse where local heroine Grace Darling lived. Currie can also tell stories of the ships that have come to grief on the rocks by the islands, and takes passengers to see the island St Cuthbert lived on until he died. If you're pushed for time there's a 30-minute 'fast blast' trip, but you really need longer to see the wildlife and islands properly. The optimum time for spotting puffins and nesting birds is from April until the end of July. The seals are there all year, but the best time for pups is the end of September and beginning of October. Visits to Holy Island are also available; phone for details. Warm clothing, waterproof jackets and trousers can be borrowed, and life jackets are supplied.

Bamburgh Castle

Bamburgh, Northumberland NE69 7DF (01668 214515/www.bamburghcastle.com). **Open** mid Mar-Oct. **Admission** £6.50; £2.50 6-15s; free under-5s. **Credit** *Shop* MC, V.
A fantastic structure dominating the local landscape, Bamburgh Castle is in impressive condition and gives a real taste of life in Britain's 'darker' ages. Inside, the huge echoey rooms yield a sobering armoury with old muskets, pikes, guns, swords and armour. Further down, a very creepy dungeon filled with rather graphic models of prisoners might cause the lips of the very young to wobble a tad. Don't miss the well, 50m deep, which used to double as an escape route; the exit from the tunnel is visible in the shrubbery outside the castle walls.

Heatherslaw Light Railway

Ford Forge, Heatherslow, Cornhill-upon-Tweed, Northumberland TD12 4TJ (01890 820244). **Open** Apr-Oct. **Admission** *Return ticket* £5.50; £4.50 concessions; £3.50 5-16s; £1 under-5s. **No credit cards.**
This 15in gauge steam railway runs from Heatherslaw, a tiny village west of Berwick-upon-Tweed, to Etal, an equally tiny village two miles away, making a return journey of 50 minutes. In Heatherslaw you can visit the corn mill, which still produces quality stoneground flour from locally-grown wheat. Mill produce is available in the gift shop, along with locally-baked bread, biscuits and cakes. There's also a coffee shop. At Etal there's a 14th-century castle and some tearooms in the village. Horse riding is available nearby at Kimmerston Riding Centre, and there are bicycles for hire at Heatherslaw Cycle Hire.

Lindisfarne Castle

Holy Island, Berwick-upon-Tweed, Northumberland TD15 2SH (01289 389244/ www.nationaltrust.org.uk). **Open** *Feb* daily; phone to check times. *Mid Mar-Oct* Tue-Fri; phone to check times. *Garden* 10am-dusk daily. **Admission** (NT) £5.80; £2.90 5-18s; £14.50 family (2+2); free under-5s. *Garden only* £1 suggested donation. **Credit** MC, V.

A romantic 16th-century castle with spectacular views, Lindisfarne was transformed into an Edwardian holiday home by renowned architect Sir Edward Lutyens. Sitting alone on a small hill on the edge of the island, the castle, seen from a distance, looks pretty much like an upturned ice-cream cone. This is probably the daintiest castle you will ever visit, and is in stark contrast to the monumental Bamburgh Castle which stands opposite on the mainland (*see above*). Inside are little rooms filled with beautiful furniture, where the children can enjoy spotting the tiny cellos and bows which hang from items of furniture as part of a quiz. It's also worth visiting the walled garden. Designed by Gertrude Jekyll, it's an oasis of colour and scent in the middle of a sheep field. Opening times depend on the tides, so call to check before planning a visit.

Pot-a-Doodle Do

Borewell Farm, Scremerston, Berwick-upon-Tweed, TD15 2RJ (01289 307107/www.pot adoodledo.com). **Open** *Easter-Oct* 10am-5pm daily. *Nov-Apr* 10am-4pm Wed-Sun. **Admission** phone for details.
This arts centre is great for rainy days and creative children, who can choose between painting figurines and glass, making mosaics or creating sand art. All the activities are designed for any age and ability, and staff are always on hand to help. Prices start from £6 for a figurine – choose which you want to paint. There's a play park outside and quad bike trekking for children aged ten and over (£16 for 30 minutes). The nearby licensed restaurant is a fine place for lunch, and you can stay the night in the Wigwam Village (*see p291*).

Warkworth Castle

Warkworth, Northumberland NE65 0UJ (01665 711423/www.english-heritage.org.uk). **Open** *Apr-Sept* 10am-5pm daily. *Oct* 10am-4pm daily. *Nov-Mar* 10am-4pm Mon, Sat, Sun. **Admission** (EH) £3.40; £2.60 concessions; £1.70 5-15s; £8.50 family (2+3); free under-5s. **Credit** MC, V.
The village of Warkworth sits in the shadow of this picturesque ruined castle and its polygonal three-storey keep, which dates from the 14th century. Although much smaller than the neighbouring Alnwick Castle (*see p296*), it's still worth a visit as the principal buildings have survived very well. If you visit on Sunday or Wednesday, a little boat will take you across the river Coquet to see the hermitage; here, the lords installed a holy man to pray for them. Carved out of the bedrock in the 14th century and originally consisting of a porch, chapel and sacristy, it's an impressive sight. The chapel is carved with rib vaulting, columns and an altar in imitation of actual masonry. No craft other than the little ferry is allowed to land there, but further down the river and nearer to the castle you can hire rowing boats and take a jaunt along the lovely river, just to round the day off.

Edinburgh

'Auld Reekie' loves the bairns.

It may be the seat of Scotland's parliament, and home to the world's most famous arts festival, but Edinburgh's real plus point for families is its manageable size. Many of the key attractions are within easy walking distance of each other, in the heart of either the Old or New Town, both of which were designated UNESCO World Heritage Sites in 1995. This architectural divide between the two parts of the city – the Old Town and the New Town – is also easy for any visitor to comprehend. For children of all ages, Scotland's capital means entertainment, in many forms, all year round. During the winter, Capital Christmas and Hogmanay provide the colour and spectacle, August means the Festival, and at other times a commendable collection of galleries, museums, expansive green spaces and living history provide the fun.

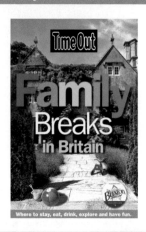

Edinburgh has been a citadel, a royal capital, the seat of philosophical debate, the crucible for the Protestant Reformation, Scotland's paean to Georgian architectural elegance and the location for some notorious murders. Unsurprisingly, she has adopted some odd nicknames over the years; perhaps the most aspirational is 'the Athens of the North', which refers to the architecture and accomplishments of her 18th-century thinkers, artists and businessmen. A less lofty moniker is 'Auld Reekie', after the fug from the coal fires that hung over the city and blackened many a monument. That name has fallen out of use in recent decades, as buildings have been cleaned and smokeless fuel controls imposed. Of course, the smoking ban of 2006, outlawing smoking in any enclosed public place in Scotland, has had a further defugging effect in cafés, restaurants and pubs, on public transport, in taxis, shopping malls and the like.

Another health-driven human rights law that exists north of the Border is the Breastfeeding Bill. Since March 2005, it has been a criminal offence for a mother to be harassed or otherwise prevented from breastfeeding her child (under the age of two years) in a public place or in licensed premises where children were previously welcomed (such as 'family friendly' pubs). This law also covers other carers bottlefeeding milk to their charges.

The charm of the Old

The original boundaries of the Old Town are fairly easy to plot, even on a modern map. To the north, the pestilential Nor' Loch (the North Loch) provided a natural city defence, until it was drained in the 18th century and Princes Street Gardens (and, much later, Waverley Station) were created. To the south, the boundary is marked by the Cowgate, but for further protection, where the Meadows parkland is now, lay the marshy Burgh Loch.

After the disastrous defeat of the Scots at Flodden in 1513, the Flodden Wall was contructed by the citizenry to defend the town from English depredations. It took 50 years to finish and effectively boxed in the town, taking in the then-separate parishes of Edinburgh and the Cowgate. The wall ran from the eastern bounds of the loch, up and over the Royal Mile, continuing south up the Pleasance and then west to the Castle Rock, along a route now marked by Drummond Street, Teviot Place, Lauriston Place and the West Port. Remnants still stand beside the private George Heriot's School, and to the east end of the Cowgate.

Hemmed in by the Flodden Wall, space in old Edinburgh was at a premium – and the citizens built upwards when they couldn't

build outwards. Between the towering Old Town buildings run gloomy-looking closes (narrow, covered alleyways that usually lead to a courtyard of some sort) and wynds (cramped, winding lanes leading off the main thoroughfares).

Many hold pleasant surprises: check out Trunk's Close, which opens into a public garden behind the Storytelling Centre (*see p313*), or go down Lady Stair's Close and read the extracts from some of Scotland's poets carved into the flagstones.

Even if you skim over the artefacts from pre-history, Viking visitations and Dark Age lives, the Old Town spans 1,000 years of history. Sights range from the millennium-old pillars housed in the High Kirk of St Giles on the High Street to the ultra-modern wood, rock and steel construction of the modish Scottish Parliament building at Holyrood. Many of the attractions in the Old Town occupy interesting buildings, so keep one eye on the façade of any place you visit. Gladstone's Land, for example, is a 16th-century equivalent of multi-storey living. The Clashach sandstone National Museum of Scotland building (*see p313*), meanwhile, manages to evoke millennia of building styles, yet retains a strong modern feel.

If you're not from Scotland – and even if you are – Edinburgh signposting can seem bizarre, particularly in the Old Town. A road may have a primary nomenclature, but it will be known by other names as you walk along it. Thus a stroll down the Royal Mile may also entail a trip along Lawnmarket, the High Street and the Canongate.

The grace of the New

The New Town was planned out with the Georgians' eye for symmetry and balance. The streets are wide here, and there is still a sense of spacious, gracious living in Moray Place, Royal Circus and surrounding areas. The New Town is home to the National Gallery of Scotland (*see p311*), the Scott Monument and the Georgian House.

Frederick Street and Howe Street take you into the realms of Stockbridge, once a distinct suburb of the city but now seen as part of the New Town. The area's delights include riverside walks, wonderful delis such as Herbies (66 Raeburn Place, 0131 332 9888) and Iain Mellis's famous cheese shop (492 Great Western Road, 0141 339 8998, www.ijmellischeesemonger.com).

Edinburgh

Here, too, you'll find the verdant expanse of Inverleith Park and access to the Royal Botanic Gardens (*see p314*).

You never need to walk too far for green space in this city. Edinburgh is built round acres of parklands, and you're seldom more than ten minutes' walk away from a green oasis, even in the heart of the city.

Some of these places are natural phenomena – such as the lofty Arthur's Seat. The 823-foot volanic peak stands at the heart of the 650-acre Holyrood Park – which with three lochs, picturesque ruins, the Salisbury Crags and miles of grassland, isn't your average city park. You can walk to the top of the Crags and Arthur's Seat, but it's not a spur-of-the-moment jaunt. You'll need decent shoes, warm clothes and a sensible attitude; people have to be rescued every year. If in doubt, enjoy the grassy expanse around Holyrood Palace and the landscaped gardens that surround the Scottish Parliament building. Other parkland areas in the city, such as Princes Street Gardens and the Meadows, are man-made – both were created by draining lochs.

Edinburgh has been the capital of Scotland for more than 500 years, and was the first-choice site for the re-establishment of a Scottish Parliament in 1999. The city has also long been a centre for the courts, civil service, banking industry and academic world, giving it a certain assured – some would say bourgeois – demeanour.

But there is another side to Edinburgh, unleashed at the biggest event of its year, when visitor numbers hit a phenomenal peak. August is, of course, the month of the Edinburgh Festival. This catch-all term encompasses the official International Festival, as well as the Fringe, Film, Book, Jazz and Blues Festivals, plus the Military Tattoo. If you're looking for a quiet time to visit the city, pick another month.

The city's sense of fun (and knack for encouraging tourism) also emerges in the winter. Edinburgh always puts on a fabulous Capital Christmas, but really goes overboard for New Year. Hogmanay builds to a massive street party on 31 December, attracting visitors from all over the world.

For something dedicated to the bairns, try visiting during the Bank of Scotland Children's International Theatre Festival in May. The event is the biggest performing arts festival for children and young people in the UK, and it's certainly easier to find a room at this time of the year. For details see **Festivals and Events** *pp330-334*.

WHERE TO STAY

Edinburgh has accomodation to suit most tastes and budgets, and recent years have seen a spate of new hotel launches. Demand is brisk, however, and places soon fill up: even outside Festival season, advance booking is highly recommended. Predictably, rates shoot up during August and Hogmanay; watch out too for rugby internationals, which push prices up.

If you prefer the flexibility of self-catering accomodation, Edinburgh has several aparthotels. Many of the smaller hotels and guesthouses also offer self-contained apartments in the city centre.

The vibe's strictly retro at **Monster Mash**. *See p307.*

Apex International

31-35 Grassmarket, EH1 2HS (0131 300 3456/www.apexhotels.co.uk). **Rates** £99-£240. **Credit** MC, V.

Stylish accommodation and children can go together very well, and here the under-12s don't have to pay for the style if they stay in their parents' room. Decor at the Apex International is sleek and contemporary, with a changing array of original artwork and photography dotted around the building. There are DVD players in every room (with a list of films to hire that includes a decent percentage of family and children's titles), hairdryers, and a take-home branded rubber duck in every bathroom; cots are provided for the tinies. In the Yu Spa complex, the stainless steel ozone pool has unrestricted access for children. Staff in the various restaurants are happy to warm baby milk and food, high chairs are available in the Metro Brasserie, and a little meal time sanity is ensured thanks to the hotel's policy of serving children immediately. The Metro also has a children's menu, which includes 'baby tapas' and a range of smoothies; it's more relaxed and informal here than at the rooftop Heights restaurant, where breakfast is served. There is a vast range of in-house menu packages, including packed lunches, express foods and an early dining option (4.30-6pm), which may suit families with younger children. Right in the heart of the Old Town, the Apex is perfect for sightseers and shoppers. The Grassmarket is busy at night, however, particularly during the summer. It's great if you like bustle, but young families who need peace and quiet may prefer to forego the views of the castle from the superior rooms, and consider a no less stylish rear facing standard room.

Balmoral Hotel

1 Princes Street, EH2 2EQ (0131 556 2414/ www.thebalmoralhotel.com). **Rates** *Room only* £345-£510. **Breakfast** £16-£18.50; £8-£9.25 under-12s. **Credit** AmEx, MC, V.

A landmark on Princes Street for over a century, the clock mounted high on the tower of the Balmoral Hotel is always set a little fast, to give panicking train commuters three minutes' grace. That clock, and the hotel itself, are part of Edinburgh's social history. Nowadays the Balmoral is part of the Rocco Forte Hotels group, offering five star luxury and a blend of bygone elegance and contemporary style. Decorated in tones of sage, cream, blue and mocha, the sumptuous rooms have top-of-the-range everything, from internet access and air-conditioning to glorious marble and ceramic bathrooms. Unlike many top of the range hotels, the Balmoral has gone out of its way to welcome families. The complimentary 'Five Star Kids' package kicks off as soon as you arrive; your child is welcomed and given their own 'check-in card'. Goodies in the room include a gift, child-sized bathrobes and slippers and children's toiletries, along with hotel-branded bathtime ducks to take home and a child-orientated room service menu. Wooden cots

and travel cots are available, and there are substantial fold-away beds for children sharing their parents' room. Interconnecting rooms, adjacent rooms with a shared main entry, and suites can also be booked for families. Under-threes go free, and rates for older children are dependent on special offers and packages. A babysitting service is available, provided by local childcare companies. The hotel encourages resident children to explore, with prizes for those who complete their quiz sheet. Breakfast is served in Hadrian's Brasserie, the informal dining option, where you'll find high chairs and a kids' menu. (The Michelin-starred Number One restaurant doesn't have a children's menu, but may suit a family with older children.) Accompanied children can use the pool at the hotel's spa at any time. The Five-Star Babies' package, devised for infant-toting parents, provides all the paraphernalia a baby could need, from bottle warmers to baby baths and more besides. Check the website for details.

Express by Holiday Inn

Picardy Place, off Leith Walk, EH1 3JT (0131 558 2300/www.ichotelsgroup.com). **Rates** £95-£169. **Credit** AmEx, MC, V.

Located close to Waverley Station, this hotel is great for families arriving in Edinburgh by train. Express hotels in the Holiday Inn chain offer families on a budget a simple, comfortable berth for the night, with en suite facilities and a telly. Young people up to the age of 19 can stay free, if sharing their parents' room. This particular branch is housed in a Georgian building, so there's no brash neon signage. Cribs and cots are available free if you make a request when booking – and subject to prior arrangement, pets can stay too. The Express on Britannia Way in Leith (0131 555 4422) is a purpose-built hotel next to the Ocean Terminal complex, where the Royal Yacht Britannia is housed. It has its own car park – a relatively rare commodity in Edinburgh.

Heriott Park Guest House

254-256 Ferry Road, EH5 3AN (0131 552 3456/www.heriottpark.co.uk). **Rates** £60-£100. *Apartments* £80-£200. **Credit** MC, V.

The Heriott Park is a traditionally-styled B&B, run by Gary Turner and Stewart Thom. Situated to the north of the city, it has a view all the way to the castle. There are seven double/twin rooms and eight family rooms, which can sleep between three and five people. All of the rooms are en suite, with shower rooms. Travel cots can be provided, and there are high chairs for use in the dining room. The guest house is handy for the Botanic Gardens, has free parking on the opposite side of the road, and is literally two minutes' walk from the 23 bus route, which runs to the centre of town. This is a no-smoking guest house. The Heriott Park also has two well-appointed, spacious self-catering apartments next door, which can each sleep five to seven people and would be an ideal choice for larger families.

SPOOKY EDINBURGH

Any number of chilling and macabre stories echo around the shadowy wynds and alleys of Edinburgh. Tours and exhibitions telling of supernatural sightings and grisly goings on aren't a three-year-old's idea of a top afternoon out, but many over-nines like nothing better than a good spooky story. Most entertainments of a creepy nature are based in the Old Town. Some concentrate on the history of the city, which can summon up enough grim facts to raise the hairs on the back of anyone's neck. Others go underground into the hidden closes and vaults of the Old Town, or visit notorious haunting hotspots. There are those that aren't above employing concealed actors to leap out and give you a fright.

Book tours in advance, as this sort of entertainment is extremely popular. Dress sensibly; it can be very cold, for all kinds of reasons, in graveyards, closes and vaults.

Black Hart Entertainments run the popular **City of the Dead Tour**, which takes you into Greyfriars Kirkyard and the tomb of 'Bluidy Mackenzie', scourge of the Covenanters, a number of whom died incarcerated in the kirkyard. The Mackenzie Poltergeist has resonated around paranormal circles for years. This is a chance, perhaps, to witness it for yourself. Scary. On a lighter note, the company also offer Edinburgh tours designed for children. The Secret City Tour brings in reference to Harry Potter, the invention of Christmas and the like – a poltergeist-free zone in short; phone for current details.

Another popular walk is the **Ghosts and Gore Tour**, which employs actors as 'jumper-ooters'. We fear it would be too scary for under-eights, but Witchery Tours leave it up to parents to decide how spooky to go. The walk concentrates on the gory joys of crime, punishment and other associated horrors practised in the city in past centuries (volunteer victims may be required to test out some of the torture instruments!). Witchery also use actors on their **Murder and Mystery Tour**, which trawls various sites of death, murder and execution around the Royal Mile.

A slightly more lighthearted view of Edinburgh's murderous past is provided by Mercat Tours, whose long-established **Ghosts and Ghouls Tour** takes in the Blair Street vaults. Mercat also use the vaults in their **Haunted Underground Experience**, exploring the paranormal and the Edinburgh Ghost Project of 2001.

You don't need to join a guided walk to frighten yourself silly. There are a couple of grim attractions lying in wait. **Edinburgh Dungeon** has exhibits that relate to Edinburgh's gorier history. There's the tale of Burke and Hare, representations of plague-ridden closes, revolting judicial punishments, or gloomy ghosts. Lots of scares around every corner, then, so this is not for the faint hearted – or the under-eights. There's also **Mary King's Close**, one of many narrow streets that were built over as Edinburgh expanded. The close, sealed during a plague outbreak in the 17th-century, is pretty spooky; dark, cold and feet below the city's modern thoroughfares. Add to this its haunted reputation (visitors have left toys and sweets for the ghost of Annie, a child who died of the plague), and the knowledge of its history, and your spine is truly chilled.

City of the Dead Tour

Black Hart Entertainment, Tron Kirk, 122 High Street, Royal Mile, EH1 1RU (0131 225 9044/ www.blackhart.uk.com). **Open** *Easter-Halloween 8.30pm, 9.15pm, 10pm nightly. Halloween-Easter 7.30pm, 8.30pm nightly.* **Tours** £8.50 (£6.50 concessions). **No credit cards.**

Edinburgh Dungeon

31 Market Street, EH1 1QB (0131 240 1000/ www.thedungeons.com). **Open** *Apr-Oct 10am-5pm daily. Nov-Mar 11am-4pm daily.* **Admission** £11.45; £7.45-£9.45 concessions. **Credit** AmEx, MC, V.

Mercat Tours

Mercat House, Niddry Street South, EH1 1NS (0131 225 5445/www.mercattours.com). **Open** *Ghosts and Ghouls Apr-Sept 7pm, 8pm, 9pm nightly. Oct-Mar 7pm, 8pm nightly. Haunted Underground Experience Apr-Sept 5pm, 6pm daily. Oct-Mar 6pm Mon-Thur, Sun; 5pm, 6pm Fri, Sat.* **Admission** *Ghosts and Ghouls* £7.50; £7 concessions; £4 under-16s; £19 family (2+2). *Haunted Underground Experience* £6.50; £6 concessions; £3 under-16s; £16 family (2+2). **Credit** MC, V.

Real Mary King's Close

entrance by Warriston's Close, EH1 1PG (0870 243 0160/www.realmarykingsclose.com). **Open** *Apr-Oct 10am-9pm daily. Aug 9am-9pm daily. Nov-Mar 10am-4pm Mon-Fri, Sun; 10am-9pm Sat.* **Admission** £8.50; £7.50 concessions; £6 5-15s. No under-5s admitted. **Credit** MC, V.

Witchery Tours

84 West Bow, Victoria Street, EH1 2HH (0131 225 6745/www.witcherytours.com). **Open** *Ghosts and Gore May-Aug 7pm, 7.30pm nightly. Murder and Mystery Summer 9pm, 9.30pm nightly (times may vary; phone to check). Winter 7pm, 7.30pm nightly.* **Admission** (includes *Witchery Tales* book) *Ghosts and Gore* £7.50; £5 under-15s. *Murder and Mystery* £7.50; £5 under-15s. **Credit** AmEx, MC, V.

Inverleith Hotel

5 Inverleith Terrace, EH3 5NS (0131 556 2745/www.inverleithhotel.co.uk). **Rates** £59-£119. *Apartment* £89-£159. **Credit** MC, V.
This family-run concern has the feel of a home rather than a hotel. Owners Steve and Adrienne Case have retained the character of the early Victorian townhouse, so there are cornices in the breakfast room, multi-paned sash windows and a relaxed sense of gentility – which more or less sums up the Inverleith area. All the comfortable rooms are en suite, and while there are two family rooms, cots can be provided for the doubles. Rooms also have a broadband connection. The staff are pleased to welcome children and go out of their way to help – warming baby food or milk at breakfast time, for example. For dinner, they're happy to point you in the direction of several good, family-friendly restaurants in the New Town, or there's a direct bus link to the city centre. Full Scottish, vegetarian or continental breakfasts are available, and special diets can be catered for. The Inverleith Hotel also let out a first floor flat in a Georgian townhouse on Brandon Street. It sleeps up to six people and has a travel cot, high chair and rather noble proportions in the triple-windowed drawing room. See the website for details.

Northumberland Hotel

31-33 Craigmillar Park, EH16 5PE (0131 668 3131/www.thenorthumberlandhotel.co.uk). **Rates** £70-£165. **Credit** MC, V.
This small hotel has 16 rooms. Six are doubles and four are family sized (under-12s share their parents' rooms at no extra cost), and cots are available free on request. It offers a full Scottish breakfast with potato scones and black pudding, vegetarian options on request, or lighter alternatives. A restaurant opens up in the evening, with an extensive menu of hearty traditional fare – which might be useful, as the hotel is around two miles outside the city centre. It's on a direct bus route to central Edinburgh, however, and the journey only takes ten minutes or so. The upside of this location is that it's a bit quieter.

Royal Garden Apartments

York Buildings, Queen Street, EH2 1HY (0131 625 2345/www.royal-garden.co.uk). **Rates** £99-£405. **Credit** AmEx, MC, V.
The Royal Garden Apartments are right in the heart of the city, and can be booked by the day or for months at a time. The one- and two-bedroom apartments can sleep between two and six people, with the use of a sofa bed. Children under 14 years old are not charged for accommodation, and if all the beds in an apartment are being used, a Z-bed can be supplied. Rates include daily maid service and breakfast (tea or coffee, muffins and fruit) in the communal lounge area. Rear facing apartments are quieter, and those on the higher floors have views towards the River Forth and Fife; forward facing apartments look onto the grand façade of the Royal Scottish Portrait Gallery (see

Edinburgh

p311) across Queen Street. What is extremely useful about the apartments is the extra equipment at parents' disposal – including cots, nappy bins, changing mats, books and games, high chairs and branded teddy bears for children to keep. There's also an on-site laundry.

WHERE TO EAT & DRINK

Families have no trouble foraging for grub to please all age groups in this city. As well as all the usual burger and pizza chains, there are scores of friendly Italian trattoria, as befits a city with such a pungent Italian connection. We list a couple of our favourites below, but there are so many on Hanover Street and Leith Walk you'll be spoilt for choice.

Café Mediterraneo

73 Broughton Street, EH1 3RJ (0131 557 6900). **Meals served** *Oct-Jun* 8am-5.30pm Mon-Sat; 9am-4pm Sun. *Jul-Sept* 8am-5.30pm Mon-Thur, Sun; 8am-9pm Fri, Sat. **Main courses** £6.50-£9.50. **Credit** MC, V.
This family-run café may just take the prize for the best coffee in Edinburgh. It looks quite dark at the front, but the room to the rear is bright and more modern in design. The menu is varied and fairly extensive, from sea bass to spaghetti, and vegetarian options are always available. There are one or two steps to negotiate, and if you have a pushchair it might be better to fold it. That said, there is room in the back room beside a couple of the tables for unfolded pushchairs.

Centotre

103 George Street, EH2 3ES (0131 225 1550/www.centotre.com). **Meals served** 8am-10pm Mon-Thur; 8am-10.30pm Fri, Sat; 11am-9pm Sun. **Main courses** £8.95-£21.95. **Credit** MC, V.
A fairly new addition to Edinburgh's great range of Italian restaurants, this place is very chi-chi. Smart dishes such as pan-fried tiger prawns and scallops are wonderful, but basic pizza and pasta are also several notches above ordinary trattoria fare. Fabulous Italian cheeses are a speciality. If you don't want to spend too much, bruschetta and afternoon scones are available. We love the gloriously thick hot chocolate and the puddings, which star prodigious helpings of top own-made ice-cream. Although the environment is very grown-up, children are made welcome.

Circle

1 Brandon Terrace, EH3 5EA (0131 624 4666). **Meals served** 8.30am-5pm Mon-Fri; 9am-5pm Sat; 9am-4.30pm Sun. **Main courses** £2.95-£6.25. **Credit** MC, V.
Friendly staff and an accommodating attitude to its clientele make Circle a great place to drop into for a coffee, snack or lunch. The stonework and

slate interior is also a nice change from the chrome and blond wood café decor which still permeates Edinburgh. The food ranges from sandwiches to full meals – the former large enough to satisfy any appetite. Children are genuinely welcome here, and half portions are available on some menu items; just ask. The soup is always vegetarian and there are several decent meat-free options on the menu. There are a couple of high chairs and enough room for folded pushchairs, but no nappy changing facility. This is a good stopping-off point en route to the Botanics, or if you've strolled along the Water of Leith pathway. Be warned that it can be busy at lunchtime, though, so you may have to wait for a table.

Elephant House

21 George IV Bridge, EH1 1EN (0131 220 5355/www.elephant-house.co.uk). **Meals served** *Summer* 8am-10pm Mon-Fri; 9am-10pm Sat, Sun. *Winter* 9am-7pm daily. **Main courses** £4.95-£6. **Credit** MC, V.
Choose between the small tables to the front of this café, or larger communal ones to the rear. But wherever you sit, you're surrounded by elephants. This jolly Old Town café serves snacks, salads, mains, cookies and cakes. Elephant was one of JK Rowling's haunts when she was writing *Harry Potter*, and you still see women of a certain age sitting in here seeking inspiration in the steam of their cappuccinos...

Giuliano's

18-19 Union Place, EH1 3NQ (0131 556 6590/www.giulianos.co.uk). **Meals served** noon-1.30am daily. **Main courses** £6-£16. **Credit** MC, V.
Towards the top of Leith Walk (opposite the Playhouse Theatre), Giuliano's was opened 16 years ago by four Italian friends, Giuliano, Angelo, Domenico and Pietrois, who now run three restaurants in the city. It's a lively, popular place, and children are made to feel very welcome during the day. There are high chairs, but the staff assert firmly 'in Italy we don't really have children's menus'. That suits us fine, with freshly prepared pizza and pasta dishes costing from £4.65 for a child-sized portion.

The Hub

Castlehill, EH1 2NE (0131 473 2067/ www.thehub-edinburgh.com). **Meals served** 9.30am-10pm Tue-Sat, 9.30am-5.30pm Sun, Mon. **Main courses** £3-£7. *Set lunch* £5 1 course, £7.50 2 courses. *Set dinner* £7 1 course, £9.95 2 courses. **Credit** MC, V.
Perfectly (and popularly) placed at the foot of the castle, the Hub has a lovely terrace where you can watch the world go by in summer. The lunch menu has some impressive global dishes such as venison carpaccio and crispy duck with Asian vegetables. Children may be more at home with Scottish salmon or steak ciabatta sandwiches, a

Dean Gallery. See p311.

plate of bread and dips, or olives and paprika crackers to share. The breakfast menu, with brioches, yoghurts and fruit compote or scrambled egg and smoked salmon, is brought to a halt at noon; pastries and cakes are served all day. As it's part of the Hub complex (home of the Edinburgh International Festival), there's full access for buggies and wheelchairs, as well as nappy changing facilities.

Living Room

113-115 George Street, EH2 4JN (0131 226 0880/www.thelivingroom.co.uk). **Meals served** noon-10.30pm Mon, Tue, Sun; noon-11pm Wed; noon-11.30pm Thur; noon-midnight Fri, Sat. **Main courses** £8.95-£18.95. **Credit** MC, V.

It might seem to take itself a bit seriously on first impressions, but this place is excellent for a leisurely family lunch. The food ranges from Asian fusion (crispy duck and pancakes – a great children's favourite) to British classics, including Sunday roast and shepherd's pie. There's a special menu for under-tens (£6 for two courses, £7.50 for three), offering fish and chips, chicken or macaroni cheese, but there are so many pleasantly picky/dippy things on the brunch and lunch menus that kids may prefer to go all grown-up. Families with younger children are made welcome – there are high chairs and nappy changing facilities – but after 8pm it's jazzy, bluesy and strictly for adults. Any children hanging about after eight are turned into pumpkins and put in the soup.

Loon Fung

2 Warriston Place, EH3 5LE (0131 556 1781). **Meals served** noon-11.30pm Mon-Thur; noon-12.30am Fri; 2pm-12.30am Sat; 2-11.30pm Sun. **Main courses** £6.50-£9.50. **Credit** MC, V.

This Cantonese restaurant in Canonmills is something of an institution, having been in situ for over 30 years. The food is great, and there's always masses of it. The speciality here is seafood, but there's plenty of choice in amongst the old favourites. Loon Fung is a good place to have an early supper if you've been visiting the Botanics in this neck of the woods.

Monster Mash & Monster Mex

47 Thistle Street, EH2 1DY (0131 225 5782/ www.monstermashcafe.co.uk). **Meals served** 10am-10pm daily. **Main courses** £5.50-£11.95. **Credit** MC, V.

With outposts in Edinburgh and Glasgow, Monster Mash is a gastronomic celebration of the classic 1970s childhood that some parents may fondly remember. There are formica-topped tables and the *Beano* to while away the time till the food comes. The main menu centres around comfort staples such as sausages (from renowned Edinburgh butcher's Crombies) and mash, pies and fish and chips. If the kids prefer a spot of spice and sombrero with their grub, chilli, tacos, nachos, ribs, and tortillas folded and cooked in all kinds of ways are on offer on the Monster Mex menu. For afters you can get ice-creams, crumbles and sponge puddings. Wash it all down with a range of soft drinks, ice-cream floats, milkshakes, Sweetheart Stout, Newkie Brown or even champagne if you so desire. Staff are entertaining and enthusiastic, and nappy changing facilities and high chairs are available. The Forrest Road site is quite small, so you might have to bagsy a space then return to claim the table when it's free.
Branch: 4A Forrest Road, EH1 2QN (0131 225 7069).

Mussel Inn

61-65 Rose Street, EH2 2NH (0131 225 5979/ www.mussel-inn.com). **Meals served** noon-3pm, 6-10pm Mon-Thur; noon-10pm Fri, Sat; 12.30-10pm Sun. **Main courses** £9.95-£15.50. **Credit** MC, V.

A lively joint in the middle of the city centre, the Mussel Inn has an informal and airy feel, even when it's busy. The menu is wholly seafood based, with oysters, king scallops and, of course, mussels taking centre stage. Classic dishes are scaled down for the children's menu (a mini-sized pot of mussels for £3.60, for example), although many of the starters are suitable for a child's main. There is always a fish-free option for vegetarians, but choice is limited – it is a fish restaurant, after all. This place is a bit of an institution, so advance booking is recommended.

Edinburgh

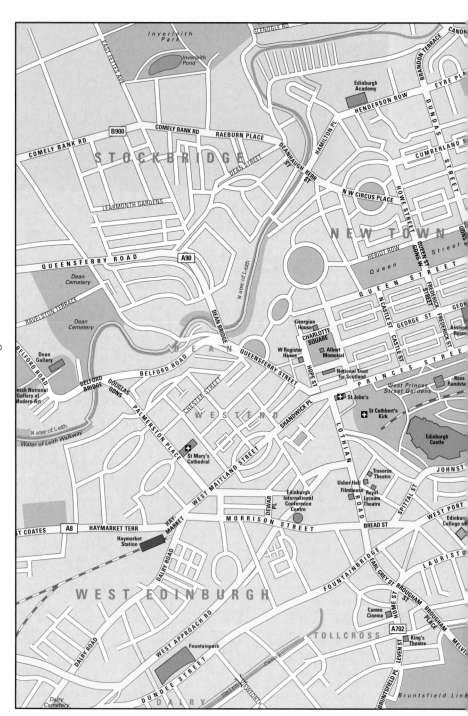

Edinburgh

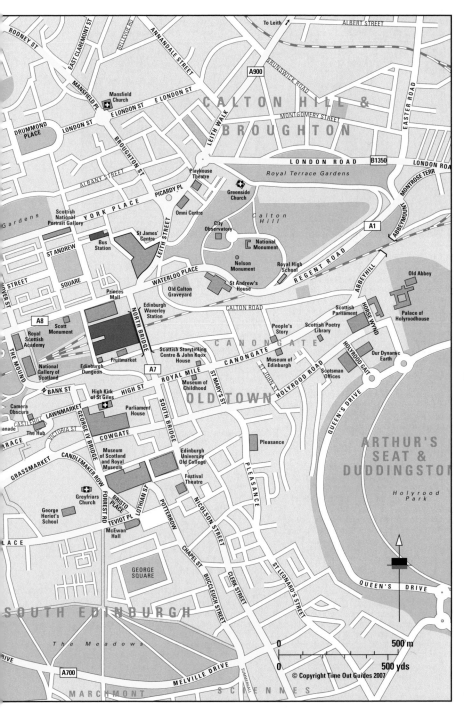

To Leith

ALBERT STREET

RODNEY ST
EAST CLAREMONT ST
ANNANDALE STREET
BELLEVUE RD
BRUNSWICK ROAD
A900
EASTER ROAD

MANSFIELD PL
MANSFIELD
Mansfield
Church
E LONDON ST
E LONDON ST
LEITH WALK

DRUMMOND
PLACE
LONDON ST
BROUGHTON ST

CALTON HILL &

MONTGOMERY STREET

BROUGHTON

ALBANY STREET

LONDON ROAD
B1350
LONDON ROA

Royal Terrace Gardens

MONTROSE TERR

Gardens
Playhouse
Theatre
PICARDY PL

Scottish
National
Portrait Gallery
YORK PLACE
Greenside
Church
Omni Centre
City
Observatory
Calton
Hill
A1

ABBEYMOUNT

ABBEYHILL

Old Abbey

ST ANDREW
Bus
Station
St James'
Centre
LEITH STREET
National
Monument
Nelson
Monument
Royal High
School
REGENT ROAD

SQUARE
WATERLOO PLACE
St Andrew's
House
Palace of
Holyroodhouse

Princes
Mall
Old Calton
Graveyard
HORSE WYND

A8
Edinburgh
Waverley
Station
CALTON ROAD
Scottish
Parliament

Royal
Scottish
Academy
Scott
Monument
NORTH BRIDGE
CANONGATE
People's
Story
Scottish Poetry
Library
Our Dynamic
Earth

THE MOUND
National
Gallery of
Scotland
Edinburgh
Dungeon
Fruitmarket
A7
Scottish Storytelling
Centre & John Knox
House
CANONGATE
Museum of
Edinburgh
HOLYROOD GAIT
HOLYROOD ROAD
Scotsman
Offices

N BANK ST
High Kirk
of St Giles
HIGH ST
ROYAL MILE
Museum of
Childhood
ST MARY'S ST
ST JOHN'S ST

Camera
Obscura
LAWNMARKET
Parliament
House
SOUTH BRIDGE
OLD TOWN
QUEEN'S DRIVE

CASTLEHILL
The Hub
GEORGE IV BRIDGE
VICTORIA ST
COWGATE
Pleasance
ARTHUR'S

TERRACE
anade
GRASSMARKET
CANDLEMAKER ROW
Museum
of Scotland
and Royal
Museum
Edinburgh
University
Old College
PLEASANCE
SEAT &
DUDDINGSTON

Festival
Theatre
Holyrood
Park

George
Heriot's
School
Greyfriars
Church
BRISTO
PLACE
FORREST RD
TEVIOT PL
LOTHIAN ST
POTTERROW
NICOLSON STREET

PALACE
McEwan
Hall
CHAPEL ST
BUCCLEUCH STREET
CLERK STREET
ST LEONARD'S STREET
QUEEN'S DRIVE

GEORGE
SQUARE

DRIVE
SOUTH EDINBURGH

The Meadows

A700
MELVILLE DRIVE
SUMMERHALL

MARCHMONT
SCIENNES

0   500 m
0   500 yds
© Copyright Time Out Guides 2007

Edinburgh

Bagpipes on the battlements at **Edinburgh Ca**

S Luca

16 Morningside Road, EH10 4DB (0131 446 0233/www.s-luca.co.uk). **Meals served** 9am-10pm daily. **Main courses** £4.20-£5.75. **Credit** MC, V.

Luca's is one of Edinburgh's most famous ice-cream makers, but there's also own-made pizza and pasta on the menu. The children's menu offers mini servings of pasta or pizza, plus egg 'n' chips, chicken nuggets and a Scottish fry-up for breakfast or brunch; selected dishes from the main menu are also available in half portions. The café is on two floors, so prams and pushchairs have to be left downstairs if you want to go upstairs. Staff will heat bottles, high chairs are provided and there are nappy changing facilities in both the male and female lavatories.

Vittoria

113 Brunswick Street, EH7 5HR (0131 556 6171/www.vittoriarestaurant.com). **Meals served** 10am-11pm Mon-Sat; noon-11pm Sun. **Main courses** £6.50-£14.95. **Credit** AmEx, MC, V.

In business for over 60 years, Vittoria still looks modern and stylish, like so many Italian ladies in their middle age. The restaurant started life as Pompa's Tearoom back in 1936, and was taken over by Alberto Crolla in 1963. It's run by Tony Crolla now. The gigantic menu features some splendid Italian specialities, including ravioli di pesce; ravioli filled with lobster and salmon cooked with butter, sage and tomato. There are no fewer than 15 vegetarian pasta options, including child favourite spaghetti Alessandro (spaghetti cooked in olive oil and garlic, with chilli and mixed vegetables). To follow, ice-cream concoctions hit the spot for children; adults might prefer the tiramisu or sherry-infused trifle. Prices reflect a friendly neighbourhood trattoria. The management have opened a new wood-fired oven pizzeria, La Favorita, on Leith Walk; here, the children's

menu includes chocolate pizza and ice-cream spaghetti, alongside more conventional pasta, gnocchi and pizza options.
Branch: La Favorita 325-331 Leith Walk, EH6 8SA (0131 554 2430/www.la-favorita.com).

Waterfront Wine Bar & Grill

1C Dock Place, EH6 6LU (0131 554 7427/ www.waterfrontwinebar.co.uk). **Meals served** noon-3.30pm, 6-10pm daily. **Main courses** £8-£24.50. **Credit** MC, V.

The Waterfront is a lovely spot for relaxed family dining, and well worth the short trip from the city centre into Leith. There's a strong emphasis on fish of all kinds, but other options are provided for dedicated carnivores and vegetarians. Children are extremely well catered for, with an appealing menu that includes fish and chips, all-organic pasta with a sausage and tomato sauce, free range scrambled eggs on toast and own-made fishcakes, all priced around £2.95, plus a goody bag of activities to keep them occupied. If you sit out in the conservatory, you look out onto one of Leith's old water systems and the Scottish Executive building.

PLACES TO SEE, THINGS TO DO

A number of Edinburgh's attractions are in the care of either Historic Scotland (HS) or The National Trust for Scotland (NTS); for details, see www.historic-scotland.gov.uk and www.nts.org.uk. These bodies have their own memberships, and if you're planning to 'do' a number of their properties on your visit, or over a series of visits, it might be worth joining to save on entry fees. Both organisations work with the likes of English Heritage and the National Trust, so check if you can gain free or reduced entry by means of any other preservation or conservation body you might belong to.

It's worth noting that the NTS doesn't permit pushchairs or backpack-style child carriers into some of its properties. More glamorous mothers take note; stiletto heels are also vetoed in some places, because of the risk of damage to old floors.

Edinburgh has no less than five national art galleries: the National Gallery of Scotland; the Royal Scottish Academy Building; the National Portrait Gallery; the Scottish National Gallery of Modern Art; and the Dean Gallery. Information on all of them can be obtained by calling 0131 624 6200 or by visiting www.natgalscot.ac.uk. Getting around the galleries is simple, as there is a free shuttle bus in operation. Of the big five, we list our children's favourite, the Dean (*see right*).

Brass Rubbing Centre

Trinity Apse, Chalmers Close, High Street, EH1 1DE (0131 556 4364/www.cac.org.uk). **Open** *Apr-July, Sept* 10am-4.45pm Mon-Sat. *Aug* 10am-4.45pm Mon-Sat; noon-5pm Sun. Last admission for brass rubbing 3.45pm. **Admission** free. *Brass rubbing* £1.50-£28. **Credit** MC, V.

Now here's a benign activity for all the family to enjoy on a rainy day. There are several different types of rubbings to attempt, some of which are quite complex. Clear guides demonstrate how to achieve a perfect image with your wax crayon and paper, and staff are happy to help out and answer any artistic queries. The cost of your brass rubbing depends on what size it is, and includes materials. The centre is housed in the atmospheric Trinity Apse, the only extant remnant of Edinburgh's Gothic Trinity College Church, founded in 1460.

Edinburgh Zoo.
See p312.

Camera Obscura & the World of Illusion

Castlehill, Royal Mile, EH1 2ND (0131 226 3709/www.camera-obscura.co.uk). **Open** *Nov-Mar* 10am-5pm daily. *Apr-Jun* 9.30am-6pm daily. *Jul, Aug* 9.30am-7.30pm daily. *Sept, Oct* 9.30am-6pm daily. **Admission** £6.95; £5.50 concessions; £4.50 5-15s; £21.10 family (2+2); free under-5s. **Credit** MC, V.

Young children are intrigued by the distorting mirrors on the exterior of this building. Older children – and accompanying adults – are more likely to enjoy the 19th-century version of CCTV on show within. The Camera Obscura works by mean of a series of mirrors, which project a periscope image on to a white disc in a darkened room. You can see many of Edinburgh's main landmarks from one tiny room, and also spy on the passers-by down below. Powerful telescopes on the building's rooftop also give great views all over the city. Three floors of exhibits, such as pin-hole cameras, morphing machines and holographs, as well as plenty of interactive technology, keep everyone busy once they've finished spying.

Dean Gallery

73 Belford Road, EH4 3DS (0131 624 6200/ www.natgalscot.ac.uk). **Open** 10am-5pm daily. **Admission** free.

Opened in 1999 to house the Paolozzi Gift – a body of work by Edinburgh-born artist Sir Eduardo Paolozzi – this is possibly the most child-friendly of the city's major galleries. The lofty 19th-century building accommodates Paolozzi's two-storey high *Vulcan*, which ticks most kids' boxes – it's a giant; it's a giant robot; it's an iron man. In addition to Paolozzi's works, there is a mock-up of his studio, and various artefacts and bric-a-brac. A number of pieces are set into the gardens around the Dean, and it's a lovely spot to while away some time on a sunny day. The gallery also has a café selling snacks and light meals. The Scottish National Gallery of Modern Art is just across the road, if you fancy combining the two.

Edinburgh Castle

Castlehill, EH1 2NG (0131 225 9846/ www.historic-scotland.gov.uk). **Open** *Apr-Sept* 9.30am-6.30pm daily. *Oct-Mar* 9.30am-5pm daily. Last entry 45mins before closing. **Admission** £11; £9 concessions; £5.50 5-15s; free under-5s. Guided tour free. *Audio guide* £3; £2 concessions, £1 under-16s. **Credit** AmEx, MC, V.

This is no fairy-tale offering. Edinburgh Castle is a grim, defensive beast, towering over the city. There have been settlements on Castle Hill for thousands of years, with the earliest evidence of habitation dating back to the Bronze Age. Once you're up on the Esplanade, where the annual Military Tattoo takes place, you can see why; the views are mightily impressive, and the site offers a superb vantage point over the surrounding area. The castle itself is a conglomeration of buildings,

Edinburgh

constructed over 900 years. Most of what you can now see dates from extensive 19th-century renovations, although the oldest building, St Margaret's Chapel, was built in the 12th century. The remains of David's Tower, built by King David I, complete with their creepy light show, are worth a peek. It's hard to imagine the scale of the entire tower, destroyed by repeated artillery pounding during the Lang Siege of 1571-3; the skeletons of men who died there were unearthed during excavations.

Crown Square, the castle's main courtyard, houses some of the most historically interesting buildings. The Royal Apartments contain the Honours of Scotland exhibition and the Stone of Scone. Scottish monarchs were crowned on the stone for centuries, until Edward I looted it in 1296 and took it to Westminster Abbey. A group of patriots stole it back in 1950; three months later a similar stone turned up outside Arbroath Abbey, and was taken back to London. The stone was finally returned to Scotland in 1996 – but opinion is divided as to whether it's the real thing. Also worth a visit are the dungeons, where reconstructions tell of the French and American prisoners who were held there during the Napoleonic war and the American War of Independence.

The castle has real soldiers to see as well as models and mannequins, as it's the regimental HQ for the recently formed Royal Regiment of Scotland. The National War Museum is also housed here, for a spot of Scottish military history. It's always worth checking Historic Scotland's website before visiting, as you may find that there are special living history events scheduled.

Finally, be aware that many of the pathways are steep and cobbled, and not all areas of the castle are accessible to wheelchairs or pushchairs.

Edinburgh Zoo

134 Corstorphine Road, EH12 6TS (0131 334 9171/www.edinburghzoo.org.uk). **Open** *Apr-Sept* 9am-6pm daily. *Oct* 9am-5pm daily. *Nov-Mar* 9am-4.30pm daily. **Admission** £10; £7.50 concessions; £7 3-15s; £35.50 (2+3), £32 (2+2) family; free under-3s. **Credit** MC, V.

About 127 types of animal are on show here, although, like many city zoos, Edinburgh draws the line at elephants and giraffes. Most children love the meercats, the ring-tailed lemurs and the chimps. Other exotic inhabitants include Asiatic lions, tigers, zebra, eagles, painted hunting dogs, bongos and always-entertaining penguins. Daily animal encounter events let children get their paws on small mammals, insects, snakes and lizards (these are free, but there's a ticket system as spaces are limited). Don't miss the famous Penguin Parade, when the birds leave their enclosure for a (supervised) stroll on the lawns. There are also brass rubbing sessions. The zoo is built on a hill, so some serious walking is in order. If it

Museum of Childhood

all seems a bit much for shorter legs, a hill-top safari vehicle operates from 10am-3.30pm every day, weather permitting, to do the hard work for you. There are two self-service cafés and a waitress-service restaurant in the Mansion House, plus kiosks and picnic areas scattered around the zoo. There are also several play areas and a maze to get lost in, but these can get extremely busy.

John Knox House & the Scottish Storytelling Centre

43-45 High Street, EH1 1SR (0131 556 9579/ www.scottishstorytellingcentre.co.uk). **Open** *Scottish Storytelling Centre* Oct-Jun 10am-6pm Mon-Sat. Jul-Sept 10am-6pm daily. *John Knox House* 10am-5pm Mon-Sat. **Admission** *Scottish Storytelling Centre* free. *John Knox House: Inside History exhibition* £3; £2.50 concessions; £1 7-17s; free under-7s. **Credit** MC, V.

John Knox House opened in 2006 after extensive renovations, and is a great example of Early Modern living in Edinburgh (another being Gladstone's Land in the Lawnmarket). The house was saved from demolition in the 1800s, thanks to a tenuous connection with John Knox, one of the founding fathers of Scottish Presbyterianism; he may have lived there towards the end of his life (he died in 1572). What is certain is that John Mossman, goldsmith to Mary, Queen of Scots, once lived here with his wife, and their initials adorn the house's marriage lintel. Inside, there's much biographical material on the preacher and the goldsmith; watch out for the trip step, which is a 16th-century burglar alarm. There are also false locks on one of the doors for added security.

Kids that like a touch of the macabre will relish the Tower of Destiny, which has representations of the final moments of Knox, Mary, Queen of Scots, James Mossman and Sir William Kirkcaldy of Grange, who defended Edinburgh Castle against Mary's enemies, and was hanged in 1573. Less gory tales can be enjoyed at the Scottish Storytelling Centre, housing the free permanent Scotland's Stories exhibition. This appeals to children of all ages, with an interactive wall that serves as an introduction to Scottish tradition and literature. Stories are presented using a series of boxes that display mini tableaux, including some toddler-friendly touchy-feely boxes. Other high-tech delights include a sound and vision display dedicated to Robert Louis Stevenson and networked access to other storytelling events throughout Scotland. During the summer, the centre hosts its own free daily storytelling sessions, where tellers adjust their yarns to suit the audience's age group. A visit here is an enjoyably entertaining way to spend an hour or so, after which you can stroll through the garden to the rear of the centre, accessed via Trunk's Close. The Storytelling Centre marks where the Netherbow Port once stood, dividing Edinburgh from the next parish of the Canongate. The old bell that rang out the curfew, warning people that the gates were about to be locked for the night, can still be seen high up on the Storytelling building.

Museum of Childhood

42 High Street, Royal Mile, EH1 1TJ (0131 529 4142/www.cac.org.uk). **Open** 10am-5pm Mon-Sat; noon-5pm Sun. **Admission** free.

Like many museums about childish things, this is bound to appeal more to nostalgic parents than their progeny. Many younger children don't really see the point of lots of toys in glass cases that they can't touch. It's a real (untouchable) treasure trove, however, and older children may enjoy seeing what their parents and grandparents once played with. Amusing automata, such as 'The Haunted House' and 'Sweeney Todd' play out gruesome little scenarios; they used to cost 1d to set in motion, but now you won't see much change out of 50p.

National Museum of Scotland

Chambers Street, EH1 1JF (0131 247 4422/ www.nms.ac.uk). **Open** 10am-5pm daily. **Admission** free.

The light and airy museum building may be contemporary, but it houses thousands of years' worth of artefacts. These tell Scotland's story, from the days of the earliest settlers to life in the 19th and 20th centuries. Touch screens accompany many of the exhibits, which range from the gruesome Maiden of Edinburgh – the city's guillotine – to a room full of gleaming Scottish silverware. Children who are too young to investigate the exhibits will have fun exploring the building: twisting stairways, reminiscent of turnpike stairs found in castles, lead to mezzanine levels, and arrow-slit-like windows offer views down into other parts of the museum. Next door is the Royal Museum (*see p314*), and the two museums interconnect and share facilities.

Our Dynamic Earth

Holyrood Road, EH8 8AS (0131 550 7800/ www.dynamicearth.co.uk). **Open** *Apr-Jun, Sept, Oct* 10am-5pm daily. *July, Aug* 10am-6pm daily. *Nov-Mar* 10am-5pm Wed-Sun. Last entry 50mins before closing. **Admission** £8.95; £6.50 concessions; £5.45 5-15s; £1.50 2-5s; free under-2s. *Annual ticket* £12; £9 concessions; £8 under-16s; £37.50 family (2+2), £45 (2+3). **Credit** MC, V.

If you thought that Geology couldn't possibly make an interesting subject for a visitor attraction, think again. Fittingly, Our Dynamic Earth is located near the former home of James Hutton, the Edinburgh-born 'Father of Geology', but its scope ventures far beyond anything Hutton could have dreamt of. Inside the ultra-modern, tent-like building, the exhibitions take you back 15 billion years into the past, then work forward to the present and into the future. There are all kinds of enjoyable interactive goodies, such as an earthquake simulation, a vertiginous virtual helicopter ride and an iceberg to touch. In the FutureDome, the 'what-if' options game puts the future of the planet in your hands. Occasional special events take place here, and the giant dome in the centre has been used for Edinburgh Festival shows.

Edinburgh

Royal Botanic Garden

20A Inverleith Row, EH3 5LR (0131 552 7171/www.rbge.org.uk). **Open** *Nov-Feb* 10am-4pm daily. *Mar, Oct* 10am-6pm daily. *Apr-Sept* 10am-7pm daily. **Admission** *Garden* free. *Glasshouses* £3.50; £1-£3 concessions, under-16s; £8 family (2+2). *Audio guide* 50p. **Credit** MC, V.

The 'Botanics' have flourished in this area for over 185 years, and have something of interest for most ages. Children love the squirrels, the pond and its resident wildfowl, the pheasants and the sheer space. While there are some typical botanic garden rules, such as no ball games, no picnics and no lying about on certain areas of grass, the good news is that there's acres of space just over the road in Inverleith Park, where any of the above is allowed. At the east entrance is the Botanics Shop, selling pocket-money toys and squirrel and duck feed. There's also a small garden centre for those shamed into doing something about their own patch at home. In the centre of the gardens, the Terrace Café serves snacks, meals and children's lunch boxes, and has indoor and outdoor seating. The gardens host children's events throughout the year, along with the odd art exhibition.

Royal Museum

Chambers Street, EH1 1JF (0131 247 4422/ www.nms.ac.uk). **Open** 10am-5pm daily. **Admission** free.

The Royal Museum is currently in the throes of a massive refurbishment that began in early 2007, and may not be complete until 2011. Museum curators say it will be a 'reinvention', and result in many more artefacts being exhibited, improved gallery displays and better social areas. It may also mean that some areas have restricted access in the interim, but there's always plenty to see and do here. One of the most recent galleries to be unveiled is the interactive 'Connect' room on the ground floor. There are robots, a light wall to test out your reflexes, a 'make your own electricity' exhibit, steam trains and a rocket. So there's no shortage of buttons to press, levers to pull and switches to turn on and off. As well as the usual animal displays, Egyptian sarcophagi, fossils and other museum standards, the Royal Museum has the unique Millennium Clock in the main hall; a phantasmagorical delight and a gem of automaton technology. Ask at the information desk for the day's display times. Permanent displays are supplemented by temporary exhibitions, some of which are free to enter and suitable for younger visitors. For quieter moments, there are two large fish pools in the main space, as well as the Art Cart – an arty drop-in event available daily in the main hall. Family-friendly facilities include well appointed toilets, a nappy changing room and lifts to the upper levels. There are two cafés; if you're visiting with younger children, the café at the rear of the museum has high chairs and booster seats.

Scott Monument

Princes Street, EH2 2EJ (0131 529 4068/ www.cac.org.uk). **Open** *Apr-Sept* 9am-6pm Mon-Sat; 10am-6pm Sun. *Oct-Mar* 9am-3pm Mon-Sat; 10am-3pm Sun. **Admission** £3; free under-5s. **No credit cards**.

It's a long way down from the top of the Scott Monument. If you venture up this Victorian Gothic construction (and brave the somewhat claustrophobic final flight of stairs to the pinnacle), you're rewarded with grand views over Edinburgh. Work on the 200ft edifice began in 1840, although the idea for a monument to Sir Walter Scott was mooted soon after his death in 1832. A vast white marble statue of the great author sits at the base of the monument, flanked by his faithful hounds.

The ultra-modern **Our Dynamic Earth**. *See p313*

Index

Index

Numbers in **bold** indicate the key entry for the topic; numbers in *italics* indicate illustrations.

Index

Index

H

I

J

K

L

Index

Index

Index

Index

Y

Z

ACCOMMODATION

Index

RESTAURANTS, PUBS & CAFÉS

Advertiser's Index

Please refer to relevant sections for addresses / telephone numbers.

Festivals & Events

Dates are given where available; for the latest information, see the relevant website.

JANUARY

London

New Year's Day Parade
1 January
If you like a good parade, the capital's New Year effort is a tough act to beat. Regally called 'a celebration of nations', it stars more than 10,000 performers from 20 different countries prancing and parading through the streets of central London.
www.londonparade.com

FEBRUARY

London

Chinese New Year Festival
(Sunday after Chinese New Year)
Chinatown, the area around Gerrard Street and Lisle Street, near Leicester Square, explodes into action and dances in the new year. In recent years the event, with its dragon parade, fireworks and children's parade, has attracted more than 200,000 spectators, so prepare to jostle.
www.chinatownchinese.co.uk

MARCH

Bath

Bath Literature Festival
Late February/March 2008 (tbc)
With the city's literary history confirmed by Jane Austen's patronage, it seems odd that Bath's bookfest has only been running for 12 years. It's now a well established ten days of literary happenings. Family events take place throughout; the last one was attended by Sue Heap, Shirley Hughes and Nick Sharrett.
www.bathlitfest.org.uk

Bognor Regis

Clowns Convention
8-9 March 2008 (tbc)
Clowns from all over converge on Butlins in Bognor for their AGM, with circus workshops and events. To obtain a day pass for the event, contact Butlins (www.butlins.co.uk), or just be in Bognor for the big parade. Note that 2008 days were not confirmed as we went to press.
www.thebestof.co.uk/bognor

APRIL

London

Flora London Marathon
22 April 2007; 13 April 2008 (tbc)
The starting point is Greenwich Park; the 13-mile halfway point is at the Tower of London and everyone grinds to a halt in St James's Park. This marathon attracts about 35,000 starters, all of whom had to apply by the previous October. It's a great spectacle, and a party atmosphere prevails all along the route.
www.london-marathon.co.uk

MAY

Padstow

'Obby 'Oss Day
1 May 2007, 2008
Padstow's world famous, 900-year-old 'Obby 'Oss Festival takes place on May Day. Two 'Osses, monstrous effigies made out of hoop-work, tarpaulin and horse hair are paraded through the streets to the sound of wild singing, drumming and accordion music. Revellers keep going until midnight. It's a celebration of the onset of summer, and possibly linked to an ancient fertility rite.
www.padstow.com

Helston

Floral Dance
8 May 2007, 2008
The annual 'Furry Dance' (also called the Floral Dance), sees the Cornish town decorated with flowers. Children and adults dance through the streets in Victorian costume to the well-known tune.
www.helston-online.co.uk/flora.htm

Edinburgh

Children's International Theatre Festival

24-30 May 2007; 2008 dates tbc
Europe's biggest and best specialist
festival for children is aimed at kids aged
three to 14 years old and their families.
An excellent programme offers an exciting
blend of story-telling, song, dance
and acrobatics, and features theatre
companies from Russia, Holland, Italy,
Canada and Belgium as well as Scotland.
With everything from Chekhov for kids to
ballet and slapstick humour, it's sure to
be a winner with parents and children.
www.imaginate.org.uk/festival

Bath

Bath International Music Festival

18 May-3 June 2007; May-June 2008 (tbc)
Inaugurated in 1948, the festival has
become a highly regarded music event,
which has many forms of the art covered,
from orchestral, chamber and contemporary
classical music to world and electronic
sounds. The programme takes place
mainly in city venues and also includes
free outdoor events.
www.bathfestivals.org.uk

Bath

Bath Fringe Festival

25 May-10 June 2007
Bath Fringe, an independently run jamboree
of arts and entertainments across the
city, is one of the oldest (it was started up
25 years ago) and largest in the country.
There are usually about 200 events over
its 17 days. As it coincides with Whitsun
half term, there's plenty for children –
shows, workshops, games and a big
parade, as well as a talent show.
www.bathfringe.co.uk

Swansea

Swansea Bay Summer Festival

May-September 2007
From summer half term right through
the school summer hols Swansea does
its level best to pull in the punters with
a weekly calendar of fairs, carnivals,
shows, productions and seaside fun.
To get your hands on a summer brochure
for 2007, check the website.
www.swanseabayfestival.net

JUNE

Stoke-on-Trent

Etruria Canal Festival, Stoke-on-Trent

2-3 June 2007 (tbc)
The Etruria Industrial Museum, which
explores the history of the Midlands
pottery industry, is the venue for the
annual Canal Festival. Boats and boat
people, many dressed in traditional gear,
converge on the site, and there are family
attractions such as trails, a fair and
traditional games.
www.stoke.gov.uk

Bognor Regis

Sands of Time Seaside Festival

9-10 June 2007
The sunniest place in Britain is just the
venue for this two-day hymn of praise to
the seaside. Alongside traditional events,
such as the all-important sandcastle
competition and donkey rides, there's
a vintage car rally. The 2007 festival has
a 'Creatures of the Deep' theme.
www.sandsoftime.co.uk

Croyde

Gold Coast Ocean Festival

15-17 June 2007
The largest single event in the month-long
North Devon Festival, the Ocean Fest
is a free sports and music extravaganza
for surf dudes and dudettes, usually
held on the summer solstice weekend.
Surfing, beach football and volleyball,
paddle racing, mountain boarding,
skateboarding and BMX jumping are all
enthusiastically pursued, and there's an
arena for live music, a shopping village,
bars and restaurants.
www.goldcoastoceanfest.co.uk

Broadstairs

Dickens Festival

16-24 June 2007
Charles Dickens went a bundle on
Broadstairs, and visited the resort every
summer for many years. The festival in
his honour was inaugurated in 1937 and,
to mark its 70th birthday in 2007, the
organiser promise an extra special
celebration. Expect lots of Broadstairs
literary types in period costume and a
good deal of Dickens-themed high jinks.
The festival's play is adapted from The
Pickwick Papers.
www.broadstairsdickensfestival.co.uk

Goodwood

Festival of Speed

22-24 June 2007
The world's biggest celebration of motor
sport – loved by men and boys, in particular
– is now in its 15th year. The theme for
the 2007 festival is 'Spark of Genius –
Breaking Records, Pushing Boundaries'.
www.goodwood.co.uk

Chichester

Chichester Festivities
29 June-15 July 2007
Now in its 33rd year, this country town's entertainment extravaganza involves 17 days of music, dance, literary luminaries, fun, frolics and fireworks.
www.chifest.org.uk

JULY

Berwick

Tweedmouth Feast
19 July 2007
The oldest festival in the borough dates back to the 12th-century festival of St Boisil. It celebrates the plentiful salmon run that was annually hauled from the River Tweed. The fishing trade may have dropped off, but the locals work hard to keep the event on the tourist map, with the annual crowning of the Salmon Queen, a parade, fishing games, musical diversions and a food fair.
www.berwick-upon-tweed.gov.uk

Ramsgate

Ramsgate Powerboat Grand Prix
7-8 July 2007
The premier event of the Grand Prix season for spectators and competitors takes place at the Royal Harbour in Ramsgate.
www.britishresorts.co.uk

Helston

RNAS Culdrose International Air Day
11 July 2007
Everyone prays for fine weather for the Royal Navy's air show at this Cornish air base. Visitors can admire daredevil flying displays and climb into cockpits.
www.airshows.org.uk

Machynlleth

Machynlleth & District Carnival
22-28 July 2007
A fun-packed week, with activities every evening leading up to the big day, when a traditional carnival including a procession through the town pulls in the revellers. Floats assemble at 12.30pm at the station. Entertainment includes children's sports, a falconry display, singing and dancing, a bouncy castle, donkey rides, a magician, refreshments and a bar.

Brockenhurst

The New Forest & Hampshire County Show
24-26 July 2007
A big jamboree held in New Park every year, the show is one of the top ten agricultural and equestrian shows in Britain. There's livestock to admire, show-jumping to inspire, rare breeds and craft workers, food purveyors and entertainers.
www.newforestshow.co.uk

Sheringham

Sheringham Carnival
28 July-5 August 2007
Talent contests, gourmet raffles, a putting competition, bowls tournament, sandcastle building... visit Sheringham during carnival week and you won't be at a loss for something to do. Children enjoy the sandcastle building and the pantomime horse race. Sheringham's shenanigans reach a peak of excitement on Carnival Day, when there's a parade of floats, street entertainments and a fair.
www.sheringhamcarnival.co.uk

AUGUST

Isle of Wight

Skandia Cowes Week
4-11 August 2007
The first organised yacht race took place at Cowes on 10 August 1826. Now the regatta attracts more than 1,000 yachts and 8,500 competitors. First-class sailing, varied shoreside activities and a (usually) sunny festival atmosphere make it a great event for all family members.
www.skandiacowesweek.co.uk

Margate

Margate Carnival
5 August 2007
One of the largest and most colourful carnivals in the South East, this knees-up by the seaside always draws big crowds.
www.britishresorts.co.uk

Salcombe

Salcombe Yacht Regatta
5-11 August 2007
Salcombe Yacht Club organise regular dinghy racing, cadet sailing, cruiser races and rallies, but their big event is the Regatta, which attracts a fleet of boats and sailors as well as onlookers from all over the country. As well as boats, there's a sandcastle building competition, fireworks, treasure hunts and crab catching fun.
www.salcombeyc.org.uk

Broadstairs

Broadstairs Folk Week
10-17 August 2007
The seven bays of Broadstairs are alive with the sound of music for this week.

The event is held on a campsite spread over two school fields only ten minutes' walk to the centre of town, where Panic Circus provide the family entertainments. *www.broadstairsfolkweek.org.uk*

Edinburgh
Edinburgh International Festival
10 August-2 September 2007
During this, one of the most famous arts festivals in the world, the old capital fills up with musicians, actors, comedians, street entertainers and loads and loads of tourists. It's three hectic weeks of big fun, with lots of other related festivals (Tattoo, Fringe, Film, Jazz and Book) going on at around the same time (note that the Edinburgh Fringe starts five days earlier). *www.eif.co.uk*
www.edfringe.com

Bognor Regis
Hotham Park Country Fair
11-12 August 2007
This big and beautiful park is an ideal setting for a conglomeration of craft stalls, food tents, music and dancing. *www.arun.gov.uk*

Whitby
Whitby Regatta
11-13 August 2007
A three-day festival of salty seadog high jinks for all the family. Whitby's summer event culminates with a carnival parade on Monday 13th, with a firework display in the evening. Vintage cars and armed forces displays take place on the West Cliff, rowing races are held in the harbour and there's a greasy pole to climb for a prize. *www.discoveryorkshirecoast.com*

Cromer
Cromer Carnival
11-17 August 2007
The week is packed full of jolly events, with crab catching and sandcastle building competitions, beach sports and treasure hunts for children, as well as air displays, fireworks and a big parade on carnival day (Wednesday 15 August). *www.cromercarnival.co.uk*

Totnes
Carnival & Orange Race
12-19, 21 August 2007
Oranges are the only fruit for this carnival, which sees this historic town all done up in its finery. There's a children's fancy dress parade and a procession on 18 August. The Orange Race on 21 August, organised by the Elizabethan Society,

---

TOP 5

DOTTY ANNUAL EVENTS

Dancing with 'Obby 'Osses in Padstow (May). *See p330.*

Birdmen getting airborne in Bognor (September). *See p334.*

Orange rolling in Totnes (August). *See below.*

Pulling faces in Egremont. (September). *See p334.*

A really gothic Hallowe'en in Whitby (October). *See p335.*

---

commemorates a visit to the town by Sir Francis Drake in the 1580s, when he gave a little boy some fruit. Contestants chase their oranges down the hill. Turn up and register on the day (the race starts at 11am). Oranges are provided. *www.totnesinformation.co.uk*

Arundel
Arundel Castle Activity Day
16 August 2007
Visit the historic castle today to try your hand at fencing and archery. The more sedentary can get creative at the arts and crafts stalls. *www.arundelcastle.org*

Arundel
Arundel Festival
24 August-2 September 2007
The festival, held at Arundel Castle, attracts visitors from all over the world. In 2006 it witnessed performances by the great Humphrey Lyttelton, Katherine Jenkins and Texas. On 24-25 August there will be picnic concerts and fireworks in the grounds of Arundel Castle, and on 26-27 August there are pop concerts (but no picnics are allowed with the pop), also in the castle grounds. Other music and opera events take place between the end of August and 2 September inside the Castle and Fitzalan Chapel. *www.arundelfestival.co.uk*

Grasmere
Grasmere Sports & Show
26 August 2007
This historic and energetic Sports Day involves Cumberland wrestling, hound trails and the Fell Race, in which musclebound men that look as if they're made of steel

and sinew run straight up the fellside. Then there are gundog and sheepdog displays, junior races, mountain bike dashes and a tug of war. You'll need the famous beer tents after that lot.
www.grasmeresportsandshow.co.uk

London
Notting Hill Carnival
27-28 August 2007
Europe's biggest street party, first thrown in 1959, has become a bit of a bunfight, attracting more than a million revellers these days. Families should come on the Sunday, traditionally children's day, when the parade is all about them.
www.lnhc.org.uk

Dartmouth
Port of Dartmouth Royal Regatta
30-31 August, 1 September 2007
This famous regatta, established in 1834, became royal when Queen Victoria sailed in unscheduled during some bad weather in 1856 and became a spontaneous patron. These days the event attracts much interest, for alongside the waterborne events, there's an air display, fireworks, market stalls lining the embankment, music and dancing and fun events all week.
www.dartmouthregatta.co.uk

Blackpool
Blackpool Illuminations
31 August-4 November 2007 (tbc)
To usher in the autumn, a chosen celebrity is given the honour of flicking the switch to light up this splendid seaside town and chase away the blues.
www.visitblackpool.com

SEPTEMBER

Bognor Regis
Birdman 2007
1-2 September 2007
This is a an annual flight competition for human-powered flying machines. Many flyers design machines to aim for the distance prizes – £25,000 is offered for the furthest flight over 100 metres. The attempt started in 1971 at resort of Selsey, until the competition became too famous and repaired to Bognor.
www.birdman.org.uk

Isle of Wight
Bestival
7-9 September 2007
One of the last festivals of the summer, Bestival is described as a 'boutique music festival' and is curated by Radio 1 DJ Rob da Bank. It is in fact, one of the most child-friendly around. It takes place in an 88-acre park of natural woodland – Robin Hill on the Isle of Wight, where there are loads of sprog-friendly play areas. You can bring your own tent, or hire a bivouac, tipi, yurt or beach hut. There's a tree top trail, maze, rabbit run tunnels and miniature village to amuse the children.
www.bestival.net

Seahouses
Seahouses Festival
8-9 September 2007
This delightful Northumbrian sea shanty festival, first put on in 1998, has become a major event in this coastal village. It's a weekend of song and nautical-themed activities, with craft and food fairs, taking place in various venues around Seahouses, including the harbour.
www.seahousesfestival.org

Egremont
Egremont Crab Fair
15 September 2007
A fair first held in 1267 has become one of the dottiest events in the English calendar. Egremeont, a market town in the Lake District, puts on a fun-filled festival in the week before the big day, but the craziness starts at 8am on the third Saturday in September, when competitors try to climb a greasy pole to win a leg of lamb. Sporting events, such as fell running, Westmorland wrestling and apple chucking, take place throughout the day, then in the evening a pipe-smoking contest and gurning (face-pulling) competition take place.
www.egremontcrabfair.org.uk

Southampton
Southampton Boat Show
14-23 September 2007
This annual marine fest fills the city with yachty types and their families. It takes place in Mayflower Park and the busy Hydropool Marina, and there's loads to do, from boat trips and scuba try-outs to pirate games on the Treasure Island beach.
www.southamptonboatshow.com

Alnwick
Alnwick Food Festival
22-23 September 2007
The town's marketplace is packed with all manner of colourful stalls selling a varied selection of local produce, including locally farmed meat, own-made baked goods, fresh vegetables, fruit, condiments, pickles and ice-cream. Stallholders let visitors taste their wares and are happy to

dispense cooking tips. Cookery demos are held in the adjacent Northumberland Hall, and the chefs use ingredients from the 40-plus food producers in the marketplace.

Newquay

British Bodyboard Surf Contest
27-28 September 2007
This is just one of a number of big surfy events taking place in the bays of Newquay. The biggest is undoubtedly the National Surfing Championships (October) – it's usually in Newquay, but the venue, sponsor and date were not confirmed as we went to press. Of most interest to grommets is the under-18s competition, the Billabong British Junior Surfing Championships, held on 15-16 September a little north of here, at Bude's Widemouth Bay.
www.britsurf.co.uk

OCTOBER

Chichester

Autumn Countryside Show
6-7 October 2007
The Weald & Downland Museum reminds all-comers of the way we used to plough the fields and scatter in this mellow and fruitful tribute to the harvest. Steam engines, threshing boxes, plough horses and vintage tractors are at work, and local craftspeople display their skills. The 2007 event incorporates the Wood Show.
www.wealddown.co.uk

Dartmouth

Food Festival
11-13 October 2007
Dartmouth enters wholeheartedly into this annual foodfest, which includes stalls from local food producers, tasting sessions, food education workshops and cookery demonstrations. Local restaurants offer special festival menus.
www.dartmouthfoodfestival.co.uk

Whitby

Whitby Goth Weekend
26-27 October 2007
One for the teens, this, though a national gathering of black-clad miserablists around this most gothic of towns, with its Dracula connections, during Hallowe'en week, is spookily entertaining for all ages. Started about ten years ago by the only goth in the village (to coin a phrase) the WGS is mainly a music festival, although there are walks, black-clad get togethers and clothing stalls. The focal point of events is the Spa Pavilion on the town's West Cliff.
www.whitbyonline.co.uk

NOVEMBER

London

Lord Mayor's Show
10 November 2007
This is when the newly elected Lord Mayor of London (*not* Ken) is presented for approval to the monarch or the monarch's justices. Amid a procession of 140 floats and 6,000 people, the Lord Mayor leaves Mansion House at 11am and proceeds to the Royal Courts of Justice. The procession takes about an hour and a quarter to pass, wherever you stand. At 5pm fireworks are set off from a Thames barge.
www.lordmayorsshow.org

Edinburgh

Capital Christmas
Atmospheric Edinburgh pulls on its best festive kilt in late November with the official switch-on of the city's Christmas lights. The fun continues for the entire month with performances, fairground rides, markets and heaps of things for the weans to do.
www.edinburghchristmas.com

London

London Christmas Tree & Lights
Oxford Street; Regent Street; Trafalgar Square
The Christmas lights are turned on by a minor celeb around the end of November. In Trafalgar Square a giant fir tree – a gift from the Norwegian people in gratitude for Britain's role in liberating their country from the Nazis – is erected, and carols are sung around the same time.
www.oxfordstreet.co.uk
www.regent-street.co.uk
www.londongov.uk

DECEMBER

Edinburgh

Hogmanay
2006's New Year's Eve street party, ceilidh and concert were cancelled because the weather was so stormy. Nevertherless, the Scots capital is traditionally the place for grand revels on 31 December.
www.edinburghshogmanay.org

London

New Year's Eve Celebrations
Trafalgar Square becomes an alarmingly crowded gathering point for revellers, but the millions of pounds worth of fireworks let off around the South Bank and the London Eye are truly spectacular.
www.londongov.uk

Useful Addresses

CAR HIRE

Alamo
0870 400 4508/www.alamo.com
Avis 0844 581 0147/www.avis.co.uk
Budget
0844 581 2231/www.budget.co.uk
easycar www.easycar.com
Enterprise
0870 350 3000/www.enterprise.com
Europcar
0870 607 5000/www.europcar.co.uk
Hertz
0870 599 6699/www.hertz.co.uk

COACHES

National Express
0870 580 8080/
www.nationalexpress.co.uk

DISABLED

Contact a Family
0808 808 3555/www.cafamily.org.uk
DisAbility Holidays.net
0845 634 5163/www.disabilityholidays.net
Holiday Care Service
0845 124 9971/www.holidaycare.org.uk
Wheelchair Travel & Access Minibuses
01483 233640/
www.wheelchair-travel.co.uk

FAMILY HOLIDAY ORGANISATIONS

British Activity Holiday Association
020 8842 1292/www.baha.org.uk
Children's Holiday Fund
020 7928 6522/
www.childrensholidays.org.uk
Family Holidays Association
020 7436 3304/www.fhaonline.org.uk
Gingerbread
0800 018 4318/www.gingerbread.org.uk

HERITAGE ORGANISATIONS

Cadw (The official guardian of the built
heritage of Wales)
www.cadw.wales.gov.uk

English Heritage
0870 333 1181/
www.english-heritage.org.uk
National Trails
www.nationaltrail.co.uk
The National Trust
0870 458 4000/www.nationaltrust.org.uk
The National Trust for Scotland
0131 243 9300/www.nts.org.uk

HOTEL CHAINS

Best Western www.bestwestern.com
Britannia Hotels www.britanniahotels.com
FJB Hotels www.fjbhotels.co.uk
Forestdale www.forestdale.com
City Inn www.cityinn.com
Intercontinental Hotels Group
www.ichotelsgroup.com
Macdonalds Hotels & Resorts
www.macdonald-hotels.co.uk
Marriott www.marriott.co.uk
Novotel www.novotel.com
Premier Travel Inn
www.premiertravelinn.com
Travelodge www.travelodge.co.uk
Von Essen www.vonessenhotels.com

TRAIN BOOKING/INFORMATION

National Rail Enquiries
0845 748 4950/www.nationalrail.co.uk
The Train Line www.thetrainline.com

WEATHER

BBC Weather Centre
www.bbc.co.uk/weather.
Check the weather in your chosen
destination. This website also gives tides
information in coastal regions, as well as
surf reports.

Met Office
0870 900 0100/www.metoffice.gov.uk.
Local, regional and international weather
forecasts, features and warnings.